Comprehensive Classroom Management

Creating Positive Learning Environments for All Students

Vernon F. Jones
Lewis and Clark College

with

Louise S. Jones
Beaverton School District
Beaverton, Oregon

ALLYN AND BACON   *Boston   London   Toronto   Sydney   Tokyo   Singapore*

Vice-President, Publisher: Nancy Forsyth
Editorial Assistant: Christine R. Nelson
Marketing Manager: Ellen Mann
Production Administrator: Annette Joseph
Production Coordinator: Susan Freese
Editorial-Production Service: TKM Productions
Composition Buyer: Linda Cox
Manufacturing Buyer: Louise Richardson
Cover Administrator: Linda Knowles
Cover Designer: Susan Paradise

This textbook is printed on
recycled, acid-free paper.

Library of Congress Cataloging-in-Publication Data
Jones, Vernon F.
   Comprehensive classroom management : creating positive learning
environments / Vernon F. Jones with Louise S. Jones. — 4th ed.
    p.   cm.
   Includes bibliographical references (p.   ) and indexes.
   ISBN 0-205-15664-9
   1. Classroom management. 2. Interaction analysis in education.
3. Motivation in education. 4. School discipline. I. Jones,
Louise S. II. Title.
LB3013.J66 1994
371.1'024—dc20   94-18167
                                    CIP

Printed in the United States of America
10 9 8 7 6 5 4 3 2   99 98 97 96 95

Credits: Text on pages 106–107 is from Vernon F. Jones, *Adolescents with Behavior Problems: Strategies for Teaching, Counseling, and Parent Involvement,* pp. 71–72. Copyright © 1980 by Allyn and Bacon. Reprinted with permission. Various quotations throughout this book are from Forrest Gathercoal, *Judicious Discipline,* 3rd ed., 1993, San Francisco, CA: Caddo Gap Press, pp. 25, 71, 72, 76–77. Reprinted by permission.
Cartoon credits: page 7 © by Sidney Harris, *Phi Delta Kappan;* pages 17, 62, 140, 286, and 332 Ford Button; pages 33 and 234 © Martha F. Campbell; pages 64 and 259 Glen Dines, *Kappan;* page 66 Douglas Blackwell; page 169 cartoon reprinted courtesy James Estes, cartoonist; page 183 reprinted with permission of cartoonist Scott Masear; page 281 Otha J. Collins; page 343 Ray Vogler; page 404 Frank Cotham.

To Vern's first mentor, Jere Brophy,
whose excellent work continues to inform us;

to the thousands of teachers whose ideas and responses
to the materials in the book have enriched its content
and been a source of professional and personal satisfaction;

and to our children, Sarah and Garrett,
who teach us so much and bring us so much happiness

CONTENTS

PREFACE

PURPOSE

In March 1984, a 10-member Panel on the Preparation of Beginning Teachers, chaired by Ernest L. Boyer, president of the Carnegie Foundation for the Advancement of Teaching, issued a report listing three major areas of expertise needed by beginning teachers:

1. Knowledge of how to manage a classroom
2. Knowledge of subject matter
3. Understanding of their students' sociological backgrounds

A publication from the Association for Supervision and Curriculum Development entitled *Effective Schools and Classrooms: A Research-Based Perspective* (Squires, Huitt, & Segars, 1983) stated that effective teachers—those whose students demonstrate consistently high levels of achievement—possess skills in three areas:

1. Planning, or getting ready for classroom activities;
2. Management, which has to do with controlling students' behavior; and
3. Instruction, which concerns providing for or guiding students' learning. (p. 10)

In his comprehensive chapter in *Handbook of Research on Teaching,* Walter Doyle (1986) explained that the classroom teacher's role involves two major functions: establishing order and facilitating learning. Regardless of changes that may be made in the education system, schooling in the United States will not improve significantly unless teachers develop skill in the widely varied teaching methods generally described as classroom management.

Faced with large class sizes, increasing numbers of students who arrive at school experiencing considerable emotional stress, and classes in which students' abilities vary widely, teachers are experiencing a heightened need for increased effectiveness in motivating and managing students. The movement toward increased inclusion of students with various disabilities has intensified teachers' needs in this area.

Fortunately, technology in classroom management has kept pace with the increasing demands placed on teachers. Research in classroom management has grown explosively in the last 25 years. Most teachers trained in the 1960s learned only such simple prescriptions as "don't smile until Christmas" or "don't grin until Thanksgiving." By the mid 1990s, however, thousands of articles and hundreds of thoughtful research projects focused on student behavior and learning. The concept of school discipline, which had concentrated on dealing with inevitable student misbehavior, was replaced by the concept of classroom management, which emphasized methods of facilitating positive student behavior and achievement.

Unfortunately, too few teachers have been provided with clear, usable materials that enable them to develop essential knowledge in classroom organization and student motivation and management. In a National Education Association special report, *Conditions and Resources of Teaching* (NEA, 1988), teachers rated undergraduate education courses and in-service training as the 2 least effective sources of job-related knowledge and skills. Graduate courses fared only slightly better, rating tenth of the 14 sources listed.

This fourth edition of *Comprehensive Classroom Management* responds to this need. The purpose of this book, however, is much more than to provide the reader with strategies for maintaining order in classrooms and schools or even to increase student achievement. As we discuss in Chapters 1 and 2, U.S. education is struggling to provide an effective educational experience to a wide range of students. We are encouraged by books such as Forrest Gathercoal's (1993) *Judicious Discipline,* William Glasser's (1990) *The Quality School,* and Curwin and Mendler's (1988) *Discipline with Dignity,* which emphasize schools as communities of caring and support in which students are helped to learn responsible behavior.

Our purpose is to provide the reader with specific strategies for creating positive, supportive, respectful environments that encourage all students to view themselves and learning in a positive light. Our heartfelt desire is that the book will increase each reader's ability to empower students to believe in themselves, understand the learning environment, and view the school as a place where their dignity is enhanced and where they can direct and take credit for their own learning. We agree with Tetreault's (1993) statement that

> to educate students for a complex, multicultural, multiracial world, we need to include the perspectives and voices of those who have not been traditionally included—women of all backgrounds, people of color, and females and males who perceive their education as not made for us. (p. 141)

We also concur with Mary McCaslin and Thomas Good (1992), who wrote:

> We believe that the intended modern school curriculum, which is designed to produce self-motivated, active learners, is seriously undermined by classroom management policies that encourage, if not demand, simple obedience. We advocate that a curriculum that seeks to promote problem solving and meaningful learning must be aligned with an authoritative management system that increasingly allows students to operate as self-regulated and risk-taking learners. (p. 4)

Although authors can provide research-proven methods and the theory that supports their use in schools and classrooms, we realize that the teacher is the decision maker. We know that making changes in the classroom is difficult and risky and that making changes in the school is even more difficult. However, we strongly believe (and the best current educational research supports) that in order to create schools that will help an increasing number of students succeed in life, educators must implement many of the methods presented throughout this book. We acknowledge and respect that teachers must consider each new approach in light of their personal styles and teaching situations; we also know that the methods in this book have proven effective for thousands of teachers. Engaging in thoughtful, reflective decision making before implementing a new approach is the sign of a competent professional; inaction is no longer professionally responsible.

AUDIENCE

This book is for preservice and in-service teachers, counselors, administrators, school psychologists, and special educators. Its comprehensive and research-based presentation offers practical ideas for creating positive classroom and school climates, organizing and managing classrooms, improving instruction, dealing with classroom discipline problems, and developing schoolwide student management programs. These ideas enable educators in their various roles to understand the broad issues and skills involved in effective classroom management, instruction, and schoolwide student management and to work collegially in responding to unproductive student behavior.

The concepts and strategies presented in this book will assist educators who work with a wide range of students. They stem from research and have been field-tested by thousands of teachers who work with students who are African American, Hispanic, Native American, Asian, Anglo, poor, rich, learning disabled, emotionally disturbed, and talented and gifted. Although educators who work with students at risk for school failure will find these methods essential to their students' success, those who work with students who are successful will find that implementing the ideas in this book will enrich their own and their students' educational experiences.

APPROACH

Materials used to train teachers and administrators have too often focused on isolated aspects of effective instruction and management. To develop a realistic, workable approach to classroom management, educators have had to seek out and integrate information from literally dozens of sources—each of which has claimed to provide "the answer." This fourth edition of *Comprehensive Classroom Management* offers a thorough research-based synthesis of current knowledge in effective classroom management, instruction, and schoolwide student management.

"Recent research makes it clear that successful classroom management involves not merely responding effectively when problems occur, but preventing problems from occurring frequently" (Brophy, 1983, p. 23). Extensive review of the research and our own experiences in classrooms highlight five major factors or skill areas involved in effective classroom management:

1. Developing a solid understanding of students' personal/psychological and learning needs
2. Establishing positive teacher-student and peer relationships that help meet students' basic psychological needs
3. Implementing instructional methods that facilitate optimal learning by responding to the academic needs of individual students and the classroom group

4. Using organizational and group management methods that maximize on-task student behavior
5. Using a wide range of counseling and behavioral methods that involve students in examining and correcting their inappropriate behavior.

This emphasis on providing a variety of specific methods to consider does not, however, imply that teachers should implement these methods by rote. We believe that teachers should (and will) implement recommendations selectively, attending to their own teaching styles, learning goals, students' needs, and other context variables. Because we have always been deeply involved in schools and in teacher training, it seems obvious that research "can extend the range of hypotheses (alternative strategies) considered and sensitize the teacher to the possible consequences of his/her actions" (Good & Power, 1976, p. 47). However, research cannot prescribe a universal set of methods that will be effective in all instances.

We have stayed away from providing a cookbook of what to do if Johnny cheats or steals because we agree with Allen Mendler (1992), who wrote:

> It will never be possible to compile a list of all possible techniques to be used when problem behaviors occur. Formulas fail to fit all situations. It is therefore more important that educators be guided by a sound set of principles and guidelines from which they can use existing strategies or develop new ones. (p. 26)

The importance of encouraging teachers to consider context variables, including instructional goals and students' age, gender, socioeconomic level, culture, and cognitive skills, has been pointed out by a number of writers and researchers. As Brophy and Evertson (1976) stated:

> Effective teaching requires the ability to implement a very large number of diagnostic, instructional, managerial, and therapeutic skills, tailoring behavior in specific contexts and situations to the specific needs of the moment. Effective teachers not only must be able to do a large number of things; they also must be able to recognize which of the many things they know how to do applies at a given moment and be able to follow through by performing the behavior effectively. (p. 139)

As mentioned earlier, our approach places a major emphasis on creating positive learning environments and empowering students to understand and be actively involved in classroom management and instruction. We strongly believe that a significant number of serious management problems are a response to the manner in which students are treated as human beings and the types of instructional tasks they are asked to perform.

Any writer (or reader) must be cautious about how research is used as a framework for making practical decisions. In determining the methods to be presented in this book and the research used to support and expand these methods, we have made numerous choices. These choices are based on extensive study of the available research; on personal and professional acquaintance with leading researchers and writers in the field; and on our own experience as regular classroom teachers, special educators, public school administrator, pre- and in-service teacher trainers, psychologist, and researcher. Our decisions are also based on Elliot Eisner's (1984) ideas about translating educational research into useful prescriptions for practitioners. Responsible use of research, according to Eisner, requires that the educator should "have examined a body of research studies, extracted generalizations, determined that the theory is supported by the evidence, and then used the theory as a tool for shaping decisions" (p. 448). He also suggested that people involved in educational research (and, we trust, in preservice and in-service teacher training) should have "an intimate acquaintance with life in classrooms" (p. 450). The material presented throughout this book meets these criteria.

The methods have been used by us and by numerous teachers whom we have taught and with whom we have worked during the past 25 years. During the past 15 years, the methods have been field-tested by teachers in hundreds of classrooms evenly divided among primary, intermediate, middle, and high school settings (Jones, 1991). These settings include classrooms in inner-city, rural, and suburban schools.

ORGANIZATION OF THE TEXT

Comprehensive Classroom Management is divided into five parts. Part I presents an overview of the history and key concepts associated with classroom management and its relationship to students' basic personal and psychological needs. This overview provides a theoretical foundation for understanding and thoughtfully implementing the practical suggestions in later chapters. Part II focuses on interpersonal relationships in the classroom and on the interaction between school and home as key factors influencing students' behavior and achievement. Part III examines motivation and instruction as major variables influencing student behavior. Part IV provides numerous research-supported, practical strategies for improving classroom organization and management. Part V presents methods for working with individual students who experience ongoing and/or serious behavior problems.

The book and chapter organization helps readers implement the content into their classroom management process. Chapter 1 presents an overview of classroom management that can help the reader understand the issue of classroom management. Each subsequent chapter begins with an overview of the chapter's topic and presents data to support the value of teachers' changing to incorporate the specific ideas presented throughout the chapter. This overview is followed by specific methods teachers can consider as alternatives to how they currently manage their classroom. Each chapter concludes with activities to help the reader implement the skills presented in the chapter and evaluate the results.

This edition of *Comprehensive Classroom Management* includes many innovative methods stemming from new research and the authors' extensive work with school staff throughout the country. Specific changes include:

- A greater focus on multicultural education and issues of gender
- An increased focus on the alignment between students' needs, learning styles, and cultures and the instructional and behavior management methods used in schools

- An increased focus on actively involving students in understanding and taking responsibility for their learning environment and for demonstrating positive behavior
- An increased number of case studies and examples from classrooms where teachers have used the methods in this book
- A new section on the key aspects of an effective schoolwide student management plan and the process for developing and implementing such a plan
- New ideas for working with students experiencing serious behavior problems who are "mainstreamed" into regular education classes

ACKNOWLEDGMENTS

We wish to acknowledge the many teachers whose application of the methods presented in *Comprehensive Classroom Management* have validated their effectiveness. Specifically, we thank Susan Foster, Mark Gaulke, Peter Grauff, Heather Lilley, Dean Long, Lisa Stevens, Marjorie Miller Tonole, and Terri Vann for allowing us to use student behavior change projects they completed in our graduate classes. We also thank Marty Voge for providing us with Figure 11.3. Our special appreciation goes to Cory Dunn for his assistance in developing Figure 1.5, his work in developing the concept of the curriculum of responsibility, his sharing of the Think–Feel–Act model to problem solving and the associated case study presented here, and his work on the systems approach. We have learned a great deal from working with Cory during the past 10 years.

Our thanks also go to the following educators for their thoughtful comments on the previous editions: Karen A. Bosch, Old Dominion University; Kathryn Castle, Oklahoma State University; Charles P. Doyle, DePaul University; Peter J. Gilman, Hardin-Simmons University; and George Miller, Western Michigan University. Additional thanks to Bernice Magnus-Brown, University of Maine at Orono, and Thomas J. Buttery, East Carolina University, whose reviews assisted us in preparing this new edition.

Foundations of Comprehensive Classroom Management

Theory and practice in classroom management have improved dramatically during the past two decades. Unfortunately, practical methods presented to teachers have often been simplistic and piecemeal. Because of public and teacher concern about student behavior, new ideas have too often been quickly marketed as panaceas. Rather than helping teachers understand the issues in effective classroom management and the relationship among various strategies, much published material has presented unidimensional approaches to small aspects of classroom management. There methods have usually failed to affect students' behavior significantly or have solved only a few of the teachers' problems with discipline. When this occurs, teachers are left with a sense of frustration and impotence. They must either blame themselves or ask if the profession has anything meaningful to offer in the way of ideas on classroom management.

Part I is directed toward alleviating the confusion associated with the topic of classroom management. It examines the major causes of unproductive student behavior and provides a theoretical and philosophical foundation from which to examine approaches that encourage positive student behavior and achievement and respond to disruptive behavior. Chapter 1 places the concept of classroom management in perspective by examining the extent of the problem, considering the reasons for an increase in problems associated with student behavior, describing the history of classroom management, defining comprehensive classroom management, and discussing the relationship between classroom management and the teacher's professional needs. Chapter 2 examines students' personal needs that must be met for them to become productively involved in the learning process. Discussions of classroom management have too often overemphasized controlling unproductive student behavior rather than creating environments that encourage productive behavior. The concepts in Chapter 2 provide a foundation for refocusing attention on preventive interventions.

After completing Part I, you should understand why discipline problems arise and the factors that can be examined and implemented in order to reduce these problems. This perspective provides a basis for employing the preventive and corrective strategies described throughout the book. Perhaps more important, this understanding will enable you to analyze your own classroom or school environment creatively and to evaluate how you might implement the ideas presented in this book or create new solutions for dealing with the behavior problems that occur in your school.

CHAPTER 1

Classroom Management in Perspective

Almost all surveys of teacher effectiveness report that classroom management skills are of primary importance in determining teaching success, whether it is measured by student learning or by ratings. Thus, management skills are crucial and fundamental. A teacher who is grossly inadequate in classroom management skills is probably not going to accomplish much.

—Jere Brophy and Carolyn Evertson (1976)
Learning from Teaching

The concept of classroom management is broader than the notion of student discipline. It includes all the things teachers must do to foster student involvement and cooperation in classroom activities and to establish a productive working environment.

—Julie Sanford, Edmund Emmer, and Barbara Clements
"Improving Classroom Management"
Educational Leadership

The findings show that teachers who approach classroom management as a process of establishing and maintaining effective learning environments tend to be more successful than teachers who place more emphasis on their roles as authority figures or disciplinarians.

—Thomas L. Good and Jere Brophy (1994)
Looking in Classrooms

Classroom management can and should do more than elicit predictable obedience; indeed, it can and should be one vehicle for the enhancement of student self-understanding, self-evaluation, and the internalization of self-control.

—Mary McCaslin and Thomas L. Good (1992)
"Compliant Cognition"
Educational Researcher

Student behavior problems have for years been a major concern of teachers, administrators, and parents. National concern about students' achievement has intensified public interest in schools and students' behavior. Although teachers face the task of educating many students whose home and community environments are disruptive, research demonstrates that teachers' skills in managing classrooms are a major factor influencing students' motivation, achievement, and behavior. In a recent meta-analysis of factors influencing student learning, classroom management was identified as the most important factor (Wang, Haertel, & Walberg, 1993). The concept of discipline, with its emphasis on dealing with inevitable misbehavior among students, has been replaced by a more comprehensive body of knowledge on how to increase students' achievement by preventing management problems.

EXTENT OF THE PROBLEM

The issue of student behavior has been a longstanding concern of laypersons and educators. Since its inception in 1969, the annual Gallup Poll of the Public's Attitudes toward the Public Schools has found school discipline to be the public's primary educational concern on 16 occasions. From 1986 through 1991, discipline was viewed as second to drug use as the biggest problem facing the U.S. public schools; in 1992 and 1993, concerns about student behavior ranked third behind concerns regarding school funding and drug use.

Teachers echo the public's concern about student behavior. In a 1987 study conducted for the Center for Education Statistics, 44 percent of public school teachers reported more disruptive classroom behavior in their schools than five years earlier, and 28 percent indicated that problems were about the same. Almost one-third of teachers (29 percent) stated that they had seriously considered leaving teaching because of student misbehavior, and teachers estimated that about 7 percent of their students were habitual behavior problems. In June 1989, the second Gallup Phi Delta Kappa Poll of Teachers' Attitudes toward the Public Schools reported that 50 percent of the teachers surveyed rated the discipline problems in their community as "very serious" or "fairly serious" (up 1 percent from 1984). Even though 93 percent of teachers in the study reported that their school had a written discipline policy, 34 percent regarded it as too lenient, 28 percent said it was not comprehensive, and 50 percent stated that it was not applied consistently. In 1991, 44 percent of teachers nationwide reported that student misbehavior interfered substantially with their teaching (Mansfield, Alexander, & Farris, 1991). This same study showed that 19 percent of teachers reported being verbally abused by a student in the previous four weeks and 28 percent of the teachers viewed physical conflicts among students as a serious or moderate problem in their school.

Reporting on a large sample of elementary and secondary teachers, Blase (1986) concluded that teachers perceive as most stressful student behavior that is aggressive and that interrupts classroom events. Feitler and Tokar (1992) reported that 58 percent of the 3,300 K–12 public school teachers in their sample "ranked 'individual pupils who constantly misbehave' as the number one cause of job-related stress" (pp. 156–157). Emmer (1994) recently reported that many of the events that evoke negative teacher emotions are related either directly or indirectly to issues of student behavior.

These findings also are no surprise, considering the amount of time teachers are involved in managing students' behavior. Gump (1967) reported that approximately half of teachers' actions involved instruction. The remainder of teachers' behavior involved such management functions as organizing and arranging students for instruction (23 percent), dealing with misbehavior (14 percent), and handling individual problems (12 percent). A study (Wragg, 1984) of 36 British teachers observed during 213 lesson hours in classes of mixed ability found that 54 percent of teachers' behavior involved management functions. Doyle (1986) presented an impressive review of research indicating the interdependence of management and instruction functions. Simply stated, students' learning is directly related to classroom order.

The current mandate to increase the extent to which students with disabilities are educated in regular classrooms requires that teachers improve their classroom management skills. Research indicates that teachers spend significantly more time instructing and managing these special students and have between 60 and 90 percent more interactions with them than with students not identified under the law (Thompson, White, & Morgan, 1982).

Also, the increasing number of students experiencing social/emotional problems places a premium on teachers using effective classroom management skills. A study conducted by the University of Washington School of Medicine (Trupin, Low, Forsyth-Stephens, Tarico, & Cox, 1988) reported that nearly 7 percent of the children in Washington (state) public schools may be seriously emotionally disturbed.

While writing this edition, one of the authors was asked by an elementary school staff to provide a workshop on working with students who have conduct disorders. When the staff was asked to provide more specificity by describing what was meant by "conduct disorders," the staff sent the author a description of the students in one of the teacher's classes (Figure 1.1). During the 1993–94 school year, the authors asked over 2,000 teacher to state whether they thought the profile given in Figure 1.1 was atypical. The most common response was that primary-grade teachers thought the description was quite similar to their own classes, whereas intermediate-level teachers indicated that, perhaps because their students were older, had experienced more life difficulties and received more testing at school, this was a very conservative list.

School administrators share teachers' and parents' concerns. In a 1986 survey conducted by the Center for Statistics, U.S. Department of Education, two-thirds of the junior and senior high school principals stated that even though school discipline was less of a problem than five years ago, it was still a major problem, and 12 percent stated that discipline problems in their schools were worse. Administrators also reported suspending an average of 10 students out of every 100 each year for disciplinary reasons. In 1990–91, 1 million students were suspended out of school and 1.4 million students were given some form of in-school suspension. According to a U.S. Department of Education's Office for Civil Rights 1993 report, 54 percent of these students were White, 32 percent were African American, and 12 percent were Hispanic. This is clearly a disproportionate suspension rate for students of color.

Regardless of whether disruptive behavior or low achievement troubles us most, students' attendance and the number of students who fail to graduate provide additional cause for alarm. In 1991, only 85.7 percent of 21- and 22-year-olds in

8 are in Chapter 1 (3 of which will test out as learning disabled)

1 is on a reading individual education plan

1 is an English-as-a-second-language student

3 are receiving assistance for speech problems

3 are receiving in-school counseling

2 are receiving out-of-school counseling

1 has a history of physical abuse

3 are from homes with a history of domestic violence

2 have been sexually abused

1 child lives in a shelter home

1 child is in his fourth school since kindergarten; several others in their third

2 students have been evicted from their apartments for setting fire to them

FIGURE 1.1
A Profile of a
First-Grade Class

Reprinted by permission.

the United States had graduated from high school. The rate for White students was 90 percent, the rate was 81 percent for Black students, and the rate was 61 percent for Hispanic students (Kaufman, McMillen, & Bradby, 1992).

Obviously, it is insufficient merely to document the severity of student behavior problems. Educators must understand why these problems arise. There are two basic reasons classroom management continues to be a major problem in U.S. schools. First, teachers are asked to instruct a wide range of students, many of whom come to school with varying degrees of emotional distress and inadequate personal skills. Second, despite significant research and the associated dramatic increase in methods for effectively motivating and managing students, many teachers have received only a limited amount of useful information about how to organize and manage classrooms in order to maximize productive student learning and behavior. The following sections examine why student behavior continues to be a major problem in U.S. schools and present a conceptual framework for understanding the steps that can be taken to reduce the problem dramatically.

SOCIAL FACTORS INFLUENCING STUDENTS' BEHAVIOR

Although teachers cannot immediately or directly alter the social factors that create students' problems, understanding these factors does enable teachers to place students' failure and disruptive behavior in perspective and to create environments that reduce rather than intensify their effects. When discussing the problem of disruptive or disturbed student behavior, teachers often ask why these problems seem to have increased during the past decade. Indeed, as education and psychology have developed an increasingly sophisticated body of knowledge, teachers have entered the classroom better trained than before. There is little question that today's teachers better understand such topics as human development and the learning process than did teachers 10 years ago. Therefore, although unproductive student behavior is often a response to factors within schools and classrooms, it seems reasonable to assume that today's school environments are, in general, more supportive of students' needs and more conducive to learning than they were 10 or 20 years ago. Consequently, though improving teachers' skills remains a major component in combating unproductive student behavior, other variables must be considered in order to develop a comprehensive understanding of the intensified problems of classroom discipline.

Divorce and subsequent single-parent households has skyrocketed in the United States in the past 40 years. Only 11 percent of children born in the 1950s experienced their parents being separated or divorced; nearly 55 percent of students born in the 1990s will experience this phenomenon (Whitehead, 1993). In addition, one in every four children growing up in the 1990s will live in a stepfamily, and it appears that, by their teens, nearly half of these children will experience a second divorce as their stepfamily breaks up. Finally, the out-of-wedlock birthrate jumped from only 5 percent in 1960 to 27 percent in 1990. These figures clearly indicate the extent of family breakup, disruption, and emotional turmoil experienced by students. In a report from the Children's Defense Fund, Haycock (1990) indicated that 12 million children (over 20 percent) live in poverty and have no health insurance. The fastest growing group of homeless people in this country is families with children. Finally, a 1994 report by the National Committee on the Prevention of Child Abuse suggests an increase in the number of reports of child abuse and neglect. The committee stated that there were nearly three million reported cases of child abuse and over one million cases verified in 1993 (Edmonds, 1994).

During the past decade, runaways have doubled from 1 to 2 million youth, and the number of suicides in the United States are eight times those of Japan. In addition, even homes that may look like safe, prosperous, nurturing environments often create stress for children as working parents expect children to take on major family responsibilities without adult supervision and encourage children to become involved in numerous out-of-school activities. Indeed, studies indicate that young people who commit suicide are often high achievers unable to handle the stress of fast-paced lives and high expectations for achievement in multiple tasks.

Family stress clearly impacts students' ability to function effectively in school. Based on the National Longitudinal Study of 1988 in which a cohort of 25,000 eighth-graders from across the nation were followed through 1990, the

"He doesn't listen to a thing we say, he's very noisy, and he's always getting into trouble. I think he's ready to start school."

data from the National Center for Education Statistics showed that students "who were from single-parent families, or who had frequently changed schools were more likely than other students to have low basic skills in mathematics and reading and were more likely to drop out regardless of their sex, race-ethnicity, or SES" (Kaufman, Bradby, & Owings, 1992, pp. 15–16).

Certainly, students' use of drug and alcohol is partially a response to the increasingly stressful lives they live. Substance abuse is another social factor that reduces the time, energy, and ability of students to attend to academic tasks. The University of Michigan's Institute for Social Research released results on January 31, 1994, indicating a sharp rise in drug and alcohol use throughout the country. This report of the nineteenth annual survey of high school seniors and the third annual survey of eighth- and tenth-graders found an increased use of marijuana, stimulants, LSD, inhalants, and cigarette smoking. Two-thirds of all eighth-graders and almost 90 percent of the seniors had tried alcohol, and 25 percent of the eighth-graders and 50 percent of the seniors had used alcohol in the month prior to the survey. Sadly, 14 percent of the eighth-graders, 23 percent of the tenth-graders, and 28 percent of the seniors reported drinking five or more drinks in a row (binge drinking) in the two weeks prior to the survey. The report also showed that in the past 12 months, 9 percent of the eighth-graders, 19 percent of the tenth-graders and 26 percent of the twelfth-graders had used marijuana. While this level of use is below the levels reported in the late 1970s, from 1991 to 1993 this study reports an increase of 50 percent for eighth-graders, 25 percent for tenth-graders, and 20 percent by seniors.

Student drug use illustrates the importance of considering both social and school variables as factors influencing student behavior and learning. Certainly, educators are not solely or even primarily responsible for this problem that affects them so profoundly. Conversely, schools often provide learning environments that fail to engage a large segment of students actively and meaningfully. This situation possibly increases the likelihood that students will abuse substances during school hours and will choose substance abuse rather than involvement in school-based activities.

SCHOOL FACTORS INFLUENCING STUDENTS' LEARNING AND BEHAVIOR

Even though social factors have made the teacher's job more difficult, studies indicate that teachers and schools make a dramatic difference in the lives of many children. In her book, *Adolescents at Risk: Prevalence and Prevention,* Joy Dryfoos (1990) examined current research on the causes and possible prevention and response to such serious problems as drug use, early pregnancy, school failure, and delinquency. She summed up the important role school personnel play:

> Many of the interventions in the other fields incorporated educational enhancement as the major program component. In fact, the prevention of delinquency appears to be embedded in the prevention of school failure. Whether delinquency prevention is actually a field in itself or whether it should be subsumed under the rubric of educa-

tional remediation is an unresolved issue. To a great degree, this may be true of prevention of substance abuse and teen pregnancy as well. The acquisition of basic skills at appropriate ages appears to be a primary component of all prevention. (pp. 236–237)

A comprehensive, realistic examination of students' behavior must consider the methods of classroom organization and management that increase students' attending behavior and basic skill acquisition. Instructional factors that provide students with a sense of meaningful involvement in the school and community as well as encouraging thoughtful and creative examination of issues presented in a meaningful, dynamic curriculum must also be considered.

Teachers have control over many factors that significantly influence the achievement and behavior of students. Schools and teachers working with similar student populations differ dramatically in their ability to help students develop desirable behavior and increase students' achievement. Mortimore and Sammons (1987) summarized their extensive research on factors that influence students' academic and social gains:

> In our measurement of reading progress, we found the school to be about six times more important than backgrounds (factors of age, sex, social class, and race). For written math and writing, the difference is tenfold. The analyses of speech and of the social outcomes also confirm the overriding importance of school. . . . It is the policies and processes within the control of the principal and teachers that are crucial. These factors can be changed and improved. (p. 6)

This finding is similar in many ways to that reported by William Wayson and Gay Su Pinnell (1982) following their studies of high schools varying in amounts of discipline problems experienced:

> When discipline problems occur in school, they can more often be traced to dysfunctions in the interpersonal climate and organizational patterns of the school than to malfunctions in the individual. In short, misbehaving students are often reacting in a predictable and even sensible way to the school as it affects them and as they have learned to perceive it and react to it. We are not blaming the teacher, the principal, or the custodian for student misbehavior. But we would have them see that the system of roles and relationships in which they engage are often to blame for misbehavior. In most cases, better behavior may be taught more easily by altering patterns of roles and relationships in the school organization than by viewing and treating the student as a pathological problem. (p. 117)

The Office of Educational Research and Improvement (OERI) publication *Review of Research on Ways to Attain Goal 6: Creating Safe, Disciplined, and Drug-Free Schools* includes a description of what school staff need to do to reach this important goal:

> In the past decade, research has demonstrated that there are important school-to-school differences across secondary schools in these important student behaviors and outcomes, differences that cannot be completely accounted for by the background of

students in a school. Three dimensions of school climate appear to account for these differences:

- Goals: a strong emphasis on academic mission in the school;
- Rules and procedures: clear disciplinary standards that are firmly, fairly, and consistently enforced;
- Climate: an "ethic of caring" that guides interpersonal relationships in the school.

Each of these aspects of schools can affect outcomes independently, but when they occur in combination and are widely accepted and practiced, researchers have found that they constitute powerful and coherent school "ethos" or culture that increases the engagement of students in the academic work of schools, decreases disruptive and violent behavior in schools, and lends to increased student achievement. (Aleem & Moles, 1993, p. 12)

To make significant changes in student learning and behavior, we must seriously look at a broad range of variables in the school setting and embrace opportunities for changing our teaching behavior and how schools are structured.

Findings from several major national studies place this matter in an interesting perspective. In his book *A Place Called School,* John Goodlad (1984) provided strong support for the necessity of viewing student behavior problems as more than a response to poorly controlled classrooms. In summarizing the findings, Goodlad (1983b) stated:

The dominant instructional practices we observed in more than 1,000 classrooms (and which most staff development programs emphasize) appear to provide few opportunities for students to engage in the behaviors implied by the more exalted academic purposes of education, to say nothing of those other goals of citizenship, civility, and creativity to which state documents claim commitment. (p. 553)

Being a spectator not only deprives one of participation, but also leaves one's mind free for unrelated activity. If academic learning does not engage students, something else will. (p. 554)

Additional observational studies have confirmed Goodlad's findings. In *Horace's Compromise,* Ted Sizer (1984) stated, "No more important finding has emerged from the inquiries of our study than that the American high school student, as student, is all too often docile, compliant, and without initiative" (p. 54). This sentiment was reinforced by Ernest Boyer (1983) in his *High School: A Report on Secondary Education in America* and by Joan Lipsitz's (1984) study of effective middle schools, presented in her *Successful Schools for Young Adolescents.*

Walter Doyle's (1983) examination of academic work suggests that teachers often select methods of instruction that, while focusing on rote learning, are easily managed in terms of maintaining control. Also, some teachers handle the problem of classroom control by excluding students of lower ability from active participation in classroom activities or by reinforcing incorrect answers by these students in order to maintain a smooth classroom flow.

Students' attitudes toward school are another strong indication that school factors contribute greatly to students' academic and behavior problems. When Jane Norman and Myron Harris (1981) surveyed 160,000 teenagers for their book *The*

Private Life of the American Teenager, they discovered that only 42 percent of the students described school as "necessary," 21 percent found it "interesting," and 27 percent said school was "boring." Additionally, 60 percent of the students said they studied primarily to pass tests rather than to learn. Another study conducted by the National Center for Educational Statistics (1988) reported that more than half of the high school seniors sampled found their part-time jobs more enjoyable than school. When John Goodlad (1983a) asked students to identify the best thing about school, 34.9 percent said "friends," 13.4 percent said "sports," 7 percent said "classes," 4.1 percent said "teachers," and 8 percent said "nothing." Given these findings, we should not be surprised that more than 55 percent of teenagers state they cheat in school (Norman & Harris, 1981).

Researchers at the Center for Research on the Context of Secondary School Teaching (CRC) at Stanford University are currently studying factors in high schools that support learning (Phelan, Davidson, & Cao, 1992). Their studies are focused on determining students' perceptions regarding the school community. In examining the impact of social versus school factors, these authors have noted:

> Of most importance to practitioners and policy makers is the fact that many of the forces students mention are not objective constraints but factors under the control of teachers and principals. Furthermore, these young people present a view of themselves that may be surprising to those who are convinced that the plethora of social problems precludes effective responses through school improvement efforts. We find that, despite negative outside influences, students from all achievement levels and sociocultural backgrounds want to succeed and want to be in an environment in which it is possible to do so. (p. 696)

Parents' concerns about education support much of what researchers are saying regarding the importance of the school and classroom environment. A colleague recently held a workshop for parents serving on local school advisory committees. He reported that the parents' main concern was that students do not experience a respectful, democratic environment in the schools. As will be discussed throughout this book, students' and parents' perspectives on the quality of relationships they experience when dealing with school staff and the extent to which they are actively and meaningfully involved in the educational process are key factors that influence students' performance and behavior.

CLASSROOM MANAGEMENT: A HISTORICAL PERSPECTIVE

Given the large number of approaches to classroom management, it is helpful for teachers to place these methods into a historical perspective. To help you develop a professional perspective, this section describes three classroom management concepts and methods presented to teachers during the past four decades.

The Counseling Approach

During the 1960s and through much of the 1970s, the emphasis in dealing with student behavior was on discipline. The little training that teachers received focused on what to do *after* students misbehaved. Because the emphasis in psychology during the late 1960s and early 1970s was on personal growth and awareness, most methods focused on understanding students' problems and helping them better understand themselves and work cooperatively with adults to develop more productive behaviors.

One of the earliest and most widely used models was William Glasser's reality therapy (1965). Glasser's model derived from the belief that young people need caring professionals willing to help them take responsibility for their behavior and develop plans aimed at altering unproductive conduct. Rudolf Dreikurs and his associates (1971) developed a somewhat more clinical model based on the belief that acting-out children made poor choices because of inappropriate notions of how to meet their basic need to be accepted. Dreikurs proposed a variety of methods for responding to children's misconduct, depending on the goal of the behavior. His model provided teachers and parents with strategies for identifying the causes of students' misbehavior, responding to misbehavior with logical consequences, and running family and classroom meetings.

Emphasis on humanistic psychology was most obvious in the models of self-concept theorists. Initially summarized by LaBenne and Green (1969) and Purkey (1970), this work focused on the relationships among positive student self-concepts, students' learning, and productive behavior. This work was extended to a more practical program for teachers by Tom Gordon (1974), whose *Teacher Effectiveness Training* provided them with techniques for responding to students' misbehavior with open communication and attempts at mutually solving problems.

The focus on problem solving and communication skills began receiving renewed attention in the late 1980s. Drawing on the work of the preceding writers, Jim Fay developed his program, "Discipline with Love and Logic," which emphasizes providing students with clear cues regarding their behavior, using effective communication skills such as sending I-messages, providing students with choices, and utilizing logical and natural consequences. In his book *Judicious Discipline*, attorney and educational psychologist Forrest Gathercoal (1993) provided educators with an excellent foundation for viewing school rules and decisions regarding student behavior based on the Bill of Rights. Gathercoal's thoughtful work provides a foundation for a democratic and responsible approach to managing students' behavior.

Behavioristic Methods

As social uneasiness rose about disruptive behavior of youth, the focus of classroom discipline moved in the direction of teacher control. This increased attention to discipline was associated with the development and popularization of behavioristic methodology. Beginning in the mid-1970s, most courses aimed at helping teachers cope with disruptive student behavior focused almost exclusively on behavior modification techniques. Teachers were taught to ignore inappropriate behavior while reinforcing appropriate behavior, to write contracts with recalcitrant students, and to use time-out procedures. This emphasis on control was most systematically presented to teachers in Lee Canter's (1976) *Assertive Discipline*. Teachers learned to state clear general behavioral expectations, quietly and consistently punish disruptive students, and provide group reinforcement for on-task behavior. Behavioral control has also been emphasized in the work of Fredric Jones (1987). Jones focuses on the teachers' effective use of body language, the use of incentive systems, and individual assistance for academic problems.

During the 1980s, behaviorists began to move away from traditional behaviorism with its emphasis on rewards and consequences and began emphasizing interventions that more actively involved the student. These interventions include such methods as self-monitoring, self-talk, and social skills training (Carpenter & Apter, 1988; Nelson & Rutherford, 1988).

Teacher-Effectiveness Research

While counseling- and control-oriented approaches vied for popularity, a new emphasis on classroom management was developing during the 1970s. This new direction emphasized not what teachers did in response to student misconduct but rather how teachers prevented or contributed to students' misbehavior. This research, later labeled *teacher effectiveness,* focused attention on three sets of teacher behaviors that influence students' behavior and learning: (1) teachers' skills in organizing and managing classroom activities, (2) teachers' skills in presenting instructional material, and (3) teacher-student relationships.

Teachers' Organizational and Management Skills

A study that initially displayed the importance of teachers' organizational and management skills was reported in Jacob Kounin's 1970 book, *Discipline and Group Management in Classrooms.* Kounin and colleagues videotaped thousands of hours in classrooms that ran smoothly with a minimum of disruptive behavior and classrooms in which students were frequently inattentive and disruptive. The videotapes were then systematically analyzed to determine what teachers in these two very different types of classrooms did differently when students misbehaved. The results showed no systematic differences. Effective classroom managers were not notably different from poor classroom managers in their ways of responding to students' misbehavior. Further analysis, however, demonstrated clear and significant differences between how effective and ineffective classroom managers behaved prior to students' misbehavior. Effective classroom managers used various teaching methods that prevented disruptive student behavior.

The Texas Teacher Effectiveness Study was a second landmark study dealing with organizing and managing behavior. In this study, reported in *Learning from Teaching* by Jere Brophy and Carolyn Evertson (1976), the researchers observed 59 teachers over two years. Teachers were selected to provide two groups whose students differed consistently in performance on standardized achievement tests. Classroom observations focused on teachers' behaviors previously suggested as being related to effective teaching. The results of the study supported Kounin's findings on effective behaviors that prevented disruption and facilitated learning by creating smoothly run classrooms.

The findings of Kounin and of Brophy and Evertson were expanded by Emmer, Evertson, and Anderson (1980) in the Classroom Organization and Effective Teaching Project carried out at the Research and Development Center for Teacher Education at the University of Texas at Austin. In the first of a series of studies, these researchers observed 28 third-grade classrooms during the first several weeks of school. The research findings showed that the smooth functioning found in effective teachers' classrooms throughout the school year mostly resulted from effective planning and organization during the first few weeks of school. Effective classroom managers provided students with clear instruction in desirable classroom behavior and carefully monitored students' performance—reteaching behaviors that students had not mastered. Effective teachers also made consequences for misbehavior clear and applied these consistently. This study was followed by research in junior high school classrooms (Evertson, 1985; Evertson & Emmer, 1982a), which verified the importance that early planning and instruction in appropriate behavior have in secondary school settings.

Instructional Skills

A second area of investigation on teachers' behavior that prevents disruptive student behavior and enhances learning examines how material is presented to students. The earliest work on this subject was conducted by Madeline Hunter. For more than two decades, her ITIP (Instructional Theory into Practice) program has attempted to translate findings in educational psychology into practical strategies that improve instruction. Though her work emphasizes some of the skills pointed out by researchers interested in classroom organization and teacher-student relationships, her major contribution is in helping teachers understand the need to develop clear instructional goals, state these to students, provide effective direct instruction, and monitor students' progress.

This research has been expanded by studies that have examined the relationship between various teacher instructional patterns and students' achievement. These studies, often called *process-product research* because they examine correlations between instructional processes and student outcomes or products, are thoughtfully reviewed by Rosenshine (1983) and Good (1983). The third edition of the *Handbook of Research on Teaching* (Wittcock, 1986) contains an excellent series of chapters on this topic. Criticism of this line of research has focused on the fact that no one group of teacher behaviors is related to students' achievement with all ages and types of students and for all learning outcomes. Subsequently, some writers warn against placing too much emphasis on specific teacher skills. These writers suggest that although teachers should be familiar with the results of process-product research, they must use these findings selectively, taking into account the unique characteristics of the students with whom they work and the educational goals they espouse.

A second field of study examines the relative merits of competitive, cooperative, and individualized instruction. This work, carried out by Roger and David Johnson of the University of Minnesota, demonstrates that cooperative learning activities are associated with many desirable learning outcomes. Students who work cooperatively on learning tasks tend to relate more positively to their peers, to view learning as more positive, and to learn more information. Additional work in cooperative team learning was carried out by Robert Slavin, who developed the Teams-Games-Tournaments approach, and by Spencer Kagan (1988), who developed a very practical book entitled *Cooperative Learning: Resources for Teachers.*

Another area of study is the variability in how students learn best and how teachers can adjust instruction to respond to students' individual learning styles. This work—carried out by Rita Dunn (Dunn, 1983; Dunn, Beaudry, & Klavas, 1989), Joseph Renzulli (1983), Anthony Gregorc (1982), and others—shows that when teachers allow students to study in environments conducive to learning and use approaches to learning that are most productive for each student, the students learn much more effectively and behave appropriately. In their *Models of Teaching,* Bruce Joyce and Marsha Weil describe many types of instructional methods that respond to different learning goals and students' learning styles. Joyce and Weil (1986) stated:

> Despite the fearsome troubles besetting education, there presently exists a really delightful and vigorous array of approaches to teaching that can be used to transform the world of schools if only we could employ them.
>
> We believe that strength in education resides in the intelligent use of this powerful variety of approaches—matching them to different goals and adapting them to the students' styles and characteristics. Competence in teaching stems from the capacity to reach out to differing children and to create a rich and multi-dimensional environment for them. (p. xxiii)

Educators are becoming increasingly aware of the importance of multiethnic-multicultural education. This work focuses on the importance of respecting the ethnicity of children and developing curricula that will utilize each child's cultural background to motivate and enhance learning. James Banks (1988) wrote that "multicultural theorists feel strongly that during the process of education the school should not alienate students from their ethnic attachments but should help them clarify their ethnic identities and make them aware of other ethnic and cultural alternatives" (p. 124). In addition to work on curriculum modification, considerable work exists to suggest that students from various ethnic groups benefit from instructional styles different from those that have typically been used in U.S. schools. Books such as Crystal Kuykendall's (1992) *From Rage to Hope: Strategies for Reclaiming Black and Hispanic Student,* Hale-Benson's (1986) *Black Children: Their Roots, Culture and Learning Styles,* and James Banks and Cherry McGee Banks's (1993) *Multicultural Education* discuss instructional strategies that may benefit students of color. Work in this area is essential not only because it is important for all children to have their cultural heritage acknowledged and respected but also because an increasing number of students in U.S. schools will be children of color. Indeed, by the year 2000, 42 percent of all public school students will be students of color (U.S. Bureau of Census, 1986), and by the year 2020, the U.S. population will be 30 percent Black and Hispanic (U.S. Census Bureau, 1990). It is also important to note that while strategies that actively involve students in interacting with others and relating instructional materials to their own lives may be of particular benefit for some students, they are helpful and desirable for all students.

Teacher-Student Relationships

The third major research area within the teacher-effectiveness paradigm focuses on the effect teacher-student interactions have on students' achievement and behavior. This field of study can be divided into two basic parts: (1) studies exploring the influence of the frequency and quality of teacher-student interactions on students' achievement and (2) studies emphasizing the personal, affective dimension of teacher-student relationships and their effect on students' attitudes and, to a lesser degree, achievement.

Robert Rosenthal and Leonore Jacobson's *Pygmalion in the Classroom* (1968) generated tremendous interest in the influence teacher-student relationships have on students' achievement. These authors reported that teachers' expectations for students' performance became self-fulfilling prophecies. In other words, students seem to perform as teachers expect them to. The important question became what specifically teachers do to communicate high or low expectations to students. This question was initially studied by Brophy and Good (1971, 1974) at the University of Texas. This research has been replicated and expanded (Wineburg, 1987), including examination of attribution theory and factors related to teachers' sense of control (Cooper & Good, 1983). Numerous writers have also examined how teacher-student interactions may handicap the achievement of girls. The 1992 American Association of University Professors (AAUP) report *How Schools Short-change Girls* provides an excellent summary of ways in which schools must change if they are to serve one-half of the school population more fairly.

The second area of study involves the affective quality of teacher-student relationships and its effect on students' attitudes and self-concepts. This research was first widely reported in the late 1960s and early 1970s in books such as LaBenne and Green's *Educational Implications of Self-Concept Theory* (1969) and William Purkey's *Self-Concept and School Achievement* (1970). Although interpersonal relationships in the classroom were emphasized less during the mid-1970s, research and practical ideas on this subject received more attention in the early 1980s (Purkey & Novak, 1984).

This topic also began receiving increased attention during the late 1980s. Reports such as the Carnegie Council on Adolescent Development's *Turning Points: Preparing American Youth for the 21st Century* (1989), the Edna McConnell Clark Foundation's *Making it in the Middle: The Why and How of Excellent Schools for Young Urban Adolescents* (Lewis, 1990), and Wehlage, Rutter, Smith, Lesko, and Fernandez's (1989) *Reducing the Risk: Schools as Communities of Support* emphasize the quality of community and the importance of building close bonds between adults and students in schools.

TEACHER TRAINING IN CLASSROOM MANAGEMENT

The wide variety of approaches to classroom management has created a situation in which training in classroom management often involves introducing teachers to theoretical approaches to classroom discipline and providing tips on how to implement these approaches in a classroom. There are, however, several major problems with this method. First, little research evidence supports many of the models presented in such texts (e.g., assertive discipline, teacher-effectiveness training, or Adlerian-based approaches). In a review of the research on several leading approaches to classroom discipline, Emmer and Aussiker (1987) reported that "results of the review provide only limited support for teacher training in the models" (p. i).

Second, methods that focus on isolated models emphasizing responding to disruptive behavior seem to suggest that unproductive student behavior is inevitable. This orientation tends to suggest a limited view of teachers' options in altering classroom environments to increase positive student behavior and learning. In summarizing their findings on popular models of discipline, Emmer and Aussiker (1987) stated, "It is concluded that training in one or more of these models should be viewed as supplemental to a more comprehensive approach to discipline and management" (p. i).

Recent research indicates that the most effective method of responding to disruptive student behavior involves combining preventive classroom management and instructional approaches with corrective methods. A major research project conducted at the Center for Social Welfare Research at the School of Social Work, University of Washington (Hawkins, Doueck, & Lishner, 1988), provides support for a comprehensive approach to classroom management. The project was designed to determine methods to improve the behavior and increase the achievement of low achievers at risk for serious and extended behavioral problems. The project involved providing teachers working with high at-risk seventh-grade students with an in-service package involving proactive classroom management methods, interactive teaching, and cooperative learning. Student attitudes, behavior, and achievement in these classes were compared to those of students taught by teachers who did not receive the training. Results indicated that low-achieving, at-risk students in the experimental classrooms had more positive attitudes toward subject matter, felt more involved in school, had greater expectations for continued school success, and had less serious misbehavior than did students in the control group. This research supports a comprehensive approach to classroom management in which the teacher uses methods to improve peer relationships, instruction, and classroom organization and management.

Research from the Institute for Research on Teaching at Michigan State University indicates that the more effective teachers accept responsibility for student learning and behavior rather than blaming students. These teachers examine their instruction to determine whether students understand and find meaning in their work. They also view aggressive student behavior not as an unmanageable psychological problem but as a behavioral problem requiring resocialization

"You'll find Classroom Discipline in Three Easy Lessons *in fiction."*

and skill training to help the student learn alternative methods for dealing with stressful or conflicting situations.

COMPREHENSIVE CLASSROOM MANAGEMENT: AN ALTERNATIVE

As discussed in the previous section, researchers and writers have approached student behavior problems from a variety of perspectives. Figure 1.2 highlights the key approaches to managing student behavior and the writers associated with each approach. The research conducted and the methods suggested by these educators have contributed much to teachers' ability to manage classrooms effectively.

Unfortunately, because schools of education are constricted in the hours available for education courses and because school districts have limited resources, both preservice and in-service education concerning classroom management too often focus on the work of one or two or these educators or provide a theoretical review of several individuals' work. In many preservice education programs, classroom management is presented as a brief unit in a methods or educational psychology class. In-service presentations on the topic also are often scheduled for only a few hours, thus requiring consultants to teach a few tricks or only one aspect of classroom management, as if they were presenting the answer to teachers' problems. This approach leaves teachers with only a piece of a complex and critical puzzle. When these limited techniques fail to help teachers significantly, the teachers must assume that something is wrong with either themselves or their use of the new methods or that no one really knows how teachers can manage classrooms effectively. The results frequently are confusion, frustration, and ineffectiveness in managing classrooms and individual students' behavior.

Research on staff development suggests that to implement new material into their classrooms, teachers need both a solid theoretical understanding of the material and practice in specific methods or strategies. Therefore, it is extremely important that before attempting to develop or improve your classroom management skills, you have a clear understanding of their scope. Extensive reviews of the research and the authors' own experience in classrooms and schools suggest five major factors or skill areas associated with effective classroom management.

First, *classroom management should be based on a solid understanding of current research and theory in classroom management and on students' personal and psychological needs.* The authors' experience in teaching classroom management courses and consulting with schools suggests that, despite extensive worry about students' achievement and misbehavior, very few teachers understand why problems exist or the relationship between the problem and their own professional behavior. An analysis of data from the 1984 Gallup Poll of Teachers' Attitudes toward the Public Schools shows that "teachers blame disciplinary problems on outside influences—specifically, the courts, lack of respect for authority, and especially lack of discipline in the home, which is mentioned by virtually all teachers (94 percent). Only about one-third of the teachers feel that teachers themselves are at fault" (Gallup, 1984, p. 99).

FIGURE 1.2 Continuum of Classroom Management Strategies

Chapters 3, 4, 5	Chapters 8, 9	Chapters 6, 7	Chapter 10	Chapter 11	Chapter 12
Interpersonal Relationships	*Classroom Organization and Management*	*Curriculum and Instruction*	*Problem Solving*	*Behavior Management*	*Schoolwide Discipline*
Jack Canfield & Harold Wells	Jere Brophy	James Banks	Rudolf Dreikurs	Wesley Becker	Lee Canter
Thomas Gordon	Edmond Emmer	Walter Doyle	Jim Fey	Lee Canter	Daniel Duke
William Purkey	Carolyn Evertson	Rita Dunn	William Glasser	Frank Hewett	Forrest Gathercoal
Richard & Patricia Schmuck	Thomas Good	Thomas Good	Thomas Gordon	Fredric Jones	William Glasser
	Madeline Hunter	Asa Hilliard III	Frank Maple	Daniel O'Leary	Randy Sprick
	Jacob Kounin	Madeline Hunter	Robert Spaulding	Hill Walker	William Wayson
	Jane Stallings	David & Roger Johnson			
		Bruce Joyce			
		Crystal Kuykendall			
		Bernice McCarthy			
		Robert Slavin			
		Jane Stallings			

Once teachers understand students' needs and how these needs are related to behavior, the next step in developing a well-managed classroom is to ensure that students' personal needs are met in the classroom. Therefore, a second factor is *classroom management depends on establishing positive teacher-student and peer relationships that help meet students' basic psychological needs.* Creating more desirable student behavior by concentrating on establishing positive, supportive classroom environments is based on a concept presented by numerous psychologists and educators: Individuals learn more effectively in environments that meet their basic personal and psychological needs.

Although the creation of positive relationships in classrooms can significantly improve student behavior and achievement, research and the authors' observations increasingly support the importance of instructional excellence. Thus, the third factor in effective classroom management is *comprehensive classroom management involves using instructional methods that facilitate optimal learning by responding to the academic needs of individual students and the classroom group.* This aspect of classroom management is based on the idea that "low motivation, negative self attitudes, and failure are largely the result of improper learning conditions. According to this learning-theory analysis, we should be able to alter a student's failure rate by changing the conditions of classroom learning and, as a consequence, increase his motivation to succeed" (Covington & Beery, 1976, pp. 12–13).

Most classrooms house 25 to 35 students. Teachers are responsible for orchestrating the movement, attention, and learning of varied students in a limited space. Therefore, regardless of how well a teacher understands students' needs, creates a positive emotional climate, and effectively provides instruction, organizational skills are critical. Consequently, the fourth factor is *comprehensive classroom management involves using organizational and group management methods that maximize on-task student behavior.* Teachers' organizational and instructional skills interact to influence students' achievement. Kounin (1970) reported that student task involvement ranged from 98.7 percent for the most successful teacher in his sample to 25 percent for the least effective. Doyle (1986) summarized this relationship between behavior control and instruction:

> The data reviewed in this chapter suggest, however, that the solution to the tension between management and instruction may require a greater emphasis on management. In other words, solving the instructional problems of low ability students cannot be done by de-emphasizing management or by designing more complex instructional arrangements for the classroom. Indeed, such "solutions" are likely to increase the problems they are designed to rectify. A more appropriate answer to the problem would seem to involve improved knowledge and training in management so that teachers can be free to concentrate on instructional solutions to learning problems. (p. 418)

Goodlad (1983a) expanded on this relationship between instruction and organizational/management skills when he wrote:

> Our data reveal that the teachers we studied were aware of the desirability of having students participate in setting their goals, making choices, solving problems, working cooperatively with peers, and so on. But these views were tempered by conflicting ones

having largely to do with maintaining control. Those time-honored practices that appeared to help maintain control won out. (pp. 469–470)

The creation of a positive classroom environment characterized by effective teaching and organizational skills will go a long way toward reducing behavior problems and increasing students' achievement. However, anyone who has taught or worked with children who have behavior problems is aware that some children will, at least for a time, behave inappropriately in even the most productive learning environments. Consequently, teachers need a repertoire of behavior management skills to support their instructional skills. The final factor in management is *classroom management involves the ability to use a wide range of counseling and behavioral methods that involve students in examining and correcting their inappropriate behavior.*

Many teachers will say that they do not have the time to use in-depth counseling strategies; this statement is generally accurate and realistic. Teachers cannot be expected to administer sophisticated psychological diagnostic instruments or use in-depth counseling strategies within the classroom. On the other hand, many relatively simple yet effective approaches are available for helping children examine and change their behaviors. Because teachers are increasingly faced with the task of teaching children who require special assistance, it has become necessary that teachers acquire problem-solving and behavior management techniques.

These five basic factors and their relationships to the chapter organization of this book are depicted in Figure 1.3. Even though teachers will want to examine methods associated with each factor, changes aimed at creating more positive student behavior should proceed in the hierarchic order suggested in Figure 1.3. When faced with problems concerning students' classroom behavior, teachers too often begin to intervene at the upper end of the hierarchy without laying a foundation by developing prerequisite knowledge and using preventive interventions. When they do, interventions will, at best, cause a limited, short-term improvement in students' behavior and may create greater student resentment and alienation.

As indicated by the topics listed in Figure 1.3, this book is designed to offer a comprehensive and hierarchic presentation of classroom management. This approach has been supported by the previously mentioned work at the Center for Social Welfare Research at the School of Social Work, University of Washington, at the Institute for Research on Teaching at Michigan State University, and the OERI research on creating safe, disciplined, and drug-free schools. In addition, studies conducted by the National Center for the Study of Corporal Punishment and Alternatives in the Schools (Hyman & D'Alessandro, 1984) to examine effective programs for training teachers to discipline students verify the importance of the skills described in this book. Their analysis of effective programs gives seven general techniques for motivating students and helping them deal with discipline problems:

1. Providing feedback to students about their behaviors, feelings, and ideas;
2. Using diagnostic strategies to better understand students and student-teacher interactions;

3. Modifying the classroom climate;
4. Applying techniques of behavior modification;
5. Using democratic procedures for solving classroom problems;
6. Expressing emotions appropriately; and
7. Using therapeutic approaches to behavioral problems. (p. 43)

Finally, the concepts and strategies presented in this book are congruent with what Good and Brophy (1991) listed as key principles in effective classroom management:

1. Students are likely to follow rules they understand and accept.
2. Discipline problems are minimized when students are regularly engaged in meaningful activities geared to their interests and aptitudes.

FIGURE 1.3
Skills the Teacher Needs to Develop Comprehensive Classroom Management

Correction	*Factor 5*	
(Chapters 10–12)	Helping students evaluate and correct unproductive behavior	Schoolwide student management programs
		Implementing behavioristic techniques
		Using problem-solving methods
Prevention	*Factor 4*	
(Chapters 3–9)	Organization and management (Chapters 7, 8)	Beginning the school year
		Implementing methods that maximize on-task student behavior
	Factor 3	
	Motivation and instruction (Chapter 6)	Incorporating teaching methods that motivate students by responding to their learning needs
	Factor 2	
	Interpersonal relationships (Chapters 3–5)	Working with parents
		Creating positive peer relationships
		Establishing positive teacher-student relationships
Theoretical Foundation	*Factor 1*	
(Chapters 1, 2)	Developing a sound theoretical foundation	Understanding students' personal needs
		Understanding classroom management

3. Management should be approached with an eye toward maximizing the time students spend engaged in productive activities, rather than from a negative viewpoint stressing control of misbehavior.

4. The teacher's goal is to develop self-control in students, not merely to exert control over them. (p. 199)

PLACING CLASSROOM MANAGEMENT IN PERSPECTIVE

A discussion of classroom management is not complete without recognizing teachers' limitations in dealing with disruptive student behavior. When unproductive student behavior is a response to lack of appropriate instructional materials, negative classroom environment, lack of peer support, or a temporary crisis in a child's life, changes in the classroom environment will often immediately and significantly change students' behavior. Unfortunately, in a few children, unproductive behaviors are an indication of serious personality disorders that cannot be immediately altered by changes in environment or limited counseling intervention. When working with these children, teachers must place their interventions in proper perspective to avoid becoming discouraged. It is important to do everything possible to provide a positive learning environment and to help such children control their behavior. Realize, however, that even psychotherapists are not always able to help children who display severe behavior disorders. Similarly, residential treatment centers are often only modestly successful in working with such children.

The Curriculum of Responsibility

The concept of a curriculum of responsibility (Figure 1.4) has helped many teachers place classroom management and instruction in its proper perspective. This concept suggests that both teachers and students have major responsibilities within the school environment. Teachers are responsible for creating positive, supportive, clearly structured learning environments. Students cannot be expected to respond responsibly in a confusing, arbitrary, irresponsible environment. However, when teachers have met this responsibility, they have the right to expect students to behave responsibly within this environment.

Teachers' Responsibilities

First, teachers are responsible for ensuring that students feel accepted and supported rather than isolated or intimidated in the classroom. This responsibility involves creating teacher-student and peer relationships that are positive and supportive for all students. Second, teachers are responsible for ensuring that students understand the school environment. Students need to know how the classroom will operate (classroom procedures) and why these procedures exist. As discussed in Chapter 8, it is important that students are actively involved in developing, learning, and committing to these procedures. Students also need to understand the academic procedures, such as what will be learned, why this learning is being presented, how their work will be assessed, and why instructional decisions are made.

FIGURE 1.4
Curriculum of
Responsibility

Relationships
Knowledge
Limits
Options   } Educators' Responsibility

Choices
Consequences   } Student's Responsibility

Third, teachers are responsible for ensuring that students know the limits within the classroom and school. Students need to know what will occur if they choose not to follow classroom and school rules and procedures. As discussed in Chapters 10 through 12, it is essential that the results of these consequences be clear, treat students with dignity, serve to teach students new skills, and include an attempt to analyze the environment to determine factors that may have contributed to a student's inappropriate behavior.

Fourth, teachers are responsible for providing students with options. When students have difficulties learning or behaving responsibly, teachers need to assist them or help them obtain assistance. In the case of academic difficulties, this responsibility might involve tutorial time from the teacher or a peer, modifications in the work presented to the student, or changes in the methods of evaluating the student's progress. For students whose home environment and/or work schedule makes it difficult to complete homework, this teacher responsibility may involve assistance in scheduling time and in finding effective places to complete work. Teachers need to help students experiencing behavioral difficulties resolve the matter through problem solving, developing new skills, or support from another peer or adult.

Within a responsible, productive environment, students are responsible for the choices they make and thus for the consequences these choices elicit. Students choose whether to be productively involved in instructional activities, to attend class, to complete homework, and to follow classroom and school rules. When students make good choices, they should encounter positive consequences. When they make poor choices, they need to receive consequences that help them develop new skills and/or make better choices.

Developing Programs That Meet the Needs of Students At Risk

Like teachers, school district personnel at all levels are increasingly being asked to clarify their roles in serving students who are at risk for school failure. The authors' reading of the research and extensive work with these children suggests the following seven major areas in which school district staff can implement program development in order to more effectively meet the needs of students at risk:

1. Create more positive, personal adult-student relationships.
2. Increase staff's skills in classroom management.

3. Increase staff's skills in utilizing diversified instructional methods that actively engage students in meaningful learning.
4. Modify schoolwide student management (discipline) to emphasize conflict resolution.
5. Alter the school schedule to involve students with fewer adults and peers over longer periods of time.
6. Create special programs for students who have special social-emotional needs.
7. Improve coordination between school staff and staff in community agencies that serve youth.

As this list suggests, although the quality of classroom instruction and management is critical to working with students at risk, there is more to meeting these students' needs than merely assisting teachers in improving their instructional and classroom management skills. Teachers must realize that the structure of the schools in which they teach and the relationships their schools have with outside agencies will increasingly impact their ability to work effectively with an increasing number of students at risk for school failure. Because of this, each of these seven areas is discussed throughout this book.

Effective Classroom Management versus Control

Some researchers on school effectiveness and some approaches to classroom management have placed almost exclusive emphasis on student on-task behavior and achievement of basic skills. Classroom management and instructional skills that enhance these student behaviors tend to emphasize a high degree of classroom structure and the use of extrinsic rewards to increase students' motivation. Research suggests, however, that an intermediate amount of control is associated with the greatest student gains in achievement. That is, too little or too much control of students' behavior or students' responsibility for the learning task limits their achievement.

Another reason for avoiding too great an emphasis on controlling students' behavior and enhancing achievement test scores is that this emphasis fails to address important issues about the goals of public education in U.S. society. Research indicates that for simple, low cognitive-level tasks, greater teacher control is desirable. Thus, if the goal is to learn the multiplication tables, greater teacher control of learning activities and students' behavior may result in increased learning. When students are involved in solving complex problems or in creative production, however, less teacher control is associated with better outcomes. Jencke and Peck (1976) reinforced this concept:

> If teachers supply immediate reinforcement, they must pay the cost of having students learn to rely on rewards that are external to the problem situation itself. This cost may be worth incurring if the teacher is merely attempting to get children to efficiently commit facts to memory. However, the price may be too high when students are learning new concepts or if they are engaged in problem-solving or pattern-searching. (p. 33)

Corno (1979) reported that although increased classroom structure was associated with student gains in achieving basic learning tasks, it was associated with lower scores in creativity. Similarly, Soar and Soar (1980) found that the degree of students' attention to a task was positively related to low cognitive-level learning but negatively related to high cognitive-level learning. Apparently, creative production requires time merely to "sit and think," as opposed to working diligently as it is normally defined by research in on-task student behavior.

These studies are supported by research suggesting that high levels of teacher praise are associated with increased basic skill achievement but with decreased creativity and less student independence, persistence, and self-confidence. When teachers use praise to reinforce on-task behavior and simple, correct answers, students respond by producing more of these responses at the expense of more creative, independent work.

If we wish to enhance students' independence, responsibility, creativity, and motivation, we must use classroom management strategies that do more than use rewards and punishments to increase on-task behavior and high scores on achievement tests. Structure, praise, and reinforcement are important tools that do help many, if not all, students in learning basic skills, yet they are not the best techniques for helping all students to reach all learning goals.

Finally, the authors' own experience strongly suggests that a focus on control often creates at least two undesirable responses. First, rather than emphasizing classroom and school factors that may be influencing student behavior, a focus on control reinforces teachers' viewing student behavior problems primarily as an issue of gaining control of recalcitrant students. This orientation seems to run counter to the large body of research indicating that some teachers and schools are very effective at facilitating student learning and positive behavior whereas some are much less effective. Second, the research on punishment clearly indicates that aggression tends to beget aggression. For many of the most difficult-to-manage students at whom a power orientation is directed, a focus on power and control tends to evoke aggressive, hostile, or withdrawal behavior. In short, the use of power is often effective at intimidating students who need control least and is seldom effective with students whose behavior is most unproductive.

Effective classroom managers use the skills suggested in Figure 1.3 to create positive, supportive, well-structured classrooms and actively engage students in meaningful learning activities. Effective classroom managers maintain order by creating warm, positive, collegial learning environments and by using problem solving and other behavior management methods that help students develop responsibility for their own behavior.

Meeting Teachers' Needs: Establishing a Systems Approach to Responding Effectively to Student Behavior Problems

Teachers' professional needs fall into three general categories: (1) possessing the skills to motivate and manage students in a manner that allows teachers to experience success and professional fulfillment, (2) receiving personal and professional support from their teaching colleagues, and (3) receiving support from administrators and other support personnel.

Whether the reader's goal is to make significant changes in his or her approach to managing a classroom or to learn a few new techniques for working with a particularly difficult student, the quality of professional support available in the school setting will significantly affect that reader's ability to reach the goal. Teaching is a demanding job, and teachers need encouragement, suggestions, and expressions of personal interest and support from their colleagues. Numerous writers have emphasized that teachers are able to work more effectively with students when the teachers themselves are treated as professionals and experience the school environment as being safe and supportive.

Support from colleagues may take the form of sharing materials, helping colleagues by taking their duty when they are not feeling well, listening with interest, providing ideas for dealing with a difficult parent or student, or reinforcing a colleague's efforts. Discussing this type of support, Schmuck and Schmuck (1974) emphasized the relationship between teachers' needs for personal and professional support and their ability to work effectively with children: "First, the security, comfort, and stimulation that teachers receive from their colleagues increase the amount of personal esteem they bring to interactions with students and the amount of energy they have for working closely with students. Second, staff interactions offer models to students that represent the actual climate of the school" (p. 124).

Despite their best intentions, teachers can become frustrated by the persistent, unproductive, or irresponsible behavior of a student or group of students. When this occurs, teachers may have difficulty analyzing the classroom situation and developing new strategies for working with the students. At this point, teachers benefit from the assistance of colleagues who can see the situation from a new and different perspective and can offer suggestions for working with the student(s). As discussed in Chapter 11, teacher assistance teams can provide teachers with ideas and support for working with students who are demonstrating ongoing and/or serious learning and behavior problems and can also increase the support teachers experience. In addition to assistance from their peers, teachers need support from administrators and specialists. This includes provision of materials and supplies, support for curriculum planning and advanced training, support for innovative instructional practices, and assistance in the form of positive feedback as well as specific, nonjudgmental professional criticism.

Some students will test even the most well designed classroom management system implemented within the most positive learning environment. When this occurs, teachers need assistance from administrators and other special support personnel as part of a well-designed schoolwide student management plan. During the 1980s, teachers became increasingly aware of the importance of formalizing such support. An example of this approach is the following 1988–89 contract between the West Linn School District No. 3Jt, Clackamas County, Oregon, and the Willamette Falls Bargaining Council:

Article 5—Student Discipline

A. *General*

Definition of duties and responsibilities of all administrators, coordinators, supervisors, and other personnel pertaining to student discipline shall be reduced to writing by the District, and presented to each teacher at the start of each school year. Such definition of the duties and responsibilities of personnel is a retained right of the District.

B. Procedure

Teachers may temporarily exclude a student from the classroom when in the judgment of the teacher the student's behavior is seriously disrupting the instructional program. When a student is so excluded, the following procedure will be utilized:

1. The student will be sent to the building office. Prior to requesting that the student be placed back in the classroom, the principal or designee will meet with the teacher to discuss the referral and the conditions for the student's return.
2. If the teacher does not agree to place the student back in the classroom at the principal's or designee's request, the student will not be allowed back in the class pending completion of this procedure.
3. In the event the teacher and principal or designee disagree, the matter will be referred as soon as possible to the Superintendent. A conference will be arranged with the teacher, principal or designee and Superintendent. The decision of the Superintendent will be final.
4. The parties agree that in such matters a speedy resolution of any disagreement is of paramount importance. The parties agree that a good faith effort will be made to arrange and meet with the Superintendent as soon as possible; even if it means meeting outside the regular workday. If the Superintendent is not available to meet as per this section, this meeting will be conducted by the Assistant Superintendent. If neither is available, it will be conducted by another certified central office administrator.

(*Source:* West Linn School District and Willamette Falls Bargaining Council. Reprinted by permission.)

Students who repeatedly violate classroom rules may need the assistance of specialists within the school setting or community. Initially, these specialists can make additional suggestions for teacher interventions in the classroom. Eventually, some students may need to be placed in a more structured setting, where they can obtain more systematic and consistent interventions to help them develop and demonstrate new skills. The model in Figure 1.5 outlines the responsibilities of various educators and support personnel at different steps of unproductive student behavior. The key concept in this model is that teachers are initially responsible for the majority of inappropriate student behavior. However, when students continue to behave unproductively, despite teachers' use of proven classroom management and instruction methods, teachers and students will be best served when the school system has developed clear guidelines concerning the assistance that will be provided to teachers.

The majority of the methods presented throughout this book focus on what teachers can do to motivate and manage students more effectively (Step 1 in Figure 1.5). Teachers and administrators should understand that implementing the concepts and methods presented in this book will be facilitated when teachers receive strong support from colleagues and administrators. As discussed in detail in Chapter 11, school systems can best support teachers and provide important services and safeguards for the children they serve when they have clearly delineated and widely disseminated procedures for obtaining assistance in responding to students with special needs.

Step	Responsibility	Procedure	Resources
#1	Classroom teacher	Regular classroom placement	The teacher uses instructional and classroom management methods that incorporate best-accepted practices.
#2	Classroom teacher and school staff	Regular classroom and referral to school resources	This step involves advice and support from colleagues, involvement of the school support staff, or student referral into a systematic schoolwide student management (discipline) system.
#3	Classroom teacher, school staff, and district staff	Regular classroom placement and request for district resources	The district provides consultation resources, such as a special educator, school psychologist, or behavior specialist.
#4	Classroom teacher, school staff, and district staff	Request for special education evaluation and eligibility decision. Placement in a special building program and/or regular classroom.	The multidisciplinary team determines eligibility, the IEP team determines the placement and programming, and the special education staff provides and coordinates services.
#5	School staff, special education, district staff, and community resources	Placement within district resources and referral to community resources	District and community resources are called in for assistance.

FIGURE 1.5
Continuum of Services for Managing Student Behavior

SUMMARY

Teachers continue to experience persistent and often serious problems managing students' classroom behavior. Given the increasing number of students who will enter U.S. schools at risk for school failure, it seems likely that during the next decade teachers will continually need to upgrade their skills in motivating and managing students.

Fortunately, research in classroom management has expanded dramatically during the past 20 years. Teachers no longer need to depend on simplistic advice for or unidimensional answers to the complex tasks of motivating and managing students. Teachers can increasingly draw on an expanding body of methods that will enable them to create more positive, supportive classroom environments, better organize and instruct their students, and more effectively respond to the behavior of students who misbehave even in supportive, well-managed classrooms characterized by clear, meaningful instruction. The efficacy of new methods can be enhanced if teachers have a clear philosophy of classroom management and understand their own responsibilities and those of their students and the school support personnel. Finally, school systems can better assist students with serious behavior problems if all educators within the system understand the methods to be followed in responding to unproductive student behavior.

Students who create classroom management and instructional challenges are, in fact, our best staff development specialists. They let us know that even though we may be very good, we can always expand our skills. Fortunately, almost without exception, the new methods we implement to assist students who are struggling with their learning and behavior will be beneficial for all students. Effective classroom management is not a zero-sum game in that efforts to assist students in need necessarily take away from other students. When we use the methods suggested in this book, we not only enhance our ability to reach the student at risk but we simultaneously enrich the learning experience of all our students.

RECOMMENDED READING

Alschuler, A. (1980). *School discipline: A socially literate solution.* New York: McGraw-Hill.

American Association of University Women Educational Foundation. (1992). *The AAUP report: How schools shortchange girls.* Washington, DC: Author.

Banks, J., & McGee Banks, C. (Eds.). (1993). *Multicultural education: Issues and perspective* (2nd ed.). Boston: Allyn and Bacon.

Brophy, J., & Evertson, C. (1976). *Learning from teaching: A developmental perspective.* Boston: Allyn and Bacon.

Carnegie Council on Adolescent Development. (1989). *Turning points: Preparing American youth for the 21st century.* Washington, DC: Author.

Dryfoos, J. (1990). *Adolescents at risk: Prevalence and prevention.* New York: Oxford University Press.

Gathercoal, F. (1993). *Judicious discipline* (3rd ed.). San Francisco: Caddo Gap.

Glasser, W. (1969). *Schools without failure.* New York: Harper and Row.

Good, T., & Brophy, J. (1994). *Looking in classrooms* (6th ed.). New York: Harper and Row.

Goodlad, J. (1984). *A place called school.* New York: McGraw-Hill.

Hacker, A. (1992). *Two nations: Black and white, separate, hostile, unequal.* New York: Random House.

Hahn, A., Danzberger, J., & Lefkowitz, B. (1987). *Dropouts in America: Enough is known for action.* Washington, DC: Institute for Educational Leadership.

Henry, J. (1963). *Culture against man.* New York: Random House.

Jones, V. (1980). *Adolescents with behavior problems: Strategies for teaching, counseling, and parent involvement.* Boston: Allyn and Bacon.

Kuykendall, C. (1992). *From rage to hope: Strategies for reclaiming Black and Hispanic students.* Bloomington, IN: National Educational Service.

Lehr, J., & Harris, H. (1988). *At-risk, low-achieving students in the classroom.* Washington, DC: NEA.

Lewis, A. (1990). *Making it in the middle: The why and how of excellent schools for young urban adolescents.* New York: The Edna McConnell Clark Foundation.

Lipsitz, J. (1984). *Successful schools for young adolescents.* New Brunswick, NJ: Transaction Books.

Maeroff, G. (1982). *Don't blame the kids: The trouble with America's public schools.* New York: McGraw-Hill.

McCaslin, M., & Good, T. (1992). Compliant cognition: The misalliance of management and instructional goals in current school reform. *Educational Researcher, 21,* 4–17.

Purkey, W., & Novack, J. (1984). *Inviting school success: A self-concept approach to teaching and learning* (2nd ed.). Belmont, CA: Wadsworth.

Rutter, M., Maughan, B., Montimore, P., Ouston, J., & Smith, A. (1979). *Fifteen thousand hours.* Cambridge, MA: Harvard University Press.

Silberman, C. (1970). *Crisis in the classroom: The remaking of American education.* New York: Random House.

Sizer, T. (1984). *Horace's compromise: The dilemma of the American high school.* Boston: Houghton Mifflin.

Sleeter, C. (Ed.). (1991). *Empowerment through multicultural education.* New York: State University of New York Press.

United States Department of Education. (1993). *Reaching the goals. Goal 6: Safe, disciplined, and drug-free schools.* Washington, DC: Office of Educational Research and Improvement.

CHAPTER 2

Understanding Students' Basic Psychological Needs

Teaching is difficult under the best educational conditions, and this failure to take into account the needs of students or teachers makes what is already a hard job almost impossible. Any method of teaching that ignores the needs of teachers or students is bound to fail.

—William Glasser (1990)
The Quality School: Managing Students Without Coercion

Teachers can augment the academic self-image by identifying and developing some of the unique cultural and social strengths Black and Hispanic youth bring to the classroom. An understanding of how the social self-image can be used to bolster the academic self-image is critical.

—Crystal Kuykendall (1992)
From Rage to Hope: Strategies for Reclaiming Black and Hispanic Students

Students behave appropriately and learn more effectively in environments that meet their basic personal and psychological needs. All students learn best in school settings in which they are comfortable and feel safe and accepted. Students' academic failure and misbehavior can be understood—and subsequently prevented or corrected—by examining classroom and school environments to determine which student needs are not being met.

Teachers are frequently frustrated by their inability to determine the source of disruptive student behavior that detracts from students' learning. When asked to describe why children misbehave, teachers often include in their responses such factors as poor attitude, poor home environment, lower-than-average IQ, lack of parental support for school, and medical or emotional problems. In a 1987 report entitled *NEA Research/Gallup Opinion Polls: Public and K–12 Teacher Members,* teachers overwhelmingly stated their belief that parents and society are responsible for discipline problems occurring in schools. Some 81 percent of the teachers polled stated that parents and society had major responsibility; only 7 percent believed that schools had major responsibility; and 12 percent thought schools shared responsibility equally with parents and society. Interestingly, only 58 percent of the public polled believed that parents and society were the major causes of student discipline problems; 21 percent believed the schools had major responsibility; and 21 percent believed responsibility was shared equally.

It is also important and somewhat disturbing to note that 64 percent of teachers polled stated that because the problem is at home, there is not much more schools can do to bring about improved student behavior. This conclusion suggests that teachers can merely coax or bribe these students into behaving more appropriately or remove or punish these children when misbehavior occurs. Teachers may thus absolve themselves of responsibility for students' misbehavior. In this scheme, teachers are merely a reactive force. They must put a finger in the dike when confronted with unpredictable forces over which they have little control.

"Mrs. Horton, could you stop by school today?"

Even though it is true that student behavior is influenced by factors outside the control of the school, studies on school and teacher effectiveness have demonstrated that teachers and schools have a major impact on how students behave and learn and on how they feel about themselves. Therefore, another approach to analyzing unproductive or irresponsible student behavior is to believe that almost all students can function productively in a classroom and to consider what classroom variables can positively affect student learning and behavior. Much of this book provides specific methods used by teachers to create such environments. However, professional educators must understand *why* these techniques are effective rather than merely use them as gimmicks that positively influence student behavior. Consider for a moment that you were taking a child with a stomachache to see a physician. How would you react if, without examining the child, the physician indicated that an appendectomy would be performed? When you asked why the physician intended to perform the operation, the doctor indicated that the previous summer he had taken a class on appendectomies, had been told the operation was helpful to all children, and had demonstrated skill in performing it. It is likely that you would seek another opinion and would perhaps even report the incident to the appropriate source. Allen Mendler (1992) placed this in perspective when he wrote:

> Most discipline programs incorrectly place their emphasis upon strategies and techniques. The latest gimmick is offered to get Johnny to behave. The problem is that there are a lot of Johnnys out there and not all respond according to how the text or technique says they should. Having worked with thousands of children and adults,

> I have concluded that it is fruitless to expect that any technique will work with all people who present the same symptom. . . . The competent teacher needs to get at the reasons or functions of a given maladaptive behavior to formulate a strategy likely to work. . . . When they [children] misbehave, they tell us that they need help learning a better way. They are telling us that there are basic needs not being met which are motivating the behavior. (pp. 25, 27)

Teachers are involved daily in creating the atmosphere in which children spend approximately one-fourth of their waking lives. Although this necessity obviously places considerable responsibility on the teacher, it simultaneously imparts a positive, creative dimension into teachers' professional lives. Teachers are not faced with the prospect of merely reacting to student behaviors over which they have no control. On the contrary, by creating environments that respond sensitively to students' needs, teachers can ensure that most student behavior will be positive and goal directed.

You may wonder whether an emphasis on students' needs means subjugating teachers' needs or expectations. It is important to realize that meeting children's needs does not mean that adults do not provide structure, expect high-quality performance, or hold students accountable for their behavior. Indeed, these factors are part of environments that meet students' needs.

The necessity for presenting a chapter on students' psychological needs and focusing a portion of this book on strategies for creating positive classroom environments is based on the unfortunate but very real fact that classroom environments often fail to meet students' basic needs. Too many children who enter school excited and eager to learn leave school feeling unliked and unsuccessful. After conducting a survey of more than 600 students in grades 3 through 11, Morse (1964) wrote:

> Eighty-four percent of the third-graders were proud of their school work, while only 53 percent of the eleventh-graders felt the same way. In the low grades, 93 percent felt they were doing the best work they could; only 37 percent of the seniors felt this way. Without regard to their achievement quotients and the fact that the failures tend to drop out, the older pupils who remained in school came to feel they were doing inadequate work. Again, over half the young children said they were doing as well in school as they would like, but only 22 percent of the eleventh-graders felt this way. About 40 percent of the pupils often felt upset in school; and with regard to achievement, 20 percent said their teacher made them feel "not good enough." Over 40 percent reported they often became discouraged in school and this discouragement too increased with age. (p. 198)

Similar results were reported by Cormany (1975), based on a study in which the Pennsylvania Department of Education surveyed students' feelings about school. Cormany reported that although 64.4 percent of the kindergarten children expressed positive feelings about school, only 12.8 percent of sixth-graders reported such feelings. A survey of more than 8,000 students in grades 5 through 9 reported a similar change in students' attitudes and behavior (Currence, 1984). Results showed that 61 percent of fifth-graders said they "try their best at school," compared with only 30 percent of the ninth-graders. Similarly, 60 percent of fifth-, sixth-, and seventh-graders said they never cheated, yet only 33 percent of ninth graders said this. This reduction in positive attitudes toward oneself as a learner appears to be even more pronounced among African American students (Silberman, 1970; Bell, 1985).

It can be argued that children simply become more critical as they grow older, but substantial evidence suggests that at least a significant amount of this negativism and the associated acting-out or withdrawal behavior is a response to school settings that fail to meet students' needs. Teachers certainly do not mean to create such environments and are often not even aware that they are doing so. Most teachers sincerely wish to provide an optimal learning environment for their students. Unfortunately, many teachers are hampered by a combination of limited skills resulting from ineffective teacher training programs and the multiple demands placed on them. This book cannot alter the latter situation, but it does provide teachers with skills that enable them to cope with these demands more effectively.

This chapter describes the basic psychological needs that must be met for students to behave in a positive, productive manner. No attempt is made to present an in-depth description of any one theorist's work or to describe child and adolescent development. Rather, the chapter highlights needs that, when met within the school setting, enhance positive teacher and student behavior and thereby facilitate learning.

The effectiveness of any teaching strategy or behavior change approach is influenced by the degree to which it responds to students' needs. When a teacher's behavior elicits an unproductive student response, it is likely that the student lacks necessary skills to respond as the teacher would like and/or that the teacher has in some way infringed on, or failed to provide a productive means of obtaining, an important student need. In a fascinating analysis of why students drop out of traditional educational settings, Quigley (1987) proposed that it is less the content of schoolwork and instead the extent to which the school environment responds to how the student has learned to view learning, meaning, and participation in his or her environment. In most cases, dropping out is related to how people relate to one another and to the quality of independence and respect provided to the student within the learning environment.

Hargreaves (1982) argued that what teachers interpret as disruptive behavior may in fact be students' legitimate criticism of schooling as it affects them. He stated that schools do not treat lower-level students with dignity and that students' response is often to reject the schooling process. This is a central issue facing schools. If we are to be successful in effectively educating a broader spectrum of students, the focus of all school change—from restructuring to curriculum and instructional advances—must be on enhancing the dignity of all students. Students must become collaborators in the educational process. They must understand the learning process, make important decisions about their own learning, and be actively involved in the learning and assessment process. When this occurs, teachers will be required to spend much less time managing inappropriate student behavior.

THEORETICAL PERSPECTIVES

When faced with unproductive student behavior, teachers may in their frustration make statements such as, "I don't understand why he does that," "She did that for no reason," or "What would you expect, given his family?" However, numerous writers have noted that all behavior is caused either by environmental factors or by the individual attempting to meet a need.

One approach to understanding children's unproductive school behavior suggests that most unproductive student behavior is a response to children not having their basic needs met within the environment in which the misbehavior occurs (Maslow, 1968). This explanation has the advantage of placing the teacher in a creative, exciting position. Rather than simply reacting to uncontrollable forces, the teacher controls a wide variety of factors that influence children's behavior.

This view of teachers as able to influence students' behavior positively is supported by research and theory presented by the behavioristic approach and by social psychology. Behaviorism views individual behavior as determined by the pattern of rewards and punishments to which the person is exposed. Teachers often experience frustration when working with students whose history at home or in school or both has included limited reinforcement for desirable school behaviors and considerable reinforcement for behaviors inappropriate in the school. Teachers can, however, learn to teach and reinforce appropriate behaviors systematically. Teachers also can enlist peers or positive adult role models in reinforcing positive behaviors. The works of Bandura (1969) and Bronfenbrenner (1970) highlight the social psychologists' view that students' behavior is heavily influenced by the values and behaviors modeled by individuals who are significant in children's lives. Children learn a great deal by modeling others' behavior. Research suggests that children are more likely to model individuals who (1) are perceived as having a high degree of competence, status, and control over resources; (2) have provided previous support and reinforcement; and (3) play a prominent role in the students' daily life. Because teachers have the potential for possessing these qualities, they can, by thoughtful modeling, significantly affect students' behavior. Similarly, by helping to create classroom norms and procedures that encourage students to behave in a positive, supportive manner, teachers can create settings in which the majority of students serve as effective role models for the few students who may initially lack desirable attitudes and behaviors.

Another way to view unproductive student behavior is to see it as a skill deficit. This model suggests that students who act aggressively on the playground lack skills to make appropriate contact with peers, to handle the inevitable frustrations and conflicts that arise, and to solve problems. Similarly, students who act out during instructional time may lack skills in understanding or organizing the work, using self-talk to handle frustration, or knowing how to obtain assistance.

This social-cognitive skill deficit model suggests that students need more than reinforcement for appropriate behavior and negative consequences for inappropriate behavior. Students need to be taught social and work skills in the same manner that they are taught reading or math skills. Indeed, it is interesting that when students have serious difficulties reading, they are referred to a specialist who works intensively with them for an extended period of time. Educators do not expect students to learn to read by being placed in time out or otherwise isolated from classmates. Likewise, teachers seldom expect students with reading difficulties to be at grade level after only a few sessions with the reading specialist. However, when students experience difficulties with their behavior, educators often isolate them, provide little or no instruction in how to behave appropriately, and expect one or two visits to a counselor or principal to resolve the problem and ensure that the child has the skills necessary to function as effectively as his or her classmates. If we accept student behavior problems as representing skill deficits, this is not realistic. Instead, educators must respond to unproductive student behavior by creating opportunities for students to develop much needed skills.

Various writers have attempted to categorize and describe basic psychological needs that exist for children at different stages of their development. Understanding these needs can help educators better understand student behavior. This understanding allows us to become less emotional and defensive about unproductive student behavior and instead to consider ways to alter this behavior by more effectively meeting students' needs within our classrooms and schools. Instead of asking, Why does he or she do this to me? we can ask, What needs are not being met for this student in my classroom? and Can I make any adjustments that will help this student better meet these needs so he or she can experience success in my class?

Rudolf Dreikurs

Basing his work on the concepts developed by the Viennese psychiatrist Alfred Adler, Rudolf Dreikurs centered his ideas for working with children on the belief that their basic need is to be socially accepted: "We should realize that a misbehaving child is only a discouraged child trying to find his place; he is acting on the faulty logic that his misbehaviour will give him the social acceptance which he desires" (Dreikurs & Cassel, 1972, p. 32).

Dreikurs described four goals associated with children's misbehavior: attention getting, power, revenge, and displays of inadequacy. He suggested that "when a child is deprived of the opportunity to gain status through his useful contributions, he usually seeks proof of his status in class through getting attention" (1972, p. 34). If adults are ineffective at responding to this attention getting, Dreikurs indicated that students will seek power. If this response is thwarted by the teachers' own power methods, students will become deeply discouraged and seek revenge. Finally, Dreikurs suggested that "a child who has tried passive destructive forms of attention-getting in order to achieve the feeling of 'belonging' may eventually become so deeply discouraged that he gives up all hope of significance and expects only failure and defeat" (Dreikurs & Cassel, 1972, p. 39). In *Discipline without Tears* (Dreikurs & Cassel, 1972) and *Maintaining Sanity in the Classroom* (Dreikurs, Grunwald, & Pepper, 1971), Dreikurs suggested methods for assisting teachers in identifying which of the four mistaken goals the child is seeking and ways teachers can respond to children to help them return to positive involvement in the regular classroom.

Erik Erikson

In his well-known conceptualization of the eight stages of man, Erikson (1963) postulated that elementary-age children are in the stage he labels "Industry versus Inferiority." During this stage, children must move away from playing make-believe and develop an ability to produce things. Children must learn to do something well and to develop a sense of their own competence. Erikson describes the essence of this stage:

> And while all children need their hours and days of make-believe in games, they all, sooner or later, become dissatisfied and disgruntled without a sense of being able to make things and make them well and even perfectly: it is this that I have called the sense of industry. . . . For nothing less is at stake than the development and maintenance in children of a positive identification of those who know things and know how to do things. (Erikson, 1968, pp. 123, 125)

In Erikson's writing we can see the dual emphasis on viewing oneself as competent and on having this competence verified and expanded through meaningful contact with other people. Teachers can assist in meeting these student developmental needs by ensuring that all students (1) understand the work they are being asked to do, (2) can successfully complete the work they are given, (3) monitor and chart their progress, and (4) receive positive feedback from other people for their efforts and accomplishments. Similarly, students need to understand teachers' behavior expectations, to be allowed to practice these when necessary, and to receive assistance in and reinforcement for developing these behaviors when they are not skills the students currently possess. Many of the ideas presented in Chapters 6 through 11 will help you create a classroom setting in which this can be accomplished.

In addition to understanding theories that deal with children's needs, upper-grade elementary or middle school teachers must be aware of the unique needs of adolescents. The physical onset of adolescence is occurring at an earlier age. In addition, children are becoming more sophisticated at an earlier age due to the availability of television and of adults' tendency to encourage sophisticated behavior in children. Consequently, fifth- and especially sixth-grade teachers find themselves dealing with students who are experiencing the early stages of adolescence.

Erikson described the next developmental stage—that experienced by young adolescents—as the search for a sense of identity. During the initial phase of this stage (ages 11 to 13), there is a dramatic increase in self-consciousness and a lowered self-esteem. Young adolescents feel onstage, as if everyone is observing them. Elkind (1967) has labeled this the "imaginary audience." Young adolescents also view themselves and their personal problems as unique and cannot understand that other people are experiencing similar feelings. Elkind labeled this concept the "personal fable."

This means that even though secondary teachers often feel pressured to cover material and complete the curriculum, student learning and behavior can be enhanced when teachers take time to create a classroom climate in which adolescents feel comfortable with their teacher and peers and engage in cooperative learning activities that allow for supportive peer interactions. This climate serves to reduce the students' sense of self-consciousness and isolation, which releases energy for productive learning.

Young adolescents are also beginning to challenge previously accepted beliefs and values. With the gradual increase in their ability to consider abstract ideas and better understand the concepts of past and future, adolescents begin to view their world more subjectively and critically. Therefore, adolescents have a basic need to examine ideas, rules, and decisions critically. They are likely to question why they must study a topic, complete an assignment, or follow a rule that does not apply to the adults who share their environment. This often frustrating behavior increases as students move through midadolescence (ages 14 to 16) and become somewhat less absorbed in egocentric, self-oriented matters and more interested in their relationship to others and in better understanding and controlling their environment. Students in grades 8 through 10 are often testing their new personal, physical, and cognitive skills by challenging rules or adult behavior they view as illogical or indefensible. During these early and midadolescent years, students need fair, clearly articulated structure and adults who are personally strong and flexible enough to become involved in openly discussing questions adolescents have about subject matter, teaching techniques, and school rules and procedures (Jones, 1980).

Stanley Coopersmith

Another useful concept on students' needs is offered by Coopersmith (1967). In his research on the factors associated with self-esteem, Coopersmith found that in order to possess high self-esteem, individuals need to experience a sense of significance, competence, and power. *Significance* can best be defined as the sense of being valued that an individual attains from involvement in a positive two-way relationship in which both parties sincerely care about each other. *Competence* is developed by being able to perform a socially valued task as well as or better than others at one's age level. For example, winning a free-throw shooting competition involving her peers would provide a fifth-grader with a sense of competence. Being able to tie her shoe or add one-digit figures would provide her with a much smaller sense of competence. Finally, *power* refers to an ability to control one's environment.

Like Erikson, Coopersmith's research indicates that students need to experience a sense of trust and personal involvement as well as a sense of accomplishment or competence if their needs are to be met. Coopersmith also noted that in order for individuals to feel good about themselves and their environment, they must experience a sense of power or control. Students who clearly understand classroom rules and procedures and who understand what is to be learned and why it might be useful to them will experience a sense of power. Likewise, students experience a sense of power when they are allowed to choose a topic of special interest to study, provide input into how the classroom is arranged, or understand their own learning style and its relationship to their learning and teacher decision making.

William Glasser

For more than three decades, William Glasser has crusaded for increasing the sense of efficacy and power students experience. In his book *Control Theory in the Classroom*, Glasser (1985) stated, "Our behavior is always our best attempt at the time to satisfy at least five powerful forces which, because they are built into our genetic structure, are best called basic needs" (p. 14). Glasser described the five basic needs as "(1) to survive and reproduce, (2) to belong and love, (3) to *gain power,* (4) to be free, and (5) to have fun." (Glasser, 1985, p. 22; emphasis added). Glasser indicated that students will function productively only in school environments that allow them to experience a sense of control or power over their learning.

In *The Quality School: Managing Students Without Coercion,* Glasser (1990) extended his ideas on enhancing students' sense of involvement and empowerment. When describing why educators see relatively high rates of off-task behavior in schools, Glasser noted:

> For workers, including students, to do quality work, they must be managed in a way that convinces them that the work they are asked to do satisfies their needs. The more it does, the harder they will work.
>
> Instead, teachers are required to stuff students with fragments of measurable knowledge as if the students had no needs—almost as if they were things. . . .
>
> Because this low-quality, standardized, fragmented approach is so unsatisfying to students (and teachers), more and more students are actively resisting and this resistance is seen as a discipline problem. (p. 22)

In order to better understand why students misbehave and the relationship between this behavior and students' needs within the school environment, the authors strongly encourage every public school educator or prospective teacher to spend an entire day every year being a student in their school. This should involve the educator either riding the bus to school or entering the school at the same time as the student and completing all activities as if he or she were a student (including lunch, physical education, recess, etc.). Having done this with over 500 teachers, the authors are aware of how often the participants are surprised at the uncomfortable seating, the lack of breaks, and the low levels of academic involvement and positive personal contact experienced by the student they are shadowing. Activity 2.1 provides additional ideas for this learning activity.

David Elkind

In *The Hurried Child,* Elkind (1981) added an interesting dimension to the topic of children's psychological needs. He stated that relationships among all individuals, but especially between children and adults, involve basic patterns of dealing with each other. He described these patterns as implicit contracts and noted that they are constantly changing. He further commented that children's needs are met when contracts change in response to changing personal and cognitive skills demonstrated by children, but that contracts must not change primarily in response to adults' needs.

Elkind described three basic contracts between adults and children: (1) responsibility-freedom, (2) achievement-support, and (3) loyalty-commitment. The freedom-responsibility contract refers to adults "sensitively monitor[ing] the child's level of intellectual, social, and emotional development in order to provide the appropriate freedoms and opportunities for the exercise of responsibility" (1981, p. 124). The achievement-support contract refers to adults expecting age-appropriate achievements and providing the necessary personal and material support to help children reach expected goals. The loyalty-commitment contract emphasizes adults' expectations that children will respond with loyalty and acceptance of adults because of the time, effort, and energy adults give. Although Elkind focused on the parent-child relationship, these contractual areas apply to all adult-child relationships.

Elkind's key concept related to contracts is that they are frequently violated by adults and that this violation causes stress for youngsters. Violation of the freedom-responsibility contract occurs when adults fail to reward responsibility with freedom. For example, when students act responsibly in making a reasonable request of a teacher or administrator and are met with disrespect, this contract has been violated. Likewise, students who have demonstrated skill in directing portions of their own learning but are not allowed to do so experience frustration and stress through violation of the responsibility-freedom contract. The achievement-support contract is violated when adults do not provide adequate support for students' achievement. The low-achieving student who receives few opportunities to respond in class, little assistance in answering questions, and less reinforcement for appropriate answers is not receiving support commensurate with desired and potential achievement. Difficulties in the loyalty-commitment contract occur when children, especially adolescents, fail to provide adults with indications of loyalty commensurate with the efforts or commitment that adults see themselves as having made. When adults respond with removal of commitment, giving up on or criticizing the student, rather than by understanding and discussing the problem, contract violation occurs. This condition is more likely to happen with low-achieving students who may not immediately repay teachers for what appear to be considerable amounts of time and effort.

Joan Lipsitz

While serving as director of the Center for Early Adolescence at the University of North Carolina at Chapel Hill, Joan Lipsitz wrote extensively on the needs of early adolescence. She noted that adults often fail to understand this age group, which leads to classroom management and instructional decisions that cause a considerable amount of the unproductive behavior that so frequently frustrates teachers who work with this age group. Lipsitz emphasized the importance of developing school environments that meet young adolescents' developmental needs. These needs include:

1. The need for diversity,
2. The need for opportunities for self-exploration and self-definition,
3. The need for meaningful participation in school and community,
4. The need for positive social interaction with peers and adults,
5. The need for physical activity,
6. The need for competence and achievement,
7. The need for structure and clear limits. (Dorman, 1981, p. 1)

Joan Lipsitz's thoughtful book *Successful Schools for Young Adolescents* (1984) examines four schools that have successfully met these needs. Schools interested in assessing their effectiveness in responding to these needs as well as in creating more productive learning environments for young adolescents can refer to Lipsitz's book as well as Dorman's *Middle Grades Assessment Program* (1981).

Abraham Maslow

Although each theoretical conceptualization described in the previous section provides a valuable increment of insight into children's needs, Maslow's concept of the basic human needs incorporates the key components of many theories in a form that allows teachers systematically to assess and respond to students' needs. Maslow has suggested that there is a hierarchy of basic human needs and that lower-level needs generally take precedence over higher-order needs. His hierarchy of needs, which has been divided in a variety of ways, includes these components:

Self-actualization
Self-respect
Belongingness and affection
Safety and security
Physiological needs

Maslow's theoretical position is that people are basically good and that they have an innate need to be competent and accepted. Unproductive behavior is therefore not viewed as an indication of a bad child but rather as a reaction to the frustration associated with being in a situation in which one's basic needs are not being met. Maslow further suggested that these basic needs cannot be met without assistance from other people. Finally, he postulated that only when the basic needs are met can the individual become motivated by self-actualization or the need to take risks, learn, and attain one's fullest potential.

STUDENTS AT RISK FOR SCHOOL FAILURE

Concern for students at risk has become a major theme in U.S. education. The term *at risk* has generally referred to students who are likely to drop out of school. The Business Advisory Commission of the Education Commission of the States (ECS) has extended this concept to include youngsters who are unlikely to make successful transitions to becoming productive adults. In discussing students who are at risk for school failure, William Morse (1985), an expert on children with emotional and behavioral disorders, wrote:

> We have observed that increasing numbers of children are coming to school at risk because their self-development remains immature. School is a place designed for children who have absorbed the lessons from an effective primary group. The normal family, by providing security, along with food, clothing, and shelter, has prepared its children for school in three major ways. Children are ready to trust because their parents have been trustworthy. They are ready to meet social expectations because the family has set and maintained standards. They have a sense of their selfhood because of their positive role in the family and the regard in which they are held. For such children, school is a new, extended world of promise for which they are ready. (p. 27)

Morse, along with almost anyone currently working in a public school setting, has also noted that an increasing number of students from grades K–12 come to school daily without basic self-needs being met. The authors' own work with students and reading of the research suggests the following six major areas in which students at risk experience major social/emotional skill deficits.

1. A history of poor adult-child relationships with an accompanying need for positive, supportive relationships
2. A tendency to lack a sense of personal efficacy or power and the associated need to experience this by better understanding the learning process and developing a sense of personal responsibility and power
3. A closely related focus on external factors that influence their behavior and the need to learn to accept responsibility for their behavior and to see how they can control their own learning and behavior
4. Low self-esteem, especially related to such school behaviors as achievement and peer friendships, and the need to develop and validate a positive self-esteem through positive social interactions and school success
5. A poorly developed sense of social cognition—an inability to understand others' feelings or points of view and take this into account when making decisions and the need to learn to understand others' responses and to work cooperatively with others
6. Poor problem-solving skills and the need to develop these skills as a means to enhance self-efficacy and self-esteem as well as to develop an important life-long skill.

Although the condition of being at risk is certainly influenced by many social factors—including poverty, racism, sexism, family dysfunction, and substance abuse—it is also related to the quality of schooling in our society. The coordinator of the At-Risk Research Project of the National Center for Effective Secondary Schools highlighted this concept when he wrote:

> We have to face the fact that the condition of being at risk is partially generated by the school. The problems these kids bring to school are exacerbated by the way they're treated by the discipline system and the ways teachers interact with them. There is also a substantially detrimental effect caused by the lack of interesting and engaging experiences to which they will be able to respond. (Turnbaugh, 1986, p. 8)

Many students are at risk for school failure, but African American, Hispanic American, and Native American students have particularly high dropout rates. In 1991, the high school completion rate for 21- through 22-year-olds was 90 percent for Whites, 81 percent for African Americans, and 61 percent for Hispanic Americans (Kaufman, McMillen, & Bradby, 1992). Sadly, about 10 percent of African American, Hispanic American, and Native American eighth-graders dropped out of school in 1990.

Crystal Kuykendall, a prominent African American educator, noted that African American and Hispanic American (and the authors would add Native American) youth are "being 'distanced' from mainstream America. The continued underachievement and isolation of such a large and growing population is nothing short of a national tragedy" (1992, p. xii). Kuykendall has pointed to a number of powerful figures:

- During the past decade, the proportion of Black men attending college suffered the largest decline of all racial and gender groups.
- One out of every four Black men between the ages of 20 and 29 and one out of every eight Hispanic men of same age is either in jail, on trial, or on parole (U.S. Department of Justice, 1991).
- The largest increases in poverty are among Blacks without a college education.
- More than two-thirds of all Black children in female-headed households are poor. For those children in homes where the Black mother is under 25 years of age, the poverty rate is 90%.
- Black and Hispanic youth are suspended from schools at a rate three times that of their White counterparts. (pp. xii–xiii)

In its 1991 report, *State of Hispanic America,* the National Council of LaRaza indicated that the future of Hispanic American youth may be even more dim than that of African Americans.

James Banks, a leading writer in the area of multicultural education, recently highlighted the problems faced by children of color when he wrote, "In the early grades, the academic achievement of students of color such as African Americans, Hispanics, and American Indians is close to parity with the achievement of White mainstream students. However, the longer these students of color remain in school, the more their achievement lags behind that of White mainstream students" (Banks & McGee Banks, 1993, p. 3).

Writers such as James Banks, Johnella Butler, Harold Dent, Geneva Gay, and Crystal Kuykendall have written extensively on the problems students of color confront in their attempt to achieve success in U.S. classrooms. Studies indicate that many African American, Hispanic American, and American Indian students are more field dependent and group oriented than the average White student and that schools are structured as highly individualistic, competitive environments (Ramirez & Castaneda, 1974; Hale-Benson, 1986). Geneva Gay (1993) wrote, "First, the sameness of educational resources for diverse individuals and groups does not constitute comparability of quality or opportunity. Teachers, materials, and teaching environments that work well for Anglo students do not necessarily work equally well for ethnic minorities" (p. 182). Gay highlighted three reasons why students of color may fare well less well than their White counterparts in traditional classrooms:

1. Most [teachers] do not know how to understand and use the school behaviors of these students, which differ from their normative expectations, as aides to teaching. Therefore, they tend to misinterpret them as deviant and treat them punitively.
2. . . . Most curriculum designs and instructional materials are Eurocentric. . . . They are likely to be more readily meaningful and to have a greater appeal to the life experiences and aspirations of Anglo students than to those of ethnic minorities. Thus, when attempting to learn academic tasks, Anglo students do not have the additional burden of working across irrelevant instructional materials and methods.

3. A high degree of cultural congruency exists between middle-class Anglo student culture and school culture. These students do not experience much cultural discontinuity, social-code incompatibility, or need for cultural style shifting to adjust to the behavioral codes expected of them in school. (pp. 182–183).

What does this mean for teachers who are concerned about improving their students' achievement and behavior? It means that effective classroom management is more than a series of behavioral strategies for controlling student behavior. The authors suggest a definition of *effective classroom management* that is virtually identical to the definition of *multicultural education* proposed by James Banks. Banks and McGee Banks (1993) defined *multicultural education* as "a total school reform effort designed to increase equity for a range of cultural, ethnic, and economic groups" (p. 6). Figure 2.1 summarizes Banks's view concerning the dimensions of multicultural education.

A discussion of students at risk would not be complete without mentioning current work on the education of girls. Although girls graduate at the same rate as boys (Kaufman, McMillen, & Bradby, 1992), studies suggest that girls receive fewer response opportunities, are confronted with lower expectations—especially in math and science, study a curriculum that focuses less on their contributions and are engaged in instructional activities less suited to their learning styles than are men. In the introduction to the report *How Schools Shortchange Girls,* the writers stated:

> The absence of attention to girls in the current education debate suggests that girls and boys have identical experiences in school. Nothing could be further from the truth. Whether one looks at achievement scores, curriculum design, self-esteem levels, or staffing patterns, it is clear that sex and gender make a difference in the nation's public and secondary schools. There is clear evidence that the educational system is not meeting girls' needs. (American Association of University Women Educational Foundation, 1992, p. 2)

The student needs presented in this chapter, particularly the needs of students at risk, can be effectively met by teachers who choose to implement the methods presented throughout this book. This belief is supported by the fact that much of the research on effective schools and teacher effectiveness on which these methods are based was conducted in schools with many students at risk. Furthermore, in order better to respond to the needs of students at risk, the materials in this book expand on the school effectiveness research by including a greater emphasis on students' personal and social skill development as well as increasing students' motivation to learn and their sense of understanding and influencing their classroom and school environment. Specifically, the book emphasizes creating classroom and school environments that meet the following criteria:

1. Provide personally supportive and engaging environments.
2. Provide diversified instruction that enables all students to utilize their preferred learning styles.
3. Engage students in creating and learning social roles and relationships within the school context.

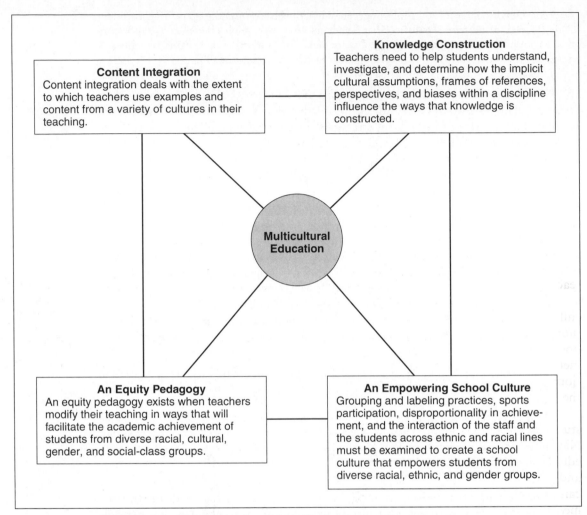

FIGURE 2.1   The Dimensions of Multicultural Education

Source: Reprinted with permission from James A. Banks, "The Dimensions of Multicultural Education," *Multicultural Leader, 1* (Winter/Spring 1991): 4.

4. Utilize problem solving and conflict management as the central theme in dealing with behavior problems.
5. Teach students strategies for setting goals and monitoring their own behavior.

STUDENTS WITH EXCEPTIONAL LEARNING AND EMOTIONAL NEEDS

The current emphasis on including the widest possible range of students in the least restrictive educational environment ensures that regular classroom teachers will increasingly be responsible for educating students with special learning and emotional needs. The use of effective classroom management methods influences all students but it has a particularly strong impact on students with exceptional learning needs. Students experiencing behavior and social/emotional problems are more negatively affected by negative teacher or peer responses and require classroom environments in which relationships are characterized by safety and support. These students also benefit from structured environments in which academic and behavioral expectations and consequences are clearly taught, monitored, and implemented. Likewise, students with learning disabilities benefit from supportive, well-structured environments and have special needs for instructional methods and materials that meet their unique learning needs.

Although often ignored, students labeled talented and gifted also have unique learning needs that are best served by teachers using the classroom management methods described throughout this book (Jones, 1983). Because many students who are gifted possess a questioning attitude, skepticism, and sense of their own power, and because they have intensified needs to learn problem-solving skills, participate in decision making, and set and evaluate goals, they are especially resentful of and harmed by classroom management methods that emphasize rigid teacher control.

In working with exceptional students who are gifted and talented, you will be called on to use a wider range of teaching skills than with students who display more normative behavior. In fact, the teaching methods presented throughout this book are those used by effective special education teachers. Interestingly, these methods not only enable teachers to manage and instruct a wide range of exceptional students effectively but they also improve the behavior and achievement of the more typical students.

Educators are understandably concerned and frustrated when they encounter students whose needs seem more extensive than those of most students. Polly Nichols (1984) developed an interesting and useful model for considering how educators need to respond differently to students who vary in their personal needs and developmental level. As shown in Figure 2.2, Nichols explained that students can generally be classified into one of four groups. Autonomous students effectively meet their personal and learning needs in school settings and are often a joy to teach. Reactive students "have the skills in their repertoire to manage life in the mainstream, but they do so inconsistently; they react to external and internal stimuli by acting out, withdrawing, or avoiding school. They will do well for one teacher and be terrors for another; they do well for three days and do battle on the fourth, all for reasons that 'were not their fault' " (Nichols, 1984, p. 53). Reactive students often do not understand their schoolwork and lack prerequisite skills for completing work. They also frequently lack skills in getting along with other students, controlling their emotions, and problem solving. Therefore, these students need assistance in understanding their environment and in developing new skills that will enable them to meet their needs in school settings.

Self-centered students lack the ability to understand others' point of view and to comprehend the impact their behaviors have on others. They have often come from abusive or drug-affected families and require considerable assistance in developing new skills and altered self-perceptions. Teachers who have these students in

FIGURE 2.2 Down the Up Staircase: Step Up/Step Down Model

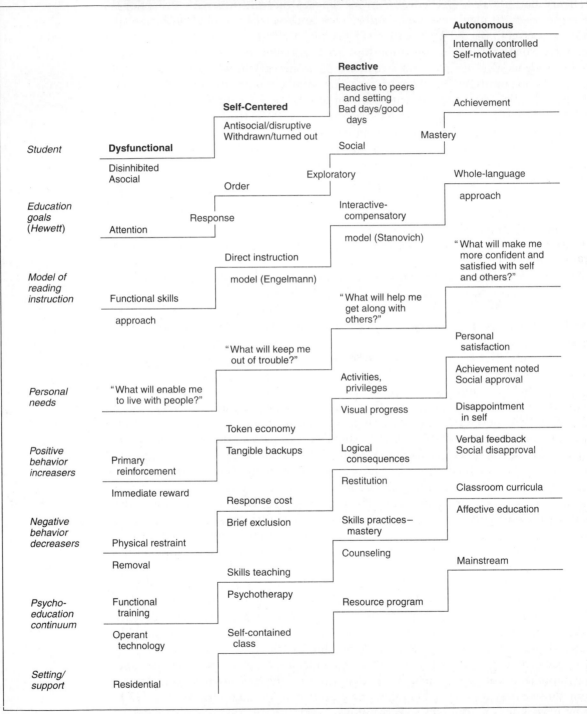

Source: Polly Nichols, Ph.D., University of Iowa. Reprinted by permission.

their classroom often require assistance from other sources, and these students are frequently candidates for special education services. Dysfunctional students are generally not served in regular education classrooms. This category includes children who are autistic and seriously emotionally disturbed.

The important point Nichols made in presenting her model is that when working with students who are experiencing behavior problems, teachers must go down the up staircase. Teachers will be most effective when they use with all students the methods described as being effective for autonomous students. When students fail to respond to these more proactive methods that place a priority on students' being internally motivated and responsible for their own behavior, teachers will need to develop the skills to use methods described as needed for reactive students. "For example, social approval is not used only with autonomous students; on level two, social approval plus activities, privileges and progress charts will be used to reinforce desired behaviors, and so on down to level four" (Nichols, 1984, p. 53). Although Nichols's model suggests that reactive students receive services in resource room settings, the authors believe that many of these students can be served in regular classroom settings with teachers using the methods presented throughout this book to meet these students' needs.

METHODS FOR DISCOVERING STUDENTS' PERSONAL NEEDS

There are three basic methods for determining students' needs. First, teachers can examine what theories and associated research results say about those needs. This approach has the advantage of providing teachers with information based on a large sample of students in varied settings. Perhaps even more important, this method is relatively free from the teachers' own biases and needs. For example, the teacher who does not feel comfortable allowing students to take an active part in the learning process may, in fact, interpret student behavior as indicating that students do not want or cannot handle even a limited amount of this responsibility. Theoretical statements that have stood the test of time and data collected using sound research designs are not influenced by such individual biases and may therefore provide a clearer picture.

The second approach to determining students' needs within the school setting is to ask students what they need in order to feel more comfortable and better able to learn. An individual is the world's best expert on himself or herself. Students basically know better than anyone what factors make them comfortable, productive, and happy. It is a fact of life that students have had fewer experiences than adults and consequently are less knowledgeable about the relationship between behavior and its consequences. Nevertheless, students are often much more sensitive and aware than teachers acknowledge. A fourth-grade child has been involved in observing and influencing human behavior for 10 years. Similarly, this child has spent 10 years attempting to manipulate the environment in order to meet personal needs. Consequently, even elementary school children have considerable expertise in understanding the variables that influence their behavior. They know which environmental factors create comfort, safety, and belongingness, and which factors elicit discomfort, rejection, and the accompanying withdrawal or aggression. Given that a teacher's goal is to create environments that facilitate students' learning, it seems reasonable that teachers should systematically involve students in providing information about the learning environment.

The third method for obtaining information about students' needs is systematic observation. By carefully monitoring how children behave in various situations, teachers can learn a great deal about unmet student needs. One of the authors recently taught a child who often appeared very sluggish, unmotivated, and slow in both speech and comprehension. At times, however, the student was quite animated and aware. Before making a referral, and following an uninformative parent conference, the author began collecting data on the relationship between the student's behavior and food consumption. The student consistently seemed more animated after lunch. Data also revealed a consistent pattern between mornings when the student seemed sluggish and those when he reported having no breakfast or merely a cookie or a similarly poor breakfast. When the mother was shown these data, she reported that the child had hypoglycemia. This realization led to a discussion that culminated in the mother's agreeing to provide the necessary morning diet, and this change was followed by significant improvement in the child's behavior.

A young teacher provided another example of the benefits associated with carefully observing students' behavior as a means of assessing students' needs. When describing a student's behavior, the teacher noted that the student did not get along well with his peers and that this unmet need was very likely to be the cause of his problem. A more thorough examination of the boy's behavior, however, indicated that he had few negative peer contacts in situations such as recess or at lunch, when fights might be expected. Instead, nearly all his negative peer contacts occurred when the class was involved in seatwork. Therefore, though it was quite possible that a need for belongingness influenced the boy's behavior, a more appropriate initial intervention involved responding to his academic needs by providing him with seatwork that he could complete successfully.

ACTIVITIES FOR EXAMINING STUDENTS' PERSONAL NEEDS

This section presents several activities that can be used to examine students' personal/psychological needs within the classroom. The first activity asks you to "walk a mile in a student's shoes" in order to understand better why students may behave as they do. The second activity helps you to consider that every incident has varied perspectives. The third activity helps you better understand students' views of their classroom by directly asking them how they react to various aspects of their classroom experience. The fourth activity helps you to analyze the data collected in the third activity and develop a plan of action for your classroom.

Select a student at the grade level you teach who is not in your classroom. Choose a student who has behavior and/or academic problems but who is not a serious behavior problem. Inform the student that you are attempting to develop a better understanding of what it feels like to be a student and that you will be following his or her schedule for the day. Follow this student for an entire day. If possible, stay within sight of the student from the time he or she enters school until he or she leaves. In order to make the day as realistic and as comfortable as possible for the student, attempt to be inconspicuous. Remember—your goal is to experience the day as a student, not to monitor the student's behavior.

When you have completed this task, take time to think and write about the experience. What feelings did you have? What made you uncomfortable? What did you enjoy most? What changes would you make to enhance the quality of the day?

When you have completed your writing, share your findings with a colleague who also went through this experience. Were there any similarities in your reactions to the experience? What were the differences in how you experienced the day? Why do you think these occurred?

ACTIVITY 2.1
Shadowing a Student

Select an incident in which a student misbehaved to such an extent that you had to send him or her to the office. Before continuing this activity, write down the punishment or consequence you would expect the student to receive for this act.

On a separate sheet of paper, write a ½- to 1-page statement indicating how each of the following individuals would describe the incident leading to the referral: (1) yourself, (2) the student involved, (3) a student-centered counselor, and (4) the administrator who heard both your and the student's points of view. At the bottom of each paper, write a brief statement indicating what you think each individual would suggest as the solution or resolution to this situation.

Having completed this exercise, write a statement concerning how you believe the situation should be responded to or resolved.

ACTIVITY 2.2
Examining Various Perspectives to a Behavior Problem

This activity provides students with an opportunity to describe the extent to which their needs are being met in the classroom. The questionnaire presented in Figure 2.3 has been used in a variety of classrooms. We encourage you to use this form or to alter it in any manner that will provide a more accurate tool for determining your students' needs.

ACTIVITY 2.3
Discovering Students' Own Thoughts about Their Needs

After developing and administering a student feedback form and summarizing the results, you should interpret the results and decide what changes, if any, need to be made. The following tasks and questions will help facilitate this process.

ACTIVITY 2.4
Interpreting and Responding to Student Feedback

(continued)

List the three statements students marked most frequently in the two most positive categories. For each of these statements, write one factor in the classroom that contributes to this positive student reaction.

List the three statements students marked most often in the lowest categories. For each of these statements, write one factor in the classroom that contributes to this negative student reaction. After completing Chapters 3 through 9, return to the activity and, following each classroom factor, list one change (including teacher's behavior) that could be made in the classroom to reduce or eliminate this factor.

Complete this activity by listing three things you learned about your students' needs based on the results of the questionnaire.

Once you have prepared an instrument for obtaining information from students, set aside a suitable amount of time for introducing and administering the questionnaire. Be sure to prepare the students adequately by briefly discussing your reasons for seeking their ideas and sincerely expressing your desire that they take the activity seriously and feel free to provide honest responses.

Many of you who have requested written feedback from students are aware of how easy it is simply to scan the material for any positive or negative comments, feel good about having asked for feedback, and file the material away. There are two problems with this approach to responding to student feedback. First, by merely scanning the feedback, you may either fail to notice subtle but consistent feedback or overreact to several negative statements that are not representative of the feelings expressed by the majority of students. If you receive a piece of negative feedback from only one or two students, you may want to discuss the findings with the students (if students have signed their names) or to consider why a few students responded as they did. (It may simply be that the student(s) had a bad experience immediately preceding the administration of the questionnaire.) It is unlikely, however, that you would want to make a major change in the classroom, or even raise the issue with the entire class. On the other hand, if three-fourths of the class respond that they would like a change, it is important that the issue be thoughtfully examined and discussed with the class. Unless student feedback is clearly summarized and tabulated, it is easy to confuse major issues that need attention with comments from a few students that are taken too personally and blown out of proportion.

A second danger associated with merely scanning student feedback is that unless the results are shared with students and obvious responses are made to their suggestions, students begin to feel that the activity is not meaningful and that their input is not valued. Consequently, it is advisable to create a method for displaying the results so that they can be shared with students. The easiest approach is often to tally the results. Figure 2.4 provides the tallied results obtained by using the first nine questions on the student feedback form presented in Figure 2.3.

A simple tally enables you to see where changes may be needed, as well as areas that students view as strengths. An interesting extension to tallying data is to determine a numerical average score for each item. When using a five-choice rating

FIGURE 2.3   Student's Psychological Needs Assessment Questionnaire

Check the
appropriate box.

Your Thoughts About Our Class	Always	Most of the Time	Sometimes	Seldom	Never
Physiological					
1. Do you eat a good breakfast each morning?					
2. Can you see the blackboard and screen from where you are sitting?					
3. Do I talk loudly and clearly enough for you to hear?					
4. Do you have time to relax during the day?					
5. Do you have enough time to complete your assignments?					
6. Do we go slowly enough in class?					
7. Do you need a study period at the end of the day?					
8. Is the room a quiet place to work?					
Safety and Security					
10. Are your grades fair?					
11. Does each day in this class seem organized?					
12. Do you understand the school and classroom rules?					
13. Is the discipline used in this classroom fair?					
14. Can you say what you'd like to in this class?					
15. Do you feel free enough to ask me questions?					
16. Can you trust your teacher?					
17. Can you get help when you need it?					
18. Are you happy when you take your report card home?					
Love and Belonging					
19. Is the room a happy place to be?					
20. Do you think that the students in this class like you?					

(continued)

FIGURE 2.3 Continued

Your Thoughts About Our Class	Always	Most of the Time	Sometimes	Seldom	Never
21. Am I friendly and do I smile at you?					
22. Do I take time with you each day?					
23. Do I show that I like you?					
24. Do you feel that I listen to you when you have a problem?					
25. Do I praise you when you deserve it?					
26. Do other students respect your property?					
27. Do other students care about how well you do in school?					
28. Do I listen to your suggestions?					
Self-Esteem					
29. Do you feel involved in this class?					
30. Do you feel proud when you share a project with the class?					
31. Do you take part in class discussions?					
32. Do you follow the classroom rules?					
33. Do you help other students learn?					
34. Are you a good student?					
35. In which subject area do you feel most successful?					
Self-Actualization					
36. Are you able to study things that interest you?					
37. Can you use what you learn in school?					
38. Do you have a chance to be creative in your schoolwork?					
39. Do you like to continue your studies at home on your own?					
40. Are you excited about what you are learning in school?					

Check the appropriate box.

Check the appropriate box					
Your Thoughts About Our Class	*Always*	*Most of the Time*	*Sometimes*	*Seldom*	*Never*
1. Do you eat a good breakfast each morning?	IIII	THL THL	THL I	IIII	
2. Can you see the blackboard and screen from where you are sitting?	THL THL IIII	THL I	II	II	
3. Do I talk loudly and clearly enough for you to hear?	THL THL THL III	THL II	II		
4. Do you have time to relax during the day?	III	THL IIII	THL III	II	IIII
5. Do you have enough time to complete your assignments?	THL II	THL THL I	III	II	
6. Do we go slowly enough in class?	THL	THL THL II	IIII	II	
7. Do you need a study period at the end of the day?	III	THL II	THL II	THL II	I
8. Is the room a quiet place to work?	II	THL IIII	THL IIII	II	III

FIGURE 2.4   Results of Administering a Student-Needs Questionnaire

scale, as in Figure 2.3, a score of 5 can be assigned for each student who marked the most positive response, a score of 4 can be given for the second response, and so on. The scores can be added and then divided by the number of students completing the form in order to achieve a class score for each item. Therefore, the results shown in Figure 2.4 indicate that the class score for item 1 in Figure 2.3 is 3.6. Obtaining a class score for each item allows you to compare students' attitudes and feelings at different times throughout the school year. For example, if you responded to a low score on item 1 by teaching a unit on nutrition or sending a letter home to all parents about students' breakfasts, you could check the results of the intervention by administering the questionnaire again after several weeks and comparing the class scores on item 1 to see whether a change had taken place.

SUMMARY

Many teachers view their lack of ability to understand and effectively respond to unproductive student behavior as a major cause of job-related stress and personal frustration. Anyone who has taught has heard a colleague say in exasperation, "I just don't understand why Johnny acts that way." This chapter presented the important concept that student behavior can be understood by considering basic psychological needs that students bring to the school setting. In many if not most cases when students act unproductively at school, they are responding to the fact that basic needs are not being met in the school setting. Unproductive school behavior is more frequent among students whose basic needs are not being met at home and in the community. Nevertheless, the problems outside of school are often not the major cause of the students' school difficulties, nor does their presence absolve us of our responsibility to create learning environments that meet students' basic needs.

Throughout much of the 1980s, school improvement projects focused heavily on improving the quality of instruction. During the 1990s, educators have become increasingly aware of the number of students who enter school without the personal support and positive self-esteem needed to succeed. All students will experience greater success when they are educated in settings that meet their basic needs, but this factor is critical for students who enter school with many needs unmet.

RECOMMENDED READING

Allers, R. (1982). *Divorce, children, and the school.* Princeton, NJ: Princeton Book Company.

American Association of University Women Educational Foundation. (1992). *The AAUW report: How schools shortchange girls.* Washington, DC: Author.

Banks, J., & McGee Banks, C. (Eds.). *Multicultural education: Issues and perspective.* Boston: Allyn and Bacon.

Coopersmith, S. (1967). *The antecedents of self-esteem.* San Francisco: W. H. Freeman.

Dreikurs, R., Grunwald, B., & Pepper, F. (1971). *Maintaining sanity in the classroom: Illustrated teaching techniques.* New York: Harper & Row.

Elkind, D. (1981). *The hurried child: Growing up too fast too soon.* Reading, MA: Addison-Wesley.

Erikson, E. (1963). *Childhood and society* (2nd ed.). New York: Norton.

Erikson, E. (1968). *Identity, youth, and crisis.* New York: Norton.

Glasser, W. (1969). *Schools without failure.* New York: Harper & Row.

Glasser, W. (1985). *Control theory in the classroom.* New York: Harper & Row.

Glasser, W. (1990). *The quality school: Managing students without coercion.* New York: Harper & Row.

Gordon, T. (1974). *Teacher effectiveness training.* New York: Wyden.

Grossman, H. (1984). *Educating Hispanic students: Cultural implications for instruction, classroom management, counseling and assessment.* Springfield, IL: Charles C. Thomas.

Holt, J. (1979). *The underachieving school.* New York: Pitman.

Jones, V. (1980). *Adolescents with behavior problems: Strategies for teaching, counseling, and parent involvement.* Boston: Allyn and Bacon.

Kukendall, C. (1992). *From rage to hope: Strategies for reclaiming Black and Hispanic students.* Bloomington, IN: National Educational Service.

Maslow, A. (1968). *Toward a psychology of being.* New York: Van Nostrand.

Morse, W. (1985). *The education and treatment of socio-emotionally impaired children and youth.* Syracuse, NY: Syracuse University Press.

Phlegar, J. (1987). *Good beginnings for young children: Early identification of high-risk youth and programs that promote success.* Andover, MA: Regional Laboratory for Educational Improvement of the Northeast and Islands.

Purkey, W., & Novak, J. (1984). *Inviting school success: A self-concept approach to teaching and learning* (2nd ed.). Belmont, CA: Wadsworth.

Strickland, D., & Cooper, E. (Eds.). (1987). *Educating Black children: America's challenge.* Washington, DC: School of Education, Howard University.

Willis, H. (1987). *Students at risk: A review of conditions, circumstances, indicators, and educational implications.* Elmhurst, IL: North Central Regional Educational Laboratory.

Wood, M. (1975). *Developmental therapy.* Baltimore: University Park Press.

Creating Positive Interpersonal Relationships in the Classroom

An ounce of prevention is worth a pound of cure: This statement is the key to effective classroom management. A large percentage of classroom problems can be prevented by creating positive, safe classroom environments. Books on classroom management too often focus on techniques for modifying individual students' behavior through a system of rewards and punishments while failing to acknowledge the vital role the social atmosphere plays in influencing students' behavior. Unfortunately, this major oversight frequently creates situations in which students are manipulated into behaving appropriately in environments that do not meet their basic psychological or academic needs. This approach is not only thoughtless and unfair to students but it also creates a situation in which the new behavior is maintained only as long as desired rewards are present. Therefore, it is easy to understand why programs based solely on behavioristic interventions have had limited success in generalizing behavior change to new environments.

Part II focuses on specific methods for preventing unproductive student behavior by creating positive interpersonal relationships in the classroom and throughout the school. These methods are important because they help create environments in which students feel happy and excited about learning. This atmosphere, in turn, tends to elicit more positive student behavior and to facilitate learning.

Educators should be aware of the dangers inherent in the completely unsubstantiated belief that time spent in creating classrooms in which students feel involved, safe, and happy could somehow be better spent in additional instructional time. As discussed in Part I, students' academic performance is enhanced when teachers take time to respond to their personal and psychological needs. Research indicates that positive affect is associated with improved student attitudes and higher-level thinking skills. Another important reason for blending academic and personal-social skill building is that if schools' goals include preparing young people to be involved citizens, activities aimed at developing a sound base of knowledge must be balanced with skills in interpersonal relations and problem solving.

Chapter 3 examines two pivotal aspects of teacher-student relationships: (1) the personal, affective quality of these relationships, and (2) how teachers communicate expectations to students. Chapter 4 focuses on the quality of peer relationships within classrooms. The chapter provides numerous activities for enhancing positive, cooperative peer relationships. Parents can do much to encourage positive student attitudes toward school, and Chapter 5 examines methods you can use to create positive, supportive relationships with parents.

CHAPTER 3

Establishing Positive Teacher-Student Relationships

Most important, students say they like classrooms where they feel they know the teacher and the other students. While students appreciate a well-organized and orderly environment, they do not like one in which the teacher is detached and treats the classroom as a whole rather than as a roomful of individuals.

—Patricia Phelan, Ann Locke Davidson,
and Hanh Thanh Cao (1992)
"Speaking Up: Students' Perspectives on School"
Phi Delta Kappan

Nowadays, to be successful in a position of authority requires an ability to connect in a caring way by inspiring hope within others and by leading one's own life in a manner that models the message.

—Allen Mendler (1992)
*What Do I Do When . . . ? How to Achieve Discipline
with Dignity in the Classroom*

The quality of teacher-student relationships dramatically affects whether students' personal needs are met in the classroom. Students spend nearly a quarter of their waking lives between ages 6 and 17 with teachers. Because teachers are responsible for evaluating students' work and controlling the quality of life in the classroom, they are powerful adult figures in students' lives. Effective teachers understand the influence they have on students and use this influence positively.

A significant body of research indicates that academic achievement and students' behavior are influenced by the quality of the teacher-student relationship. Students prefer teachers who are warm and friendly. More important, positive teacher-student relationships, in which teachers use the skills described in this chapter, are associated with more positive student responses to school and with increased academic achievement. Davidson and Lang (1960) reported that students who felt liked by their teachers had higher academic achievement and more productive classroom behavior than did students who felt their teachers held them in lower regard. Similarly, Morrison and McIntyre (1969) reported that 73 percent of the students in their study who were low achieving perceived their teachers as thinking poorly of them, but only 10 percent of high achievers held such beliefs. When examining students' adjustment, Truax and Tatum (1966) found that children adjusted more positively to school, teachers, and peers when teachers displayed empathy and positive regard for children.

An excellent example of the importance of combining acceptance with respect for students was reported by Kleinfeld (1972) in a powerful analysis of teachers' interactions with Eskimo and Native American students who had recently moved to urban settings. Kleinfeld found that teachers who were effective with these children were able to combine showing a personal interest in the students with demands for solid academic achievement. Summarizing her findings, she stated:

> The essence of the instructional style which elicits a high level of intellectual perform-ance from village Indian and Eskimo students is to create an extremely warm personal relationship and to actively demand a level of academic work which the student does not suspect he can attain. Village students thus interpret the teacher's demandingness not as bossiness or hostility, but rather as another expression of his personal concern, and meeting the teacher's academic standards becomes their reciprocal obligation in an intensely personal relationship. (p. 34)

In an ongoing study at the Center for Research on the Context of Secondary School Teaching at Stanford University, researchers are examining the factors in high school environments that support positive student attitudes and learning. The study is designed to determine students' perceptions regarding factors that influence their school performance. In a review of their work, the researchers stated, "A recurring them in students' comments is the tremendous value they place on having teachers who care. . . . In fact, the number of student references to 'wanting caring teachers' is so great that we believe it speaks to the quiet desperation and loneliness of many adolescents in today's society" (Phelan, Davidson, & Cao, 1992, p. 698).

In their extensive study of school environments that meet the needs of students at risk for school failure, Welhage, Rutter, Smith, Lesko, and Fernandez (1989) reported the following four common impediments to students developing a sense of school community:

1. *Adjustment:* Students at risk need a more personal and supportive relationship with adults than schools typically provide.

2. *Difficulty:* "Although we found literal inability to do the work a relatively rare characteristic of at-risk students, it is the case that increased time and more intensive tutoring were required for many. . . . The educational situation students complained most about was the ubiquitous 'lecture-discussion' based on reading assignments" (p. 124).

3. *Incongruence:* This related to the lack of personal-social match between the student and the institution.

4. *Isolation:* "We found that students who had persistent conflicts with adults or who found no teacher with whom to establish a personal relationship were at risk of dropping out" (p. 131).

The authors also stated that "there are four teacher beliefs and/or values, accompanied by corresponding sets of behaviors, that together constitute a positive teacher culture facilitating membership and engagement for students" (p. 135). These beliefs are the following:

1. Teachers accept personal responsibility for student success.
2. Teachers practice an extended teacher role.
3. Teachers are persistent with students.
4. Teachers express a sense of optimism that all students can learn.

Support for the importance of improving teacher-student relationships can also be found in numerous studies indicating that teachers demonstrate a low rate of positive statements when working with children (Brophy, 1981; Greenwood & Hops, 1976; Luce & Hoge, 1978; Thomas, Presland, Grant, & Glynn, 1978; White, 1975). "In general, praise for appropriate and desired behavior is a rare event, particularly between adult and child. Studies of natural rates of teacher praise and approval to individual children have shown them to be extremely low in an absolute sense and also in relation to other categories of teacher behavior" (Walker, 1979, p. 95).

In her *Successful Schools for Young Adolescents,* Joan Lipsitz (1984) remarked that successful schools for this age group provide a warm, personal environment. Describing these schools, Lipsitz wrote:

> Gradually, students gain increasing amounts of independence. They remain, however, in a highly personalized environment. The nature of the schools' organizational structure establishes continuity in adult-child relationships and opportunities for the lives of students and adults to cross in mutually meaningful ways. In each school, students . . . are actively aware of being liked, which is notable only because, in most schools, young adolescents are generally disliked. (p. 181)

Taken together, this research points to a need for teachers to learn and conscientiously apply skills in relating those positively to their students.

Fortunately, research (Aspy & Roebuck, 1977) demonstrates that teachers' behavior in the area of interpersonal relationships can be significantly changed by in-service training. Furthermore, these changes can positively affect students' attendance, achievement, and self-concept.

THE TEACHER AS A MODEL

Modeling theory provides another reason to be concerned about the quality of the teacher-student relationship. Children learn a great deal by watching adults. Much of children's behavior is developed by emulating the behaviors of adults who play significant roles in their lives. "One of the most salient developments in American social psychology during the past decade has been what for many laymen appears as a demonstration of the obvious; namely, children learn by watching others. Or, to put the issue in more provocative form: the behavior of others is contagious" (Bronfenbrenner, 1970, p. 124).

"Of course I believe that a teacher should offer a positive role model; however . . ."

Social learning theorists have shown that individuals learn many things primarily by observing and modeling the behavior of others. Research (Bandura, 1969, 1977) indicates that individuals are more likely to model the behavior of people whom they view as possessing competence and control over resources, and who are a major source of control, support, and reinforcement.

We must realize that our influence as models continues throughout the school year. In many schools, student turnover is high, and the many students who transfer into the school have their initial and most influential contacts with the teacher at times other than the first days of school. Teachers frequently comment that transfer students often gravitate to a less-than-ideal group of students. If we wish to have new students accept our values, we must make a special effort to provide them with an adult model who demonstrates competence and warm care for the new student. A few minutes of extra time spent going over classroom procedures and meeting privately with the students to discuss their work and offer assistance can dramatically increase the likelihood that they will model us rather than the behavior of any potentially negative group of peers.

Bronfenbrenner also reported that young people are more likely to model behavior that is exhibited by several adults. Furthermore, youngsters tend to model behaviors if they think adults benefit from the performance of these behaviors. These factors suggest the importance of creating schools in which a large percentage of adults demonstrate the skills and attitudes described in this chapter and in which teachers are reinforced by their peers and administrators for exhibiting these skills.

In his book *Judicious Discipline,* Forrest Gathercoal (1993) wrote:

Professional ethics are the conscience of a school community; they serve as acceptable standards of moral and proper conduct. Ethics are sometimes referred to as "beginning where the law stops." For example, there is no law against a teacher confronting a student with, "Why can't you be as good as your sister was in this class?" But, viewed through professional ethics, the comparing of students is considered poor educational practice, one that will often precipitate attitudinal problems that negatively affect the level of student achievement.

The foundation of professional ethics lies in the manifestation of educators always acting in the best interests of their students. (p. 25)

Because teachers are the models for how members of the school community will interact, it is essential that their relationships consistently demonstrate a positive regard for those who work in and visit the school.

Before presenting specific approaches for improving teacher-student relationships, we must place this issue in a proper perspective. The quality of teacher-student relationships has great influence on the amount of productive or disruptive behavior students display in a school setting. We must be careful not to confuse the importance of establishing positive teacher-student relationships with the belief that all classroom problems can be solved by love and understanding. Regardless of how concerned, positive, and fair a teacher is, students frequently misbehave in classes that are poorly organized and in which students are not provided with appropriate and interesting instructional tasks.

ESTABLISHING EFFECTIVE RELATIONSHIPS WITH STUDENTS

As anyone who has taught for very long realizes, students need and want positive teacher behavior to be associated with firmness, realistic limits, and competent teaching. The ability to blend warmth and caring with realistic limits is frequently a difficult task for young teachers. Unfortunately, this confusion is occasionally intensified by advice suggesting that beginning teachers should be less warm toward and more distant from their students. The main issue is not whether teachers should be less warm or friendly, but that they must simultaneously assert both their right to be treated with respect and their responsibility for ensuring that students treat each other with kindness. Warmth and concern can exist side by side with firmness. Indeed, effective teaching involves blending these vital ingredients.

Before presenting specific communication skills that help teachers develop open, effective relationships with students, it is important to consider the general issue of how teachers can most effectively relate to their students. In his classic book *Teacher Effectiveness Training*, Thomas Gordon (1974) wrote:

> The relationship between a teacher and a student is good when it has (1) *Openness* or *Transparency*, so each is able to risk directness and honesty with the other; (2) *Caring*, when each knows that he is valued by the other; (3) *Interdependence* (as opposed to dependency) of one on the other; (4) *Separateness*, to allow each to grow and to develop his uniqueness, creativity, and individuality; (5) *Mutual Needs Meeting*, so that neither's needs are met at the expense of the other's needs. (p. 24)

The Issue of Power and Control

Perhaps the most important decision we make as educators relates to the issue of power within the classroom. Many years ago, John Holt discussed the concept of natural as opposed to arbitrary role-bound authority. He stated that virtually all teachers have natural authority, which is the authority based on their knowledge of the subject matter, their ability to develop effective and exciting learning activities, their control of important resources, and their ability to manage effectively and facilitate the classroom group. Students are impressed with this type of authority. One need only observe young people at athletic camps to see how extremely impressed they are with natural authority and how it can motivate positive, on-task behavior. Teachers also possess role-bound authority. This is the authority based on their role as teacher and includes their ability unilaterally to reward and punish student behavior. Holt suggested that these two types of authority are in opposition; that is, the more natural authority one uses, the less one needs to use role-bound authority. Conversely, the more role-bound authority one uses, the less students can observe or will be responsive to one's natural authority.

In his book *The Quality School: Managing Students without Coercion*, Glasser (1990) made a similar point when he wrote, "The real power comes from students' perceptions of the teacher as competent to do the job, which is to show and model what is to be done and to create a good environment in which to work. Students appreciate the fact that the lead-teacher never threatens or punishes but says that if there are problems, 'We will work them out' " (p. 54).

The topic of multicultural education has provided another important forum for discussing the issue of power and control in the classroom. Sleeter (1991) wrote, "For me, and for many other advocates and theorists of multicultural education, empowerment and multicultural education are interwoven, and together suggest powerful and far-reaching school reform" (p. 2). In discussing the relationship between multicultural education, empowerment, and social change, Sleeter (1991) stated:

> The multicultural education approach, or cultural democracy, attempts to redesign classrooms and schools to model an unoppressive, equal society which is also culturally diverse. Explicitly this approach does not strongly teach social criticism and social change, but implicitly it does so in that a multicultural classroom or school implementing this approach is clearly different from the existing society. Students are empowered as individuals by achieving and receiving validation for who they are, and are empowered for social change by having lived a pluralistic model. (p. 11).

Numerous writers (Banks, 1993; Bennett, 1986; Sleeter, 1991) have argued that multicultural education must also include a focus on constructive social change. In discussing the goals of multicultural education, Bennett (1986) argued, "In view of the fact that certain ethnic groups are unable to gain, maintain, and effectively use political power, to ignore this goal is to make a sham out of the goals" (p. 212).

The authors' view is that students must be taught to understand and effectively influence their environment. Furthermore, they must at all times be treated with dignity. As discussed in Chapters 3, 10, and 11, this means being taught how to communicate needs and feelings effectively and being provided permission to express these feelings in acceptable ways. As noted in Chapter 8, it includes being involved in and understanding how the classroom will operate and how to learn the skills necessary to function in this manner. As discussed in Chapter 6, empowerment in an educational setting also means understanding why curriculum and instruction decisions are being made and being able to make some of these decisions. Finally, as outlined in Chapters 9, 10, 11, and 12, it means being actively involved in developing strategies for changing behaviors that are inappropriate in a school setting.

Creating Open, Professionally Appropriate Dialogue with Students

Although the specific decisions teachers make concerning their relationships with students vary depending on their students' age, the basic themes related to teacher-student relationships are similar across grade levels. One important question involves deciding how open and involved a teacher wishes to be with students. In an earlier work (Jones, 1980), one of the authors wrote that teachers can select from among three general types of teacher-student relationships. Although teacher-student relationships vary on numerous dimensions, a primary factor involves the level of openness chosen. We can choose a teacher-student relationship characterized by:

1. Almost complete openness, in which we share a wide range of personal concerns and values with students
2. Openness related to our reactions to and feelings about the school environment, with limited sharing of aspects reflecting our out-of-school life
3. An almost exclusive focus on a role-bound relationship; that is, we share no personal feelings or reactions, but merely perform our instructional duties

Not surprisingly, beginning teachers often grapple with whether they should be involved in very open, personal relationships with their students. They may wonder about the extent to which they should join in with students, share students' interests, use student slang, and so on. The authors' experience suggests that students respond best to adults who are comfortable with themselves, their values, and their personal preferences and who, when appropriate, can share these non-judgmentally with students. Consequently, if a teacher enjoys the same music as many students do, discussing it with students offers a format for relaxed, personal interaction. Likewise, when preferences or values of a teacher differ from those of students, encouraging a two-way exchange of ideas can prove stimulating and educational to both the students and the teacher.

However, you should avoid becoming overly involved in students' interests or activities outside of school, particularly if you are a secondary teacher. Adolescents are working at developing their own identity and generally view adulthood as a positive stage in which individuals have reached desired personal and social adjustment. Consequently, adolescents are confused by adults who show intense interest in students' social activities and interests. It confuses them to see adults who appear

"It's great how Mr. Watson's able to communicate with kids on their own level!"

to want to be similar to young people or a part of their peer group. If adults do not have something more interesting or valuable to offer, a major goal of adolescence—moving toward partnership in the adult community—is devalued. Students need to know that we have interesting lives apart from them and that we find life stimulating and challenging in some ways that are different from theirs. At the same time, they need us to be interested enough in them and open enough with our own values to share our ideas with them and engage them in discussions of personal as well as academic matters.

These issues highlight the value of establishing the second type of teacher-student relationship—one in which we share our reactions to and feelings about occurrences within the school setting and share with students limited aspects of our out-of-school life. Teachers who choose this type of relationship will often share with students occurrences involving their children, recreational activities, or cultural events they have attended. These teachers will also show considerable openness in discussing their feelings about events in the classroom.

The importance of being open enough to allow students to know us as people was highlighted for one of the authors during his experiences teaching junior high school students who had behavior disorders. Discussions with students indicated that a number of them were involved in shoplifting from a large chain store near the school. However, these same students frequently visited a leather shop where the proprietor kept money, tools, and leather on the outer counter while he worked in a back room. When asked why they stole from the chain store but not the leather worker, the students expressed some surprise and indicated emphatically that they knew this man and they did not steal from "real people." This incident emphasized an important issue in dealing with young people. They often react negatively to and abuse people whom they view as merely roles, but they less often create problems for individuals whom they know and understand.

In addition to letting students know us as people, we can model a degree of openness to our own students' verbal expressions of concerns and feelings in our classrooms. An excellent example of effective modeling occurred several years ago when one of the authors visited the classroom of an extremely effective teacher. The eighth-grade students in his class were actively involved in a science project and the room buzzed with noise and interest. A boy called across the room to his friend, John, and requested that John throw him the scissors. John immediately obliged, and the airborne scissors narrowly missed hitting another student. Rather than shouting at John, the teacher walked over to him and put his hand on John's shoulder. He proceeded to share with John the fact that the near miss had frightened him because he cared about and felt responsible for the students in his class. He then asked John if in the future he would carry the scissors across the room. The teacher then spoke briefly with the boy who had requested the scissors and with the student who had narrowly missed being hit. At the end of the period, the teacher took time to review the importance of the classroom procedure regarding scissors and had students demonstrate the correct procedure.

After class, the teacher explained why his intervention had been so calm and personal. He stated that young adolescents are involved in so many changes that their egos are very fragile and they personalize almost everything. He went on to say that his goal was to provide the student with information in a manner that would enhance the likelihood that the student would listen. Had he yelled at the student or made an example of him in front of the class, the student probably would have responded by focusing on the teacher's mean behavior rather than by examining his own behavior. The teacher stated that by admitting to his own feeling and sharing it with the student, he had provided the student with valuable information without making him defensive.

This incident is an excellent example of a skilled teacher's ability to synthesize spontaneously a working knowledge of adolescent development with practical communication skills. The result of this synthesis was that the teacher was able to respond in a way that facilitated the student's personal growth while modeling emotional control and sensitivity to the student's feelings.

While working on the current edition of this book, the authors saw another poignant example of the benefits of openness. An intern teacher consulted one of the authors regarding her problems with a high school biology class. The intern had taken over for a very dynamic and popular teacher and the students were behaving poorly and at times even being cruel to the intern. The author suggested that the intern openly discuss her feelings with the class while also acknowledging her appreciation for the students' feelings and sense of loss. Several educators advised the intern against this, indicating that she might be opening a "Pandora's box." The intern chose to have the discussion with the class and reported that students were very open in thoughtfully sharing their frustration. Indeed, one student indicated that her grade had dropped from an A to a C since the intern took over and that she was very frustrated. The intern noted that this was her first experience grading high school work and that she would be glad to meet with students to discuss their grades. Many students expressed appreciation for the intern's openness and the intern reported that the tenor of the class changed dramatically.

As educators, we must realize that feelings and perceptions about individuals in the classroom and classroom events are an important, legitimate issue of concern that affects students' motivation and achievement. If we are to be successful teaching students in the 1990s and beyond, we must be willing to deal with the affective component of the classroom milieu as well as with the cognitive content. A central theme of this book is that effective classroom managers are aware of classroom processes and are willing and able to engage students in assessing and adjusting classroom procedures and instructional methods. This act involves not only our own awareness and self-analysis but also involving students in open dialogue and problem solving.

A final example of the decision we must make about openness to student feedback occurred when a student-teacher being supervised by one of the authors was challenged by a student in his sophomore biology class. Frustrated by his inability to understand a lecture, the student stood up at the back of the class and stated loudly, "This class stinks!" Rather than sending the student to the office, the teacher responded by stating that, though he wished the student would share his frustration in a more polite manner, he was glad that he was able to state his anger rather than not come to class. The teacher proceeded to inform the student that he would like to discuss the student's concern, but that first he needed to determine whether it was shared by a majority of the class or only by a few students. The teacher's inquiry indicated that only three students shared this concern. Therefore, the teacher indicated that it made more sense for him and the three students to work together to consider how to make the class better for them. The student responded positively, and several discussions led to a positive resolution.

An interesting sidelight to this story involved the supervising teacher's reaction. This teacher strongly supported the third approach to teacher-student relationships. He stated that teachers cannot afford to be open with students or to discuss classroom instructional or behavioral matters. Instead, he believed that teachers must always be in authoritarian command of the classroom and that students must be required to do what teachers expect with no questions asked. The student-teacher who very effectively used an open response experienced considerable pressure from the school setting to become socialized to accepting the third type of response.

An optional manner for handling this situation within the context of the second type of teacher-student relationship was offered by a skilled middle school physical education teacher. She indicated that even though she supports the concept of teachers being open about their reactions to classroom events, she believes students can be taught that the teacher will not allow abusive language or direct confrontation of a teacher in front of a class. She believes that students should know ahead of time that when this occurs, they will be politely but firmly required to leave the class, knowing also that at a later time they will have an opportunity to discuss their concerns and behaviors with the teacher.

The different reactions chosen by the teachers in this example exemplify the decision we must make concerning the type of openness to students' input we select. Certainly, each teacher must operate at a degree of openness that is personally comfortable. Nevertheless, the second type of openness enhances students' sense of ownership in, and impact on, the classroom environment and thus can improve classroom management and student motivation.

Systematically Building Better Relationships

Even though using the second type of teacher-student relationship will generally enhance the rapport teachers can establish with students, it is sometimes desirable for teachers to act more systematically in developing positive teacher-student relationships. We can express our interest in and concern for students by (1) monitoring the quality of our relationships with students, with a focus on maintaining a high rate of positive statements; (2) creating opportunities for personal discussions with them; and (3) demonstrating our interest in activities that are important to them.

Maintain a High Ratio of Positive to Negative Statements

Children are sensitive to praise and criticism given by adults. Unfortunately, many teachers find that disruptive behavior is more noticeable and therefore respond to it more frequently than to on-task behavior. As indicated in Figure 3.1, frequent negative remarks by the teacher are usually accompanied by students' dislike for school. Though we often fall into the trap of believing that critical remarks will improve students' behavior, research suggests that the opposite is true.

> In one study we took a good class and made it into a bad one for a few weeks by having the teacher no longer praise the children. When the teacher no longer praised the children, off-task behavior increased from 8.7 percent to 25.5 percent. The teacher criticized off-task behavior and did not praise on-task behavior. When the teacher was

	Pre 2 Weeks After Start of School (September 20–27)			Post January 22–24		
Teacher	Pos.	Neg.	Students Responding Yes to: "Do You Like School?"	Pos.	Neg.	Students Responding Yes to: "Do You Like School?"
1	.72	28	90%	.76	24	90%
2	.34	66	90%	.33	67	20%
3	.66	34	80%	.70	30	70%
4	.69	31	90%	.65	35	80%
5	.54	46	100%	.61	39	20%
6	.80	20	100%	.87	13	100%
7	.22	78	90%	.19	81	20%
8	.64	36	70%	.64	36	40%
9	.79	21	100%	.77	23	100%
10	.92	08	80%	.89	11	90%
11	.52	48	100%	.63	37	60%
12	.73	27	90%	.65	35	90%
13	.45	55	90%	.61	39	80%
14	.67	33	80%	.73	27	80%
15	.58	42	90%	.60	40	70%
16	.51	49	60%	.58	42	10%
17	.76	24	70%	.77	23	70%

FIGURE 3.1
Influence of Positive and Negative Teacher Statements on Students' Feelings about School

Source: Personal correspondence with Bud Fredericks, Teaching Research, Monmouth, OR. Reprinted by permission.

asked to increase her criticism from 5 times in 20 minutes to 16 times in 20 minutes, the children showed even more off-task behavior. Off-task behavior increased to an average of 31.2 percent, and on some days was over 50 percent. Attention to that off-task behavior increased its occurrence when no praise was given for working. Introduction of praise back into the classroom restored good working behavior. (Becker, Engelmann, & Thomas, 1975, p. 69)

An excellent example of the effect of teachers' negative or positive statements occurred several years ago in a school district in Oregon. Much to their credit, district administrators became worried about what they perceived as a negative attitude among a significant number of their young schoolchildren. The district subsequently sought the services of an outside agency to examine the situation. The consultants decided initially to examine the ratio of positive to negative statements made by teachers. They began their intervention by simply asking children in second-grade classrooms to answer yes or no to the question, Do you like school? As indicated in the fourth column of Figure 3.1, at the beginning of the school year, most students in all classes responded yes to this question. The consultants discovered, however, that, for students who experienced classrooms characterized by a low rate of positive teacher verbalizations, these positive feelings about school changed dramatically within the first 15 weeks of school.

More specifically, in the eight classes in which teachers provided less than 65 percent positive statements, the percentage of students responding that they liked school dropped an alarming 48 percent during the 15 weeks. In the seven classrooms in which 70 percent or more of the teachers' statements were positive, though, students' responses to the question of whether they liked school remained, on the average, exactly the same after 15 weeks of school. These data suggest that children are much less comfortable in classroom environments characterized by a low rate of positive teacher statements.

The data in Figure 3.2, taken from a school with whom one of the authors consulted, show a dramatic pattern of students who have spent more time in the school perceiving teachers as less understanding, caring, helpful, and fair professionals. Though slight decreases in students' attitudes might be expected as youngsters move into early and mid-adolescence, our work in middle schools suggests that

FIGURE 3.2
Students' Perceptions of Teachers: Percentage of Students Responding "Nearly Always" or "Most of the Time"

Question	6th Grade	7th Grade	8th Grade
Teachers understand the problems of students	37	33	20
Teachers care about students	76	43	41
The principal and vice-principal help the students	43	32	21
Teachers pick on some students	25	40	51
Teachers give most of their help and attention to the good students	31	36	51
A student can get help from a teacher	50	43	25

significant changes are unusual. When such changes do occur, they are inevitably associated with lower achievement and greater student misbehavior.

In their book *Inviting School Success,* Purkey and Novak (1984) set forth four types of teacher behaviors toward students:

1. Intentionally disinviting
2. Unintentionally disinviting
3. Unintentionally inviting
4. Intentionally inviting

In defining these terms, Purkey stated, "As used here, an invitation is a summary description of message—verbal and nonverbal, formal and informal—continuously transmitted to students with the intention of informing them that they are responsible, able, and valuable. Conversely, a disinvitation is intended to tell them that they are irresponsible, incapable, and worthless" (p. 3). An example of an intentionally disinviting behavior would be the teacher who on the first day of school privately singles out a student whose sibling had been a particular problem several years earlier and informs the child that if he is anything like his brother, this will be a very difficult year for him. Even though this teacher statement is intentional and intended to motivate the student to behave properly, the student receives it as punitive, unfair, and disinviting. An example of an unintentionally disinviting statement was provided by a high school vice-principal. He stated that the day before final exam week began, he observed a student requesting assistance from a teacher. The teacher's response, "Don't worry, you haven't got a chance of passing the test anyway," was devastating but probably unintentionally disinviting.

Teachers make many inviting comments to students. For example, teachers often greet students at the door, state how glad they are to see a student, and respond positively to the quality of student work. Some of this inviting behavior occurs unintentionally because teachers are positive people who care about their students. On other occasions, teachers consciously consider the impact of positive invitations and intentionally invite students to be positively involved in their classes. An excellent example of intentionally invitational behavior and its relationship to teacher openness with students was shared with the authors by a high school English teacher. One day, the teacher experienced a small crisis before arriving at school. The first two periods went fairly well. However, the teacher became tired and anxious as the day went on and was concerned about teaching his unruly third-period class. At the end of the second period, one of his better junior English students asked for some assistance. The teacher stated that he was not feeling well and asked the student if he would assist the teacher. The student was glad to help and the teacher suggested that they both stand at the door, greet the incoming students, and make a statement about what an interesting class this was going to be. The teacher reported that when the bell rang and he turned to the class, every student was seated and attentively focused on the front of the class—an unheard of reaction from these students. The teacher then noticed two sets of students who were not in his third-period class. They informed him that they had heard this was going to be an interesting class and had decided to attend. Two of the students had even obtained permission from their third-period teacher. The English teacher reported that after clarifying the issue of the additional students, he had one of the most rewarding instructional experiences in some time.

In addition to their value in increasing positive student attitudes, invitational interactions provide the basis for creating teacher-student relationships that facilitate the use of corrective interventions described in Chapters 9, 10, and 11. An excellent example of this concept was provided by a student-teacher with whom one of the authors was working during the final editing of this book. The student-teacher was working with one of the most disruptive third-graders the author had encountered. Each day, the boy was involved in many instances of aggressive behavior toward peers and insubordination to adults. Because the school's assertive discipline program had only increased the student's acting-out behavior, and because the boy's parents would not allow the school to provide special education services, the principal was considering expelling the student.

The student-teacher decided to work with the student as part of her assignment in a classroom management course. In so doing, she was asked to attempt many of the methods described throughout this book and was encouraged to work consistently (and persistently) on establishing rapport with the student. The student's initial responses were extremely negative. He frequently and vividly informed the student-teacher that he hated teachers (a value reinforced by his parents) and that he wanted nothing to do with her. But the teacher persisted. She discovered that the boy's mother raised show dogs, and she watched a cable television show from New York in which the mother's dog took second place in a national competition. The student-teacher discussed this event with the student and attempted to discover other aspects of the boy's life. One day when a professional athlete with the same name as the boy's was traded, the teacher laminated the article in plastic and placed it on the bulletin board with a large red arrow pointing to it. The class was understandably curious, and the boy received considerable attention. Gradually, he increased his willingness to work cooperatively with the teacher. Although he would not become involved in problem solving, he did agree to a contract that was associated with considerable changes in behavior. Although the dramatic improvement in the student's behavior required behavioristic methods, these were not effective until the student was willing to work with the teacher. The improved relationship made possible other interventions that led to important changes.

An elementary school principal recently shared an outstanding example of how an administrator utilized invitational relationships. During a workshop presented for a state principals' association, the principal asked one of the authors if he could share something he had done based on his attending a similar workshop with the author. He told his colleagues that his background had caused him to be a very authoritarian person and that when he became a principal, he informed teachers that they could be guaranteed of firm support from the office. He noted that his most common intervention with students sent to his office for discipline was to intimidate and threaten the student. He proceeded to note that after attending the workshop, he carefully considered his reactions and realized that they were seldom associated with positive, long-term changes in student behavior and that he had received some negative comments from parents. He decided to try an experiment in which he selected 12 students who were experiencing ongoing behavior problems. He divided these students into three groups, and each day all three groups of 4 students began their day by spending approximately four minutes with him during which all 4 students shared a positive thing that had happened to them the previous day, one thing they were looking forward to in school that day, and anything adults at school could do to help them that day. At the end of each session, each student gave the principal his or her "sign" ("high 5," hug, etc.) and went to class. The principal noted a dramatic improvement in these students' attendance, work completion, and on-task behavior. He shared with the audience that from that point on, he decided to alter the manner in which he worked with students.

Communicating High Expectations

How teachers communicate their expectations about how well students will do in the classroom is an important and well-documented factor in teacher-student relationships. School effectiveness research has consistently pointed to teachers' high expectations of students' performance as a key factor associated with students' achievement. In a variety of subtle and not-so-subtle ways, we communicate to some students that they are bright, capable, and responsible, while other students receive the message that they are dull, incapable, and irresponsible.

Our expectations of students are influenced by a variety of factors other than actual performance or behavior. Frericks (1974) found that teachers viewing a group of students labeled low in ability described the students' behavior more negatively than did teachers who viewed the same students but were told they were observing "regular students in a normal classroom." Spencer-Hall (1981) reported that some students nominated for a citizen-of-the-year reward had misbehavior rates as high as that of any student in the class. Teachers are obviously influenced by how students present themselves or are labeled, as well as by students' behavior.

Unfortunately, gender and ethnicity also influence how teachers respond to students. Studies suggest that boys receive more teacher attention than do girls. For example, in preschool classrooms, boys receive more academic instruction, hugs, and teacher attention (Serbin, 1973; Ebbeck, 1984). David and Myra Sadker have conducted extensive studies that indicate that boys call out almost eight times as often as girls and teachers' responses to call outs is to listen to and comment about the boys' statements while correcting the girls for not raising their hand (Sadker, Sadker, & Thomas, 1981). In addition, teachers also appear to favor boys in terms of calling on students to volunteer (Sadker & Sadker, 1985). Studies also indicate that boys receive more praise than girls and that they are more likely to receive detailed feedback associated with their praise. Studies also suggest that boys receive particularly partial treatment in science classes (Kahle, 1990; Lee, 1991).

Students' ethnic background also appears to influence teacher expectations and treatment of students. In the 1992 *AAUW Report: How Schools Shortchange Girls,* the committee stated:

> Evidence also suggests that the attention minority students receive from teachers may be different in nature from that given to white children. In elementary school, black boys tend to have fewer interactions overall with teachers than other students and yet they are the recipients of four to ten times the amount of qualified praise ("That's good, but . . .") as other students. Black boys tend to be perceived less favorably by

their teachers and seen as less able than other students. The data are more complex for girls. Black girls have less interaction with teachers than white girls, but they attempt to initiate interaction much more often than white girls or than boys of either race. Research indicates that teachers may unconsciously rebuff these black girls, who eventually turn to peers for interaction, often becoming the class enforcer of go-between for other students. Black females also receive less reinforcement from teachers than do other students, although their academic performance is often better than boys.

In fact, when black girls do as well as white boys in school, teachers attribute their success to hard work but assume that the white boys are not working up to their full potential. This, coupled with the evidence that blacks are more often reinforced for their social behavior while whites are likely to be reinforced for their academic accomplishments, may contribute to low academic self-esteem in black girls. (pp. 70–71)

Results from classroom interaction studies indicate that teachers generally respond more favorably to students they perceive as high achievers. High achievers receive more response opportunities; are given more time to answer questions; receive more positive nonverbal feedback such as smiles, nods, and winks; and are less likely to be ignored. Cooper and Good (1983) provided this list of common ways in which teachers respond differently to students who are high achieving versus those who are low achieving:

1. Seating low-expectation students far from the teacher and/or seating them in a group.
2. Paying less attention to lows in academic situations (smiling less often and maintaining less eye contact).
3. Calling on lows less often to answer classroom questions or to make public demonstrations.
4. Waiting less time for lows to answer questions.
5. Not staying with lows in failure situations (i.e., providing fewer clues, asking fewer follow-up questions).
6. Criticizing lows more frequently than highs for incorrect public responses.
7. Praising lows less frequently than highs after successful public responses.
8. Praising lows more frequently than highs for marginal or inadequate public responses.
9. Providing lows with less accurate and less detailed feedback than highs.
10. Failing to provide lows with feedback about their responses as often as highs.
11. Demanding less work and effort from lows than from highs.
12. Interrupting performance of lows more frequently than highs. (p. 10)

In reviewing the research on expectation effects, Brophy (1983) cited studies suggesting that "teacher expectations do have self-fulfilling-prophecy effects on student-achievement levels, but that these effects make only a 5 to 10 percent difference, on the average" (p. 635). Brophy went on to state:

These conclusions clearly imply that even ideal teacher education related to the topic of teacher expectations will not work miracles in our schools, but they do not imply that the topic is unimportant. Even a 5 percent difference in educational outcomes is an important difference, the more so as it is compounded across school years. Furthermore, the presentation so far has been confined to consideration of the average effect across all teachers of expectations concerning student achievement. The story becomes much more complicated, and the implications for teacher education much more obvious, when we turn attention to other kinds of expectations and to differences among teachers in predisposition to expectation effects. (p. 635)

We must realize that the concept of holding high expectations for all students does not mean that we should provide identical treatment for all students. To a considerable extent, the differential treatment students receive from teachers is a logical and often thoughtful response to individual student needs. Nevertheless, teachers should become aware of the potential for allowing successful students to dominate classroom interactions.

It is often desirable that we initiate a higher percentage of our academic contacts with students who are low achieving during individual or small-group instruction. Similarly, especially when introducing new material to younger children, we should try to maximize the percentage of correct responses so that students do not become confused by competing, inaccurate information. The critical issue is that we must become aware of ways in which we respond differently to various types of students and thoughtfully and systematically implement differential interaction patterns that support individual student and group learning. Figure 3.3 presents guidelines teachers can follow to minimize the negative effects of teacher expectations.

As teachers, we need to be aware of the importance of communicating positive expectations to all students. Periodically, we need to (1) collect data about how we interact with students in our classes, (2) analyze the data to see if we are using primarily supportive or critical statements, (3) determine whether we are responding differently (more critically or less often) to some students, and (4) attempt to alter our patterns of interaction so that we communicate high expectations to all students. Several of the activities at the end of the chapter will assist you with this. In addition, teachers can develop creative, fun ways of ensuring that students receive equal opportunities. You can write each student's name on a tongue depressor, popsicle stick, or chip, and draw from a can to determine who will answer each question. (Remember to replace the name back into the can following each draw.) This keeps students alert and ensures that, over time, all students will receive an equal number of questions to answer.

Creating Opportunities for Personal Discussions

As in any relationship, it is helpful to have time to get to know one another without the interruptions occasioned by day-to-day events. The following sections discuss ideas for creating such opportunities within the context of the teacher-student relationship. Your decision about which activities to use will depend on the grade level you teach and the time and energy you wish to employ in developing positive teacher-student relationships.

Demonstrating Interest in Students' Activities
An important way to indicate our concern for students and to enjoy our relationships with them is to take time to attend the activities in which they are involved.

FIGURE 3.3

Guidelines for
Avoiding the
Negative Effects
of Teacher
Expectations

- *Use information from tests, cumulative folders, and other teachers very carefully.*
    - Some teachers avoid reading cumulative folders for several weeks at the beginning of the year.
    - Be critical and objective about the reports you hear from other teachers, especially "horror stories" told in the teachers' lounge.
- *Be flexible in your use of grouping strategies.*
    - Review work of students in different groups often and experiment with new groupings.
    - Use different groupings for different subjects.
    - Use mixed-ability groups in cooperative exercises when all students can handle the same material.
- *Make sure all the students are challenged.*
    - Avoid saying, "This is easy, I know you can do it."
    - Offer a wide range of problems, and encourage all students to try a few of the harder ones for extra credit. Try to find something positive about these attempts.
- *Be especially careful about how you respond to low-achieving students during class discussions.*
    - Give them prompts, clues, and time to answer.
    - Give ample praise for good answers.
    - Call on low achievers as often as high achievers.
- *Use materials that show a wide range of ethnic groups.*
    - Check readers and library books. Is there ethnic diversity?
    - Ask your librarian to find multiethnic stories, filmstrips, etc.
    - If few materials are available, ask students to research and create their own, based on community or family resources.
- *Be fair in evaluation and disciplinary procedures.*
    - Make sure equal offenses merit equal punishment. Find out from students in an anonymous questionnaire whether you seem to be favoring certain individuals.
    - Try to grade student work without knowing the identity of the student. Ask another teacher to give you a "second opinion" from time to time.
- *Communicate to all students that you believe they can learn—and mean it.*
    - Return papers that do not meet standards with specific suggestions for improvements.
    - If students do not have the answers immediately, wait, probe, and then help them think through an answer.
- *Involve all students in learning tasks and in privileges.*
    - Use some system for calling on or contacting students to make sure you give each student practice in reading, speaking, and answering questions.
    - Keep track of who gets to do what job. Are some students always on the list while others seldom make it?
- *Monitor your nonverbal behavior.*
    - Do you lean away or stand farther away from some students? Do some students get smiles when they approach your desk while others get only frowns?
    - Do you avoid touching some students?
    - Does your tone of voice vary with different students?

Source: Anita Woolfolk, *Educational Psychology,* 3/e, © 1987, pp. 340–341. Reprinted by permission of Prentice-Hall, Inc., Englewood Cliffs, New Jersey.

As a rule, parents are extremely appreciative of and impressed with teachers' attendance at student activities. Additionally, such attendance often is associated with dramatic improvement of the students whose activities were attended.

Eating Lunch with Students

Most teacher-student contact occurs in the presence of 25 to 30 other children. Unless they take the initiative by staying after school, students may never have individual private time with their teacher. One way to provide this personal time is to have lunch in the classroom with individual students. This time can be arranged by providing a sign-up sheet so that students who are interested can reserve a time to eat lunch alone with you. You and the student can use the lunch period to share personal interests. You should be willing to listen to the student's concerns about personal or school problems, but the time together should not be used as a conference in which you discuss the student's schoolwork or behavior.

Arranging Interviews

Anyone who has taught young children for several years has experienced an instance in which a student appeared surprised to see the teacher in a nonschool setting, such as the grocery store. Children often view the teacher solely as a teacher and are quite unaware of his or her interests and life outside the school setting. One approach for making you seem more real is to allow the children to interview you. You can expand this activity by having your spouse or older children visit the classroom and be interviewed by the class.

Sending Letters and Notes to Students

Beginning the school year with a personal letter from you is an effective technique for establishing rapport with students. A positive individualized letter placed on each student's desk informs each student that you are happy to have him or her in class, eager to get to know him or her, and excited about the upcoming school year. Notes given to students throughout the school year can enhance the personal relationship between you and the student. Appropriate times for expressing thoughts or providing information by notes or letters include when a student has been successful at a new or difficult task, when a student's behavior has improved, when a personal matter seems to be worrying a student, and on a student's birthday. Students also appreciate receiving a note or a get-well card along with their homework when they are sick and must miss school for several days.

Using a Suggestion Box

Students often perceive their teacher as relatively uninterested in their ideas about the classroom. Although we may view this situation as undesirable, it is to some degree an understandable response to the reality that we have primary responsibility for creating an appropriate classroom environment. One method that indicates our interest in students' ideas is to display a suggestion box and encourage students to write ideas for making the class a better place in which to learn. This approach can be expanded to include holding class meetings in which students discuss their ideas and concerns about the classroom. When classroom meetings are used, having students place agenda items on the board can replace the suggestion box. Either way, our willingness to request, accept, and respond to students' suggestions can be an effective method for improving teacher-student rapport.

Joining in School and Community Events

Schools often organize special events such as hat days, carnivals, and bike rodeos. Similarly, communities have picnics, carnivals, and other social events. We can demonstrate our interest in students and our own enjoyment of a good time by becoming involved in these activities. Schools can also organize special events or displays that give students a chance to view teachers in a personal light and increase positive teacher-student interaction. Both authors have worked in buildings where a childhood picture of each staff member was displayed and students attempted to match the teachers with the childhood pictures. Similarly, the authors have taught in schools where a bulletin board was arranged so that teachers and students could publicly write positive statements to other students or teachers. Involvement in activities such as these helps create a positive school atmosphere and thereby significantly reduce unproductive student behavior.

Joining in Playground Games

Students enjoy having teachers participate in their playground activities. Occasionally sharing recess time with the children is an excellent way for us to show our humanness and to demonstrate that we enjoy our students. Not only can this activity enhance teacher-student relationships but it can also provide us with an excellent form of relaxation. The physical activity and the opportunity to interact with children in a relaxed and nonacademic setting can provide a refreshing break in the school day. One way to formalize this type of teacher-student interaction is to develop several opportunities for friendly athletic competition between students and teachers.

Making Birthday Cards

A birthday is a special day for children. A thoughtful way to respond to children's excitement is to make a card when each student has a birthday. The card can include a birthday greeting as well as a positive statement about some aspect of the student's work or behavior.

Introducing New Students to Adults in the School

Several schools with which the authors work have developed a creative method for introducing new children to school personnel. A new student is given a booklet in which he or she is to obtain the signatures of key adults in the building, such as the principal, secretary, librarian, custodian, cook, and playground assistant. When each adult signs the book, he or she gives the child a gift, such as an eraser, pencil, cookie, or a positive note. By the end of the second day, the child has met a variety of caring adults, and these adults know there is a new student who will need special invitations for a few weeks as he or she makes the adjustment into a new school setting.

USING EFFECTIVE COMMUNICATION SKILLS

Teachers who choose to discuss classroom issues with students and to elicit student feedback about classroom events will benefit from a variety of specific communication skills that enhance open interpersonal relationships. Teachers can use the communication skills described in the following sections regardless of the type of teacher-student relationship they choose. If you choose a more open, interactive classroom management style, however, you will find these skills particularly important in effectively developing your classroom management skills.

The importance of using effective communication skills cannot be overemphasized. They are the foundation for good classroom management. Unless we use effective communication skills, all other attempts at creating a well-managed, positive learning environment will be severely limited and usually short-lived. Caring interpersonal interactions are essential in meeting such important individual needs as safety and security, belongingness, and self-esteem.

In addition to creating relationships that meet essential student needs, using effective communication skills benefits us by allowing us to meet our own needs more effectively and simultaneously to achieve our professional goals. Using the skills presented in this section enables us to:

1. Be warm and friendly and enjoy relationships with students.
2. Express our own needs and wants clearly within the classroom.
3. Better understand and accept students and experience more positive feelings toward them.
4. Create situations in which students feel understood and cared for and therefore respond more positively to us and to their peers.

Communication skills can be divided into the two categories of sending skills and receiving skills. Sending skills are commonly used when speaking to someone. Receiving skills are techniques that can be used to become a more effective listener.

Before examining the communication skills presented in this section, realize that the effective use of these skills is based on specific beliefs about children and the goals and roles adults choose to follow when working with children. The use of communication skills is based on these four premises:

1. We wish to share with students responsibility for resolving problems.
2. We believe that students are, for the most part, responsible individuals when the atmosphere is conducive to their being so.
3. We accept that there can be more than one perspective to a problem and consider perspectives other than our own to be valid.
4. We do not perceive our objective in a teacher-student confrontation as being "to win."

When considering whether to use the methods described in the following sections, you must realize that they are skills intended to help teachers implement open, type-two interactions with students. These methods will be of little value to teachers who wish to establish or maintain closed, authoritarian, type-three relationships with students.

Placing Communication Skills in Cultural Context

It is important that educators place these suggestions within a cultural context. For example, Wei (1980) noted that Vietnamese students may feel uncomfortable with American teachers' friendliness and openness, and may initially respond shyly and withdraw when asked to be involved in open adult-student relationships. Some Asian students may also find it uncomfortable to make direct eye contact with their teachers, viewing this as a sign of disrespect. Cambodian, Laotian, and Vietnamese students may find a teacher's straightforwardness rude and attacking (Nguyen, 1987).

Similarly, some studies indicate that, as a sign of respect, African American students are more likely than Anglo students to avoid eye contact with those in authority (Gilliam & Van Den Berg, 1980). African American students may maintain less physical distance between themselves and others (Aiello & Jones, 1971; Bauer, 1973), may be more sensitive to praise and criticism (Cooperman, 1975; Ferrell, 1971), and may be more sensitive to nonverbal cues (Hale, 1981). Teachers must also be aware that their positive behavior may initially be received with some skepticism by African American students. In describing the attitudes Black students may have toward White teachers, Gay and Abrahams (1973) wrote, "The most important dimension of the Black stereotype of whites is that Black children are taught early to be suspicious of whites" (p. 332).

Like Southeast Asian students, Hispanic students may find direct and informal relationships with adults in the school to be uncomfortable. An open discussion in which the teacher seeks to ascertain both sides of the situation and facilitate a dialogue may be seen as hostile (Grossman, 1984; Burger, 1972). Indeed, some Hispanic students may find a direct approach as indicating a lack of respect for the student—the opposite of what many professional adults in the Anglo community would expect. Hispanic students may tend to be accepting of physical contact and may respond well to a supportive touch (Grossman, 1984). Hispanic students may also have experienced in their community that it is acceptable for more than one person to speak at a time during a group discussion. Therefore, teachers need to be particularly careful in ensuring that Hispanic students understand and have an opportunity to practice the typical school expectation that one person speaks at a time.

The real key is that we all need to be sensitive to the differences between our own preferences or the recommendations of others and our students' particular communication patterns. Although all students benefit from developing communication skills that will be used and valued in a wide variety of settings in this society, teachers also need to realize the confusion of experiencing several different norms regarding communication. Therefore, when using communication skills that may vary from those used by students in the home, teachers must realize the importance of carefully explaining and teaching these skills. In addition, teachers must be alert to the need to adjust communication patterns when students appear uncomfortable or confused by them.

Sending Skills

Sending skills fall into three general categories: (1) skills in confronting students about behaviors they need to change, (2) skills in providing students with feedback about their academic performance, and (3) skills in presenting positive expectations to students. To highlight their most common use, each skill is presented separately. It is obvious, however, that the three skills are interrelated and particularly that the skills for confronting student behavior will, in most interactions, enhance the quality of the teacher-student relationship.

Skills for Confronting Inappropriate or Disruptive Behavior

The following methods will assist the teacher in improving relationships with students.

1. *Deal in the present.* Information is more useful when it is shared at the earliest appropriate opportunity. Young people are very "now" oriented. It is unfair and ineffective to bring up issues after several days have elapsed. Therefore, though it may be necessary to wait until you can speak with the student alone or until the student has better control of his or her emotions, it is best to discuss important matters as soon after they occur as possible.

2. *Talk directly to students rather than about them.* Adults have a tendency to talk to parents or colleagues about students rather than talking directly to the student. The assumption seems to be that students could not understand or would be overpowered by the information. The authors' experiences strongly contradict these beliefs. Indeed, it appears that students suffer more from worrying about what has been said about them than they do from receiving skillfully presented direct feedback. By talking directly to students, we show respect for them while ensuring that they receive accurate (rather than secondhand) information about adults' feelings.

3. *Speak courteously.* Nothing does more to create positive interactions than using simple courtesy statements such as *thank you, please,* and *excuse me.* Because teachers serve as important models for students, their interactions with them should include more (certainly not less) frequent use of courtesies than do their interactions with other adults.

4. *Make eye contact and be aware of nonverbal messages.* An old saying states that children often respond more to what adults do than to what they say. Because young people are so dependent on adults, they become adept at reading adults' nonverbal messages. It is therefore important that we attempt to make our nonverbal messages congruent with our verbal messages. If you are talking to a student but looking over his or her shoulder, the student will find it difficult to believe that you feel positive about her or him and are sincerely concerned. Similarly, when we shout that we are not angry with a class, the students will be more likely to listen to the tone of voice than to the words.

5. *Take responsibility for statements by using the personal pronoun* I. It is hard to underestimate the importance and value of I-messages. Students who experience consistent and/or serious behavior problems are often deficient in social cognition skills. Simply stated, they are not as capable as their peers of understanding and appreciating others' points of view. For example, they may not understand why a teacher is bothered by their talking out or why, despite their aggressive or rude behavior, their peers do not wish to play with them.

Just as many students learn to read before entering school, many children learn to understand others' perspectives through the use of language employed at home. Students who have not had these opportunities will, just like students who enter school unable to decode letters and sounds, need learning experiences that help them develop important social cognition skills. I-messages are one method of providing this important assistance.

In their *Discovering Your Teaching Self,* Curwin and Fuhrmann (1975) provided a succinct and sensitive statement about this skill:

> Meaningful communication between people (the communication between adults and children is of special interest to us) often breaks down because one party (or both) continually tells the other what's wrong with him rather than identifying how he himself is feeling in the situation. When I tell someone what's wrong with him, I virtually take away from him all responsibility for himself. Since I know what is wrong, I also know how to "correct" it. Thus I leave him powerless and probably defensive. (p. 196)

If we say to a student, "You are being disruptive" or "You're late again!" the student is likely to feel attacked and defensive. If, however, we say, "It distracts me and I feel uncomfortable when you talk while I am talking (or when you come in late)," the student has been provided with some useful information about his or her effect on other people. Similarly, using the pronoun *we* is unfairly ganging up against a student. When confronted with statements beginning with "we feel" or "the entire class believes," the student is likely to feel attacked and defeated. Though they are flexible, children are also very sensitive and need to be confronted by one person at a time. Furthermore, because each of us is an expert on only our own feelings, it appears reasonable that each of us should share our own feelings and dispense with the pronoun *we.*

In his *Teacher Effectiveness Training* (TET), Thomas Gordon (1974) wrote that when expressing a concern about students' behavior that affects the teacher, the teacher should employ an I-message consisting of three components: (1) the personal pronoun *I,* (2) the feeling the teacher is experiencing, and (3) the effect the student's behavior is having on the teacher. For example, a typical teacher's response to a student's interruption might be, "If you can't stop interrupting me, you can leave the room." If an I-message is used in this situation, the teacher might say, "When you interrupt me, I become frustrated because I get distracted and have difficulty helping the other students."

Because I-messages express personal feelings and often deal with student behaviors that require change, it is best to send them privately. We should do so especially when we are dealing with adolescents. Adolescents, being particularly sensitive to peer pressure, will often respond to even the most thoughtful public criticism defensively. Because most adolescents value being treated as adults, though, they will usually respond positively to private expressions of our concern.

Another, less open, way to send an I-message involves politely yet firmly expressing a demand using the first person singular. Therefore, if a student began talking to another student during a teacher's presentation, the teacher might say in a nonthreatening manner, "I expect students to listen quietly while someone in this class speaks." Although this type of I-message will more likely elicit a defensive response from older students, it is a clear, straightforward way to present your expectations.

Sending an I-message seems like such a simple intervention and is something many adults initially find somewhat unnatural. Over the past 20 years, however, the authors have taught this simple skill to thousands of in-service and preservice teachers and have received literally hundreds of comments from teachers on how surprised they were at the effectiveness of this strategy. The day before writing this section of the fourth edition, a young high school teacher in one of the author's classes shared with her colleagues that she had quietly sent an I-message to one of her most disruptive students. She was amazed that the student stopped by after class to apologize to her and that during the following week his behavior had dramatically improved. When asked why she thought he had apparently responded so well, she noted that he was probably used to being criticized for his behavior and he was appreciative that someone would treat him courteously.

6. *Make statements rather than ask questions.* When children misbehave, they are frequently bombarded with questions. This approach leaves the child feeling intimidated and defensive. Questions such as Are you feeling all right? Would you like to leave the room for a few minutes? or Can I help? can be extremely productive. Teachers should, however, be aware of opportunities for replacing questions with statements. Consider the different feelings a child might have on coming late to class and hearing *Where have you been?* compared to *I was concerned when you were late because we have to leave on our field trip in five minutes.* It is important to keep in mind that questions are often important tools for helping children understand and change their behavior. Asking students what they were doing or how their behavior helped them is an important component in solving problems. Questions often misdirect students from taking responsibility for their own behavior, however, while creating defensiveness. Therefore, when dealing with students' behaviors, use questions sparingly and in the context of a problem-solving approach.

Skills for Giving Specific, Descriptive Feedback

Studies indicate that teachers are not particularly effective at using feedback to students. When providing students with feedback about their academic performance it is useful to ask ourselves three questions: How much? To whom? and What type? The answer to the first question is probably somewhat more but not too much.

Based on results of a three-year study involving data collection in more than 100 fourth-, sixth-, and eighth-grade classrooms, Sadker and Sadker (1985) expressed concern about the quantity and quality of teachers' feedback to students. These researchers found that teachers demonstrated low rates of specific positive feedback or criticism and high rates of acceptance. "Acceptance included teacher comments that implied that student performance was correct and appropriate . . . (Examples include: 'O.K.,' 'uh-huh,' 'I see,' or simply teacher silence)" (Sadker & Sadker, 1985, p. 360). The Sadkers' main interpretation of their findings was that teacher feedback was too bland. They found that "in two-thirds of the classrooms observed, teachers never clearly indicated that a student answer was incorrect"

(p. 360). Similarly, only 11 percent of teacher feedback involved praise, and in more than one-fourth of the classrooms, teachers never praised students' answers. These findings regarding the general lack of critical or specific feedback are reinforced by data reported by Goodlad (1984) indicating that 20 percent of both elementary and secondary students stated that they were neither informed nor corrected following a mistake.

The answer to the second question, To whom should effective feedback be provided? is closely related to the issue of expectation effects. Positive, prescriptive feedback needs to be more evenly distributed so that it is provided not only to high achievers or to students with the social skills to elicit this feedback. In fact, research (Brophy & Evertson, 1976; Good, Ebmeier, & Beckerman, 1978; Stallings, 1975) indicates that positive feedback is more effective with students of lower socioeconomic status and low achievement—the students who research suggests receive the least positive feedback.

The answer to the question, What type of feedback is most effective? is the key question. One of the most important communication skills teachers can use is specific, clear, descriptive feedback that helps students take responsibility for their successes. Research on attribution theory (Anderson & Prawat, 1983; Weiner, 1979) indicates that students attribute their success or failure to ability, effort, luck, or difficulty of task. If students attribute their success or failure to effort, they are able to view their performance as influenced by factors within their control (an internal locus of control) and are therefore able to expect success in similar situations if they make the effort. When failure is attributed, however, to ability, luck, or difficulty of task, students feel less control over results and begin to believe that making a concerted effort in the future will have little effect on the outcome. Praise that helps students focus on factors within their control that influenced performance allows students to develop an internal locus of control.

Unfortunately, on occasions when they are successful, low achievers tend to credit luck or the ease of task for this success. High achievers, however, tend to credit their effort and ability for their success. Teachers can alter children's perceptions of their control over success or failure by using feedback more effectively. In an interesting study, Dweck (1975) showed that elementary students who viewed school learning as extremely hopeless could change this belief by receiving training sessions in which they were given both success and failure, and, when failing, were informed that their failure was due to lack of effort. Students who received this training responded to failure by persisting and implementing problem-solving strategies to resolve their dilemma. Schunk (1983) studied elementary students' responses to positive feedback and stated that simply providing students with statements about their effort may suggest to students that they do not have the ability to complete the task without extensive effort. It seems that the most effective feedback provides students with information that they possess the ability to achieve success and that they will need to expend effort to do the task well.

By becoming more skilled in providing students with useful positive feedback, teachers can help students take credit for their successes and develop a better appreciation for their ability to control the school environment in positive ways. O'Leary and O'Leary (1977) stated that to serve as an effective reinforcer, feedback (they use the term *praise*) to students must have three qualities:

1. *Contingency.* Praise must immediately follow desired behaviors rather than be applied simply as a general motivator. Anderson and colleagues (1979) found that teachers failed to use praise contingently because the rate of praise following reading turns that contained mistakes was similar to the rate following correct responses.
2. *Specificity.* Praise should describe the specific behavior being reinforced. Again, Anderson and colleagues (1979) suggested that teachers needed improvement in this area. Their data showed that teachers were specific in only 5 percent of their praise for academic work and in 40 percent of their praise for behavior.
3. *Credibility.* Praise should be appropriate for the situation and the individual. Older, high-achieving students are aware that praise is used primarily for motivation and encouragement and may find praise unnecessary and even insulting.

Perhaps the most useful information on the effective use of positive feedback to students was presented by Brophy (1981). Figure 3.4 presents Brophy's summary of research findings on the effective use of feedback (he also uses the word *praise*).

Receiving Skills

Listening skills are extremely important; when used effectively, they create relationships that allow students to feel significant, accepted, respected, and able to take responsibility for their own behavior. By effectively using listening skills, adults help youngsters clarify their feelings and resolve their own conflicts. Unfortunately, adults all too often provide quick answers for children rather than carefully listening in order to help the youngsters clarify the problem and then aid them in developing a solution.

William Glasser (1988) stated that students' attempts to have someone listen to them is the source of nearly 95 percent of discipline problems in school. Speaking of student behavior problems in schools, Glasser wrote, "I believe that frustration of the need for power, even more than the need for belonging, is at the core of today's difficulties" (p. 40). Glasser noted that there are three levels at which students can satisfy their need for power of involvement in the school environment. First, students simply need to believe that someone whom they respect will listen to them. At the second level, someone listens and accepts the validity of the student's statement or concern. The third and highest level involves an adult's stating that the students idea may be worth implementing.

Stop for a moment and reflect on the last several situations when a student came to you with a problem or expressed a strong emotion. What did you do? If you are like most adults, you provided a quick answer to the problem or attempted to stop the expression of emotion by providing assurances or by suggesting that the student should not be expressing the emotion. Both of these responses are commonly used because they require a minimum of time and effort and prevent adults from having to deal with a youngster's emotions. When adults consistently provide answers, however, they subtly inform students that they do not care enough really to listen to them and do not trust their ability to resolve their own conflicts.

FIGURE 3.4

Guidelines for
Effective Praise

Effective Praise	Ineffective Praise
1. is delivered contingently	1. is delivered randomly or unsystematically
2. specifies the particulars of the accomplishment	2. is restricted to global positive reactions
3. shows spontaneity, variety, and other signs of credibility: suggests clear attention to the student's accomplishment	3. shows a bland uniformity that suggests a conditioned response made with minimal attention
4. rewards attainment of specified performance criteria (which can include effort criteria)	4. rewards mere participation without consideration of performance processes or outcomes
5. provides information to students about their competence or the value of their accomplishment	5. provides no information at all or gives students information about their status
6. orients students toward better appreciation of their own task-related behavior and thinking about problem solving	6. orients students toward comparing themselves with others and thinking about competing
7. uses student's own prior accomplishments as the context for describing present accomplishments	7. uses the accomplishments of peers as the context for describing students' present accomplishments
8. is given in recognition of noteworthy effort or success at difficult (for this student) tasks	8. is given without regard to the effort expended or the meaning of the accomplishment (for this student)
9. attributes success to effort and ability, implying that similar successes can be expected in the future	9. attributes success to ability alone or to external factors such as luck or (easy) task difficulty
10. fosters endogenous attributions (students believe they expend effort on task because they enjoy it and/or want to develop task-relevant skills)	10. fosters exogenous attributions (students believe they expend effort on the task for external reasons—to please the teacher, win a competition or reward, etc.)
11. focuses students' attention on their own task-relevant behavior	11. focuses students' attention on the teacher as an external authority figure who is manipulating them
12. fosters appreciation of, and desirable attributions about, task-relevant behavior after the process is completed	12. intrudes into the ongoing process, distracting attention from task-related behavior

Source: From "Teacher Praise: A Functional Analysis" by Jere E. Brophy, 1981, *Review of Educational Research, 51,* p. 32. Copyright 1981 by American Educational Research Association. Reprinted by permission.

Before examining the major listening skills, we must clarify an important point. There are numerous instances (perhaps even a significant majority) during a school day when a student is merely requesting information. If a student requests permission to leave the room or asks for clarification of directions, it is appropriate simply to provide the information. However, when students share personal problems, express confusion with their work, or display emotions, it is often most effective initially to use one or more of the listening skills discussed in this section.

The primary goal of using listening skills is to help students express their real concern, need, or want. Students often initially make general, angry statements that disguise their real concerns. A student who says "I hate this class" might be feeling frustration at his or her inability to understand the material or concern over lack of acceptance by peers. By using the methods described in the following pages, you can help the student clarify the underlying problem. Once the problem has been exposed, you must switch from merely listening to an active role in helping the student examine and solve the problem.

Empathic, Nonevaluative Listening

This skill involves providing the speaker with a sense that she or he has been clearly heard and that the feelings expressed are acceptable. Several major benefits can be derived from using these skills. First, students learn that their feelings are acceptable, which reduces the tension and anxiety associated with having to hide one's true feelings. This act in turn makes students feel more accepted. Second, when thoughts and feelings can be expressed openly and are received nonjudgmentally, students are much less likely to express feelings through unproductive behaviors. Acting-out in the classroom, vandalism, and truancy are often indirect methods of dealing with feelings that could not be expressed openly and directly. Third, when adults listen nonevaluatively, they provide young people with an opportunity to examine and clarify feelings that are often confusing and frightening. This exchange frequently enables youngsters to understand a situation and to consider approaches to coping with the situation effectively.

One of the authors was recently given an interesting example regarding active listening. A special education director with whom the author works shared his recent conversations with a student in a high school program for students with behavior disorders. The boy approached the director (who had been the boy's special education teacher seven years earlier) and stated in a somewhat derogatory tone that the director looked older since he had lost some of his hair. The special education director noted that rather than chastise the boy for his rudeness, he acknowledged the boy's perceptive observation, shared his own feelings about losing hair, and asked the boy how he was doing. The director reported that the boy responded calmly and asked whether people still thought he was the dumbest, most cruel student who had ever attended the district. This allowed the director an opportunity to discuss the boy's behavior, his abilities, and his responsibility for his behavior. He reported that the boy was very surprised by the discussion, thanked him, and left pensively. The director indicated that had he not listened carefully to the boy, the boy would not have had an opportunity to have some important misconceptions corrected.

This is an excellent example of our need to guard against our vulnerabilities. Most of us have certain key behaviors or words from children that "set us off." However, most of these stem from a belief that children should not be allowed to challenge or criticize adults. Instead, we may want to consider that the issue is *how* students challenge us. If students are unskilled in providing us with important information regarding their feelings, needs, and concerns, rather than punishing their ineffectiveness, we may want to model for them and teach them how to do this in an effective, acceptable manner.

There are two basic approaches to nonevaluative listening. First, the listener can simply acknowledge the speaker's statement by looking at him or her and making oral responses such as "M-hm," "Yes," "Uh-uh," "I see," and "I understand." This form of listening encourages the speaker to continue talking by indicating that the listener is attentive and involved. Obviously, this type of response is least effective when used in isolation; most children wish to hear more than a simple acknowledgment.

The second method for using empathic, nonevaluative listening is commonly called *paraphrasing, active listening,* or *reflecting.* In their *Learning Together and Alone,* Johnson and Johnson (1975) presented seven guidelines for using this skill.

General Guidelines for Paraphrasing

1. Restate the sender's expressed ideas and feelings in your own words rather than mimicking or parroting her exact words.
2. Preface paraphrased remarks with, "You think . . . ," "Your position is . . . ," "It seems to you that . . . ," "You feel that . . . ," and so on.
3. Avoid any indication of approval or disapproval.
4. Make your nonverbal messages congruent with your verbal paraphrasing; look attentive, interested, and open to the sender's ideas and feelings, and show that you are concentrating upon what the sender is trying to communicate.
5. State as accurately as possible what you heard the sender say and describe the feelings and attitudes involved.
6. Do not add to or subtract from the sender's message.
7. Put yourself in the sender's shoes and try to understand what it is he is feeling and what his message means. (p. 102)

Paraphrasing has the advantage of making the speaker feel listened to while allowing the listener to be somewhat more involved than is possible when using only acknowledging responses. Furthermore, by providing a summary of the speaker's statement, the listener may help the child clarify his or her thoughts or feelings. If the paraphrased statement is not congruent with what the speaker wanted to say, the speaker has an opportunity to correct the listener's paraphrase and thereby clarify the initial statement.

One word of caution about the use of paraphrasing: Students may say that they do not like having someone repeat what they have just said. This response is more common in the upper elementary and secondary grades than among young children. If students frequently indicate that they view your statements as parroting their own, you will either need to reduce the amount of paraphrasing used or try to use responses that vary slightly from the student's original statement. Activity 3.8 provides several methods for helping you improve and diversify skills in empathic, nonevaluative listening.

Activities for Improving Sending Skills

It is easy to react positively to ideas and yet never take the time or risk to incorporate these into our repertoire. The following activities can help you practice the sending skills discussed in this section. Even teachers who frequently use these skills will find that the structured practice will improve their awareness of and fluency in implementing these skills.

ACTIVITY 3.1
Monitoring Courteous Remarks

1. Make a tally of the courteous remarks you make to students during a one-day period. You may want to carry a counter or a small note pad.
2. If you used fewer than 25 such statements (research indicates that elementary teachers have approximately 1,000 interactions with children each day and that secondary teachers have nearly 500), try to double the number the next day.
3. Briefly write (or discuss with a colleague) how it felt to increase the number of courteous statements. Did your students respond any differently the second day?

ACTIVITY 3.2
Sending I-Messages

To test your knowledge of I-messages, change each of these five statements into an I-message:

1. Late again! What's the matter with you?
2. I don't want to hear another word out of anyone.
3. No book again? How do you expect to learn anything?
4. How can you be so inconsiderate as to stand there drinking water for so long when you know other children want a drink?
5. If you get in trouble on the playground one more time, you can miss the rest of your recesses this month!

If you have difficulty with this task, consult a colleague or refer to Thomas Gordon's (1974) *Teacher Effectiveness Training.*

ACTIVITY 3.3
Giving Useful Oral Feedback

Change each of these general statements into a statement that provides the student with specific, nonevaluative feedback.

1. That's a nice picture, Susan.
2. Jimmy, your behavior on the playground was terrible.
3. Class, you were very rude during the assembly.
4. Erin, your penmanship has improved a lot since the last writing assignment.
5. Bill, if you keep disrupting the class, I will send you to the principal's office.

Write a specific example of effective and ineffective praise for each of the 12 aspects of praise listed in Figure 3.4.

From the list of 12 aspects of effective praise, select 3 you believe would be most helpful in improving the quality of your praise. If you are currently working with students, use each of these at least once a day over a five-day period.

ACTIVITY 3.4
Improving Your
Positive-Negative
Ratio

1. Have a student or colleague tally the positive and negative statements you make during a minimum of two hours of instructional time. Try to include several types of lessons and do not code more than 30 minutes at a time. Especially when using students to tally remarks, it is helpful to define positive and negative statements and to provide the coder with a list of commonly used positive and negative remarks. Neutral remarks such as statements related to instruction or comments such as "Okay," "All right," or "Yes" should not be coded.

2. If your ratio of positive-to-negative statements was less than 3 to 1, repeat the activity and try to focus on responding positively to productive student behavior. Following a period in which your ratio was very high, ask students to evaluate the lesson.

3. Write 10 inviting statements that you could use in your teaching. During the next two teaching days, make at least 10 inviting statements each day.
   Examples of Inviting Statements:
   a. I really enjoyed your presentation. Would you be willing to share it with the other fifth-grade class?
   b. I'm really glad you're back and feeling better.
   c. I'm very glad you are in my class this year.
   d. Those are two good causes; can you think of any more?
   e. Would you like some help with that work?
   Your List of Inviting Statements:

a.	f.
b.	g.
c.	h.
d.	i.
e.	j.

Activities for Monitoring Teacher's Expectations

The activities that follow are examples of methods we can use to examine our interactions with low- and high-achieving students. You can use these data as a reference for considering whether your differential interactions are supporting optimal learning for all students or are inadvertently disadvantageous to low-achieving students.

Additional information and activities dealing with communication of teachers' expectations can be found in a packaged in-service program entitled *Teacher Expectations and Student Achievement (TESA)* (Kerman & Martin, 1980). Many teachers with whom the authors have worked have found this material extremely valuable both in increasing their positive expectations for lower-achieving students and for enhancing professional dialogue and sharing among staff members within the school.

Before beginning the next three activities, you should know that research indicates that when teachers are made aware of how they treat students differentially and are involved in monitoring their teacher-student interactions, inequitable interactions can be eliminated (Good & Brophy, 1974; Sadker & Sadker, 1985).

List the four highest- and four lowest-achieving students in your class. Place these students' names in the form provided in Figure 3.5. Have a colleague tally your interactions with these students during at least two half-hour periods when the class is involved in group instruction.

This activity can also be completed by presenting the observer with a seating chart and a label for each type of teacher-student interaction on which you wish to obtain data. An observer might be asked to observe several students and to tally the number of times they were asked a question, given assistance in answering a question, criticized, praised, or volunteered an answer. Figure 3.6 is a sample of the data you might collect using this procedure.

After examining the results, respond to these statements:

Two things I learned about my interactions with these students are . . . .
Two things I will try to do differently the next time I teach a large group lesson
  are . . . .

Draw a map of your classroom, including location of the furniture. Ask a colleague to come into your classroom during a period of at least half an hour when the class will be involved in seatwork and you will be free to assist students. Have the observer mark your movement with a solid line during the entire observation. The observer should write a number by each place where you stop. To record the amount of time spent at each spot, have the observer place a tally mark next to the number for every 15 seconds that you remain in that spot.

After examining the walking map, answer these questions:

1. Where did you spend the most time? Least time?
2. Were any students ignored? Were there specific reasons for not interacting with these students?
3. Did the classroom arrangement influence your movement? How?
4. What changes, if any, would you make in your walking pattern during this type of instruction?
5. What changes, if any, would you make in your classroom arrangement?

Teachers who frequently use lecture or large-group discussions almost inevitably look at one area of the class much more than others. Almost all teachers have some blind spot. While teaching, one of the authors almost always sits with his left leg on his right knee. Because this position twists the body to the right, students on the left side of the class are often ignored. The author periodically asks his students to tally the number of contacts he has with students from each side of the class in order to make him more aware of (and accountable for) his behavior.

FIGURE 3.5 Monitoring Teaching-Student Dyadic Interactions

| Student's Name | Student Volunteers Answer | Teacher Asks Student a Question | Student Response | | | Teacher Assists Student | Teacher Praises Student | Teacher Criticizes Student | Teacher Calls on Another Student |
			Correct	Partially Correct	Incorrect				

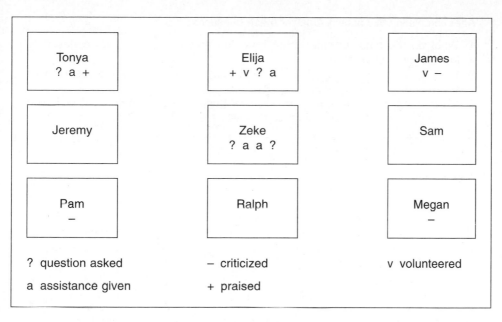

? question asked   – criticized   v volunteered

a assistance given   + praised

FIGURE 3.6
Monitoring
Teacher-Student
Interactions

ACTIVITY 3.7
Balancing
Positive
Statements

For three days, make one inviting statement to each child in your class. In order to ensure that each child receives such a statement, make a class list and place a check by each child's name when he or she has been given an inviting statement. After completing the activity, answer these questions:

1. Were there some students whom you had to consciously remind yourself to provide with an inviting statement? If so, did these students have anything in common?
2. Did students respond any differently during the three days? If so, how?
3. Did any students make a positive comment to you about your behavior during these three days?

A good supplement to this activity is again to list your four highest- and lowest-achieving students. Ask a colleague, an aide, or even the principal to tally the number of positive and negative statements you make to each of these students during two half-hour instructional periods.

Student's Name	Positive Comments	Negative Comments
High achievers		
1.		
2.		
3.		
4.		
Low achievers		
1.		
2.		
3.		
4.		

(continued)

ACTIVITY 3.7
Continued

After completing this activity, answer these questions:

1. What do the data indicate about how you respond to high- as opposed to low-achieving students?
2. Did you find yourself behaving differently because you were being observed? If so, what did you do differently?
3. Did any of the eight students appear to respond differently than usual while you were observed? If so, how did their behavior change?

Activities for Improving Receiving Skills

The demanding pace of the schoolday places real demands on teachers' ability to listen carefully to student concerns. Nevertheless, the act of carefully listening to students can considerably reduce classroom problems and is imperative as a prerequisite to effective problem solving. The following activity is designed to help you take time to implement effective listening skills.

ACTIVITY 3.8
Practicing
Listening Skills

To examine and improve your skills in using paraphrasing, imagine that each of the following statements has just been said to you. Write two responses to each of the 10 statements. In the first response, simply paraphrase the statement without mimicking the student's words. In the second response, add a feeling component.

1. Someone stole my lunch ticket!
2. This work is too hard.
3. Can we have ten extra minutes of recess?
4. Bill has had the book for two days.
5. I hate you!
6. I didn't get into trouble in music class today.
7. Nobody in the class likes me.
8. Do I have to take my report card home?
9. I never get to take the roll.
10. Mary is always picking on me.

During one schoolday, list five statements children make to you and five questions they ask you that could best be responded to by empathic, nonevaluative listening. When the list is complete, write a response to each of the 10 student statements.

EVALUATING THE QUALITY OF TEACHER-STUDENT RELATIONSHIPS

Before implementing any of the varied behaviors that you can use to create more positive teacher-student relationships, you should evaluate the current quality of your own interactions with students. Just as effective teaching involves both a diagnostic and a prescriptive component, any decision to alter our behavior can be helped by first assessing the students' reaction to the current behavior. This approach enables us to focus changes in areas in which students' feedback suggests that changes may be needed in order to improve teacher-student relationships. Figures 3.7, 3.8, and 3.9 present forms that many teachers have found useful in assessing the quality of their relationships with their students.

SUMMARY

Positive, supportive teacher-student relationships are important for all students. However, they become a critical factor influencing the behavior and achievement of

FIGURE 3.7 Elementary School Teacher Feedback Form

	😊	😐	☹️
1. Do I listen to you?			
2. Do I help you enough?			
3. Do I care about you?			
4. Do I help you feel good about learning?			
5. Do I seem happy when I teach?			
6. Do I think you can do your work?			
7. Can you share your good and bad feelings with me?			
8. Am I polite?			
9. Am I fair?			
10. Do you know what I want you to do?			
11. Do I help you understand why we are doing each activity in class?			
12. Do I call on you enough in class?			
13. Do I let you know when you have done good work?			
14. Are you excited about what I teach you?			

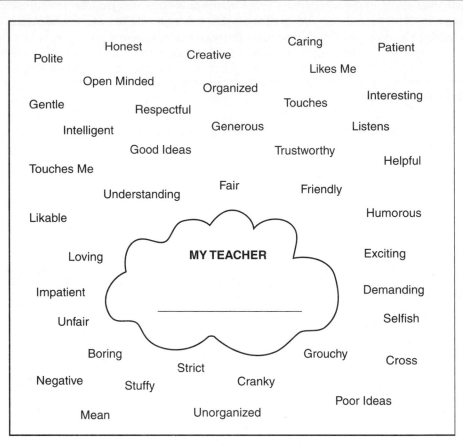

Circle the words that describe your teacher.

Circle in red if the words describe your teacher most of the time.
Circle in blue if the words describe your teacher sometimes.
Circle in green if the words seldom describe your teacher.
Circle in orange if the words never describe your teacher.

FIGURE 3.8
Teacher-Student
Relationship
Evaluation Form

students who are experiencing academic and behavioral difficulties. These at-risk students come to school with greater needs for adults who model positive adult behavior and who provide students with positive, inviting statements, high expectations, and feedback that helps them learn to take credit for their successes.

The learning process is a highly interactive, personal, and ego-involving activity. Students cannot reach their potential in school unless adults positively invite them to do so. In summarizing her findings on particularly effective middle schools, Joan Lipsitz (1984) wrote:

> Most striking is the level of caring in the schools. In the careful assignment of students to teachers and houses, in counseling, on school-sponsored trips, in home visits, in teachers' use of personal time with students. . . , hours upon hours are spent in and

FIGURE 3.9   Student's Assessment of Teacher's Instructional Skills

I believe students are knowledgeable both about how they learn best and in describing effective teaching. Therefore, I am asking you to give me some feedback on what I believe to be important aspects of my teaching. Please be serious, fair, and honest when completing this form. Also, please do not put your name on the form. Place an *X* in the column that best describes the question.

What's the Score?	Hole in One	Birdie	Par	Bogey	Out of Bounds
1. Are the goals and objectives for each lesson clear?					
2. Do you value what you are learning in this class?					
3. Do I use different ways to teach lessons (films, projects, discussions, guest speakers, and so on)?					
4. Do you get to study subjects or ideas that interest you?					
5. Is there a good balance for you in the amount of time spent in large- and small-group activities?					
6. Do you think the skills taught in this class are useful in some other areas of your life?					
7. Do you accomplish goals you set in this class?					
8. Do tests give you information about what you have learned?					
9. Do tests help you to see what skills still need to be practiced?					
10. Do you feel pressured to finish work in this class?					
11. Are you comfortable sharing your ideas with other students in this class?					
12. Are the goals of each new assignment clear?					
13. Are you aware of how you are doing in this class?					
14. Are most of the assignments challenging but not too hard for you?					
15. Do I allow enough time for questions and discussion?					
16. Does the class allow you to express yourself creatively?					
17. Do you think the grading is fair?					
18. Do you feel you have a chance to be actively involved in learning?					

(continued)

FIGURE 3.9   Continued

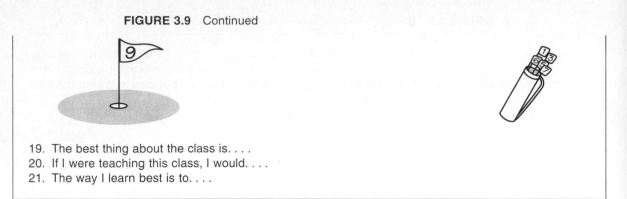

19. The best thing about the class is. . . .
20. If I were teaching this class, I would. . . .
21. The way I learn best is to. . . .

outside of school on behalf of the personal welfare of the students. This level of caring, which we all need and flourish under, is especially important for a vulnerable age group. (p. 181)

Although not all teachers wish to be as involved as those in the middle schools Lipsitz found to be most supportive of student personal growth and achievement, we can all work to improve the quality of adult-student relationships in schools. In so doing, we can make schools more positive and enjoyable learning environments for both adults and young people.

RECOMMENDED READING

American Association of University Women Educational Foundation. (1992). *The AAUW report: How schools shortchange girls*. Washington, DC: Author.

Brophy, J., & Good, T. (1986). Teacher behavior and student achievement. In M. Wittrock (Ed.), *Handbook of research on teaching* (3rd ed.). New York: Macmillan.

Combs, A. (1992). *A personal approach to teaching beliefs that make a difference*. Boston: Allyn and Bacon.

Dusek, J. (Ed.) (1985). *Teacher expectations*. Hillsdale, NJ: Erlbaum.

Ginott, H. (1972). *Teacher and child*. New York: Macmillan.

Glasser, W. (1990). *Quality school: Managing students without coercion*. New York: Harper & Row.

Gordon, T. (1974). *Teaching effectiveness training*. New York: Peter H. Wyden.

Haugen, S. (1993). *Ladder of success: Problem solving skills*. P.O. Box 4368, Salem, OR.

Johnson, D. (1993). *Reaching out*. Boston: Allyn and Bacon.

Jones, V. (1980). *Adolescents with behavior problems: Strategies for teaching, counseling, and parent involvement*. Boston: Allyn and Bacon.

Mendler, A. (1992). *What do I do when . . ." How to achieve discipline with dignity in the classroom*. Bloomington, IN: National Educational Service.

Purkey, W., & Novack, J. (1984). *Inviting school success: A self-concept approach to teaching and learning*. Belmont, CA: Wadsworth.

Rogers, C. (1961). *On becoming a person*. Boston: Houghton Mifflin.

Schmuck, R., & Schmuck, P. (1983). *Group processes in the classroom*. Dubuque, IA: William C. Brown.

Seiler, W., Schuelke, D., & Lieb-Brilhart, B. (1984). *Communication for the contemporary classroom*. New York: Holt, Rinehart and Winston.

Wehlage, G., Rutter, R., Smith, G., Lesko, N., & Fernandez, R. (1989). *Reducing the risk: Schools as communities of support*. Philadelphia: Falmer Press.

CHAPTER 4

Creating Positive Peer Relationships

Classrooms that have a climate of competitiveness, hostility and alienation cause anxiety and discomfort and do not facilitate the intellectual development of many students. Classrooms in which students and teachers support one another facilitate the development of self-esteem and the satisfaction of fundamental motives. They also provide the opportunity for students to use their intellectual capacities to their fullest.

—Richard Schmuck and Patricia Schmuck (1983)
Group Processes in the Classroom

Positive interpersonal relations among students are necessary both for problem solving in groups and for general classroom enjoyment of instructional activity. The psychological security and safety necessary for open exploration of instructional tasks is based upon feelings of being accepted, liked, and supported by fellow students. Class cohesion is based upon positive interpersonal relationships among students.

—David Johnson and Roger Johnson (1975)
Learning Together and Alone:
Cooperative, Competition, and Individualistic Learning

Peers play an important role in determining the quality of the learning environment. With today's increased emphasis on students' achievement, teachers are often hesitant to allocate time for creating positive peer relationships in the classroom. In addition, teacher education programs seldom provide teachers with specific skills for developing positive, supportive group norms. A considerable body of research indicates, however, that time spent creating a positive peer group can eliminate much misbehavior and can provide a classroom climate that enhances students' achievement.

Peer relationships influence students' achievement in several ways. First, peer attitudes toward achievement affect students' academic aspirations and school behavior (Coleman, 1966; Lewis & St. John, 1974; Rutter, Maughan, Mortimore, Ouston, & Smith, 1979; Sharan & Sharan, 1976). Second, the quality of peer relationships and personal support in classrooms affects the degree to which students' personal needs are met and, subsequently, their ability to be productively involved in the learning process (Lewis & St. John, 1974; Schmuck, 1963, 1966).

Third, peer relationships can directly affect achievement through cooperative learning activities (Johnson & Johnson, 1987; Johnson, Marayama, Johnson, Nelson, & Skon, 1981; Slavin, 1983a, 1988). Finally, at-risk students are more likely to feel alienated from school and have low rates of participation in school as early as third grade (Finn, 1989). It is likely that the quality of peer relationships students experience in the classroom and throughout the schoolday dramatically influence the extent to which students become involved in school.

Anyone who has worked with groups of students has witnessed the role peers play in influencing students' behavior. When discussing the differences between confronting an adolescent in front of the group and having a private talk with the student, teachers frequently remark that it seems as if they are dealing with two completely different students. We should not be surprised that students' feelings and behaviors are significantly influenced by their classmates. During the school year, students spend more than 1,000 hours with their classmates. Also, because most elementary school classrooms are composed of children who live near one another, friendships and conflicts that develop in the classroom often influence youngsters' lives outside the school. Peer pressure is somewhat less complex and extensive for early primary-grade children whose egocentricity reduces the influence of their peers. Nevertheless, at all grade levels, the values, norms, and behaviors of the group significantly affect individual students' feelings of safety, belongingness, respect for others, and self-esteem.

In their *Group Processes in the Classroom,* Richard and Patricia Schmuck (1983) wrote of the classroom group's importance:

> The classroom clearly offers a setting in which high levels of feeling exist daily and wherein covert psychological dynamics often come into play. As students interact, and students and teachers relate, they communicate—however indirectly—their feelings about one another. Such gestures of affect influence how students view themselves, their abilities, their likability, and their general worth. Morever, feelings, evaluations, or defenses about oneself make up students' self-esteem and have impact on the degree to which they use their intelligence and the manner in which they form their current educational aspirations. (p. 24)

UNDERSTANDING THE CLASSROOM GROUP

The classroom by nature elicits many interactions and feelings. By placing 25 to 35 individuals in a 30-by-30-foot room, schools create a highly interactive environment. Peer interaction is a natural and desirable aspect of almost all learning environments. Group instruction is used both because it is frequently more expedient and because a good education involves learning how to function as a group member. The group's influence is intensified by the competition found in most classrooms. Students compete for the highest test scores, strive to earn high grades, or run for class office. Even when we use individualized programs that deemphasize competition, students have numerous opportunities to compare their work to that of their classmates. It is understandable and perhaps unavoidable that classrooms are characterized by a fairly high level of interaction and the accompanying spontaneous interchange of feelings.

Although teachers often express concern and frustration over the negative aspects of peer pressure, the peer group can be a positive and supportive factor in the classroom. When students feel liked by their peers and when interactions are characterized by thoughtfulness and helpfulness, students experience a sense of safety and security, belongingness and affection, significance, respect of others, and power. Students are then able to concentrate more fully on learning and are willing to take greater risks in attempting to master new skills. Consequently, it is extremely important that we implement strategies that encourage the development of positive, supportive peer interactions in the classroom.

It is beyond the scope of this book to examine group dynamics thoroughly, but it is important to realize that groups, like individuals, have needs that must be met before the group can function effectively. If the classroom group is to function in a supportive, goal-directed manner, teachers must initially set aside time for activities that enable students to know each other, develop a feeling of being included, and create diverse friendship patterns. Only after these feelings have been developed can a group of students proceed to respond optimally to the learning goals of the classroom.

A large body of both theory and research supports these observations. Several major theories of group development support the concept that interpersonal issues must be clarified before groups can begin to function effectively in meeting their task goals. Tuckman (1965) and Schmuck and Schmuck (1983) observed that the functions groups serve can be divided into interpersonal and task functions. This two-stage theory of group development and functioning is supported by work with classroom groups (Runkel, Lawrence, Oldfield, Rider, & Clark, 1971). Schutz's theory (1966) states that during the early stages of a group's development, members care primarily about being included in the group. Discussing this aspect of group dynamics in their *Group Processes in the Classroom*, Schmuck and Schmuck (1975) stated, "Issues of interpersonal inclusion characterize the beginning of a group's life. In the classroom, the students and teacher confront one another's presence and raise questions such as: How will I fit in here? Who will accept me? Who will reject me? What do I have to do to be accepted? Academic work cannot easily be accomplished until these questions of inclusion are answered satisfactorily" (p. 171). Gibb's (1964) theory of group dynamics also supports the importance of initially dealing with interpersonal issues. Gibb stated that groups begin to function effectively only after members feel accepted and develop a sense of interpersonal trust. He also stated that, following resolution of this primary issue, groups move on to the issues of making decisions and group norms and goals.

Much research also suggests that group norms greatly influence individual students' behavior. The Coleman Report (1966) is perhaps the best-known study of the effect of peer norms. This study, commissioned by the U.S. Office of Education and directed by James Coleman, was an attempt to determine the factors that influenced school achievement among high school students. Coleman's data suggest that factors such as funds available for equipment and salaries, the racial makeup of the school, and the teachers' educational level make little difference in determining students' achievement. Instead, the major factors are the socioeconomic composition and achievement orientation of fellow students. When students attend schools in which academic achievement is valued, their interest in academic endeavors and their academic achievement increase. Similarly, attendance at schools in which academic performance is not valued tends to decrease students' academic interest and achievement. Coleman's study has been criticized on several grounds, yet it appears that peers' attitudes do account for a significant amount of variance in students' achievement.

In a closely related study, Lewis and St. John (1974) attempted to determine the variables that influenced achievement of African American students in classrooms in which the majority of students were White. Their research showed that higher achievement among African American students was related to norms that stressed both achievement and acceptance of such students within the classroom. The results indicated that the presence of high-achieving White students was not significantly sufficient to enhance academic achievement among the African American students. It appeared that this factor has to be combined with White students accepting their African American peers as friends. This powerful influence of peer conformity is partially explained by the fact that "individuals rely on group norms to guide them, especially when they are unsure about social reality. . . . For students especially there is a pull toward the peer group to make the complex world of the school more understandable. . . . Students feel insecure when their personal response is in opposition to a group norm" (Schmuck & Schmuck, 1975, p. 121).

Group values and norms so deeply influence the individual student's behavior that we can expect that the student's self-esteem will be significantly affected by the group, and that the student's self-image will mirror the group's attitudes about the student. Indeed, research (McGinley & McGinley, 1970; Stevens, 1971) suggests a correlation among the student's popularity, self-esteem, and achievement. Although the influence of these factors undoubtedly is complex, most teachers would agree that students who are well liked by the group generally feel better about themselves and tend to function more productively in the classroom. The influence of positive group feelings on learning is directly supported by studies from various grade levels indicating that students' achievement is higher in classrooms characterized by diverse, positive peer relationships (Muldoon, 1955; Schmuck, 1966; Walberg & Anderson, 1968).

This work has been supported by studies on cooperative learning. Students who are involved in cooperative learning activities in which they study with peers and in which their efforts produce benefits for peers as well as for themselves perform higher on standardized tests of mathematics, reading, and language and also do better on tasks involving higher level thinking than when they study alone (Slavin, Madden, & Leavey, 1984). Slavin (1987) summarized the results of studies on the benefits of students working cooperatively: "When cooperative learning methods provide group goals based on the learning of all members, the effects on student achievement are remarkably consistent. Of 38 studies of at least four weeks' duration comparing cooperative methods of this type to traditional control methods, 33 found significantly greater achievement for the cooperatively taught classes, and 5 found no significant differences" (p. 10).

Similarly, researchers at the National Center on Effective Secondary Schools at the University of Wisconsin–Madison synthesized the research on cooperative learning and students' academic success in secondary schools. With the exception of one technique (the jigsaw method), cooperative learning was found to be more successful in more than 75 percent of the studies. The authors' own work in helping teachers implement cooperative learning suggests that cooperative learning is very effective, especially in increasing the motivation and learning of at-risk students when teachers (1) take time to help students understand the reasons behind their decision to implement this new method, (2) help students become better acquainted, and (3) assist students in developing skills for working in groups.

Studies also indicate that cooperative learning can be an effective technique for helping students be accepted into and function effectively in classrooms. Good and Brophy (1991) highlighted the social/affective benefits associated with cooperative learning:

> Effects on outcomes other than achievement are even more impressive. Cooperative learning arrangements promote friendship choices and prosocial patterns of interaction among students who differ in achievement, sex, race or ethnicity, and they promote the acceptance of mainstreamed handicapped students by their nonhandicapped classmates. Cooperative methods also frequently have positive effects, and rarely have negative effects, on affective outcomes such as self-esteem, academic self-confidence, liking for the class, liking and feeling liked by classmates, and various measures of empathy and social cooperation. (p. 416)

Achievement effects appear to be positive for all types of students, although there are some indications that African American and possibly Hispanic students gain even more from cooperative learning arrangements than do Anglo students.

The relationship among positive group norms, diverse liking patterns, and productive student behavior and achievement is a major incentive for teachers to develop skills in creating positive peer relationships in the classroom, but we have a second important reason for acquiring these skills. Today's students live in a world that is increasingly urban and in which people are more and more interdependent. The time when the average person lived in relative isolation and was basically self-sufficient is long past. Individuals depend on others for needed goods and services as well as for meeting emotional needs. Likewise, individuals are rediscovering the importance of coming together in order to combat social problems ranging from burglary to an energy crisis. This increased interdependence can also be seen in the move away from the Renaissance scholar toward increased specialization. In producing anything from automobiles to ideas, individuals focus on an ever more specialized aspect of their work and must cooperate with other people in order to create increasingly sophisticated products.

If schools are to prepare students for a society characterized by interdependence and cooperative effort, they must provide students with frequent and meaningful experiences in functioning cooperatively in groups. Rather than continually stressing competition and individual learning, teachers must use cooperative group work in the classroom. More than three decades ago, John Dewey emphasized that life in a classroom should mirror the processes students will face in society. He wrote too that the goal of schooling is to provide students with skills that will enable them to create a better living situation.

Figure 4.1 presents a summary of what employers want from individuals entering the workplace. It is interesting how many of these skills relate to working effectively with others. In its 1982 report *Basic Skills in the U.S. Workforce,* based

FIGURE 4.1 What Employers Want

What Employers Want: A Summary

Once upon a time, bank tellers counted out cash, deposited checks, and made sure the balance sheet added up at quitting time.

The typical bank teller these days must also be able to advise customers on a wide range of financial services, make "spot" decisions, and use a wealth of database information previously available only to managers.

The transformation of the teller's role, argues a report issued jointly by the American Society for Training and Development and the U.S. Department of Labor, is indicative of the extraordinary changes in the workplace—changes with important consequences for the education of students in grades K–12. "To be effective in the workplace, the new bank teller may not need to have the same degree of skills in a narrow area of expertise, but instead must have good knowledge of a wide range of skills," the report argues.

As part of a major research project examining the skills needed for work, the report, *Workplace Basics: The Skills Employers Want,* identifies seven skill groups. They are:

Learning to Learn.

Employers are more frequently shifting employees between jobs and responsibilities, "putting a premium on the ability to absorb, process, and apply new information quickly and effectively."

Listening and Oral Communication.

Fifty-five percent of time spent in communicating is spent listening, but schools offer "scant instruction" in oral communications or listening.

Competence in Reading, Writing, and Computation.

"Most employers today cannot compete successfully without a workforce that has sound basic academic skills." Although schools frequently teach isolated reading, writing, or computational skills, use of these skills on the job will require additional proficiency in summarizing information, monitoring one's own work, and using analytical and critical thinking skills.

Adaptability: Creative Thinking and Problem Solving.

An organization's ability to succeed depends on using creative thinking to solve problems and overcome barriers, thus placing a premium on workers who develop such skills.

Personal Management: Self-Esteem, Goal Setting/Motivation, and Personal/Career Development.

Taking pride in work accomplished, setting goals and meeting them, and enhancing job skills to meet new challenges are necessary characteristics of employees. "Unfortunately, the educational system provides little formal training" to develop such attributes.

Group Effectiveness: Interpersonal Skills, Negotiation, and Teamwork.

The ability to work cooperatively in teams is increasingly important for workplace success.

Organizational Effectiveness and Leadership.

Employers want employees to "have some sense of where the organization is headed and what they must do to make a contribution . . . and who can assume responsibility and motivate co-workers."

Source: Workplace Basics: The Skills Employers Want, American Society for Training and Development and U.S. Department of Labor, Employment and Training Administration, 1988. Reprinted by permission.

on a nationwide survey of businesses, labor unions, and educational institutions, the Center of Public Resources reported that 90 percent of people fired from their jobs were fired not for lack of technical skills but for problems with interpersonal relationships and behavior. Likewise, employers want to hire individuals who understand the organization, who can set personal and work goals and monitor their own progress, and who can solve both interpersonal and cognitive problems. The materials in Chapters 6, 9, and 10 emphasize methods for helping students develop these very skills.

It is likely that many teachers who read this chapter will be concerned that the time taken to help students know and work effectively with their peers is time taken away from instruction. This is an important issue. As teachers, our primary responsibility is to help students develop skills in the subject matter for which we are responsible. We must also realize, however, that we are responsible for understanding and implementing the most current research and instructional methodology for helping all students develop mastery of the content. The evidence clearly indicates that taking time to establish a safe, supportive classroom group in which students know each other and support each other's learning will significantly enhance student learning. We can either take a small but significant amount of time to help the relationships in our classrooms run smoothly or we can risk spending extensive time and energy on responding to problems caused by students feeling isolated, unable to receive assistance, uninvolved, and unwanted.

The activities presented throughout the remainder of the chapter can help the reader create a more positive, supportive classroom environment. They can also help students develop work norms and personal skills that will serve them well in their future roles as parent, spouse, friend, and worker.

ACQUAINTANCE ACTIVITIES

You can undoubtedly recall experiencing discomfort when walking into a party or other group setting when you know very few individuals there. Compare this feeling with those elicited when you walk into a room filled with acquaintances and friends. People usually feel more relaxed and comfortable in discussions or other activities with people they know. Students experience similar feelings. The new student who is confronted by 30 unfamiliar faces is likely to respond either by withdrawing until the environment becomes more familiar or by acting-out as a means of controlling the environment by eliciting an expected response.

Several years ago, one of the authors was contacted by a teacher who was experiencing much frustration because the students in his sophomore English class were not becoming involved in group discussions. Furthermore, the teacher said absenteeism in class was relatively high and students were not handing in the number of assignments he had expected. The teacher, a hardworking, dynamic young man, indicated that the material being read and discussed seemed to be of high interest and that he had made a special effort to relate aspects of the literature to students' lives. Students were seated in a circle and open discussion was encouraged.

While discussing this situation, I asked the teacher whether students in the class knew each other. The teacher seemed surprised by the question and indicated that because the students came from only two feeder schools and had been in his class for nearly six months, he assumed they were well acquainted. The students' behavior suggested, however, that they felt some discomfort, and the teacher agreed to assess how well they knew one another. He was surprised to discover that only a quarter of the students in his class knew the first names of more than half of their peers. He discussed this figure with the class and explained his decision to allocate time to activities that would help students become better acquainted. Following these activities, he again collected data on attendance, percentage of assignments handed in, and students' participation in class discussions. All three variables showed changes that were statistically significant at the .01 level. These results were so striking that the teacher's English department decided to incorporate a peer-acquaintance unit into the first nine weeks of the school year.

The peer-acquaintance activities described here include several that were used by the teacher described in the previous paragraph. These activities are designed to help students get better acquainted with one another so that they will feel safe and secure and will therefore become more actively engaged in the learning process. As students become better acquainted, the likelihood that they will interact with and be influenced by a wider range of students increases and that cliquish behavior decreases.

The Name Chain

A name chain is the most effective method for helping students learn each other's names. The following steps can make this activity run smoothly:

1. Ask the students to sit in a circle so that each one can comfortably see all the students in the group.
2. Clearly explain the reasons for being involved in the activity. You might say that one benefit of knowing everyone's name is that this increases their knowledge of the environment and thereby makes them more comfortable and more likely to become actively involved. Similarly, you may indicate that knowing other students' names will enable students to greet each other in a friendlier, more relaxed manner, which will have a tendency to make both the classroom and the school a more positive place.
3. Ask the students if they have any questions about why they are being asked to do the activity.
4. Explain to the students that each person will be asked to say his or her first name and tell the group one thing about himself or herself. They may choose to tell the group something they like to do, something interesting that happened to them recently, how they are feeling, and so on. Inform the class that they will be asked to repeat each student's name and the statement he or she has made. They will begin with the person who spoke first and stop when they have given their name and have said something about themselves. The first student may say, "I'm Bob, and I went to the beach this weekend." The next would say, "That's Bob (or you're Bob), and he (or you) went to the beach last weekend. I'm Sandy, and I enjoy backpacking." Because we are faced with the difficult task of learning a large number of names and because having an adult remember their names seems particularly important to

adolescents, it is best to have you be the last person to speak. You will therefore be able to list each student's name and what they have shared with the class.

5. Have everyone take a paper and pencil and change seats. Ask the students to start with a designated individual and go clockwise around the circle, writing down each person's name. It is not necessary to have them list what each student shared.

6. Ask for a volunteer who will begin with the person designated as the starting place and slowly give the name of each person in the circle. This recital serves as an opportunity for students to check the accuracy of their list and to learn the names of any students they might have missed. (Jones, 1980)

It is important to provide follow-up for this activity. For example, for several days following the activity, you may want to attempt to go around the class listing each student's name or ask for a volunteer to do so. We must continue to be aware of whether students are remembering names and continue to emphasize the value of knowing names. If you ask students to work in groups, you may suggest that they make sure they know each member's name before beginning the group activity. Teachers too often involve students in activities and then fail to follow up with behavior that reinforces the learning derived from and the values implied by the activity.

What's in a Name?

This activity is excellent as a first-acquaintance activity or as an activity following a name chain. Students are placed in groups of five or six. Briefly lead a discussion on the value of names. You might include comments about how names may reflect a cultural heritage, refer to a loved relative, or be chosen because a parent liked the name. The discussion can also focus on how names may evoke positive or negative feelings, depending on how each of us likes our name or what people do with the name. Then, tell the class that the activity involves sharing some things about the students' names as a way of becoming better acquainted. Ask students to tell these facts about their name:

1. State their full name.
2. How did they get their name? For example, were they named for someone? Does the name represent a family heritage or nationality?
3. Do they have any nicknames? Who calls them by this name? Do they like the nickname(s)?
4. Do people change their name in any way? For example, is it often shortened and so on? How do they feel about this?
5. Do they like their name? If not, what name would they prefer?
6. What name do they want used in the class?

After all groups have finished, one student in each group can volunteer to introduce each member of the small group to the entire class. They do so by giving the name each student wants to be called in the class.

Know Your Classmates

Each student will need a ditto sheet entitled Know Your Classmates (see Figure 4.2) and a pencil or pen. Ask students to find a person in the class who fits each description listed on the sheet and to obtain the person's signature on the line in front of the description. To encourage students to interact with numerous peers, inform them that they cannot have the same person sign their sheet more than twice. The descriptions can be adapted to fit the specific interests of children at different ages and in different settings.

Interviews

Interviews are an excellent means for students to become better acquainted with each other. This activity will often foster new friendships and feelings of self-importance. Lack of information about others is often a major barrier to establishing new friendships. When children do not know their peers, they tend to make assumptions and develop unrealistic fears or unfounded biases. As students interview each other,

FIGURE 4.2
Know Your
Classmates

Name _____

Collect the signatures of the appropriate persons:

_____ 1. A person whose birthday is in the same month as yours.
_____ 2. A person who has red hair.
_____ 3. A person whom you don't know very well.
_____ 4. A person who has an interesting hobby. What is it? _____
                        _____
_____ 5. A person with freckles.
_____ 6. A person whose favorite color is yellow.
_____ 7. A person who loves to read.
_____ 8. A person who takes gymnastic lessons.
_____ 9. A person who is left-handed.
_____ 10. A person with naturally curly hair.
_____ 11. A person who has a dog. The dog's name is _____.
_____ 12. A person who belongs to a Scouting troop.
_____ 13. A person shorter than you.
_____ 14. A person taller than you.
_____ 15. A person with the same color shirt or dress as you are
                        wearing.
_____ 16. A person who plays an instrument. What instrument? _____
                        _____
_____ 17. A person who traveled out of the state this summer. Where?
                        _____
_____ 18. A person who wants to play professional sports when he or
                        she grows up. Which one? _____
_____ 19. A person with more than four children in the family. How
                        many? _____
_____ 20. A person who plays soccer.
_____ 21. A person with braces on his or her teeth.
_____ 22. A person who rides horseback.

they learn new and exciting information about their peers. This knowledge, in turn, promotes diversified friendship patterns in the classroom.

We can use interviews in the classroom in many ways. One method involves introducing the interviewing process by having students list 10 questions that would help them know a classmate better. This list provides some examples of questions that might be asked by 9-year-olds:

1. What is your favorite color?
2. What is your favorite sport to play? to watch?
3. What are you proudest of?
4. Do you have any pets? If so, what are their names?
5. What is your favorite professional team in football? basketball? baseball?
6. What kinds of foods do you like to eat?
7. If you could go anyplace on a vacation, where would you go? Why?
8. Do you take any lessons?
9. Do you have any hobbies?
10. Do you like your first name? If not, what would you change it to?

Write these questions on the chalkboard and tell the students each to choose a person whom they do not know very well and, using the 10 questions as a guide, learn as much as they can about their partner. After 10 minutes, ask each pair to separate but stay within viewing distance and draw their partner. These portraits are later shared and displayed. The next step consists of the pairs drawing a map of how to walk to each other's homes (used only for students old enough to understand the streets in their neighborhood). The final step is for each student to share the information about their partner with the rest of the class. Because you are a group member, you should participate in this activity.

Another approach to interviewing also begins by developing a list of questions students might ask each other. These questions are written on the board and referred to as students interview each other in pairs. After these questions have been asked, each pair of students joins with another pair. The four children share the new information they have learned about their partners. After a few minutes, ask the class to reconvene and request each person to share five things about his or her partner with the class.

A third interviewing technique has a student sit in a place of honor at the front of the classroom. The student is asked questions by the other class members. Students enjoy being in the limelight and often state that this is their favorite approach to interviewing.

A final interviewing approach has several students serve as reporters. They interview their peers and obtain such information as where students were born; the number of members in their family; a student's favorite television show, food, color, or animal; a special hobby or pet; any unusual places they have traveled to; and students' future goals. The teacher tabulates the information and either duplicates it and gives it to each student or makes a large chart in the hall for other classes to read.

The results of these interviewing activities can often be seen in new friendships and more open communication in the classroom. This atmosphere in turn makes the classroom a safer and more relaxed learning environment for students.

Guess Who?

An acquaintance activity used by a number of secondary teachers gives students an opportunity to discover how well they know their peers. The steps for setting up this activity are the following:

1. Briefly describe the activity to the students and elicit their willingness to take part in the activity.
2. Ask students to write brief (two- or three-line) statements about themselves, which can include facts about their personal history, family, hobbies, and so forth.
3. Collect all the autobiographical statements.
4. Ask each student to take out paper and pencil. Read each description and ask the students (you, too, should be involved) to write the name of the student who they believe wrote the description.
5. After all the descriptions have been read, reread them and ask the authors to identify themselves. Ask the students to indicate on the list whether they made the correct choice. Upon completing the task, you can ask students to indicate the number of their peers whom they correctly identified. These results can be used to initiate a discussion about the degree to which class members have become acquainted.
6. An interesting alternative to this activity is to have students write brief statements that include one false statement about themselves. Then give the class the student's name and personal description and ask them to decide which statement is false. This activity can be performed by the entire group or can be developed as a contest between two groups.
7. A second variation of this activity is to have each student write a poem or riddle about himself or herself. These poems are put into a box. Each student draws a poem from the box and reads it aloud to the class. From the information on the poem, the class tries to identify the author of the poem. As a follow-up, each student could draw a self-portrait that could be placed on a bulletin board with his or her poem below it.

Having students know and feel supported by their peers is valuable at all grade levels, but it may be particularly critical as young people move through early adolescence. Students in grades 6 through 8 are experiencing rapid cognitive and physical changes. This is a time of heightened self-consciousness and decreased self-esteem. Consequently, students learn much more effectively in environments in which teacher-student and peer relationships are characterized by warmth, support, and stability. Schools for young adolescents should not only use a wide range of acquaintance activities but should also be organized so that students spend a sizable portion of the school day with students and teachers whom they know. Lipsitz (1984) described successful schools for young adolescents:

> The groups of students are small enough that, as the teachers and paraprofessionals in the schools say, they know the students' moods and do not make the interpersonal mistakes that would be unavoidable in large, more impersonal settings. The students are secure in being known, and staff members are relaxed because of their deep

familiarity with the students and their confidence in dealing with them. . . . The schools have adopted policies that strengthen and stabilize peer groupings by extending the time students remain together, both during the day and also over a period of several years. . . . Antisocial behavior that results from the randomness and brevity of student groupings in most secondary schools is substantially reduced in these schools. (p. 182)

If you are interested in incorporating additional acquaintance activities into your lesson plans, you can find numerous resources. Especially useful are Borba's *Esteem Builders* (1989), Canfield and Siccone's *One Hundred Ways to Develop Student Self-Esteem and Responsibility* (1992), Gibb's *Tribes: A Process for Social Development and Cooperative Learning* (1987), Nicherson, Lollis, and Porter's *Miraculous Me* (1980), Schniedewind and Davidson's *Open Minds to Equity* (1983), and Whittington, Crites, Moran, Kreidman, and Beck's *Peace Begins with Me* (1989).

ACTIVITIES FOR ESTABLISHING A COHESIVE GROUP

Group cohesiveness refers to the extent to which a group experiences a sense of identity, oneness, and esprit de corps. Cohesive groups are characterized by warm, friendly interactions among all members rather than by positive interchanges limited to small cliques within the group. Cohesive groups provide settings in which students feel safe, experience a sense of belonging, and view themselves as being liked and respected by others. Research (Lewis & St. John, 1974; Schmuck, 1966) indicates that students who are accepted by their classmates have more positive attitudes toward school and are more likely to achieve closer to their potential than are students who feel rejected and isolated. These findings are supported by research (Combs & Taylor, 1952) that indicates that students perform less effectively when they feel threatened by the environment.

> Cohesiveness is correlated with the productivity of a group, provided the norms are supportive of production. Cohesive groups are more goal-directed than noncohesive groups, and as long as the goals of the individuals are in line with productivity, cohesiveness is a facilitating factor. Classroom groups which have strong goals have satisfied students. Moreover, students who know what is expected of them and who are involved and close to their peers in pursuing educational goals are more satisfied than students in classrooms that are disorganized and fragmented. (Schmuck & Schmuck, 1974, p. 31)

Group cohesiveness and a positive group identity do not develop simply because students spend time together. Rather, positive feelings about being a group member are developed by making the group seem attractive, distinguishing it from other groups, involving the group in cooperative enterprises, and helping students view themselves as an important component in the group. The activities described in this section are designed to accomplish these goals. The activities are most effective when used in association with acquaintance activities and with activities for creating diverse liking patterns.

Activities aimed at creating a cohesive classroom group will be most effective when introduced at the beginning of the school year. One important reason for developing group cohesion early in the school year is that cohesive groups are desirable only if the group's norms support your learning goals. If you can begin the year by establishing a positive group feeling while creating norms that support academic achievement and productive behavior, the school year will be pleasant and productive.

Activities for Elementary School Classrooms

Ways of Having a Happy Classroom
Focusing on the positive qualities of a classroom sets a tone for the entire year. In the fall, ask students to list things they can do to make the classroom a happy place to be. Students can be encouraged to describe ways of positively interacting with each other, ideas for having fun in the classroom, and so on. The students' ideas can be written on a large sheet of paper and posted in the classroom. Every month, students can be asked whether they are acting in accordance with the ideas expressed on the chart and they can evaluate each item to see if it is still applicable. New ideas may be added at any time.

Group Contributions
To establish a cohesive classroom it is important that students focus on their contributions to the group. This theme can be enhanced by creating a bulletin board. Give each child paper, pencil, and crayons and ask him or her to draw a picture of himself or herself. After these have been completed, ask students to think about what contribution they can make to the group. After you have led a short discussion to clarify the concept and provide students with ideas, give them a strip of paper and tell them to write down their contribution. Collect the pictures and contributions and mount them on a bulletin board for all to see. This is an excellent way of reinforcing the facts that everyone can contribute to the classroom and that the classroom will be a better place if all contribute some of their special talents.

Classroom Arrangements
Developing a comfortable classroom environment can enhance students' motivation and provide opportunities for increasing their sense of competence and power. It is desirable to involve students in decisions about the classroom arrangement whenever possible. Give them a basic floor plan of the room, including all built-ins. Then ask them to sketch in the desks and any other movable furniture. The arrangements can be displayed and the students and you can choose the floor plan with which all would be most comfortable. By giving students responsibility for a room arrangement, we indicate our respect for their judgment and they gain a sense of significance, competence, and power.

Students can also be active in decorating the room. They can be encouraged to bring posters from home, take part in designing bulletin-board displays, and determine the types of plants they would like in the room. Increased student involvement in organizing and decorating the room is almost always associated with an intensified group feeling, higher motivation, and reduced vandalism.

Class Spirit

At the beginning of the school year, most students are excited and motivated. Teachers can take advantage of this excitement by establishing a class spirit that creates a bond among the students. Many activities throughout the year can revolve around this class spirit.

To create a class spirit, teacher and students discuss the kinds of group identity they would like to develop and formulate a list. The list might include a class animal, name, flower, insect, song, flag, color, cheer, game, cartoon character, sport, bird, and poem. Suggestions are welcomed, and eventually students vote to determine their choices in each category. When the class spirit is completed, it is displayed proudly in a prominent place in the room.

It is very important to reinforce this activity by using parts of the class spirit whenever possible throughout the year. For example, when sending a newsletter to parents, we might draw several of the class symbols on the letter and mimeograph the newsletter onto paper that is the class color. Similarly, stating the class cheer before special sporting events or singing the class song at the close of each week continues to enhance class spirit.

Class History

An effective activity that helps mold students into a cohesive group is development of a class history or class yearbook. When approached with this idea in the fall, students are always overwhelmingly in favor of making a class history.

Four to six students are chosen either by the teacher or by their peers to write the history, and all students are encouraged to contribute ideas. Every month, the history writers meet and decide what events, assemblies, new lessons, and so on they wish to incorporate into their class history. The historians then divide the writing assignments. At the end of the year, students have a collection of the year's events. In addition to these events, the class history can include poems written by students, a student directory of addresses and phone numbers, an autograph page, a page about students' thoughts on the year, and a letter written to the students by the teacher. The class history helps create a sense of group purposefulness and commitment and is a memorable treasure for each student.

Photo Album

Whenever a special event occurs, capture the moment in a photograph. Students can become actively involved by learning to use a camera. Pictures taken by students can be accompanied by written statements and put on the bulletin board until replaced by a picture and description of a new event. The old material can then be placed in the class photo album and some of the written material can be incorporated into the class history.

The photo album can be shown to parents during scheduled conferences or when a parent drops by the school. Parents enjoy seeing pictures of their children involved in special school activities. This sharing enhances parent interest in their child's school experience and increases parental support for the teacher and the school. When a particularly good picture of a child is obtained, the teacher can make a copy and send it to the parents along with a short note. Parents appreciate this thoughtful gesture, and their increased interest in their child's classroom experience helps their child develop a sense of pride and commitment.

When there are a few moments left in a day, it is enjoyable to recall several of the special events by looking at the pictures in the class photo album. This is an effective means of reinforcing a sense of identity and creating positive feelings about the class.

Opening and Closing Questions

Students arrive at school with many different feelings and needs. Some students may arrive in an irritable mood resulting from an argument with a younger brother or a lack of a proper breakfast. Another student's favorite goldfish may have died, while another child may be happy because it is his or her birthday. It is often hard for students to make the transition from home to school. Therefore, it is important that students be given a few minutes at the beginning of each day to share any events that are significant to them.

Students are asked to meet in a circle. The teacher then asks whether any person needs or wants to share anything. A student who has just broken his or her foot may need someone to carry his or her lunch tray, while another student whose dog just died may need some care and understanding. Teachers also have days when they are tired or not feeling well and therefore would like the students to be particularly quiet and helpful during the day. When students are treated kindly and their needs are accepted and respected, they will respond to your needs and desires.

For students who are less comfortable sharing their needs in a group, an optional activity is to have them write down their needs and place them in a box or bag. You can check several times during the day to see whether any child has put a need in the box.

The end of the school day can be an important time to establish closure on any issues that occurred during the day. Questions such as What did you learn today? How do you feel about the day? or What did you like and dislike about today? often evoke serious discussion. It is advisable to allow at least 10 minutes for this session. Taking time at the end of each day encourages students to examine what they have accomplished and also helps to ensure that the day will end on a positive note.

Special Days

Creating special days allows students to have some influence over their environment while enhancing a sense of group identity. Special days might include a day on which everyone wears the same color; a day for wearing favorite buttons; a day when students wear their baseball, soccer, ice skating, or Scout uniforms; a day for dressing as students did during the 1950s; and a day when everyone wears his or her favorite hat. You can add to the special day by relating various subjects to the day's theme. Math problems to solve batting averages could be included on uniform day, music of famous singers during the rock'n'roll era might be discussed and listened to during music class on 1950s day, or students might read stories involving hats on hat day.

My School Bulletin Board

Creating a cohesive group is very important, but it is often useful to expand this concept beyond the classroom. One way to do so is to have students make a hall display or bulletin board with the theme What I Like about My School. Use pictures, essays, or a collage. This activity enhances school spirit and focuses on the positive aspects of a school. This concept can be extended to include a large hall mural with the same theme to which each class contributes their ideas about why they like their school.

Baby Pictures Bulletin Board

An activity that enhances group or school cohesiveness is the display of teachers' or students' baby pictures. A contest can be held to determine which students can correctly identify the teachers' or students' baby pictures. Students enjoy this activity and it often leads to increased dialogue between students and teachers and among students.

A somewhat similar activity is to display samples of students' or teachers' hobbies in the main showcase. Students and teachers can try to match the hobby with the person involved. This activity can be used to generate positive feelings and a sense of esprit de corps either within the classroom or throughout the school.

Activities for Secondary Classrooms

Because secondary school students spend considerably less time in one classroom group, most secondary teachers will choose to incorporate only one or two of the types of activities described in the previous section. A teacher of Junior Writing and American Literature recently shared a technique for incorporating group cohesiveness activities. During the first week of school, she has the class brainstorm ways in which individuals contribute to the class as a whole. These are listed on the chalkboard and may include such statements as:

Breaking the ice
Listening carefully and quietly
Making perceptive observations
Contributing their own experiences
Bringing the group back to the topic being discussed
Asking someone to clarify a point
Summarizing
Asking questions

This material is used to stimulate a discussion about how there are many ways of contributing to a class and how students will differ in their contributions. About a week later, pass out slips of paper with the name of a student on each slip. Each student in the class receives one slip and is asked to write one positive comment about a contribution the student listed on the slip has made to the class. The slips are handed in, and students volunteer to read several of them.

Because they have limited time with their students, most secondary teachers emphasize cooperative learning or other academic learning activities as the basis for creating positive peer relationships that enhance students' motivation and achievement. It is important to keep in mind, though, that these activities will be more successful when students know their classmates and have first been taught basic group skills.

The authors have found several activities and processes particularly valuable in helping secondary students develop skills in functioning as supportive, effective group members. The process includes involving students in an activity that requires cooperation to reach a goal, followed by systematically discussing the behaviors that facilitated the group activity. The game Five Squares (Figure 4.3) is perhaps the best activity for stimulating this student learning. As described in Figure 4.3,

FIGURE 4.3
The Five-Square Game

Preparation of Puzzle

A puzzle set consists of five envelopes containing pieces of stiff paper cut into patterns that will form six-inch squares, as shown in the diagram. Cut the squares into parts and lightly pencil the letters *a* through *j* as shown below. Then mark the envelopes *A* through *E* and distribute the pieces thus:

        Envelope A—j, h, e
                 B—a, a, a, c
                 C—a, i
                 D—d, f
                 E—g, b, f, c

Erase from the pieces the lowercase letters and write instead the envelope letters *A* through *E,* so that the pieces can easily be returned for reuse.

Several combinations of the pieces will form one or two squares, but only one combination will form five squares.

Instructions for Students

Each person should have an envelope containing pieces for forming squares. At the signal, the task of the group is to form five squares of equal size. The task is not complete until everyone has before him or her a perfect square and all the squares are of the same size. These are the rules: (1) No member may speak, (2) no member may signal in any way that he or she wants a card, and (3) members may give cards to others.

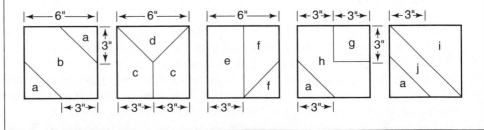

students are placed in groups of five, and each group is given the task of passing puzzle pieces until each group member has an equal-sized square in front of him or her. Tell students that groups who complete their task can quietly observe groups still at work. Finally, if one or more groups has difficulty completing the task, members of these groups can raise a hand, signaling that they would like to be replaced by a student from a group that has completed the task. This student then joins the group still working and continues to follow the rules. The addition of a new member who has seen the correct pattern will usually facilitate quick task completion.

When all groups have completed the task, you can involve students in discussing the groups' functioning. On a chalkboard or butcher paper, make columns labeled "Behaviors That Facilitated Task Completion" and "Behaviors That Hindered the Group." Then ask students, without mentioning names, to describe behaviors that helped their group complete their task. Next, students can list behaviors that blocked their group. Then lead a discussion on group behavior. Interestingly, this activity may also highlight additional factors related to establishing effective learning environments. For example, when using the activity recently, a student in one of the author's classes indicated that he had experienced considerable anxiety when other students began watching his group. This comment led to a productive discussion on the advantages and disadvantages of anxiety in learning and a further discussion on how anxiety could be limited in the class.

Even though this activity requires most of a class period, the authors and dozens of secondary teachers with whom the authors have worked have found that the benefits in terms of students' understanding how groups operate and appreciating the value of involving everyone in group activities far outweigh the time cost.

Group skill-building activities have the advantage of serving several functions. While teaching students the behaviors associated with effective group work, they help students become better acquainted and can increase the feeling of group cohesiveness. Additional group skill-building activities can be found in the books listed in the Recommended Reading at the end of this chapter.

Group cohesiveness may also be enhanced by involving students in shared decision making about classroom organizational factors or problems. As discussed in Chapter 9, students can cooperatively develop classroom rules and procedures. Also work with students to resolve problems that arise. Recently, a friend reported that he had been working with his junior English class to resolve the problem of student papers being late. The teacher stated that more than half his class worked part time and several teachers were requiring that major projects be due on the same day. The teacher and his students collected data on due dates for each student's assignments and developed a series of due dates that was approved by all students in the class.

Utilizing Base Groups

One method the authors have found particularly helpful is the formation of base groups. As defined here, a *base group* is a group of four students who support each other for either a term or a year. Like a cooperative group, a base group is heterogeneous in regard to how successful students are with the course content, gender, and ethnicity. Since the base group will stay together for an extended period of time, many teachers have found that it is worth the time to allow students some input into the makeup of their group. This can be done by asking students to list three or four students they would like to have in their group and perhaps one student with whom they would prefer not to work. Although developing groups takes longer when this information is used, the groups initially function much more smoothly and it appears well worth the initial investment.

The group is not intended to be a cooperative group that works together on specific course projects. Instead, the group meets several times a week for 5 to 15 minutes to check on everyone's content mastery and progress. If someone is absent, a member of the base group collects assignments and is prepared to assist the absent student. If a student is absent for several days, a member of the base group might call and tell the student that he or she is missed and ask if any help is needed. If a member of the base group is having difficult with content, the group can help tutor the student. This may take place during a lengthened base group session or at times arranged by the students. If a student fails to respond to this assistance or is failing to make a good effort in class, the base group can ask for the teacher's assistance.

Base groups can also be used to check homework assignments, to ensure that everyone has adequate notes or materials prior to a test or major assignment, and even to provide study groups for test or daily assignments. At the very least, the base group provides a setting in which at least three members of the class are concerned about each student's learning. This helps create a sense of each student being known and valued in the class—a key prerequisite to learning for many students.

Prior to using base groups, it is important that the teacher clearly outline the group's roles and assist the students in getting to know each other. Second, the teacher must initially provide some structure for the base groups. For example, base groups can be asked to go over each student's assignment sheet or to examine each student's goal sheet or portfolio to ensure that everyone is understanding the work or making adequate progress. Base groups are particularly valuable for field-dependent learners and students new to a class, but they help all students learn to work as a team and to develop empathy and communication skills.

ACTIVITIES FOR ENHANCING DIVERSE LIKING PATTERNS

You have undoubtedly been involved in groups in which everyone was comfortable with and enjoyed every group member. Whether it was an extended family, school staff, religious group, or group of close friends, you probably looked forward to being with this group and found that the group supported personal and intellectual growth. Compare this experience with working in a group characterized by cliques and numerous isolated individuals. Anyone who has been unfortunate enough to work in such a group knows that it is much less supportive of creativity, risk taking, and productivity.

Students are similar to adults in that they are happier and more productive in environments that provide warmth and friendship. The Lewis and St. John (1974) study discussed earlier in this chapter indicated that the presence of high-achieving students was not in itself enough to increase achievement among lower-achieving students. In addition to being exposed to norms that supported academic achievement, the lower-achieving students needed to be accepted as friends by their classmates. When students feel liked by their peers, they experience a sense of significance, belonging, safety, and respect of others. Unless these basic personal needs are met, students will have less energy to expend in learning.

The activities described in this section increase the likelihood that all children in the classroom will be liked and accepted by their peers. Though it is important to use several of these activities early in the school year, we should reinforce positive peer interactions by using activities such as these at least two or three times a month throughout the school year.

As with the activities connected with group cohesiveness, elementary and middle school teachers will be most likely to use the specific activities described in this section. Because teachers in grades K–8 work with groups of students longer, it is appropriate that they spend more time involving students in activities encouraging positive peer relationships and improved self-esteem. Secondary teachers will find that by incorporating the methods described in the previous section, student friendships will become more widespread and cliquishness will be reduced. These results are more likely to occur if elementary and middle school teachers have used activities such as those found on the following pages.

Friendship Bulletin Board

The Only Way to Have a Friend Is to Be One—this can be the theme of a bulletin board in the hall. This bulletin board can take many forms. One method is to have students draw pictures of friends doing things together and to share with the class what they are doing. A second approach is to make a collage of friends and write words around the collage about the qualities a friend has. Another method is to have students draw self-portraits or to pair students and have each person draw or make a silhouette of his or her partner. Students can then put feelings that describe themselves or their partner into words in the heart of the silhouette. Thoughts and ideas the students have can be put in the brain. By the hands and feet of the silhouette, students can draw in things they can do well. These can be mounted and each person can write a paragraph about why the partner is a friend.

This activity introduces the concept that children in the class can be friends. It also encourages children to begin to consider positive characteristics of their classmates. These concepts provide a basis for establishing a safe, positive environment characterized by diverse liking patterns.

Good Deeds Tree

To build on the theme of helping others, a large paper tree or branch is placed on the bulletin board. Students are asked to pay special attention to the nice things people say and do. Whenever they see something nice being done, students write down what happened on a leaf made of green paper and pin it to the tree. The result is a tree full of leaves and a room filled with happy children.

Variations of this activity can be created by using pumpkins in a pumpkin patch at Halloween or shamrocks in a field near St. Patrick's Day. When working with children who cannot write their responses, set aside several times a day to ask children to list nice things they have seen or heard. Write these on the appropriate paper and allow the children to pin them on the bulletin board.

Wanted Posters

Another activity that helps create an environment of warmth and friendship is construction of Wanted posters. Students are given a piece of parchment paper. They burn the edge of the paper to make it look like a poster from the old West and print the word "WANTED" on the paper. Next, the student mounts a picture of himself or herself in the center and writes the phrase FOR A FRIEND BECAUSE . . . underneath the picture. Around the picture each student writes words describing the qualities that make him or her a good friend. A piece of tagboard or brown construction paper can be used as a backing or support. A discussion about friendship and an opportunity to share the posters should follow this activity.

Warm Fuzzies

People enjoy receiving compliments. Everyone likes to receive positive attention and recognition in the form of a warm smile, physical touch, or kind word. Unfortunately, children often receive more criticism and frowns than compliments and smiles. In response to this situation, Claude Steiner (1977) wrote a children's book entitled *The Original Warm Fuzzy Tale*. This delightful story can be read to students of all ages. After reading the story, you can lead a discussion that helps students clearly understand the concepts of warm fuzzies and cold pricklies and how they make people feel. Following this discussion, students will often initiate the idea of giving warm fuzzies to each other.

One approach to helping children learn to be more positive with their classmates is to make warm fuzzies. Warm fuzzies can be made by wrapping yarn around one's fingers several times. The wrapped yarn is then tied in the middle and the ends are cut off. The ends are then fluffed up and a warm fuzzy has been created. After students have made a warm fuzzy, they are asked to think of a reason they deserve a warm fuzzy. Students are encouraged to share their reasons. Each student then keeps his or her first fuzzy. The class should continue making fuzzies until each child has between 5 and 10 fuzzies. To conclude this activity, students can be asked to give a fuzzy to a friend. When giving a fuzzy, students are asked to tell the reason it is being given. Even though the teacher may choose to set time aside daily to hand out fuzzies, students should also be encouraged to give a fuzzy whenever they wish.

Another way to give warm fuzzies is to have a Fuzzy Box where students place positive notes about their peers (students often choose to attach a warm fuzzy to their note). These notes can be read aloud during the last few minutes of the day. Students enjoy receiving compliments in front of their peers.

Friendship Kites

This activity is an opportunity for students to share some positive thoughts about other students. Spring is usually kite season, and so students make personal paper kites. To implement this activity, students will need four sheets of construction paper: one 12-by-18-inch white sheet for the kite and three 9-by-12-inch sheets of any other color. The three colored sheets can be used to make paper flowers or other designs. Students will also need crepe paper streamers cut and twisted and stapled to the kite. To complete the project, they will need string, glue, scissors, a ruler, a pencil, and felt pens or crayons.

Once the kites have been constructed, they are passed around the room and each student writes a positive statement about the designer on each kite. The kites can then be displayed for several days. In addition to reinforcing a diverse liking pattern, this activity helps increase students' feelings of worth and self-esteem.

Valentine Booklets

Another activity that encourages sharing positive feelings is creating Valentine booklets. Give each child a Valentine's Day booklet cut in the shape of a heart. The front and rear covers are red hearts, and the inside pages are white hearts. There should be as many white heart pages as there are members in the class (including the teacher). A booklet is created by punching each heart and attaching the pages with string.

Students sit in a circle with their Valentine booklets on their laps. Ask the children to pass their books to the person on their right. Students then write a nice phrase about the person whose booklet they receive. When you or the time-keeper see that each child has finished writing, speak the phrase, "Pass to the right" again. This activity continues until each individual has his or her own booklet. It takes about one hour to complete, but the results are worth the time spent. Students enjoy this activity and are often seen reading through their booklets when they need a lift.

This activity can be used in association with a variety of special days. Shamrock books can be used on St. Patrick's Day, and the words *I am lucky to know Scott because* . . . written on the outside. Similarly, booklets can be developed around the theme of being thankful at Thanksgiving, and special qualities each student possesses that will help him or her succeed can be used as a theme on a holiday celebrating the birthday of a famous person.

Secret-Pal Books

Positive communication is vital in a classroom. The secret-pal book activity is a strategy for increasing positive communication. Every Monday, each child draws the name of another student. During the week, the students observe the nice things that they see their secret pal doing and write these in their secret-pal book. These books can be made of colored construction paper cover and plain newsprint pages. Students can be encouraged to decorate the books by drawing pictures, writing positive adjectives that describe their secret pal, or writing a word that begins with each letter of the child's name (e.g., Brian: B = brave, R = responsible, I = interesting, A = athletic, N = neat). On Friday, students reveal their secret pals and present them with their books. Students enjoy this activity very much and always look forward to finding out who will be their new secret pal.

A daily variation in the week-long secret-pal books involves having children write their own names on a "secret-pal smiley face." These faces are placed in a basket and each child draws one, making sure that it is not his or her own name. Throughout the day, each child watches his or her secret pal and writes down two or three friendly or helpful things he or she observes the secret pal doing. At the end of the day, the secret pals are revealed and the smiley faces may be taken home.

Discovering Me

This activity gives students an opportunity to interact positively with each other and enhances their self-esteem. Each student draws a class member's name from a hat. Beneath the drawn name, the student writes a positive adjective to describe the class member. When everyone has finished writing an adjective, the papers are pinned to students' backs. Each student may ask another student three questions that can be answered only with yes or no. Each child continues asking questions until he or she has guessed the adjective pinned to his or her back, at which time the child sits down. Students enjoy this type of peer involvement.

I-Booklet

Each child cuts eight capital *I* letters out of colored construction paper. The student uses the first *I* to decorate a cover using his or her name in colored cutout pieces of construction paper. On the first page of the book, the child focuses on his or her name by writing it in as many unusual ways as possible. On the second page, the student illustrates favorite things such as food, toys, colors, friends, television shows, and so on. On the third page, the students draw pictures of things they like to experience with each of their five senses. On page 4, ask students to think about the seasons and what they enjoy doing on the weekends during the various seasons. They can either cut out pictures or draw favorite activities for each season. The next page is devoted to pictures of family, their house, a special friend, pets, and something special their family enjoys doing, such as camping. On the sixth page of the book, the *I* is divided into black and white, representing night and day. Students draw several things they do during the day and several things they do in the evening. Page 7 focuses on facts about the student, such as age, height, address, brothers and sisters, or pets. On the last page, students write a poem about themselves, list positive words that describe them, or write a story about themselves. When all the *I* pages are completed, they can be assembled to form an I-booklet. These booklets should be shared with other classmates. Unlimited topics can be chosen to form these booklets, and topics should be adjusted according to the grade level. For primary students, you could have a laminated person in jeans but without hair or eye color. Each week a student's name is drawn and the child colors in his or her eyes and hair on the laminated figure. The chosen child adds patches to the jeans with titles such as height, weight, favorite color, favorite food, phone number, address, or friends, and fills in the patch with the designated information.

Positive Bombardment

Positive self-concepts are sustained and strengthened in an atmosphere of trust and security. When this type of environment has been established, a positive bombardment can be effectively used. This activity can be implemented in a variety of ways. One technique is to have a child seated on a stool in a circle. The students take turns sharing reasons they like or respect the person being bombarded. Once students have become familiar with this activity and have learned how to give specific positive feedback, the positive bombardments can take place in small groups. Students can now assume greater responsibility for the activity, and more children can become involved in a shorter time.

Another alternative is to choose a theme such as *I felt really happy when you . . .* or *You really are a friend because . . .* and have students complete this phrase as they talk to the person being bombarded. Positive bombardments can also be used as an ending to class discussions or class meetings. For example, children can be asked to make one nice statement to the person seated on either side of them.

Good Citizen Award

One special award that helps students focus on the nice things that are done for others is the Good Citizen Award. Students are asked to pay attention to the sensitive and thoughtful responses their peers make to each other. At the end of the day, students share their observations and the class decides who should receive the honor of Good Citizen for the day. The chosen citizen receives a special certificate, and the child's name is added to the Good Citizens' list. This is a simple way to build strong positive feelings within a classroom.

Student Directory

Almost all students have special interests and abilities about which they feel confident. When students feel comfortable in the classroom, they will often be excited about sharing their expertise with their peers. The creation of a student directory is an activity designed to help students identify their strengths and encourage them to use each other as resources.

Students are asked to identify the activities or skills they believe they perform effectively enough to teach another child. These topics should not be limited to school subjects. They may include skills such as basketball dribbling, downhill skiing, working with dogs, model rocketry, borrowing in subtraction, organizing desks, writing a report, or calligraphy. These lists are collected, tabulated, and placed in alphabetical order with the name(s) of the student(s) listed after each skill. The student directory is typed and mimeographed, and each student receives a copy. A directory is also placed in the front of the room for use by the students. The directory can be a valuable tool for a child who needs assistance with a topic.

Students will often use this directory as a way to improve their skills by asking an expert to help them.

The "I Can" Can

This activity provides students with a visible means of becoming aware of their successes and achievements. Give all children a soup or coffee can and ask them to decorate the cans in some way that represents themselves, such as favorite color, activities, or hobbies. Next, students write the words *I CAN* on their can. Each time a student masters a new skill, he or she writes the mastered skill on a piece of paper, rolls it up like a scroll, ties it with ribbon, and places it in the can. Periodically, the students should take their cans home and share their successes with their parents.

Social Skills Training Programs

Another increasingly popular approach to creating positive peer relationships and integrating isolated or aggressive children into their peer group involves implementing social skills and problem-solving training activities with the entire class. In its simplest form, social skills training can be accomplished by instructing students in many of the skills described in Chapters 3, 4, and 10 of this book. For example, we could instruct children in sending I-messages and warm fuzzies. Students could practice these skills as a group and be encouraged to use them frequently in their daily classroom interactions. Similarly, we can teach students active listening (Chapter 3) and problem-solving skills (Chapter 10).

Social skills training can also be implemented with one of several curricular programs now available. The recommended readings at the end of the chapter include several good resources. Recently, the authors heard about an inner-city middle school that needed to reduce suspensions of minority students. Investigating the cause of suspensions, the administration discovered that most were in response to students' fights. Further investigation suggested that most fights began with students becoming involved in verbal put-downs. The staff decided to approach this problem by teaching all students in the school some basic communication and problem-solving skills. Each homeroom was scheduled for one full day of training in a program developed by the school district. Teachers joined their students and also received special training so that they could encourage students to use the new skills. Follow-ups after six months and one year showed a nearly 50 percent reduction in suspensions for fighting. Chapter 11 provides a more detailed description of specific methods for social skills training.

Rose (1983) stated several advantages to using social skills training in the classroom or other school-group setting. First, youngsters generally find a group setting more attractive than individual work. Second, a group makes better use of the teacher's or counselor's time. Third, the group provides diverse models and an opportunity for students to receive feedback from peers. Fourth, the group provides an opportunity for students to teach each other, thus facilitating development of their own social competence.

The authors have worked with numerous schools whose faculties have chosen to implement social skills training in their curriculum. Most frequently, these have been middle schools and junior high schools whose faculties were interested in reducing the anxiety and conflicts that occur when students from several small neighborhood schools are combined into a larger school.

SCHOOL CLIMATE

Improving the classroom climate by systematically monitoring and improving the quality of teacher-student and peer relationships will do much to create positive student behavior and increased achievement. Students' and teachers' attitudes and behavior are also affected, however, by the quality of life in the school at large. An increasing body of research points to the importance of school climate (Anderson, 1982).

The importance of classroom and school climate was emphasized by John Goodlad (1984). He and his colleagues studied 38 schools in seven regions across the country. The study involved interviews with all 38 principals, 1,350 teachers, 8,624 parents, and 17,163 students, as well as intensive observations in 1,016 classrooms. Analyzing the results of this study, Goodlad reported that schools differed very little in the type of instruction found within classes. He reported, though, that differences in student achievement were found. Goodlad (1983b) summarized these findings.

> I have used the adjectives, "healthy," "satisfying," and "renewing" to describe schools in our sample that pay more than average attention to the quality of interactions among those inhabiting the school and to the physical and social context in which those interactions occur. . . . Schools differed in their ability to create an academic ambience, but the differences appear to be more related to school and classroom climate factors than to methods of teaching per se. (p. 555)

More specifically, Wayson and Pinnell (1982) cited a variety of studies to support their contention that "eight features of schools have a strong relationship to the quality of discipline" (p. 118).

1. Patterns of communication, problem solving, and decision making.
2. Patterns of authority and status.
3. Procedures for developing and implementing rules.
4. Student belongingness.
5. Relationships with parents and community forces.
6. Processes for dealing with personal problems.
7. Curriculum and instructional practices.
8. The physical environment. (p. 118)

In their study of 12 London high schools, reported in *Fifteen Thousand Hours,* Rutter and his colleagues (1979) reported that a variety of schoolwide factors differentiated schools with positive student behavior and high achievement from schools facing serious problems in these areas. Factors within the school's control that significantly influenced students' behavior and performance included the degree to which teachers emphasized academic achievement; teachers' organizational, instructional, and classroom management skills; high teacher expectations about students' performance; teachers' willingness to see students about problems at any time; an emphasis on rewards rather than punishments; teachers' involvement in decision making and the associated consistency in teachers' expectations and behavior; and students' involvement in positions of responsibility within the school. Rutter and his associates concluded that "the pattern of findings suggested that not only were pupils influenced by the way they were dealt with as individuals, but also there was a group influence resulting from the ethos of the school as a social institution" (p. 205).

The factors described by Wayson, Pinnell, and Rutter and his colleagues have also been reported in three books whose authors conducted ecological analyses of effective secondary schools. Joan Lipsitz's (1984) analysis of four high-quality middle schools reported in *Successful Schools for Young Adolescents,* Sarah Lawrence Lightfoot's (1983) study of six high schools, *The Good High School,* and Wehlage, Rutter, Smith, Lesko, and Fernandez's (1989) *Reducing the Risk: Schools as Communities of Support,* a study of secondary school programs successful for serving high at-risk youth, offer thoughtful portraits of secondary schools that are serving youths well.

Educators interested in assessing their school's climate can turn to a large number of instruments and procedures (Dorman, 1981; Howard, 1981; Kelley, 1980, 1981; Lindelow & Mazzarella, 1981; Squires, 1983; Wood & Johnson, 1982). We have used Dorman's (1981) *Middle Grades Assessment Program* with several schools and found it to be extremely helpful in assisting middle-school staff in determining directions for improving the quality of their school's climate.

The important point is that teachers should work together to consider not only how their classroom management and instruction influence students' behavior and achievement but also how the school environment can be altered to encourage positive student attitudes. This can prove to be an exciting, cooperative project that effectively and creatively uses teachers' creativity and concern for students. The authors have taught in and worked with schools in which a committee consisting of students and teachers was established to generate ideas for improving school climate. Figure 4.4 offers some examples of positive school climate activities instigated by these committees.

ACTIVITIES FOR EXAMINING PEER RELATIONSHIPS IN THE CLASSROOM

There are two basic methods of determining the degree to which children in the class are accepted by and feel involved in the classroom group. One method is the sociometric test for determining which students are most frequently chosen by other students as desired work or play partners. To collect these data, students can be asked to list (younger children may tell you their choices) the two students in the classroom with whom they would like to eat lunch, work on a school project, or do some other activity.

In *Group Processes in the Classroom,* Schmuck and Schmuck (1992) provided more methods for collecting this type of sociometric data. A sociogram can also

1. Take pictures of students (including those with a history of school problems) involved in positive behavior. Enlarge these and post them in the hallway.
2. Hold assemblies at least each quarter to reinforce positive student accomplishments. Emphasize improvement as well as standard excellent achievement.
3. Involve students in beautifying the school. Plant flowers around the outside of the school.
4. Provide a space in the hallway where teachers can post positive comments about students and students can write positive statements about their teachers.
5. Create an award (a stuffed turtle or giraffe works nicely) to be presented each week to the staff member who "stuck their neck out" to help students. The award can initially be given by the school climate committee with subsequent selection made by the previous recipient.
6. Involve students and staff in a fund-raising activity, such as a jog-a-thon, with proceeds going to a local charity or other worthy cause.
7. Rather than have an attendance officer call absent students, have an adult with whom the student relates well call.
8. Involve the entire school in a day-long evaluation of the school, with ideas generated to resolve problems and make the school even better.
9. Set aside some time each day or week when everyone in the school stops what they are doing and reads quietly.
10. At the end of each day, have everyone in the school write on a 3-by-5-inch card one positive experience they had that day.
11. Release teachers to spend a day experiencing the same schedule as a student who is having an unsuccessful school experience. Have the teachers report to the faculty what they saw, how they felt, and any suggestions they have for making the school a better place for their student to learn.
12. Encourage the school staff to write notes to their colleagues whenever they observe a colleague involved in an especially helpful or thoughtful interaction with a student or staff member.

FIGURE 4.4
Activities for Creating a Positive School Climate

be developed by observing a class for a time and recording every instance in which a child has a positive or negative interaction with another child. This method has the advantage of providing an indication of the actual interaction patterns in a classroom.

The second method for determining students' feelings about their position in the classroom group as well as their general feelings about the group is to develop a questionnaire that allows them to report their feelings about the group. The advantage of this approach is that is can provide more detailed information than is available through a sociometric test or observation. The main problem with this approach is that students must experience fairly high trust before they will accurately report the information. Even during the initial stages of group development, however, this approach will often reveal useful information. Figure 4.5 is an example of a questionnaire that can be used at several grade levels.

Once you have discovered the dynamics in the classroom, the next step is to implement activities that create more positive peer relationships and group norms. There are several methods for developing positive peer relationships in the class-

FIGURE 4.5
Group
Assessment
Questionnaire

Please answer these questions as carefully as you can.

1. Do you like being in this class? _____ _____
                Yes   No
 Why? _____

2. Would you say that you are a leader or a follower in this class?
 (Circle your answer in red) Leader Follower

3. Would you rather be the opposite of the answer that you gave in question 2?
 (Circle your answer in green) Yes No Maybe

4. Do you listen to people in our class?
 (Circle your answer in yellow) Usually Sometimes Seldom

5. Do other children listen to you when you are talking? _____ _____
                      Yes   No

6. Are you comfortable helping people in this class?

        _____   _____   _____
         Yes   No   Sometimes

7. Are you comfortable asking for help from class members?

        _____   _____   _____
         Yes   No   Sometimes

8. Name three things that you contribute to our group.
 a.
 b.
 c.

HELP?!!

9. Name two things you would like to contribute to our group.
 a.
 b.

10. How do you feel about the students in your class?
         _____ I like all the students
 (check in blue) _____ I like most of the students
         _____ I like only a few students

11. Do the students like you?
         _____ Most of the students like me.
 (check in orange) _____ Some of the students like me.
         _____ I don't think the students like me very much.

12. Do you have friends to sit with at lunch? _____ _____
                 Yes   No

13. When you are at recess, do members of this class let you play with them?

    _____ _____ _____
    Yes   No   Sometimes

14. If you could change one thing about the people in this class, what would you change? _____

Thank you for filling out this questionnaire for me.

room. You can begin the school year by helping students become better acquainted with their peers. This endeavor can be accompanied by activities that create a class spirit and positive group identity. Throughout the year, support these activities by involving students in other activities aimed at building friendships. You can also enhance positive peer relationships by implementing instructional strategies, such as peer tutoring and group projects, which reinforce the value of supportive, cooperative learning. Finally, use problem-solving approaches focused on helping peers resolve their own conflicts.

ASSESSING THE EFFECT OF CLASSROOM ACTIVITIES FOR IMPROVING PEER RELATIONSHIPS

Whenever a teacher implements a new academic or behavior change program, it is important periodically to assess its effectiveness. Educators too often use new ideas because they appear interesting or educational and fail to determine whether the new program meets its stated goals. The following activity will help you assess the outcomes of implementing the procedures described throughout this chapter.

ACTIVITY 4.1
Assessing the Effect of Implementing New Peer-Relationship Activities

Select and implement at least three activities from each of the three approaches to improving peer relationships. These activities can be selected from those described in this chapter or from the resources listed at the end of the chapter. Secondary teachers will want to select several acquaintance activities and to involve students in several cooperative activities.

Both prior to and after implementing these activities, administer Figure 4.5 (or a similar figure) or use a sociogram. Compare the results obtained earlier with the new data. Summarize this comparison by completing these statements:

The number of students who were not selected by any of their peers changed
   from _____ to _____ .
I was surprised to find that . . .
I was happy that . . .
More students stated that they . . .
Fewer students stated that they . . .
My thoughts about improving peer relationships in the classroom are that . . .

SUMMARY

Prior to the recent focus on cooperative learning, the quality of peer relationships was perhaps the most underestimated factor influencing student behavior and achievement. The emphasis on achievement test scores and the associated concern with covering content led even those teachers who valued and were comfortable with their role in creating positive peer relationships to view time spent on building positive, supportive peer relationships as a luxury they could not afford. Many lessons learned in school programs for at-risk children and youth during the late 1960s and 1970s were apparently forgotten with the focus on on-task behavior, direct instruction, and achievement test scores.

Fortunately, recent research on cooperative learning has again provided impetus for teachers to consider the creation of positive peer relationships as an important variable influencing student behavior and learning. Hopefully, today teachers are increasingly provided with information about the importance of selecting a range of methods for creating classroom environments supportive of high student achievement. The recent concern about at-risk students should help ensure that a greater emphasis is placed on meeting students' personal needs both as a critically important goal in itself and as a prerequisite to higher achievement.

RECOMMENDED READING

Beane, J., & Lipka, R. (1984). *Self-concept, self-esteem and the curriculum*. Boston: Allyn and Bacon.

Borba, M. (1989). *Esteem builders; A K–8 curriculum for improving student achievement, behavior and school climate*. Rolling Hills Estates, CA: Jalmer.

Borba, M., & Borba, C. (1978). *Self-esteem: A classroom affair. 101 ways to help children like themselves*. Minneapolis: Winston Press.

Borba, M., & Borba, C. (1982). *Self-esteem: A classroom affair (Vol. 2)*. Minneapolis: Winston Press.

Canfield, J., & Siccone, F. (1992). *One hundred ways to develop student self-esteem and responsibility*. Boston: Allyn and Bacon.

Chase, L. (1975). *The other side of the report card*. Pacific Palisades, CA: Goodyear.

Daniel, B., & Daniel, C. (1978). *Warm smiles, happy faces*. Carthage, IL: Good Apple.

Dinkmeyer, D. (1973). *Developing an understanding of self and others (DUSO)*. Circle Pines, MN: American Guidance Service.

Eberle, B., & Hall, R. (1975). *Affective education guidebook: Classroom activities in the realm of feelings*. Buffalo, NY: DOK.

Farnette, C., Forte, I., & Loss, B. (1977). *I've got me and I'm glad: A self-awareness activity book*. Nashville, TN: Incentive.

Foyle, H., Lyman, L., & Thies, S. (1991). *Cooperative learning in early childhood education*. Washington, DC: NEA.

Gibb, J. (1987). *Tribes: A process for social development and cooperative learning*. Santa Rosa, CA: Center Source.

Goldstein, A. (1980). *Skillstreaming the adolescent: A structured learning approach to teaching prosocial skills*. Champaign, IL: Research.

Huggins, P. (1990). *Helping kids handle anger: Teaching self-control*. Longmont, CO: Sopris West.

Huggins, P., Moen, L., & Manion, D. (1993). *Teaching friendship skills: Primary version*. Longmont, CO: Sopris West.

Johnson, D., & Johnson, F. (1987). *Joining together: Group theory and skills,* 3rd ed. Englewood Cliffs, NJ: Prentice Hall.

Johnson, R. (1993). *Reaching out.* Boston: Allyn and Bacon.

King, C., & Kirschenbaum, D. (1992). *Helping young children develop social skills: The social growth program.* New York: Brooks-Cole.

Lalli, J. (1984). *Feelings alphabet: An album of emotions from A to Z.* Rolling Hills Estates, CA: B. L. Winch.

McElmurry, M. (1983). *Belonging.* Carthage, IL: Good Apple.

McElmurry, M. (1981). *Feelings.* Carthage, IL: Good Apple.

McGinnis, E. (1990). *Skillstreaming in early childhood: Teaching prosocial skills to the preschool & kindergarten child.* Champaign, IL: Research Press.

Nickerson, C., Loilis, C., & Porter, E. (1980). *Miraculous me.* Seattle: Comprehensive Health Education Foundation.

Pincus, D. (1990). *Feeling good about yourself.* Carthage, IL: Good Apple.

Purkey, W., & Novak, J. (1984). *Inviting school success: A self-concept approach to teaching and learning* (2nd ed.). Belmont, CA: Wadsworth.

Rainbow activities: Fifty multi-cultural human relations experiences. (1977). South El Monte, CA: Creative Teaching Press.

Richards, J., & Standley, M. (1982). *Dealing with feelings.* Santa Barbara, CA: Learning Works.

Schniedewind, N., & Davidson, E. (1983). *Open minds to equity: A sourcebook of learning activities to promote race, sex, class and age equity.* Englewood Cliffs, NJ: Prentice Hall.

Schwartz, L. (1976). *The month to month me.* Santa Barbara, CA: Learning Works.

Stanish, B. (1982). *Connecting rainbows.* Carthage, IL: Good Apple.

Stanish, B. (1988). *The giving book: Creative classroom approaches to caring, valuing and cooperating.* Carthage, IL: Good Apple.

Thayer, L. (Ed.). (1976). *Affective education: Strategies for experiential learning.* La Jolla, CA: University Associates.

Vacha, E. (1979). *Improving the classroom social climate.* New York: Holt, Rinehart and Winston.

Waksman, S., & Messmer, C. (1979). *Social skills training: A manual for teaching assertive behaviors to children and adolescents.* Portland, OR: Enrichment Press

Walker, H. (1987). *The ACCESS program (Adolescent Curriculum for Communication and Effective Social Skills).* Austin, TX: Pro-Ed.

Whittington, R., Crites, L., Moran, G., Kreidman, N., & Beck, B. (1989). *Peace begins with me: A non-violent values curriculum for K–6th grade students.* Honolulu, HA: Family Peace Center.

CHAPTER 5

Working with Parents

Research has shown that parents and family are critical factors in children's education, particularly for those who are at risk of dropping out of school. Numerous studies demonstrate that the influence and support given by the family may directly affect the behavior of children in school, their grades, and the probability that they will finish high school.

—Paul Haley and Karen Berry (1988)
Home and School as Partners

What are optimal conditions for a parent-teacher conference? A quiet corner, protection from interruptions and a teacher who listens. The words exchanged during the conference may be forgotten, but the mood of the meeting will linger on. It will decide the subsequent attitudes and actions of the parents.

—Haim Ginott (1972)
Teacher and Child

Parents are the most important and influential adults in students' lives. Even at the secondary level, parents' attitudes toward school dramatically affect students' feelings and behavior. With few exceptions, parents want to know about their children's progress and to have them be successful in school. Parents are delighted to hear that their youngsters are performing well and they expect to be informed immediately when problems arise. Effective teachers accept the important role parents play in students' lives and implement methods for communicating positively with parents. Based on the National Longitudinal Study of 1988, data from the National Center for Education Statistics showed that "parental involvement in school activities had a consistent effect on all three measures of school failure, even after holding constant the student's sex, race-ethnicity, and socioeconomic status. . . . The frequency of discussions between the parent and the child about school-related concerns also had a consistent impact on whether or not the student dropped out. Students were particularly at risk if their parents never talked to them about these matters" (Kaufman, Bradby, & Owings, 1992, p. 22).

Although a teacher's primary role is to work with students, for several reasons, teachers find that an important and rewarding role includes their work with parents. First, children's attitudes about school are influenced by their parents (Coleman, 1966; Simpson, 1962). When parents feel good about their child's teacher and school, the youngster is more likely to receive encouragement and reinforcement for desirable school behavior. Second, because parents are, most often, legally responsible for their children, they should be kept informed about their children's behavior and academic performance. Third, parents can be valuable resources for teachers. They can volunteer time to tutor students, assist teachers by typing or mimeographing materials, or share their expertise on special topics with students. Finally, in a limited number of instances, the rewards and punishments available in school are not powerful enough to elicit desirable behavior from a youngster. When this occurs, school personnel need to involve parents in developing a behavior change program for the student.

Even though teachers can derive numerous benefits from interacting with parents, many teachers indicate that parent contacts are a difficult and relatively undesirable aspect of teaching. Teachers' discomfort in working with parents is based on several factors. First, parent contacts are often time consuming and energy draining. When teachers have worked with students for seven hours and had approximately 1,000 interchanges (Jackson, 1968), it is understandably difficult to be enthusiastic about additional school-related interactions. Similarly, by the end of the day, teachers are usually tired and face several hours of grading and planning. Time spent contacting parents means that a larger amount of this work must be completed at home in the evening. Teachers also find parent contacts difficult because local funding of education makes parents aware that they pay for their children's education and they therefore believe they should be able to monitor teachers' performance. This situation is intensified because the teaching profession has never been viewed with the awe or respect bestowed on such professions as medicine or law. Perhaps because all parents have been students, they believe themselves knowledgeable about what their youngster needs in order to function effectively in school. These factors cause many teachers to be somewhat intimidated by parents and therefore to minimize their parent contacts.

These factors increase the likelihood that contacts with parents will be seen as a necessary task rather than an enjoyable sidelight. Teachers can, however, develop attitudes and skills that will make parent contacts much more enjoyable and productive. This chapter provides methods for making positive contacts with parents throughout the school year, implementing effective parent conferences, and handling parent confrontations. Chapter 11 presents methods for involving parents in helping teachers deal with students' consistent or extremely disruptive behavior.

As with most classroom management methods, each of us must decide how much time and effort we wish to invest in working with parents. Elementary school teachers are expected to maintain frequent contact with parents, and children at this age generally respond well to parents' encouragement. At the middle school and junior high school level, most teachers work with between 80 and 150 students and thus will choose to implement only a few of the ideas presented in this chapter.

However, the authors and most secondary teachers with whom we have worked have found that the benefits of teacher-parent communication can be obtained with minimal contact and by using methods that are pleasant and not very time consuming. As students move into the upper middle school and high school grades, they can and should become more responsible for their own behavior, and parent contacts can become primarily informational in nature. Nevertheless, most students enjoy having parents informed of their activities and successes, and parents of students at every grade level should be informed when students are experiencing serious or persistent problems.

KEEPING PARENTS INFORMED

Importance of Early Contacts

Obtaining parental support is facilitated by familiarizing parents with the teacher's instructional goals and classroom methods as soon as possible. Parents are no different from children or teachers. They are more likely to feel positive about and support issues they clearly understand and have had an opportunity to discuss. Parents who perceive themselves as being treated warmly and respectfully by us and who are familiar with our instructional goals and classroom management procedures are much more likely to encourage student achievement and support us if problems arise.

By introducing parents to the curriculum and major classroom procedures early in the year, we are also able to work with the parents before any worries about their child's achievement or behavior make contacts less positive. A major reason for teachers' concerns about parental contacts is that, except for parent-teacher conferences, most teacher-parent contacts focus on negative student behavior. When our initial interaction with the parents is positive, we are more likely to feel comfortable contacting the parents as soon as their involvement appears necessary. Relationships based on infrequent interactions are seldom as warm and comfortable as those in which contacts are more frequent. Therefore, if we wish to feel comfortable in our contacts with parents, we must instigate relatively frequent, positive contacts with them. Contacts with parents are an excellent example of the idea that an ounce of prevention is worth a pound of cure. Several suggestions are offered here for initiating such contacts.

Methods for Obtaining Parental Support

There are many approaches to developing parental support for student achievement and positive classroom behaviors. The ideas presented here are among those that the authors and teachers with whom the authors have worked have found particularly useful. You are encouraged to modify these methods creatively in order to develop an approach best suited to your situation.

An Introductory Letter

Perhaps the easiest approach for making the initial contact is to send a letter to each student's parent(s). Because the letter will include information that you will want to present personally to students, it is best to send the letter so that it arrives one or two days after school begins. In the letter, you can introduce yourself, state your interest in developing positive teacher-parent contacts, and invite the parents to attend a back-to-school night or a similar event in which you and they have an opportunity to meet and discuss the school year. Figure 5.1 is an example of an introductory letter.

The Initial Meeting

It is very important to try to meet parents as soon as possible. The most expedient approach to meeting between 30 and 150 parents seems to be to provide an evening when parents are invited to visit their child's classroom(s) and discuss the teacher's approach to instruction and classroom management. It is helpful if the school supports this concept by arranging a formal back-to-school night. If this opportunity is not available, though, it is worth the effort to arrange such an event for ourselves and any colleagues who may be interested. It is sometimes necessary to arrange an alternative meeting time for parents who are unable to attend or uncomfortable attending an evening session. Information about the times that are most convenient for parents can be obtained by requesting this information in the initial letter sent to parents.

Prior to the initial meeting with parents, it is important for elementary teachers to make a telephone contact in which something positive about the child is reported, and to obtain the parents' commitment to attend the parent orientation

---

FIGURE 5.1
Introductory
Letter to Parents

(Date)

Dear Parents,

With school under way, I'd like to take a moment of your time to welcome you to the fourth grade and to introduce myself. My name is Mrs. Louise Jones and I have taught in the Beaverton School District for 23 years in both open and self-contained classrooms. I completed my undergraduate work at Oregon State University and received my master's degree from Lewis and Clark College.

I am very interested in making this a successful and happy school year for you and your child. To ensure this success, we must keep the lines of communication open. I respect the fact that you know your child very well, and so when either you or your child feel worried, please contact me. Likewise, if there is an activity or project that you enjoy, please let me know. I am available at school until 4:00 P.M. each day. I will be contacting you throughout the year about projects, upcoming events, the nice things I see your child doing, and problems, if any arise.

In a few weeks our school will have its annual Back-to-School Night. At that time I will discuss in detail the academic program, my discipline procedures, grading, and my goals and expectations for this year. There will also be a display of books and materials that your child will be using during the year. I encourage you to attend this special evening because it will give you an opportunity to understand the fourth-grade program and to become better acquainted with the room and materials that your child will be using throughout the coming year.

Sincerely,
Mrs. Louise Jones

meeting. This telephone contact also breaks the ice and sets the stage for future telephone conversations.

First impressions are extremely important—especially when a relationship involves sporadic and somewhat role-bound interactions—and it is imperative to do everything possible to create a positive initial meeting. In addition to the obvious factors of being well groomed and personable, the teacher should be well organized and the classroom should look interesting and include a personal touch. Parents are very impressed by competence. You may start the meeting on a positive note by placing an outline of the evening's topics on the board. Figure 5.2 provides an example of an outline for a parent orientation meeting. This outline can be accompanied by a folder for each parent, including:

1. A description of the curriculum for the grade level
2. An introductory letter about yourself that includes professional background and a philosophy of education
3. A class schedule
4. A handout describing the emotional and social characteristics of a child at the grade level
5. A list of special projects that may require some parental assistance
6. A statement of your classroom-management procedures
7. Book ideas for book reports
8. A parent resource form eliciting information about what parents can offer to the class

By providing parents with written information, you indicate that the information is important. A folder also creates ready-made notes and thus increases the likelihood that parents will learn and recall the information presented.

Another popular idea is to display the textbooks the students will be using throughout the year. This exhibit is most effective if you place a card beside each book indicating the subject, an overview of the topics covered in the book, and why the book is being used.

You can also facilitate a positive meeting by providing a personal touch; obviously, there are many ways to do this. One activity that is fun is to have each child make a silhouette of her or his head or a life-size outline of her or his body. The silhouette can be placed on the desk, and the outline seated in the child's chair. The parent(s) can then be asked to find their child's seat. Children can also write a note to their parent(s) to indicate several things they would like their parent(s) to see in the classroom.

During the parent orientation, your approach to classroom management can be discussed. Parents can be provided with copies of the classroom rules, and you can discuss how both minor problems and consistent behavior problems will be handled. For example, outline the use of class meetings, describe the problem-solving approach that will be used, and discuss behavior contracts. You should also make a clear statement on when parents will be contacted about students' behavior.

Similarly, you should clearly outline the instructional methods that will be used to help the students. Discuss the class schedule and indicate the types of instruction that will be used in teaching each topic. You might inform the parents

I. Introducing the Teacher
   A. College training and degrees earned.
   B. Professional experience:
      1. length of teaching experience
      2. type of classroom—open vs. self-contained
II. Social and Personal Expectations for Students during the Year
   A. Students will develop responsibility:
      1. for themselves
      2. for their property
      3. for their assignments
   B. Students will learn to respect their peers' successes and weaknesses.
   C. Students will develop a feeling of pride for their accomplishments.
   D. Emphasis will be placed on maintaining and improving self-concept:
      1. focus on the positive at school
      2. encourage parents to reinforce positive behavior at home
   E. Students will learn to work harmoniously in groups: emphasis on sharing.
   F. Emphasis will be placed on teaching students the skill to communicate openly with each other and adults.
III. Academic Curriculum and Goals
   A. Students will increase their learning by one grade level in all subject areas by the end of the school year
   B. A short discussion on the major topics covered in each academic subject:
      1. reading
      2. math
      3. language arts
      4. handwriting
      5. spelling
      6. social studies
      7. science
      8. physical education
      9. music
     10. library
IV. Emphasis Will Be Placed on Organizational Skills
   A. Notebooks will be organized by subjects and returned papers will be filed under the proper heading.
   B. Spiral notebooks will contain students' creative-writing work.
   C. Desks will remain neat and orderly.
V. Grading System
   A. Students' grades are determined by the marks: O—outstanding; S—satisfactory; N—needs improvement.
   B. Report cards are given four times a year.
   C. Conferences are held in the fall and spring quarters.
VI. Students Will Have Homework under These Conditions:
   A. To reinforce a weak skill area.
   B. To reinforce a new concept: short practice on the multiplication factor or weekly spelling word list.
   C. When students have failed to use their academic time wisely in school.
   D. Students are encouraged to read for a few minutes each night.
VII. Students Will Be Assigned Three Major Projects during the Year
   A. Parents will be informed by letter.

FIGURE 5.2
Outline for Parent Orientation Meeting

(continued)

FIGURE 5.2
Continued

          B. The date on which the project is due will be set realistically so that it will
             not interfere with family obligations.
          C. Students are encouraged to start the projects when they are assigned.
   VIII. Discipline Procedure
          A. Parents will be contacted when necessary.
          B. Parents are given a copy of the Class Rules.
    IX. Teachers' Comments on the Student's Study Habits So Far This Year
     X. Miscellaneous Comments
          A. Mark all clothing with the student's full name.
          B. Keep emergency card current.
          C. Please send a note when your child has been ill, is riding a different bus
             home, or is leaving before the end of the school day.

that during reading, their children will be grouped by ability and will receive numerous homework assignments. Discuss the types of homework students will be assigned and describe how parents can best respond to the homework. You may want to state that should students ever be confused and overly concerned about a particular homework assignment, the student or parent is welcome to call you at home for assistance. Experience indicates that though parents appreciate and are impressed by this offer, teachers receive very few evening phone calls about assignments.

When discussing academic work, you may want to describe the various special services, such as reading or gifted programs, that are available for providing students with individualized instruction outside the classroom. Similarly, you should discuss how individual differences are attended to in the classroom. Along these lines, it is helpful to outline the grading system that will be used and to discuss such issues as whether grades will reflect improvement or performance measured against some external standard. You may also want to describe any special instructional methods such as peer tutoring, individual goal setting, or group projects. Finally, parents can be informed that they will receive letters announcing any special projects or assignments that may require that they provide their child with some assistance. By clarifying the academic program and informing parents when and how they will be involved in helping their children, teachers can begin to create an accepting, supportive parent response.

You should also inform parents that they can expect to receive telephone calls and notes when their child has had a particularly good day or done something new or especially interesting. Similarly, the parents should be informed that they will also be notified when problems arise so that they are aware of what is happening. Teachers can make this process easier and more comfortable for themselves and parents by obtaining information concerning the most convenient time to contact each parent. Indicate that although you accept the responsibility for providing an exciting educational experience and helping the students to learn social skills and responsibility, the most effective approach to motivating student learning and dealing with any problems that arise is for the home and school to work together effectively.

Follow-Up

Do not wait too long before reinforcing the ideas presented in the orientation meeting. You may do so by arranging to involve parents in an instructional activity within a week or two following the meeting. The involvement may include an assignment in which parents are asked to help their children obtain information. You might ask the students to develop a family tree or to interview their parents for a career day. Another follow-up activity involves sending positive notes to parents about improvements or achievements their children have made in the specific areas discussed during the orientation meeting.

An additional aspect of follow-up is contacting parents who did not attend an orientation session. One approach is to send the parents their folder along with a letter stating that they were missed and inviting them to schedule a time to visit the classroom and discuss the material in the folder. It is helpful to call parents who do not respond and ask them whether they had any questions about the material they received. Although such contacts do require additional time, they are worth the effort, for they create a foundation for increased parental support.

Continuing Teacher-Parent Communication

All parents care about their children, and virtually all parents want their children to be successful at school. Therefore, it is important to keep parents continually informed about their child's progress in your class.

Teachers should also contact parents when a child consistently begins to act-out in class, falls behind in schoolwork and may need special assistance, or needs to complete some work at home. As in any relationship, it is better to deal with problems when they first arise than to wait until a crisis has occurred. Parents are justified in their annoyance when they attend a conference and discover that their child has been behind for six or eight weeks. Though it is true that some parents either do not care or cannot provide assistance in working with their child, it is important to hold positive expectations. It is surprising how often parents with a reputation for lack of concern or for ineptness in helping their child can respond productively when contacted early and treated thoughtfully. There is an important distinction between teachers' constantly calling parents for support and calling parents to provide them with information. Parents have a right to expect teachers to handle minor problems and seek professional assistance in coping with major problems. Parents should be informed, however, when minor problems such as incomplete assignments or failure to bring supplies become frequent occurrences. Similarly, parents should be informed when major behavior or academic problems arise.

One method of communicating with parents is to send informational letters about upcoming areas of study, field trips, long-term projects their child will be asked to complete, or newsletters about class happenings. Parents appreciate receiving information regularly, and a bimonthly or monthly letter seems most appropriate.

Another approach is to have students make personalized stationery during the first weeks of school. They can design their own patterns and decorate their stationery using felt pens, charcoal, paint, or any other art medium. Teachers can use this stationery to send positive notes home about the student. It is best if elementary teachers send a positive note home at least twice a term. Most teachers find it helpful to record when notes were sent as well as the content of the notes. In this way, you can send notes to all students and focus on different positive events each time a note is sent for each child.

Phone calls are another method for contacting parents. Teachers who call each child's parent(s) at least once before scheduling the initial conference and at least once a term thereafter find that parent-teacher contacts are more relaxed and enjoyable. Teachers often shy away from parents who have a reputation for being difficult. These, however, are the parents whom we should make the most effort to know. Parents appreciate knowing that their child's teacher cares enough to make a phone call, and the most critical parent will frequently become a supporter of the teacher who takes time to call. When making phone calls, always begin and end the conversation with a positive statement about the child. Also ask the parent how the child is reacting to school and whether the parent has any information that might assist you in making the school experience more productive for the child. Like children, parents respond more positively when given a sense of competence and power.

Parents can also be contacted informally when you attend extracurricular activities in which their child is involved. This strategy is particularly effective with the parents of students who are doing poorly in school. On a number of occasions, the authors have made concerted efforts to attend athletic performances of students involved in persistent school misbehavior and have found that when the parents saw concrete evidence of the authors' concern for their child, they became much more involved in encouraging the student to behave responsibly in school.

A final method for keeping parents informed is to ask them to serve as volunteers in the classroom. Parents are more likely to support us if they understand and feel a part of what goes on at school. Many parents of students with behavior problems had negative experiences when they were in school. Consequently, they respond negatively to and are often intimidated by teachers. Involving these parents in a positive manner in the classroom can do a great deal to alleviate these negative feelings. Parent volunteers who are treated with respect by teachers almost always become strong supporters of the teacher. As anyone who has worked with parent volunteers knows, the teacher will initially need to spend time discussing the volunteer's role and helping volunteers understand and respond consistently to our instructional and discipline style. It is important to recognize situations in which a parent's style of interacting with children may contradict

"Wilson sometimes has a little difficulty handling parent conferences."

the teacher's methods. In such cases, perhaps the volunteer's efforts can be channeled into support activities that involve minimal contact with students.

PARENT CONFERENCES

For most teachers, parent conferences are a required form of parent contact. Parent conferences can play a vital role in eliciting parents' support for us and can help us work with students who are experiencing difficulties. Unfortunately, a poorly organized or otherwise negative conference can create or intensify parental dissatisfaction. This dissatisfaction will frequently be reflected in students' behavior. Furthermore, coping with parental criticism diverts valuable teacher time and energy. Therefore, parent conferences have a real influence on classroom discipline.

By thoughtfully preparing for a conference and implementing a well-organized conference, we can reduce our own anxiety about conferring with parents while increasing the likelihood that parents will leave the conference feeling positive about and supportive of us. This section offers suggestions for improving skills in conferring with parents.

Preparing for a Conference

Because teacher, parent, and student all care about the outcome of a teacher-parent conference, it is important to consider how best to prepare each of these individuals for the conference. A conference will be more comfortable and productive when each person involved (the student is integrally involved even if he or she is not present) is prepared for the conference.

Preparing Students

The first steps in preparing students are to discuss the goals of conferences and to allow children to ask questions and express their concerns. Students need to know why their parents are being given a report and what will happen at the conference. The next step is to provide students with an opportunity to evaluate their own work. Because the primary goal of periodic teacher-parent conferences is to clarify and communicate students' accomplishments, it is logical that students should be involved in this process. Providing students with an opportunity to evaluate their own work also reduces their anxiety about the type of information their parents will be receiving. Self-evaluation provides children with a sense of significance, competence, and power.

There are several approaches to involving students in self-evaluation. The most specific and valuable method is to allow students to fill out a report card on themselves. The easiest and most effective method of developing a self-evaluation report card is to ask students to rate themselves on the same items on which the district or school requires you to rate students. Figure 5.3 is an example of such a form. Once the student has completed a self-evaluation form (younger children or students who have difficulty with reading will require assistance in completing a form), you can schedule time to discuss the results individually with each student.

FIGURE 5.3
Self-Evaluation
Report Card

Name _____

Reading

1. Approximately how many pages of outside reading have you done this term?
   _____

2. Have you done as good a job on outside reading as you could have?
   _____

3. Have you kept up your daily assignments in your literature book or reading text?
   _____

4. What grade do you deserve in reading?
   grade: _____   effort: _____

Math

1. Have you worked hard to get all your assignments done on time?
   _____

2. Are there any of the multiplication tables that you are not sure of?
   _____ If so, which ones? _____

3. Are there any areas of math that you are not clear about or need more help in?
   _____

4. What grade do you deserve this term in math?
   grade: _____   effort: _____

Spelling

1. Have you studied your list words each week? _____
2. Have you been completing your workbook assignments each week on time?
   _____

3. Do you think you remember the words that you learn to spell each week?
   _____

4. How well do you spell your words in your creative writing and on daily assignments?
   superior   very good   fair   poor   (Circle one)
5. What grade should you receive for spelling this term?
   grade: _____   effort: _____

Cursive Writing

1. What grade do you feel you have earned this term in cursive writing?
   grade: _____   effort: _____
2. What do you need to work on? _____

Science, Social Studies, and Art

What grade would you give yourself in each of these areas for this term?
Please give a reason for each grade.

Science: grade: _____   effort: _____
Reason _____

Social Studies: grade: _____   effort: _____

Reason _____

Art: grade: _____   effort: _____
Reason _____

What areas are you doing well in at school? _____

What do you need to work on? _____

In what ways do you feel you have grown personally this year?

_____

Please evaluate your study habits and personal growth, using these ratings.

   + = outstanding growth
   = = okay or satisfactory growth
   ✔ = need to improve in this area.

Put the appropriate mark on each line below.

Study Habits

____ Following directions
____ Completing assignments on time
____ Working well in (your) a group
____ Working well alone
____ Listening well to whomever is speaking
____ Showing neatness in your work and desk
____ Assuming responsibility for your work

Personal Growth Areas

____ Considering other people's feelings
____ Follow school rules in a positive way
____ Taking care of your personal belongings
____ Controlling your own behavior
____ Being able to accept responsibility for your own actions
____ Being able to get along well with others

Is there anything that you would like to share with me about yourself or your work?

_____

Is there anything you would like me to write on your report card or share with your parents? _____

Do you have any comments about my teaching this term? _____

_____
_____

Other comments that might be helpful for me to know? _____

_____

Thank you for your help!

Inform the students that this conference will allow the teacher and student to discuss any discrepancies between the teacher's and student's evaluation. It is extremely important to discuss these differences. Student resentment and hostility are often the outcomes of a conference in which parents are given negative information about a student before this information has been systematically discussed with the student. The implications for classroom management are obvious and dramatic. Students will treat their teacher and peers with greater kindness and respect when they feel they have been treated fairly.

Another method that can be incorporated with a self-evaluation report card is to have students examine their behavior and academic achievements compared with their stated goals. If students have been involved in writing goals for the grading period, they can be asked to write a short statement about the degree to which they have met these goals. This procedure not only places their learning and subsequent grade in perspective but it also reinforces the concept of students' responsibility for their own learning.

Preparing Parents

There are two basic methods for preparing parents for a teacher-parent conference. First, as discussed earlier, you should already have had several positive contacts with the parents. These contacts ideally include a back-to-school night, a phone call, and several notes sent home on their child's progress. Second, about one week before the conference, you should send the parent(s) a note reminding them of the conference and providing them with an agenda for the conference. Figure 5.4 provides an example of such a note and outline.

Teacher Preparation

Teachers are responsible for providing the parent(s) with clearly presented information in the context of a positive, comfortable interaction. There are three basic steps in accomplishing this goal: First, as discussed in the preceding paragraphs, we should adequately prepare the student and parent(s) for the conference. Second, we should acquire and clearly organize important information about the student. Third, we should create a comfortable, relaxed environment.

Parents are impressed with data. Data indicate that we have invested time and energy in preparing for a conference. Data also testify directly to our professional competence. By focusing on specific data, we quickly move ourselves out of the parents' conception of teachers as professional babysitters and into the category of skilled professional educators. Data also have the obvious advantage of objectifying a discussion. The presence of data greatly diminishes the likelihood that a conference will turn into a debate over whether a student's grade is fair or whether a student's behavior really warrants concern.

Data also provide protection for the teacher by furnishing a record of a student's academic progress and behavior as well as of our attempts to make thoughtful interventions aimed at improving skills and behaviors. The availability of data prevents us from being accused of exaggerating a problem, picking on a

FIGURE 5.4
Agenda for a
Parent
Conference

Dear Mr. and Mrs. Smith:

I am looking forward to our conference on Wednesday, November 6, at 3:30 P.M. In order to help us use the time most effectively, I will try to follow the agenda listed below. I hope that this list will cover all areas you would like to discuss. If you have any special questions, it might be helpful to jot them down prior to the conference.

Conference Agenda

1. Share positive personal qualities about the student.
2. Read student's self-evaluation.
3. Discuss the report card and examine samples of the student's work.
4. Discuss the student's behavior and peer relations.
5. Time for any final parent questions or concerns.
6. Summarize the conference by discussing the student's strengths, weaknesses, and areas that need improvement.

Sincerely,

Mrs. Johnson
3rd-Grade Teacher

---

student, or not having attempted to solve the problem ourselves. Regardless of how competent we may be, lack of specific information significantly undermines our position when working with parents. Consequently, well-organized data are a necessary component of any parent conference and are especially important when a conference focuses on dealing with inappropriate student behavior or poor student achievement. The four major types of data that are useful in a parent conference are:

1. Data on the students' and parents' feelings about the class
2. Data on the students' behavior and the results of attempts to improve the behavior
3. Data on the students' academic work
4. Data on conferences with colleagues and specialists aimed at developing a solution to any matter that is a problem

It is helpful to acquire information about how the parents view the school year as progressing for their child. By requesting this information, we acknowledge the importance of the parents' concerns and ideas. Information about the parents' perceptions of their child's reactions to school and the parents' own wishes can also enable us to be better prepared for the conference. Figures 5.5 and 5.6 provide an example of a cover letter and parent questionnaire used by intermediate-grade teachers.

> Dear Parents,
>
> I am attempting to make parent conferences more productive for myself, your child, and you.
>
> In order to do so, I would like to have as much information as possible for the conference. You can help me by responding to the questions on the attached sheet. If there are any questions that you do not care to answer, please feel free to leave them blank. I would very much appreciate your returning this questionnaire to me at least one day before the conference. If that is not possible, please bring it to the conference with you.
>
> I appreciate the time you are taking to help make this a rewarding conference for all of us.
>
> I look forward to seeing you next week.
>
> Miss Wilson

FIGURE 5.5
Cover Letter to Preconference Parent Questionnaire

Data on a student's behavior will be necessary only when conferring with parents whose child is having serious behavior problems. In such cases, the parents should be presented with specific data on the child's behavior and our approaches to helping the child in improving the behavior.

Because the school's primary function is to provide students with basic academic skills, the teacher-parent conference should heavily emphasize informing parents about their child's academic progress. You should prepare for each conference by providing a folder that includes samples of the student's work in each major subject. The folder should include specific examples that will help the parent understand any areas in which the student is having particular difficulties.

If the data on the student's academic progress indicate that the student is not functioning well, be prepared to provide the parent(s) with examples of ways in which the student's academic program has been adjusted in order to meet the student's special needs. If you have worked with specialists in developing an individualized program, it is helpful to provide information about these conferences. This can be done by using a standard form to record the results of such conferences. Figure 5.7 is an example of a form you can use for this purpose.

There are several advantages to presenting this type of data. Data concerning professional consultation speak to the teacher's concern and resourcefulness. Furthermore, they indicate to the parents that their child's problem is not simply a personality conflict with a teacher or the result of an incompetent teacher's having difficulty teaching their slightly energetic student. Another advantage to having consulted with specialists is that this procedure should present the parents with clearer and more thorough data. Especially in the area of academic difficulties, classroom teachers often have limited skills in diagnosing the specific factors that may be causing a student's problems. By consulting specialists, not only can the teacher provide the parents with more detailed information but the teacher can also simultaneously acquire information that can assist in developing a more appropriate academic program for the student.

Please complete this questionnaire and return it as soon as possible. Thank you.

Name: _____

1. My child's general attitude toward school this year is _____
   _____

2. My child expresses most interest in school in _____
   _____

3. My child's greatest concern in school seems to be _____
   _____

4. Some things my child does very well are (these do not have to pertain to school)
   a. _____   d. _____
   b. _____   e. _____
   c. _____   f. _____

5. An area I would like to see my child work especially hard in is _____
   _____

6. Please list some positive qualities that you child has so that we can discuss good
   qualities at school (such as trustworthy, patient, understanding, punctual) _____
   _____

7. Something I have wondered about this year is _____
   _____

8. Some things my child would like to do but has never done are _____
   _____

9. Some things that seem difficult for my child are (not necessarily school work:
   example, doing small tasks with fingers) _____
   _____

10. Something my child would like to do in school is _____
    _____

11. Several subjects that my child seems to enjoy are (include interests and hob-
    bies) _____
    _____

12. I would appreciate any suggestions or comments you have that would help me
    work more effectively with your child. _____
    _____
    _____
    _____

Thank you for taking time to complete this questionnaire.

FIGURE 5.6
Preconference
Parent
Questionnaire

It is helpful to provide parents with a conference summary. This review can focus the conference and can also serve as a reminder, for teachers often hold several consecutive conferences. The parent should be given the summary sheet at the end of the conference. Figure 5.8 is an example of a conference summary form.

Once we have prepared students and parents and have collected and developed the important data, the final preparation involves creating a comfortable conference setting. If possible, the conference should be held at a round table so that neither party is in a dominant position. The atmosphere can be made more

Consultant's Name _____   Date _____

Consultant's Position or Role _____

Reasons for holding the conference:

Goals for the conference:

Information obtained:

Decision(s) reached:

Additional comments:

FIGURE 5.7
Teacher-
Specialist
Conference Form

Source: From Vernon F. Jones, *Adolescents with Behavior Problems: Strategies for Teaching, Counseling, and Parent Involvement,* p. 274. Copyright © 1980 by Allyn and Bacon. Reprinted with permission.

relaxed by placing some flowers on the table and having cookies and coffee available. The agenda should be placed on the board or on a large sheet of butcher paper as a reminder for both parties. Parents also appreciate knowing what topics and skills have been covered during the term. A piece of paper listing these skills can be placed next to the agenda for reference during the conference. Pencil and paper should be provided so the parent(s) can take notes during the conference.

Providing an Effective Conference

If you have prepared effectively, the actual conference will usually be quite easy and comfortable. After greeting the parent(s) warmly and chatting for a moment about any positive topic, begin the conference by sharing several positive personal qualities the child displays at school. Encourage the parent(s) to discuss any aspects of the student's behavior they have enjoyed or been particularly pleased with recently. The next step is to ask the parent(s) to read the student's self-evaluation report card and any other material the student has written about his or her progress during the term. Students often are so critical of their own work that this is an interesting and

Student's Name: _____

Academic Achievement

Reading
Doing well in: _____
Needs to work on: _____

Math
Average of math scores: _____   _____
                              tests   daily work

Strong areas: _____
Needs to improve on: _____

Other subjects: _____
_____

Behavior and Personal Characteristics

Positive personal qualities that I see in your child: _____ _____
_____

Improvement needed in: _____
_____
_____

Comments about how your child is relating to his or her classmates: _____
_____

Final Comments

You could help at home by: _____
_____
_____
_____

Any additional comments: _____
_____
_____
_____

FIGURE 5.8
Conference
Summary Form

sensitive preparation for any critical comments that you may need to make. Once they have read their child's own critical evaluation, parents are less likely to question your statements about areas in which their child needs improvement.

Many parents are concerned about their child's report card, so the next step is usually to discuss the actual report card and examine specific examples of the student's work. When doing so, initially focus on positive aspects of the student's work. Parents respond well to the "sandwich theory of feedback" in which critical comments are sandwiched between positive comments about their child. Another strategy is to introduce an area that needs improvement with the statement, "I would like to encourage your child to. . . ." By focusing on the positive, you can minimize parental defensiveness and criticism.

Once academic matters have been discussed, focus on the student's behavior and peer relationships. It is important to discuss positive aspects of the student's behavior as well as aspects that require improvement. Also, if the student has experienced serious behavior problems, provide the parent(s) with specific data on the student's behavior and efforts to assist the student in changing behavior. During this portion of the conference, it may be appropriate to invite the principal or any other specialists to join in the discussion. (The last section in this chapter provides specific strategies for conferring with parents of seriously acting-out children.)

After you have discussed the student's academic progress and behavior, the parent(s) should be encouraged to ask questions and make comments. If the parents do not have any questions, you can help them focus on their thoughts and concerns by referring to any pertinent items on the preconference parent questionnaire (Figure 5.6).

Conclude the conference by summarizing the student's academic and behavior strengths and weaknesses. Goals for improvement can be written down (Figure 5.9), and you can discuss any ways in which the parents can assist the child at home. These should be listed on the conference summary form (Figure 5.8). Discuss any follow-up contacts that appear desirable based on the information discussed during the conference, and express sincere appreciation for the parents' efforts and input.

The final step in implementing an effective conference is to ask parents to evaluate the conference (Figure 5.10). This evaluation provides us with valuable information about aspects of the conference that parents find most and least beneficial. Perhaps equally important, by requesting an evaluation, you conclude the conference with an activity that acknowledges the parents' value and provides them with a sense of competence and power.

METHODS FOR SECONDARY TEACHERS

As stated at the beginning of this chapter, secondary teachers usually have fewer direct parent contacts than do their elementary school counterparts. Most secondary schools do not require parent conferences for all students, nor do they expect teachers to maintain continuing contact with their students' parents. Nevertheless, experience and reports from numerous teachers suggest that secondary teachers too often underestimate both the value and feasibility of steady parent contacts. Teachers who have placed an emphasis on positive, proactive interactions with parents by using the following cost-effective methods for communicating with parents report increased parental support and improved student attitudes toward academic activities.

Introductory Letters

Teachers can provide parents with a wide range of information by sending home a form letter describing selected aspects of learning goals, instructional methods, and classroom procedures. A letter might include a course syllabus or similar list of topics to be covered and specific skills the students will learn. Teachers may also

PLAN FOR IMPROVEMENT

STUDENT'S NAME: _____

TEACHER'S NAME: _____

PARENT'S NAME: _____

DATE: _____

AREA TO BE IMPROVED: _____

_____

THE TEACHER WILL: _____

_____

THE STUDENT WILL: _____

_____

THE PARENT WILL: _____

_____

LONG-RANGE GOAL: _____

_____

FIGURE 5.9
Plan for
Improvement

comment on the specific teaching methods that will be used during the course. For example, if you use group work or projects, you might describe the activities in which students will be involved as well as the educational rationale for using these methods. Teachers may also comment on grading procedures, decisions on when to inform parents about lack of student progress, and methods that will be used in responding to disruptive student behavior. This material should be prefaced by suggesting that such behavior is not anticipated, because the combination of interesting and effective instruction and the commitment to assist students will make it unlikely that these methods will prove necessary.

Would you please take a moment to evaluate our conference? This review helps me as I plan our next one.

Excellent   10   ____

                9   ____

                8   ____

                7   ____   Please check the appropriate line.

                6   ____

Average   5   ____

                4   ____

                3   ____

                2   ____

Poor   1   ____

Was there a subject that you especially appreciated my sharing or that was very helpful to you?

Was there an area we neglected to discuss that you feel I should have brought up?

Do you have any other comments to share?

FIGURE 5.10
Conference
Evaluation Form

Newsletters

A newsletter is an expedient way to keep large numbers of parents informed. Because most secondary teachers have three separate preparations, a newsletter sent every three weeks for each class requires a teacher to write one newsletter each week. The newsletter can involve less than a page, describing subjects currently being taught, projects due, films being shown, and so on. You can also use this opportunity to jot a personal note on newsletters to parents whose child is experiencing noteworthy success or problems.

Progress Reports

Many schools require that teachers notify parents at midterm of each nine-week period if their child is earning lower than a C grade. You can readily develop your own form for immediately contacting parents whose children are beginning to experience academic or behavioral problems. Because this form should be sent when students are just beginning to experience a problem, you should summarize the steps you will be taking to help the student. This form need not initially require you to write; you can simply list the methods you systematically use.

DEALING EFFECTIVELY WITH PARENTS' CRITICISM AND CONFRONTATION

Anyone who has taught for several years has had to deal with an angry or critical parent. Many teachers state that, along with classroom discipline, this type of confrontation is perhaps the least desirable aspect of teaching. Although there is no foolproof method for dealing with an angry parent, there are several strategies that can be used to cope with such situations in an effective, professional manner.

1. Greet the parent in a pleasant manner. It is more difficult for parents to remain critical and aggressive if you seem glad to see them.

2. Use active listening to defuse the parent's emotions. Becoming defensive or initially arguing with the parent will usually only intensify the parent's emotions. By using phrases such as "I appreciate your concern" or "I can see that you are really concerned about this," you can help the parent feel understood. This tactic will gradually enable the parent to calm down and replace angry or frightened feelings with more positive and productive feelings.

3. Look genuinely interested and listen carefully. This attitude also helps the parent feel accepted and will gradually reduce negative or intense feelings.

4. Present a calm, professional manner. Stand erect, look at the parent, and remain calm. Just as students respond more effectively to teachers who remain calm and in charge during a crisis (Brophy & Evertson, 1976; Kounin, 1970), parents need the structure provided by a calm response.

5. Ask the parent what he or she wishes to accomplish. One method of structuring a confrontation conference is by questioning the parent: "I appreciate your concern. What would you like to accomplish with our discussion today?" This approach helps focus the parent's energy and moves the conference away from a gripe session into a potentially productive problem-solving conference.

6. Set a time limit if necessary. If your time is limited, it is important to inform the parent. Do so by stating, "I have 20 minutes before I have to be back with my class. Let's see how far we can get in solving the problem in that time. If we need more time, I will be glad to schedule a conference as soon as possible."

7. Ask the parent whether the student is aware of the problem. Because the student is the most important person involved, it is important to clarify how he or she feels about the issue being raised by the parent. This question also slows the parent down and creates a more productive focus for the conference. Furthermore, the question helps introduce the issue of the student's responsibility for any problem that may exist.

8. Be honest. When confronted by parents, it is easy to understate the seriousness of a problem or to accept too much responsibility for a problem that is largely something the child must work on. Maintain your professional integrity and set the stage for future conferences by initially presenting an honest and clear statement of the problem.

9. Emphasize specific data. Data are simultaneously one of your best professional tools and your best defense. If a parent angrily states that his daughter did well in math last year but is having difficulty this year, the most logical and effective approach is to examine data on the student's math skills.

10. Tell the parent specifically what will be done to deal with the problem. Parents have a right to know what the teacher will do to alleviate a difficulty. Furthermore,

critical parents can often become strong supporters if they learn that they will be listened to, shown data, and presented with a plan. If the parent's worry was not justified, the plan may involve a follow-up conference to examine the results of the current program. If, however, the parent highlighted an area that required attention, developing a plan shows respect for the parent's concern and competence on your part.

INVOLVEMENT WITH PARENTS OF CHILDREN WHO HAVE DISABILITIES

With the passage of PL 94-142, teachers became more frequently and formally involved in working with parents of children who have disabilities. As awareness about various conditions increased, more students with disabilities were placed in public schools, more services became available to help them, and teachers found themselves referring more students for these services. Referral forms vary from district to district, but usually include requests for this information:

> Date of referral
> Name of person making referral
> Parent's name, address, and phone number
> Student's current placement
> Reason for referral
> Examples of attempts to correct problem
> Responses of student to such efforts. (Meyen, 1982, p. 69)

Although parents need not be contacted until their permission is required for the educational evaluation, they should be notified as soon as you perceive a problem, so that teacher-parent communication will be open throughout your efforts to assist the student and during the referral process. Steady communication with the parents better prepares them to participate productively in the decision on placement and in creating an individualized education program (IEP). "They are also able to share information that can be of value, and can allow insight into any cultural and language differences that may be contributing to the student's difficulty. Effective communication between home and school is an effective way to help gain a total picture of the child's needs and to prevent disagreements and misunderstandings that too often have led to delays in needed services" (Meyen, 1982, p. 70).

In addition to involvement in the referral process, PL 94-142, Section 121a. 344, states that the student's teacher(s) will, along with the parents, other school personnel, and, when appropriate, the student, be involved in an IEP conference to determine the specific special services needed to assist the student. The formats employed vary from state to state, but most IEPs include:

1. A statement of the child's present levels of educational performance, including academic achievement, social adaptation, prevocational and vocational skills, psychomotor skills and self-help skills;
2. A statement of annual goals which describes the educational performance to be achieved by the end of the school year under the child's individualized education program;

3. A statement of short-term instructional objectives, which must be measurable, intermediate steps between the present level of educational performance and the annual goals;
4. A statement of specific educational services needed by the child (determined without regard to the availability of services), including a description of:
   a. all special education and related services needed to meet the unique needs of the child, including the type of physical education program of the child, and
   b. any special instructional media and materials which are needed;
5. The date when those services will begin and length of time the services will be given;
6. A description of the extent to which the child will participate in regular education programs;
7. Objective criteria, evaluation procedures, and schedules for determining, at least annually, whether the short-term instructional objectives are being achieved;
8. A justification for the type of educational placement that the child will have; and
9. A list of the individuals who are responsible for implementing the individualized education program. (Heward & Orlansky, 1980, pp. 20–21)

The teacher's involvement does not end with participation in developing an IEP. In many cases, a portion of the student's special educational program will be carried out in the regular classroom. It is likely that this placement will involve us in periodic contacts with the student's parents and school support personnel. Although we need to be aware of these requirements, we need not be intimidated by them. If you use the skills presented in this chapter, you will find most relationships with parents to be a positive and productive aspect of your professional role.

PLACING SCHOOL-HOME INTERACTION IN PERSPECTIVE

A chapter on teacher-student contacts is not complete without clarifying the parameters of school-home contacts. As mentioned throughout this chapter, when teachers take a proactive approach by providing early positive and informative contacts with parents, teacher-parent interactions can be a positive, enjoyable aspect of a teacher's job. Similarly, when teachers develop skills for calmly and professionally responding to parents' concerns, even potentially negative interactions with parents can become less stressful and can serve to initiate greater parent understanding and support.

Unfortunately, the high rate of divorce, substance abuse, poverty, family mobility, and two working parents have all created a society in which an increasing number of at-risk students live in homes characterized by ineffective parenting and stress. Many parents lack the preparation, emotional stability, time, and support to provide effective parenting. This means that many students come to school anxious or upset about situations that have occurred at home.

Our responsibility as teachers is to use methods such as those described throughout this book that create positive, caring, supportive, well-structured environments for all students. As discussed in Chapter 12, teachers are also responsible for obtaining the help of other teachers and school support personnel in developing special methods for working with students who experience ongoing problems. This is the extent of our responsibilities as teachers. Teachers are not mental health specialists and cannot be expected to provide parent training or to help parents obtain resources for resolving family problems.

Even though teachers' responsibilities in working with parents are limited, school staffs can provide varied assistance to parents. Schools are the one societal institution with which all children and parents come into contact. School personnel thus are often the first to become aware of problems, and parents may be more likely to seek assistance from schools than from social service agencies. Schools can provide an important service to parents and children by offering limited direct services and by referring families to other community resources. School counselors are an obvious source of direct services to parents and children. Many elementary schools have child development specialists who work with the most seriously at-risk children and their parents. Unfortunately, many elementary schools do not have counselors. Given the frequency and depth of personal problems facing many elementary children, it seems critical that elementary schools provide counselors who can help children work through emotional conflicts and develop personal-social skills they have not learned at home. Unless these services are available, some of the most needy children will be hampered by emotional problems that will seriously limit their obtaining essential learning.

Another type of assistance to families can be classes on parenting skills. Many schools offer parents periodic seminars or classes on methods of effective parenting. Because virtually all parents have some contact with their child's school, and because for most parents the stigma of attending a session at their child's school is less than attending a mental health clinic class, the schools are an important resource for providing parenting skills. Schools with whom the authors have worked have successfully used the *Parent Effectiveness Training and Systematic Teaching for Effective Parenting (STEP)* materials as tools for helping parents develop basic parenting skills. The authors have provided numerous parent training sessions and classes and have consistently found parents to be appreciative and pleased with the applicability of their new skills.

Schools can provide another important support service for parents and families in turmoil. Many schools have begun to contract a social worker or other social service professional to serve as a liaison between the home, family, and community for children who are experiencing ongoing school problems in association with serious home problems. Mental health agencies employ systems and language different from those used by school personnel; therefore, someone familiar with these systems can use these resources more effectively. A school-community liaison can serve as a resource for educators and parents and can help obtain much needed community services for children and their families. Even though schools are not responsible for resolving all problems faced by the students they help educate, they do have an obligation to identify and provide effective referrals for children experiencing stress and trauma that are influencing their ability to benefit from the educational environment. Additional suggestions and references for increasing home-school cooperation and support can be found in *Home and School as Partners: Helping Parents Help Their Children* by Paul Haley and Karen Berry (1988).

Reporting child abuse is a special issue in home-school relationships. An educator's responsibility for reporting child abuse is an example of the coordination of school and community resources to help children and their families. "Child abuse and neglect is recognized as a problem of epidemic proportions, both nationally and in Oregon. The number of identified child victims in Oregon has grown at an alarming rate; more than 385 percent increase from 1980 to 1985. In spite of the skyrocketing numbers of reports, national studies indicate that only a small percent of maltreated children are reported to child protection agencies" (Roberts, 1986, p. 7).

To help abused children, states have enacted legislation that requires educators to report child abuse. In Oregon, educators are required to report suspected physical abuse, neglect, mental injury or emotional abuse, sexual abuse, and sexual exploitation. Oregon law also provides the professional who makes the report with safeguards against legal prosecution, as in the following:

418.762—Immunity of Persons Making Reports in Good Faith.

Anyone participating in good faith in the making of a report pursuant to ORS 418.750 to 418.760 and who has reasonable grounds for the making thereof, shall have immunity from any liability, civil or criminal, that might otherwise be incurred or imposed with respect to the making or content of such report. Any such participant shall have the same immunity with respect to participating in any judicial proceeding resulting from such report.

All teachers and administrators should become familiar with the child-abuse laws in their state and the reporting and follow-up procedures used by their district. Many districts have developed working relationships with community children's service agencies responsible for handling reported child abuse to ensure that proper follow-up is provided and to coordinate efforts to help the child cope with the temporary emotional stress often associated with this type of report.

ASSESSING PARENT CONTACTS

Awareness is almost always the first step in changing one's behavior. Before deciding whether to take the time and risks involved in trying new behaviors, most people choose to examine their present behavior. Activity 5.1 provides you with an opportunity to examine your current parent contacts. It also offers several ideas for systematically improving these contacts.

ACTIVITY 5.1
Assessing and Improving Parent Contacts

Assessing Your Parent Contacts

To assess the current level of your contact with parents, answer these questions:

1. How many informational letters have you sent out to every parent so far this year? _____

2. What percentage of your students' parents have received a positive phone call about their child's work or behavior? _____

3. What percentage of your students' parents have received a positive note about their child's work or behavior? _____

4. How many students in your class are experiencing what you would define as significant academic or behavior problems? _____

(continued)

5. How many parents of these students have you talked to about the problem and your approach to dealing with it? _____
6. How many parents have served as volunteers in your classroom this year? _____
7. How many hours a week is a parent present in your classroom? _____

Improving Your Parent Contacts

1. Send an informational letter to your students' parents. After two weeks, evaluate this effort by answering these questions:
   a. How many parents made a positive comment about the letter? _____
   b. How many students said something positive about the letter? _____
   c. List two advantages to sending the letter:
      (1) _____
      (2) _____
   d. List any disadvantages associated with sending the letter.
2. Over a two-week period, send a positive note home with each child in your class. After two weeks, evaluate this effort by answering these questions:
   a. How many parents made a positive comment about the note? _____
   b. How many students said something about the note? _____
   c. List two advantages to sending the note:
      (1) _____
      (2) _____
   d. List any disadvantage associated with sending the note.

IMPLEMENTING AND ASSESSING NEW METHODS

Having examined a variety of methods for preparing and implementing parent conferences, the next step is to select specific methods you believe would make your next set of conferences more productive and enjoyable. Activity 5.2 will assist you in assessing methods you decide to implement. If you are somewhat tentative about a new method, you might wish to use it with several parents with whom you are most comfortable.

Select one method for improving student, parent, and teacher preparation for your next conference. Write these on a sheet of paper and make a specific statement about how you will implement each method. Next, select one method from the section on implementing an effective conference.

During your next series of parent conferences, implement each of the methods you have selected. After the conferences are completed, evauate the new methods by completing these statements for each new approach:

The most beneficial aspect of this new approach was . . .
Another advantage was that . . .
Parents' response to this approach was . . .
Students' response was . . .
One difficulty with this new approach was . . .
I felt more comfortable when using this method because . . .

SUMMARY

Teachers often underestimate the power parents give to teachers. As teachers who have children in school, the authors are acutely aware of the value of parent-teacher contacts. Like virtually all parents, the authors are deeply concerned about their children's progress in handling new social and academic expectations. Teachers provide parents with input concerning how intelligent and skilled their children are and how well they are getting along with others. These are extremely important facts to almost all parents. Indeed, the defensiveness you may experience when working with parents of children who are struggling in school is due in large part to the importance parents place on the information you are giving them and to the difficulty they have accepting negative information about their child.

Because information about their children's school progress is so important to parents, it is necessary that this information be shared on a regular basis. As teachers, we can establish more positive, supportive teacher-parent relationships when we initially inform parents about the curriculum, instruction, and classroom management to which their child will be exposed. This needs to be followed by periodic updates about classroom activities and student progress. In addition, any time a student begins to have an academic or behavioral problem, we should contact the parent as soon as it appears that the matter cannot be quickly and smoothly resolved between us and the student.

Teacher-parent contacts can be time consuming and, like all aspects of our profession, require practice before we become comfortable and adept at them. They can, however, be among the most rewarding aspects of our teaching experience and can have a significant impact on the most important and rewarding aspect of our job—seeing improvement in the quality of student behavior and learning.

RECOMMENDED READING

Books on Teacher-Parent Contacts

Bailard, V., & Strang, R. (1964). *Parent-teacher conferences*. New York: McGraw-Hill.

Epstein, J., & Connors, L. (1992). School and family partnerships. *Practitioner, 18,* 1–10.

Flaxman, E., & Inger, M. (1992). Parents and schooling in the 1990s. *Principal, 72,* 16–18.

Gordon, I., & Breivogel, W. (1976). *Building effective home-school relationships*. Boston: Allyn and Bacon.

Heffernan, H., & Todd, V. (1969). *Elementary teachers' guide to working with parents*. West Nyack, NY: Parker.

Hoover-Dempsey, K. (1992). Explorations in parent-school relationships. *Journal of Educational Research, 85,* 287–294.

Jones, V. (1980). *Adolescents with behavior problems: Strategies for teaching, counseling, and parent involvement*. Boston: Allyn and Bacon.

Kelley, E. (1974). *Parent-teacher interaction: A special education perspective*. Seattle, WA: Special Child Publications. A Division of Bernie Straub Publishing Company.

Losen, S., & Diament, B. (1979). *Parent conferences in the schools: Procedures for developing effective partnership*. Boston: Allyn and Bacon.

Martin, J. (1992). *The schoolhome: Rethinking schools for changing families*. Cambridge, MA: Harvard University Press.

McLoughlin, C. (1987). *Parent-teacher conferencing*. Springfield, IL: Charles C. Thomas.

Procidano, M., and Fisher, C. (Eds.). (1992). *Contemporary families: A handbook for school professionals*. New York: Teachers College Press.

Rich, D. (1987). *Schools and families: Issues and actions*. Washington, DC: National Education Association.

Rutherford, R., & Edgar, E. (1979). *Teachers and parents: A guide to interaction and cooperation*. Boston: Allyn and Bacon.

Sartain, H. (1989). *Nonachieving students at risk: School, family and community intervention*. Washington, DC: NEA.

Swap, S. (1993). *Developing home-school partnerships: From concepts to practice*. New York: Teachers College Press.

Vandergrift, J., & Greene, A. (1992). Rethinking parent involvement. *Educational Leadership, 50,* 57–59.

Wilson, G., & Wingate, B. (1974). *Parents and teachers: Humanistic educational techniques to facilitate communication between parents and staff of educational programs*. Atlanta, GA: Humanities Press.

Books on Parenting Skills

Blechman, E. (1985). *Solving child behavior problems at home and at school*. Champaign, IL: Research Press.

Dinkmeyer, D., McKay, G., & McKay, J. (1987). *New beginnings: Skills for single parents and stepfamily parents*. Champaign, IL: Research Press.

Ehly, S., Conoley, J., & Rosenthal, D. (1985). *Working with parents of exceptional children*. Columbus, OH: Merrill.

Faber, A., & Mazlish, E. (1982). *How to talk so kids will listen and listen so kids will talk*. New York: Avon.

Faber, A., & Mazlish, E. (1987). *Siblings without rivalry*. New York: W. W. Norton & Co.

Ginott, H. (1965). *Between parent and child: New solutions to old problems*. New York: Macmillan.

Gordon, T. (1970). *Parent effectiveness training: The tested way to raise responsible children*. New York: Wyden.

Haley, P., & Berry, K. (1988). *Home and school partnerships: Helping parents help their children*. Andover, MA: The Regional Laboratory for Educational Improvement of the Northeast and Islands.

Kroth, R., & Otteni, H. (1985). *Communicating with parents of exceptional children* (2nd ed.). Denver, CO: Love.

Pogrebin, L. (1980). *Growing up free: Raising your child in the 80s*. New York: Bantam Books.

Rich, D. (1987). *School and families: Issues and actions*. Washington, DC: National Education Association.

Rotter, J., Robinson, E., & Fey, M. (1988). *Parent-teacher conferences* (2nd ed.). Washington, DC: NEA.

Sloane, H. (1979). *The good kid book: How to solve the 16 most common behavior problems*. Champaign, IL: Research Press.

Swick, K., & Duff, E. (1979). *Parenting*. Washington, DC: National Education Association.

Wagonseller, B., & McDowell, R. (1979). *You and your child: A common sense approach to successful parenting*. Champaign, IL: Research Press.

Increasing Student Motivation and Learning by Implementing Instructional Methods That Meet Students' Academic Needs

Effective classroom management is closely related to effective classroom instruction. When students fail to attend school or classes or when they act-out or fail to be productively engaged in classroom activities, teachers must carefully examine whether the curricular content and instructional methods are actively and meaningfully engaging students at an appropriate level of difficulty and in ways that respect their cultural heritage and relate to their own lives. Part III presents current theory and practice on student motivation and effective instruction. Chapter 6 begins with a brief examination of current research on motivation to learn and indicates the relationship between this research and classroom practice. The chapter continues with a discussion of and practical suggestions for implementing a variety of instructional methods proven effective in increasing student motivation and learning. This chapter responds to the large body of data indicating that many students find schools confusing, boring places in which to learn. Methods are presented for altering this situation by clarifying instruction, increasing meaningful student involvement in the learning process, and using teaching methods that respond to individual students' needs.

CHAPTER 6

Enhancing Students' Motivation to Learn

Thus low motivation, negative self-attitudes, and failure are largely the result of improper learning conditions. According to this learning theory analysis, we should be able to alter a student's failure rate by changing the conditions of classroom learning and, as a consequence, increase his motivation to succeed. Actually there is considerable experimental evidence on this point.

—Martin Covington and Richard Beery (1976)
Self-Worth and School Learning

Typically, the information offered to teachers about motivational strategies focuses on controlling performance rather than on stimulating motivation to learn, and emphasizes the use of incentives, rewards, and grades rather than strategies designed to stimulate students to generate learning goals and the cognitive and metacognitive strategies to accomplish them.

—Jere Brophy (1986)
Socializing Students' Motivation to Learn

This important work of several decades ago, as well as much of what has since been in the forefront of educational thought, stresses the importance of teachers finding ways to make subject matter relevant to students, to involve students in setting their own goals, to vary the ways of learning to use approaches that employ all of the senses, and to be sure that there are opportunities for relating the knowledge to experiences or actually using it.

—John I. Goodlad (1984)
A Place Called School: Prospects for the Future

Recent studies have demonstrated that students learn best and behave more appropriately in classroom settings that meet their learning needs. Students' misbehavior and failure can often be traced to failure to create an educational environment conducive to learning. Educators have also begun to appreciate that students vary in the type of classroom structure and instruction that best facilitate their learning. Understanding the instructional needs of an individual child or group of children provides teachers with information essential for creating a positive learning environment.

KEY ISSUES IN STUDENT MOTIVATION TO LEARN

Although meeting students' personal needs (as discussed in Chapter 2) provides a foundation for creating environments supportive of personal growth and learning, closely related and equally important needs exist within environments that are specifically designed to help children acquire academic knowledge. Many students meet their needs for autonomy, competence, self-esteem, and self-actualization by successfully completing classroom activities and assignments. Understanding the research on motivation and its relationship to student academic needs enables teachers to implement instruction that results in students' obtaining feelings of worth within the school setting.

When frustrated by students' failure to pay attention, complete assignments, or attend class, it is tempting to blame factors outside the classroom. As discussed in Chapter 1, studies indicate that teachers generally blame family and community factors for students' lack of motivation to learn. Personal experience and reading of the research suggests another explanation, however. The authors have never met a student who was unmotivated to learn. The authors have met many students who were unmotivated in certain settings but highly motivated in others, as well as many students who were motivated when their learning needs were met but appeared unmotivated when they were not. Consider how you would feel if you were placed in a third-year, second-semester medical school program and told that your future success would be influenced by how you performed. Most people would search for ways to withdraw from or deny the value of this anxiety-provoking, stressful situation. More concretely, consider how you respond in a college course, in-service workshop, or meeting in which the content seems irrelevant or boring or when you are not asked to be actively involved. In nearly 50 years of attending faculty meetings, the authors have seen numerous examples of teacher behavior that looked similar to the behavior of the students at risk about whom there is much concern.

Like many other writers, the authors' view of motivation incorporates the expectation × value theory (Feather, 1982). This model suggests that the extent to which people become actively and productively involved in an activity is based on (1) whether they believe they can be successful at the task and (2) the degree to which they value the rewards associated with successful task completion. The authors add a third variable—climate, or the quality of relationships within the task setting during the time the people are engaged in the task. Thus, the formula becomes:

$$\text{motivation} = \text{expectation} \times \text{value} \times \text{climate}$$

Because it is described as a multiplicative function, this model suggests that students will not be motivated unless all three components are present—that is, they (1) expect they can accomplish a task, (2) find value in the task, and (3) complete the task in an environment supportive of their basic personal needs.

The second concept that organizes the authors' thinking about motivation is Eccles and Wigfield's (1985) idea that three types of value may be associated with a task: (1) intrinsic value—the simple interest or enjoyment associated with engaging in a task; (2) attainment value—the value of obtaining achievement, notoriety, or influence through accomplishing a task; and (3) utility value—the benefits to one's career or other personal goals associated with performing a task successfully. This threefold concept suggests that teachers need to ensure that at least one type of value is present if students are to be motivated by the task.

STUDENTS' ACADEMIC NEEDS

Figure 6.1 provides a list of student academic needs that, when met, enhance student motivation and achievement. The list is based on the authors' own categorization of research and has been validated and expanded by lists generated by more than 600 teachers. It is informative to compare the academic needs in Figure 6.1 to a summary of research on strategies for motivating students to learn by Jere Brophy. Figure 6.2 presents 33 principles of motivation based on Brophy's research review. In parentheses beside each motivation principle is the student academic need to which the principle lends support or can be presented as an example. Brophy's review provides a strong validation for the 12 academic needs that are the basis for this chapter.

Additional validity for the list of academic needs can be found in Wehlage's (1983) analyses of a number of programs particularly successful with marginal students. According to Wehlage, programs for marginal students should do the following:

1. Offer "optimal challenge with manageable conflict."
2. Provide the student with an opportunity to exercise initiative and responsibility.
3. Provide the student with a task that has integrity (i.e., is not "make-work") and thus reinforces the person's sense of dignity.
4. Provide the student with "a sense of competence and success."
5. Engage the student in reflection about his or her experiences (pp. 38–40).

---

1. Understand and value the learning goals.
2. Understand the learning process.
3. Be actively involved in the learning process and relate subject matter to their own lives.
4. Take responsibility for their own learning by setting goals and following their own interests.
5. Experience success.
6. Receive realistic and immediate feedback that enhances self-efficacy.
7. Receive rewards for performance gains.
8. See learning modeled by adults as an exciting and rewarding activity.
9. Experience a safe, well-organized learning environment.
10. Have time to integrate learning.
11. Have positive contact with peers.
12. Receive instruction matched to their cognitive and skill level and learning style.

FIGURE 6.1
Students'
Academic Needs

FIGURE 6.2

Highlights of
Research on
Strategies for
Motivating
Students to
Learn

(The numbers in parentheses are added and refer to the 12 student academic needs in Figure 6.1)

Essential Preconditions

1. Supportive environment (1)
2. Appropriate level of challenge difficulty (2)
3. Meaningful learning objectives (2)
4. Moderation/optimal use

Motivating by Maintaining Success Expectations

5. Program for success (5)
6. Teach goal setting, performance appraisal and self-reinforcement (4, 6)
7. Help students to recognize linkages between effort and outcome (6)
8. Provide remedial socialization (4, 6)

Motivating by Supplying Extrinsic Incentives

9. Offer rewards for good (or improved) performance (7)
10. Structure appropriate competition (7, 9, 11)
11. Call attention to the instrumental value of academic activities (1, 3, 4)

Motivating by Capitalizing on Students' Intrinsic Motivation

12. Adapt tasks to students' interest (4)
13. Induce novelty/variety elements
14. Allow opportunities to make choices or autonomous organizers (4)
15. Provide opportunities for students to respond actively (3, 4)
16. Provide immediate feedback to student responses (6)
17. Allow students to create finished products (9, 10, 12)
18. Include fantasy or simulation elements
19. Incorporate game-like features (3, 4)
20. Include higher-level objectives and divergent questions (12)
21. Provide opportunities to interact with peers (11)

Stimulating Student Motivation to Learn

22. Model interest in learning and motivation to learn (8)
23. Communicate desirable expectations and attributions about students motivation to learn (1, 8)
24. Minimize students' performance anxiety during learning activities (1, 4, 5, 10, 11, 12)
25. Project intensity (8)
26. Project enthusiasm (8)
27. Induce task interest or appreciation (3, 4, 8)
28. Induce curiosity or suspense
29. Induce dissonance or cognitive conflict (1, 9)
30. Make abstract content more personal, concrete or familiar (1, 2, 3, 4, 11, 12)
31. Induce students to generate their own motivation to learn (1, 2, 3, 4, 11, 12)
32. State learning objectives and provide advance decisions (4)
33. Model task-related thinking and problem solving (8)

Source: From Jere Brophy, "Synthesis of Research on Strategies for Motivating Students to Learn," *Educational Leadership* 45 (November 1987): 45. Reprinted with permission of the Association for Supervision and Curriculum Development and Jere Brophy. Copyright © 1987 by the Association for Supervision and Curriculum Development. All rights reserved.

The first section of this chapter briefly overviews these needs that serve as a basis for implementing the instructional methods described in the remainder of the chapter.

Understand and Value the Learning Goals

Walter Doyle (1983) wrote that "the quality of the time students spend engaged in academic work depends on the tasks they are expected to accomplish and the extent to which students understand what they are doing. It is essential, therefore, that direct instruction include explicit attention to meaning and not simply focus on engagement as an end in itself" (p. 189). Unfortunately, many students do not really understand why they are involved in a learning activity. They study to obtain good grades, please their parents or teacher, or avoid punishment. Research suggests that this lack of understanding and meaning begins early in school. Anderson, Brubaker, Alleman-Brooks, and Duffy (1984) interviewed first-grade students about the seat-work they had done. They found that many low-achieving students did not know how to complete the tasks and that few students at any level really understood why they had done them. Nevertheless, rather than ask important questions of the teacher, low-achieving students seemed concerned about completing the assignments and often used rather random methods of completing their tasks. As one first-grader told the researchers, "I don't know what it means, but I did it." (Anderson et al., 1984, p. 20). Even though high-achieving students completed the work, they gave little evidence of understanding the purpose of the assignments. They described the purpose of the assignments as "It's just our work" but consistently failed to indicate specific material they were learning or skills they were practicing. In discussing this study, Brophy (1986b) stated:

> Analysis of the teachers' presentations of assignments to the students suggested that teacher failure to call attention to the purposes and meanings of these assignments was a major reason for the students' low quality of engagement in them. Most presentations included procedural directions or special hints (Pay attention to the underlined words), but only 5 percent explicitly described the purpose of the assignment in terms of the content being taught. (p. 11)

In another study, Rohrkemper and Bershon (1984) asked elementary students to describe what they were thinking about while they completed their assignments. Of the 49 students, 2 mentioned their concern with finishing (perhaps so they could go to recess); 45 were trying to get the right answer; and only 2 mentioned anything related to understanding the content. Unfortunately, this is characteristic not only of elementary students who lack formal operational thinking and thus require considerable assistance in understanding the reason for the work they are asked to complete. For many secondary school students, school becomes a game. As one adolescent stated, "School is just like roulette or something. You can't just ask: Well, what's the point of it? The point of it is to do it, to get through and get into college. But you have to figure the system or you can't win, because the odds are all on the house's side" (Silberman, 1970, pp. 146–147). It is no surprise that 55 percent of 160,000 teenagers sampled by Norman and Harris for *The Private Life of the American Teenager* (1981) stated that they cheated in school.

One time, the authors observed an eighth-grade boy working on an English assignment involving selecting adverb phrases embedded in a paragraph. His strategy was to find a phrase, look back at the model, check for similarity, and then, if it matched, write the phrase on his paper. When asked what he was doing, the boy responded, "I have absolutely no idea, but I had better have it done tomorrow when class starts."

These observations are not surprising in light of research on how teachers present learning tasks to students. Brophy and his colleagues (Brophy, Rohrkemper, Rashed, & Goldberger, 1983) examined teacher statements while presenting new assignments in six intermediate classrooms. During the presentation of 165 tasks, not once did a teacher indicate that the task would help the children develop skills that would be useful or enjoyable. In only 3 percent of the introductions did the teachers express personal enthusiasm for the task; in only 3 percent did they relate the material to students' personal lives or interests; and only 1 percent of the task introductions included a statement about the teacher's personal experiences or beliefs that illustrated the importance of the task. In analyzing these teacher presentations of instructional tasks in intermediate-grade mathematics and reading groups, Brophy stated:

> The task introductions made by teachers observed in this study probably did not have much impact on student motivation to learn because: a) statements likely to stimulate student motivation to learn did not occur often enough; b) when they did occur, they were usually too short and sketchy to do much good; and c) whatever good they might have done was probably negated by other statements likely to undermine motivation to learn. (Brophy, 1986b, p. 13)

In one study, Roehler, Duffy, and Meloth (1987) reported that teachers could learn to give students specific explanations concerning the purpose of instructional activities. Results indicated that students taught by these teachers demonstrated significantly greater understanding of and appreciation for the purpose of the instruction.

Understand the Learning Process

The vast majority of students believe that effective learning means doing well on homework assignments, in-class assessment methods, and standardized tests. Unfortunately, in every class and every school, 25 percent of the students are in the bottom quartile on any of these tasks (statistically, they must be). If teachers continue to allow students to define learning as the process of "winning," we will continue to have a significant percent of students acting out and dropping out in response to their perceived failure.

In order to increase students' motivation to learn, teachers should place a major focus on teaching students about the learning process. This can begin during the first few days of school by assisting students in developing a functional definition of what it means to be an effective learner (e.g., making a good effort, asking for assistance when one does not understand material, making progress toward meaningful goals, etc.). Students can then hold themselves accountable to these standards rather than the current standard of being one of the top students in the class.

Maher (1987) found that when inner-city high school students who were experiencing persistent behavior and academic problems were given opportunities to meet with teachers and discuss the material and methods to be used in the classroom each week, the students completed significantly more work. Roehler and colleagues (1984) found similar results when teachers were taught to call students' attention to the purpose of the learning material. Jones (1986) found that after being introduced to the concept of teaching students about the learning process and requesting students' feedback about how effectively teachers were implementing designated instructional methods, 80 percent of teachers indicated they used this process, and 87 percent stated that it had a positive effect on student learning.

Be Actively Involved in the Learning Process and Relate Subject Matter to Their Own Lives

In his *A Place Called School,* Goodlad (1984) found that across all grade levels, teachers talked three times as much as students. Goodlad's study painted a clear picture of uninvolved students who sit listening to the teacher or who are involved in seatwork. Research also indicates that students' feelings are seldom dealt with in classroom settings. Adams and Biddle (1970) reported that less than 0.5 percent of verbalizations in the classrooms they studied focused on feelings or interpersonal relations. Similarly, after collecting data in a large number of classrooms, Flanders and Amidon (1967) reported that the acceptance of feelings accounted for only 0.005 percent of the verbal exchanges in classrooms. Goodlad's (1983a) data support these findings. He concluded that "affect—either positive or negative—was virtually absent. What we observed could only be described as neutral, or perhaps 'flat' is a better adjective" (p. 467).

Summarizing his extensive, systematic study of education in a sample of 38 schools, Goodlad (1983a) wrote, "Teachers appear to teach within a very limited repertoire of pedagogical alternatives, emphasizing their own talk and the monitoring of seatwork. The customary pedagogy places the teacher very much in control. Few activities call for or even permit active student planning, follow-through and evaluation" (p. 467). In lamenting the lack of exciting instruction in U.S. schools, Theodore Sizer (1984) wrote, "No more important finding has emerged from the inquiries of our study than that the American high school student, as student, is too often docile, compliant, and without initiative" (p. 54). Piaget (1977) emphasized that, especially for young children, learning must involve doing. Children tend to learn what they do

"In arithmetic, we're studying 'guzintas'—three guzinta nine three times, two guzinta four two times. . . . . ."

rather than what they see or hear. "Good pedagogy must involve presenting the child with situations in which he himself experiments, in the broadest sense of that term—trying things out to see what happens, manipulating things, manipulating symbols, posing questions and seeking his own answers, reconciling what he finds one time and what he finds at another, comparing his findings with those of other children" (Duckworth, 1964, p. 2).

A number of writers have indicated that students of color respond more effectively to an instructional style that permits active student involvement. Kuykendall (1992) wrote that "educators who are serious about enhancing the achievement and motivation of Black and Hispanic youth must be willing to use a variety of activities to stimulate interest and facilitate student growth. . . . Black and Hispanic youth are likely to respond favorably to think-pair-share activities, lively group discussions, cooperative learning, group projects, and telling of stories about personal experience" (p. 39). Writers such as Banks (1988, 1993), Hale-Benson (1986), Kuykendall (1992), Ramirez and Castanada (1974), and Shade (1989) have noted that African American, Hispanic, and Native American students tend to be field-dependent learners who need to be more actively involved in the learning process.

More recently, work in multicultural education has emphasized the importance of including materials incorporating the contributions and perspectives of diverse racial, ethnic, and gender groups. Diaz-Rico (1993) presented an interesting example of how student behavior in an interracial classroom was dramatically improved and how student motivation and achievement was enhanced by the teacher responding to her students' diverse skills and interests. Stinchcombe (1964) highlighted an important concept for students of color when he wrote, "When a student realizes that he does not achieve status increment from improved current performance, current performance loses meaning. The student becomes hedonistic because he does not visualize achievement of long-run goals through current self-restraint. He reacts negatively to a conformity that offers nothing concrete. He claims autonomy from adults because their authority does not promise him a satisfactory future" (pp. 5–6).

In their book, *Women's Ways of Knowing*, Belenky, Clinchy, Goldberger, and Tarule (1986) indicated that women benefit from learning environments that emphasize quality personal relationships and that value the learner's voice. Women seem to be more motivated and effective when they are able to relate material to their own lives, use their own experiences as valid contexts for interpreting and expanding information, and work collaboratively with others. This work has been expanded by others (Butler, 1993; Tetreault, 1993) who argue for a more personal and less competitive learning environment.

It is interesting to note that during the 1930s, a team of educators and psychologists carried out a major study to assess the value of active student involvement in the learning process (Aikin, 1942; Chamberlain, 1942). The program, called The Eight Year Study, involved working with 30 secondary schools to increase interdisciplinary study and the use of diverse teaching methods such as small groups, cooperative learning, and simulation. The results of the comparison showed that, in college, students from the experimental schools:

1. Earned a slightly higher total grade average;
2. Earned higher grade averages in all subject fields except foreign language;
3. Specialized in the same academic fields as did the comparison students;
4. Did not differ from the comparison group in the number of times they were placed on probation;
5. Received slightly more academic honors in each year;
6. Were more often judged to possess a high degree of intellectual curiosity and drive;
7. Were more often judged to be precise, systematic, and objective in their thinking;
8. Were more often judged to have developed clear or well-formulated ideas concerning the meaning of education—especially in the first two years in college;
9. More often demonstrated a high degree of resourcefulness in meeting new situations;
10. Did not differ from the comparison group in ability to plan their time effectively;
11. Had about the same problems of adjustment as the comparison group, but approached their solutions with greater effectiveness;
12. Participated somewhat more frequently, and more often enjoyed appreciative experiences in the arts;
13. Participated more in all organized student groups except religious and "service" activities;
14. Earned in each college year a higher percentage of non-academic honors (officeship in organizations, election to managerial societies, athletic insignia, leading roles in dramatic and musical presentations);
15. Did not differ from the comparison group in the quality of adjustment to their contemporaries;
16. Differed only slightly from the comparison group in the kinds of judgments about their schooling;
17. Had a somewhat better orientation toward the choice of a vocation;
18. Demonstrated a more active concern for what was going on in the world. (Aikin, 1942, pp. 111–112)

In his examination of the impact of demographic changes on education and its implications for an increasing number of at-risk students in our schools, Hodgkinson (1985) highlighted the importance of helping students understand the relationship between their schoolwork and the world outside school. In commenting about successful dropout programs he noted, "When the relation between education and work becomes clear, most of these potential drop-outs can be motivated to stay in school and perform at a higher level" (p. 12).

An interesting approach to assisting students in making the important connection between their own lives and classroom content is the creation of future plans. This involves students in writing about what they want to do when they grow up (e.g., when they are 25 years old). This includes not only the job they would like to have but also what they would do with their leisure time, their roles in a family and community group, and so on. As students study various content areas, they are asked to discuss how what they are learning will help them enjoy these activities or perform adult tasks more successfully. This assessment and discussion can be incorporated on a weekly basis in secondary school base groups and in middle school advisory sessions, and on a daily basis in elementary school classrooms.

Take Responsibility for Their Own Learning
by Setting Goals and Following Their Own Interests

The concept of locus of control further reinforces the importance of increasing students' active involvement in the learning process. White's (1959) theory of competence motivation and DeCharms's (1976) work relating this theory to the educational setting indicate that when students are involved in directing their own learning, they will produce better work and enjoy the work more than when they are merely responding obediently to obtain rewards. Rotter's (1966) theory and research on locus of control has been followed by studies indicating that students can develop an internal locus of control by being involved with learning environments in which they are provided with responsibility and choice.

In two interesting studies, DeCharms (1976, 1984) involved teachers of sixth- and seventh-grade minority students in setting their own goals and making decisions about how to reach these goals. A major emphasis was on students' feeling a sense of personal responsibility for meeting or failing to meet their goals. Results of these studies indicate that student achievement gains were greater for students in the goal-setting classes than in the control group and that despite the fact that no follow-up interventions occurred during the following years, students in the experimental group continued to have a higher achievement rate and had a higher rate of graduation from high school. Similar results have been found when providing a similar experience to mainstreamed high school students (Maher, 1987). Wlodkowski (1978) mentioned several benefits associated with academic goal setting:

> The advantage of this method is that it brings the future into the present and allows the student to become aware of what it is necessary to do in order to have a successful learning experience. . . . With the goal-setting model, the student knows that she/he is in command and can calculate what to do to avoid wasting time or experiencing self-defeat. Thus, before even beginning the learning task, the student knows that his/her effort will be worthwhile and has an actual sense that there is a good probability for success. (p. 54)

One probable factor leading to students' decreased satisfaction with school as they progress through the grades (Flanders, Morrison, & Brode, 1968) is that students learn that they must study what they are told rather than what interests them. Morris (1978) provided a similar analysis: "The reasons for this are complex. However, the drop might be minimized by a careful examination and involvement of children's interests (not what teachers think children's interests are) in the curriculum" (p. 242). Swift and Spivack (1975) presented a similar prescription for teaching at-risk students: "Relating children's interests and ideas to classroom activities is probably a useful procedure for all children. However, for inattentive youngsters such an interplay of interest and classroom is paramount for decreasing the distraction caused by preoccupation with thoughts, ideas, interests, or activities which pull their attention away from the classroom" (p. 21).

In an interesting study, Asher and Markell (1974) found that even though fifth-grade girls were much better readers than boys when reading low-interest materials, boys read as well as girls when both were given high-interest material.

Students' motivation to learn seems related to their sense of feeling in control of the learning environment. Deci, Nezlek, and Sheinman (1981) reported that students in classrooms in which teachers are less controlling score higher on intrinsic motivation. Pascarella, Walberg, Junker, and Haertel (1981) found that greater student control over the learning environment is associated with greater interest in subject matter.

Mahoney (1974) found that students enjoy school more and achieve better when they are allowed to make choices during their school day. Matheny and Edwards (1974) evaluated the impact of increasing students' choices and responsibility for learning in 25 classrooms in grades 1 through 7. Teachers were provided with in-service training to (1) allow students more choice in deciding when assignments would be completed, (2) have students score their own work, (3) use individual conferences with students to evaluate progress, (4) develop learning centers, and (5) use learning contracts with students. The results indicated that teacher implementation of these strategies was associated with higher student reading gains and increased student perception of controlling their learning outcomes.

Experience Success

No one enjoys being in a setting in which he or she consistently fails. Most adults can recall situations in which they responded to failure by dropping an activity and attempting something at which they were more adept. To a large degree, this behavior was influenced by the need to view oneself as competent. Success experiences are instrumental in developing feelings of self-worth and confidence in attempting new activities. "It is through achievement that academic self-confidence grows, and increased confidence in turn promotes achievement through inspiring further learning. In short, confidence and competence must increase together for either to prosper. When they do not grow apace, students are likely to suffer" (Covington & Beery, 1976, p. 5).

Teacher effectiveness research suggests that students' learning is increased when they experience high rates of success in completing tasks. When the teacher is available to monitor and assist students, success rates of 70 to 80 percent are desirable (Brophy & Evertson, 1976). When students are expected to work on their own, success rates of 95 to 100 percent are desirable (Fisher, Berliner, Filby, Marliave, Cahen, & Dishaw, 1980). Studies suggest that when students are given inappropriate tasks, the tasks are much more likely to be too difficult than too easy. Following successful experiences, individuals tend to raise their expectations and set higher goals, whereas failure is met with lowered aspirations. Success or failure also influences individuals' self-evaluations. Studies also indicate that praising students' work produces greater performance gains than does criticism and that the positive effects in self-rating and performance tend to spread to areas related to those in which praise was provided for success experience.

Students who have a history of school failure and are concerned about future failure are at a distinct disadvantage. Tobias (1979) suggested that highly anxious students divide their attention between the material being taught and their concerns about failure, or being criticized or embarrassed. These students are involved in a downward spiral because they miss considerable amounts of information due to their anxiety (Hill & Wigfield, 1984). Covington has characterized this situation as a "double-edged sword." If these students try, they look stupid. However, if they do not try, they are viewed negatively by the teacher. The power associated with preventing feelings of humiliation and incompetence is supported by the fact that many students choose a teacher's frustration and criticism about their behavior rather than risk another academic failure (Covington, Spratt, & Omelich, 1980). Students who experience a low rate of school success are more likely to have an external locus of control. Students who believe that their past failures were caused by lack of ability are less likely to anticipate future success and are therefore less likely to exert effort. In extreme cases, this can lead to learned helplessness, in which the students feel that nothing that they do matters.

One of the authors recently worked with a talented high school teacher in a district serving approximately 85 percent Chapter 1 students. In order to increase student motivation, the teacher incorporated four key methods. First, he utilized peer-relationship activities to help create a more cohesive group. Second, he established base groups so students had peer invitations and accountability. Third, he expanded his use of cooperative learning. Fourth, he utilized the goal setting and monitoring form seen in Figure 6.3. He discovered that students were particularly unskilled at specifying strategies they could use to complete their work. The form provided an impetus to work with students on their planning skills and for students to hold themselves and their peers accountable. He reported that student work completion and attendance increased dramatically and that many students commented on the chance to set their own goals and evaluate their progress.

Receive Realistic and Immediate Feedback That Enhances Self-Efficacy

Closely associated with the need for success experiences is the need to receive immediate and specific feedback. Because students care about being successful, it is important that they receive feedback clearly designating the extent to which they have succeeded at a task. Several studies (Burrows, 1973; Collins, 1971) show that students' achievement is enhanced by providing them with information about their current level of performance (based on results of diagnostic tests), followed by specific learning tasks aimed at mastering the material.

In fact, students most concerned about failing are most in need of immediate feedback; without it, they tend to judge their performance as unacceptable. Page (1958) found that supportive comments, accompanied by statements about specific strengths and weaknesses in students' work, were more effective in improving students' performance than were either grades or brief positive comments. Butler and Nisan (1986) compared student responses to papers with either substantive comments and no grade or grades with no comments. Students who received comments more frequently stated that they (1) found the task more interesting, (2) worked on the task because they were interested in the material, and (3) attributed their success on the task to their interest and effort.

The quality of feedback is important because it affects students' perceptions of themselves as learners. Stipek (1988) stressed the importance of students receiving feedback that helps them see their progress: "Unless students actually perceive

FIGURE 6.3 Homework Plan

Subject	Homework Assignment	Due Day/Date	Study Strategy (Where-When-How)	Target Grade	Date Completed	Strategy Grade	Grade

The study strategy that I found most helpful this week was: _____

themselves to be making process in acquiring skills or new knowledge, they will not feel efficacious, even if they are rewarded for their efforts and even if their performance is better than others" (p. 94).

Not all feedback is effective in improving students' performance. Studies show that hostile or extensive criticism creates negative attitudes and lowers achievement, creativity, and classroom control. Praise is often overused and is not a powerful reinforcer for many children (Brophy, 1981; Ware, 1978). Praise can be an effective form of feedback when it provides students with specific information about the quality of their work and the effort made to complete the work. However, praise is often misused. Teachers frequently praise incorrect answers, and this false praise is more often given to lower-achieving students. "To the extent that praise is important, the key to its effectiveness lies in its quality rather than its frequency. Effective teachers know both when and how to praise" (Good & Brophy, 1984, p. 193).

Rosenholtz and Simpson (1984) examined classroom variables that affect how students view their ability. They categorize classrooms as unidimensional (creating a sense that ability is a stable characteristic and in which students know who has and does not have ability) and multidimensional (in which ability is not nearly as stratified). In unidimensional classrooms, feedback is provided in such a way that students can easily compare their work with others. For example, charts indicating the level of student performance are placed on the walls, and exemplary work and the names of students whose work is missing or needs redoing are prominently displayed. Rosenholtz and Simpson suggest that to encourage students to see ability as a trait or factor that is flexible and related to effort, teachers should make feedback and evaluation a more private matter.

Effective feedback provides students with important benchmarks. It enables students to understand where they are in relation to achieving goals, the amount of progress they have made toward a goal, and what they need to do to continue or improve on their progress. Effective feedback also communicates that the teacher believes the student can reach predetermined goals, that the student's effort is a major factor influencing the outcome, and that how a student's progress compares to that of other students is not a major factor.

The material on praise in Chapter 2 provides helpful hints on how to apply positive feedback effectively to enhance student motivation. The section in Chapter 8 on providing useful feedback and evaluation and the section on goal setting later in this chapter offer additional suggestions for increasing student motivation by meeting this academic need.

Receive Appropriate Rewards for Performance Gains

"Rewards are one proven way to motivate students to put forth effort, especially when the rewards are offered in advance as incentives for striving to reach specified levels of performance" (Good & Brophy, 1994, p. 225). When considering the value of rewards for performance gains, however, educators need to consider several important problems associated with the use of rewards. First, numerous studies indicate that external rewards can reduce intrinsic interest in a task (Morgan, 1984). Children who receive a reward for participating in an activity may show less interest in the activity. Therefore, rewards should be used only when other attempts such as altering the approach to presenting the material, individual goal setting, and other motivational and instructional strategies have failed. Good and Brophy (1987) summarized this concern:

> Extrinsic motivational strategies can be effective in certain circumstances, but teachers should not rely on them too heavily. If students are preoccupied with rewards or competition, they may not pay much attention to what they are supposed to be learning or appreciate its value. The quality of task engagement and of ultimate achievement is higher when students perceive themselves to be engaged in a task for their own reasons rather than in order to please an authority figure, obtain a reward, or escape punishment. (p. 227)

A second issue concerning rewards is that they appear to be most useful when they simultaneously reinforce performance and provide feedback about mastery of the material. Lepper (1981) stated that rewards used to obtain control (e.g., "Do what I say and you will be rewarded") tend to reduce intrinsic motivation. However, when rewards are provided based on a student's reaching a designated performance criterion (e.g., "Let's agree on a goal and when you reach this you will be rewarded"), they are less likely to undermine interest. Nevertheless, as suggested by reinforcement theory, even this is dependent on the student's being able to obtain the reward. Rewards that are offered but not obtained have a negative impact on motivation and effort.

Chapter 11 offers specific methods for using rewards to enhance student performance and improve student behavior. The recommended readings at the end of Chapter 11 cite additional sources that emphasize this approach to motivation.

See Learning Modeled by Adults as an Exciting and Rewarding Activity

As mentioned in Chapter 3, teachers possess many characteristics that make their behavior likely to be modeled. Therefore, teachers should carefully consider how they model an interest in and excitement about learning. Of the 33 strategies Brophy (1987) listed for motivating students (see Figure 6.2), 4 of these support the value of effective teacher modeling: (1) model interest in learning and motivation to learn, (2) project intensity, (3) project enthusiasm, and (4) model task-related thinking and problem solving.

Experience a Safe, Well-Organized Learning Environment

Given the number of students who come from home environments characterized by a lack of support, safety, and consistency, it is imperative that teachers develop clear expectations about student behavior and academic performance. These expectations should include the statement that the teacher will fulfill her or his responsibility to ensure that other students will not interfere with a student's right to feel safe, supported, and able to learn in a calm learning environment. Students also need to understand how the classroom will operate, how problems will be resolved, and how they will be involved in influencing classroom structures—including curricular and instructional decisions. The skilled teacher balances the value of structure in creating a safe, clearly understood classroom environment with the costs associated with too much teacher dominance or control. Chapter 8 presents methods for creating well-structured classrooms. Chapters 9 through 12 offer methods for increasing classroom order and safety by helping students modify their unproductive behavior.

Have Time to Integrate Learning

Students need time during the school day to slow down and integrate what they have learned. All too often, students are rushed from one activity to another, with no time allotted for summarizing the learning that has taken place in each activity. When this hurry occurs, students begin to feel confused and often experience a sense of failure, for they frequently have not understood what it was they were supposed to have learned from the preceding activity. As teachers, we are often lulled into believing that everyone has understood because several of our students who learn quickly indicate that the material has been learned and understood. Students learn at varying rates, however, and in different ways, and it is important to slow down and provide all students with an opportunity to organize the new ideas that have been presented. Effective teachers develop specific instructional activities designed to help students summarize new learning and relate this new knowledge to previous and future learning and the students' own lives.

During the past decade, many elementary, middle, and secondary schools have moved toward scheduling lessons and classes for extended blocks of time so teachers have greater flexibility in incorporating interactive, interdisciplinary instruction and students have more time to explore and integrate new learning.

Have Positive Contact with Peers

As discussed in Chapter 2 and expanded upon in Chapter 4, having support from peers is a major factor influencing students' motivation to learn. The increased use of activities to help students know their peers, develop a sense of being part of a group, and develop improved group skills are essential aspects to motivating all students to learn.

Receive Instruction Matched to Their Cognitive and Skill Level and Learning Style

Even though the personal and academic needs described throughout this chapter apply to all children, it is important to be aware that children differ considerably in their levels of cognitive development and learning styles. On the issue of teachers' responding to differences in students' achievement and ability levels, Stipek (1988) wrote, "The importance of tasks being matched to each child's skill level cannot be overemphasized. This is necessary for intrinsic motivation, and it is necessary for learning. As difficult a principle as this is to implement, it is the most important principle of motivation and learning" (pp. 55, 57). Teachers who use the same instructional methods with every student or who use a limited range of instructional activities will create a situation in which some students become frustrated, experience failure, and respond by misbehaving.

Learning Style

In addition to attending to students' current level of cognitive development, teachers can increase students' motivation and success by responding effectively to students' learning styles. Students differ in their approaches to learning. Every student has a cognitive or learning style that represents the general approach he or she takes to learning and organizing material. Reisman (1964) wrote that teachers too often examine students' failure by considering personal and social problems and do not focus on the child's learning style and determine the best approach to providing instruction.

Research (Dunn & Dunn, 1987) suggests that students' learning can be enhanced by providing them with material that enables them to use the sensory modality with which they are most comfortable. In addition, Bernard (1973) commented that, though teachers have generally been aware of students' individual needs in amount of time needed to complete various tasks, they have generally ignored other aspects of students' learning styles. As mentioned earlier, a number of authors suggest that students differ according to whether they depend on personalized, social factors in learning (field-dependent students) or on more impersonal, abstract factors (field-independent students). Ramirez and Castaneda (1974) suggested that field-independent students are less concerned about relationships within the classroom and prefer abstract material. They enjoy independent work and competition. Conversely, field-dependent students seek teacher and peer approval and want learning material to be concrete and related to their own interests. Students also differ on such factors as their ability to attend to relevant cues and ignore inappropriate stimuli, to accept new ideas and surroundings, and the ability to reflect on questions before responding.

Extensive research conducted by Rita Dunn and colleagues provided support for the studies cited in the previous paragraph. Dunn's research demonstrated that a variety of elements differentially affect individuals' learning. Figure 6.4, a chart designed by Kenneth and Rita Dunn, demonstrates these variables or elements. Dunn (1983; Dunn & Dunn, 1987) reported various studies demonstrating that allowing students to work in classroom settings in which environmental, physical, and sociological factors were similar to those preferred by the student dramatically enhances student learning.

For example, studies, primarily by doctoral students working with Rita Dunn (Dunn & Dunn, 1987), suggest that many students learn material more effectively and score higher on tests when allowed to sit on comfortable materials rather than at standard desks and when allowed to work in noisy environments, and that some students, especially elementary children, learn more effectively and are less fidgety in low rather than in bright lights. In one study, half of all seventh-grade students in one junior high school learned more effectively when allowed to move about during learning activities. Student learning can also be enhanced by allowing students to eat when they need to, study material at a time of day best suited to

FIGURE 6.4 Diagnosing Learning Styles

Source: Rita Dunn and Kenneth Dunn. The Center for the Study of Learning and Teaching Styles, St. John's University. Reprinted by permission.

their learning preference, and learn through modalities they prefer. Chapter 7 presents a number of methods teachers can use to respond to students' learning preferences within the context of regular classroom operation.

Researchers including Anthony Gregorc (1982), David Kolb (1978), Joseph Renzulli (1983), and Bernice McCarthy (1987; McCarthy, Leflar, & McNamara, 1987) categorized individual learning styles and found that when instructional methods match students' learning-style preference, student achievement is significantly enhanced. McCarthy developed the 4-MAT system, a cycle of learning that identifies four distinct styles of learning and four matching instructional roles that facilitate learning for each learning style. Figure 6.5 presents a model of learning styles based on these researchers' findings.

As discussed later in this chapter, McCarthy did not suggest that teachers need to individualize each lesson in order to incorporate the learning-style preference of each learner. Learning-style theory and research do suggest, however, that students will be more highly motivated and will learn significantly more when instructional

FIGURE 6.5 Learning Styles

Innovative Learner	Analytic Learner	Common-Sense Learner	Dynamic Learner
The Learner:	*The Learner:*	*The Learner:*	*The Learner:*
Seeks meaning	Wants to know the	Needs to know how	Needs to use the
Wants reasons for	facts	things work	self-discovery
learning new material	Perceives information	Seeks usability	method
Needs to be	abstractly,	Enjoys solving	Takes risks
personally involved	processes it	problems	Is flexible
in the learning	reflectively	Desires hands-on	Relishes change
process	Can create concepts	experiences	Seeks action
Desires to work with	and build models	Wants ideas to be	Follows through with
people	Enjoys collecting data	practical	plans
Is highly imaginative	Needs to know what	Needs to know how	Enjoys the
Has good divergent	the experts think	things that they are	trial-and-error
thinking skills	Values sequential	asked to do will help	method
Perceives information	thinking	in real life	Receives information
concretely,		Likes to practice ideas	concretely,
processes it reflectively	*The Teacher:*	Perceives information	processes it actively
	Provides information	abstractly,	
The Teacher:	by direct instruction	processes it actively	*The Teacher:*
Is a motivator	Sees knowledge as		Is a resource
Uses the discussion	increasing	*The Teacher:*	Becomes an evaluator
approach	comprehension	Becomes a coach	Serves as a facilitator
Incorporates a great		Models	Encourages a variety
deal of		Involves the student	of learning
teacher-student		Gives immediate	approaches
interaction		feedback	

methods are diversified so that opportunities exist for all learners to be regularly involved in instructional activities that emphasize their own learning-style preference.

It is interesting but not surprising that students can provide useful information about how they learn best. As part of a required audit, the Little Rock School District asked a random sample of 566 students in grades 7 to 12 to state what classroom factors helped them learn. The results (Mosley & Smith, 1982) showed the top five factors to be:

1. Clear, complete explanations and concrete examples
2. Positive, relaxed learning environments in which students could talk to and learn from other students
3. Individualized instruction, in which teachers know that the students are different, occasionally divide students into groups, check on students' progress, and assign varied tasks
4. Adequate academic learning time in class
5. Motivation and interest by using a variety of instructional methods and teacher's enthusiasm

Learning-style inventories can also provide teachers with information about students' learning-style preferences. The recommended readings at the end of this chapter include several learning-style inventories. The use of these inventories can support several important student learning needs. Assessment of learning styles can (1) increase students' sense of efficacy by helping them better understand the learning process (how they learn and why teachers make key instructional decisions), (2) increase student involvement in the learning process, (3) help students establish goals, and (4) encourage teachers to increase the amount of instructional activities that have meaning to the student.

The concept of brain hemisphericity is closely linked to the work on students' learning styles. During the past few years, considerable research has been done supporting the notion that people who tend to be left-brain dominant learn in different ways and have different environmental and organizational needs in the classroom than do right-brain dominant people (Dunn, Cavanaugh, Eberle, & Lenhausern, 1982). Right-brain dominant people in general are bothered by noise when working; prefer dim lighting; are less persistent and motivated when doing detailed, logical, sequential kinds of tasks; prefer a tactile mode of learning; and like to learn while working with peers. Left-brain dominant students tend to learn best when it is quiet, and they like bright light, prefer to work by themselves, and learn visually, auditorily, or both. These students enjoy analyzing situations, like tasks to be logical and sequential, and pay attention to detail.

Most of the curriculum in the public school deals with facts and knowledge: logical, sequential, linear concepts; systems, rules, and symbols. "In elementary and many secondary classes, students spend two-thirds of their time doing seatwork with printed worksheets" (Doyle, 1983, p. 180). Durkin (1981) analyzed five basal reading programs and reported that they emphasized practice and assessment and included little instruction in comprehension. Findings from national studies by Boyer (1983), Goodlad (1984), Lipsitz (1984), and Sizer (1984) all reinforce the fact that most instruction is teacher dominated and fact oriented. This type of instruction favors field-independent left-brain dominant students. Many students are field-independent right-brain dominant, however, and learn best when they are actively involved in the realm of creativity, imagination, intuitiveness, spatial concepts, and inventiveness. Therefore, as discussed in the remainder of the chapter, when designing curriculum and instruction, it is important to create a balance of activities that focus on the learning-style preferences of right- and left-brain dominant students.

INSTRUCTIONAL METHODS THAT ENHANCE STUDENT MOTIVATION AND LEARNING

Research and practice focusing on the quality of instruction have followed two general paths. First, a group of researchers (Anderson, Evertson, & Brophy, 1979; Good & Grouws, 1979) have examined the specific instructional skills and amounts of time spent on various instructional tasks displayed by teachers whose students achieved higher scores on standardized tests. Stimulated by these process-product studies relating students' acquisition of basic skills to a variety of teacher behaviors that increase students' engaged learning time, several leading educators—including Thomas Good (1979), Madeline Hunter (1981), and Jane Stallings (1984)—have developed teacher training programs aimed at increasing students' achievement by improving teachers' skills in providing direct instruction to students. Because recent national studies indicate that many students are not mastering fundamental knowledge in basic skills, it is imperative that teachers learn instructional skills that will increase students' gains in acquiring basic skills. Furthermore, attaining higher-level cognitive goals depends heavily on students' having mastered basic skills.

A second group of educators—including John Goodlad (1984), David and Roger Johnson (1987), Bruce Joyce and Marsha Weil (1986), Bernice McCarthy (1987), Barbara Presseisen (1988), and Robert Slavin (Slavin, Karweit, & Madden, 1989)—emphasize instructional approaches that actively involve students in instructional activities aimed at acquiring not only important basic skills but also higher level cognitive skills and interpersonal skills. This work coincides with increasing interest in student responsibility and self-control. Thomas Good (1983) summarized the focus on students' involvement: "In particular, researchers should examine how teachers' classroom management styles influence student initiative and self-control. Students need structure and purposeful direction, but they must also have opportunities to learn to determine their own objectives and to develop strategies for evaluating progress in self-chosen goals" (p. 63).

Taken together, the research suggests that teachers must possess the skills (outlined in Chapters 7 and 8) for organ-

"Sorry, but my right brain just took over."

izing and managing classrooms and for systematically presenting material to students. Teachers must also, however, have skill in helping students establish learning goals, initiate and evaluate their own learning, work cooperatively in the learning process, and develop skills in higher-level cognitive processes such us analysis, synthesis, and research methodology. "Since no single teaching strategy can accomplish every purpose, the wise teacher will master a sufficient repertoire of strategies to deal with the specific kinds of learning problems he or she faces" (Joyce & Weil, 1986, p. 20). This concept is echoed by Thomas Good (1983, p. 62): "Effective managers in the research reviewed here thought about the needs of their students and adjusted their teaching to particular classes. These teachers appeared to be good decision makers." As professionals, teachers must be introduced to a broad range of knowledge and be provided with assistance in learning to make thoughtful decisions about how to integrate various methods of instruction and classroom management.

The remainder of this chapter provides a practical overview of several instructional skills that can improve students' acquisition of basic skills and increase their motivation, interest, and higher-level cognitive skills. It is obviously not possible in one chapter to describe in detail the increasing amount of excellent work available for helping teachers improve and diversify the quality of their instruction. We have chosen to present general instructional strategies that can be implemented in a wide range of grade levels and curriculum areas. The emphasis in these strategies is on increasing students' sense of metacognitive understanding and empowerment of the learning environment.

Demystifying Learning

As mentioned earlier, most students see learning as a series of unrelated activities and a game to be won or lost. Thematic curriculum, portfolio assessment, cooperative learning, and other curricular and instructional methods are doing much to help students better understand their learning, but it is important to make a direct, clear, and concerted effort to assist students in better understanding the meaning of learning and the learning process.

The authors have found it helpful to teach students six key concepts. First, as discussed earlier in this chapter, it is important to begin the school year by having students develop a functional definition of learning. Second, especially for students beyond the third grade, it is important to teach students the basic concepts of motivation described in this chapter. Third, it is helpful for students to understand Howard Gardner's (1983, 1993) concept that individuals have different learning strengths. Students must understand that classmates will vary in the speed or ease with which they master material, but, with assistance, everyone can be an effective learner. This concept is particularly easy for one of the authors to teach since he rates in the 5th percentile in musical ability and the 17th percentile in spatial relations. He could certainly be more proficient in each category and his life could be enriched had he not avoided these areas in order not to experience failure. Students as young as the primary grades can learn this concept by discussing their strengths and areas in which they are less skilled. The authors have also used several activities to demonstrate this concept. One activity is presented in

Appendix A. Other activities can be found in Pat Huggins's (1993) work on multiple intelligence.

Fourth, it is important that students learn about learning styles. Students can be given learning-style inventories and assisted in discussing the results. More importantly, however, students must understand that everyone has different strengths and limitations regarding how they process information and how they prefer to learn. A positive, productive learning environment accepts and responds to these differences by creating opportunities for all students to utilize their strengths. Fifth, students become more motivated learners when they understand the various levels of learning and why they are being asked to study various materials. As discussed in the following section, this involves teaching students some taxonomy of learning and helping students understand when and why they are working at each level. Sixth, students benefit from learning how to study effectively. As discussed later in this chapter, students can learn how to work effectively in groups. They can also learn how to study various types of materials. As a seventh-grader, the authors' daughter frequently found herself studying all material as if she were trying to memorize virtually all the content. In seven years of schooling, no one other than her parents had helped her to understand how to read a novel differently than a history text or an original source being used as a reference for a report. Students need to learn various study skills if they are to feel control of their own learning.

During the past five years, the authors have worked with hundreds of teachers who have attempted to clarify the learning process in order to empower students and thereby increase students' motivation, achievement, and positive behavior. Our findings (Jones, 1991) have suggested that teachers who work with students to demystify learning find that student learning and behavior improve dramatically.

Figure 6.6 provides a list of 26 ways to demystify the learning process by helping students develop a clearer understanding of what learning is and why curriculum and instructional decisions are made. Activity 6.6 at the end of the chapter will assist you in examining your current practice and possible goals related to these methods.

Teaching More Than Facts

The teaching of factual material is certainly one function of the public schools. Schools serve society by transmitting information and providing children with basic skills in reading, writing, and arithmetic. The acquisition of basic factual information and skills is, especially in the primary grades, an important component of a child's learning. In a society characterized by rapid changes in technology and information processing, the acquisition of facts is increasingly a means to an end rather than an end in itself. Schools must begin early to help children use their basic skills for more analytic and creative purposes. Basic skills are important prerequisites to higher-level cognitive functioning. Especially at the secondary level, though, curriculum and instructional techniques used with students who possess basic skills too often focus on memorization and low-level cognitive skills.

Respondents to the 1984 Gallup Poll of the Public's Attitudes Toward the Public Schools (Gallup, 1984) gave high rankings to numerous goals other than

1. Work with students to clearly and explicitly define learning.
2. Celebrate students' successes based on this definition.
3. Write and verbally explain the goals and objectives for each lesson and why these have been chosen.
4. Relate learning to students' own lives and interests.
5. Teach students a taxonomy of learning.
6. Teach students some basic concepts about student motivation.
7. Explain to students why you choose each instructional method to reach your stated goal.
8. Have students establish learning goals.
9. Use "experts" from the community to evaluate student performance and demonstrate and discuss its value.
10. Teach students about learning styles.
11. Teach students about types of special abilities (Howard Gardner's concepts).
12. Teach students about learning disabilities (differences) and how students can work with these differences.
13. Use peer tutoring and teach students how to be tutors.
14. Teach students key instructional methods being used by large number of staff and involve students in providing teachers with feedback on how these are being implemented.
15. Involve students in teaching small lessons to the class so they can learn to appreciate the skills involved in effective teaching and the prerequisites for effective learning.
16. Have students provide ongoing feedback to the teacher regarding how she or he is using effective instructional and management methods.
17. Explain to students your philosophy of assessment.
18. Be very specific in clarifying when assessment will occur, how it will be used, what to study, and how to study.
19. Have students monitor their own learning gains and grades.
20. Have students develop test questions.
21. Provide alternative methods for assessing students' knowledge.
22. Involve students in assessing their own effort in reaching learning goals.
23. Teach students a variety of study skills.
24. Provide students assistance in how to study specific types of materials.
25. Involve students in developing classroom rules and procedures.
26. Involve students in assessing how well they are following the rules and procedures.

FIGURE 6.6
Methods for
Demystifying the
Learning Process

acquisition of basic skills. Slightly more than half of the respondents gave a 10 (the highest rating) to the education goal "to develop the ability to live in a complex and changing world." John Goodlad reported similar findings from his *A Study of Schooling* (1983a): "Analysis of documents regarding goals for U.S. schools reveals a steady evolution from narrow academic skills to a far wider array of concerns—and to citizenship, vocational, and personal goals as well. All 50 states endorse them, as did most of the 8,600 parents surveyed in *A Study of Schooling*. Are we to brush these aside as impractical idealism simply because, for the most part, they elude our ability to measure them?" (p. 553). Incorporating material that goes beyond the factual level also greatly influences students' motivation and behavior. Students enjoy acquiring factual information; they also have a strong need to become emotionally involved in the learning process.

Levels of Instruction

In their *Clarifying Values through Subject Matter*, Harmin, Kirschenbaum, and Simon (1973) suggested that instruction can take place at the fact, concept, or personal application level. Additional models were presented by Bloom (1956) in his *Taxonomy of Educational Objectives, Handbook I: Cognitive Domain* and Krathwohl, Bloom, and Masia (1964) in their *Taxonomy of Educational Objectives, Handbook II: Affective Domain.* In developing curricula, it is helpful to categorize instruction into the four levels: facts, concepts, generalizations, and personal application. The relationship between these four levels and Bloom's taxonomy is shown in Figure 6.7.

The *facts* level involves providing students with basic information. When developing a unit on ecology, information on the chemicals that are associated with pollution, what causes pollution, and the effects various pollutants have on the human body would be included. This level is similar to the *knowledge* level described by Bloom (1956).

The *concepts* level focuses on the relationships among facts and examines major themes associated with facts. An ecology unit might examine the concept of people's relationship to their environment, the benefits and costs associated with progress, or responsibility to future generations. This level incorporates what Bloom describes as *comprehension* and *analysis*.

The *generalizations* level provides students with an opportunity to use the information they have obtained and the concepts they have developed to solve problems or interpret situations. In the context of an ecology unit, students might be asked to write legislative proposals dealing with ecology or to develop a model city. The educational objectives associated with these activities are similar to those Bloom labels *application, synthesis,* and *evaluation*.

At the final level is *personal application*. Here, students are asked to relate their learning to their own beliefs, feelings, and behaviors. In an ecology unit,

Teaching More Than Facts	Bloom's Taxonomy
Facts	Knowledge
Concepts	Comprehension analysis
Generalizations	Application Synthesis Evaluation
Personal application	Affective domain

FIGURE 6.7
Comparison of Bloom's Taxonomy of Educational Objectives and Teaching More Than Facts

students might be asked to discuss their own behavior regarding such topics as litter, recycling, or water usage. This level relates to the learning objectives in the affective domain described by Krathwohl and associates (1964). Because it is at this level that students relate learning directly to their own lives, teachers should, whenever possible, incorporate this level into their instruction. No other level has greater potential for stimulating students' interest and increasing on-task behavior.

It is obvious that older students will be better able to become involved in instruction associated with higher levels. Nevertheless, primary teachers should attempt to help children develop simple concepts, think creatively about generalizations and applications, and, most important, view learning as something that relates to their own lives. Failure to incorporate higher levels indicates to children that learning is merely the acquisition of often unrelated facts. When this failure occurs, it is more difficult for teachers in subsequent grades to introduce higher levels of instruction.

An Example

An example of a lesson used by one of the authors in a fourth-grade class can help to clarify how each level can be incorporated into an instructional unit. The example, involving a unit on the Northwest Indians, begins with students learning numerous *facts* about the lives and history of these Native Americans. Individual student interests are accommodated by having each student choose a topic of special interest, obtain relevant material, and make a presentation to the class. As students learn about the beliefs Native Americans held and how their lives have changed over the years, discussions take place on *concepts* such as prejudice, progress, and "might makes right." In this lesson, instruction at the *generalization* level takes two forms. First, students are asked to discuss such topics as what legislators could do to assist the Native Americans, how society should handle such current problems as salmon-fishing rights and whether Native Americans should live their own life-style separately or be integrated into society. Second, students design and perform a *potlatch*. This performance involves creating costumes, learning authentic songs and dances, making dried food, and decorating the room.

One of the authors and a colleague have also developed a method for incorporating the *personal application* level by providing students with an intense personal experience related to this unit. The activity has one class move out of the classroom on the pretext that the other class needs the room to complete some useful research. The displaced class is placed in a corner in the hall behind a chalkboard. When students become uncomfortable and complain, it is suggested that they petition the principal to change the situation. The principal's refusal almost inevitably provokes anger associated with a sense of impotence. Once students have been allowed to experience these feelings, they return to their classroom and are assisted in sharing their feelings with the class that displaced them. The teachers then help the students draw the analogy between their experience and that of Native Americans. The activity ends by the two classes having a small party to reduce any negative feelings that may have been created by the experience.

It is likely that students will remember this activity and the basic concept taught. Although this example provides a rather dramatic approach to incorporating students' feelings into a lesson, there are numerous less time-consuming approaches. Figure 6.8 outlines a high school unit that incorporates all four levels. If you are interested in obtaining additional suggestions, consult Harmin, Kirschenbaum, and Simon's (1973) *Clarifying Values through Subject Matter.*

Incorporating Students' Interests

One of the authors recently observed a high school physics teacher introduce a difficult concept. The teacher asked the class how many of them had, at the beginning of the year, listed understanding flight as an interest and learning goal for the class. Most students raised their hands, and the teacher reinforced this response by providing the data that had been generated during the first week of class. He then informed the class that the next two weeks would be spent on some difficult material that, by itself, had little meaning. He noted, however, that when combined with one additional skill, this material would allow them to figure trajectories and other factors associated with flight. He then asked how many of the students were interested in delving into this difficult but important material. All the students in the class raised their hands, and the stage was set for a productive series of lessons.

As teachers, we are making a major mistake and creating many problems for ourselves when we fail to provide productive outlets for students' interests. Although teaching at more than the facts level will stimulate students' interest and involvement in the learning process, we can increase their motivation and learning by using a wide range of strategies that directly incorporate students' interests into the curriculum. The following methods suggest various approaches to incorporating students' interests.

Methods

1. *Early in the school year, have students build a list of things they would like to learn about each major curriculum area to which they will be exposed.* This activity provides you with valuable information and stimulates students' interest by showing that some of their learning will relate directly to their interests. You may choose to create a unit on one or more topics that received widespread interest. Topics of interest can also be incorporated into the regular school curriculum. Finally, you may integrate these interests into several of the other strategies presented in this section.

2. *When introducing a unit, have the students list questions they have about the topics that will be covered.* In addition to providing you with useful information, this activity creates for the students an association (often lacking) between their interests and the material they are asked to learn.

3. *Teach students how to order films on topics that interest them.* Students can watch these films during study times when they have completed their work, in place of recess, or when you structure time for exploring individual interests. If a film is of particular interest because it relates to a topic being examined by the entire class or because many students share an interest, it can be shown to the entire class.

FIGURE 6.8

Teaching More
Than Facts: A
Lesson Design
for Teaching
Romeo and Juliet

Factual Level

Activities

1. Read the play aloud, with students taking parts and the teacher reading the more difficult parts and explaining as the students progress through the play.
2. Discuss what happens in each act, using a guide sheet.
3. Introduce students to the structure of a Shakespearean tragedy.
4. Introduce major themes and elements of a Shakespearean tragedy.
5. Give quizzes after the completion of each act and at the end of the play.

Concept Level

Activities

1. Relate the plot of *Romeo and Juliet* to movies the students have seen or books they have read. (A shortened version of *West Side Story* might be taught at the end of this unit in which character-by-character and scene comparisons are done.)
2. Discuss the problems Romeo and Juliet had in communicating with their parents. (Relate to Romeo's tragic flaw—impetuousness.)
3. Discuss the effects of hate and prejudice.
4. Discuss the concept of fate.
5. Introduce students to Elizabethan concepts relevant to a greater understanding of the play.
6. Point out universality of themes, characters, and situations to show their relevance to students.
7. By reading the play in class students will study it as a literary work and dramatic performance but they also will be viewing the Franco Zepherelli version of *Romeo and Juliet* to analyze his interpretation.
8. Discuss the plot complication of Juliet's impending marriage to Paris.

Generalization Level

Activities

1. Relate the specific problem of Romeo and Juliet to adolescents today.
2. Discuss alternatives to the outcome of Romeo and Juliet.
3. Discuss examples of hate and prejudice today.
4. Help students realize that reading Shakespeare's plays, like reading any great works of literature, is both a demanding and a rewarding experience.
5. Do environmental situations influence prejudice? Would there be more prejudice against gays in a small rural town or San Francisco?
7. Give examples of prejudice against nationalities, beliefs, appearance, and values.

Personal Application Level

Activities

1. What could Romeo and Juliet have done differently?
2. Do you think their death justifies the ending of the feud? (Do the means justify the end?)
3. Are Juliet's parents hypocrites?
4. How do you view the nurse's relationship to Juliet and did she betray Juliet?
5. Has the friar done the right thing for Romeo and Juliet?
6. What prejudices do you think you have?
7. How did you arrive at those prejudices? Did anyone or any situation influence you?
8. What can you and society do to help eliminate or lessen prejudice?

4. *Teach students how to invite guest speakers (including parents) to discuss a topic of interest to students.* You will, of course, always want to confirm younger students' contracts, but they can learn to take major responsibility for obtaining interesting guests.

5. *Create a unit on biographies.* Students can be asked to choose a person about whom they would like to know more and acquire information about this person. Each student can then dress up like the person they have researched and make a presentation to the class as that person.

6. *Allow individual students to choose special topics they would like to study.* When presenting a unit, have students choose different aspects of the topic and report their findings to the class.

7. *Create opportunities for structured sharing.* Each day of the week can be designated as a time for sharing what students have read or accomplished in a particular area. Monday might be set aside for sharing written compositions, Tuesday for newspaper articles, Wednesday for something positive students did for someone else, and so on.

8. *Have students develop special-interest days or weeks.* Students can decide on a topic they would like to study. All subject matter for the day (or week) can be related to this topic. If they selected whales, lessons in math, reading, creative writing, science, and social studies could be constructed around whales.

9. *When involving students in creative writing, do not always assign topics.* At times, allow students to write stories related to experiences that have been meaningful to them.

10. *Use learning logs.* In their learning logs, students write in their own words what they are learning, what it means to them, and how it relates to their own life.

11. *Begin a unit by having students write what they already know about the topic.* In addition to providing diagnostic information, you can use these data to involve students who have special interest and knowledge in instructing small groups or the entire class.

12. *Allow students to develop their own spelling list.* Teachers who use this approach often find that students who have previously learned very few spelling words make dramatic gains and select words more difficult than those they had been misspelling.

Responding to Students' Individual Learning Styles

A less obvious and relatively new approach to involving students in the learning process is to let students use an approach to learning that they find most beneficial. As mentioned earlier, individual students vary considerably in the manner in which they learn most effectively, and several authors have attempted to list the factors that influence students' learning and to categorize individual learning styles.

Writers disagree on how effectively teachers can diagnose students' learning styles. Knowing the quality of knowledge available in this area and the demands individualization places on teachers, it seems reasonable that rather than attempt to individualize according to each student's preferred learning style, we should use instructional methods that respond to obvious differences in students' learning styles. Although teachers often view this as a herculean task, there are two reasonable and realistic approaches to accommodating various student learning styles.

Adjusting Environmental Factors to Meet Students' Learning Needs

As discussed earlier in the chapter, one approach to responding to students' learning styles has been developed by Rita and Kenneth Dunn. Research (Dunn, 1989) indicates that most students are significantly affected by approximately 6 of the 26 factors that influence students' learning (Figure 6.4). By adjusting the classroom environment and some instructional methods, teachers can easily create a learning environment more conducive to many students' unique learning needs. The following methods have been implemented by the authors and by many teachers with whom they work.

Methods

1. *When presenting material, use visual displays, such as writing on the overhead projector, to assist students who are visual learners.* Dunn (1983) stated that approximately 40 percent of students learn more effectively when they can read or see something. Interestingly, Price (1980) suggested that most children are not good visual learners until they reach third or fourth grade.

2. *Allow students to select where they will sit.* Students vary in the amount of light, sound, and heat they prefer and may, in fact, self-select seats that provide more productive learning environments for them. Teachers often comment, especially during junior high school, that some students may abuse this privilege. The authors have found that they seldom do so if they are taught the concept of learning styles and if classroom procedures such as allowing students to select their own seats are presented as part of a procedure to make learning more personalized and effective for all students.

3. *Permit students to choose where they wish to study.* Some students work most effectively at a table, others in a soft chair, and others seated at a traditional school desk. The authors have even taught children who worked best when they could move around the room and do their work on a clipboard.

4. *Be sensitive to individual students' needs to block out sound or visual distractions.* Discuss differences in learning style with the class and allow students to select a quiet study carrel. Also, observe students to see whether they appear easily distracted during seatwork. Teachers frequently move easily distracted students nearer to the teachers desk; however, because this is often the busiest place in the classroom, this move may aggravate the problem by creating more distractions for the student.

5. *Make healthy snacks available to students or allow them to bring their own.* Because many students fail to eat an adequate breakfast, midmorning is a key time for allowing them to have a snack. Teachers who try this tactic generally find that initially all students take a cracker, carrot, or celery stick. Soon, however, only students who are hungry or who work best when they can eat will choose to eat.

6. *Provide opportunities for students to select whether they will work alone, in pairs, or with a small group.* Students can work with peers to complete assignments, study for tests, work on long-term projects, or critique each other's work.

7. *Provide adequate structure for both short-term and long-range assignments.* Students learn more effectively when seatwork is preceded by substantial direct instruction. Likewise, students need the structure provided by periodic conferences with the teacher or an assignment checklist and timetable for longer assignments.

8. *Give students instruction in study skills.* Both reflective and impulsive learners can benefit from learning to organize material prior to writing a formal paper. Some students organize material best using an outline format. More right hemisphere-oriented students may prefer to organize by mapping—a process of making connections in nonlinear fashion. Likewise, visual and kinesthetic learners profit from learning how to take notes.

9. *Provide learning activities that require use of both sides of the brain.* Figure 6.9 lists a variety of traditional instructional activities that emphasize use of either the right or left hemisphere as well as activities that tend to require use of both hemispheres.

10. *Employ individual goal setting, self-monitoring, and contracts.* These devices can assist students who require structure and concrete evidence to enhance motivation.

11. *Realize that some students require more frequent breaks than do others.* Teach students how to take short breaks without disrupting the class.

12. *Consider that students doing poorly in a subject might perform better if that subject were taught at a different time of day.* It is somewhat difficult to make this adjustment, but dramatic results can be obtained by switching a student's basic-skill lesson from morning to afternoon. Secondary school schedules that rotate the periods at which classes are taught allow students to study all subjects at a time when they work best.

13. *Increase the length of time you wait before calling on a student to answer a question.* This added time assists more reflective learners. Again, it is important to explain and teach this procedure to the class before implementing it.

14. *Develop learning centers that incorporate a variety of learning modalities.* Learning centers can be created that allow students to learn visually, auditorially, and kinesthetically. Learning centers also enable students to make decisions concerning light, sound, and design preferences, whether to work independently or with other students, and to select activities that allow them to deal with the material supportive of their own cognitive learning-style preference.

Incorporating a Variety of Instructional Techniques

A second approach to accommodating various student learning styles has focused on training teachers to use a wide range of instructional methods when presenting information to students. A number of models have been developed to help create more diverse instructional methods; of these, the authors have found three approaches most useful.

194

FIGURE 6.9 Learning Activities Related to the Right and Left Hemispheres of the Brain

LEFT

workbooks, worksheets
drill and repetition
repetitive learning games
demonstrations
copying
following directions
collecting facts
computations
record keeping

RIGHT

creative art activities
guided imagery
creative writing
use of metaphors & symbols
designing
solving old problems new ways
mythology
open-ended discussions
self-expressive activities

INTEGRATIVE

dramatic presentations/
reader's theater
design technology
interpreting data
hypothesizing
simulation games
problems of logic

word problems/
integrated mathematics
brainstorming
oral reports
independent research
directed art activities
research methods

role-plays
evaluating alternatives
"show and tell"
developing plans
group projects
organizing and directing

group sharing
writing essays
being read to
whole language
designing an experiment
personal journals, logs

Before presenting these methods, a word of caution is offered. The methods described in the remainder of this section are quite complex, and it is likely that only the experienced teacher will be able to incorporate them from the limited exposure that can be provided here. These methods are offered because experience indicates that their use can increase students' motivation and learning. Most readers, however, will want to consult the original source material or take a workshop on these methods in order to incorporate them consistently and effectively into their instructional repertoire.

First, in their book *Models of Teaching,* Bruce Joyce and Marsha Weil (1986) presented 22 models of teaching. The presentation of each model includes a description of the instructional goals the model is best suited to meet, the student and teacher roles and relationships encouraged by the model, and the special conditions and materials needed to implement the model. Teachers have reported that the addition of several models to their repertoire has had dramatic effects on their enjoyment of teaching as well as on students' motivation and behavior.

Second, Anthony Gregorc has described four types of learners. His work suggests that students learn best when teachers include optional approaches that students can select for practicing material or demonstrating their understanding. Figure 6.10 provides a lesson plan with options for students who have each learning-style preference described by Gregorc (1982). If you are interested in additional ideas, consult work by Kathleen Butler (1984).

Like Gregorc, Bernice McCarthy (1987) stated that students' learning styles can be described by four categories (see Chapter 6). Rather than emphasizing the importance of determining each student's preferred category, McCarthy encouraged teachers to develop lesson plans that include learning activities that systematically respond to all four student learning styles. In each unit, this approach provides some instruction matched to each student's preferred approach to learning, but it also requires that students experience and hopefully develop further skills in the other three styles of learning. Figure 6.11 offers activities for each of the four quadrants or learning styles as well as for right- and left-brain-dominated learners within each style.

Involving Students in Academic Goal Setting

As discussed earlier in this chapter, students will be more motivated by instructional tasks when they experience a sense of control over their environment and perceive themselves as mastering material. Students who perceive themselves as directing their own learning work harder and take greater pride in the outcome than do students who are less involved in decision making.

Individual goal setting is perhaps the most effective method for enabling students to experience a sense of understanding and controlling their own learning while incorporating their own interests. This method also has potential for helping students select learning activities that are congruent with their learning style. Teachers need to help students develop goals that are both realistic and directed at improving skill deficits revealed by diagnostic testing and observation, but students' involvement in establishing goals and recording progress can also significantly enhance their motivation and reduce acting-out or withdrawal behavior.

FIGURE 6.10
Adjusting to
Students'
Learning Styles

Unit: Advertising
Goals: Students will:

1. Become aware of propaganda techniques.
2. Learn how to introduce and market an item.
3. Understand the five myths of advertising.
4. Become more aware of consumerism.
5. Become aware of careers in the field of advertising.

Possible Learning Activities for Each Learning Style
Presented by Anthony Gregorc

Abstract Sequential

1. Describe the history and growth of the advertising field in the past fifty years.
2. Interpret the meaning of the phrase *honesty in advertising.*
3. List myths about advertising.
4. Devise a theory for the recent changes in commercials that are viewed during prime time.
5. Research each advertising technique.
6. List careers in the field of advertising.

Abstract Random

1. Create a taste test for the public on a new product.
2. Devise and conduct a survey about what consumers want in fast-food restaurant.
3. Write a jingle for a product.
4. Write, then role play a commercial.
5. Design a bulletin board about advertising.

Concrete Random

1. Brainstorm many ways in which advertising influences people in their daily lives.
2. Create and design a new product and its logotype.
3. Describe the types of products consumers might buy in the year 2000.
4. Write a poem or story about how toothpaste became popular.
5. Design a board game to teach facts and information about advertising.
6. Identify 25 products by their logotypes.

Concrete Sequential

1. Design a storyboard using sequential procedures.
2. Write a computer game about advertising.
3. Design a wall display showing a past advertisement for a product, a current advertisement, and a future advertisement for the same product.
4. Make a collage of advertisements from various magazines by classifying them according to an advertising technique.
5. Take a field trip to an advertising agency.

FIGURE 6.11 Sample Activities for a Unit on Water Supply

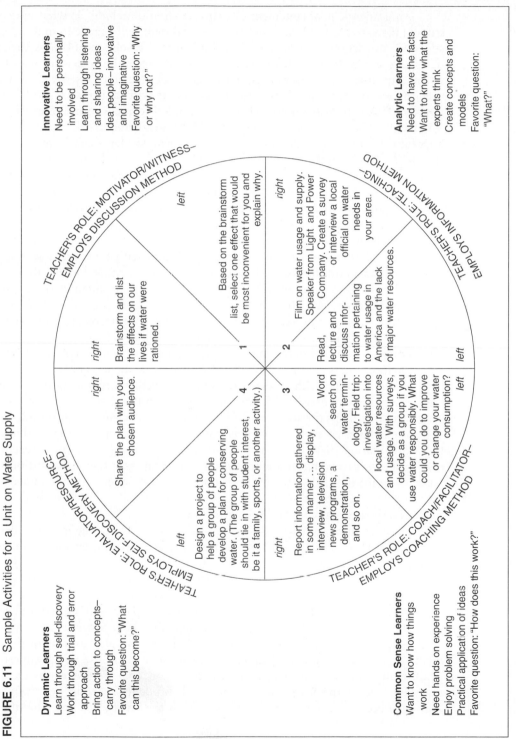

Innovative Learners
Need to be personally involved
Learn through listening and sharing ideas
Idea people–innovative and imaginative
Favorite question: "Why or why not?"

Analytic Learners
Need to have the facts
Want to know what the experts think
Create concepts and models
Favorite question: "What?"

Dynamic Learners
Learn through self-discovery
Work through trial and error approach
Bring action to concepts–carry through
Favorite question: "What can this become?"

Common Sense Learners
Want to know how things work
Need hands on experience
Enjoy problem solving
Practical application of ideas
Favorite question: "How does this work?"

TEACHER'S ROLE: MOTIVATOR/WITNESS–EMPLOYS DISCUSSION METHOD

TEACHER'S ROLE: TEACHING–EMPLOYS INFORMATION METHOD

TEACHER'S ROLE: EVALUATOR/RESOURCE–EMPLOYS SELF-DISCOVERY METHOD

TEACHER'S ROLE: COACH/FACILITATOR–EMPLOYS COACHING METHOD

1 Brainstorm and list the effects on our lives if water were rationed.
Based on the brainstorm list, select one effect that would be most inconvenient for you and explain why.

2 Film on water usage and supply. Speaker from Light and Power Company. Create a survey or interview a local official on water needs in your area.
Read, lecture and discuss information pertaining to water usage in America and the lack of major water resources.

3 Word search on water terminology. Field trip: investigation into local water resources and usage. With surveys, decide as a group if you use water responsibly. What could you do to improve or change your water consumption?
Report information gathered in some manner ... display, interview, television news programs, a demonstration, and so on.

4 Share the plan with your chosen audience.
Design a project to help a group of people develop a plan for conserving water. (The group of people should tie in with student interest, be it a family, sports, or another activity.)

Source: McCarthy, Bernice, *The 4-MAT System.* Barrington, IL: Excel, Inc., 1980. Reprinted by permission.

197

An academic goal statement or contract should include (1) what material the student plans to learn, (2) what activities the student will engage in to develop these skills, (3) the degree of proficiency the student will reach, and (4) how the student will demonstrate that the learning has occurred. Several approaches may be used when implementing academic goals. Each student can be involved in working toward one or more academic goals associated with a personal skill deficit or interest. This emphasis on goals can be expanded to incorporate term-length goal statements. Because most schools provide an academic report to parents (and, hopefully, to students) following a nine-week term, students can be aided in setting several academic goals on a term basis. Nine weeks will be too long for primary children, but most intermediate-grade and secondary students find nine-week goal setting provides a sense of direction and commitment. At the beginning of each term, you and the student can examine the student's current performance level and the material he or she will study during the term. The student can be helped to write several goals for the term, perhaps stating that by the end of the term he or she will be able to solve two-place multiplication problems with 80 percent accuracy. It is obviously important that you help each student choose goals that are attainable but that will require some additional effort by the child. Although children are motivated to achieve goals that require some real effort, they are also frequently intimidated by goals that seem impossible to reach. Furthermore, continued failure tends to reduce students' achievement orientation and self-concept. Figure 6.12 is an example of a high-interest form an elementary or middle school teacher could use to help students commit themselves to specific academic goals.

When working with students who have difficulty organizing their work and who have a history of school failure, it is often helpful to use a detailed goal-planning sheet that helps the students make very specific decisions. Figures 6.13 and 6.3 present examples of such forms. It is important that teachers support this process by clearly stating their goals in terms of student learning outcomes. Teachers can also help by providing students with forms that ask specific questions about students' learning goals. Student responses should be collected, responded to, and returned to students as soon as possible. Teachers should confer with students whose goals seem unrealistically high or low.

Another approach to employing academic goal setting involves designing assignments that allow students to choose the type of work they will complete, and, if appropriate, the grade they will earn for completing the designated amount of work. The most common format for using this method involves listing assignments for earning each grade and having students sign a contract indicating which assignments they plan to complete. This approach is particularly effective when you wish to involve all students in an assignment on which lower-achieving students might experience considerable difficulty with more complex aspects of the assignment. A contractual approach enables each student to choose an appropriate level of difficulty, and you can ensure that the basic concepts are learned by incorporating them within the lowest acceptable level. Students respond positively to this approach because it is a clear statement of what they will learn and what they must accomplish.

The benefits of this approach were highlighted in a study involving behavior problem adolescents (Maher, 1987). In this study, 49 high school students identified

FIGURE 6.12   Goal-Setting Form

under special education classification as behavior disordered were placed in mainstream classes. Half the students and their mainstream teachers were involved in jointly setting academic goals and specifying the instructional methods that would be used to reach these goals. The remaining students were placed with teachers who were required to set instructional goals but who did not work with students in setting these goals or discussing instructional methods. Results indicated that students involved in goal setting and a discussion of instructional methods learned more, felt more positive about school, and felt that this approach would be useful with other students who have behavior problems. Teachers involved in the experimental group used a greater diversity of instructional methods, were positive about the approach, and stated that they could incorporate the approach within their normal planning.

Implementing Self-Evaluation

Involving students in self-evaluation not only saves much time and energy but it also provides students with an opportunity to understand their academic performance better and to experience a sense of personal responsibility. When students evaluate and record their own work, they are more likely to develop an internal locus of control and view their progress as based on their own efforts. Similarly,

```
┌─────────────────────────────────────────────────────────────────────┐
│  Name _____  Class _____  Date _____       │
│  1. Goal: _____  │
│     _____   │
│  2. Reason(s) for working on goal: _____   │
│     _____   │
│  3. Where will you work on the goal: _____   │
│     _____   │
│  4. Time needed to finish goal: _____   │
│  5. Materials needed: _____   │
│     _____   │
│  6. Steps used to reach goals:                                         │
│     a. _____    │
│     b. _____    │
│     c. _____    │
│     d. _____    │
│     e. _____    │
│     f. _____    │
│  7. Prediction of my success:                                          │
│     Choose one:  Grade _____    Points _____         │
│                  Percent (70) _____   Other _____         │
│  8. Records:                                                           │
│     Goal Sheet _____    Checklist _____              │
│     Graph/Chart _____    Timeline _____              │
│     Products _____    Other _____              │
│  9. Reward: _____   │
└─────────────────────────────────────────────────────────────────────┘
```

FIGURE 6.13
Goal Planning
Worksheet

Source: Van Reusen, A. K., & Bos, C. S. (1988). The Goal Regulation Strategy. Reprinted by permission.

self-evaluation enables students to acknowledge areas that need improvement. In working with third-grade students from an inner-city public school, Klein and Schuler (1974) found that when students were allowed to evaluate their own performance contingent on passing skill tests in math, their performance improved markedly. Apparently, the ability to be autonomous was motivating to these students. Allowing students to score their own work also demonstrates the teacher's respect for them, which in turn enhances students' sense of significance and competence, and the associated increase in self-esteem often has a positive effect on students' behavior.

Students are impressed with displays of data, especially when the data deal with their own performance. Data provide immediate, concrete reinforcement for learning. Students often fail to associate their seemingly herculean efforts with actual increased knowledge or changes in behavior. Data make the learning or behavior change a concrete experience, which alone often provides more reinforcement than any free time or praise from the teacher. Surprisingly, the benefits associated with monitoring progress may be particularly great for students who are progressing slowly. These students often view themselves as making no progress or actually falling behind (as indeed they may be when the basis for comparison is their peers' work). Providing these students with specific data that demonstrate their progress is perhaps the most effective and honest motivational strategy.

Student goal setting provides an ideal opportunity for introducing regular data collection into the classroom. Students need periodic checks to determine how they are progressing toward their goals. One method for monitoring students' progress is to teach them to chart their own improvements. This can be done by instructing them in using graph paper to display results. Because bar graphs involve simple counting, students will have little difficulty in acquiring this skill. In fact, one of the authors worked with a teacher who successfully taught children in a primary grade who had emotional problems to use six-cycle graph paper.

Once students have learned how to chart data, they can begin to monitor their own progress. The graphs can be kept in their desk or notebook and should be attached to the associated contract or statement of goals. Students can be asked to contact the teacher or a peer with whom they are working if their graph suggests that they are having difficulty reaching their goal. You should, of course, periodically check students' results to see whether they are making satisfactory progress in reaching their goals. Figures 6.14 and 6.15 are examples of charts students can use to record their academic progress.

Students can use the form in Figure 6.15 to combine goal setting and self-evaluation. Each week, students take a spelling pretest (students of varying ability have different numbers of words and therefore use a longer or shorter form). The students record the pretest score and, based on this score, select a goal for the number of words they will spell correctly on the posttest. A visual image also is provided by having the students color in the number of words spelled correctly on the pretest and (in a different color) the posttest. On a separate chart students record the number of words they have learned each week and the cumulative total for the year. It is possible that some of the least-skilled spellers will learn more spelling words (based on formal spelling tests) than the better spellers in the class, who miss very few words on their pretests.

Finally, the students list the strategy they would use for learning spelling words and rate their daily use of the strategy. When one particular teacher began using this approach, she indicated her surprise at how limited students were in their strategies. She assisted the students by having the class brainstorm strategies they could use and allow students to select one of these or develop their own strategy of the week. She also had students daily rate their use of the strategy on a 0–2 scale, with 0 indicating they forgot to use the strategy, 1 meaning they used it a little but not as they had planned, and 2 indicating they had used it as planned. At the end of the week, students who met their goal would stand up, tell the class the strategy they used, and read off their scores for strategy use. This facilitated students in developing an internal locus of control by helping them learn the relationship between strategy use and achievement.

Another approach to student self-evaluation is to involve students either in pre-parent conferences or to include students in parent-teacher conferences. Teacher-student conferences held prior to parent-teacher conferences can be a

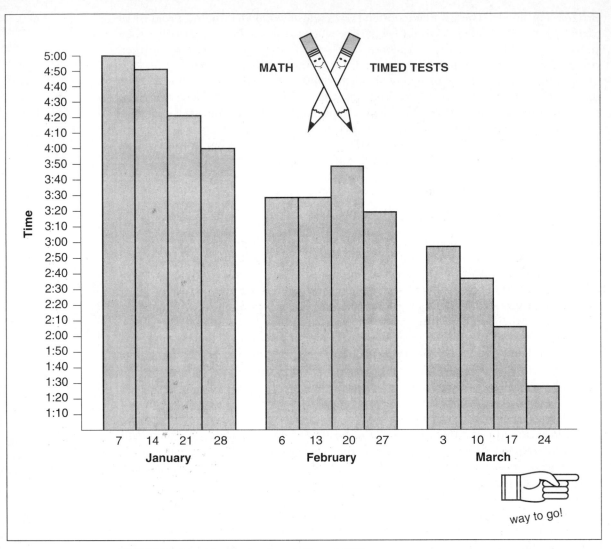

FIGURE 6.14   Monitoring Acquisition of Skills

chance for students to evaluate their own behavior and academic performance and compare this to the marks the teacher has prepared. The teacher and student can discuss any differences, which can lead either to a compromise or to our helping the student better understand his or her marks and setting specific goals for obtaining the desired marks during the next marking period. Another obvious advantage to this type of teacher-student conference is that it can reduce the anxiety many students experience in parent-teacher conferences. The fear of the unknown is eliminated when students know their marks and the issues we plan to discuss with their parents.

FIGURE 6.15   Spelling Goals and Strategies

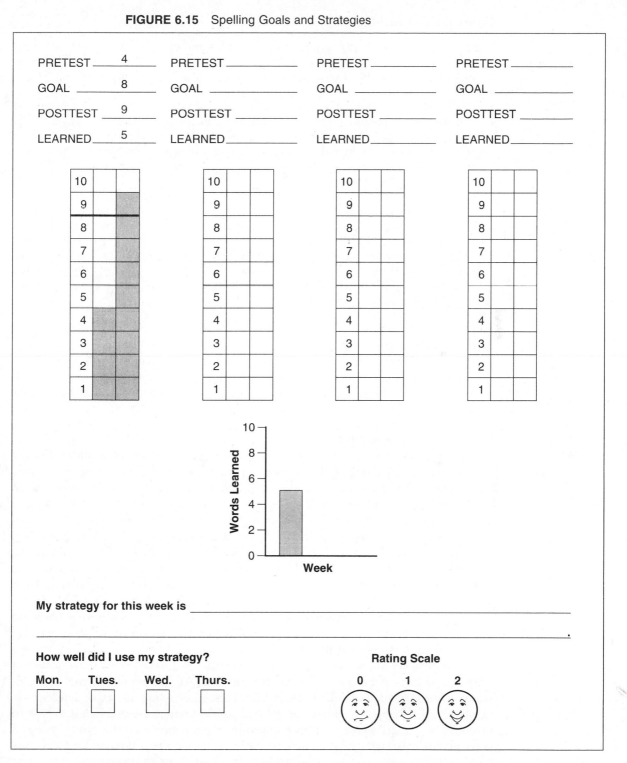

Cooperative Learning

Cooperative learning is perhaps the most popular and effective method for meeting students' varied learning styles and actively involving students in the learning process. Johnson (1979) discussed the advantages of this approach when he wrote:

> The successful mastery, retention, and transfer of concepts, rules, and principles is higher in cooperatively structured learning than in competitive or individualistic learning. . . . Members of cooperative groups evolve superior strategies for conceptual learning, seek and utilize others' information more effectively, cognitively rehearse and formulate in their own words the material being learned, and cover more material in a shorter period of time. . . .
>
>   The more cooperative students' attitudes and experiences, the more they see themselves as being intrinsically motivated, persevering in pursuit of clearly defined learning goals, believing it is their own efforts that determine school success, wanting to be good students and get good grades, and believing that ideas, feelings and learning new ideas are important and positive . . . students experiencing cooperative instruction like the teacher better and perceive the teacher as being more supportive and accepting (academically and personally) than do students experiencing competitive or individualistic instruction. (pp. 149–151)

Working cooperatively with peers also creates positive peer relationships and enhances students' self-esteem.

Teachers interested in implementing cooperative learning can choose from a wide variety of methods. Cooperative learning methods, however, generally fall into three types or approaches: (1) simple structure, (2) process, and (3) extended structure.

Simple Structure Activities

Simple structures refer to activities teachers can use periodically to stimulate discussion and review materials. In his book *Cooperative Learning: Resources for Teachers,* Kagan (1989) presented a number of simple structure activities that can be used in any subject matter. Roundtable is one activity in which the teacher asks a question that has numerous possible answers—such as to list all the possible causes of the Civil War or all the common denominators for 24 and 42. Students then make a list on one sheet of paper, with each student adding one answer and passing the paper to the left. Numbered Heads Together is another activity. Students are again asked a question and placed in small groups to develop an answer. Each student in the group is assigned a number. The students work until the teacher signals them to stop. The teacher then calls out a number and each student assigned that number raises his or her hand. This student is the group's representative and can be called on to present the group's answer.

Another simple structure activity called Stars is used to review material and prepare students for a quiz or test. After the teacher has presented the material, study groups of three or four students of mixed abilities are assigned. Each group is asked to develop five questions related to the material being studied and to provide the correct answer for each question. Each member of the group makes a copy of this material. The next task (usually occurring the following day) involves creating quiz groups consisting of students from different study groups. In the quiz group one person at a time reads a question from his or her list and the other students write down the answer they think is correct. The person who read the question then provides the correct answer and the person to the right asks the next question. This process continues until each person has read all the questions prepared by the study group. The questions are then collected and the teacher prepares a test from these questions.

Teachers interested in developing simple structure cooperative activities can find excellent ideas in *Cooperative Learning: Resources for Teachers* by Spencer Kagan (1989) (available by writing Resources for Teachers, Suite 201, 27402 Camini Capistrano, Laguna Niguel, CA 92677) and in Johnson and Johnson's (1985) *Cooperative Learning: Warm-Ups, Grouping Strategies and Group Activities.*

Process Approach

David and Roger Johnson have conducted numerous research studies and written extensively on cooperative learning. Their approach highlights a *process* or series of steps teachers can apply to implement cooperative learning with any subject matter. The Johnsons have stated that there are five basic elements of this process (Johnson, Johnson, & Johnson-Holubec, 1988):

1. *Positive interdependence.* This element involves structuring goals and activities so that students must be concerned about the performance of all members of the group. This can be accomplished through such methods as providing only one copy of the material (materials interdependence), assigning each group member a role (role interdependence), making success dependent on all members' reaching a specified goal (goal interdependence), assigning the same grade or reward to each group member (reward interdependence), or providing each member only a portion of the information necessary to complete the task (resource interdependence). The key is that the group members know that they are in it together and that they sink or swim together.

2. *Individual accountability.* This means that every student is accountable for mastering the material. This can be accomplished through the traditional means of having each student take a quiz or otherwise demonstrate competence. It can also be created by indicating to students that any group member can be asked to demonstrate mastery of the content by being called to the overhead or by being called on in some other way.

3. *Face-to-face interaction.* Students are arranged in such a manner that they are knee to knee and eye to eye and are involved in actively sharing and discussing the content.

4. *Teaching collaborative skills.* To function effectively in groups, students must learn how to work cooperatively in a small group. Figure 6.16 lists specific group skills the authors have found it important to teach students. Figure 6.17 presents the steps Johnson and Johnson (1987) have outlined for teaching students cooperative skills.

5. *Processing group skills.* Once students have been introduced to cooperative group skills, it is necessary to monitor and reinforce these skills consistently. This

FIGURE 6.16
Group
Collaborative
Skills

1. State the assignment.
2. State the group process goal(s).
3. Call attention to the time limit.
4. Assign group roles (if used).
5. Proceed with the assignment.
6. Summarize the activity.
7. Evaluate the group process skills.

task will initially be accomplished by the teacher, but it can be transferred to students as they develop proficiency in the skills. When initially teaching and monitoring group skills, it is best to focus on one or two skills at a time. As students become more familiar with group skills, they can be monitored on three to five skills at a time. Figure 6.18 provides an example of a form the authors have found helpful for monitoring group skills.

Figure 6.19 presents the steps Johnson, Johnson, and Johnson-Holubec (1988) suggested for teachers who are interested in incorporating cooperative learning into their classroom. Teachers interested in incorporating the Johnsons' approach to cooperative learning into their classrooms can find a variety of materials available and can also attend well-designed workshops to develop the needed experience and skills. The materials the authors have found most helpful are *Learning Together and Alone, Circles of Learning, Cooperation in the Classroom,* and *Cooperative Learning: Warm-Ups, Grouping Strategies and Group Activities.* (These materials can be ordered through Interaction Book Company, 7208 Cornelia Drive, Edina, MN 55435. Additional information can be obtained through the Cooperative Learning Center, the University of Minnesota, (612) 624-7031.)

Extended Structure Approach

Robert Slavin and his colleagues at Johns Hopkins University have produced several approaches and a variety of methods that combine cooperation and competition with a game or tournament activity. These methods are referred to as Student Team

FIGURE 6.17
Helping
Students
Develop
Collaborative
Skills

1. Do students believe the skill is needed and useful?
2. Do students understand what the skill is, what the behaviors are, what the sequence of behaviors is, and how it looks when it is all put together?
3. Have students had an opportunity to practice the skill?
4. Have students received feedback that is immediate, descriptive, and specific?
5. Have students persevered in practicing the skill?
6. Have students had the opportunity to use the skill successfully?
7. Have students used the skill frequently enough so that they have integrated the skill into their natural behavior?
8. Do the classroom norms support the use of the skill?

Tally the number of times student demonstrate a skill.

Skill	Group One				Group Two		
	Bob	Nancy	Tariq		Rolando	Marissa	Beryl
Contributes ideas							
Encourages others							
Listens							
Participates							
Checks for understanding							
Organizes the task							

FIGURE 6.18   Teacher Observation Sheet

Learning. The most popular are Teams Games Tournament and Student Teams–Achievement Division.

Teams Games Tournament (TGT) includes four steps. First, the teacher presents material to the whole class. Second, students study together in heterogeneous groups of four or five to master content and prepare for a tournament at the end of the week. Third, students are assigned to tables comprising three students of similar ability and from different teams. The three students compete at academic games (usually questions on cards or dittos prepared by the teacher) to demonstrate mastery of material covered that week. By answering questions, students earn points for their team. Fourth, the points earned by team members at their various tables are totaled to determine the team's weekly score. These scores are often published in a weekly newsletter as a means to provide students with recognition for their efforts. In addition, depending on individual performance in the weekly tournament, the teacher may rearrange the groups to ensure that all groups have an opportunity to experience success.

Student Teams–Achievement Division (STAD) is a modified form of TGT. In this approach, weekly individual quizzes replace the tournaments, but points are still totaled for the group and recognition is provided for group scores. STAD has become increasingly popular because it is easier to implement than TGT. Also, because it does not include face-to-face competition, it is less competitive; this is important for some students. (Information on the use of these methods can be

FIGURE 6.19
The Teacher's
Role in
Cooperation

Make Decisions

Specify Academic and Collaborative Objectives. What academic and/or collaborative skills do you want students to learn or practice in their groups? Start with something easy.

Decide on Group Size. Students often lack collaborative skills, so start with groups of two or three students; later advance cautiously to fours.

Assign Students to Groups. Heterogeneous groups are the most powerful, so mix abilities, sexes, cultural backgrounds, and task orientations. Assign students to groups randomly or select groups yourself.

Arrange the Room. The closer the students are to each other, the better they can communicate. Group members should be "knee to knee and eye to eye."

Plan Materials. Materials can send a "sink or swim together" message to students if you give only one paper to the group or give each member part of the material to learn and then teach the group.

Assign Roles. Students are more likely to work together if each one has a job which contributes to the task. You can assign work roles such as Reader, Recorder, Calculator, Checker, Reporter, and Materials Handler or skill roles such as Encourager of Participation, Praiser, and Checker for Understanding.

Set the Lesson

Explain the Academic Task. Prepare students by teaching them any material they need to know, then make certain they clearly understand what they are to do in the groups. This might include explaining lesson objectives, defining concepts, explaining procedures, giving examples, and asking questions.

*Structure Positive Interdependence. Students must feel that they need each other to complete the group's task, that they "sink or swim together." Some ways to create this are by establishing mutual goals (students must learn the material and make certain group members learn the material), joint rewards (if all group members achieve above a certain percentage on the test, each will receive bonus points), shared materials and information, and assigned roles.

*Structure Individual Accountability. Each student must feel responsible for learning the material and helping the group. Some ways to ensure this feeling include frequent oral quizzing of group members picked at random, giving individual tests, having everyone in the group write (pick one paper at random to grade), or having students do work first to bring to the group.

Structure Intergroup Cooperation. Having groups check with and help other groups and giving rewards or praise when all class members do well can extend the benefits of cooperation to the whole class.

Explain the Criteria for Success. Student work should be evaluated on a criteria-referenced rather than a norm-referenced basis. Make clear your criteria for evaluating the groups' work.

Specify Expected Behaviors. The more specific you are about the behaviors you want to see in the groups, the more likely students will do them. Make it clear that you expect to see everyone contributing, helping, listening with care to others, encouraging others to participate, and asking for help or clarification. Younger students may need to be told to stay with their group, take turns, share, ask group members questions, and use quiet voices.

*Teach Collaborative Skills. After students are used to working in groups, pick one collaborative skill they need to learn, point out the need for it, define it carefully, have

students give you phrases they can say when using the skill, post the phrases (praise, bonus points, stars), and observe for and encourage the use of the skill until students are doing it automatically. Then teach a second skill. Consider praising, summarizing, encourageing, checking for understanding, asking for help, or generating further answers.

Monitor and Intervene

Arrange Face-to-Face Interaction. The beneficial educational outcomes of cooperative learning groups are due to the interaction patterns and verbal exchanges that take place among students. Make certain there is oral summarizing, giving and receiving explanations, and elaborating going on.

Monitor Students' Behavior. This is the fun part! While students are working, you circulate to see whether they understand the assignment and the material, give immediate feedback and reinforcement, and praise good use of group skills.

Provide Task Assistance. If students are having trouble with the task, you can clarify, reteach, or elaborate on what they need to know.

Intervene to Teach Collaborative Skills. If students are having trouble with group interactions, you can suggest more effective procedures for working together or more effective behaviors for them to engage in. You can ask students to figure out how to work more effectively together. If students are learning or practicing a skill, record on an observation sheet how often you hear that skill, then share your observations with the groups.

Evaluate and Process

Evaluate Student Learning. Assess how well students complete the task and give them feedback on how well they did.

Process Group Functioning. In order to improve, students need time and procedures for analyzing how well their group is functioning and how well they are using collaborative skills. Processing can be done by individuals, small groups, or the whole class. To start, have groups routinely list three things they did well in working together today and one thing they will do better tomorrow. Then summarize as a whole class.

Provide Closure. To reinforce student learning you may wish to have groups share answers or paper, summarize major points in the lesson, or review important facts.

*Essential Elements of Cooperative Learning Groups

Source: From *Cooperation in the Classroom* (pp. 2-38–2-39) by D. Johnson, R. Johnson, and E. Johnson-Holubec, 1988, Edina, MN: Interaction Book Co. Reprinted by permission.

obtained by writing The Johns Hopkins Team Learning Project, Center for Research on Elementary and Middle Schools, The Johns Hopkins University, 3505 N. Charles Street, Baltimore, MD 21218.)

Summary of Cooperative Learning

In general, research seems to indicate that cooperative learning activities that include some form of competition and group rewards are more effective than those that depend on the benefits of students' working together. However, the benefits of cooperative learning are considerable even when these variables are not a major focus of the activity. Given the problems associated with competition and rewards, teachers are encouraged to focus as much as possible on the benefits of improved learning for all students, to help individual students and the class keep records of learning gains, and to emphasize the joy in assisting one another. Also, teachers should emphasize social and activity reinforcement and minimize the use of concrete, tangible rewards for achievement gains.

It is also important to realize that none of the authors or trainers involved in cooperative learning believes it should replace teacher-directed instruction. Even though cooperative learning can be used to generate ideas or can serve as a pretest to determine students' knowledge, students need to learn material from teachers and in many cases do not have the skill to develop new information or a new concept. Therefore, cooperative learning is most effective when it is used to practice or work on the application of material first introduced by a teacher. As noted earlier in this chapter, cooperative learning can be used in the context of different learning activities intended to meet the needs of students with varying learning styles. Cooperative learning is a technique that supports and enhances a number of instructional decisions, but it is not intended to be an end in itself. Nevertheless, the benefits of using cooperative learning are considerable, and we encourage readers not currently using this method to consider incorporating it into their instructional repertoire. Good and Brophy (1987) effectively summarized the value of cooperative learning:

> Achievement effects appear to be positive for all types of students, although there are some indications that black and Hispanic students gain even more from cooperative learning arrangements than Anglo students do. Effects on outcomes other than achievement are even more impressive. Cooperative learning arrangements promote friendship choices and prosocial patterns of interaction among students who differ in achievement, sex, race, or ethnicity, and they promote the acceptance of mainstreamed handicapped students by their nonhandicapped classmates. Cooperative methods also frequently have positive effects, and rarely have negative effects, on affective outcomes such as self-esteem, academic self-confidence, liking for the class, liking and feeling liked by classmates, and various measures of empathy and social cooperation. (p. 416)

When implementing cooperative learning, teachers should realize that having students work in groups, even when the teacher has structured the activity to encourage positive interdependence and individual accountability, will not ensure a productive learning environment. As with any other activity (see Chapter 8), teachers need to instruct students in the classroom procedures to be followed when involved in cooperative learning activities, such as the following:

1. Do the students clearly understand their task and the associated learning goals?
2. Do the students understand why you have chosen to use group work to facilitate their learning the content?
3. Do the students find intrinsic, achievement, or utility value in the material?

4. Do the students possess the skills necessary to complete the task; that is, do they know how to use the materials, and can at least several students in each group read any written material associated with the task?

5. Are all materials readily available, and has a procedure been established so they can be easily obtained?

6. Do the students know how much time they have to complete the task?

7. Do the students know what they should do if they require assistance?

8. Do the students know what to do if they finish early or what options are available if they cannot complete the task in the allotted time?

9. Have you established a method for gaining the students' attention should it be necessary to add an instruction, clarify a problem, or ask the groups to stop their work?

10. Do the students know the behaviors that will be expected of them while they work in the group?

Using Peer Tutoring

A number of benefits can be derived from implementing peer tutoring in a classroom. First, tutoring fosters the concept that asking for and offering help are positive behaviors. This act encourages cooperation and concern for peers and thereby creates a more supportive, safe learning environment. Second, the opportunity to instruct another child can provide a student with a sense of competence and personal worth. Third, in assisting another student, the student frequently learns the material more thoroughly. The combination of increased understanding and the act of instructing another student frequently makes a student a more excited and confident learner. Finally, peer tutoring helps the teacher monitor and individualize instruction. By allowing students to serve as resources for other students, the teacher increases the availability of individual attention and thereby reduce students' frustration and the accompanying acting-out behavior.

Although peer tutoring has many benefits, it can become a frustrating and counterproductive activity if students are not provided with skills in how to assist each other. Therefore, it is important that if you plan to implement peer tutoring, then provide your students with instruction in how to assist another student. Do so by listing and discussing the dos and don'ts of helping someone with the work. You can then model appropriate behavior and then allow students to practice this behavior and receive feedback. If the equipment is available, students can be videotaped while assisting other students, and the tape can be viewed and discussed. An exciting aspect of providing students with instruction in how to teach another student is that this activity helps them better understand the learning process.

There are numerous approaches to implementing peer tutoring. Students can be provided with green and red 8½-inch square cards attached to their desks so that they can be displayed in front of the desk. Students who need help during seatwork can display a red card, and students who understand this material and are willing to assist other students can display a green card. This procedure can be particularly helpful when you are busy working with a small group and are not available to assist students. A similar approach involves listing on the board the names of students who are able to assist their peers on a project.

Assigning individual students to work with a student who needs assistance is another common approach to peer tutoring. This activity may involve students in the same class or students from higher grades. Another method involves arranging students' desks in groups of four and informing students that they may assist their peers as long as they follow previously learned procedures for effective teaching.

One of the authors observed a young teacher presenting an art lesson to a group of eighth-grade students. The teacher was working with a particularly difficult class, The class included several students whom the school had characterized as behavior problems, as well as a boy who was very withdrawn and who had emotional problems. The teacher indicated that she was somewhat concerned about the day's lesson because she had a very limited background in the material she was presenting. She also said that the last period of the day on a particularly nice spring day was not the ideal time to be teaching eighth-graders a concept as difficult as depth perception. With this introduction, the author was prepared to observe chaos and to have numerous opportunities for observing the teacher's skills in dealing with behavior problems.

The teacher began the lesson by briefly reviewing the material she had presented on the previous day. She appeared comfortable responding to a variety of students' questions. On one occasion, a student pointed out a major flaw in something she had presented. The teacher indicated that she did not see his point and asked the student if he would be willing to come up to the board and clarify his point for both her and the class. The student did so, and the class responded politely to his brief instruction.

After perhaps 10 minutes of instruction, the teacher indicated that the students should continue working on their assignments. She commented that some students were finding the tasks more difficult than others and suggested that when they had a problem, they find another student to help them. As students began working on their projects, the teacher circulated around the room answering students' questions and reinforcing students' work. It soon became apparent, however, that she could not possibly answer all the questions that were being fired at her. Her interventions then changed from direct work with students to serving as a clearing center for resources available within the classroom. As she moved around the room, she made comments such as, "Why don't you ask John? He does a good job with two-point perspective," "It might help, Bill, if you could explain to Maria why you . . . ," "I really appreciate your helping, Sue. You did a really good job of teaching because you helped him to discover the answer for himself."

The author was impressed with the extremely high percentage of on-task behavior displayed by the students. In addition, the teacher's role as facilitator freed her to spend much time with her most severely disturbed student. Because she had structured students' responses to be positive and supportive, students' interactions throughout the class period were extremely positive. In addition to assisting each other, students frequently showed their work to their peers and almost always received either compliments or constructive suggestions.

In examining the dynamics of this class period, it is interesting to recall Postman and Weingartner's (1969) statement that teachers should perhaps teach subjects outside of their area of academic preparation. When teaching subjects they understand extremely well, teachers often do all the teaching while the students are forced into the role of passive learner. On the other hand, when teachers are learning the material or are somewhat unsure of the content, it may be easier to allow students to become involved as co-learners and team teachers. It may appear that material is being covered more slowly (and perhaps more noisily) when using this format, but the theoretical considerations and research results presented earlier in this section point to many advantages associated with this form of instruction.

An increasingly popular approach to peer tutoring involves creating support groups outside the classroom for students who have the ability to complete their work but who have experienced serious and persistent achievement problems. Sullivan (1988) reported the results of a special study groups program for middle school students whose ability levels indicated that they could pass their courses but who were failing one or more courses. Students were involved in weekly study skills meetings with the vice-principal, met with their group to work on assignments several times a week, and received a progress report every Friday. Results indicated that 50 percent of the total number of grades received by students in the study skills groups went up at least one grade, and only 10 percent of the grades went down. Results for a control group showed that only 14 percent of the grades went up.

A Case Study

This case study, taken verbatim from a project completed by a high school English teacher as part of her work in a graduate education course, typifies how you can incorporate ideas found throughout this book to help individual students reach their potential. The authors chose this example because:

1. It was carried out and written by a teacher who deals with 140 students each day.
2. The teacher developed and carried out the project with no assistance.
3. The teacher has just completed a course using this text as the major source-book.

> At first I didn't take much notice of Bill in my freshman and sophomore-level writing class. He's one of those quiet, unobtrusive students, the kind you love to use in a seating chart as a barrier between the class clown and a social butterfly. Rarely, if ever, did he call attention to himself. He never raised his hand to volunteer an answer, and when called on, would struggle so to come up with an appropriate response that I would too frequently—to avoid his obvious embarrassment—cut short his efforts and recognize one of the hands waving excitedly around him. He is never late to class; he has never asked for a hall pass; he never questions directions or instructions for an assignment; he seldom visits in class with his neighbors; he always appears to listen attentively to lectures. Therefore, next to the 140 other students who come to me daily with varying levels of ability and enthusiasm for "creative writing," Bill, at first, didn't demand a lot of my attention.
>
> A couple of weeks into the term, however, I began to notice that in fact Bill was becoming a problem of the subtler type; he was not doing his assignments. In fact, his pattern of behavior seemed suspiciously close to what has been categorized as "failure

syndrome"—a feeling of defeatism and helplessness resulting from repeated failure. Therefore, after three weeks of inconsistent, below-class-average performance, I decided to investigate Bill's history as a student in our district.

I discovered that in his elementary years he was apparently a pleasure to his teachers. Their comments on his conduct and citizenship grades suggested he was a model of exemplary behavior, and his academic marks were "satisfactory" or better. In junior high school, however, his grades began to slip, notably, those earned in English dropped to a "D" average throughout his seventh and eighth grades. As a result, his junior high English teachers recommended that he be placed in Sentences (our low-level remedial-writing class) during the first term of his freshman year in high school. Let there be no doubt that, as well-intentioned as this program may be, a stigma is attached to this placement as surely as if these students wore a badge that proclaimed their lack of proficiency and their below-average performance. At any rate, in Sentences he earned a term grade of "C minus" and was promoted the next year to Paragraphs. That is where our paths crossed.

Next, I checked into Bill's current C.A.T. scores. The grade-level score for overall comprehension for his age group is 9.7; Bill's score was 7.7—two years below grade level. On the Gates Reading Test he had scored 8.3 on comprehension; the grade-level score is 9.3. He scored about a year below grade level, no small consideration in a class such as writing, which is a complex activity requiring mature, advanced mental operations. Therefore, his scores indicated that many of the writing tasks I required of him were quite possibly beyond his level of competence.

I wondered about his other classes. So I sent a Progress Report form to his other teachers to determine how successful he was in his other courses. The results were that in classes requiring incremental, concrete, mechanical exercises he was doing above-average work. But in the majority of his classes—those requiring more abstract, complex cognitive processes—his grades were below average. Unfortunately, the beginning of a pattern seemed to be developing that, without intervention, sooner or later would probably lead to resignation on his part.

Glasser's theory indicated what my first move should be: provide a caring atmosphere. I decided to make a point of casually noticing him, smiling and saying hello as he entered the classroom daily. I routinely do this to my students at random, and so this notice didn't cause him to be unduly curious. But each day I made sure I spoke to him until it became a habit for both of us. The next step he provided. He received the "Outstanding Athlete of the Week" award, for which I, of course, complimented him and placed his newspaper picture on a bulletin board in my room where "Class Heroes" who have received such an honor get recognition of some sort. On seeing his picture in this spot and receiving accolades from his classmates, I believe his chest size must have expanded three inches.

While he was feeling more comfortable and "invited" in the classroom, he seemed to be gaining confidence in himself, which was reflected in his assignments. (And was I also—albeit unconsciously—giving him more credit as a struggling student who deserved the benefit of the doubt?) I used as many opportunities as possible to reaffirm these signs of success—praised his improved writing, included a well-written narrative paper (on soccer, naturally) as a class model for effective writing. As research on attribution theory suggests, low-achieving students need to be reminded that their success is due to their efforts. A "Happy-Gram" sent home mentioning specifically his particularly good narrative paragraph, followed two weeks later by his "Goal Completion Award" seemed to be the turning points that altered his downward slide in my class.

During this intervention I made some academic changes as well as the social ones. First, I allowed more flexibility in the topics I assigned for writing projects so that Bill (and the other students) had more options to choose from. The more interested he was in a topic, the more knowledgeable he was about it, and the more motivated he became to write. I also began to assess his learning style—both by analyzing the type of assignments he did well on and by conversations with him when I asked for feedback. As a result, after giving directions for an assignment, I used my "roaming" time for private contact with him to clarify his understanding and review his independent work, making solicited suggestions so that I could spot misunderstandings and frustrations and offer followup assistance. I also began to use a different approach to grading his writing. Martin and Lauridsen (1974) suggest in *Developing Student Discipline and Motivation* that students needs to be graded on an individual basis. Consequently, I allowed him to compete against himself and not his more academically mature class-mates, so that his continuous progress merited praise. Then, because he was growing in confidence and self-esteem, the next step seemed to be to try the suggestions of Johnson and Johnson (1987) and allow Bill to work in a group. Their research suggests that successfully orchestrated group work increases confidence in one's ability. And so I arranged for Bill to participate in a peer editing group in which he was both academically and socially compatible. In this setting, a feeling of interdependence grew between him and members of the group, fostering sociability, responsibility, and self-esteem.

Meanwhile, research by Jones (1980) suggests that students should share the respon-sibility in behavior modification by some type of self-monitoring. Therefore, it became Bill's responsibility to keep personal records on a weekly Progress Report form I filled out. He also continued to keep a class notebook in which he copied daily assignments from the board and kept them in front of his notebook as a type of table of contents. The completed assignment then, after it was graded and returned, was kept chrono-logically in his notebook and a check mark was made on the assignment page. As a back-up reminder, in case an assignment did not get turned in by the deadline, we agreed that a "Homework Alert" notice was to be sent home, signed by his parent, and returned to me within two days. If the card was not returned within the time limit, Bill was aware I would be calling home to discuss the situation with his parent. This back-up strategy was never necessary, however. In fact, during the past five weeks, Bill has missed only one assignment (because of a late soccer game and a long bus ride home).

A statement by Jere Brophy (1982b) summarizes my intervention best:

> For example, in dealing with failure-syndrome students who have essentially given up attempts to cope with classroom demands, effective teachers refuse to cave in by reducing task demands and treating these students as if they are really unable to succeed in the classroom. Instead, they approach such students with a mixture of sympathy, encouragement, and demands. These teachers reassure the students that they do have ability and that work given will not be too difficult for them. Then, the teachers help them to get started when they are discouraged or need some support, reinforce their progress, and perhaps offer contracts providing rewards for accomplishments and allowing opportunities for students to set goals. In general, the emphasis is on encouragement and help rather than prodding through threat of punishment. Failure-syndrome students are not merely *told* that they can succeed, but *shown* convincingly that they can, and helped to do so. (p. 23)

These suggestions seemed to have worked in providing more realistic expectations, building self-confidence, and in creating a more comfortable classroom in which Bill could become the student he can be.

IMPLEMENTATION ACTIVITIES

As discussed in Chapter 2, students' needs may be discovered by analyzing the classroom environment in light of theories and research, by asking students to provide specific feedback, or both. This section provides six activities you can use to consider how effectively you are meeting student's academic needs.

ACTIVITY 6.1
Evaluating a Classroom Environment in Light of Students' Academic Needs

For each of the 12 student academic needs listed in Figure 6.1, list two ways in which you currently meet the need within the classroom. Be specific. For example: I use interest centers to respond to students' needs to follow their own interests. If you are not currently teaching, select a classroom that you have observed recently.

Next list two specific ways in which you could alter your teaching methods in order to meet these needs more effectively.

ACTIVITY 6.2
Analyzing Students' Behavior Problems

If you are having problems with the behavior of a student or group of students, it is important to consider instructional factors that may be causing the problem. First, write the name of the student or students who are creating the most difficulty for you in class. Next, complete the form in Figure 6.20 for each student you have listed. After carefully examining your responses, answer these questions:

One reason this student(s) may be acting out in my class is . . . .
This activity made me realize that . . . .
In order to help this student(s) behave more appropriately in this class, I will need to . . . .
Two specific things I will change in this class or with this specific student are . . . .

ACTIVITY 6.3
Assessing Instructional Factors Related to Student Motivation

Select a recent lesson you taught. For the lesson you have selected, write a brief statement describing what you did or said to introduce the lesson. For this same instructional activity, write a brief statement indicating how you taught the material to the students. On a 1- to 5-scale (5 being the highest), rate how effectively this lesson responded to the academic needs listed here.

Students' Academic Needs
____ Understand and value the learning goals
____ Understand the learning process
____ Be actively involved in the learning process
____ Relate subject matter to their own lives
____ Control the learning environment by setting goals or following their own interests
____ Experience success

_____ Receive realistic and immediate feedback that enhances self-efficacy
_____ Receive rewards for performance gains
_____ See learning modeled by adults as an exciting and rewarding activity
_____ Experience an appropriate amount of structure
_____ Have time to integrate learning
_____ Have positive contact with peers
_____ Receive instruction matched to their skill level and learning style

---

ACTIVITY 6.4
Using Student's Input to Determine the Extent to Which Their Academic Needs Are Being Met in a Classroom

Students can provide us with helpful information on how well the classroom environment is meeting their academic needs. The questionnaire in Figure 6.21 is an example of an instrument that can be administered to discover how students feel about their classroom.

To complete this activity, administer the questionnaire provided or modify it to fit the skill level of the children completing the form. Tally the results as suggested in Figure 2.4. When the results have been tallied, analyze the data by completing these items:

1. List all the statements that more than five students responded to with the responses "Always true" or "Most of the time."
2. List all the statements to which a majority of students responded with the responses "Occasionally" or "Never true."
3. Write three responses to the statement: I learned that . . . .
4. Based on this new information, write three statements about changes you would like to make in your classroom.

ACTIVITY 6.5
Responding to Variations in Learning Styles

Create a chart like the following: List the instructional activities you have used (or those you have seen used if you are currently observing a classroom rather than teaching) during the past two days. Behind each activity, indicate the type of cognitive skill it emphasizes.

Instructional Activity	*Right Brain (RB)* *Left Brain (LB)* *Integrative (I)*	*Abstract Sequential (AS)* *Abstract Random (AR)* *Concrete Sequential (CS)* *Concrete Random (CR)*
1.		
2.		
3.		
5.		
6.		
7.		

Tally the responses to provide yourself with an indication of the number of activities that fell into each category (e.g., 10 left-brain activities, 2 right-brain, and 7 integrative).

(continued)

ACTIVITY 6.5
Continued

> Within the lessons you have planned (if you are not in a classroom, design a set of lesson plans), attempt for two days to use instructional activities that fall into each category. You may wish to design a lesson that incorporates Bernice McCarthy's four learning-style types.
>
> After teaching these lessons, answer these questions:
>
> Did you notice any differences in students' behavior during the two days in which the lessons were more balanced? Describe these differences.
> Were any particular students noticeably more involved or better behaved or both during these two days? If so, which students were they?
> How did you feel during these two days?
>
> Complete these sentences:
>
> I learned that . . . .
> I was surprised that . . . .
> In the future I will try to . . . .

ACTIVITY 6.6
Demystifying
Learning

> Turn to Figure 6.6. Circle the number of each method you currently utilize in your classroom or a classroom in which you are observing. Place a box around the number of each activity you would like to implement in your classroom. Finally, place an X through any activities you believe are simply not appropriate for your teaching style or students at your grade level. After completing this, meet with two or three other teachers or members of your class and review each item on the list. Each time someone has a box around one of the numbers, see if the others in your group can share how they or someone they know implements this method.

SUMMARY

Until recently, research, theory, and in-service education in the area of classroom management and school discipline ignored the relationship between student behavior and students' attitudes toward learning. Classroom management focuses on how to increase on-task behavior with relatively little attention paid to whether the curriculum and instructional methods motivated students to learn. Fortunately, educators are becoming increasingly aware of the relationship between student motivation and students' behavior. Such well-known educators as Jere Brophy, William Glasser, John Goodlad, Joan Lipsitz, Ted Sizer, and Ernest Boyer emphasize that the motivational quality of the learning environment is a key factor influencing student learning and behavior. This chapter examines the key factors that influence the degree to which students are motivated to learn and will become positively engaged in instructional activities. When these factors are ignored, teachers find themselves spending much time attempting to control student behavior. When these student needs are met, however, a greater portion of students' classroom behavior becomes directed toward completing learning tasks.

FIGURE 6.20
Analyzing the
Classroom
Environment

As you present you next lesson or assignment in an area in which a student or group of students has had trouble, notice:

	Almost Always	Sometimes	Almost Never
1. Is the subject area one in which the student has always failed?			
2. Can the student read at whatever level the material is presented?			
3. Is the assignment clear enough so the student knows exactly what is expected?			
4. Is the task at a level of difficulty that is challenging but which offers a chance of successful completion for the individual (rather than for the class average)?			
5. Is the material presented in a manner which seems to interest the student: written, lecture, audiovisual, programmed workbook, independent work, group assignments, etc? Is the material content of interest?			
6. Is enough time allowed to get into the assignment and develop an interest and complete the task satisfactorily?			
7. Will the student be graded on an individual basis so that successful completion will get a good grade?			
8. Is there a pleasant consequence that you know appeals to the student (possibly chosen by the student) that will follow successful completion of the task?			
9. Is there some motivating consequence to at least complete part of the assignment, even if the student cannot complete all of it?			
10. Do you give the student another chance to do the assignment correctly and to improve the grade?			
11. Do you give more attention to the student when he tries a task than you do when he refuses to try?			

Source: From *Developing Student Discipline and Motivation* by Reed Martin and David Lauridsen. © 1974 by Research Press, Champaign, IL 61820. Reprinted by permission.

FIGURE 6.21   Student Academic Needs Questionnaire

Please check the appropriate box	Always True 100%	Most of the Time 75%	Half of the Time 50%	Occasionally 25%	Never True 0%
Understand the teacher's goal					
1. Do you understand the goals for each lesson?					
2 Do you know the purpose of or reason assignments are given?					
3 Do I explain new material well enough to you?					
4. Are the directions in class clear?					
Actively involved in the learning process					
5. Do you frequently raise your hand to answer a question?					
6, Do you get a chance to share your ideas in class?					
7. Have you suggested changes for our classroom?					
8. Is there a good balance for you in the amount of time spent in small- and large-group activities?					
Relate subject matter to their own lives					
9. Do you see the skills taught in this class as being useful in some other area of your life?					
10. Are you asked to collect information or materials from outside of school to use in school assignments?					
Follow own interests					
11. Are you able to study subjects or ideas that interest you?					
12. Do you get to make choices about the topics you study?					
Experience success					
13. Do you feel good about how much you are learning?					
14. Do you experience success in your academic work?					
15. Do you accomplish academic goals that you set?					

Please check the appropriate box	Always True 100%	Most of the Time 75%	Half of the Time 50%	Occasionally 25%	Never True 0%
Receive realistic and immediate feedback					
16. Are my comments on your work help-ful?					
17. Do tests give you information about what you have learned?					
18. Do tests and assignments help you see what skills you still need to prac-tice?					
Experience an appropriate amount of structure					
19. Does this class seem organized?					
20. Do you know when work is due?					
21. Are deadlines reasonable?					
22. Are you aware of your progress in this class?					
23. Do you understand the class rules and procedures?					
Time to integrate learning					
24. Do I allow enough time for questions?					
25. Is there enough review time before a test?					
26. Is there enough practice on each skill before going on to a new one?					
Have positive contact with peers					
27. Are other students accepting of your ideas?					
28. Do people listen carefully to whoever is speaking?					
29. Do students in this class help each other?					
Receive instruction matched to skill level and learning style					
30. Are most of the assignments in class challenging to you?					
31. Do you feel that you have a variety of choices for exhibiting your knowledge?					
32. Does the way I teach help you learn the material?					

RECOMMENDED READING

Ames, C., & Ames, R. (Eds.). (1984). *Research on motivation in education. Vol. I: Student motivation.* New York: Academic Press.

Ames, C., & Ames, R. (Eds.). (1985). *Research on motivation in education. Vol. II: The classroom milieu.* Orlando, FL: Academic Press.

Andrini, B. (1991). *Cooperative learning and mathematics: A multistructural approach.* San Juan Capistrano, CA: Resources for Teachers.

Belenky, M., Clinchy, B., Goldberger, N., & Tarule, J. (1986). *Women's ways of knowing: Development of self, body and mind.* New York: Basic Books.

Bernstein, B. (1993). *Cooperative learning in math: Skill-oriented activities that encourage working together.* Carthage, IL: Good Apple.

Breeden, T., & Mosley, J. (1992). *The cooperative learning companion: Ideas, activities, & aids for middle grades.* Nashville, TN: Incentive Publication.

Butler, J. (1993). *Transforming the curriculum: Teaching about women of color.* In J. Banks & C. McGee Banks (Eds.), *Multicultural education.* Boston: Allyn and Bacon.

Bybee, R., & Sund, R. (1982). *Piaget for educators.* Columbus, OH: Charles E. Merrill.

Cantlon, T. (1991). *Structuring the classroom successfully for cooperative team learning.* Portland, OR: Prestige Publishers.

Cantlon, T. (1991). *The first four weeks of cooperative learning: Activities and materials.* Portland, OR: Prestige Publishers.

Carin, A., & Sund, R. (1978). *Creative questioning and sensitive listening techniques.* Columbus, OH: Charles E. Merrill.

Deci, E., & Ryan, R. (1985). *Intrinsic motivation and self-determination in human behavior.* New York: Plenum.

Dewey, J. (1963). *Experience and education.* New York: Macmillan.

Diaz-Rico, L. (1993). From monocultural to multicultual teaching in an inner-city middle school. In A. Woolfolk (Ed.). *Readings in Applied Educational Psychology.* Boston: Allyn and Bacon.

Dishon, D., & Wilson O'Leary, P. (1984). *A guidebook for cooperative learning.* Holmes Beach, FL: Learning Publications.

Dunn, R., & Dunn, K. (1978). *Teaching students through their individual learning styles: A practical approach.* Reston, VA: Reston.

Edwards, B. (1979). *Drawing on the right side of the brain.* Boston: Houghton Mifflin.

Gardner, H. (1993). *Multiple intelligence: The theory into practice.* New York: Basic Books.

Gibbs, J., & Allen, A. (1978). *Tribes: A process for peer involvement.* Lafayette, CA: Center for Human Development.

Good, T., & Brophy, J. (1994). *Looking in classrooms* (6th ed.) (Chap. 6). New York: Harper and Row.

Harmin, M., Kirschenbaum, H., & Simon, S. (1973). *Clarifying values through subject matter.* Minneapolis, MN: Winston Press.

Hart, L. (1983). *Human brain and human learning.* New York: Longmans.

Huggins, P. (1993). *The assist program: Multiple intelligence lessons.* Longmont, CO: Sopris West.

Johnson, D., & Johnson, R. (1987). *Learning together and alone: Cooperative, competitive, and individualistic learnings* (2nd ed.). Englewood Cliffs, NJ: Prentice Hall.

Johnson, D., & Johnson, R. (1984). *Cooperation in the classroom.* Edina, MN: Interaction Book Company.

Johnson, D., Johnson, R., Bartlett, J., & Johnson, L. (1988). *Our cooperative classroom.* Edina, MN: Interaction Book Co.

Johnson, D., Johnson, R., & Johnson-Holubec, E. (1986). *Circles of Learning: Cooperation in the classroom.* Edina, MN: Interaction Book Co.

Johnson, R., & Johnson, D. (1985). *Cooperative learning: Warm-ups, grouping strategies and group activities.* Edina, MN: Interaction Book Co.

Johnson, R., & Johnson, D. (Eds.). (1984). *Structuring cooperative learning: Lesson plans for teachers.* Edina, MN: Interaction Book Co.

Joyce, B., & Weil, M. (1986). *Models of teaching* (3rd ed.). Englewood Cliffs, NJ: Prentice Hall.

Kagan, S. (1985). *Cooperative learning: Resources for teachers.* San Juan Capistrano, CA: Resources for Teachers.

Kagan, S. (1987). *Cooperative learning: Resources for teachers.* Printed by the author—Suite 201, 27402 Camino Capistrano, Laguna Niguel, CA 92677.

Kagan S. (1991). *Cooperative learning: Transparencies for teachers.* San Juan Capistrano, CA: Resources for Teachers.

McCarthy, B. (1987). *The 4-MAT system: Teaching to learning styles with right/left mode techniques.* Barrington, IL: Excel.

McCarthy, B., & Leflar, S. (1983). *4-MAT in action: Creative lesson plans for teaching to learning styles with right/left mode techniques.* Barrington, IL: Excel.

McCarthy, B., Leflar, S., & McNamara, M. (1987). *The 4-MAT workbook: Guided practice in 4-MAT lesson and unit planning.* Barrington, IL: Excel.

McElmurry, M. (1985). *Cooperating: Alternatives to competition in the home and classroom.* Carthage, IL: Good Apple.

Rotalo, S. (1982). *Right-brain lesson plans for a left-brain world—A book of lesson plans for English and speech.* Springfield, IL: Charles C Thomas.

Slavin, R. (1980). *Using student team learning.* The Johns Hopkins University, 3505 N. Charles Street, Baltimore, Md.: The Center for Social Organization of Schools.

Slavin, R. (1983a). *Cooperative learning.* New York: Longman.

Slavin, R. (1983b). *Working together and learning together.* Saskatchewan Department of Cooperation and Cooperative Development, The Stewart Resources Center, S.T.F. Box 1108, Saskatoon, Saskatchewan, S7K3N3.

Sonnenberg, J. (1991). *Cooperative learning, thinking and problem solving.* Minneapolis, MN: T. S. Denison & Co.

Stanish, B. (1981). *Hippogriff feathers: Encounters with creative thinking.* Carthage, IL: Good Apple.

Stone, J. (1991). *Cooperative learning and language arts: A multistructural approach.* San Juan Capistrano, CA: Resources for Teachers.

Tetreault, M. (1992). *How schools shortchange girls.* Washington, DC: NEA.

Tetreault, M. (1993). Classrooms for diversity: Rethinking curriculum and pedagogy. In J. Banks & C. McGee Banks (Eds.), *Multicultural education.* Boston: Allyn and Bacon.

PART IV

Minimizing Disruptive Behavior and Increasing Learning by Effective Classroom Organization and Management

In his chapter on classroom organization and management in the third edition of *Handbook of Research on Teaching,* Walter Doyle (1986) wrote, "Broadly speaking, classroom teaching has two major task structures organized around the problems of (a) learning and (b) order. Learning is served by the instructional function. . . . Order is served by the managerial function, that is, by organizing classroom groups, establishing rules and procedures, reacting to misbehavior, monitoring and pacing classroom events, and the like" (p. 395). In the previous section, we examined some important findings on instructional methods that teachers can use to increase the likelihood that students will be motivated by learning tasks and will benefit from instruction. Section IV focuses on the second major task associated with classroom teaching: maintaining order in the classroom.

Studies indicate that the amount of time students are engaged in instructional activities vary from less than 50 percent in some classes to more than 90 percent in others (Fisher, Filby, Marliave, Cahen, Dishaw, Moore, & Berliner, 1978). This section helps you increase the time students spend actively engaged in learning. More effective teachers use their management time wisely and thereby enhance the time available for instruction and monitoring student work. In a study of eight secondary schools, Stallings and Mohlman (1981) found that effective teachers spent less than 15 percent of their time organizing and managing their classes. Teachers who effectively use the time needed to organize and manage classrooms can minimize the time required for these important functions.

Chapter 7 lists in detail strategies that effective teachers use when presenting material to students and monitoring students' seatwork. Researchers have demonstrated that use of these strategies is associated with higher rates of on-task student behavior and greater academic achievement.

While the methods described in Chpater 7 have been gleaned primarily from research in classes using a direct instruction and seatwork approach to teaching and learning, many of them apply to classes in which students are more actively engaged in learning. The authors and many of their students (both beginning and veteran teachers) have found these methods to apply in a wide range of instructional settings—including those in which students are actively involved in construction their own knowledge and meaning.

Chapter 8 presents the methods effective teachers use at the beginning of the school year. The text emphasizes strategies for teaching classroom rules and ensuring that all students learn such key classroom procedures as what to do during the first few minutes of class, how to request assistance with seatwork, when it is appropriate to talk, and how to request permission to leave the room.

Classroom Management Skills That Increase Learning by Maximizing On-Task Behavior

We also found that student engagement in lessons and activities was the key to successful classroom management. The successful teachers ran smooth, well-paced lessons with few interruptions, and their students worked consistently at their seatwork.

—Jere Brophy and Carolyn Evertson (1976)
Learning from Teaching

This intrinsic tension between the demand for order and the need for students to have unstructured opportunities to explore, solve authentic problems, and construct their own meanings is at the center of any conception of a disciplined educational environment. Clearly, school policies that define order as silence and conformity can force teachers to focus on drill and practice and preclude valued curriculum experiences. At the same time, the demands of loosely structured settings and open-ended tasks must be acknowledged and teachers provided a supportive environment to solve the problems these types of curricular patterns often impose.

—Diane Aleem and Oliver Moles (1993)
Review of Research on Ways to Attain Goal Six: Creating Safe, Disciplined, and Drug-Free Schools

More than two decades ago, Jacob Kounin discovered that effective teachers could be distinguished not by their way of dealing with students' misbehavior but by the classroom management strategies they used to prevent classroom disruptions. Subsequent studies have reinforced and elaborated on Kounin's findings. To increase students' on-task behavior and achievement and to minimize disruptive behavior, you can consider implementing many proven methods of classroom management discussed in this chapter.

The importance of teachers using the skills described in this chapter was emphasized by Kounin's (1970) research on classroom discipline. Kounin began his study by collecting several thousand hours of videotapes, both from classrooms of teachers who were acknowledged to be extremely effective in managing their classes and from classrooms of teachers who had serious, continuing management problems. Kounin expected to find significant differences in how teachers from these two groups handled discipline problems that occurred in their classrooms. Surprisingly, the results indicated that the successful teachers responded to control problems in much the same manner as did the teachers whose classrooms were often disorderly.

Based on these findings, Kounin and his colleagues reexamined the tapes, seeking any real differences between the teaching methods of teachers who were successful and those who experienced major management problems. They discovered that the differences lay in the successful teachers' ability to prevent discipline problems. These teachers used many types of management skills to ensure that students were more consistently and actively engaged in instructional activities. Successful teachers were better prepared and organized and moved smoothly from one activity to another. These teachers also maintained students' involvement in instructional activities by initially stimulating the students' interest and effectively holding their attention throughout the lesson. Similarly, successful teachers used seatwork that was individualized and interesting. Kounin also discovered that the more effective teachers had greater classroom awareness, constantly scanning the classroom so that they were aware of potential problems and could deal with these before any real difficulties arose. These teachers anticipated students' needs, organized their classrooms to minimize restlessness and boredom, and effectively coped with the multiple and often overlapping demands associated with teaching.

Research on teachers' effectiveness in producing gains in students' learning (Brophy & Evertson, 1976) indicates that the same teacher behaviors that reduce classroom disruption are also associated with increased student learning. In describing the findings of the two-year Teacher Effectiveness Project, which examined the relationship between various teacher behaviors and gains in students' learning, Brophy and Evertson (1976) stated, "Our data strongly support the findings of Kounin (1970). . . . That is, the key to successful classroom management is prevention of problems before they start, not knowing how to deal with problems after they have begun" (p. 127). Brophy and Evertson also wrote, "Of the process behaviors measured through classroom observation in our study, the group that had the strongest and most consistent relationships with student learning gains dealt with the classroom management skills of the teachers. By 'classroom management,' we mean planning and conducting activities in an orderly fashion; keeping students actively engaged in lessons and seatwork activities; and minimizing disruptions and discipline problems" (p. 51).

In their study of 12 inner-London secondary schools reported in *Fifteen Thousand Hours,* Rutter, Maughan, Mortimore, Ouston, and Smith (1979) found teachers' classroom-management skills to be a key factor influencing students' achievement and behavior. They wrote, "The measures we used touched on only a few aspects of classroom management and there are innumerable ways in which good management may be achieved. What is important is that teachers learn the skills involved" (p. 186).

The research on academic learning time (ALT) supports the idea that teachers should incorporate teaching methods that increase on-task student behavior. "If 50 minutes of reading instruction per day is allocated to a student who pays attention about one-third of the time, and only one-fourth of the student's reading time is a high level of success, the student will experience only about four minutes of ALT-engaged reading time at a high success level" (Berliner, 1984, p. 62). Rosenshine (1983) summarized specific teacher behaviors found to be associated with students' achievement gains and included many of the skills presented in this chapter.

METHODS FOR INCREASING ON-TASK BEHAVIOR

This chapter will provide you with a wide variety of effective teaching methods that prevent students' misbehavior. If you are an experienced teacher, you will undoubtedly find that many of these methods are already a part of your teaching behavior. However, many new methods can easily be added to this repertoire. These additions can be expected to significantly reduce disruptive student behavior and thereby make teaching more enjoyable while increasing students' achievement.

The chapter is organized around the eight general instructional management skills listed in Figure 7.1. Following a brief statement about each skill, numerous specific teaching strategies will be presented that will help improve your classroom management.

It is critical to understand how to use the methods in this chapter. They are not offered as gimmicks for increasing students' time on-task or your control. Instead, they are methods that can assist you in helping students better understand their schoolwork and enhance the quality of learning time. Neither are these methods offered as a cookbook of behaviors to be routinely followed. Like the neophyte cook, the beginning teacher may choose to implement many of these methods. Much as a cook alters and discards recipes depending on the outcome, the skilled teacher seasons standard methods with their own experiences and action research. Teachers constantly need to monitor their own behavior and its relationship to students' learning in order to develop teaching methods that are maximally effective in the classrooms. In addition to the ideas and activities presented in this book, you will find Good and Brophy's (1994) *Looking in Classrooms* particularly

1. Giving clear instructions
2. Beginning a lesson
3. Maintaining attention
4. Pacing
5. Using seatwork effectively
6. Summarizing
7. Providing useful feedback and evaluation
8. Making smooth transitions

FIGURE 7.1
Instructional Management Skills That Facilitate On-Task Behavior and Academic Achievement

useful in helping monitor and adjust classroom organization and management behavior.

Giving Clear Instructions

A key step in presenting a lesson is to provide clear instructions for the activities in which students will be engaged. A significant amount of disruptive student behavior stems from students' not knowing how they are to proceed or what they are to do when they require assistance or complete their work. Students are often poorly prepared for seatwork assignments. Teachers frequently fail to provide adequate information on why assignments are given or how work relates to past or future learning. Students often do not get enough procedural directions. Because seatwork accounts for nearly 70 percent of students' time in class (Doyle, 1983; Good, 1983), and students tend to take seriously only work for which they believe they will be held accountable (Doyle, 1983), it is critical that we improve our skill in providing students with clear directions on academic work. The following methods suggest ways of eliminating disruptions caused by lack of clear instructions.

Methods

1. *Give precise directions.* Instructions should include statements about (a) what students will be doing, (b) why they are doing it, (c) how they can obtain assistance, (d) what to do with completed work, and (e) what to do when they finish. It is also helpful to indicate how much time they will be spending on the task. This direction may include a statement about when the work can be completed if it cannot be finished within the designated time limits. Research (Brophy & Evertson, 1976; Kounin, 1970) clearly indicates that a significant amount of disruptive student behavior stems from students' not having enough information on these matters. Students respond to this uncertainty by interrupting the teacher with multiple requests for information or by expressing their boredom or anxiety by acting out. Teachers also should specify the aspects of the assignment that are most important, and perhaps even want to post these factors where students can refer to them. This information is valuable in reducing students' anxiety and helps them pace themselves. Some of these instructions are best taught as continuing procedures. For example, students should understand the procedure for obtaining assistance, handing in work, and selecting alternative activities after they complete seatwork.

2. *Describe the desired quality of the work.* This can increase students' sense of accountability and decrease their anxiety. Accountability without clarity, however, is often confusing and anxiety provoking, and it is important to provide specific guidance on your expectations. A teacher of talented and gifted students recently reported that she tells students that there are three types of work: (1) "throw-away"—material that is for practice only and not to be handed in; (2) "everyday learning"—work that should be neat because it will be graded by the teacher, but not a perfect copy because the main purpose is to check students' understanding; and (3) "keepers"—work that will be displayed or that the student may wish to keep.

3. *Vary your approach to giving instructions.* Though clear instructions must be provided consistently, it is useful to employ different approaches in giving them. For example, changing one's voice from a soft to an excited tone (or vice versa) can heighten students' attention. You can also use different media, such as the chalkboard, overhead projector, or butcher paper, for writing instructions.

4. *Employ attending and listening games to improve students' receiving skills.* Students must have clear instructions, but it is equally important that they develop skill in listening to and understanding instructions.

5. *After giving instructions, have students paraphrase the directions, state any problems that might occur to them, and make a commitment.* After giving instructions, ask such questions as, What is one thing you will be doing? What will you do if you finish early? and What do I want you to do? It is often useful to ask key questions of several students who normally have difficulty in following instructions. This tactic not only increases the likelihood that they will listen to instructions but also provides reinforcement for their attending skills. The next step is to ask students whether they see any problems that might arise. Students are very adept at listing potential difficulties, which can then be alleviated. Finally, look at various groups of students and ask, "Are you ready to start and follow these directions?" By obtaining a nod or verbal commitment from each student, you increase the likelihood that they will attempt to complete the activity in a satisfactory manner. If some students indicate that they are not interested in attempting the task, accept this statement and indicate that you need to meet briefly with them after the class has begun their work. Then proceed to obtain a commitment from the remaining students.

6. *Positively accept students' questions about directions.* Employing the strategies described in this section will vastly reduce the number of questions about directions, but situations will arise in which students have questions. To create a safe, supportive atmosphere, it is important to respond positively to student questions. Reprimanding students in front of the class only creates a negative atmosphere. If one or more students consistently ask questions about directions that have already been clearly stated, we should discuss this problem privately with the student(s). This discussion should use the problem-solving approaches described in Chapter 10. Examples of solutions that might result from discussing the problem include having the student write the directions, having the student choose a classmate to assist in clarifying directions, or calling on the student to paraphrase a portion of the directions.

7. *Place directions where they can be seen and referred to by students.* Accessibility is particularly useful when directions are complicated, when students will be working on an assignment over an extended period, or when students frequently repeat an activity. For nonreaders, use pictures to describe the directions.

8. *Have students write out instructions before beginning an activity.* This method provides students with much-needed practice in thinking through the steps they should take before they begin their work. Students can be told that their directions must be checked by the teacher or aide before they begin the assignment.

Though checking requires time and effort and should not be used with every lesson, it is especially useful when students will be working on a long-term project.

9. *When students seem to be having difficulty following directions, consider breaking tasks down into smaller segments.* Young children often have difficulty following a series of directions. Therefore, it is often necessary to give only one or two directions at a time or to have students complete one portion of a task before going on to the next activity.

10. *Give directions immediately prior to the activity they describe.* One of the authors recently observed a student teacher give excellent directions about seat-work, then proceed to present 15 minutes of direct instruction. By the time students were released for seatwork, most of them had forgotten the directions.

11. *Model the correct behavior.* If students have been asked to raise their hand before answering, you can raise our hand while asking the question.

12. *Hand out worksheets or outlines before taking a field trip.* Anyone who has visited British schools has seen excellent examples of this strategy. British children are frequently provided with worksheets to complete during a field trip. By helping students focus on relevant materials, this method reduces acting-out behavior and simultaneously helps students understand what they can learn from the activity.

Beginning a Lesson

Teachers frequently have difficulty in attracting students' attention and getting a lesson started. The reason is at least partly that students often attempt to postpone the beginning of a lesson by socializing or moving about the room. Students quite accurately realize that the best time for buying time is before the lesson begins. The material presented in this section suggests approaches you can use to reduce disruptions that occur while you are introducing a lesson. Before implementing any of these methods, however, you should carefully examine such factors as whether the previous lesson has been satisfactorily summarized so that students are ready to move on to a new lesson, and whether the problem may lie more in the transition between lessons than in the beginning of the new lesson. We refer you to sections later in this chapter for suggestions in summarizing lessons and facilitating smooth transitions.

Methods

1. *Select and teach a cue for getting students' attention.* Students benefit from having a consistent cue indicating that it is time to focus their attention. They hear standard phrases such as "Okay, we are ready to begin" so often that these statements are often ineffective for eliciting attention. One of the authors has her class select a new cue each month. Students enjoy being involved and choose catchy phrases. During a recent year, students chose "Boo" for October, "Gobble Gobble" for November, and "Ho Ho Ho" for December. While teaching a summer institute on classroom management, the value of using a catchy phrase was demonstrated by recording the time it took 40 teachers to pay attention quietly following the phrase "May I please have your attention?" The average time for five such requests was nearly two minutes (in each instance, students were involved in group work). The class was presented with this figure and asked to develop a less common phrase. They chose "Rain Rain Go Away." This phrase was practiced until the class could attend within 10 seconds. Follow-up data gathered during the next two weeks showed that the group never took more than 10 seconds to become completely quiet.

2. *Do not begin until everyone is paying attention.* Almost every teacher has heard this suggestion, and yet most teachers find it very difficult to follow. Worried about wasting time, we often begin a lesson even though we do not have several students' attention. Unfortunately, numerous disadvantages are associated with this decision. First, teachers inevitably spend much more time reprimanding students or repeating directions than they would waiting for students to be quiet. Second, it is impolite to talk over other people, even if they are talking when they should be listening. Third, talking over students is poor modeling because it suggests that this is an acceptable method of gaining attention. Fourth, by beginning a lesson while students are talking or not paying attention, we indicate that we are not in control of the class. Finally, both we and the students who are behaving appropriately will be distracted by inappropriate student talk and consequently the lesson will be less effective. Because of these multiple disadvantages, it appears obvious that we will do well to delay our introductory comments until every student is quiet and attentive.

3. *Begin the lesson by removing distractions.* Many students—especially those with behavior problems—find it difficult to screen out distracting stimuli. You can help students focus on the lesson by closing the door if noise is coming from the hallway or by asking students to clear their desks of everything except items they will need for the assignment.

4. *Clearly describe the goals, activities, and evaluation procedures associated with the lesson being presented.* Students are more highly motivated and learn more when they are aware of the specific goals toward which they are working (Bryan & Locke, 1967; Kennedy, 1968). Clear statements about the learning process meet students' needs for safety and control over their environment. Because students are often extremely concerned about such factors as whether they can complete the work on time and how it will be evaluated, teachers should respond to these issues at the beginning of the lesson. If these issues are not discussed, some students will be worrying about these factors rather than devoting their attention to the lesson.

5. *Stimulate interest by relating the lesson to the students' lives or a previous lesson.* It is extremely important to place content in perspective. Students often feel that they are being asked simply to learn a series of unrelated facts or concepts. Students' motivation can be increased dramatically by indicating why the material is being learned and by suggesting ways in which the learning can influence their lives. For example, division can become much more interesting if it is viewed as a method for determining a Little League batting average. We can reduce anxiety associated with learning a new skill by relating this material or its components to skills students already possess or information that has been learned previously. This approach increases students' sense of safety and enables them to approach the new task with greater confidence.

"First, you have to get their attention."

6. *Start with a highly motivating activity in order to make the students' initial contact with the subject matter as positive as possible.* One of the authors begins a unit on the Lewis and Clark expedition by dressing up as Meriwether Lewis and collaborating with a colleague to present a skit summarizing the lives of these two noteworthy explorers. Students find the skit entertaining and are motivated to learn more about the expedition. Students' interest can be similarly stimulated by a good film, an experiment, or by presenting interesting questions, such as, Why can birds fly though people cannot?

7. *Hand out an outline, definitions, or study guide to help students organize their thoughts and focus their attention.* This material can be made more interesting by embellishing it with humorous cartoons or scattering thought-provoking questions or comments throughout.

8. *Challenge students to minimize their transition time.* Children enjoy games and are impressed by data. Draw on this knowledge by presenting students with data indicating the amount of time it requires them to settle down and asking them to try to reduce this time. There are six basic steps to implementing this approach. First, collect baseline data (see Chapter 11) and record them on a large and easy-to-read chart. Second, the data should be discussed with the students and their assistance requested. Third, help the students choose an appropriate and reasonable goal. Fourth, define exactly what you mean by being ready for class. Fifth, the class must develop a system for collecting and recording data. Finally, it may be necessary to determine a reward for reaching the stated goal.

Maintaining Attention

The amount of time students spend involved in instruction is significantly related to their achievement (Denham & Lieberman, 1980; Fisher et al., 1978). Classes vary dramatically in the percentage of time students are engaged in instructional tasks, with rates ranging from consistently less than 50 percent to 90 percent (Fisher et al., 1978).

Many teachers state that one of the most frustrating tasks associated with teaching is maintaining students' attention during group instruction. Although children and young adolescents do in fact have a somewhat shorter attention span than do adults, their ability to attend quietly to an interesting television program or video game suggests that the skilled teacher can stimulate more consistent attention to task than is seen in most classrooms.

Methods

1. *Arrange the classroom so that students do not have their backs to the speaker.* When a lesson involves the teacher as the center of attention, students should be seated so that everyone is facing the teacher. This arrangement can be accomplished using rows, a circle, or a U-shape. When students are seated in small groups, request that all students face you before beginning a lesson. Similarly, if you wish students to talk to each other, desks must be arranged in a circle, square, or U-shape so that students can comfortably see and hear each speaker. Teachers who use a variety of instructional activities should consider teaching students a procedure for quickly and quietly moving desks. With a small amount of instruction, students in all grades can learn to rearrange desks in approximately one minute. Figure 7.2 presents a seating arrangement that is particularly useful in elementary school classrooms because it allows for easy monitoring of seatwork as well as for effective group discussion.

2. *Employ a seating arrangement that does not discriminate against some students.* Teachers spend nearly 70 percent of their time in front of the classroom (Adams & Biddle, 1970). Therefore, it is no surprise that students at the back of the room contribute less to class discussions (Adams & Biddle, 1970; Delefes &

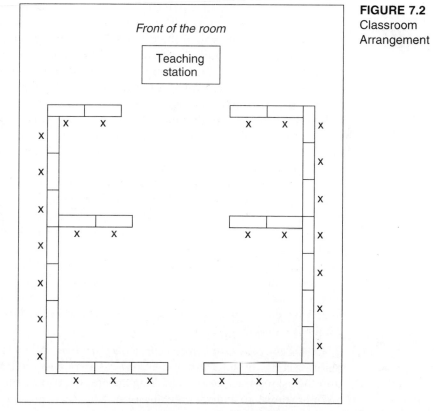

FIGURE 7.2
Classroom Arrangement

Jackson, 1972), are less attentive and less on-task (Schwebel & Cherlin, 1972), and achieve less (Daum, 1972) than do students seated near the front of the class.

Considering these findings, it is interesting that teachers tend to place higher-achieving students nearer the teacher and provide them with more contact (Rist, 1970). Fortunately, research also indicates that teachers can encourage more evenly distributed student responding. Daum (1972) demonstrated that when low-ability students were moved to the front of the room, their achievement improved more than that of low-ability students who remained at the back of the room. Interestingly, the high-achieving students' achievement did not suffer when they were moved farther from the teacher. Similarly, Adams and Biddle (1970) discovered that students' involvement is more evenly distributed when high- and low-achieving students are interspersed throughout the room. These studies suggest that teachers can increase on-task student responses by adjusting seating arrangements and moving around the room so that all students become actively involved in meaningful classroom interaction.

3. *Use random selection in calling on students.* When you call on students by progressing up and down rows or around a circle, students who have just responded or who know they will not have to respond for several minutes often become bored and disruptive. Students can be kept attentive if you select them randomly and occasionally return to a student who has recently answered a question. When employing random selection, be careful not to provide significantly more response opportunities to high-achieving students. Research (Brophy & Good, 1974; Cooper & Good, 1983) indicates that teachers provide high-achieving students with more response opportunities than their low-achieving peers. One strategy for preventing this bias is to place a tally beside each child's name as he or she is called on. It is a good idea periodically to explain to students why you choose to call on every student. Students who always volunteer answers have probably received numerous response opportunities during their school career and may become frustrated when these opportunities are distributed more equally. This frustration may be reduced by informing the class that calling on all students allows you to find out whether most people understand the material and helps everyone to learn by giving everyone a chance to respond.

One danger in involving all students is that you are less likely to receive an immediate correct answer to every question. Studies (Brophy & Evertson, 1976; Stallings, 1976; Ward & Tikunoff, 1976) indicate that, especially in the primary grades and when working with children from lower socioeconomic classes, students' achievement is enhanced when you provide information, ask focused questions, and receive correct answers from students. Therefore, you should carefully consider when to involve lower-achieving students. For example, these students might be called on when they raise their hands during skill-acquisition lessons and might be encouraged to become actively involved during lessons that involve personal issues or opinions.

4. *Ask the question before calling on a student.* When teachers select the student before asking the question, other students may become less interested in the question. By asking the question, looking around the room, and providing students with an opportunity to consider the question, you create greater interest and anticipation

and thereby increase attending behavior. Also take this opportunity to reinforce the procedure of students' raising their hands to answer questions (e.g., "Raise your hand if you can answer this question," or "John, you have your hand raised. What is the answer?").

5. *Wait at least five seconds before answering a question or calling on another student.* Most teachers are surprised to learn that research (Rowe, 1974) indicates that, on the average, teachers wait only one second for a student to respond before answering a question themselves or calling on another student. To make this finding more believable and relevant, consider a typical question you might ask in your classroom and silently count to 10 in order to experience a 10-second wait. You may be surprised at how long 10 seconds is. Consider, however, the process students must go through when asked a question. First, they must hear the question and decide whether they understand it. Second, they must search for the information. Third, they must consider whether their response will be accepted. Fourth, they must decide whether they will receive reinforcement or rebuke for their response (in some situations a correct response will be reinforced by the teacher but punished by peers). This process may occur very rapidly for bright students, but most students require considerably longer than one second to complete it.

As with most strategies, teachers need to consider the context when increasing their wait time. For example, during a whole-class oral drill review on math facts, a teacher would probably wait only one or two seconds before calling on a student. Perhaps the main reason we fail to wait following a question is that many students' hands are raised before we complete the question and the class moves along smoothly if we simply call on a student whose hand is raised.

Research (Rosenthal, 1973) indicates that teachers tend to wait longer for answers from students they view as brighter. The study also suggests, though, that when teachers do wait longer for lower-achieving students, they are rewarded with greater responsiveness from the students. Rowe (1978) reported that when teachers increase their waiting time, a variety of positive things occur. Figure 7.3 summarizes her findings. In a review of studies involving wait time, Tobin (1987) found that when average teacher wait time was greater than three seconds, teacher and student discourse changed and higher cognitive level achievement occurred at all grade levels.

---

1. Length of students' responses increases.
2. Number of unsolicited but appropriate answers increases.
3. Failure to obtain a response decreases.
4. Children's confidence increases.
5. Teacher-centered teaching decreases.
6. Students' questions increase.
7. Lower-achieving students contribute more.
8. Students' proposals increase.
9. Students give more evidence to support their answers.
10. The variety of students' responses increases.

FIGURE 7.3
Advantages of Increasing Teachers' Wait Time

If you wish to maintain students' attention and increase their willingness and ability to answer questions, you must provide all students adequate time to answer. When teachers fail to provide this time, students soon learn that they can maintain their uninvolvement simply by failing to respond immediately.

6. *Use games that encourage attentive listening.* Children often find it difficult to sit quietly and listen when the teacher or their peers are talking. This important skill can be taught by involving students in activities that encourage listening. One strategy that students enjoy is the yarn activity. Before leading a group discussion, inform the class that they will use a ball of yarn to facilitate the discussion. The students are told that only the person holding the ball of yarn can speak. When a student finishes speaking, he or she is to roll the yarn to another student who has raised his or her hand. Before releasing the ball, the speaker holds on to the yarn. This act indicates that he or she has been involved in the discussion; as the yarn is passed from student to student, a sociogram-like matrix is created by the yarn. Another good activity is to use paraphrasing during a group discussion. Before stating a point, each speaker must accurately paraphrase the point made by the previous speaker. Students quickly learn that they are often thinking about their own response rather than listening to the speaker, and they quickly learn to become better listeners.

7. *Ask students to respond to their classmates' answers.* Teachers often inadvertently reinforce the idea that students do not need to listen to their classmates' answers. By asking students a series of independent (though often related) questions, teachers create a situation in which students can, with no immediate consequences to themselves, become inattentive to their peers' responses. This problem can be alleviated by occasionally asking students to comment on an answer provided by a classmate. It is important, however, that you do not use this approach as a method for catching and embarrassing inattentive students. When calling on such a student, ask a question that he or she can answer, such as, "John says that when we do not give this plant any light it will die. Do you agree, Bill?"

8. *Do not consistently repeat students' answers.* Many teachers parrot nearly every answer provided by a student. This practice is intended to ensure that all students hear the correct answer. But it also teaches students that (a) they do not need to speak loudly because the teacher is the only one who needs to hear their answer, (b) they do not need to listen to their peers because the teacher will repeat the answer, and (c) the teacher is the source of all learning in the classroom. All these negative side-effects reduce students' motivation, involvement, and attention.

9. *Model listening skills by paying close attention when students speak.* Children model their behavior after adults who have a significant role in their lives. If you want students to listen attentively to their peers, you must model good listening skills. Concentrate on looking at the speaker and using nonverbal cues that indicate sincere interest. Unfortunately, teachers often find that their attention is distracted by disruptive student behavior. Initially attempt to deal with this distraction by employing a quick glance or gesture to indicate displeasure. If the behavior requires a more extensive diversion of attention from the speaker, you may wish to apologize to the speaker by making a statement such as, "I'm sorry that I did not hear the last

part of your answer, Melissa, but I had to ask several students to check themselves. Would you mind repeating your answer?"

10. *Be animated.* In his classic work on classroom discipline, Kounin (1970) wrote, "Teachers who maintain a group focus by engaging in behaviors that keep children alert and on their toes are more successful in inducing work involvement and preventing deviancy than are teachers who do not" (p. 123). Studies indicate that not only do students like enthusiastic teachers but that teachers' enthusiasm facilitates students' achievement (Coats & Smidchens, 1966; Mastin, 1963; Rosenshine & Furst, 1973). Demonstrate enthusiasm and animation by moving around the room, varying your voice level, using interested facial expressions, and maintaining a high energy level. If you wish to examine your behavior periodically to see whether it appears animated, use audio- or videotape recordings of your teaching. Though every teacher must develop a personal style and few teachers want to put on a performance all day every day, some animation is extremely helpful in keeping students' attention.

11. *Reinforce students' efforts and maintain a high ratio of positive to negative verbal statements.* Students will feel safer and more willing to be involved in a classroom characterized by warmth and support. Though they do not want overly affected or unrealistically positive feedback, they are motivated by straightforward and sincere praise. When teachers fail to provide frequent, clear, and varied reinforcement, students begin to lose interest and often attempt to acquire more interesting responses by engaging in inappropriate behavior.

12. *Vary instructional media and methods.* Anyone who has sat through a two-hour monotone lecture is aware of the need to vary the stimuli used during instruction. Because they spend a great deal of time watching television, youngsters may be particularly sensitive to changing stimuli. Though teachers cannot match television's diversity, we should nevertheless concentrate on adding diversity to instruction. We can use various media—such as an overhead projector, chalkboard, butcher paper, and film—as we move from lesson to lesson. Similarly, different instructional approaches can be used for different lessons. We may use seatwork for math, small groups for social studies, and a presentation during science. Teachers and students can also invite guests into their classrooms. During a recent school week, guests in one of the author's classes included a local folk-singing group, an ambulance driver who demonstrated the equipment in her ambulance as well as mouth-to-mouth resuscitation and cardiopulmonary resuscitation, and a mother who spoke about nutrition. Students enjoy and are almost always attentive to adults from their community. Finally, teachers can add surprises such as using different-colored chalk or writing larger and smaller in the same sentence to attract students' attention.

13. *Create anticipation.* Create a sense of interest by making statements such as, "This is a tough one" or "I'm not sure we've talked about this but maybe someone can answer it." Anticipation can also be created by leaving an interesting lesson without attaining closure. People tend to recall unfinished tasks and are more likely to forget completed tasks. By stimulating interest but moving on to a new activity, you can increase students' interest. This increased interest may also generalize to other subjects. When using this approach, however, you will want to attain some closure by examining possible answers and will also want to assure students that they will be able to return to the subject the following day.

14. *Use silences effectively.* Research on teachers' waiting time suggests that most teachers are uncomfortable with silence—we seem to believe that silences will be filled with disruptive behavior. Silences, however, offer several advantages that enhance students' learning and may reduce disruption. Silence can create suspense and anticipation. It can also give students time to slow down and assimilate material. Similarly, silence often clarifies information by breaking it into smaller segments. Finally, it can be used to emphasize an important point or to signal students to attend to the next statement or action. If you fall into the habit of employing rapid, nonstop talking to prevent students from interrupting, they often develop strategies for taking their own breaks. Unfortunately, these strategies often include disruptive, attention-getting behavior. Students who are poor auditory learners will find rapid, uninterrupted talk frustrating and will frequently respond by tuning out or acting out. It is helpful to inform students why silences are being used and to provide them with assistance in using silences productively, such as, "Before answering, I would like each of you to think about the question and see if you can find the answer" or "Please sit quietly for a minute and think about the slide we just saw."

15. *Ask questions that relate to students' own lives or similar situations.* Students find learning more meaningful when it can be related to their own lives and interests. Therefore, include questions such as, "Have you ever felt this way?" "How would your parents feel about this?" or "Do you believe that it is right to . . . ?" Similarly, incorporate aspects of students' daily lives into our instruction. During creative writing, students can write stories in which others in the class are characters.

16. *Provide work of appropriate difficulty.* Students' misbehavior is often a response to work that is either too easy or too difficult. Students prefer work that is moderately difficult over tasks that are too easy (Kleinfeld, 1975; Maehr & Sjogren, 1971). When work is too difficult, though, students become discouraged. Failure also causes students to lower their expectations of their own performance.

Research (Brophy & Evertson, 1976) suggests that when the teacher is available to provide assistance (as during monitored seatwork or recitation), students should be able to answer 70 to 80 percent of questions correctly. When students must work independently (as on independent seatwork or homework), students should be able to answer 95 percent correctly (Brophy, 1982; Fisher et al., 1980). Seatwork must not only allow for these high success rates but must also be different enough from previous work to challenge students.

Similarly, teacher questions to students should also elicit a relatively high rate of correct responses. Brophy (1986a) states that approximately three-fourths of teachers' questions should elicit correct responses and the remainder should elicit some form of incorrect or incomplete answer rather than failure to respond. Success rates can be expected to be lower when new material is being introduced but higher during reviews. Brophy noted, "Consistently low success rates (below about 65 percent), however, suggest that the teacher is 'teaching over the students' heads' or has not prepared them effectively for the questions" (p. 9).

17. *Provide variability and interest in seatwork.* Seatwork can be made more interesting by developing units that relate to current events, such as sports or students' other interests (animals, entertainment figures, etc.), or by creating seat-work that is based on some form of board game. Students can also be involved in working cooperatively with peers or presented with a competitive situation.

18. *When presenting difficult material, clearly acknowledge this fact, set a time limit for the presentation, and describe the type of follow-up activities that will clarify the lesson.* Students are less likely to become discouraged and subsequently act out when teachers provide this type of information. Though we must not create a self-fulfilling prophecy, students benefit from knowing that the presentation involves a new and complicated concept. We can simultaneously stimulate interest and acknowledge the difficulty of the material by comments such as, "We're going to work on a new math skill today. I'll talk about it for fifteen minutes and then give you some problems. If you have difficulty, I will help you with the problems."

Pacing

Undoubtedly, you have experienced many examples of both effective and ineffective pacing. People who have sat through a dull movie or a long meeting in which they were neither interested in the topic nor asked to be involved have experienced ineffective pacing. Conversely, teachers have all experienced lessons that presented an ideal blend of active involvement and presentation of new ideas. Take a moment and recall a specific situation in which you felt the pacing was optimal. Now, recall an instance in which the pacing was very poor. Reflect on how you felt and behaved in each situation. If you are like most people, you were much more comfortable and attentive in the well-paced setting. Students' behavior is also dramatically influenced by the quality of their teacher's pacing. Disruptive student behavior can often be linked directly to poorly paced lessons.

Methods

1. *Develop awareness of your own teaching tempo.* Students' behavior and performance are affected by their teacher's tempo (Yando & Kagan, 1968). We can learn to generate interest and enthusiasm effectively or to create a calming effect by adjusting our own personal pace in the classroom. The best method for examining your own pace is to videotape yourself during large-group instruction. As you watch the replay, ask yourself questions such as Did I talk too fast? Was I animated? Did I repeat myself too often? and Would I enjoy listening to my own presentations?

Another method for obtaining feedback on pacing involves incorporating questions about pacing into questionnaires given to students to assess the teacher's instruction. Students can respond to questions such as Do I speak slowly enough? Do I notice when you are not understanding the material and stop to explain? and Do you have time to complete the work I require? Following a workshop presented by one of the authors, an experienced high school teacher decided to improve his pacing by teaching his students several signals they could use to provide him with feedback. Students were asked to make the common chattering movement with their hand to indicate that the teacher was repeating himself, place their hand up in a stop motion when he was going too fast, and make a circle with their index finger when they were confused. The teacher reported to his colleagues that students thoroughly enjoyed providing him with feedback and that he believed his teaching was more effective.

2. *Watch for nonverbal cues indicating that students are becoming confused, bored, or restless.* We often become so involved in presenting our material that we fail to attend to indications that several or even many students are becoming increasingly inattentive. Kounin (1970) discovered that teachers who had fewer discipline problems effectively scanned their rooms and responded to potentially disruptive student behavior before it became a major problem. When students appear restless, teachers have several options. First, you can state your perception and ask the children to express their feelings, such as, "A number of you seem to be having difficulty paying attention. Can someone tell me what is causing the problem?" If students have become accustomed to sharing feelings and solving problems, it is likely that one or more can pinpoint the problem. Another option that may be used separately or may follow the intervention above is to speculate about the cause of the problem and change the pace accordingly. Therefore, you might decide that too much material is being covered and may shorten the lesson and incorporate several personalized questions to increase students' involvement and attention. The teacher who continues undaunted in the face of students' restlessness is inviting further disruptive behavior.

3. *Break activities up into short segments.* The use of films as instructional aids helps demonstrate this strategy. Teachers almost always allow a film to run all the way to the end before discussing its content. There are, however, several advantages to stopping the film at important points and discussing the ideas being presented. First, major points of information can be highlighted. Second, this procedure allows students to assimilate smaller amounts of information at a time. Many students simply cannot process the material offered in a half-hour film. Third, this method differentiates viewing a film at school from watching a movie or viewing television. Students can begin to learn that movies shown in school are meant to convey specific information and ideas rather than simply to entertain.

4. *Provide structured short breaks during lessons that last longer than 30 minutes.* Disruptive behavior is sometimes merely students' method of obtaining a short respite from the rigors of a long schoolday. Because many students do not have the skill to refresh themselves quietly and productively during extended periods of study, teachers can reduce disruptions either by providing structured breaks or by teaching children how to take their own breaks. You can also provide a break by asking the students to put their pencils aside and take a minute to stand and stretch. You can also create a break by involving students in a short (three to five minutes is the optional length for such break activities) game such as Twenty Questions, Seven-Up, or Simon Says. It is important to inform the students that this activity is being used to provide a brief break and that they will be expected to return to work as soon as the activity is completed. Students can be taught how to relax using deep

muscle relaxation. You can then encourage them to respond to the need to wander around the room or disrupt another student by taking a moment to relax themselves before continuing with their work. This approach may be reinforced by occasionally employing it as a structured break activity.

5. *Vary the style as well as the content of instruction.* Students often become restless when faced with extended instructional periods using only one type of instruction. If students have completed a large-group discussion in social studies, it is best not to move directly to a large-group science presentation. Teachers with good classroom management skills learn to move smoothly among a variety of instructional approaches.

6. *Do not bury students in paperwork.* At times, students' misbehavior may be an attempt to add a little entertainment and relief to a day filled with innumerable worksheets. Students may act out because they are given 30 problems to complete when only 5 were needed to indicate mastery of a new skill or when they are confronted with a continuous procession of worksheets.

Using Seatwork Effectively

Research in hundreds of elementary school classrooms shows that students spend more than half their time working privately at seatwork (Angus, Evans, & Parkin, 1975; Good & Beckerman, 1978; McDonald, 1976). Data from some of the classes of the Beginning Teacher Evaluation Study (Fisher et al., 1978) also show that in some classes students make nearly 100 percent errors during 14 percent of the time they are involved in seatwork. Given findings suggesting that during seatwork students learn best when experiencing approximately 90 percent success rates (Rosenshine, 1983), it is critical that we learn to structure seatwork effectively to ensure students' involvement and success.

Methods

1. *Make seatwork diagnostic and prescriptive.* Seatwork should be designed to provide students with meaningful practice while enabling teacher and student to assess the student's progress. Therefore, seatwork should be checked by the teacher or student, recorded and filed by the student, monitored by the teacher, and discussed in periodic teacher-student conferences. When this procedure is followed, students view seatwork as meaningful and are much less likely to act out during instructional periods designated for seatwork.

2. *Develop a specific procedure for obtaining assistance.* Students will inevitably require assistance when engaged in seatwork assignments. Because teachers are often engaged in small-group instruction or helping other students while all are doing seatwork, it is necessary to establish a procedure whereby children can obtain assistance without interrupting the teacher. If such procedures are not established and students are instructed not to disturb the teacher, they will become frustrated when they need assistance and are likely to respond by acting out. The most effective method of providing assistance is peer tutoring.

3. *Establish clear procedures about what to do when seatwork is completed.* It is helpful to display a poster reminding students what to do with their completed

work (e.g., remind them to score, record, and file their work), and what alternatives are available once these tasks have been completed. Learning centers and puzzles or other challenging activities provide useful and necessary alternatives for students.

4. *Add interest to seatwork.* Include cartoons, puzzles, or personalized questions on worksheets.

5. *Monitor seatwork by moving around the room systematically.* Teachers often inadvertently spend a disproportionate amount of time in one or more areas of the classroom. During seatwork instruction, it is important to monitor each student's work. You can ensure that this is done by carrying a clipboard and noting when each student's work is monitored or by having a colleague or student draw a map of your walking pattern during a seatwork period. When involved with a small group, assign the group a task and leave briefly to monitor students involved in seatwork. By teaching a procedure for obtaining assistance, you can reduce the need to provide lengthy assistance to students involved in seatwork and can simply remind them to follow the procedure.

6. *Monitor students' seatwork and make needed adjustments.* One of the authors recently observed a student teacher in a fifth-grade class. Students in the class completed seatwork at varying rates, and the teacher's failure to adjust seatwork or provide optional learning activities meant that many students were free to wander and disrupt the class. To bring out this point for the teacher, I coded at five-minute intervals the number of students who had completed one-quarter, half, three-quarters, or all their work. The results (Figure 7.4) clearly indicate the inappropriateness of giving all students the same seatwork task. In addition to monitoring the time required to complete seatwork, monitor the percentage of students who complete their work with at least 75 percent accuracy (a higher percentage should be selected if you are not available to monitor the seatwork). This information, as well as a group average score, should be recorded as a basis for determining future seatwork assignments for individual students or the class as a whole.

7. *Work through the first several seatwork problems with the students.* All students will then understand the procedure to be followed and will be able to ask questions if they do not understand the work.

8. *Spend considerable time in presentation and discussion before assigning seatwork.* Students learn more effectively when they have been well prepared for this work.

FIGURE 7.4
Number of Students Who Had Completed Various Amounts of Seatwork at Five-Minute Intervals

	Percentage of work complete			
	0–25%	*26–50%*	*51–75%*	*76–100%*
5 minutes	11	12	8	2
10 minutes	6	10	10	7
15 minutes	4	6	13	10
20 minutes	3	4	7	9

9. *Relate seatwork directly to material presented immediately prior to it.* Students will have more difficulty with seatwork assignments related to material discussed on the previous day or stemming from individualized work.

10. *Keep contacts with individual students relatively short (30 seconds or less).* Longer contacts minimize your ability to scan the room or to provide assistance to all students.

11. *Provide short segments of seatwork.* Rather than making one long presentation followed by an extended period of seatwork, break the instruction into smaller segments and follow each with a short period of seatwork.

12. *Have students work together during seatwork.* Students can jointly develop solutions or cooperatively prepare for group competition.

Summarizing

Many children view the schoolday as a series of tasks to be completed and do not understand what they have learned or how the learning relates to specific learning goals or their own lives. Try to recall a course you found particularly difficult. Take a moment to consider how you went about studying for the course and how well you understood the material. It is likely that you studied specific facts and that you did not fully understand the central concepts of the discipline or the relationship between what you were studying and your own life. It is also very likely that you found the course frustrating and confusing. Unfortunately, many students experience similar feelings about much of the schoolday. We should not be surprised that acting-out behavior replaces appropriate on-task behavior. Many of the methods presented in this chapter are effective in producing more positive student behavior precisely because they reduce students' frustration. Helping students understand what they have learned is a key factor in clarifying the school experience. When combined with clearly stated goals and useful feedback, the methods presented in this section provide students with a sense of accomplishment and meaning in their school experience.

Methods

1. *At the end of a lesson or a schoolday, ask students to state or write in a journal one thing they have learned.* Not only does this activity help clarify what they have learned but it also provides each student with a sense of accomplishment. Students should be informed that if they have difficulty stating what they have learned, they can seek assistance from the teacher or a peer.

2. *Have students play the role of a reporter and summarize what has been learned.* We can introduce a student as a news reporter who will highlight the information from a lesson. We might say, "This is NBC reporter Billy Williams, who will report on the Nez Perce conflict that caused the tribe's flight to Canada. Come in, Billy."

3. *Have students create a skit to act out what they have learned.* In a unit on fur trappers, students can play the role of trappers building a bull boat. During their work, the trappers can discuss how the boat is built and how it applies to their livelihood. Similarly, when studying parts of speech, students can be given cards listing various parts of speech and asked to organize themselves into meaningful sentences.

4. *Ask students to create learning displays.* Students can develop a collage, outline, newspaper article, and so on, to display their learning. They might write an article reporting on how plants grow. Students could also draw a chart that demonstrates this process.

5. *Encourage students to present their learning to others.* Students can share what they have learned with their classmates, other classes, or their parents. This sharing can take the form of reporting results of science experiments, performing skits, showing the results of art projects, and so on. Students can also share their learning by actually teaching their newly acquired information to other students.

6. *Display students' work.* Displaying students' work provides students with a sense of pride and accomplishment and also provides closure to an activity. Students can view the result of a unit or lesson, which reinforces the fact that the various steps led to an observable final product.

7. *Relate material to students' lives and interests.* An effective summary involves clarifying how the new material relates to students' lives or can be useful to students. When completing a unit on division, students can be asked to calculate their Little League batting averages, their teams' won-lost percentages, or whether they would save money on certain items by purchasing them in larger quantities. Similarly, at the completion of a unit on how plants grow, students could be asked to list the ways in which their new knowledge will help them to grow a better garden or keep their house plants alive longer.

8. *Provide frequent review sessions.* It is helpful to review previous learning and relate this information to current or future lessons. When presenting a daily, continuing lesson, you should begin the day's lesson with a brief review of the material covered on the previous day. This refresher not only enhances retention but also reinforces the concept that learning builds on previous learning. Students too often perceive each lesson as an isolated hurdle to be jumped rather than a step in a sequential learning process. Frequent reviews increase the likelihood that learning will be seen as a connected series of events.

9. *Use tests as tools for summarizing learning.* Teachers should treat tests like any other summary or learning experience. Students need to be informed that tests are a means for discovering how much they have learned and what material may need to be covered more thoroughly. When they have completed a test, answers should be discussed so that students receive a review of the correct answers.

Providing Useful Feedback and Evaluation

Evaluation of students' performance is an area that causes much worry among students, teachers, and parents. Teachers worry about their ability to evaluate students accurately and whether their feedback is fair and helpful. Students worry not only about what evaluations indicate about their own competence but also about their parents' reactions to teachers' evaluations. Finally, parents worry about reports on their child's performance, not only because they hope their child will be successful and happy and because a good evaluation reflects favorably on them but also because consistently poor evaluations may suggest either poor parenting or limited academic potential. Because of the interest and potential anxiety associated with evaluation, it is clear that by using effective methods in this area you can create greater clarity and safety and thereby reduce disruptive behavior. Many years ago, Regan (1966) wrote in *Modern Elementary Curriculum* that the six basic purposes of evaluation are:

1. To reveal to teachers what is happening to each child.
2. To motivate learning through furnishing pupils with information concerning success in various areas of the curriculum.
3. To furnish teachers with a means of appraising teaching methods, textbook, and other instrumentalities of the educative process.
4. To provide a basis for continuous improvement of the curriculum.
5. To give pupils experience in evaluating their own progress.
6. To reveal the progress the school program is making toward the achievement of the accepted objectives. (p. 452)

The methods presented next reinforce these purposes and offer practical ideas for effectively using evaluation in the classroom.

Methods

1. *Help students view evaluation as part of the learning process.* We need to place no greater emphasis on tests or report cards than on any other instructional activity. Children should be encouraged to view evaluation as simply an integral part of learning. This understanding can be enhanced by employing many of the methods described in this section.

2. *Tell students the criteria by which they will be evaluated.* When working with specific skills, students should know what they are to learn and what level of performance is acceptable. Similarly, when they are assigned projects in subjects from art to social studies, they should be informed about the specific goals for the lesson, and, if their work will be evaluated, what specific criteria will be used. The importance of sharing information with children was powerfully stated by Herbert Kohl (1967):

> The easiest way to bring this up in class was to tell the children exactly where they stood. I braced myself, and defying all precedent as well as my own misgivings, I performed the unforgivable act of showing the children what their reading and IQ scores were according to the record cards. I also taught a lesson on the definition of IQ and of achievement scores. The children were angry and shocked; no one had ever come right out and told them they were failing. It was always put so nicely and evasively that the children never knew where they stood. (p. 176)

3. *Relate feedback directly to individual or teacher goals.* Feedback should help students understand how effectively they are progressing toward clearly specified goals. This clarification makes the learning process much more concrete and clear. Studies (Burrows, 1973; Collins, 1971) indicate that providing students with the results of diagnostic tests and then providing instruction aimed at achieving mastery of specific objectives leads to dramatic increases in learning.

4. *Record data so that students can monitor their progress.* Students can benefit immensely from the realization that they are able to learn. One of the authors once worked with a seventh-grade boy who viewed himself as a totally inept learner. One day while he was working in a room that included a two-way mirror, he was videotaped during a period in which he worked diligently for 50 consecutive minutes. When the videotape was shown to the student, he responded with disbelief. He simply could not believe that he could study for 50 minutes. The student asked to have the principal and his own mother view the tape. This incident proved to be a watershed in the boy's school life.

Students should be taught how to record their academic progress. You can do so by teaching simple graphing skills. You may also wish to provide interesting data displays, such as a football field with strings to which cardboard football players are attached. The players can be moved down the field to represent individual or group acquisition of skills. Chapter 6 provides specific techniques for employing academic goal setting and student self-monitoring.

5. *Provide immediate and specific feedback.* Page (1958) found that students' learning was enhanced when they were provided with specific positive and negative information about their performance. Generalized feedback such as a grade or comments like "Good" or "Nice work" do not tend to improve students' performance on subsequent tests.

6. *Attempt to focus on positive accomplishments.* Whenever possible, help students record their accomplishments rather than focus on their failures. Initially focus on the items students have answered correctly and then help them correct mistakes. Effective feedback encourages students to describe both the strengths and weaknesses of their work.

7. *Provide honest feedback.* It is important to focus on students' success, but students' performance is not aided by feedback that is inaccurately positive. Students resent feedback they perceive as fake (Travers, 1967). Furthermore, providing students with too much praise for work that does not meet acceptable standards only confuses them and reduces their motivation and performance.

8. *Ask students to list factors that contributed to their success.* Students need assistance in specifying behaviors that enabled them to succeed. Low-achieving students often view their successes as based on luck or outside forces rather than on their own efforts. Helping children focus on the relationship between their effort and performance can help them feel a greater sense of competence and power. This confidence will in turn increase the likelihood that they will begin to accept greater responsibility for their own behavior.

9. *Deemphasize comparisons between students and their peers.* Though it is helpful for students to know how they stand in relation to grade-level norms, teachers should not evaluate how well they perform in relation to their peers. In addition to placing some children in a no-win situation, comparative evaluations suggest that the goal of learning is to outperform one's peers rather than to master

the material. Students should be evaluated on criterion-referenced tests and their performance compared to their own earlier work.

10. *Deemphasize grades as feedback on students' work.* Grades by themselves provide almost no useful information. When it is important or necessary to provide students with information about the quality of their performance as compared to an external criterion such as grade-level norms, it is best to have a teacher-student conference and outline specific skills the student will need to improve in order to score at grade level. Detailed teacher's comments and supportive statements are much more effective than grades in motivating students' performance.

> Grades tend to motivate those students who least need it; that is, those who are already successful; while, perversely, the very students who need motivating the most (poor students) are most put off and threatened by grades. . . .
>
> When it comes to motivating school achievement, it appears that the type of learning structure is by far the more important factor, with grades playing a secondary, even negligible, role. (Covington & Beery, 1976, pp. 116, 117)

Making Smooth Transitions

A surprisingly large amount of classroom time is spent in transition from one activity to another. The approximately 30 major transitions each day in elementary classrooms account for nearly 15 percent of classroom time (Gump, 1967; Rosenshine, 1980). Most experienced teachers acknowledge that the beginning and end of class periods, or the transition between subjects or activities during the period, are the times when students are most likely to be disruptive. Therefore, as we would expect, the handling of transitions distinguishes skilled from less-skilled classroom managers (Doyle, 1984).

Students' disruption during transitions often leads to extended periods of off-task behavior, which drains teachers' energies and reduces students' achievement. Because students' learning is directly related to the amount of time they spend studying a subject (Borg, 1980; Rosenshine, 1976; Sirotnik, 1982), teachers must develop skill in making smooth transitions. It is equally important, however, to realize that the quality of learning time is more important than time itself (Berliner, 1979; Doyle, 1983; Good, 1986; Peterson & Swing, 1982). Therefore, the goal of an effective transition is not so much getting students immediately on task as it is preparing students to be productively involved in the coming instruction.

Methods

1. *Arrange the classroom for efficient movement.* The classroom should be arranged so that areas through which students move frequently are wide and cleared of materials. Desks should be arranged so that students and teacher can move around the room without disturbing students who are working. You are encouraged to make a detailed map of your classroom and mark areas where students frequently move or congregate. Are these large enough to prevent overcrowding and its accompanying disruption? Are pathways clear and wide? Is space used so that the classroom has a sense of openness?

2. *Create and post a daily schedule and discuss any changes in schedule each morning.* Numerous low-level discipline problems arise when students are confused over scheduling issues, such as a change in their violin lesson or not attending reading due to the specialist's absence. These difficulties can be minimized by discussing the classroom schedule each morning. This activity also provides a clear and task-oriented transition into the schoolday.

3. *Have material ready for the next lesson.* It is often helpful to have an outline of the lesson written on the chalkboard or on butcher paper. Similarly, having a filmstrip or film set up and ready to go or having materials ready for distribution allows us to make a smooth transition rather than attempting to prepare materials while monitoring students' behavior and dealing with disruptions that often occur during transition periods. Students' behavior is dramatically affected by the teacher's behavior. If you are well prepared, relaxed, and make smooth transitions, students will almost always follow by moving calmly from one activity to the next. Conversely, if you become frustrated or anxious while attempting to arrange an activity, students will inevitably follow suit.

4. *Do not relinquish students' attention until you have given clear instructions for the following activity.* Numerous problems can be prevented by moving from a summary of one lesson immediately into a transition activity (such as a brief game of Seven-Up) or the next lesson. All too often, teachers allow the class to become disruptive while teachers prepare for the next lesson, only to find that it requires considerable time and energy to regain the students' attention.

5. *Do not do tasks that can be done by students.* Free yourself to monitor the class and reduce the demands on your own time and energy by having students do a wide variety of tasks, such as handing out and collecting materials, running filmstrips, and taking the roll. In addition to freeing you for more important instructional and management tasks, involving students in organizational tasks can provide them with a sense of competence and power.

6. *Move around the room and attend to individual needs.* Being prepared and allowing students to handle many small tasks can free you to scan the classroom more effectively and handle any minor problems that, if ignored, could expand into major disruptions. Having a moment to notice and say a few words to a student who is frustrated by an inability to complete the previous activity may prevent a major disruption by that student during the next lesson.

7. *Provide students with simple, step-by-step directions.* Younger students especially benefit from being given specific directions that ask them to do one thing at a time. Rather than asking students to "get ready for lunch," you might break this task into the smaller steps of clearing their desks, sitting quietly, one group at a time getting their lunches, and so forth.

8. *Remind students of key procedures associated with the upcoming lesson.* If the next lesson requires some students to work independently while you instruct a small group or have conferences with students, remind students of the procedures they should follow during this type of activity. This is best handled by first describing the learning activity and its goal and then asking students to describe the procedures they are to follow during this type of activity.

9. *Use group competition to stimulate more orderly transitions.* We can involve the class in attempting to reduce the amount of time required to make a transition. Similarly, small groups or rows of students can be involved in competition to see who can make the quietest and fastest preparation for the next lesson.

10. *Develop transition activities.* Students often find it difficult to make the transition from home to school or from lunch or physical education back to a quieter setting. Smooth transitions can be facilitated by implementing structured activities that help students make these transitions. Ask them to begin the schoolday by writing in their journals or by discussing the daily schedule. Transitions from active periods such as lunch into quieter learning activities can be facilitated by transition activities such as reading to the students or leading students in deep muscle relaxation. When these activities are used consistently, students not only find safety and comfort in this structure but also learn how to monitor transitions for themselves.

IMPLEMENTING AND ASSESSING NEW TEACHING METHODS

A major problem associated with reading a long list of methods is the tendency to acknowledge their value but not slow down long enough to implement any one method systematically. You may feel stimulated or overwhelmed by the many methods presented in the previous section. Unfortunately, neither of these feelings has a direct, positive effect on students' behavior. To improve students' learning and behavior, you must take time to use several of these methods thoughtfully in the classroom.

ACTIVITY 7.1
Implementing and Assessing New Teaching Methods

Label each of eight sheets of paper with one of the eight approaches to reducing disruptions during a lesson (see Figure 7.1). Next, under each topic, write one specific method you do not currently use and that you believe would help you reduce classroom disruptions. For example, on the page labeled *Giving clear instructions,* you might write: Place directions where they can be seen and referred to by students. The next step involves writing and completing these statements on each page:

I will begin using this method (give a specific date) _____ .
I will know that I have implemented this method when I have . . . .
After _____ days I will evaluate this method by . . . .

After thoughtfully and specifically completing these statements for each of the eight methods, write the following statement near the bottom of each page and complete it after you have implemented and evaluated the new method.

Based on my evaluation, I believe the new method . . .

In addition to selecting specific methods that will help improve students' learning and behavior, you will develop professionally by attempting the following activity that helps to demonstrate the value of collecting data on your use of new teaching methods.

ACTIVITY 7.2
Monitoring Students' Hand Raising

Part I

During a question-and-answer period, select five questions varying in difficulty. When asking these, stop approximately two-thirds of the way through each question and quickly count the number of hands that are raised. Also, try to notice which students have their hands up. It may help to involve a colleague or parent in collecting these data. After the lesson, complete these questions:

How many students had their hands raised when you stopped during each question?
Were considerably more hands raised for the less difficult question?
What did you notice about the students whose hands were raised? Did they tend to be your higher-achieving students?

Part II

During a question-and-answer period in the same subject with the same students, select five questions varying in difficulty. Wait five full seconds after completing each question. Count the number of hands that were raised to answer each of these questions. Again, try to notice which students raised their hands. After the lesson, complete these questions:

How many students had their hands raised to answer each question?
Were considerably more hands raised for the less difficult questions?
What did you notice about students who raised their hands?

Now compare the results of your two experiments. Make the task easier by completing this form for each set of questions.

Question	Number of Students' Hands Raised	Type of Student Raising Hand
1. Most difficult		
2.		
3.		
4.		
5. Least difficult		

Finally, complete these sentences.

I learned that . . . .
I was surprised that . . . .
When I waited longer . . . .

This is only one example of how you can collect data to assess the results obtained by implementing new teaching methods. Whenever possible, we encourage you to generate some form of evaluation to assess the results of using new methods.

SUMMARY

The original research on classroom management focused on the noninstructional aspects of teacher behavior that prevented disruptive student behavior. Jacob Kounin discovered that what differentiated effective from less effective classroom managers was what these teachers did before, not after, students became involved in unproductive behavior. This chapter presents eight areas of teacher behavior that are related to student behavior and achievement. For each area, a brief overview of the research findings and a number of specific suggestions teachers can use in order to increase positive student behavior are presented. Even though we now know that this is only one aspect of effective classroom management, you will find that by using a variety of the methods presented here, you can create a more smoothly run, efficient classroom in which student behavior is significantly more goal directed.

RECOMMENDED READING

Brophy, J., & Evertson, C. (1976). *Learning from teaching*. Boston: Allyn and Bacon.

Good, T., & Brophy, J. (1994). *Looking in classrooms* (6th ed.). New York: Harper and Row.

Hosford, P. (1984). *Using what we know about teaching*. Alexandria, VA: Association for Supervision and Curriculum Development.

Kounin, J. (1970). *Discipline and group management in classrooms*. New York: Holt, Rinehart and Winston.

Smith, D. (1984). *Essential knowledge for beginning educators*. Washington, DC: American Association of Colleges for Teacher Education.

Squires, D., Huitt, W., & Segars, J. (1984). *Effective schools and classrooms. A research-based perspective*. Alexandria, VA: Association for Supervision and Curriculum Development.

Wlodkowski, R. (1978). *Motivation and teaching: A practical guide*. Washington, DC: National Education Association.

CHAPTER 8

Developing Productive Student Behavior by Effectively Teaching Rules and Procedures

Although the rules and procedures used by effective classroom managers vary from teacher to teacher, we do not find effectively managed classrooms operating without them.

—Edmund Emmer, Carolyn Evertson, Julie Sanford, Barbara Clements, and Murray Worsham (1982)
Organizing and Managing the Junior High School Classroom

Until students are allowed to have and begin to feel a proprietary interest in school and classroom rules, classroom control and a good learning environment will always be at risk.

—Forrest Gathercoal (1993)
Judicious Discipline

And teachers can't expect students to follow rules they perceive only as arbitrary challenges to their freedom and dignity. When teachers take the time to explain the rationale underlying rules, student compliance increases.

—*Today's Education,* 1983–1984 Annual Edition

Teaching is a demanding, fast-paced job. Each day, the typical elementary school teacher has more than 1,000 teacher-student interactions and teaches 10 subjects. Secondary teachers often teach 150 or more students with only four minutes between classes. Those demanding working conditions can cause confusion and frustration and limit students' learning time. Research indicates that effective teachers take time early in the school year to develop classroom rules and procedures that help their classrooms run smoothly and minimize disruptions, and thus maximize students' learning time.

Research in teacher effectiveness has increasingly stressed that effective teachers organize their classrooms so as to prevent disruptive behavior. More than 20 years ago, Good and Brophy (1973) wrote, "Teachers who take time early in the year to listen to students and to explain carefully the rationales underlying rules and assignments are making a wise investment. This ultimately will establish teacher credibility and reduce the students' tendencies to continue to test the teacher throughout the year" (p. 168). Three years later, Brophy and Evertson (1976) reported a similar result: "Much of the behavior that distinguished the most effective teachers from the less effective ones was behavior that could be called 'proactive.' That is, it was behavior initiated by the teachers themselves, often prior to the beginning of the school year or the beginning of a particular school day" (p. 142). Research reviews by Soar and Soar (1979, 1980) also suggest that students' learning is enhanced by teachers' developing basic classroom structure. Soar and Soar (1979) wrote that "unless a teacher has established a minimum of structure, relatively strong interactions that are not functional for pupil learning are likely to occur" (p. 117).

Research conducted at the Research and Development Center for Teacher Education at the University of Texas at Austin (Emmer, Evertson, & Anderson, 1980; Evertson & Emmer, 1982a, 1982b) provides specific information on techniques that effective teachers use during the first few weeks of school. Effective classroom managers at both the elementary and junior high school level spend time teaching students classroom rules and procedures. Emmer, Evertson, Sanford, Clements, and Worsham (1981) described *rules* as "written rules which are either posted in the classroom, given to students on ditto or other copy, or copied by students into their notebooks" (pp. 18, 19). *Procedures* were defined as, "Procedures, like rules, are expectations for behavior. They usually apply to a *specific* activity, and they usually are directed at accomplishing, rather than forbidding some behavior" (p. 19). Effective teachers do more than post rules or present procedures. Especially in elementary classrooms, teachers work with students to ensure that they understand and can demonstrate rules and procedures. This is an important point. Students' behavior needs to be dealt with much like their academic skills. Teachers spend considerable time during the first few weeks of school assessing students' knowledge, reviewing material, and reteaching academic skills students have forgotten. Similarly, when effective teachers first introduce important academic material, they attempt to provide clear instruction, carefully monitor students' progress, and provide immediate corrective feedback if a student or group of students are having difficulty with the material. In the same manner, teachers must begin the school year by teaching the classroom rules and procedures, carefully monitoring students' behavior, informing students of mistakes, and reteaching rules or procedures that students are frequently failing to follow.

The initial studies involving teacher behavior at the beginning of the school year were correlational; teachers whose students made greater achievement gains were observed establishing rules and procedures and carefully monitoring student work. Following these discoveries, however, several studies were conducted to determine whether teachers trained in the materials in this chapter were more effective in increasing student on-task behavior and learning than were teachers who did not receive this training and implement these new teacher behaviors.

Results from these studies (Evertson, 1985; Evertson, Emmer, Sanford, & Clements, 1983) clearly demonstrate that providing training in these methods can lead to changes in teacher behaviors that are associated with improved student behavior. In addition, Evertson (1985) found that even when provided to teachers who had recently received systematic training to improve their instructional skills, training in effectively developing, monitoring, and reinforcing classroom rules and procedures was associated with improved student behavior. Figures 8.1 and 8.2 outline the content presented in the elementary and secondary teacher training sessions.

Teachers must keep in mind that many behaviors that are undesirable in the classroom are not inherently bad and in fact may be encouraged in other settings. For example, neither student chatter nor attention-seeking behavior is bad or destructive in itself. One would expect 30 children placed in close quarters to make a considerable amount of noise. Similarly, children often show off in front of adults or their peers. In fact, adults encourage children to seek the limelight in sporting events or other competitive activities. Therefore, we should not be surprised to discover that we must help children develop attitudes and skills that support behavioral norms that are most adaptive for specific school activities.

FIGURE 8.1
Major Components Presenting in Beginning-of-Year Treatment

1. *Readying the classroom.* Be certain your classroom space and materials are ready for the beginning of the year.
2. *Planning rules and procedures.* Think about what procedures students must follow to function effectively in your classroom and in the school environment: decide what behaviors are acceptable or unacceptable; develop a list of procedures and rules.
3. *Consequences.* Decide ahead of time consequences for appropriate and inappropriate behavior in your classroom, and communicate them to your students; follow through consistently.
4. *Teaching rules and procedures.* Teach students rules and procedures systematically; include in your lesson plans for the beginning of school sequences for teaching rules and procedures, when and how they will be taught, and when practice and review will occur.
5. *Beginning-of-school activities.* Develop activities for the first few days of school that will involve students readily and maintain a whole-group focus.
6. *Strategies for potential problems.* Plan strategies to deal with potential problems that could upset your classroom organization and management.
7. *Monitoring.* Monitor student behavior closely.
8. *Stopping inappropriate behavior.* Handle inappropriate and disruptive behavior promptly and consistently.
9. *Organizing instruction.* Organize instruction to provide learning activities at suitable levels for all students in your class.
10. *Student accountability.* Develop procedures that keep the children responsible for their work.
11. *Instructional clarity.* Be clear when you present information and give directions to your students.

Source: C. Evertson, E. Emmer, J. Sanford, and B. Clements. "Improving Management: An Experiment in Elementary School Classrooms," *Elementary School Journal,* 84 (1983): 173–188. Copyright © 1983 by The University of Chicago.

I. *Planning* (before school starts)
   A. Use of space (readying the classroom)
   B. Rules for general behavior
   C. Rules and procedures for specific areas
      1. Student use of classroom space and facilities
      2. Student uses of out-of-class areas
      3. Student participation during whole class activities/seatwork
      4. Student participation in daily routines
      5. Student participation during small-group activities
   D. Consequence/incentives for appropriate/inappropriate behavior
   E. Activities for the first day of school
II. *Presenting Rules, Procedures, and Expectation* (beginning of school)
   A. Teaching rules and procedures
      1. Explanation   3. Feedback
      2. Rehearsal   4. Reteaching
   B. Teaching academic content
   C. Communicating concepts and directions clearly
III. *Maintaining the System* (throughout the year)
   A. Monitoring for behavioral and academic compliance
   B. Acknowledging appropriate behavior
   C. Stopping inappropriate behavior
   D. Consistent use of consequences/incentives
   E. Adjusting instruction for individual students/groups
   F. Keeping students accountable for work
   G. Coping with special problems

FIGURE 8.2
Outline of Workshop Content for Secondary Teachers in the Experimental Group

Source: Carolyn M. Evertson, "Training Teachers in Classroom Management: An Experimental Study in Secondary School Classrooms," *Journal of Educational Research,* 79 (1): 54, 1985. Reprinted with permission of the Helen Dwight Reid Educational Foundation. Published by Heldref Publications, 1319 Eighteenth St., N.W., Washington, D.C. 20036-1802. Copyright © 1985.

Several words of caution are offered before discussing approaches to establishing productive classroom rules and procedures. Rules and procedures should be developed in conjunction with teaching strategies that help students meet their personal and academic needs. In his *Culture against Man,* Jules Henry (1963) vividly depicted an example of a classroom procedure that violates students' personal needs.

> Boris had trouble reducing "12/16" to the lowest terms, and could only get as far as "6/8." The teacher asked him quietly if that was as far as he could reduce it. She suggested he "think." Much heaving up and down and waving of hands by the other children, all frantic to correct him. . . . She then turns to the class and says, "Well, who can tell Boris what the number is?" A forest of hands appears, and the teacher calls Peggy. Peggy says that four may be divided into the numerator and the denominator.
>
>   Thus Boris' failure has made it possible for Peggy to succeed; his depression is the price of her exhilaration; his misery the occasion for her rejoicing. This is the standard condition of the American elementary school, and is why so many of us feel a

> contraction of the heart even if someone we never knew succeeds merely at garnering plankton in the Thames: because so often somebody's success has been bought at the cost of our failure. (pp. 295, 296)

Unfortunately, students are often expected to behave in compliance with rules and procedures even though the learning environment does not respond sensitively to their needs and interests. When this condition is found in a classroom, it is understandable that students' behavior begins to oppose the classroom rules. The educational exchange must function effectively in both directions. Students can be expected to support rules and procedures that enhance learning only if the learning process shows respect for students and their needs.

Jerome Freiberg (Freiberg, 1993; Freiberg, Huang, Stein, & Waxman, 1994; Freiberg, Prokosch, & Treister, 1990) has recently presented exciting data indicating that his Consistency Management program is associated with improved achievement and behavior in inner-city elementary classrooms. The program emphasizes providing students with opportunities to be responsible for meaningful organizational tasks within the classroom and throughout the school. In addition, rather than the teacher developing the classroom rules, teachers are encouraged to have students create their own set of behaviorial expectations. Freiberg's program places a major emphasis on treating students and staff with dignity and enhancing their sense of responsibility for the creation of a postive learning environment. In a similar vein, Mary Kay Tetreault (1993) found four themes in her study of teachers who are "committed to improving the education of women and minorities" (p. 141). These themes are: (1) allowing mastery of content to move away from comprehension of what the teacher or expert thought was essential and to include the student's construction of knowledge as a central issue in the classroom, (2) including the student's voice in asking questions and bringing her or his perspective to bear, (3) modifying the role of authority so that teachers become facilitators of learning and shared decision makers with students, and (4) authenticating the contributions of those from various cultural groups and from women as well as men.

Crystal Kuykendall (1992) made a similar point in her book *From Rage to Hope: Strategies for Reclaiming Black and Hispanic Youth.* She noted that classrooms have historically been established to focus on order and have deemphasized or punished a personal, interactive approach to learning. Kuykendall argued that this passive type of learning environment disadvantages students of color who are likely to have a more field-dependent, interactive, personalized mode of learning.

These comments are presented here to highlight the importance of considering the learning needs, interests, and styles of all learners when developing classroom structures. As indicated throughout this book, the authors are deeply concerned that management techniques not become viewed as strategies for maintaining simple obedience, especially when this obedience is focused on behaviors related to very traditional ways of teaching and learning. Instead, it is hoped that the reader will use the materials in this and subsequent chapters as a basis for collaborating with students to develop classroom expectations and procedures that help create mutual respect and shared decision making and responsibility between all students and their classroom teacher.

Another concept that can help you thoughtfully develop classroom rules is that rules should not be designed to catch children misbehaving so that they can be punished. Instead, rules should provide guidelines or benchmarks that help children examine their behavior, considering its effect on themselves and others. Consequently, behavior that violates accepted rules should be dealt with by discussing the matter with the child. This does not mean that reasonable punishments should not be used, but when dealing with unproductive behavior, teachers must help children examine both their motivations and the consequences of their actions. Overemphasis on punishment often obscures the issue of motivation and attitude and simultaneously limits the child's attention to the immediate negative consequences of his or her behavior. This pressure tends to limit thoughtful consideration of either the effect the behavior has on others or the long-term

"And then, of course, there's the possibility of being just the slightest bit too organized."

consequences associated with continuing the behavior. In a real sense, a punishment orientation reinforces a low level of moral development and does not help children develop a higher, more socially valuable level of morality.

DEVELOPING CLASSROOM RULES AND EXPECTATIONS

Several factors increase the likelihood that students will accept and consistently follow classroom rules. First, students need to be involved in developing the rules that apply in the classroom. Second, rules need to be clearly stated. Students have difficulty responding to glittering generalities such as "behave appropriately." Third, although it is important to state expectations clearly, it is just as important to keep the rules as few as possible. Fourth, students must clearly indicate their acceptance of the rules agreed on by the classroom group. Fifth, because rules established in the school setting may conflict with rules children experience outside of school, it is important that student behavior be monitored and frequently discussed to ensure that it is consistent with the classroom rules. Finally, students will be more likely to behave in accordance with rules if they know that the rules are accepted by significant others, such as their parents and peers.

In his book *Judicious Discipline,* Forrest Gathercoal (1993) has developed a method of developing rules that stems from the Bill of Rights. In her creative book *Practicing Judicious Discipline,* Barbara McEwan (1991) presented a number of practical strategies for helping students understand their rights and responsibilities and for developing positive school communities where students accept responsibility because they understand such issues as their constitutional rights; compelling state interest; limits of time, place, and manner; and so on.

The specific methods presented in the remainder of this chapter apply most directly to elementary school classrooms or other relatively small, self-contained settings, such as a special education class or a small alternative school. The basic ideas, however, describe the essential ingredients in establishing classroom rules and responsibilities. Whenever significant variations are needed for secondary classrooms, they are included.

Discussing the Value of Rules

The first step in developing classroom rules is to help students discuss why it is important to develop rules that all members of the class agree to follow. You may want to introduce or stimulate the discussion by asking students why adults have rules such as obeying traffic signals, paying their taxes, and not crowding in lines. Throughout this discussion, reinforce the concept that the classroom group and the school are a society, and, like larger societal groups, it will function more effectively when people decide to create and follow rules. Help students consider how rules benefit people who must work together. This topic places the focus clearly on the advantages each child derives from class members' accepting the rules. For example, students may state that rules are important because if everyone did whatever he or she wanted, the classroom might become too disruptive for effective studying.

Students' statements on why it is important to develop classroom rules can be written on the chalkboard or a large piece of butcher paper. The latter approach has the advantage of making the list easier to save and discuss later should the group have difficulty in following its rules. Secondary teachers generally use a less elaborate discussion of why rules are needed. Nevertheless, teachers should elicit students' comments about why rules are needed when a group of people work for some time together in a relatively small space.

Developing a List

The next step in developing functional classroom rules is to have the students list all rules they believe are important. These can include rules related to academic as well as behavioral expectations. An academic rule might include working quietly during study periods or attempting to complete all homework on time. During this stage, help the students state all rules in a positive manner. If a student states, "Don't talk while others are talking," help the student phrase this rule thus: "Each student should listen quietly while another person is talking." Similarly, "Students should not steal from each other, the teacher, or the school" could be stated as, "If anyone needs something, he or she will ask to borrow it." Once the students and you have completed their list of rules, help them cross out any that do not apply and combine as many as possible.

Secondary teachers may not want to develop a separate list for each of five or six classes; two optional strategies are available. First, some teachers have each class select one rule. These rules are combined to form the teacher's class rules. Second, some teachers present their own rules and ask each class if they believe one or two additional rules might help their class.

Figure 8.3 lists classroom rules that can be used in either an elementary or secondary classroom. Rules need to be general and all encompassing. When developing such a list with young children, teachers can increase students' understanding by discussing, role-playing, and initially displaying (pictorially or in writing) several specific behavioral examples of following and violating each rule. Activity 8.1 (at the end of the chapter) offers you an opportunity to practice developing classroom rules that would be appropriate and effective with the students with whom you work.

Getting a Commitment

When the final list has been developed, lead a discussion to clarify each rule and ask students to state whether they can accept each rule. During this important stage, several students may state that they do not believe they can abide by a particular rule. You can then ask the students whether the rule seems to be one that does not help people or whether they agree that it is a good rule but do not believe they can consistently act in accordance with it. If they express the latter, you can explain that they are not expected to be able to act perfectly all the time. Just as they will learn how to solve new math problems and read more efficiently, they will also learn how to behave in ways that are more effective. The initial question is not whether the students can already solve all their math problems or consistently behave appropriately, but whether they believe that these skills are helpful to them and if they will attempt to improve these skills. If the students state that a rule is not acceptable, you can help them clarify why they believe it to be undesirable. In most cases, students will quickly acknowledge the basic value of the rule. If one or more students persist in stating that a rule is unacceptable, however, you have the option of deleting the rule or asking to postpone further discussion of the item until you have had an opportunity to discuss it with the small group of students who disagree.

A number of teachers have their students take the list of rules home (usually with an accompanying statement about how the teacher will handle persistent rule violation) for parents to sign and return. This strategy is particularly useful when working with young adolescents or a group of students who a teacher expects may

---

1. Speak politely to others.
2. Treat each other kindly.
3. Follow teacher requests.
4. Be prepared for class.
5. Make a good effort at your work and request help if you need it.
6. Obey all school rules.

FIGURE 8.3
Classroom Rules

have difficulty consistently demonstrating responsible behavior. The fact that everyone responsible for the students' behavior understands the rules and consequences can have a positive effect on student behavior and can minimize the confusion and tension associated with instances when parents must be contacted about a student's inappropriate behavior.

When sending a list of rules and consequences home, it is important to include a general philosophy statement about your classroom management and instruction. This lets you present the issue of rules in a positive manner that indicates their relationship to effective instruction and student learning. For example, your statement might begin:

> As an educator, I believe all students can learn, demonstrate concern for others, and choose to act responsibly in the classroom. My goals as a teacher are to help all students learn to the best of their capabilities and to assist students to work effectively with others. My goal is to create a classroom environment that encourages mutual respect and cooperation and that provides opportunities for students to make choices regarding their behavior. In order to create a positive and productive learning environment in which all students can achieve and learn to take responsibility for themselves, I have worked with the students to create a list of rules and procedures that will guide our behavior. Because I know you share my deep concern for the quality of your child's learning, I would appreciate your discussing the attached material with your child, signing it, and returning it to me by _____. I look forward to working with your child and to communicating with you concerning his or her progress, special achievements, and any concerns that may arise.

Monitoring and Reviewing Classroom Rules

Once students have developed reasonable rules and agreed to behave in accordance with them, the next step is to help them recognize and monitor their behavior. One approach helpful with primary-age children is to have them take turns acting out the rules. Each child can be asked to role-play both the appropriate and inappropriate behavior, and you can ask their peers to raise their hands whenever the student is behaving appropriately and place their hands in their lap when the student is behaving inappropriately. This activity is helpful in ensuring that every child clearly understands the rules.

Especially in elementary school classrooms, it is important to review the rules frequently for several weeks. A good approach is to review them every day for the first week, three times a week during the second week, and once a week thereafter. It is also helpful to have the rules displayed in a prominent place in the classroom. During the first week, it is desirable to discuss them briefly at the beginning of each day and to end the day by having the class evaluate their behavior and consider whether improvement in any area is needed. If the entire class consistently displays appropriate behavior or shows considerable improvement over the previous day, you may want to send a positive note or award home with each student. Significant individual improvements can be similarly rewarded. After the first month of school, there are several occasions on which the rules should be brought to the class's attention. First, it is a good idea to review these rules every two weeks to determine whether they are still meaningful and whether any rules need to be added or deleted.

Classroom rules also need to be reviewed with each new student who enters the class. Many students who transfer during the school year come from highly mobile families. Some of these students have often had a pattern of difficulties in school. It is important that these students get off to a good start, which can be facilitated by their knowing the expectations for classroom behavior. A student who does well in class and is respected by other students can be assigned to help new students learn classroom rules and procedures.

Rules should also be discussed when a student or the teacher indicates that violation of one or more of the rules is detracting from learning or is infringing on a student's rights. Recently, a secondary intern teacher met with one of the authors to express concern about a sophomore class he viewed as very difficult to manage. The intern noted that students talked incessantly while peers were answering questions and that there was a very high rate of put-downs. The intern, who had been skeptical of some of the materials presented in this book, decided that things were going so badly that he had nothing to lose by taking several class periods to discuss the problem with the students and attempt to establish some expectations and procedures for the class. The teacher discussed his concern with the class and allowed them to brainstorm a set of expectations they thought would be realistic. Students edited these as a whole class and signed an agreement to attempt to follow their new expectations. The teacher then asked students to give input on what should occur if students chose to violate these expectations. Students developed the procedures they believed the teacher should follow. The next day, the intern presented a typed copy of the decisions to students and everyone signed it. The expectations and procedures for responding to violations were posted on the wall. The intern commented that he simply could not believe the difference in the class. Indeed, he shared with his colleagues that on the following day, when two of his most disruptive students started to talk out, he simply nodded toward the posted lists and the students apologized and returned to their work.

CLASSROOM PROCEDURES

As mentioned earlier in this chapter, research indicates that effective teachers not only work with students to develop classroom rules but also teach the procedures they expect students to follow during specific classroom activities. This research also provides specific information on the types of classroom activities for which effective teachers develop procedures. In their research in elementary classrooms, Evertson and Emmer (1982b) found five general areas in which effective teachers taught students how to act:

1. Students' use of classroom space and facilities
2. Students' behavior in areas outside the classroom, such as the bathroom, lunchroom, drinking fountain, and playgrounds
3. Procedures to follow during whole-class activities, such as whether to raise a hand to speak, where to turn in work, and how to get help during seatwork
4. Procedures during small-group work
5. Additional procedures, such as how to behave at the beginning and end of the school day, and when a visitor arrives

Effective Procedures

Figure 8.4 outlines the major classroom activities for which elementary teachers who are particularly effective managers develop and teach procedures. For junior high school classrooms, researchers found four key areas in which effective teachers developed procedures:

1. Beginning the class
2. Whole-class activities
3. Procedures related to academic accountability
4. Other activities, such as the end of the class period, interruptions in the class, and fire drills

FIGURE 8.4
Elementary
Classroom
Procedures

    I. *Room Areas*
      A. Student desks, tables, storage areas
      B. Learning centers, stations
      C. Shared materials
      D. Teacher's desk, storage
      E. Fountain, sink, bathroom, pencil sharpener
    II. *School Areas*
      A. Bathroom, fountain, office, library
      B. Lining up
      C. Playground
      D. Lunchroom
    III. *Whole-Class Activities/Seatwork*
      A. Student participation
      B. Signals for student attention
      C. Talk among students
      D. Making assignments
      E. Passing out books, supplies
      F. Turning in work
      G. Handing back assignments
      H. Make-up work
      I. Out-of-seat policies
      J. Activities after work is finished
    IV. *Small-Group Activities*
      A. Student movement into and out of group
      B. Bringing materials to groups
      C. Expected behavior of students in group
      D. Expected behavior of students out of group
    V. *Other Procedures*
      A. Beginning of school day
      B. End of school day
      C. Student conduct during delays, interruptions
      D. Fire drills
      E. Housekeeping and student helpers

Figure 8.5 outlines the major classroom activities for which secondary teachers who effectively manage their classrooms develop and teach specific procedures. Figure 8.6 outlines the areas in which effective classroom managers teach specific procedures related to student accountability for academic work.

An example from junior high school can clarify the concept of procedures. Most junior high school students have only four or five minutes between classes. Therefore, they usually enter the classroom excited or agitated, having had little time to review what they learned in their previous class or to get mentally prepared for the coming class. The teacher discussed this problem with the students in his class and worked with them to develop procedures for making a smooth transition when entering the classroom. First, the class and the teacher listed warm-up activities for the first four minutes of class. These activities, which changed every month, included:

1. An instructional warm-up activity
2. Sharing something you had learned in school during the past day
3. A relaxation activity
4. Listening to music selected by the teacher
5. Listening to music selected by the students

Students daily selected the transition activity, each activity being used once each week. The teacher also developed a procedure for tardy students to report to

I. *Beginning Class*
   A. Rollcall, absentees
   B. Tardy students
   C. Behavior during PA
   D. Academic warm-ups or getting ready routines
   E. Distributing materials
II. *Instructional Activities*
   A. Teacher-student contacts
   B. Student movement in the room
   C. Signal for student attention
   D. Headings for papers
   E. Student talk during seatwork
   F. Activities to do when work is done
III. *Ending Class*
   A. Putting away supplies, equipment
   B. Organizing materials for next class
   C. Dismissing class
IV. *Other Procedures*
   A. Student rules about teacher's desk
   B. Fire drills
   C. Lunch procedures
   D. Bathroom, water fountains
   E. Lockers

FIGURE 8.5
Secondary Classroom Procedures

I. *Work Requirements*
  A. Heading papers
  B. Use of pen or pencil
  C. Writing on back of paper
  D. Neatness, legibility
  E. Incomplete papers
  F. Late work
  G. Missed work
  H. Due dates
  I. Make-up work
II. *Communicating Assignments*
  A. Posting assignments
  B. Requirements/grading criteria for assignments
  C. Instructional groups
  D. Provisions for absentees
  E. Long-term assignments
III. *Monitoring Student Work*
  A. In-class oral participation
  B. Completion of in-class assignments
  C. Completion of homework assignments
  D. Completion of stages of long-term assignments
IV. *Checking Assignments in Class*
  A. Students' exchanging papers
  B. Marking and grading papers
  C. Turning in papers
V. *Grading Procedures*
  A. Determining report card grades
  B. Recording grades
  C. Grading stages of long-term assignments
  D. Extra credit
VI. *Academic Feedback*
  A. Rewards and incentives
  B. Posting student work
  C. Communication with parents
  D. Students' record of their grades

FIGURE 8.6
Accountability
Procedures

class, a procedure for taking roll, and a signal for gaining the students' attention at the end of the transition activity. Similar procedures were developed for summarizing the day's lesson and leaving the classroom. Activity 8.2 gives you an opportunity to consider the procedures you wish to establish in your classroom.

Teaching and Monitoring Classroom Procedures

A procedure is best taught by:

1. Discussing the need for the procedure
2. Possibly soliciting student ideas

3. Having students practice the procedure until it is performed correctly
4. Reinforcing the correct behavior

When introducing the procedure of developing a signal to obtain students' attention, you might work with the class to develop the signal, set a goal (everyone facing the teacher and quiet within five seconds), use the procedure while students are engaged in an activity, and reinforce them when they respond within the determined time limit. For a procedure such as lining up, you might elicit ideas for behaviors students display when lining up, practice lining up, and reinforce the class when they line up in the desired manner.

Classroom procedures must be carefully monitored during their initial acquisition. Early in the school year, teachers should respond to almost every violation of a rule or procedure. When you notice that the class or an individual student is not correctly following a procedure, the best approach is to ask the student to state the correct procedure and then to demonstrate it. If a class lines up poorly after having once demonstrated the correct procedure, you should politely comment that you know the class can line up more effectively and ask them to return to their seats so that they can practice the procedure. You might then ask students to describe the behaviors associated with lining up correctly. The class could then be asked to demonstrate their skill and be reinforced for their improved effort. Effectively teaching procedures to students is similar to good athletic coaching. The skilled coach first demonstrates the new procedure—often having the athlete perform the maneuver in slow motion. The athlete is then asked to perform the task and receives feedback on the performance, sometimes in the form of videotape replay. The coach has the athlete practice until the feat is performed satisfactorily. Later, perhaps under game conditions, if the athlete performs the task incorrectly, the coach reteaches it in a subsequent practice session. Figure 8.7 lists a number of interesting and fun methods for teaching classroom rules and procedures to students.

One teacher recently found that her classroom was becoming quite noisy during an afternoon study period. Despite several clear I-messages from the teacher as well as several students, the classroom continued to be unproductively loud during this time. Consequently, at the beginning of the study period the next day, the teacher asked the class to discuss the rule of maintaining a noise level that was conducive to studying. The class decided that they often became too loud and agreed to reduce their noise level. At the end of the period, the teacher asked the students to examine the amount of work they had completed. Most students acknowledged that they had accomplished much more work. The teacher brought the issue to the attention of the class again the next day and every other day for six days. Because the noise level appeared to maintain an acceptable level, the discussions were terminated. The rule had been reestablished.

Although it is obvious to any veteran teacher that there were other factors involved—including the teacher's respect for his students and his attempt to actively engage them in the learning material—the teacher himself noted that he believed the key variable was his actively involving students in solving the problem and committing to their decisions.

FIGURE 8.7
Creative Ways to
Teach Rules and
Routines

1. *Puppet Plays:* Use puppets to role-play responsible behaviors. Have students discuss what was appropriate. Have students identify what behaviors were not appropriate, what rules relate to the behaviors, and what behaviors should have happened instead.
2. *Storytime:* In September, read books to students that teach lessons on following rules and procedures and the rewards from self-discipline.
3. *Posters:* Have students make good behavior, good study habit, safety rules, etc. posters for the classroom, school hallways, cafeteria, and so on. Hang them where appropriate to remind students of your expectations.
4. *Letters:* Teach how to write friendly letters. Have students write letters to playground aides, bus drivers, cooks, custodians, the principal, etc., regarding the rules and their plans to be self-disciplined in the area of interest to whom the letter is written.
5. *Oops, I Goofed!:* Conduct a class discussion on student experiences when they broke a rule. Have students share a personal experience when they goofed in their behavior. Have students share what they should have done instead. Focus in on the idea that we all make mistakes and it is OK if you learn from the mistake and don't repeat it.
6. *Create a Play:* Have students write and produce a play on rules and procedures. Have students present the play to other classes in the school.
7. *School in Relation to Community Rules:* Have students share how school rules and the reasons for following them relate to community rules and their responsibilities as citizens.
8. *Rule Unscramble:* Have your class/school rules stated in phrases. Mix up the words in the phrase. Have students put the words in correct order so they make sense. Or mix up the letters of the words in a rule and have students put the letters of each word back in order so rules make sense.
9. *Rule Bingo:* Make bingo cards with classroom/school rules listed in each square. Have a student or the teacher act out the rule. Students cover the square if they have the rule listed that is being acted out.
10. *Wrong Way:* Have students role-play the wrong way to behave or the wrong way to follow procedures. Videotape the role-playing and have the whole group review and discuss not only what was done wrong but also how to do it the right way.
11. *Hug or Handshake:* When the teacher or students "catch" others following the rules, ask them if they want a hug or handshake and reward them with their wish.
12. *Contract for Success:* Have students write a letter to their parents listing the rules for the class and their plan for successful behavior and self-discipline for the school year. Have students take the letter home and review it with their parents. All persons sign the Contract for Success. Student returns the contract to school the next day.
13. *Picture Signals:* Have pictures as signals for each classroom rule. For example, ears for the rule "We listen politely." or chair for "Sit correctly in your chair." Then use the pictures to signal students if they are not following the rule. The picture signals allow silent management rather than having to stop teaching to tell students what they are doing wrong.
14. *Rules in the Sack:* Write rules on cards and put them into a paper sack. Have a student draw out a rule from the sack and explain it to the rest of the class.

15. *Hidden Rules:* Fold paper. On the inside write the class rule. On the outside of the folded paper give clues to the rule. Students read clues and guess the rule. They open the folded paper to see if they are correct. This also works well for a bulletin board display.

16. *Numbered Rules:* Give each classroom rule a number. When a student is following a rule correctly, ask students to hold up the number of fingers which related to the rule being followed. Or when teaching rules, give clues for a specific rule and students hold up the correct number of fingers for the correct numbered rule.

17. *Discrimination:* Develop a list of correct and incorrect behaviors relating to the rules and routines of the classroom and school. Have students read through the list and separate the correct from the incorrect, thus making two lists from the one. Use this discrimination activity during a reading class.

18. *Wheel of Fortune:* Play *Wheel of Fortune* where rules are the puzzles to be solved. Students guess letters of the puzzle and try to guess the rule in the puzzle.

19. *Awards:* Design certificates or bookmarker awards for classroom rules. Give students the awards when their behavior reflects appropriate behavior in relation to the specific rule.

20. *Picture Posters:* Have students bring a picture of themselves to school. Use student pictures on posters to highlight a school rule. "The following students believe it is important to respect all teachers." Show their pictures listing their names and grades. Post the posters throughout the school. Use positive peer pressure for pride in school.

Source: Deborah Johnson, Lidgerwood Elementary School, Spokane, Washington. Reprinted by permission.

CREATIVE EXAMPLES OF TEACHING RULES AND PROCEDURES

Case Study: Dealing with the Dilemma of Gum Chewing

In his thoughtful book *Judicious Discipline*, Forrest Gathercoal presented a marvelous true story about how one administrator handled the issue of gum chewing. Gathercoal (1993) wrote:

> Instead of using rules and punishments as a means of banning gum, for example, why not approach the matter as an educator would—teach students how to use gum properly. Students are far more likely to develop good character and become accountable for their behavior when they are respected as student/citizens capable of learning personal responsibility.
>
> I remember an anecdote an elementary principal shared with me about his experience with "the gum problem." He had been a teacher in his building before being appointed principal and was familiar with the problems they had with gum damage. The custodian was constantly complaining about the wrappers on the floor and gum under the furniture. The punishments for chewing gum were harsh, but the problem continued.

When he became an administrator, one of his first acts was to revise some of the rules. One change in particular reversed the ban on gum chewing. His new plan suggested that the faculty spend some time during the first day of class teaching students how to use gum properly. Teachers instructed their classes in the appropriate way to chew gum, how to wrap it in paper when out of their mouths, where to discard the gum, and how to care for the empty wrapper.

Curious about the effect of this educational approach, a few weeks into the school year the principal asked the custodian if there was a problem with gum in the building. The custodian replied that he was surprised by the fact there was no gum anywhere around school, not even the wrappers on the floor. "I don't know what you did," he said, "but you are the toughest principal we ever had here."

Another three weeks passed. The conversation again surfaced and still no evidence of gum damage was found. "You really are tough," the principal was told. "What did you do?" The principal explained that the old rules were replaced by a more positive educational approach to teaching responsibility. The custodian listened in disbelief and, without a word, walked away shaking his head. (p. 76)

Case Study: Developmental Recess

A number of years ago, one of the authors was asked to assist an elementary school staff in solving the problems of repeated referrals for playground misbehavior. The staff was concerned that their responses to continued misbehavior were not severe enough and wondered if they needed a more progressive approach to disciplining the repeated offenders. The author took two approaches to assisting the staff with their concern. First, the staff involved in playground supervision, along with the schoolwide student management committee, examined data to determine the type and frequency of misbehavior leading to a referral. This was done to determine whether there were key procedures (such as how to use a particular piece of equipment or how to play a game) that needed to be taught or retaught.

Following this, the committee was asked to consider how they were defining discipline. When confronted with continued behavior problems, it is more effective to consider what procedures or skills need to be taught to the students involved. Based on the belief that many behavior problems can be dealt with by providing students with new skills (see social skills training in Chapter 11 for further information), the author assisted the staff in establishing a developmental recess. Developmental recess removes students who have had a designated number of behavior problems on the playground and provides them with an opportunity to learn and practice the procedures for successful participation. After demonstrating acceptable behavior for a designated number of days in the developmental recess, the student may return to the normal recess activities. Physical education teachers, parent volunteers, instructional assistants, and principals have staffed this activity.

One of the authors recently worked with a staff who implemented a developmental lunch in which they provided students who had difficulty using acceptable cafeteria manners with an opportunity to learn and practice these behaviors. Figure 8.8 presents an outline of a developmental recess procedure developed by a state director of special education.

FIGURE 8.8
Developmental
Recess

The Concept

Developmental recess is one technique for helping children learn the specific skills they need to behave successfully while at recess. Since successful recess experience requires skills important to success in many other areas of life, developmental recess is viewed by many as an important component of comprehensive school curriculum.

If a child is having difficulty behaving appropriately during recess, it is very likely that the child has social skill or other playground skill deficits. Although appropriate consequences for irresponsible choices can be valuable teaching tools, the application of negative consequences as a "stand-alone" intervention does little to remediate playground skill deficits. When a child has difficulty reading, schools teach specific reading skills. The child is not placed in time-out with the hope that reading will be better in the future. When a child has difficulty with playground behavior, it is just as essential that appropriate replacement behaviors be taught and rehearsed.

This concept may be used with activities and situations other than recess. Such structured teaching of prosocial skills may be of value in relation to cafeteria behavior, school assembly behavior, and so on.

Sample Developmental Recess Model

Development recess is a relatively new concept, and a number of developmental recess models are being developed. All derive from the basic concept of teaching prosocial replacement behaviors. One model gaining popularity in a number of Oregon schools involves the following:

1. Teaching prosocial skills in small groups just prior to recess
2. Monitoring student choices during recess
3. Positive debriefing with those students immediately following recess

The following specific steps may be useful to those implementing this model for the first time:

1. Identify two school adults who are skilled and willing to work with students who have behavior difficulties at recess. One of these adults might be a school counselor, school psychologist, behavior consultant, child development specialist, and so on. The other could be a classroom teacher, administrator, playground assistant, and so on.
2. Identify a small group of students who could benefit from involvement in developmental recess.
3. Inform parents of the purpose and nature of developmental recess and obtain written authorization from parents to include the selected children in the group.
4. Assess the selected students to determine skill deficits and gather appropriate instructional materials needed for teaching prosocial skills. Assessment strategies could include the use of behavior rating scales, student self-report instruments, direct observation, and the like.
5. Schedule developmental recess in consultation with the classroom teachers of the selected students. It is recommended that students participate in developmental recess at least three or four times per week for four to six weeks. Many schools have developmental recess occur during recess.

(continued)

FIGURE 8.8
Continued

6. As children demonstrate appropriate behavior during developmental recess (usually for three to five consecutive days), they return to the regular recess.
7. For several days following their return, students check with the developmental recess facilitator prior to recess to discuss their goals and after recess to evaluate their behavior. As students experience success, they can report less frequently.

Case Study: Teaching Students to Respect Physical Space

One of the authors recently worked with a staff whose elementary students were frequently involved in inappropriate (violent or sexual) touch. A staff committee developed a plan for teaching students about individuals' personal space. In a large assembly followed by work in classrooms, students were shown (by a flashlight hanging over a student in a darkened room) that everyone has some physical space. Students were then asked to use yarn to circle themselves with the physical space they needed in various situations. This was then utilized during classtime and recess for several days. The staff reported that students quickly learned the procedure of not invading another person's physical space and that inappropriate touch on the playground, while still present, occurred at a much lower rate.

Case Study: Teaching Students Hallway Behavior in a Middle School

One of the authors recently worked with a staff who was concerned about student behavior in the hallways. Some teachers were concerned that students were not punished enough when caught being unsafe in the halls and other teachers pointed to the lack of staff consistency in responding to inappropriate student hallway behavior. The author asked the staff to discuss where the problems occurred. It soon became obvious that students were having problems in two specific areas of the building. Someone suggested that the staff involve the students in examining the problem and determining a solution. The staff and students developed a series of traffic signs (such as "yield right," "merge left," etc.) that were placed in the necessary areas. Students were then given instruction in how to move in the congested areas. Results indicated that referrals for student misconduct in hallways decreased dramatically once the procedures were collaboratively developed and effectively taught.

Changing Teachers' Procedures

Although most attention is focused on teaching students to follow selected school and classroom procedures, student behavior can often be more quickly and dramatically improved by altering the procedures adults follow. For example, one of the authors recently worked with an elementary school staff that expressed concern about student behavior both at the end of recess and in the hallways. After considerable discussion about how to teach students to behave more responsibly in these settings, one of the teachers noted that if teachers would develop the procedure of meeting their students outside at the end of recess and walking their students to physical education, music, and lunch, there would be much less chaos and many happier students. The teachers discovered that although it took approximately four minutes more each day to follow this procedure, they were saving at least five times that much instructional time because of the decrease in disruptive student behavior during and following transition times.

In a similar vein, one of the authors worked with a school staff that was concerned about how rudely students responded to adults. Again, the staff was engaged in very positive discussions about how to teach students improved communication skills. After implementing this social skills training, however, the staff remained frustrated by the level of rude responses. With some outside assistance, the staff began to realize that a significant amount of this "rudeness," or failure to respond positively to adult statements, occurred when adults were correcting students. The staff discovered that when instead of criticizing or correcting students, they validated the students' feelings and asked students how else they could respond, the amount of negative student behavior was dramatically reduced.

A final example comes from a high school program with a student experiencing serious behavioral and emotional problems. The student had received numerous office referrals and several suspensions for his aggressive responses to adults. As part of his treatment plan, the special education teacher worked with the boy and his teachers to determine ways the teachers could provide correction in a manner the boy perceived as more respectful and less confrontational. When the teachers began utilizing this new procedure, the student's aggressive responses to adults were almost eliminated. As in the previous example, although it was important to teach new procedures to the student, it was equally important to alter the teachers' procedures for responding to inappropriate student behavior.

ACTIVITIES FOR EXAMINING YOUR METHODS OF ESTABLISHING CLASSROOM RULES AND PROCEDURES

The activities in this section give you an opportunity to work with several of the major skills presented in this chapter. The value of these activities can be enhanced if you discuss them with a colleague. These activities may suggest changes you wish to incorporate in your classroom. If you make changes, keep a record of them. One week after implementing the change(s), take time to write about and share with a colleague the results of these changes.

ACTIVITY 8.1
Selecting Your Classroom Rules

List five classroom rules you would choose for your class. When you are satisfied with the rules, discuss them with a colleague who teaches or has recently taught at your grade level.

ACTIVITY 8.2
Deciding on Your Key Classroom Procedures

For this activity, refer to Figures 8.4 and 8.6 if you are an elementary teacher and Figures 8.5 and 8.6 if you are a middle school or high school teacher. For each area in which effective teachers teach classroom procedures, list a procedure you would feel comfortable using in your classroom. The material below provides an example of this activity.

(continued)

ACTIVITY 8.2
Continued

General Area	Needed Procedures	Specific Procedure
Beginning the class	1. Getting students' attention 2. Entering the class 3. Obtaining materials 4. What to do if tardy 5. Where to put slips that need signing 6. 7.	Students determine a signal.
Whole-class activities	1. How to leave the room 2. What to do when work is completed 3. Voice level 4. How to get help on an assignment 5. Using the pencil sharpener 6. When students can leave their seats 7. 8. 9.	Sign your name and the time you leave and return.
Student assignments	1. How to find work missed while absent 2. How late work will be handled 3. Heading papers 4. Where to hand in work 5. Credit for late work 6. 7.	Refer to the notebook on the back table.
Other activities	1. Dismissing 2. Public address system and announcements 3. Fire drill 4. Guest entering the class 5. 6. 7.	Everyone must be seated and quiet.

ACTIVITY 8.3
Examining Your
Methods of
Establishing
Rules and
Procedures

Evaluate your use of various methods of developing classroom rules and procedures by completing the following form. If you are not currently teaching, respond by recalling a classroom in which you previously taught or observed.

Yes   Somewhat   No

1. Do clear classroom rules apply in your class?
2. Are the rules listed in the form of positive statements?

Yes   Somewhat   No

3. Are there five or fewer rules?
4. Can every student list these rules from memory?
5. Are the rules clearly displayed in your room?
6. Are students involved in developing the rules?
7. Does each student make a clear commitment to follow these rules?
8. Do you discuss these rules frequently when they are first developed?
9. Do you review the rules every three weeks?
10. Do students clearly understand your approach to handling rule violations?
11. Do you teach students the important procedures related to classroom activities?
12. Do you teach students the major procedures related to behaviors outside the classroom?
13. When students fail to follow a procedure do you immediately reteach the procedure?
14. Does every parent know the classroom rules that apply in your class?
15. Does every parent know your methods of handling discipline problems?

Carefully examine your responses to the above questions and then complete the following statements:

> I learned that. . . .
> I am pleased that I. . . .

Three approaches I will implement in order to develop more productive classroom rules and procedures are:

1.
2.
3.

I will also consider the possibility that next year I could. . . .

SUMMARY

Successful teachers create procedures involving both proactive and corrective approaches to student behavior. In the proactive area, teachers whose students have higher rates of on-task behavior spend time early in the school year developing and teaching classroom rules and procedures. This provides students with a much needed sense of structure and security. More effective classroom managers also view their role less as disciplining students and more as reteaching appropriate behaviors when students have difficulty demonstrating these behaviors. Simply stated, the teaching of appropriate behavior has become an additional curriculum in schools.

There are situations in which you will need to do more than provide additional instruction to ensure that an individual or class follows a procedure. The key concept to keep in mind is that your response should help students take responsibility for their behavior. The next chapter examines methods for responding to situations in which students continue to violate classroom rules and procedures despite your efforts to teach and monitor these.

RECOMMENDED READING

Emmer, E., Evertson, C., Sanford, J., Clements, B., & Worsham, M. (1984). *Classroom management for secondary teachers.* Englewood Cliffs, NJ: Prentice Hall.

Evertson, C., Emmer, E., Clements, B., Sanford, J., & Worsham, M. (1984). *Classroom management for elementary teachers.* Englewood Cliffs, NJ: Prentice Hall.

Fellers, P., & Gritzmacher, K. (1985a). *Alphabet soup: A curriculum for your first week of school.* Canby, OR: Tops Learning Systems. (10970 S. Mulino Rd., 97013)

Fellers, P., & Gritzmacher, K. (1985b). *A summer start: How to organize your best school year ever.* Canby, OR: Tops Learning Systems.

Fellers, P., & Gritzmacher, K. (1987). *Peaceful procedures: A master teacher's approach to peaceful classroom management.* Canby, OR: Tops Learning Systems.

Fox, R., Luszki, M., & Schmuck, R. (1966). *Diagnosing classroom learning environments.* Chicago: Science Research Associates.

Good, T., & Brophy, J. (1994). *Looking in classrooms* (6th ed.). New York: Harper and Row.

Jones, V. (1980). *Adolescents with behavior problems: Strategies for teaching, counseling, and parent involvement.* Boston: Allyn and Bacon.

Schmuck, R., & Schmuck. P. (1983). *Group processes in the classroom* (4th ed.). Dubuque, IA: William C. Brown.

Weinstein C., & Mignano, A. (1993). *Elementary classroom management.* New York: McGraw-Hill.

PART V

When Prevention Fails: Methods for Altering Unproductive Student Behavior

When sensitively and consistently used, the methods presented in Parts II, III, and IV can result in increased student achievement and the elimination of a significant amount of disruptive student behavior. A few students, however, will cause major or consistent behavior problems despite our efforts to create positive, supportive, well-organized, and stimulating learning environments. Furthermore, the pressures and inevitable frustrations of learning and working in a relatively small area with 30 or so classmates create a situation in which some students will occasionally misbehave and require assistance in controlling and improving their behavior.

Part V presents many types of intervention strategies that teachers, counselors, child development specialists, and administrators can use to help pupils better understand and control their behavior. When examining and implementing these strategies, educators should keep in mind that these methods will be more effective when used in conjunction with the methods discussed in the previous chapters. In fact, the authors believe that adults harm youngsters by implementing behavior control strategies to ensure that young people act passively and positively in environments that do not meet their basic psychological and academic needs.

Several key concepts underlie the materials presented in Chapters 9, 10, 11, and 12. First, teachers will be most effective in their efforts to help students develop new skills and demonstrate responsible behavior when everyone in the school understands his or her responsibility and works cooperatively. As discussed in Chapter 1, the term *systems approach* is used to describe this coordination of efforts. Chapter 12 presents a detailed look at this concept.

Second, all interventions made in response to student behavior problems should be educational in nature. As educators, we will be most effective in assisting students if we view student misbehavior as based on the dual factors of student responses to the environment and skill deficits. Therefore, once we have made every attempt to adjust the environment, the next step is to assist students in developing new skills.

Third, a hierarchy exists for responding to irresponsible, unproductive student behavior. This hierarchy (presented in Figure 9.1) suggests that it is most beneficial to students if we first implement interventions emphasizing the creation of positive learning environments followed by interventions that focus primarily on student involvement and responsibility for resolving problems. Methods that depend on external reinforcers or that place outside restrictions on students' behavior are used as a last resort.

Fourth, underlying the behavior change interventions presented in Part V is the belief that students should be actively involved in all attempts to alter their behavior. Students should be involved in solving problems, helped to collect and understand data about their own behavior, and be instrumental in developing contracts aimed at altering their behavior. Finally, although it may not be desirable to have students present during all discussions of their behavior, they should be included in many such discussions and should always be aware of the problems being discussed and the programs being implemented.

When you use the methods presented in Chapters 10 and 11, be careful not to view problem-solving and behavioristic interventions as mutually exclusive. Problem-solving approaches do emphasize students' involvement in the behavior change process, but it is important to recognize that with some students it may be necessary to incorporate a behavioristic approach such as self-observation or the creation of a contract.

CHAPTER 9

Responding to Violations of Rules and Procedures

Teachers and administrators must move away from the appearance of a teacher-imposed, "hard-line" method to an educational approach emphasizing our skills and abilities as professional educators.

—Forrest Gathercoal (1993)
Judicious Discipline

Having seen that teaching is perhaps the most difficult of all management jobs, we are now ready to take a detailed look at the crucial factor in educational reform: replacing boss-management with lead-management so that we can begin to move to quality.

—William Glasser (1990)
The Quality School

One question the authors are frequently asked during workshops and classes is, What should I do when students misbehave? The authors' first response is to ask teachers to consider their goals related to classroom management. Hosford (1984) reported that when hundreds of teachers and administrators were asked to rate the most important objectives of education, they consistently listed the following as the top four objectives:

1. Desire for learning
2. Improved self-concept
3. Basic skill acquisition
4. Respect for others

Similarly, in collecting data for *A Place Called School*, Goodlad (1984) and colleagues examined educational goal statements from every state and interviewed 8,600 parents. Statewide statements consistently included numerous goals related to personal and civic skills, and parents voiced their support for these goals. Therefore, it seems ironic that teachers so often accept classroom management methods such as assertive discipline (Canter, 1976) that emphasize immediate control and order but fail to provide children with skills needed to become responsible citizens. These control-oriented solutions also fail to help teachers examine the possible causes of misbehavior or to adjust the learning environment to prevent future student failure and misbehavior. If teachers sincerely wish to help students become motivated learners and responsible citizens, we must respond to their misbehavior in a manner that encourages students' participation and responsibility.

Figure 9.1 presents the methods teachers can use to develop an effective and professionally responsible response to inappropriate student behavior. Figure 9.1 is divided into interventions that can be applied with individuals or groups of students and institutional structures that support these interventions. This chapter, as well as Chapters 10 and 11, examine the interventions used with individuals and groups. Chapter 12 examines institutional structures that facilitate the consistent and effective implementation of these interventions.

This chapter examines the first two interventions: how teachers can most effectively respond to inappropriate student behavior in the classroom and how to conduct an environmental analysis to determine possible causes of the behavior problem. Prior to reading further, you are urged to complete Activity 9.1. This will help you assess your current response to unproductive student behavior in light of the standards suggested in this chapter.

APPROPRIATE AND EFFECTIVE RESPONSES TO STUDENT MISBEHAVIOR: PUNISHMENT OR LOGICAL, INSTRUCTIONAL CONSEQUENCES?

How do teachers respond to inappropriate, irresponsible student behavior? The answer most often seems to be, with punitive responses. Punitive responses refer to the use of verbal threats and put-downs, a loud voice, sarcasm, the placing of a student's name on the board, removal of a privilege, assignment of additional work or writing sentences, time out or other isolation with no associated skill development activity, or physical punishment or suspension. Englander (1982) conducted two studies to determine how teachers responded to disruptive student behavior. In the first study, 40 teachers were observed for one week to determine their responses to three rule-violating behaviors. Of the 120 incidents, teachers responded puni-

FIGURE 9.1
Sequence of Interventions

Interventions with Individuals	Schoolwide Procedures and Programs
Contracting	Collaboration with community agencies
Social skills training	Building at-risk plan
Self-monitoring	Schoolwide student management plan
Problem solving	Personalized education plan (PEP)
Environmental analysis	Teacher assistance team
An effective response to inappropriate behavior	

tively 108 times while ignoring the other 12 behaviors. In another study, Englander asked 176 teachers to select from 15 responses to misbehavior those they would use for 20 specific student misbehaviors. In 78 percent of the cases, teachers listed punitive responses to student misbehavior. The popularity of assertive discipline with its focus on controlling students through punishments and rewards is another indication that teachers support the use of punishment as a major response to irresponsible student behavior.

The focus on punishment in schools is further supported by the frequency with which corporal punishment is used. Rose (1984) surveyed 324 principals randomly selected from 18 states to examine the extent of corporal punishment in school. Some 74 percent of the principals stated that corporal punishment was used in their schools. Reardon and Reynold (1979) found widespread support for corporal punishment from samples of parents, principals, teachers, and school board members. Finally, the rate at which students are suspended from school in the United States supports the focus on punishment.

Disadvantages of Punishment

Punishment for misbehavior has several serious problems. First, and perhaps foremost, it does not teach the student alternative methods of behavior that can be used to prevent future behavior problems. Because schools are educational institutions, it seems contradictory that children who have difficulty would be punished rather than receive instruction in how to behave more productively. Second, and perhaps of equal importance in school settings, punishment appears to inhibit learning (Englander, 1986). Kounin and Gump (1961) conducted a study involving competent first-grade teachers who differed in their use of punitive behavior with students. The findings indicated that the students of the more punitive teachers expressed less value in learning, were more aggressive, and were more confused about behavior problems in school. This finding was substantiated by the work of Kounin (1970). Studies suggest that schools in which students learn more effectively are characterized by high rates of positive reinforcement and also by somewhat lower rates of punishment (Mortimore & Sammons, 1987; Rutter, Maughan, Mortimore, Ouston, & Smith, 1979). Nash (1963) has reported on a study of corporal punishment in British schools: "It is notable that the schools where corporal punishment was absent had the best records of behavior and delinquency, despite being in areas with the lowest average ratable value. It is also notable that behavior deteriorates and delinquency increases as corporal punishment increases" (p. 401).

Third, research suggests that punishment is not an effective method for changing student behavior. Emmer and Aussiker (1987) examined the literature on the results of research evaluations associated with four approaches to discipline—teacher effectiveness training, reality therapy, assertive discipline, and Adlerian-based approaches. They also contacted 120 school districts in the United States and Canada to obtain evaluation studies about these programs. Their findings indicated that the most punitive-oriented approach (assertive discipline) was ineffective. They summarized the results on assertive discipline: "Evidence on *student* behavior and attitudes is *not* supportive of AD training; that is, many more studies found no effects, or mixed and negative effects, than found that AD training resulted in improved student behavior and attitudes" (pp. 15, 16).

Similar findings concerning the impact of punitive responses to student misbehavior were reported by Becker, Engelmann, and Thomas (1975). These researchers found that, when teachers were asked to increase their use of punitive control methods of responding to disruptive student behavior, misbehavior in the classes actually increased from 9 to 31 percent of student behavior.

Fourth, punishment allows the student to project blame rather than to accept responsibility for the behavior. Punishment tends to create a situation in which the student becomes angry or blames the individuals responsible for the punishment rather than examining personal responsibility for the problem. Glasser (1988) stated that 95 percent of all student discipline problems in schools are caused by students' lack of power and that misbehavior is an attempt to gain some sense of power. Punitive responses to student misbehavior detract from rather than enhance students' sense of power and efficacy and often lead to withdrawal or actively destructive and confrontational responses.

Fifth, using such activities as writing sentences, assigning additional homework, and lowering a student's grade as punishment may create a negative attitude regarding these activities. Activities and settings in which one is involved when receiving punishment tend to become aversive. Teachers do not want this connection made with homework or writing.

Englander (1986) stated that even though responding to student misbehavior with punishment is both common and natural, it is nonetheless impractical. Based on his extensive background in the field and his thorough review of the research, he summarized his assessment of punishment: "If punishment works it does so only under very precise and complicated conditions, much too complicated for us to consistently use in classrooms. The controls that one must utilize to optimize the effectiveness of punishment are not possible in day-to-day operations either within families or schools" (pp. 40–41).

Corporal Punishment

The disadvantages of punishment apply to all forms of punishment—particularly to corporal punishment. Corporal punishment allows the student to place blame outside himself or herself rather than to accept responsibility for a problem and learn to develop new skills. Also, corporal punishment is extremely poor modeling; research has consistently shown that aggression tends to beget aggression. It is interesting how often the authors have heard someone respond to a criticism of corporal punishment by stating that this is what the student experiences at home and thus this is what needs to be implemented at school. Would educators apply the same logic to a child whose family is illiterate and who has never been read to or learned to read? Schools are educational institutions; their goal is to provide students with new skills that can open healthy and productive options for future life. Educators cannot justify using any method that demeans and hurts children while failing to provide them with healthy alternatives.

It is interesting to note that public opinion has gradually moved during the last 25 years toward a less favorable view of physical punishment. Gallup and Elam (1988) noted that in 1988, 50 percent of those surveyed for the Annual Gallup Poll of the Public's Attitudes Toward the Public Schools responded *yes* and 45 percent responded *no* to this question:

> Spanking and similar forms of physical punishment are permitted in the lower grades of some schools for children who do not respond well to other forms of discipline. Do you approve of this practice? (p. 42)

This response compared with 62 percent who favored such actions and 33 percent who opposed physical punishment in 1970. It is also interesting to note that the poll question suggests that other forms of discipline have been tried and that this practice is used only with young children. Therefore, it is likely that there is considerably less public support for physical punishment with upper elementary and older children and for the use of physical punishment when other methods have not been effectively and systematically employed.

If the use of corporal punishment, time out with no task assigned, screaming, threatening, and ridiculing are not recommended by current research and theory, what options are available to help teachers cope effectively with the increasing number of at-risk students whose school behavior negatively effects their own learning and that of other students?

Figure 9.2 presents a comparison of two ways to view problematic student behavior. School personnel have too often viewed inappropriate behavior as an attitude rather than as a skill issue and have responded using the sequence suggested on the right-hand side of Figure 9.2. We further believe that current research and theory clearly support viewing and responding to student behavior problems using the paradigm suggested on the left hand side of Figure 9.2. By treating behavior problems similarly to academic problems, teachers are allowed to use their considerable expertise in analyzing environments and assisting students in developing alternative strategies. The next section presents classroom management procedures teachers can use to handle classroom disruptions calmly and productively. The final section in this chapter presents a model for how teachers can handle situations in which students' behavior does not improve despite the teachers' use of an effective classroom management procedure.

TIPS FOR HANDLING MINOR DISRUPTIONS

Misbehavior often occurs because students find acting out to be more interesting than a boring lesson or a better option than another failure experience. Similarly, unproductive student behavior often occurs because students do not understand a task, are not involved in the learning activity, or are unable to obtain assistance when it is needed. Therefore, most minor discipline problems can be alleviated by implementing the instructional methods discussed in Part III of this book. Nevertheless, when 30 people are required to work for approximately 6 hours a day in a 30-×-30-foot area, minor problems will inevitably occur. As Kounin (1970) discovered, a major factor in effective classroom management is teachers' ability to deal with minor disruptions before they become major problems.

FIGURE 9.2 A Comparison of Approaches to Academic and Social Problems

It is a common practice among educators to approach academic problems differently from social problems. Essentially, instructional principles are used to remediate academic problems, whereas negative consequences typically are used to manage social problems. The differences are summarized here.

Kind of Error	Procedures for Academic Problem	Procedures for Social Problem
Infrequent	Assume student is trying to make correct response.	Assume student is not trying to make correct response.
	Assume error was accidental.	Assume error was deliberate.
	Provide assistance (model-lead-test).	Provide negative consequence.
	Provide more practice.	Practice not required.
	Assume student has learned skill and will perform correctly in future.	Assume student will make right choice and behave in future.
Frequent (chronic)	Assume student has learned the wrong way.	Assume student refuses to cooperate.
	Assume student has been taught (inadvertently) the wrong way.	Assume student knows what is right and has been told often.
	Diagnose the problem.	Provide more negative consequences.
	Identify misrule or determine more effective manner in which to present the material.	Withdraw student from normal context.
	Adjust presentation. Focus on rule. Provide feedback. Provide practice and review.	Maintain student removal from normal context.
	Assume student has been taught skill and will perform correctly in future.	Assume student has "learned" lesson and will behave in future.

Source: Reprinted by permission from Geoffrey Colvin.

The following sections present ideas for responding to persistent student misbehavior or situations in which students do not respond to teachers' effective initial interventions. The eight methods presented here provide techniques for initially responding to minor classroom disruptions.

Methods

1. *Arrange seating patterns so that you can see and easily move to be near all students.* During small-group work, the students should have their back to the class and you should face the class. By maintaining awareness of what is going on and being able to move around the room without disturbing children, you can solve minor problems more quickly.

2. *Scan the class frequently in order to notice and respond to potential problems or minor disruptions.* One of the most difficult tasks for beginning teachers to learn is how to attend to more than one thing at a time. Teachers frequently become so engrossed in working with a group or an individual student, they fail to notice potential problems stemming from a frustrated student or a minor argument. Though it is important to attend to the student(s) being taught, teachers must learn to scan the room quickly.

3. *The disruptive influence of the teacher's intervention should not be greater than the disruption it is intended to reduce.* Teachers often create more disruptions with their attempts to discipline students than the students are causing themselves. Whenever possible, ignore such minor disruptions as a dropped book or overuse of a pencil sharpener. If an individual student continually creates minor disruptions, this problem can be dealt with more effectively by discussing the issue privately with the student. If many class members are involved in low-key disruptive behavior, the behavior should be discussed during a class meeting.

4. *An inappropriately angry teacher response creates tension and increases disobedience and disruptive behavior.* Both Kounin (1970) and Brophy and Evertson (1976) found evidence of a "negative ripple effect" associated with harsh teacher criticism. Rather than improving student behavior, students tend to become more anxious and disruptive in classes characterized by overly harsh discipline. Therefore, though firmness can have a positive effect on classroom behavior, it should be associated with teacher warmth, politeness, and explanations.

5. *A positive ripple effect is associated with a calm and immediate response to a problem.* When teachers react calmly and quickly to a student's disruptive behavior, other students respond by improving their own behavior.

6. *When misbehavior occurs, the first step is to make contact quietly with the student.* This can be done with a glance, by moving close to the student, by touching the student on the shoulder, or by asking the student for an on-task response. When asking the student to respond, always ask a question the student can answer. If the student has obviously not been listening to the discussion, you will embarrass the student by asking "Sam, what do you think about Tom's answer?" Asking Sam a new question, however, or paraphrasing Tom's statement and asking Sam for his opinion can productively reintegrate Sam into the mainstream of the classroom activity. Another approach to making a positive initial contact with the student is

"Cheer up. Not everyone gets the hang of class control the first time."

to praise a positive behavior that competes with the negative behavior. Rather than criticize a student's off-task behavior, praise the student the moment he or she begins to work on the assignment or focus on the class discussion.

7. *Remind students of the classroom rule or procedure they are not demonstrating.* Rather than yelling, "Chris, stop bothering Mary while she is working!" simply walk over to Chris and ask quietly, "Chris, do you know which rule you are not following?" Similarly, if an entire class is becoming disruptive or lining up without having cleared their desks, ask the class to describe their behavior and mention any classroom procedures that are being neglected.

8. *When one or two students are being extremely disruptive, it is best to focus the other students' attention on their task and then talk privately with the disruptive students.* You might say, "Would you all please help me by working quietly on your spelling sentences while I help Tom and Bob solve their problems?" By handling the situation calmly and positively, you indicate your competence, which in turn will have a calming effect on the other students.

Even though these methods are very effective, every teacher knows there are instances when, even in the most positive and effectively instructed and managed classrooms, a student does not respond productively to these methods. To handle this inevitability positively, teachers must develop a procedure for responding to serious or continuous disruptive student behavior. The next section presents methods for such situations. It also discusses the use of punishment in school settings.

A CLASSROOM PROCEDURE FOR RESPONDING TO DISRUPTIVE BEHAVIOR

Before discussing a specific approach to handling student violations of rules, the authors stress that students should be clearly informed about any approach you select. Students do not respond well to surprises. They rebel against arbitrary, unexpected consequences. The teacher must take time to discuss and even practice with students his or her response to disruptive student behavior. This is particularly true for middle school and high school teachers. Adolescents are sensitive to issues of equality and justice. They are experiencing the developmental task of becoming responsible for their own behavior and demonstrating their competence. When approaches to classroom management directly conflict with these needs, they will be met with varying degrees of resistance.

As indicated earlier, the responses to disruptive, irresponsible student behavior are most effective and professionally responsible when they serve the dual function of (1) ensuring a safe and orderly classroom and school environment and (2) providing an educational intervention that helps students develop new skills. Additionally, the response to student misbehavior is most effective when it maintains or enhances the student's dignity and self-esteem and invites the student to be responsible for his or her behavior and to become a productive member of the classroom group. Methods that focus primarily on control and punishment do not help youngsters develop new skills and tend to alienate and isolate rather than invite students.

Several key factors are involved in developing professionally responsible, effective responses to unproductive, irresponsible student behavior:

1. Students must be clearly aware of the rules and procedures and the consequences for violating them.
2. Students must be given clear cues indicating that continuation of a behavior will evoke the specified consequences.
3. It is important to be as consistent as possible in employing consequences.
4. Students should be informed that they are choosing the consequence.
5. The consequence should be educational in nature.

Figure 9.3 outlines a procedure for responding to a rule or procedure violation that the authors have used as teachers and have taught to hundreds of teachers. This method involves first using a predetermined signal to help the student become aware of his or her behavior. If the student does not see this action or fails to

Step	Procedure	Example
1.	Nonverbal cue	Raised index finger
2.	Verbal cue	"John, please follow our classroom rules."
3.	Indicate choice student is making	"John, if you continue to talk while I am talking, you will be choosing to develop a plan."
4.	Student moves to a designated area in the room to develop a plan	"John, you have chosen to take time to develop a plan."
5.	Student is required to go somewhere else to develop a plan	"John, because you are choosing not to be responsible, you will need to see Mrs. Johnson to develop your plan."

FIGURE 9.3
Steps in Responding to Students' Violation of Rules and Procedures

respond to it, say the student's name and politely request that he or she follow your classroom rules. If the student continues an unacceptable behavior, inform him or her that should this behavior continue, the student will be choosing to take time to develop a solution to the problem. Ideally, this work will occur in the classroom, where the student can benefit from instruction and also realize that the problem can be resolved among those involved. Students who have adequate writing skills can be provided with an area in which to work and materials necessary for them to complete a problem-solving form.

Figure 9.4 is an example of a problem-solving form that elementary and secondary teachers can use in their classrooms. Once a student has completed the form, it is placed in a designated spot or shown to the teacher; the student then returns to his or her seat. It is, of course, important to have a brief discussion with the student about the responses on the form. This can be done near the end of class or at the beginning of the next class period. With elementary school students, it is particularly important that they feel invited back to the class and that they realize that even though you could not accept the behavior that necessitated the problem solving, you care about them, respect their ability to be respon-

FIGURE 9.4
Problem-Solving
Form

Choose to be Responsible

Name _____   Date _____

Rules we agreed on:

1. Speak politely to others.
2. Treat each other kindly.
3. Follow teacher requests.
4. Be prepared for class.
5. Make a good effort at your work and request help if you need it.
6. Obey all school rules.

Please answer the following questions:

1. What rule did you violate? _____
   _____

2. What did you do that violated this rule? _____
   _____

3. What problem did this cause for you, your teacher, or classmates? _____
   _____

4. What plan can you develop that will help you be more responsible and follow this classroom rule? _____
   _____

5. How can the teacher or other students help you? _____
   _____

I, _____, will try my best to follow the plan I have written and to follow all the other rules and procedures in our classroom that we created to make the classroom a good place to learn.

---

sible for their behavior by completing the form, and are glad that they have rejoined the class. The next chapter provides an extended discussion and examples of how to implement problem solving in the classroom, and Chapter 12 presents methods for incorporating problem solving into a schoolwide student management plan.

It is essential that students clearly understand each step in this sequential process. This can be accomplished by role-playing each step in Figure 9.3 and then asking a student to violate a classroom rule (such as talking to a neighbor while you are talking). You then ask the student to stop the inappropriate behavior when you employ the second step. This procedure can be continued until several students are involved in responding to each of the first three steps. You can then instruct the students in writing solutions and plans. Each student writes a plan; you check these and subsequently discuss them with the class.

Several years ago during a graduate seminar, one of the authors commented that it was probably not necessary to teach the problem-solving step to students in college preparatory junior and senior high school classes. A seminar participant who had been in a course one of the authors taught five years earlier disagreed with this statement. He said that he role-played the procedures with all his juniors and seniors in chemistry and physics. He noted that students and parents frequently commented on the value of this process. This teacher was convinced that despite needing to use the fourth step only about a dozen times each year, it was a vital aspect of an effective classroom-management program.

As with all methods suggested in this book, you should carefully consider its applicability to your own teaching setting and should critically assess results when you use the new method. Should you choose to implement the preceding method for responding to rule violations, it is critical to ensure that it is not used in a manner unduly emphasizing disruptive behavior. Studies show that teachers often attend more frequently to disruptive than to on-task behavior, and that this action tends to increase off-task student behavior. Therefore, when implementing this method, attend to desired student behavior frequently and monitor behavior to assess whether the new approach was indeed associated with an increase in on-task behavior.

Should a student refuse to go to the designated area or to complete the form, the teacher needs to express a belief that the problem can be resolved and that he or she sincerely wishes the student to remain. For example, you might say, "Sam, I'm sure we can work this out and I would like to have you remain in the class. If you will start work on the form, I'll come over as soon as I can and I'm sure we can work this out together." If the student continues to be defiant, the teacher needs to indicate that the student is making a choice. For example, you might say, "Sam, if you choose not to work this out here, you are choosing to do it in the office. I would like to have you remain here, but it is your choice." Some students will continue to view this as a challenge and defy the teacher; this will almost never happen in classrooms in which the teacher has consistently demonstrated concern and respect for students and in which students have been made aware of the sequence of consequences to be followed.

Perhaps you are wondering if this method adequately allows for individual differences, for it suggests that teachers respond to disruptive behavior by using the same consequence for every child and for every rule violation. The authors believe that students want and need consistency and fairness. It is also believed that establishing clarity and incorporating an educational component in the procedure for responding to classroom disruptions are so important that it is best to use a single method. This does not mean, however, that the teacher is limited to this one intervention when helping students develop more responsible behavior. As discussed in Chapter 11, there exist a number of exciting and effective methods for working with individual students to help them develop or increase the frequency of behaviors critical to their success in school and the community.

RESPONDING TO DEFIANT BEHAVIOR

Perhaps the most demanding situation adults face in working with children is responding to defiant behavior. Many adults in U.S. society have been raised in homes in which challenging an adult was not acceptable. Therefore, a common adult response is to use power to gain control. This often results in the adult yelling at the child, threatening, putting a name on the board, removing the child from the room, or even grabbing and striking a child. Although removal may ultimately be necessary, there are a series of steps we can take prior to or along with removal. The importance of learning these methods was recently highlighted when one of the authors was asked by a major school district to address all district staff on the topic of responding to student confrontation. The request was based on the alarming number of teachers who had been involved in violent behavior toward children.

Ready Yourself for the Situation

Prepare yourself and your students for situations that might lead to conflicts. As discussed in detail in Chapter 7, this means teaching key procedures for handling new or demanding situations such as group work, test taking, playground confrontations, and the like. As it relates to communication, it means teaching students and ourselves a model for effectively dealing with our feelings. Figure 9.5 presents a model called the Ladder of Success. The authors have found this to be highly effective in providing a basic language and schema for responding to feelings in school settings. The model, which is supported by a series of 12 lessons, graphically indicates that when problems occur, we all have the choice of going "up ladder" and responding in a way that follows school rules and would be acceptable on most jobs, or "down ladder" and violating school rules and jeopardizing one's ability to maintain a job.

Build a Positive Relationship Bank Account
with Known Power Strugglers

This involves being intentionally inviting and using many of the methods described in Chapter 3. As noted earlier, students abuse roles, not people.

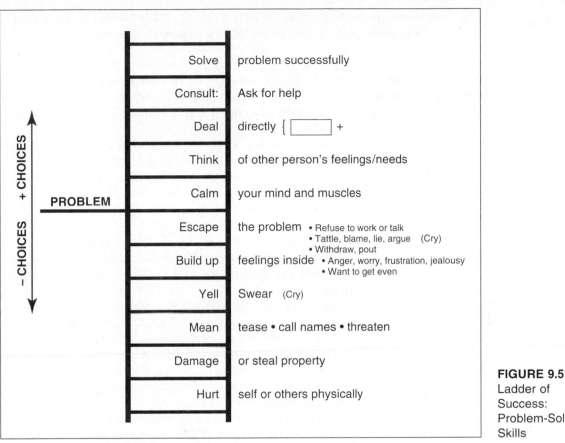

FIGURE 9.5
Ladder of
Success:
Problem-Solving
Skills

Source: Sharon Haugen, Ladder of Success: Problem-Solving Skills. Reprinted with permission.
© 1991, 1993 Sharon Haugen.

Model Self-Control

This requires us to guard against our vulnerabilities and be "smarter than a trout." Like the wily trout who knows better than to strike at every imitation lure, we must be careful not to become snared by students' attempts to gain control or negative attention by making inappropriate comments.

Respond Thoughtfully and with Purpose to Deescalate the Behavior

This requires being aware of such early warning signs as the student stopping her work, refusing to talk, looking angry or upset, making comments under her breath, looking anxious or depressed, or disengaging from the group by turning away or looking distracted. When a student shows one of these signs or initially confronts you with statements such as, "This stuff is boring!", "Who wants to learn this?", "You don't care about me!", and so on, you have several options:

1. Expand on the active-listening technique and *identify the feelings* the student may be experiencing. For example, you might say, "It sounds like you're frustrated with how easy the work is" or "I would be angry too if I thought I was asked to do something I didn't think had been explained very well."

2. *Send an I-message* to let the student know the behavior is creating discomfort for you. This will work especially well if you have placed some deposits in your positive relationship bank account. An I-message can also include a clear, positive statement about your expectations. For example, you might say, "Reggie, I expect all students to make only positive comments to their classmates."

3. *Offer assistance.* You might say, "It looks like I didn't explain that so you could understand. Would you like me to go over that again?" or "It sounds like you're frustrated with the assignment. Let's see if we can work it out so it is more interesting to you."

4. *Provide options.* You might say, "If Melinda is bothering you, it might be better to work at the science center for awhile" or "Can you use one of the strategies we agreed to use when we studied the Ladder of Success?"

5. Especially with younger children, you can *predict a positive choice and its consequence.* For example, you might say, "I think if you tried two problems and then asked your partner for help, you would know what to ask for and you'd get help before you become too frustrated."

6. Another option is to *state the expectation in a positive manner.* Therefore, if a student spoke out of turn, you might say, "Keith, remember our agreement that during class discussions students will talk only when called on so it is easier for everyone to understand each other."

7. You can briefly *review available options and consequence and give the student space and time to make a choice.* For example, you might say, "Jeremy, remember our procedure for sharing ideas. I will call on you soon when your hand is raised, but if you talk out, we'll need to do some practice during recess."

8. Sometimes it is best to just *walk away* and give the student space. Although this is usually not desirable in cases where a major confrontation has taken place, it can be used occasionally when a student seems agitated and you know it is likely he or she will settle down if given some space.

9. Ultimately, you may have to *clarify that the student must make a choice.* If a student continues to disrupt a discussion, you could say, "Celeste, I'd like you to stay because we have some interesting things planned, but you need to choose either to follow our procedure for talking during discussions or to go to the problem-solving center until we can solve this."

These are all "up-ladder" responses that help maintain the student's dignity while still indicating the teacher's expectation that all students follow the agreed-upon behavioral standards. Experience clearly indicates that teachers who use these responses have a very low number of situations where student misbehavior escalates to where it must be dealt with as a serious behavior problem.

Handling Violent Student Behavior

Even though most teachers are not confronted with violent student behavior, all teachers should be prepared for this possibility. When such behavior occurs, the teacher first needs to make a firm yet polite statement that he or she expects the behavior to stop. You might say, "I understand that you two are angry, but we have other ways to solve problems here. I expect you to stop immediately." If the student(s) fail to respond, send a student for assistance. If the behavior involves a student throwing a temper tantrum or a classroom fight between two students, ask other students to leave the room and go to a supervised area such as the library or even the hallway. Sometimes students act aggressively in order to impress other students, and they may calm down much more easily when no audience is available.

In his material on playground discipline, Randy Sprick (1990) suggested a procedure for common areas such as playgrounds in which the adults responsible for supervising these areas carry a card indicating that immediate assistance is needed. If they need assistance, this is given to a student who takes it immediately to the office. The office staff know that this card indicates that a serious situation exists and assistance must be sent immediately.

In rare cases when a teacher must restrain a student, it is important that the teacher not step between the fighting students. Instead, the teacher can select the student with whom he or she has the better rapport and physically attempt to remove that student from the fight. This is best done from the side of or behind the student by grabbing a belt or shirt, which leaves the student's hands free for self-protection. While doing this, the teacher should talk to the student, stating that he or she may have a right to be angry and will have an opportunity to resolve the conflict as soon as he or she calms down. Talking to students helps to calm them down and can help them save face by indicating that they will be involved in solving the problem. With some students, it is also helpful to remind them that this behavior is against agreed-upon rules and to note the consequence they will be choosing if they continue the fight. Even some angry high school students quiet down considerably when reminded that their parents will have to become involved if they cannot calm down and settle the problem in a more productive and acceptable manner.

In those rare instances in which a student must be restrained, it is helpful if the teacher has had some training in methods of restraint. In addition, the teacher should continue to talk calmly to the child, saying that it is all right to be upset and that he or she can be released and have a chance to talk about the frustration or anger as soon as he or she can stop struggling and talk calmly.

METHODS FOR SOLVING MAJOR AND CONTINUING STUDENT BEHAVIOR PROBLEMS

The previous methods are designed as responses for individual incidents of disruptive classroom behavior. A more serious concern involves the student who continues to disrupt the classroom despite the use of professionally responsible responses. When this occurs, several options are available to the teacher:

1. Examine the classroom environment to determine what factors may be causing the misbehavior and what, if any, adjustments can be made to increase the likelihood that the student will behave productively in the classroom.
2. Meet with the student to discuss the problem and attempt to generate a solution.
3. Contact the parent(s) and inform them of the problem and of the attempts being made to improve the student's behavior.
4. Implement some form of behavioral intervention to help the student improve his or her behavior.
5. Refer the student to the office for consequences associated with the school-wide student management program.

Whenever possible, you are urged to take these steps in the order listed.

The last section in this chapter examines methods for assessing the environment. Chapter 10 focuses on methods for problem solving with students. Chapter 5 provides ideas for contacting parents about a student's behavioral problem. Chapter 11 presents methods for implementing behavioral interventions to alter students' behavior. Finally, Chapter 12 presents methods for ensuring that building level support is available, consistent, and effective in responding to persistent or extremely disruptive student behavior.

Completing an Environmental Assessment

In a study of suspension and expulsions from various schools serving similar student populations, Galloway and Goodwin (1987) stated:

1. Whether a pupil is considered disruptive or maladjusted depends at least as much on factors within the school as on factors within the pupil or the family.
2. In general, schools that cater successfully for their most disturbing pupils also cater successfully for the rest of their pupils. (p. 132)

In his book *What Do I Do When . . . ? How to Achieve Discipline with Dignity,* Mendler (1992) highlighted the importance of examining the environment in order to determine specific interventions for each child when he wrote, "Most discipline programs incorrectly place their emphasis upon strategies and techniques. The latest gimmick is offered to get Johnny to behave. . . . The competent teacher needs to get at the reasons or functions of a given maladaptive behavior to formulate a strategy likely to work" (p. 25).

As discussed in Chapter 2, students seldom misbehave or choose to fail in classroom or school settings in which their academic and learning needs are being consistently met. Therefore, when faced with continuing disruptive classroom behavior by one or more students, it is our responsibility as teachers to (1) assess our use of effective classroom management and instructional methods, (2) determine which classroom factors seem to be associated with the student's irresponsible behavior, and (3) describe the interventions we have made to modify the environment or provide the student with assistance. Figure 9.6 is a form that has been used with hundreds of teachers to help them examine their own classroom management and instructional responsibilities as a factor in the unproductive behavior of an individual student or group of students. This form is not intended to be used as an evaluative instrument. Instead, it is to be used by a teacher or a teacher and

Level 1: Classroom Management and Instruction	Yes	Somewhat	No
1.1 The teacher interacts positively with the student.			
1.2 The teacher communicates high expectations to the student.			
1.3 The student is actively involved with peers either through cooperative learning or peer tutoring.			
1.4 Classroom procedures are taught to students and this student demonstrates an understanding of the procedures.			
1.5 There is a consistent routine in the classroom that is understood by the student.			
1.6 The student's instructional program is appropriate to his or her academic needs.			
1.7 The student has been involved in some form of academic goal setting and self-recording.			
1.8 Rules for managing student behavior are posted in the classroom.			
1.9 Rules are appropriate, succinct, stated positively, and all-inclusive.			
1.10 Consequences for inappropriate behavior are clear to all students.			
1.11 Consequences are appropriate, fair, and implemented consistently.			
1.12 The student demonstrates that she or he understands the rules and consequences.			
1.13 The teacher has met privately with the student to discuss the problem and jointly develop a plan both parties agree to implement in order to assist the student.			

Level 2: Individual Behavior Program

2.1 An academic and/or behavior program has been developed and consistently implemented and corresponding data collected for at least four weeks.

2.2 An alternative program was implemented if the original plan (2.1) proved to be ineffective.

FIGURE 9.6
Interventions before Removing a Student from the Classroom or Referring a Student for Special Education Services

colleague/consultant to consider whether changes may be warranted in one or more general area(s) related to management and instruction. Activity 9.3 provides an opportunity for you to use this form.

In addition to examining your own behavior, it can be extremely valuable to analyze a student's classroom behavior systematically and specifically. Figure 9.7 presents a form the authors have used with hundreds of teachers to assist in determining the classroom factors that may be influencing a student's behavior. Teachers have found this to be extremely helpful and on a number of occasions have adopted it as a model for providing information to colleagues at staffings held to develop intervention plans for students. Activity 9.4 provides an opportunity for you to use this form for obtaining information on a particular student whom you have observed or with whom you work. The elementary case study presented in the following section used this form to obtain the data necessary to develop the successful interventions described.

Finally, it is important to examine the interventions you have made to modify the learning environment and provide the student with special assistance in meeting the multiple demands of the classroom setting. Figure 9.8 presents a form one of the authors assisted a large elementary school district in developing in order to help teachers assess their interventions prior to making a referral to a Teacher Assistance Team.

Case Study: Middle School

Several years ago, one of the authors was asked to help a first-year band teacher in an inner-city school. The teacher was having serious problems with a last period eighth-grade beginning band class. The class met in a portable building, and the teacher worked in an elementary building until the last two periods of the day. The class consisted of 33 students, including 11 drummers (there were 4 drums in the classroom). Students were extremely disruptive, and the on-task rate was less than 30 percent.

After discussing the situation, the teacher agreed to involve the students in presenting their concerns about the class. Students were very open about their frustration with a variety of classroom procedures. For example, the teacher often worked for an extended period with one section of the band while expecting all other students to sit quietly. Students also expressed confusion about a variety of procedures, including obtaining their instruments, warm-ups, music selection, and discipline. The author and teacher spent five days working with students to establish and practice procedures for each of the 25 areas the students and teacher determined needed clarity. This included changing the discipline system from assertive discipline to the use of a form similar to those in Figure 9.3.

Pre- and postobservations showed dramatic changes in on-task behavior and an almost complete reduction in serious acting-out behavior. By involving students in the process and by creating clarity and consistency in classroom procedures, students felt a sense of safety, security, and belonging that had been lacking. They responded dramatically to this change by demonstrating more responsible behavior.

FIGURE 9.7

Analyzing
Environmental
Factors That
Influence
Students'
Behavior

Student _____

Date _____

Staff member _____

Part I   Student's Misbehavior(s)

1. Describe misbehavior(s)
   a.
   b.
   c.
2. How frequent is each type of misbehavior?
   a.
   b.
   c.
3. What time of day does it occur?
   a.
   b.
   c.
4. In what physical surroundings?
   a.
   b.
   c.
5. With which peers or adults?
   a.
   b.
   c.
6. In what kinds of activities is student engaged before misbehavior occurs?
   a.
   b.
   c.

Part II   Teacher (Or Other) Actions

1. What do you do when student misbehaves?
   a.
   b.
   c.
2. How does student respond?
   a.
   b.
   c.
3. When are your actions most successful?
4. When are these actions least successful?

Part III   Student Motivation

1. What responsibilities (assignments, tasks, or orders) does student fulfill?
2. What types of reinforcement (positive and negative) does student receive?
   a. positive (and/or encouragement)
   b. negative (and/or logical consequences)

(continued)

FIGURE 9.7
Continued

3. How does student respond to reinforcement?
   a. positive (and/or encouragement)
   b. negative (and/or logical consequences)
4. How does student relate to the group (physical aggression, verbal aggression, passivity, or other behaviors)?

Part IV   When Student Is Not Misbehaving

1. Describe positive behaviors.
   a.
   b.
   c.
2. How frequent is each type of positive behavior?
   a.
   b.
   c.
3. What time of day does each behavior occur?
   a.
   b.
   c.
4. In what physical surroundings?
   a.
   b.
   c.
5. With which peers or adults?
   a.
   b.
   c.
6. In what kinds of activities is student engaged before positive behavior occurs?
   a.
   b.
   c.

Part V   Additional Questions

1. What does student enjoy doing (hobbies or subjects)?
2. What does student do well (hobbies or subjects)?
3. Are there any reasons to suspect health or physical disabilities?

Case Study: Elementary School

This case involved a fourth-grade girl who transferred into a new school in February. Within seven weeks, she had been involved in 15 serious incidents of physical violence with peers and had on several occasions been suspended from school. The school used assertive discipline, and the severe clause had been invoked on numerous occasions.

STUDENT: _____   I.D.#: _____   BIRTHDATE: _____

Circle Specific Interventions Utilized	*Person Responsible*	*Specific Interventions and Date Initiated*	*Outcome and Specify Duration*

I. Classroom Environment
  A. Provide preferred seating (i.e., carrel, dividers, move with peer model/tutor).
  B. Alter location of school supplies for easy access or to minimize distractions.
  C. Assign to quiet area in classroom for short periods.
  D. Post and explain rules and consequences for classroom behavior.
  E. Increased teacher proximity for targeted student.
  F. Other:			

II. Instructional Modification
  A. Assess student's prerequisite skills.
  B. Provide small group and/or one-on-one instruction by:
    1. Teachers
    2. Instructional assistant
    3. Peer tutor
    4. Cross-age tutor
    5. Volunteer
  C. Modify materials:
    1. Address only essential skills
    2. Simplify vocabulary of presented materials
    3. Reduce workload
    4. Alter pacing
    5. Use programmed materials (i.e., SRA, computer drill, math kits, etc.)			

FIGURE 9.8

Observation and Assessment in the Learning Environment

(continued)

FIGURE 9.8
Continued

Circle Specific Interventions Utilized	Person Responsible	Specific Interventions and Date Initiated	Outcome and Specify Duration
6. Repeat and reinforce skills (i.e., tape lesson, games, activity centers)			
7. Change basal text			
8. Provide assignments and tests in segments			
9. Use calculator/computers			
10. Provide study aids (i.e., highlight main ideas, outlines, study guides, number line, concrete materials, etc.)			
D. Organize materials (i.e., folder, notebook, assignment sheet).			
E. Set time expectations (i.e., use timer, set time allotment, etc.).			
F. Use cues or gestures to indicate appropriate or inappropriate behaviors.			
G. Vary student responses (i.e., writing on chalkboard, art projects, verbal response alone, taping, use manipulatives, etc.).			
H. Modify instructions:			
1. Preview questions/tests			
2. Provide rewards/reinforcers			
3. Ask student to repeat directions and then restate what he's going to do to ensure understanding			
I. Modify grades:			
1. On specific reduced work load			
2. Reflecting performance on essential skills			
3. On report cards			
J. Other:			

Circle Specific Interventions Utilized	Person Responsible	Specific Interventions and Date Initiated	Outcome and Specify Duration
III. Motivation/Behavior Strategies			
A. Assess appropriateness of task.			
B. Prioritize tasks to be completed.			
C. Privately discuss and explain behavior and resulting consequences.			
D. Use behavior modification techniques (i.e., reinforcing appropriate behaviors, use cueing, gestures, etc.).			
E. Alter frequency of grouping changes to maximize or minimize child's movements.			
F. Change of schedule/group.			
G. Adapt assignments (i.e., reduced work load, verbal responses, etc.).			
H. Refer child to social worker/counselor/ psychologist.			
I. Provide individual assignments/behavior sheets, charts, checklists, etc., monitored by teacher, student, and administrator.			
J. Set up reward/ consequence system:			
1. Goal Setting—target individual behavior			
2. Set up a contract			
3. Provide reinforcers chosen from a menu (i.e., social praise, tangible/stickers, activity/free time, games, good news notes)			
K. Daily/weekly progress reports.			

(continued)

FIGURE 9.8
Continued

Circle Specific Interventions Utilized	Person Responsible	Specific Interventions and Date Initiated	Outcome and Specify Duration
L. Parent/teacher/principal/ child conferences, weekly, bimonthly, etc. M. Other:			

IV. Parent Contact/Support
    A. Notes sent home (i.e., daily or weekly progress report, good news notes).
    B. Parent/teacher check in (i.e., mutually signed assignment sheets/notebooks).
    C. Telephone contact (i.e., weekly, monthly, or as needed).
    D. Home/school learning/behavior contracts.
    E. Suggested in-district resources (parent group/TAP).
    F. Other:			

Date	Signature of Teacher	Date	Signature of Principal, CST Member or Peer Consultant

Source: Schaumburg School District 54, Schaumburg, Illinois. Reprinted by permission.

When asked to be involved in helping the school in working with this student, one of the authors first asked the teacher to complete the environmental analysis form found in Figure 9.7. Much to everyone's surprise, the results suggested that all but one of the student's physical assaults on peers had occurred during periods of reading or math. Further analysis showed that these two periods were consecutive and involved 1 hour and 50 minutes of continuous seatwork and small-group work. Additionally, the student was completing her work at only 24 percent accuracy, was only in a small group 21 minutes during this time, and no procedures existed for students to obtain help if they experienced difficulty with seatwork. Interviews with students suggested that the pattern preceding the attacks was that the student became frustrated with her seatwork and sought to obtain answers from another student (often using inappropriate methods such as grabbing the paper or looking over a student's shoulder). Because the girl had a serious body odor, was not as well dressed as most of her peers, and had not been accepted into the classroom group, these attempts at obtaining assistance were frequently met with rebuffs, put-downs, and complaints to the teacher. Finally, the teacher indicated that she had a very low rate of positive contact with the student.

Before the author's involvement in the class, the use of assertive discipline and a behavior contract were the only interventions employed to alter the child's behavior. Before reading any further, set the book aside and jot down the possible interventions you might make based on the information you have about this situation.

The author suggested that the teacher consider six interventions. First, the student's seatwork was altered so she could successfully complete more than 80 percent of her assignments. Second, the student was asked if she would like to work with a peer tutor. She selected three students, two of whom agreed to work with her. The girl was taught several statements to use when requesting assistance, and the tutors were given instruction in methods for providing help. Third, in order to help the student feel more accepted in the classroom, a number of acquaintance activities were implemented. In addition, the teacher agreed to make five inviting statements to the student each morning and each afternoon. Fourth, after obtaining the mother's permission and asking the student if she wished to attend the meeting, the teacher held a class meeting to discuss how students could help the girl have a more positive experience. The students decided to have a friend for the day who would greet the girl in the morning, play with her at morning recess, and eat lunch with her. Fifth, the school nurse worked with the mother and Children's Services Division to attempt some changes in the hygiene conditions at home. Although this was not successful, the nurse did teach the girl some hygiene skills she could use at school and obtained some new clothes for the girl (that were subsequently washed by staff). Finally, the teacher was asked to consider a change in the daily schedule.

With the exceptions of modifying the home environment and the daily schedule, all interventions were successfully implemented. The results showed that the girl had only one aggressive behavior during the remaining three months of school—and this occurred when she was intentionally tripped on the playground. The following year, the girl did not have a physically aggressive school behavior before transferring out of the school near the end of the first semester.

This case study provides an excellent example of the importance of analyzing the classroom environment and of developing proactive interventions before using control methods (such as the assertive discipline and the behavior contract that the school was using). The authors' experience in working with dozens of similar cases is that when provided with proactive methods for creating a more positive learning environment for a student, teachers can and will implement these methods, and that these methods are almost always associated with significant positive changes in the student's behavior.

ACTIVITIES FOR ASSESSING YOUR CLASSROOM ENVIRONMENT

ACTIVITY 9.1

Take a moment to recall several recent incidents in which students have been involved in minor misbehavior in your classroom. When you have these pictures clearly in mind, write down how you responded to these incidents. Next, write down

(continued)

ACTIVITY 9.2
Continued

your general policy for responding to student misbehavior. Having accomplished these tasks, use the following series of questions to rate your response to inappropriate student behavior.

Please rate your response to inappropriate behavior on a scale of 1 to 5 in the five categories below. A score of 5 indicates the highest degree of clarity, sequence, and so on, whereas a score of 1 indicates that these criteria are lacking. Each category is accompanied by a brief description to help you understand what the authors are asking you to rate.

5 4 3 2 1

1. **Clear**   If we asked a large sample of your students to describe how you respond, how close would their answers match what you have written? If almost all students would say something similar, rate yourself high.
2. **Sequential**   Do you follow a sequence when responding to inappropriate behavior (i.e., do you first use a quiet, unobtrusive response followed by a firmer response)?
3. **Dignity**   Do your responses consistently treat students with dignity? Would you use similar responses in a faculty meeting, in your home, or in a meeting at church?
4. **Educational**   Do your responses assist students in learning and demonstrating the behaviors you would like them to use? Do you provide students with some cueing or instruction as you respond?
5. **Environmental Analysis**   Does your response include taking time (perhaps later in the day or with a colleague) to consider what was occurring in the setting that may have caused the student's misbehavior? Do you consider which of the student's personal or academic needs may not have been met at that point in time and what adjustments might be made in the future?

There is obviously no objective standard for evaluating your management approach using this instrument. What we hope is that it will assist you in considering areas in which you may want to fine-tune your response to unproductive student behavior. After having scored yourself, list one or two of the five criteria on which you scored yourself high and what you do to earn this high score. Next, list one or two areas in which you scored a 3 or below and in which you may want to make a change. After reading this and the following chapter, return to this activity and write what you could do to improve your score in the two areas you listed as needing some improvement.

ACTIVITY 9.2
Responding to
Confrontation

Select two other colleagues who teach or are planning to teach students similar in age to those with whom you work or want to work. Have one person agree to be an upset student, one person a teacher, and the third person an observer. Role-play a classroom situation (perhaps assisting students in groups or with individual work) in which the student becomes upset and confronts the teacher (possibly calling her a name or criticizing the assignment). After the role-play, have the person who played the teacher discuss how he or she felt when confronted, why he or she selected the response(s) given, and how he or she felt about the interchange. Next, have the student discuss how he or she felt about the teacher's response. Finally, have the observer discuss his or her response to the intervention.

Switch roles and try this several more times. You may find it productive to videotape the role-plays and play examples back to the class or faculty.

Think of a student whose behavior has created a problem for himself or herself and/or for the class. With this student in mind, complete the interventions form in Figure 9.6 and then answer the following questions.

1. What changes could you make in your classroom that would create a more clearly structured, inviting environment for this student?
2. What interventions have you already attempted to assist this student in behaving more responsibly?
3. Based on the data you have collected, how effective do you believe you have been in assisting this student?

ACTIVITY 9.3
Assessing Your Classroom Management Behavior

Think of a student whose behavior has created a problem for himself or herself and/or for the class. With this student in mind, complete the form in Figure 9.7 and then respond to the following items.

1. List as many specific things as possible that you learned about this student's unproductive behavior.
2. Based on these discoveries, what changes could you make in the classroom to assist this student in behaving more responsibly?

ACTIVITY 9.4
Completing an Environmental Assessment

For the student you considered in either Activity 9.3 or 9.4, complete the form in Figure 9.8 by (1) circling the interventions you have implemented (or, if you are observing in a class, the interventions you have seen implemented), (2) placing a box around those that you believe would assist the student and you would like to try, and (3) placing an X through the number in front of those interventions that do not seem appropriate or feasible given your teaching situation. After you have completed this, sit down with one or more teachers or students in your college class and share what you have done and the items you selected as possible new interventions.

ACTIVITY 9.5
Assessing Your Prereferral Interventions

SUMMARY

Teachers who are effective classroom managers develop and teach clear methods for responding to unproductive student behavior that emphasize helping students take responsibility for their own behavior and learn alternative ways for handling frustrating situations. These more successful teachers are also able to analyze their classroom environment and implement changes that allow students more readily to meet their personal and academic needs in the classroom. As teachers are asked to work with greater number of students who come to school with negative emotional states and poor problem-solving skills, we will need to become more skilled at implementing the methods presented in this and the following chapters.

RECOMMENDED READING

Epanchin, B., & Paul, J. (1982). *Casebook for educating the emotionally disturbed.* Columbus, OH: Charles E. Merrill.

Kauffman, J., Hallahan, D., Mostert, M., Trent, S., & Nuttycomb, D. (1993). *Managing classroom behavior.* Boston: Allyn and Bacon.

Mendler, A. (1992). *What do I do when . . . ?: How to achieve discipline with dignity in the classroom.* Bloomington, IN: National Educational Service.

Walker, H., & Walker, J. (1991). *Coping with noncompliance in the classroom: A positive approach for teachers.* Austin, TX: Pro-Ed.

CHAPTER 10

Reducing Unproductive Student Behavior with Problem Solving

Philosophically, there is little question about the desirability of extending autonomy and freedom of choice to everyone; the problem is determining when and how much. The ability to act independently and make wise and appropriate choices is learned just like any other facet of behavior. . . . A child needs not only experience but the right kind of experience. And he needs a wise guide who can steer him clear of danger and who encourages, prompts, and reinforces behavior that is adaptive and successful.

—Garth Blackham and Adolf Silberman (1975)
Modification of Child and Adolescent Behavior

People take time. Dealing with discipline takes time. Children are not fax machines or credit cards. When they misbehave, they tell us that they need help learning a better way. They are telling us that there are basic needs not being met which are motivating the behavior.

—Allen N. Mendler (1992)
What Do I Do When . . . ? How to Achieve Discipline with Dignity in the Classroom

Regardless of how effectively we create positive learning environments and implement varied instructional methods, some disruptive student behavior is almost inevitable. At all grade levels, students' developmental needs conflict with an environment that requires large groups of students to engage in learning new skills for an extended time. Skilled teachers prevent most disruptions by using methods of classroom management and instruction that encourage positive interpersonal relationships and academic success. They also, however, possess a repertoire of methods for helping students responsibly solve minor conflicts that arise.

The ultimate goals of implementing methods to reduce unproductive or disruptive student behavior are (1) to increase the achievement of both the individual student and his or her classmates and (2) to help youngsters develop positive social skills. As stated in the introduction to Part V, the fact that schools group 30 or more students for instruction creates a situation in which some minor conflicts are likely to occur. Unfortunately, many teachers lack training and skill in helping students solve their problems. Teacher training programs have frequently failed to provide teachers with either prerequisite communication skills or specific methods for involving students in solving problems. Consequently, teachers all too often find themselves resorting to the authoritarian models they experienced as students. This point was brought home recently when a young teacher told one of the authors, "My voice is one octave lower than it was at the beginning of the year. I really hate myself for yelling at the students, but I don't know what else to do."

Regardless of the approach we take, working with students whose behavior is disruptive requires time and energy. Research (Walker & Buckley, 1973; Walker, Hops, & Fiegenbaum, 1976) indicates that teachers spend considerable time attempting to control acting-out students. Teachers often, however, misdirect their energies: "It often appears that the harder a teacher tries to control an acting-out child's behavior, the less effective she/he is. This process can be physically draining and emotionally exhausting" (Walker, 1979, p. 18). Teachers will be more effective if they spend less energy attending to and trying to control disruptive behavior and considerably more energy implementing the methods described in Parts II, III, and IV. When disruptions occur in spite of our using effective interpersonal, organizational, and instructional strategies, we should focus our energies on involving students in examining their behavior and developing mutually agreed on methods for changing the behavior.

Whenever confronted with the decision to use an authoritarian or problem-solving approach to discipline, one of the authors is reminded of a comment made by a veteran junior high school teacher. When talking to a group of young teachers about the teaching profession, the teacher stated that it was impossible to be a teacher and not go home tired every night. The teacher said, however, that there were two ways to go home tired. The first was to leave the school building and sigh with relief that another day was over and the students had been kept in line relatively well. He stated that this feeling usually stemmed from teachers' taking an authoritarian, power-oriented approach to discipline; this type of teacher frequently spent evenings worrying about whether the students would behave the next day and what could be done if they did not. The second type of fatigue, he stated, was based on using a problem-solving approach to discipline. He described it as caused by having interacted openly with students all day. Because he experienced the latter type of fatigue, he almost always felt good about his work and generally looked forward to seeing the children the next day.

In his *Teacher Effectiveness Training,* Gordon (1974) stated the issue in a similar manner in discussing the problems associated with teachers' attempting to control students by using power methods of influence:

> Teacher-student relationships at the upper-elementary and secondary levels are much more strained and stressful because teachers relied so heavily upon power (backed up by rewards and punishment) when the children were younger. Then, when students are older, they begin to react to these techniques to an ever-increasing degree with anger, hostility, rebellion, resistance, and retaliation. . . .

> Students do not naturally have to rebel against adults in the schools. But they will rebel against the adults' use of teacher power. Drop the use of teacher power, and much of the student rebellion in schools disappears. (Gordon, 1974, p. 198)

Allen Mendler (1992) placed the concept of discipline in a current social context when he noted:

> What we must realize is that, while obedience models of discipline always had a down side, in today's world they simply no longer work. The only kids who behave as a result of "obedience" methods are those who have "respect" or fear authority. And most of them will stop obeying unless they feel respected by those in authority. . . . Nowadays to be successful in a position of authority requires an ability to connect in a caring way by inspiring hope within others and by leading one's own life in a manner that models the message. (p. xl)

A basic assumption that teachers must accept before using a problem-solving approach is that they can reduce their authoritarian control and replace it with natural authority. Natural authority is the logical and readily accepted leadership associated with obvious competence, interest, and concern.

Veteran teachers often ask why students today fail to respond to authoritarian methods of discipline when these methods worked years ago when the teachers were students. The authors believe this is due largely to the way students view authority. First, students today are much more aware of their own rights. The idea that children should be seen and not heard is much less common than it used to be. Second, the way children see authoritarian adult behavior implemented in their homes is different today than for the typical student 20 years ago. The authors themselves and many teachers with whom the authors have spoken were raised in very authoritarian homes that were also highly stable, loving, supportive environments. Authoritarian control was therefore associated with stability and support. Unfortunately, many students today see authoritarian discipline associated with physical and psychological abuse and abandonment. Therefore, when confronted with authoritarian methods of student management, rather than comply, these students experience fear, anxiety, anger, and rebellion. This is exacerbated by the fact that they correctly believe that the authoritarian methods used by school personnel will not be as physically or psychologically damaging as those experienced at home.

There are three basic situations in which teachers must make a decision regarding the type of authority they will use: (1) in responding to student concerns about issues of curriculum, instruction, and matters of classroom operation; (2) in efforts to alter persistent problems concerning student behavior and learning; and (3) in attempts to stop disruptive or inappropriate student behavior. In all three situations, natural authority will be more effective because students are more likely to accept it. In addition, natural authority allows the teacher to serve as a role model for students, an increasingly important factor as schools are responsible for working with many youngsters who have not been exposed to effective adult role models. Arbitrary, authoritarian, role-bound authority should never be used in the first two situations listed above. In serious instances of aggressive student behavior toward another student, however, a teacher may need to assert authoritarian control if methods based on natural authority have failed. As discussed in the previous chapter, however, the teacher should continue to talk to the student in a manner that indicates a focus on caring for the student and the teacher's desire to be involved in problem-solving activities.

An important point to consider when deciding whether to give up authoritarian control is that this approach becomes noticeably less effective as students become older. Authoritarian control can be effectively used in the primary grades (although the effects on children are often destructive), but it is less effective with older students, who are beginning to enter a developmental stage whose main task is developing an individual identity and sense of independence.

As suggested by the teacher who discussed the two ways in which teachers can go home tired, giving up authoritarian control can have benefits for teachers as well as students. As teachers begin to involve students in solving classroom problems, the teacher's role changes from that of an all-knowing, totally responsible adult to that of an effective facilitator. Although teachers cannot abdicate their ultimate responsibility, they can create classroom settings in which they do not have to be constantly and totally in charge of every decision. The difficulty of maintaining an authoritarian role and the number of teachers who continue to accept it are two reasons for continuing high teacher turnover.

A year after taking a course from the authors, a teacher with over 30 years' experience suggested that when presenting the material in this book, the authors should tell the readers that the ideas in the book are as beneficial to teachers as they are to students. This teacher indicated that she had just completed the best teaching year of her career due to her decision to *work with* the students rather than to constantly attempt to *control* them.

There are several advantages to initially using fewer teacher-directed, behavioristic interventions. First, though some young people will, in fact, respond only to very structured, controlling interventions, others will respond surprisingly well to effective problem-solving approaches presented in a safe, caring environment characterized by effective teaching. Because it is impossible to determine which students will respond to less control-oriented methods, it is always desirable to try these first. Second, students know when they are being singled out from their peers. Students view adults as powerful and knowledgeable, and so they internalize much of what adults' words and actions say about them. Consequently, when adults use behavioristic methods for controlling a student's behavior, students may learn that they are different from and less capable than their peers. Although this situation is sometimes inevitable, its influence can be reduced by initially employing problem-solving interventions with all students. Students who perceive that a more behavioristic intervention is a response to their inability to respond to a problem-solving approach will understand more clearly why they are being provided with a structured program than will students who are initially confronted with such a program. Third, by providing acting-out students with an introduction to problem-solving approaches, educators increase the likelihood that the youngster who must be temporarily removed or controlled by a structured behavioristic program will be more knowledgeable about and able to adjust to less controlled methods when these become appropriate. Finally, because they are quite effective in controlling behavior, teachers sometimes use behavioristic interventions without first examining such important variables as the quality of teacher-student and peer relationships or the instructional materials and techniques being used in the classroom. Therefore, behavioristic approaches are sometimes used to manipulate pupils into behaving passively in environments that are not meeting their basic needs. Because problem-solving approaches give students an opportunity to discuss the environment, they are an important precursor to behavioristic interventions.

PLACING PROBLEM SOLVING IN CONTEXT

When considering when and how to implement problem solving, teachers must answer three important questions: (1) What do I want to accomplish in responding to inappropriate student behavior? (2) Where does problem solving fit into my responsibilities for managing student behavior and my classroom management plan? and (3) How does problem solving relate to other corrective behavior management interventions I may choose to employ? In answering the first question, most teachers state that in addition to wanting to maintain a positive, supportive learning environment, they want to teach students to be responsible for their own behavior. By involving students in examining their own behavior and developing alternative responses, problem solving allows students to accept greater responsibility for their behavior.

Figures 9.1 and 10.1 can help teachers answer the questions regarding their responsibility in implementing effective responses to inappropriate behavior and the relationship between problem solving and other interventions. As indicated in Figure 10.1, problem solving is used one or more times when a student continues to act unproductively in the classroom despite the teacher's best efforts to create a positive, well-structured learning environment. As discussed in Chapter 9, problem solving may take the form of having the student complete a problem-solving form as a consequence for violating a classroom rule or procedure. It may also involve the teacher's taking time to meet with the student and verbally problem solve with the student. Additionally, as discussed in Chapter 12, effective schoolwide student management programs also involve the student in problem solving when a persistent or serious misbehavior has led to an out-of-class or office referral.

Even teachers skilled in involving students in solving their own problems find that some students have major skill deficits or personality disorders that prevent them from responding to interventions requiring the establishment of a trusting relationship and an ability to evaluate one's behavior in light of its effect on others. When faced with such students, teachers need to provide greater structure than is provided by the problem-solving methods presented in this chapter. Problem solving is the intervention teachers should use following or in conjunction with attempts to alter the classroom environment in order to create a more positive, supportive learning environment. However, teachers may also need to incorporate other individualized intervention methods when problem solving does not have the desired results. In addition, teachers cannot be effective in helping students with serious behavior problems unless the school incorporates a variety of methods to provide assistance and support to teachers.

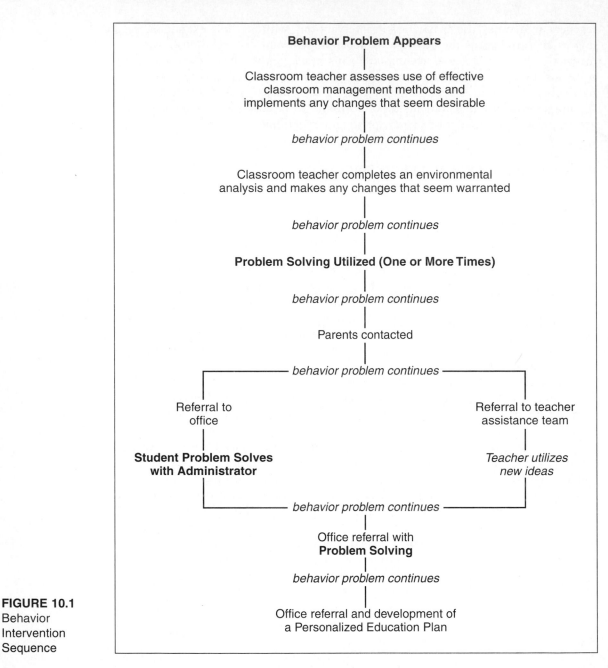

FIGURE 10.1
Behavior
Intervention
Sequence

METHODS FOR SOLVING PROBLEMS
WITH INDIVIDUAL STUDENTS

Several writers have developed methods for helping students resolve problems and take responsibility for their own behavior. In his *Teacher Effectiveness Training*, Tom Gordon (1974) offered a six-step approach to problem solving. Frank Maple's

(1977) *Shared Decision Making* describes a variety of skills needed to resolve problems effectively. Curwin and Mendler's (1988) book *Discipline with Dignity,* and Mendler's (1992) follow-up book *What Do I Do When . . . ?: How to Achieve Discipline with Dignity in the Classroom,* provide good information on helping students develop an ability to solve their own problems. Jim Fey's workshops on Discipline with Love and Logic provide another good opportunity for teachers to examine this practice as, of course, do workshops offered through the Glasser Institute. For teachers working with students who have serious problems, the method of life space interviewing developed by Fritz Redl and expanded by William Morse and Nicholas Long (Long, Morse, & Newman, 1971; Wood & Long, 1991) provides a method for helping the student understand and resolve conflicts within a structured, supportive approach. Similarly, Mary Wood's (1975) *Developmental Therapy* and Betty Epanchin and James Paul's (1982) *Casebook for Educating the Emotionally Disturbed* offer methods for working with seriously disturbed students.

Although at various times the authors have used each method described above, the remainder of this chapter presents the approaches the authors have found most useful in their own teaching and counseling experiences. If you are interested in examining other methods, refer to the recommended readings at the end of this chapter.

Glasser's Seven Steps to Effective Discipline

Many teachers find the issue of dealing unsuccessfully with persistent student behavior problems to be one of the most frustrating and time-consuming aspects of teaching. Though most teachers are well trained in subject-matter methods, many are untrained or feel uncomfortable with the role of problem solver and classroom manager. Furthermore, with the increased emphasis on competencies and achievement-test scores, some teachers frequently feel anxious about time spent solving problems. We are, however, confronted daily with individual problems that must be resolved in order for students to benefit from our instruction. Therefore, we need to develop skills in solving problems in a positive and rapid manner. Recently, a teacher in Lincoln, Nebraska, shared a concept she had found helpful in her thinking about working with behavior problems in her classroom. She noted that she believed that although teachers were not responsible for counseling students, teachers were increasingly responsible for doing what they do best—teaching students a wide variety of behaviors as well as academic skills. She noted that defining her responses as teaching new behaviors had given her a new perspective and enthusiasm for working with students experiencing behavior problems.

The simplest and most effective method of helping children solve their problems and alter their behavior was described by William Glasser (1965, 1969) in his *Reality Therapy* and *Schools without Failure.* Though Glasser provided several step-by-step approaches to discipline, the method found by the authors to be most effective involves these seven steps: (1) be warm and personal and be willing to get emotionally involved; (2) deal with specific, current behavior; (3) help the youngster make a value judgment about his or her behavior; (4) work out a plan for changing the behavior; (5) get a commitment from the student to carry out the plan;

(6) follow up by checking to see how the plan is working; (7) do not punish the student by being negative or sarcastic, and do not accept excuses if the inappropriate behavior continues. Figure 10.2 outlines Glasser's seven steps.

Advantages of Glasser's Method

Four factors make Glasser's model extremely useful for school personnel. First, the problem solving can be accomplished in a short time. Most conflicts can be resolved in less than five minutes, and frequently a solution can be developed in only a minute or two. Therefore, though it is often desirable to remove the student from the group so that the discussion can take place privately, you do not need to become involved in a lengthy discussion that diverts your attention from other instructional or supervisory duties. Second, because the model employs a step-by-step procedure, it is easy to learn. Furthermore, if a problem-solving session does not go well, you can analyze each step and discover what needs to be improved to make the session more effective.

Third, by actively involving the student in the problem-solving process, the model responds to a variety of students' needs. Rather than establishing a teacher-versus-student debate or a situation in which you manipulate the student by offering rewards for changed behavior, the student is meaningfully involved in examining his or her behavior and developing a plan for changing the behavior. Finally, because the model focuses on specific, observable behavior, data can be collected and the student is accountable for the results. The focus on observable

FIGURE 10.2
Glasser's
Problem-Solving
Method

Step 1:	Be warm and personal and be willing to become emotionally involved. "I am glad you're here and I care about you as a person and a learner."
Step 2:	Deal with the present behavior. "What did you do?"
Step 3:	Make a value judgment. "Is it helping you?" "Is it helping others?" "Is it against a rule?"
Step 4:	Work out a plan. "What can you do differently?" "What do you need me to do to help?" "Do you need any assistance from others?"
Step 5:	Make a commitment. "Are you going to do this?"
Step 6:	Follow up. "Let's check later and see how the plan worked."
Step 7:	No put-downs but do not accept excuses. "It's O.K. Let's keep trying. I trust that you can develop a plan that will work." "I know things happen, but you made a plan. Do we need a new plan?"

behavior also enables you and the student realistically to analyze the effectiveness of the plan. To become competent at using Glasser's approach, you need to understand each step and then frequently use the approach with students.

Step One

The first step is presented in Chapter 3. If you employ the communication skills and other strategies for improving teacher-student relationships described in Chapter 3, students will sense that you care and will almost always be willing to examine and attempt to change their behavior.

Step Two

The second step is to ask the student to describe his or her behavior. Awareness of actions is an important component in any behavior change program. Indeed, a simple increase in children's awareness of their behavior is often accompanied by major changes in their behavior. You can help students describe their behavior by asking questions such as, "What did you do that upset Sally?" It is important to focus the student's attention on what he or she did, not on what the other person did. The emphasis should be placed on specific, observable behavior. If a student states that he or she was bad or didn't obey us, help the child specify what request he or she did not obey and what he or she said or did when rejecting the request. If the student begins to answer the question by discussing what the other person did, you should indicate that, although this subject can be discussed later and the other person may even become involved, the student knows what he or she did and you would like to discuss this act.

Students will sometimes respond to your question about what they did by saying, "Nothing" or "I don't know." You then have several options. First, you may respond by stating, "John, I'm not trying to blame you or get you in trouble. What I want to do is help you solve the problem, and I need to know what you did so I understand what happened." When you focus on the problem rather than threaten the student or focus on the punishment, students are often willing to discuss their behavior. A second approach is to ask if the student would be willing to hear what you observed or, if you were not present, to have someone else share what he or she saw. It is important that this option be presented positively and not as a threat. When confronted with this option, students will normally discuss their behavior.

A teacher recently solved this problem by asking students, "If I had a video camera on that was taping what happened, what would I have seen?" She says that students find this nonthreatening because while they describe their own behavior, they are allowed to describe the entire event as they perceived it. If a student does not respond positively to any of these options, it usually means that he or she is quite emotional and may need time to calm down and think about the problem. You can deal with this situation by saying, "John, it seems you don't feel comfortable talking about the problem right now. Why don't we talk about it during recess." Providing the student with time to relax often facilitates a positive resolution of the problem.

Teachers often note that they doubt whether students will honestly tell them what happened. If you have a sibling within several years of your age, consider for a moment several situations in which you did something you knew was not acceptable in your home but that no one could prove you had done. If you are like most people, there were several occasions in which your parent(s) asked you whether you had done the act and you said, "No," knowing that this would make your parents either become detectives (which they were too busy to do) or punish an innocent person. The number of times you utilized this strategy was quite likely related to the severity of punishments used in your home. Like most people raised in fairly large families with strict punishments, most students who have persistent behavior problems become political experts in knowing how to avoid punishment. If you want students to be willing to problem solve with you, you must make it clear that discipline does not mean being punished or hurt but rather means being asked to take responsibility for one's behavior and to learn new methods for solving problems.

Step Three

Once the student has described his or her behavior, you should help him or her determine whether the behavior is desirable. Students will not make meaningful, lasting changes in a behavior unless they decide that the behavior should be altered. When directing a program for seventh- and eighth-grade students who exhibited serious behavior problems, one of the authors was surprised when a number of the students stated that when they changed their behavior to earn the rewards offered by a contract, they thought they were being bribed and earned the rewards only to "play the system." The students resented not being involved in assessing their behavior. Consequently, behavior changes occurred only as long as the staff could devise adequate rewards or punishments. Based on this information subsequent behavior change interventions used more dialogue and a less unilateral approach to solving problems. Research results (Jones, 1973) indicate that this approach was more successful.

Glasser suggests that, when helping youngsters make a value judgment about their behavior, you ask them: "Is the behavior helping you? Is it helping me? Is it helping the other students?" When children are involved in obviously unproductive behaviors, they will almost always answer *no* to these questions. If they answer, *yes,* you can ask, "How is it helping you?" or "How is it helping the others?" Finally, if the student insists that the behavior is helping him or her and his or her peers, you can describe how the behavior is causing problems for you or others in the school or that it violates a school rule. If you have established a positive relationship with the student, this will often provide the impetus for the student to acknowledge that the behavior needs to be changed.

Another approach to helping youngsters make a value judgment is to have them list the advantages and disadvantages or payoffs and costs of their behavior. When working with older students, we can ask them to put the payoffs and costs in writing. Figure 10.3 provides a form that can be used to facilitate this process.

If a student continues to state that an unproductive behavior is helping him or her and that he or she wishes to continue the behavior, it is likely that he or she is feeling backed into a corner or are testing your resolve. It is usually best to postpone the discussion for a short time. If a student continues to insist that an unproductive behavior is acceptable, you may need to confront the student with

	Short Term	Long Term
Payoffs		
Costs		

FIGURE 10.3
Payoff-Cost
Model of
Behavioral
Counseling

Source: From Vernon F. Jones, *Adolescents with Behavior Problems: Strategies for Teaching, Counseling, and Parent Involvement*, p. 200. Copyright © 1980 by Allyn and Bacon. Reprinted with permission.

the logical consequences of the behavior. We should be very careful not to rush to this point without exhausting all possible approaches to helping the student decide to alter the behavior. If it is necessary to use this intervention, however, it should be discussed in a matter-of-fact, nonthreatening manner, and you should clearly explain to the student why the behavior must be altered. You might say, "I am sorry that you do not see the behavior as harmful. It is my job, though, to make sure that students follow school rules. Therefore, if you do not choose to be responsible for your behavior, I must take responsibility." If the student continues to insist that the behavior does not need to change, you should inform the student of the specific consequences that will occur if the behavior continues.

Step Four
After the student has decided that the behavior really does need to be changed, the next step is to help him or her develop a workable plan for making the change. Start by asking the student a question such as, "What do you think you can do so that you can study without bothering other students?" or "What kind of plan or strategy could you use so that you don't get in trouble in music?" Do not accept a superficial plan such as the statement, "I won't do it again" or "I'll try harder." You might be relieved to hear these promises, but they do not provide the student with a specific approach for dealing more effectively with the situation. Consequently, you can respond to promises by saying, "I'm glad that you are going to try not to do it. That will certainly help. But what else can you do? What can you do when you start to get frustrated with your work?"

Students are refreshingly creative at devising useful plans/strategies for solving their own problems. Nevertheless, students sometimes state that they cannot think of a solution. Your first response should be to encourage them to think about the situation and report back to us at a designated time. Students have frequently become so accustomed to having adults provide answers that at first they are confused by having the burden placed on them. When given time to think about the situation, though, they often devise thoughtful plans. If the student is unable to develop a workable plan, you can offer several ideas for the student to consider. Offer several suggestions so that the student will make the final decision. This involvement in choosing the solution increases the likelihood that the student will accept and follow through on the plan.

With elementary and middle school students, it is helpful to teach several lessons on developing plans or strategies for responding to various situations in which problems frequently arise. This will always occur after students have been taught the problem-solving approach outlined in Figure 10.2. The class can be asked to describe common situations in which students become engaged in inappropriate behavior and then list alternative behaviors for dealing with the situation. These can be posted in the classroom and students can refer to them if they violate a school rule and become involved in problem solving.

Plans should initially be relatively simple and unstructured, such as a student's decision to work with another student in order to stay on task and complete his or her work. Plans may, however, involve a somewhat more structured approach. In fact, when less structured solutions have failed, many of the procedures described in Chapter 11 can serve as methods for implementing a plan to help a child alter his or her behavior. For example, students might be involved in writing a formal contract or self-monitoring their behavior.

Step Five

The next step is to ensure that both you and the student clearly understand the plan and to ask the student to make a commitment to the plan. You can say, "All right, that seems like a good plan. Now, just to be sure that we both understand it, what are you going to do when you become frustrated with your work?" After the student describes the plan, you can paraphrase the student's decision and acknowledge your role in the plan. You might say, "Okay, whenever you get frustrated you're going to raise your hand. If I'm busy and can't help you, you're going to quietly walk over and ask Sally for help. Then, it is my responsibility to come over and check your work as soon as I get a chance." Although it is often adequate simply to obtain an oral agreement, it is sometimes helpful to put the plan in writing. This contract is especially valuable when students are first introduced to problem solving or when the final plan is developed in the form of a contract in which both parties agree to behave in a specified manner.

Once the plan has been clarified, the student should make a commitment to try the plan. This *compact* can be accomplished by asking, "Do you believe this is a good plan? Will you give it a try?" Although this step is often part of the final negotiation of a plan, it is important to elicit a clear commitment to the plan.

Step Six

The sixth and seventh steps involve follow-up. In devising a workable solution to a problem, it is necessary to designate a time when the two parties will meet to discuss how the plan is working. This step provides you with an opportunity to reinforce the student's efforts and to discuss any problems that might arise. If the plan involves a behavior that occurs frequently throughout the day, you should meet briefly with the student on the same day as the plan is made. Furthermore, if you see the student successfully implementing the plan, praise the student for his or her efforts. If the plan involves a behavior that occurs only occasionally—as during the student's music class—you can agree to meet the student as soon as possible following the class. Follow-up sessions need not take long. You can simply ask, "How did your plan work?" If the plan worked well, express your pleasure and ask the student how he or she felt about the results. If it would reinforce the student, you may choose to provide additional follow-up by asking the principal to praise the student or by sending a positive note home with the student.

Step Seven

The final step in Glasser's plan deals with what to do if a plan does not work. First, do not be critical or sarcastic or punish the student. A major assumption underlying the use of a problem-solving approach is that in a positive, supportive environment students will want to be responsible and behave appropriately. Therefore, the student's inability to carry out a plan should not be punished. At the same time, you should not accept excuses. Students often defend their failure to change their behavior by blaming other people. Rather than allowing the student to describe what other people did that caused her or his failure to follow her or his plan, you should begin another problem-solving conference. Because the student will already have examined the behavior and made a decision to change it, the first three steps will usually take only a minute or two to complete. The conference should then focus on asking the student to consider why the plan did not work and helping her or him develop another plan. If the behavior is one that is harmful to other students, such as pushing children on the playground, you may need to inform the student of the consequences that will be incurred should the behavior continue. Although the emphasis should always be on devising a plan rather than on punishing the student, situations in which it is necessary to incorporate a punishment into a plan do occur.

Examples

The following examples of first an upper elementary and then a middle school teacher using Glasser's model with a student indicates how effective communication skills can be combined with Glasser's step-by-step procedure to create a positive resolution to a problem.

Example 1: Upper Elementary School

STEP 1. TEACHER: Darby, can I talk to you by my desk for a little bit?

DARBY: Okay.

STEP 2. TEACHER: After we corrected math today, I went over everyone's paper. Can you tell me what I found on your paper?

DARBY: I didn't get finished.

STEP 3. TEACHER: That's right. Is it helping you to not get your work done on time?

DARBY: I guess not.

TEACHER: What happens when you don't have your work ready?

DARBY: Jon doesn't have a paper to correct.

TEACHER: Yes, can you think of any other things that happen?

DARBY: I'll get a bad grade and have to do my work again.

TEACHER: Okay, and does it make it even harder for you to have to complete this assignment and then begin working on the one for tomorrow?

DARBY: Yeah.

TEACHER: Well, Darby, would you like to start having your work done on time, so that you don't get behind and so that you can feel good about giving Jon a completed paper to correct?

DARBY: Yeah.

STEP 4.   TEACHER: All right. Can you think of a plan that can help you get your work done on time?

DARBY: No—I'll just try to get it done.

TEACHER: Well, that's super to hear, but can you think of some way really to succeed in getting this work completed?

DARBY: Oh, I guess I could do it after I get home from school, before my mom gets home from the beauty shop each night. But I like to play, too.

TEACHER: Well, let's plan it out. What time does your mother get home?

DARBY: 5:30.

TEACHER: And what time do you get home from school?

DARBY: 3:15.

TEACHER: Now, do you think you can play for a while . . .

DARBY: Oh, I know. I'll play until 4:30 and then do my work from 4:30 to 5:30!

STEP 5.   TEACHER: Darby, that sounds like a great idea! I'm sure that most days you won't even need a whole hour to finish your work, especially when you get into such a good habit! And won't it be nice to be all done when your mother gets home! How long do you think you could make this plan work?

DARBY: Forever!

TEACHER: Oh, whoa!! I'm excited, too, but let's take it a little at a time!

DARBY: Okay. I will do it tonight and tomorrow night.

TEACHER: Great! Then Jon and I can expect to see completed assignments on Thursday and Friday!

Thursday

STEP 6.   DARBY: It worked! I played, got my math done in 30 minutes (it was easy!), and was watching TV when Mom got home. Boy, was she surprised when I showed her my work!

TEACHER: Oh, Darby. I knew you could do it! I really am proud of you! Keep up the good plan!

Example 2: Middle School

STEP 1.   TEACHER: Horace, may I please speak with you for a few minutes?

HORACE: Okay.

STEP 2.   TEACHER: What did you do that upset Larry?

HORACE: I didn't do anything.

TEACHER: Horace, I'm not trying to blame you or get you in trouble. What I want to do is try to help you solve the problem. But before we can solve it, I need to know what you did so that I understand what happened.

HORACE: Well, I pushed Larry's books off his desk and onto the floor and his papers got all messed up.

STEP 3.   TEACHER: Thank you for being honest with me. It sounds like you are really making an attempt to try to figure this problem out. Is this helping you or Larry in any way?

HORACE: No, but he marked in ink on my assignment sheet that I was just about to hand in, and he ruined it. And so, now I have to do it all over again.

STEP 4.   TEACHER: I will talk to Larry about this problem after we get finished dealing with your part of the problem. What kind of plan do you think you could work out so that you won't retaliate against anyone the next time something like this happens to you?

HORACE: I won't do it again.

TEACHER: I'm glad that you are going to try to not do it again. That will certainly help. But what else can we do?

HORACE: I don't know.

TEACHER: Well, how about if I make a few suggestions and you pick one of my plans to try to work with?

HORACE: Well, okay.

TEACHER: How about sending that person an I-message telling them how you feel. Like, "It upsets me when you ruin my homework and I have to do it over again." Or you could just get up and move away from that person, showing them that you don't appreciate what they've done. Do you like either one of these plans, Horace?

HORACE: Well, because we've worked on I-messages and you want us to work out our own problems, I will try an I-message next time.

STEP 5.   TEACHER: Great; now, just to be sure we both understand, what are you going to do the next time somebody bothers you and your work?

HORACE: Send that person an I-message.

TEACHER: Good; I'll check back with you in a couple of days to see how your plan is working.

A couple of days later:

STEP 6.   HORACE: It worked!! Gary ripped one of my papers yesterday and I sent him an I-message, and he actually apologized to me. I couldn't believe it.

TEACHER: I'm proud of you for working out your plan. I can see by your reaction that you are happy with your results.

Implementing Glasser's Model in the Classroom

As discussed in Chapter 8 and 9 and earlier in this chapter, problem solving should be an integral part of a teacher's classroom management plan. You must decide for yourself how this method will be incorporated into your plan. Some teachers choose to focus almost exclusively on a written form of problem solving. Other teachers prefer to have students go to a problem-solving area, think about the problem, generate a plan, and share the plan verbally when time permits. Many teachers use a combination of these methods in which written responses are the consequence for continued rule violation and verbal problem solving is used to deal with problems that do not involve serious violation of classroom rules or when the student misbehaves frequently but always responds to warnings and thus infrequently chooses to receive the consequence of a written problem-solving form.

As with any procedure used in the classroom, it will be dramatically more effective and efficient if students are taught how to use the procedure. The following 10 activities are those the authors and many teachers with whom the authors work use in teaching Glasser's method to students:

1. Provide the students with a handout and write the steps on the overhead.
2. Discuss each step and provide an example.
3. Role-play several situations in which a student misbehaves and the teacher uses this method for assisting the student in taking responsibility for his or her behavior.
4. Lead a discussion following each role-play.

5. Have the students practice by taking the role of both student and teacher and role-playing several situations.
6. Process these interactions.
7. Provide the class with an example of a violation of a classroom rule and have each student write a problem-solving plan on a form such as that in Figure 9.4.
8. Have students share and assist the class in evaluating and if necessary modifying several plans.
9. Explain how the problem-solving process relates to the classroom management plan and the difference between verbal and written plans.
10. Quiz students on the steps in the sequence and the classroom management plan.

When implementing Glasser's approach, it is important not to skip any of the seven steps listed in Figure 10.2. The authors often see teachers working with a student to develop a plan when the student has yet to make a value statement about his or her behavior. Regardless of the student's age or the nature of the problem, it is critical that the adult involved use each step and proceed in the order presented. The authors have used this method (embedded in the curriculum of responsibility) with their own children beginning at age 2, with students at every age and grade from 4-year-olds to high school seniors, and with students ranging from talented and gifted to incarcerated delinquents. The authors firmly believe that it is a central factor in creating positive learning environments and helping students learn personal responsibility. The teacher who uses Glasser's approach will find that student attitudes about the teacher and school in general will improve and that students will learn to take more responsibility for their behavior.

METHODS FOR SOLVING PROBLEMS BETWEEN STUDENTS

Teachers too seldom allow students to work out their own solutions to conflicts involving two or more students. By the third or fourth grade, most children have considerable experience in resolving interpersonal conflicts. Furthermore, students' disagreements are often short-lived. It is not unusual to see younger children who were fighting one minute playing happily together several minutes later. Indeed, adults' attempts to involve children in extensive problem solving about peer conflicts often tend to extend, compound, and intensify the problem. Similarly, when adults punish children for peer conflicts, they often inadvertently intensify the conflict. Rather than being forgotten, conflicts may linger on as students recall the punishment they received.

Teachers' involvement in solving peer conflicts may also reinforce the undesirable behavior. Students often enjoy the attention they receive when the teacher or counselor spends time helping them solve a peer conflict. This reinforcement may be especially powerful if the discussion takes place during time the students would normally be involved in academic tasks.

Excessive teacher involvement in resolving peer conflicts also suggests that students are unable to resolve their own conflicts. By reinforcing the concept that teachers alone possess the knowledge and skill for solving problems, we inadvertently encourage students to be more dependent. This situation affects both teacher and student negatively. Students are prevented from developing a sense of industry, competence, and power. This interference negatively affects their self-esteem, and students will often find less productive means of demonstrating their power. The effect on teachers is less pronounced but nevertheless notable. Teachers who attempt to solve every minor problem are often inundated with student concerns. This flood not only drains energy but also detracts from the teacher's ability to assist children with their academic tasks.

Knowing the considerable disadvantages associated with teachers' too frequent interventions in peer conflicts, it is useful to examine how to increase students' involvement in this process. The first factor to consider before encouraging students to solve their own conflicts is the degree to which students in the classroom know and like one another. If you have employed a variety of peer relationship activities such as those presented in Chapter 4, and if you have implemented cooperative learning, students will be much more likely to work together to solve their own problems. If students are highly competitive, however, or have not been assisted in establishing a positive peer culture, they will normally be much less effective in solving their own problems. Similarly, even when positive peer relations have been established, you should be careful about having two students resolve a conflict if one student has considerably more power or prestige than the other. Unless the more powerful student is very sensitive and willing to use his or her power to help facilitate a positive solution, the situation may be characterized by negative manipulation. When there is good reason to question the students' ability to obtain a positive resolution, it may be best for you to serve as a third-party facilitator during the discussion.

The actual process of involving students in solving their own conflicts is quite simple. The first step is to discuss the procedure with the class. You can introduce the topic by asking students how they think problems are solved most effectively. When working with older students, you may wish to incorporate a brief discussion of the ways in which nations or individuals in the larger society solve their differences of opinion. The purpose of a discussion is to increase students' involvement in the process while making the point that disagreements are usually most effectively solved by direct communication between the parties. Even when a third party is involved, this person's role is merely to facilitate a productive dialogue between the disagreeing parties. Once the students have discussed this issue, you should inform them that whenever a student comes to you with a problem or you are required to intervene temporarily in an angry interchange between students, they will be asked to set a time to meet to resolve their differences.

It is important to provide adequate structure for these student meetings. You should designate an area of the room where such meetings will take place. The authors know a teacher who tapes two lines on the floor so that students will discuss their differences while remaining far enough apart so that physical contact is discouraged. You may also wish to designate a time when conflict-resolution conferences will take place. Students can be informed that these will occur during recess periods, lunch breaks, or after school. Similarly, especially if students are allowed to meet during classroom activities, you may wish to set a time limit for such meetings. You can also provide students with a worksheet that helps them structure their meeting and clearly report their solution. Figure 10.4 is a form that has been used with children in grades 4 through 8. Finally, you can help students develop the skills necessary for productive conflict resolution. Students can be taught to use I-messages and active listening. You can also model an effective

FIGURE 10.4
Problem-Solving Form

WORKING
TOGETHER
to
Solve
Problems

1. What happened that caused the other person to become upset?

   Before   *During*   *After*

   _____   _____   _____
   _____   _____   _____
   _____   _____   _____
   _____   _____   _____

2. Did the behaviors described above violate a school or classroom rule?

   _____ _____ If so, which one? _____
     no   yes   _____

3. Did the behaviors help you to positively resolve the problem?

   _____ _____
     no   yes

4. What agreement or plan can you create to resolve the problem? Complete the sentence.

   We have decided that we will _____
   _____
   _____

5. What plan can you develop for preventing future problems? Complete the sentence.

   The next time one of us does something that bothers the other, we will
   _____
   _____

   _____   _____   _____
   Student #1 signature   Student #2 signature   Date

conflict resolution and can involve the class in role-playing several typical conflicts. This skill building takes very little time, is an enjoyable activity for students, and significantly increases the percentage of conflict-resolution meetings that result in two happy students and a positive solution.

During the past decade, much progress was made toward implementing peer conflict resolution in the schools. This progress stemmed from the work in the area of community mediation. Finding the courts glutted with cases, lawyers and concerned citizens established community mediation programs to reduce court cases dealing with minor neighborhood disputes. Today, there are more than 400 dispute resolution programs in existence. Concern about world peace is another factor that stimulated interest in student-conflict resolution. Organizations such as Educators for Social Responsibility and programs such as Brooklyn Community School District 15's Model Peace Education Program have extended the concept of world peace to conflict resolution in schools.

Many school districts have begun implementing conflict manager programs. In the spring of 1987, the Chicago School District introduced a curriculum on dispute resolution in all of its high schools. The 6-week unit includes a focus on interpersonal as well as global conflict resolution. The Conflict Manager Program developed by the Community Board Center in San Francisco is another widely used program. It provides students with 16 hours of training in communications and problems-solving skills. Students then serve as mediators in their schools. In elementary school buildings, student mediators wear bright Conflict Manager T-shirts to designate their role. Cahoon (1988) reported developing a similar program in her elementary school that, while using less training time, has had positive results. Roderick (1988) has presented a thoughtful discussion of the history and direction of student mediation programs.

The authors' 10-year-old son is a conflict manager at his elementary school. The program uses a model developed by the Classroom Law Project associated with the Lewis and Clark College Northwestern School of Law in Portland, Oregon. Figure 10.5 shows the sequence of interventions elementary students are taught to use when responding to peer conflicts, and Figure 10.6 provides a list of ways to nonviolently resolve a conflict. Figure 10.7 provides an outline on conflict management used in training middle school and high school conflict managers. A number of additional materials on conflict management are provided at the end of this chapter.

Although it is often possible for students to resolve their own conflicts, there are times when teachers will be involved either because students have not yet been trained or because the conflict cannot be resolved by the students—either with or without a student mediator. When this occurs, teachers will benefit from developing skill in mediating conflicts.

Most teachers find that when first implementing a new approach, it is helpful to have a model to follow. A useful model in helping teachers resolve peer conflicts with students is the Think–Feel–Act model, introduced by Cory Dunn, coordinator for the Program for Emotionally Handicapped Students in Linn and Benton Counties, Oregon. Figure 10.8 illustrates this method. In implementing this approach, the teacher's role is to allow each student to state his or her account of what happened, how he or she felt, and what he or she believes needs to be done, and to

1. Introduce yourselves: "Hi, my name is _____. I'm conflict manager and this is my partner _____."
2. Ask the parties: "Do you want to solve the problem with us or with a teacher?" If necessary, move to a quiet place to solve problem.
3. Explain to the parties: "First you have to agree to four rules":
   a. Agree to solve the problem.
   b. No name calling.
   c. Do not interrupt.
   d. Tell the truth.
4. Conflict Manager #1 asks Person #1: "What happened? How do you feel?"
   Conflict Manager #1 repeats what Person #1 said, using active listening: "So, what you're saying is . . ."
5. Conflict Manager #2 asks Person #2: "What happened? How do you feel?"
   Conflict Manager #2 repeats what Person #2 said, using active listening: "So, what you're saying is . . ."
6. Ask Person #1: "Do you have a solution?"
   Ask Person #2: "Do you agree with the solution?"
   If no: "Do you have another solution?" and so on until disputants have reached a solution agreeable to both of them.
7. Have disputants tell each other what they have just agreed to: "So will you tell each other what you've just agreed to?"
8. Congratulate them both: "Thank you for working so hard to solve your problem. Congratulations."
9. Fill out Conflict Manager Report Form.

FIGURE 10.5
Elementary School Conflict Management Process: Steps for Problem Solving

Source: Classroom Law Project, 6318 S.W. Corbett, Portland, OR 97201. Reprinted with permission.

FIGURE 10.6
Eight Modes of Conflict Resolution

Share
    WE CAN BOTH DO IT

Take Turns
    WE CAN DO IT YOUR WAY THIS TIME, MY WAY NEXT

Compromise
    GIVE UP SOME—GET SOME

Chance
    FLIP A COIN

Outside Help
    LET'S ASK A TEMMATE, CLASSMATE, TEACHER

Postpone
    LATER—WHEN WE COOL DOWN

Avoid
    AGREE TO DISAGREE—WITH RESPECT

Humor
    IS THIS IMPORTANT TO JOE'S TURTLE?

Source: Classroom Law Project, 6318 S.W. Corbett, Portland, OR 97201. Reprinted with permission.

FIGURE 10.7
Secondary
Mediation
Process

Mediation is a method of conflict resolution which stresses compromise and agreement between two parties rather than one party winning and the other losing. It also gives an opportunity to the parties to come to their own solution to a problem rather than having someone impose a solution on them.

I. INTRODUCTORY PHASE

Purpose: Explain Ground Rules and Procedures
Introduce yourself as a mediator and explain that your role is to help the parties in conflict come to a workable solution that resolves their conflict. Each person will have opportunity to tell his/her side of the story and to address issues raised by other party. Explain that you are not here to judge guilt or innocence or to find fault. Emphasize that everything said during the session will be confidential.

   Ask them to agree to ground rules:

1. Don't interrupt
2. No name calling
3. Agree to work towards a solution together
4. Respect each other
5. Remain seated during session
6. Keep everything said during session confidential

Note: Be sure that you have agreement from all parties that they will follow ground rules before you proceed.

II. IDENTIFY THE PROBLEM AND ISSUES

Purpose: Parties Tell What Happened
   Mediator #1 asks first party what happened and how they feel. Mediator paraphrases what the first party said.
   Mediator #2 asks second party what happened and how they feel.
   Mediator #2 paraphrases what the second party said.
   Mediators ask any clarification questions necessary to get additional information about the conflict.

III. UNDERSTANDING THE PROBLEM

Purpose: Parties Talk to Each Other
   Ask parties to paraphrase the other's position and how they feel.
   Ask parties to tell each other what they could do differently to avoid this conflict in future.

IV. SOLUTION SEARCH

Purpose: Parties Brainstorm Solutions
   Mediator #1 asks one party if s/he has a solution to the problem.
   If yes, then mediator asks other party if s/he agrees with that solution.
   If no agreement, other mediator asks other party if s/he has another solution. If yes, ask other party if s/he agrees.
   Continue searching for a solution going back and forth between parties until they find a solution to which both parties can agree.
   Ask parties to repeat to each other what they have just agreed to.

V. AGREEMENT

Purpose: Confirm and Write Agreement
>Ask parties to sign written agreement specifically articulating what each party will or will not do.
>
>If mediators think follow-up will be needed to ensure that agreement is completed, set up another meeting time to get back together to check in to see how things are going.

VI. FOLLOW-UP

Purpose: To Change Agreement or to Check In to See How It's Going

VII. DEPARTURE

Purpose: End the Mediation Session
If possible, have parties shake hands. Thank them for working so hard to solve their problem and tell them they are free to contact you if problems occur or just to let you know how it's going.

Source: Classroom Law Project, 6318 S.W. Corbett, Portland, OR 97201. Reprinted with permission.

have the other student paraphrase each statement so each person experiences a sense of having been heard and understands the other student's point of view. This process will be much easier to implement if students have been taught and practiced the method prior to its implementation.

The following dialogue occurred on the playground following an incident in which a small third-grader who had emotional problems was accidentally hit in the face with a ball and had his glasses knocked off. When teaching students to use this method and, whenever convenient when using it with students, it is useful to draw the arrows (as seen in Figure 10.8) to indicate who is speaking and to demonstrate that each student has had an opportunity to speak and be heard.

Teacher Facilitating a Student Problem

PETER: (Crying) He hit me with the ball and broke my glasses.

TEACHER: (Puts arm around Peter) I'm sorry you're hurt. That must have been a surprise to have that ball fly over and hit you. Let's talk to Bill and see what happened. Bill, would you please come here for a minute? (Bill leaves his game and joins the teacher and Peter.) Peter, can you tell Bill what happened?

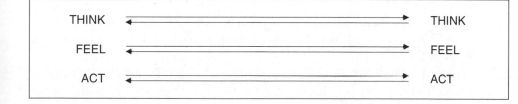

FIGURE 10.8
Think–Act–Feel Method of Conflict Resolution

PETER: You threw a ball and broke my glasses.

TEACHER: Bill, what did Peter tell you he thinks happened:

BILL: I didn't break his glasses. He's just being . . .

TEACHER: (interrupts Bill) Remember our method for problem solving, Bill. What I need you to do is tell us what you heard Peter say.

BILL: He said I threw a ball and it hit him in the face and broke his glasses.

TEACHER: Thank you, Bill. I appreciate your being responsible and helping us by using the problem-solving method. Now, Bill, would you please tell Peter what you thought happened.

BILL: We were playing catch with the football and John threw it over my head and it hit Peter. I jumped as high as I could to catch it, but it was too high.

TEACHER: Peter, can you tell us what Bill just said?

PETER: He said he didn't hit me with the ball.

TEACHER: What did he say happened?

PETER: He said John threw it over his head and he tried to catch it.

TEACHER: Peter, that was a very good job of stating what Bill said. Now, Peter, can you tell me how you are feeling?

PETER: I'm sad that my glasses are broke and I'm mad that someone broke them.

TEACHER: Bill, can you state back to us how Peter is feeling?

BILL: He's feeling mad and sad because his glasses are broken.

TEACHER: Thank you, Bill. Now, can you tell Peter how you are feeling?

BILL: I don't know.

TEACHER: Well, are you happy, sad, angry?

BILL: I guess I'm sad that his glasses got broken, but I didn't do it.

TEACHER: Peter, can you tell us how Bill said he is feeling?

PETER: He said he is feeling sad but that it's my fault the glasses are broken.

TEACHER: You're right that he said he was sad that your glasses were broken, but he didn't say it was your fault; he said that he did not break them. O.K., Peter, can you tell us what you think we need to do to solve this problem?

PETER: Yes, somebody has to buy me new glasses. My mom will kill me if I come home with broke glasses.

TEACHER: Bill, what did Peter say about what we need to do?

BILL: He said I have to buy him new glasses, but I didn't even break them.

TEACHER: Well, he said someone ought to pay for new glasses. I will take care of checking on the glasses. Bill, what do you think will help to solve this problem?

BILL: Well, I think John and me could apologize and I think we could be more careful about where we throw the ball. But Peter needs to be more careful about where he stands.

TEACHER: Peter, what did Bill just say?

PETER: He said him and John would apologize and be more careful.

TEACHER: Anything else?

PETER: Yah, he said I should look where I stand.

TEACHER: Peter, does that sound like a fair solution to the problem?

PETER: Yah, as long as someone pays for my glasses.

TEACHER: Bill, do you think we've solved the problem?

BILL: Yah.

TEACHER: O.K., boys, why don't you shake hands and then Bill will go over and get John so they can apologize to you, Peter.

The boys shook hands and Bill walked over to explain the situation to John. At this point, Peter took his glasses and started to bend them. In doing this, he realized that he had flexible stems and the stem popped back into place.

PETER: Hey look, they're not busted. They just got bent.

TEACHER: That's great, Peter. I'm really glad. Let's tell Bill and John that when they come over.

Even though using this method takes some time, it is very effective. Not only does this approach allow students to feel heard and help them develop problem-solving skills but it also helps students understand others' points of view and develop skill in identifying their feelings. As mentioned earlier in this chapter, all interventions in response to behavior problems should be educational in nature. This approach helps students develop a number of skills in which most students with behavior problems are deficient.

METHODS FOR GROUP PROBLEM SOLVING

Class Meetings

Class meetings allow both teacher and students to resolve problems openly and before they become major issues that negatively affect learning. Whenever people live close together for many hours every day, it is mandatory that time be taken to resolve minor conflicts openly. Like an automobile engine that may appear to run smoothly but will suddenly boil over unless properly lubricated, classrooms require proper maintenance checks and minor tune-ups. When implemented in a positive, supportive atmosphere, class meetings serve as the lubricant for a smoothly running classroom.

Class meetings are an integral part of a program designed to involve students in solving their own problems. Class meetings not only support the use of individual problem-solving conferences but can also provide students with opportunities for improving their social and problem-solving skills. When a youngster is positively reinforced for a behavior, another student is more likely to model the behavior

"This is Wally. He's representing us in our homework negotiations."

(Bandura, 1969; Kazdin, 1973). Class meetings provide a setting in which this type of positive modeling can be encouraged.

The use of class meetings will vary with grade level. The ideas presented in the following section are most appropriate for relatively self-contained classrooms in which teachers have major responsibility for the social and academic skill development of 25 to 35 students. Class meetings can also be an important component in middle and high school classrooms. Because students at this age spend less time with one group of students, however, and are more sensitive to peer responses, it is generally best to focus on instructional or behavioral matters affecting the entire class, while handling individual student problems in private meetings with the teacher and one or a few students. Class meetings will generally be held less often in secondary classrooms, and the agenda will usually be presented by the teacher. Students can be encouraged, though, to bring problems to our attention and request that the problem be discussed by the class.

Guidelines for Implementing a Class Meeting

The first step in implementing class meetings is to discuss the concept with students. Students should be informed that class meetings will provide them with an opportunity to discuss things they like about the class as well as things that may need to be changed in order for the class to run more smoothly. Ask students to develop their own list of reasons they think meetings are important. It is important to display enthusiasm and express interest in holding class meetings.

Once students have discussed why class meetings are helpful and are excited about holding their first meeting, present the general guidelines for class meetings. You may add your own guidelines; the authors have found the following guidelines to be useful for elementary and middle school class meetings:

1. Class meetings will be held in a tight circle with all participants (including the teacher) seated in the circle. The circle must not be too large or it will detract from students' involvement and encourage off-task behavior.

2. All problems relating to the class as a group can be discussed. Problems between two or three individuals, however, will be resolved outside the class meeting unless this problem has an effect on the class.

3. An agenda will be created prior to every class meeting. The agenda is created by students' writing the topic on the chalkboard. Students must sign their name behind the agenda item. (If the children cannot write, they can tell you the item and you can place it on the board.) The items will be discussed in the order in which they appear on the board. If an agenda item no longer applies when the meeting is held, however, it will be deleted from the list.

4. Discussions during class meetings are always directed toward arriving at a solution that is not a punishment. The goal of class meetings is to find positive solutions to problems and not to criticize people or occurrences in the classroom.

5. If an individual student's behavior is listed on the agenda, the item will not be discussed without the student's permission. If the student agrees to have his or her behavior discussed, you should emphasize that the goal of the meeting is to help the student. Be sure that students' statements focus on the youngster's behavior and are presented as I-messages rather than as judgmental statements about the youngster or his or her behavior. The focus should always be on providing the student with sensitive, thoughtful feedback and positive suggestions for altering behavior.

Students should be informed that several options are available to those who choose not to have their behavior discussed at a class meeting. First, the student may leave the room while the other students attempt to devise an approach for helping the student. You may then wish to tape-record the discussion and share it with the student during an individual conference. Second, the student may choose to discuss the problem with you and a small group of concerned students. With the student's permission, the results of this discussion can be shared with the entire class at the next class meeting. Finally, the student can discuss the problem with you and design a plan for alleviating the problem.

6. Students' responsibilities during class meetings include (a) raising hands and being called on to speak, (b) listening to the speaker and not talking while someone else is speaking, (c) staying on the topic until it has been completed, and (d) being involved by sharing ideas that will help the group.

7. The teacher will initially serve as facilitator for the class meetings.

Meeting Frequency and Length

It is best to hold class meetings whenever the agenda indicates that a meeting is necessary. Students should be assisted in listing only issues that are important to the smooth functioning of the classroom. Nevertheless, it is possible that a class meeting may be held every day. Because unresolved issues will only create problems that will significantly detract from students' learning, time spent in class meetings is usually rewarded with increased on-task behavior and the associated academic gains. A class meeting should be held at least once a week regardless of whether an agenda exists. A weekly meeting is necessary to maintain students' interest and skills as well as to reinforce the concept that the group is a valuable source of ideas and solutions. If no agenda exists, you can involve the class in a discussion of the positive aspects of the week. Similarly, you may wish to instigate a positive sharing activity and praise the class for having a positive, problem-free week.

The length of class meetings will vary according to the students' attention spans. Most primary-grade teachers find that their meetings can last between 10 and 30 minutes, and intermediate-grade teachers find between 30 and 45 minutes optimal. Middle school teachers or specialists in elementary schools who meet with a class 5 hours or fewer a week often choose to hold class meetings on a biweekly basis or to limit weekly meetings to 15 minutes so that meetings will not take up a significant portion of instructional time.

Starting Class Meetings

Begin the first class meeting by reviewing the purpose and general guidelines for class meetings. During the initial meetings, it is very important to monitor students' behavior carefully to ensure that general procedures and responsibilities are followed so that meetings run smoothly and students develop good habits. In order to ensure that initial meetings are viewed as positive and useful, be sure each agenda item is clearly resolved. Do so by asking several students to paraphrase the solution and ask for the group's commitment to carry out any plans that are developed. You may even initially wish to record each decision and post it in a prominent place in the room so that the class is reminded of their decision. A positive feeling can also be enhanced by closing each meeting on a positive note. You can do this by asking each student to state one nice thing that has happened to him or her or that he or she did for someone since the last meeting. Similarly, the group can be asked to say one nice thing about each member of the group.

Reinforce the value of students' solutions by beginning each meeting with a discussion on the results of solutions developed at the previous meeting. Unless students feel that their solutions are useful, they will understandably soon lose interest in class meetings. Furthermore, because class meetings are designed to teach problem-solving skills, it is important to reinforce students' successful efforts, analyze their failures, and help them develop increasingly effective solutions.

Increasing Students' Involvement in Class Meetings

Because a major goal in implementing class meetings is to teach students skills involved in functioning effectively in a problem-solving group, it is desirable to increase gradually their responsibility for facilitating class meetings. This is difficult to do with primary-grade children, but third-grade students can be taught to run their own class meetings. The authors have found that these four steps provide a successful approach to having students take over the class meeting:

1. After leading approximately 10 class meetings, present students with a handout describing the major functions a leader serves when facilitating a group meeting (Figure 10.9). Discuss each function and behavior with the class and inform them that they will soon be asked to lead their own meetings by having students serve these important functions.

2. Introduce an agenda item or classroom problem. While the class discusses this situation, point out and define each intervention you make. Because you continue to serve all three functions, the discussion will be interrupted on numerous occasions. Students are usually excited about learning the new skills, however, and enjoy your instructional interventions.

3. After running three or four actual class meetings in which you consistently point out the function of each intervention, meet with and teach one student the role of discussion leader. At the next meeting, this student serves as the discussion

Discussion Leader
1. Make sure everyone is comfortable and all distracting things are out of the way.
2. Make sure everyone can see all others in the circle.
3. Give the speaker time to get his or her point across.
4. Give the speaker a nod or a smile.
5. Ask clarifying questions:
   a. Are you saying that . . . ?
   b. Do you feel that . . . ?
6. Summarize:
   a. Is there anything else you would like to say?
   b. Would someone briefly summarize what has been said?

Task Observer
1. Make sure the task gets finished on time.
2. Watch the time.
3. Make suggestions of alternatives to solve the problem.
4. Point out behaviors that don't help in solving a problem.
5. Listen carefully and understand what the discussion leader is doing.
6. Understand the agenda and call out each agenda item.

Behavior and Feeling Observer
1. How did this discussion make you feel?
2. What could we do now? What might help us?
3. Was anything asked that caused you _____ (name of person) to be concerned?
   Can you tell us what it was and how you felt about it?
4. _____ (person's name) you usually help us out. Do you have any ideas for this problem?
5. Has anyone thought of new ideas for improving our discussions?
6. How many of you feel that the discussion was of value to you? Why?

FIGURE 10.9
Class-Meeting
Jobs

leader while you maintain the other roles. Prior to the next meeting, you meet with another student who learns the role of task observer. At the following meeting, the student serves this function. After this meeting, you instruct a third student in the role of behavior and feeling observer, and at the following meeting you become a group member who abides by the group responsibilities while the students run the meeting.

4. Each student should function in a role for five or six meetings so that he or she can master the skills associated with the role and effectively model it for other students. If a student has difficulty with a role, take time between meetings to instruct the student in the skills associated with the role. Providing students with this type of experience requires a small amount of time and considerable restraint and patience, but students respond to their new skills by becoming more positive, productive class members. Indeed, behavior-problem children often respond especially well, for they gain self-esteem and peer acceptance when serving as productive participants in class meetings.

Case Study: The Bad, The Good, and The Ugly—A Young Teacher's Attempt to Utilize Glasser's Approach

Chapter 12 presents detailed ideas and examples about schoolwide student management and the support teachers need in order to implement effective classroom management methods. This following example suggests why this is so important and indicates how even an effectively implemented problem-solving sequence can be undermined if the staff has not decided to consistently support such an approach. This example was presented to one of the authors by a young, very skilled intern who was enrolled in a classroom management course, and is intended to provide an example of how problem solving can both work effectively and be undermined by the lack of an effective schoolwide student management plan. The account is presented exactly as written except the names have been changed.

Ironically enough, I had an opportunity to utilize Glasser's problem-solving approach the day after we had our classroom discussions and role-playing concerning this procedure. On Wednesday morning, I was finishing some math preparation at school while most of the students were gone from the classroom. When the students returned from band, I watched them enter and talked with them in order to see how they were doing. Transition times can sometimes be a problem for them, so, whenever possible, I like to try and get a jump on any grievances. Suddenly Jeremy stormed into the classroom, sat down loudly in his chair, stood up again, and approached Rolando very aggressively. Rolando attempted to retreat, but Jeremy kept following him. At this point, I intercepted the two boys and asked them what the problem was. Jeremy, who has a difficult time controlling his anger, pushed me aside and punched Rolando on the shoulder. I was forced to restrain Jeremy, lest he inflict any more punches on Rolando, but I did tell him that he had chosen this action of mine as a result of his actions. I also told him repeatedly that when he had calmed down I could release him and we could talk about what had happened. A few seconds later, Jeremy was somewhat diffused so I took the two boys down to the office. Using Glasser's method, I talked with Jeremy first since he had been the aggressor within the classroom. Our conversation went something like this:

> TEACHER: I'm glad you feel able to talk about what happened and I'm sure we can figure out a plan that will help you. I like having you in class, especially since you have many special interests to share with the class, so I'd like us to try to solve this problem together.
>
> JEREMY: (Nods)
>
> TEACHER: What happened in the classroom? What did you do that is against a school rule?
>
> JEREMY: I hit Sam, but I was mad because . . . [Since Jeremy infrequently has a voice in these matters, I had him tell me the story of what had led up to the classroom confrontation. Jeremy said that he and Rolando had been "playing around," but then Rolando pushed him away and kicked him repeatedly, even after Jeremy told him to stop.]
>
> TEACHER: I'm glad you first told him to stop kicking you. That is a good, nonviolent way to deal with a problem. What happened then?
>
> JEREMY: I was really mad, so I went after Rolando. He tried to get away, but I was really mad, so I hit him.

TEACHER: Yeah, I saw that part. How did hitting Rolando help you solve the problem?

JEREMY: I was mad, so I hit him.

TEACHER: But did that resolve your problem? How did you feel after you hit Rolando?

JEREMY: Not very good. I feel sorry about it. I thought I might have hurt him.

TEACHER: Yeah, I felt that way too. It must feel a little scary to be out of control like that too, huh?

JEREMY: Nods and starts to cry a little.

TEACHER: Do you think that hitting Rolando helped him see your point of view?

JEREMY: No. He probably felt scared.

TEACHER: And hitting is against one of our school rules, isn't it?

JEREMY: Yes.

TEACHER: O.K. Thanks for being honest about all of that and for telling me about what happened. That helps me to see the whole picture. I also like the way you told Rolando to stop kicking you rather than just hitting him right away. We need to think of a plan for what you can do when it doesn't work to just tell someone to stop.

JEREMY: I could run away and calm down. [Jeremy does this already, but he tends to run away from school, dashing out the door and into the neighborhood during the middle of the school day. I think he feels unwanted and finds the school environment so stressful that he needs to escape.]

TEACHER: That's a good strategy, to just walk away from the situation. But that might be a bit hard to do sometimes. Can you think of another idea, in case you find it hard to just walk away?

JEREMY: I could tell someone about it.

TEACHER: That's a good idea! Who do you think you could talk to?

JEREMY: I don't know. No one really. I could talk to you but you're not always here.

TEACHER: Yeah, that's a hard thing isn't it? I would be glad to help because I enjoy working with you. Can you think of two other adults you can work with when I'm not here?

JEREMY: I guess I could talk to either the gym teacher or the science teacher.

TEACHER: That sounds like a good plan. What are the strategies we've talked about so far?

JEREMY: Well, first I tell the person to stop. If that doesn't work, then I can walk away or tell you about it.

TEACHER: And what if I'm not here?

JEREMY: Then I tell the science teacher or the gym teacher.

TEACHER: Do you feel that you can agree to this plan?

JEREMY: Yes.

TEACHER: I'm glad to hear that. Thank you very much for being so honest and for helping so much. You are really being responsible for your behavior. Is there anything you need me to do in order to help?

JEREMY: Talk to Rolando, too.

TEACHER: Yes, I have planned to do that. I'll do that right now, and then I'll bring us all together and we can talk about it, OK?

JEREMY: OK.

At this point, I had a similar discussion with Rolando who provided me with a few more details surrounding the story. Evidently Rolando and another students were having a contest to see who could open their lockers the fastest, and this other student asked Jeremy to hold Rolando. Jeremy obliged, much to Rolando's displeasure, and Rolando told Jeremy to stop. When Jeremy did not, Rolando pushed him away and kicked him a few times. In this case, Rolando's response to the problem warranted a discussion similar to the one I had just completed with Jeremy. Rolando came up with a plan similar to Jeremy's: He would first give a verbal warning, making sure the person heard it (Rolando admitted that it had been loud in the hall, and that Jeremy may not have heard him), and then he would tell a teacher about it.

After this individual conference with Rolando, I brought the two boys together and we talked about what had happened, how they felt about it, and what plans they had developed to prevent future problems. We all agreed that it had been a productive meeting. I told them both that in a few days I would ask them how their plans were proceeding. The two boys shook hands to conclude the meeting.

Throughout this process of problem solving, I had been communicating with the principal in order to make sure I was not overstepping his jurisdiction. He told me to handle the situation as best I could, but when the meeting was over, he wanted to know exactly what I had done. Therefore, after I was finished talking with Jeremy and Rolando, I told the principal how the problem had been solved and how positive I felt about it. At this point, the principal said, "Well, you know they'll have to be punished for their actions." I felt very frustrated by this comment, because it seemed to carry the implicit message: "Well, now that you've done the 'cute' problem-solving stuff, let's get down to the *real* solution." I did not agree with this idea, because I did not feel that a punishment would help them to solve future problems. In talking with the boys, it was obvious to me that both of them needed appropriate strategies and skills for solving their problems, not token punishments. I was not sure how to say this to the principal, however, since his conversational tone left me feeling rather intimidated. He offered a few "acceptable" punishments and left me to choose one for the two boys. I decided to have them stay inside with me during their 15-minute lunch recess. Besides being on the principal's "acceptable" list, this would allow us to spend time talking about a variety of topics that would give the boys an opportunity to learn more about each other. In addition, I would have a chance to see how the two would interact together in a more informal setting.

After lunch, I noticed that something was amiss when the principal called me into his office. He stated that he had heard some "new information" pertaining to the altercation between the boys, and he asked me to restate what had happened. After he heard the story from me again, he called the boys down to his office and basically gave them a rather emotional lecture, using sarcastic language and demeaning statements. The principal then said that both boys would be getting referrals, which meant a parent contact for Rolando and an in-school suspension for Jeremy. The principal also told Jeremy, "Now you'll be just one step away from a week-long suspension. Wasn't it just two weeks ago when I had to suspend you from the bus? When are you going to get the message, Jeremy?"

At this point the principal dismissed Rolando back to class and Jeremy to the office chair. He then told me to fill out the two referral forms. He said, "No need to be real extensive about it, just write down what basically happened." I completed the forms and asked if he at least could record that I had held a problem-solving conference with the two boys, during which they had developed thoughtful individual plans for preventing further problems. He agreed.

As discussed in Chapter 12, this type of situation can be prevented by a staff working collaboratively to develop a schoolwide student management plan.

IMPLEMENTATION ACTIVITIES

As mentioned earlier, one advantage to using a systematic approach to solving problems is that the adults can evaluate their use of the process. Activity 10.1 can help you analyze your effectiveness in employing Glasser's model.

ACTIVITY 10.1
Analyzing a
Glasser
Problem-Solving
Dialogue

Choose a student who is acting inappropriately in the classroom and solve the problem using Glasser's model. Do not choose the most disruptive student, for the model will be learned more effectively if it is initially used to solve less serious problems. At a later time it may be useful to employ this approach with an extremely disruptive youngster and incorporate one or more of the strategies presented in chapter 11 into the plan.

Analyze your problem-solving interaction by answering the questions listed below. This examination will help clarify exactly how the interchange progressed. Although it will be impossible to report the dialogue verbatim, summarize the essence of each stage as specifically and accurately as possible.

Step 1 What activities or approaches have you used to help the student feel that you care about him or her?

Step 2 Record the dialogue that occurred as you attempted to help the student describe his or her behavior. Try to recall accurately the questions you asked and the answers you received.

Step 3 Record the dialogue that occurred as you attempted to help the student make a value judgment.

Step 4 Record the dialogue that took place while you helped the student make a plan, and write the plan that was finally developed.

Step 5 Record the manner in which you asked the student to make a commitment to the plan. Was the student's agreement enthusiastic? Why or why not?

Step 6 How soon after the plan was made did you follow-up? Record the interaction that took place during the followup.

Step 7 Did you use sarcasm or punish the student? If so, explain the circumstances. If the plan was not effective, record the dialogue that occurred when you confronted the student with the problem. Did you start at Step 1? Were you nonpunitive?

If your intervention was successful, write three reasons you think the model worked for you and the student.

If the use of this method was not effective, carefully examine your analysis of each step. Also, ask yourself these questions:

(continued)

ACTIVITY 10.1
Continued

> Do you accept the basic assumptions presented at the beginning of this chapter?
> Were you helping the students solve the problem or were you solving the problem for him?
> Were positive and nonpunitive?
>
> Having analyzed the dialogue and answered these questions, list three reasons the approach did not work for you in this case. Do not list factors involving the student; focus on your own behavior.

ACTIVITY 10.2
Assessing Your
Classroom
Meetings

> If you currently use class meetings, complete these evaluation items. If you do not currently use class meetings, use the general guidelines presented above to implement class meetings in your classroom. Hold at least five class meetings before evaluating the results.
>
> > List two classroom problems that have been positively resolved using this approach.
> > List two ways in which class meetings have helped to improve students' attitudes or behavior in your classroom.
> > Write a brief statement about how your students have responded to or feel about class meetings.
> > Write a brief statement about your reactions to class meetings.
> > List two problems you see associated with class meetings.
> > List two things you could do to improve your class meetings.
> > If you are having difficulty with class meetings, ask a colleague who uses them effectively to observe at least one meeting and give you suggestions.

SUMMARY

The concept of problem solving as a major focus for responding to inappropriate student behavior has existed for more than 30 years. However, experience as well as reviews of the research suggest that it has been systematically implemented into a surprisingly small percentage of teachers' classroom management plans and schoolwide student management systems. This is unfortunate because, when properly applied, problem solving responds to a number of important socioemotional needs of students and helps remediate a wide range of skill deficits experienced by many students who consistently behave unproductively in school.

Fortunately, an increased emphasis on conflict resolution and the continued efforts of leaders like William Glasser have helped create a positive climate for the use of problem solving. This chapter describes several specific methods for incorporating problem solving into a classroom management plan as well as ideas for using this approach to resolve peer conflicts. The authors' experience indicates that teachers who use these approaches are impressed with the positive student attitudes they generate as well as with their students' ability to solve problems and take more responsibility for their behavior.

RECOMMENDED READING

Dreikurs, R., Grunwald, B., & Pepper, F. (1982). *Maintaining sanity in the classroom: Classroom management techniques* (2nd ed.). New York: Harper and Row.

Fagan, S., Long, N., & Stevens, D. (1975). *Teaching children self-control: Preventing emotional and learning problems in the elementary school.* Columbus, OH: Charles Merrill.

Glasser, W. (1965). *Reality therapy.* New York: Harper and Row.

Glasser, W. (1969). *Schools without failure.* New York: Harper and Row.

Glasser, W. (1986). *Control theory in the classroom.* New York: Harper and Row.

Glasser, W. (1990). *The quality school: Managing students without coercion.* New York: Harper and Row.

Gordon, T. (1974). *Teacher effectiveness training.* New York: Wyden.

Haughen, S. (1993). *The ladder of success.* Under review for publication.

Katz, N., & Lawyer, J. (1985). *Communication and conflict resolution skills.* Dubuque, IA: Kendall/Hunt.

Kreidler, W. (1984). *Creative conflict resolution.* Glenview, IL: Scott, Foresman.

Kreidler, W. (1990). *Elementary perspectives #1: Teaching concepts of peace and conflict.* Cambridge, MA: Educators for Social Responsibility.

McGarr, M., Rain, B., & Walker, J. (1993). *RAPP (Resolving All Problems Peacefully).* Ferguson Middle School, Ferguson-Florissant School District, 701 January Avenue, Ferguson, MS 63135.

Maple, F. (1977). *Shared decision making.* Beverly Hills, CA: Sage.

Mendler, A. (1992). *What do I do when . . . ? How to achieve discipline with dignity in the classroom.* Bloomington, IN: National Educational Service.

Schmidt, F., & Friedman, A. (1985). *Creative conflict solving for kids.* Miami, FL: Grace Contino Abrams Peace Education Foundation.

Schrumph, F., Crawford, D., & Usadel, H. (1991). *Peer mediation: Conflict resolution in schools.* Champaign, IL: Research Press.

Vernon, A. (1991). *Thinking, feeling, behaving: An emotional education curriculum for children and adolescents.* Champaign, IL: Research Press.

Wood, M., & Long, N. (1986). *Community board program: Training middle school conflict managers.* San Francisco: CA: The Community Board Program.

Wood, M., & Long, N. (1989). *Second step: A violence prevention curriculum, Grades 1–3 and Grades 3–5.* Seattle, WA: Committee for Children.

Wood, M., & Long, N. (1991). *Life space intervention: Talking with children and youth in crisis.* Austin, Texas: Pro-Ed.

CHAPTER 11

Behavioristic Management Procedures

The classroom teacher is the most powerful influence in any classroom. One reason for this is that the teacher has such direct control of the antecedents and consequences that precede and follow child behavior. . . . Further, the more deviant and disruptive a child's behavior, the more likely it is that reinforcement and punishment will be required to effectively change the child's overall behavior.

—Hill Walker (1979)
The Acting-Out Child: Coping with Classroom Disruption

Students occasionally need highly structured programs to help them change specific behaviors. A few students require our continuing efforts to help them acquire and demonstrate acceptable behavior. We cannot be expected to spend large amounts of time implementing behavior change programs, but to be effective, we must be able to implement behavior management methods that have proven effective in the classroom. When implemented in classroom settings characterized by supportive interpersonal relationships and instruction matched to students' needs, these methods frequently have dramatic effects on students' behavior.

The increased emphasis on inclusion of students experiencing behavior problems and the increasing number of students living in families that are experiencing serious turmoil or adjustment problems have created a situation in which teachers face an increasing number of children who require considerable help in developing appropriate behaviors. Therefore, we, as teachers, need the skills described in this chapter. Teachers should not, however, use these methods unless they have first created a classroom in which all students are accepted by the teacher and their peers, classroom rules and procedures have been carefully taught and consistently monitored, students are involved in interesting work at which they can succeed, and problem solving is taught and consistently used. Employing behavioristic interventions to manipulate students into behaving docilely in an environment that does not meet their personal-psychological and academic needs is unprofessional. Employing behavioristic interventions to help students adjust to a positive learning environment, on the other hand, is an important part of being a competent teacher.

This chapter begins with a brief presentation of the key assumptions associated with behavior modification and a discussion of the advantages and disadvantages of using behavioristic methods. In the remainder of the chapter, specific techniques are offered for collecting and recording data, involving young people in monitoring their own behavior, and writing contracts with pupils.

BEHAVIOR MANAGEMENT IN PERSPECTIVE

Behavioristic interventions have, in many ways, been misunderstood by teachers. On the one hand, some teachers have viewed behavioristic methods as a complex, time-consuming approach that nevertheless held the answer to all their discipline problems. Conversely, many teachers have viewed behaviorism as a manipulative, overly repressive approach to working with students. The answer lies somewhere between these extremes. Behavioristic methods cannot and should not solve all discipline problems. There is no substitute for effective teaching in a caring environment. Behaviorism, though, is also not necessarily a mechanistic, manipulative science. Rather, it can be used to help teachers better understand students' behavior and improve it by applying consistent positive and logical consequences to students' behavior. Furthermore, many behavioristic interventions are relatively simple and can be applied quickly and comfortably in a classroom setting.

Keep in mind that the methods described in this chapter need not and, indeed, should not be used with most students. Most teachers will find that at any given time these methods will be used with only 5 to 20 percent of their students. Moreover, most teachers indicate that these techniques are extremely helpful in assisting students with serious or persistent discipline problems positively alter their behavior. The time spent in developing an effective behavioristic intervention is almost always repaid many times over by reduction in the student's disruptive behavior.

Basic Assumptions Underlying Behavioristic Interventions

Behaviorism is really more a rationale and a methodology than a specific set of procedures. It is based on examining specific data and applying experimentally validated procedures in order to alter behavior. Quite simply, behaviorism is a scientific approach to changing behavior. This approach is based on three major

"Actually, it's a rather old form of behavior modification therapy."

assumptions: (1) behavior is influenced by the consequences following the behavior; (2) behavior change programs must focus on specific, observable behavior; and (3) data collection is necessary in order to alter behavior thoughtfully and systematically.

Behavior Is Influenced by the Consequences Following the Behavior

Behaviorists acknowledge the importance of antecedent conditions (the stimulus), but they emphasize the consequences of a behavior. This emphasis can be seen in three basic rules of behaviorism developed through careful studies of human behavior: (1) a behavior followed immediately by a reward will occur more frequently, (2) a behavior will be extinguished when it is no longer reinforced, and (3) a behavior followed closely by a punishing consequence will occur less often. Although behavioristic interventions emphasize changing behavior by systematically influencing the rewards or punishments that follow a behavior, behaviorists do not ignore antecedent or stimulus conditions. Students cannot be reinforced for producing a behavior unless they possess the ability to emit the behavior. Therefore, we must create positive environments in which students will risk trying new behaviors and must systematically provide children with assistance in gradually developing new skills.

Behavior Change Programs Must Focus on Specific, Observable Behavior

If we wish to help students develop new skills or eliminate undesired behaviors thoughtfully and systematically, we must deal with specific, observable behavior. It is not helpful to either teacher or student to state that the student is disruptive and incorrigible. It is much more helpful if we state that the student will learn more and be better liked by peers if he or she can reduce the number of times he or she interrupts the teacher and other students, and can decrease the number of times he or she hits others. Focusing on observable behavior that can be counted is the first step in developing a program for systematically altering a student's behavior.

Data Collection Is Necessary in Order to Alter Behavior Thoughtfully and Systematically

It is surprising that this basic approach is so often criticized by teachers who state that data collection is too time consuming. Effective teachers base their academic instructional program on pretests that indicate the specific skills their students possess. This step is followed by activities specifically designed to develop new skills. Finally, another test is given or an observation is made to determine how well the skill has been learned and what activities should follow. Collecting data on students' behavior serves a similar purpose. It allows us to determine whether a problem exists, how serious the problem is, and whether the interventions being used are significantly affecting the behavior. When teachers fail to collect some form of data, they often fail to assess a student's behavior accurately. Without data, we cannot objectively determine whether a student's behavior is in reality significantly different from that of his or her peers, or what behavior most needs changing.

Data collection also allows us to evaluate a treatment designed to change a student's behavior. Unless we collect data, it is easy to become frustrated when a new program or intervention does not bring about an immediate change in the behavior. By collecting data, we can notice small but significant changes in a student's behavior. Because behaviors often change slowly, we may misinterpret the effect of our interventions. An excellent example is found in the criticism trap (Becker, Engelmann, & Thomas, 1975): Teachers use criticism or reprimands because these cause an immediate, although usually temporary, change in students' behavior. In the long run, however, the negative behavior often increases because it is reinforced by the teacher's attention. Collecting and analyzing data can prevent teachers from continuing an ineffective behavior change strategy or terminating an approach that is having significant but gradual success.

Advantages of Behavioristic Interventions

There are several advantages to using behavioristic interventions to alter students' behavior. First, some youngsters need special assistance in controlling their behavior. Anyone who has worked extensively in special education or child psychotherapy is aware that a few youngsters do not initially respond to the types of interventions that are effective in helping most children change their behaviors. Although the research suffers from failure to examine the quality of the teacher-student relationship, it does indicate that some children do not respond to adults' praise (Sgan, 1967; Thomas, Becker, & Armstrong, 1968; Walker, Hops, Greenwood, Todd, & Garrett, 1977). Similarly, though the studies have examined the presentation of rules but not students' involvement in the development or monitoring of these rules, research suggests that some students do not change their behavior when presented with rules (Madsen, Becker, & Thomas, 1968; O'Leary, Becker, Evans, & Saudargas, 1969). Therefore, research suggests that there are situations in which it is necessary to provide structured, concrete reinforcement or a systematic monitoring of behavior to help some youngsters change their behavior.

A second advantage of behavioristic interventions is that extensive research clearly demonstrates these interventions can be effective. Research shows that, when systematically applied, reinforcers ranging from simple teacher praise (Hall, Lund, & Jackson, 1968) to a combination of praise, token reinforcers, and response cost (Walker, Hops, & Fiegenbaum, 1976) can effectively alter students' behavior.

Third, although behavioristic intervention does require our time and effort, it frequently requires less time than we anticipate and less time than we currently spend attempting to control the student's behavior. Furthermore, the behavioristic intervention may have a positive effect on other students in the classroom (Drabman & Lahey, 1974; Kazdin, 1973), whereas reprimands often create a negative ripple effect that increases classroom disruption (Kounin, 1970).

Teachers who are especially worried about students' self-concepts and peer relationships often state that behavioristic interventions isolate and alienate children. However, research (Drabman & Lahey, 1974) suggests that, by helping students improve their behaviors, behavioristic treatment programs may improve students' relationships with their peers.

Disadvantages of Behavioristic Interventions

The major disadvantage associated with behavioristic interventions is that, because the focus is on changing students' behavior by systematically manipulating consequences, teachers are less likely to examine their own teaching methods or other classroom factors as possible causes of students' unproductive behavior.

One of the authors recalls a teacher who referred 17 of her students for special assistance because they were emotionally disturbed. Even though students were placed in classes randomly, only 1 student from the classroom across the hall was referred. Observations indicated that the referred children were significantly more active and aggressive toward their peers than their counterparts across the hall. The observations suggested, however, that the frequency and intensity of the teacher's critical statements to students was a major factor influencing the students' behavior. Before teachers attempt to modify students' behavior with behavioristic methods, we should carefully examine how extensively our own teaching strategies and style of interacting with students are negatively affecting their behavior.

A second disadvantage to behavioristic strategies for changing students' behaviors is that, except for self-management and social skills training interventions, behavioristic approaches emphasize external controls. This emphasis is in opposition to children's need for a sense of competence and power and dramatically conflicts with adolescents' desire to be autonomous. The use of external rewards also tends to reinforce lower levels of moral development. Therefore, particularly when working with adolescents, overemphasis on behavioristic methods may detract from the important developmental tasks of understanding others' perspectives and learning to make decisions based on the effect one's behavior has both on oneself and on others (Selman, 1980). Working with youngsters who are experiencing serious behavior problems can be viewed as a reparenting process. These young people have not learned the social skills or acquired the positive feelings about themselves that enable them to function effectively. Like caring, effective parents, adults who work with these students need to provide them with love and self-respect and with skills in controlling their own environment. Although this may need to be supplemented by behavioristic interventions aimed at controlling the students' behavior, these interventions should never become the major treatment program. If emphasis on behavioristic interventions sidetracks us from incorporating a wide range of less restrictive, less control-oriented treatment interventions that help students to accomplish important developmental tasks, behaviorism can have a negative effect on students' ability to become competent and positive individuals.

A final disadvantage associated with behavioristic interventions is that they may place a negative connotation on the very goal they are intended to make more desirable. Several studies have found that when people are offered an extrinsic reward for performing a task they view as interesting, the task soon becomes perceived as less interesting and on-task behavior and task performance decrease (Deci, 1971, 1972; Lepper & Greene, 1975). Consequently, whenever possible, we should use the least externally control-oriented approach to changing a student's behavior. In the long run, this restraint will encourage a greater sense of personal competence and a more internalized commitment to the values inherent in the desired behaviors.

SELF-MANAGEMENT

As discussed throughout this book, the approach that is most beneficial in helping students change their behavior is one that provides the greatest amount of student involvement and helps students develop new skills that can be transferred to other settings. The behavioristic strategies that best fulfill these criteria involve students in monitoring their own behavior. In addition to the problem-solving approaches discussed in Chapter 10, there are two basic approaches to helping students monitor and control behavior. The first method is to help them count and record their own behavior. A second approach is to implement cognitive-behavior therapy.

Self-Monitoring

Students have a basic need to be viewed positively and to demonstrate their competence and power by controlling their own behavior. Often, however, students are not aware of the extent of their unproductive behavior. Some youngsters have difficulty controlling their emotions and behaviors without the assistance of external cues (Patterson, 1971). Involving students in collecting data on their own behavior can, in some instances, provide enough external structure to produce dramatic improvements in their behavior. This procedure not only involves students in their own behavior change program but it also significantly reduces the amount of time spent in collecting data. Furthermore, perhaps because self-monitoring helps create an internalized locus of control, changes in behavior associated with this approach seem more likely to generalize both to other situations and to other behaviors (Johnson, 1970; Johnson & Martin, 1973).

Self-monitoring procedures have proven effective in a variety of settings and with a variety of children (McLaughlin & Gnagey, 1981). McKenzie and Rushall (1974) reported that having youngsters record their behavior on a bulletin board was effective in improving the behaviors of those who were consistently late, absent, or uninvolved in activities at a swim club. Broden, Hall, and Mitts (1971) demonstrated that self-recording attending and nonattending behavior and receiving praise for improvement was an effective intervention with an eighth-grade girl who was failing history. The girl's attending behavior increased from 30 percent to 80 percent under this treatment condition. Hutzell, Platzek, and Logue (1974) reported similar success in reducing head jerking and distracting guttural vocal sounds in an 11-year-old boy.

Procedures

When first instructing students in counting their own behavior, you must ensure that they can accurately describe the behavior. You can teach this skill by asking them to demonstrate the desirable and undesirable behaviors. The next step is to develop a method for tallying the data. Especially when working with young children, it is helpful to start by incorporating a visual display of the behavior being counted. A *countoon* can serve this purpose. A countoon includes a picture of the behavior being tallied and a place for the student to make a tally each time the behavior occurs. Figure 11.1 is an example of a countoon used to help a student

COUNTOON

1	2	3	4	5	6	7	8	9	10
11	12	13	14	15	16	17	18	19	20
21	22	23	24	25	26	27	28	29	30
31	32	33	34	35	36	37	38	39	40
41	42	43	44	45	46	47	48	49	50

Count your hand raising

1	2	3	4	5	6	7	8	9	10
11	12	13	14	15	16	17	18	19	20
21	22	23	24	25	26	27	28	29	30
31	32	33	34	35	36	37	38	39	40
41	42	43	44	45	46	47	48	49	50

Count your talk outs

FIGURE 11.1 Countoon

become aware of how often he talks out without raising his hand. Older students may not be willing to make checks on a chart each time they emit inappropriate behaviors. A talented junior high school counselor uses the form shown in Figure 11.2 to help students take more responsibility for their behavior.

Although most students will accurately monitor their own behavior after these two steps have been accomplished, seriously acting-out students will usually require more assistance. There are two additional steps that you can implement to encourage students to count their own behavior accurately.

Start by reinforcing the student for obtaining data that closely match those you or another adult coder obtain. As they learn to record their behavior accurately, reinforcement for accuracy can be replaced by rewarding decreases in the unproductive behavior. This procedure can be effective in reducing disruptive behavior in seriously acting-out children (Drabman, Spitalnik, & O'Leary, 1973).

Another procedure involves initially having the student receive reinforcement for improving behaviors that are being recorded by an adult. As the student's behavior improves, he or she can be allowed to monitor his or her own behavior and receive designated reinforcements for improved behavior. Finally, the reinforcement is withdrawn and the student simply receives praise for controlling and

Student's name _____

Time	What the Class Is Supposed to Be Doing	What (Student's Name) Is Doing . . . (+ or o)
9:55		
10:00		
10:05		
10:10		
10:15		
10:20		
10:25		
10:30		
10:35		

_____
Teacher's signature

FIGURE 11.2
Student Self-
Monitoring Form

recording his or her behavior. Bolstad and Johnson (1972) demonstrated that this approach could be effectively used with disruptive first- and second-grade children.

Regardless of the methods you use to encourage students to monitor their own behavior accurately, the student must record his or her own data and the results must be placed where the student can refer to them. In a creative study in which junior high school students with emotional disorders were taught to influence their teachers' behaviors positively, Gray, Graubard, and Rosenberg (1974) reported that students' involvement in collecting data was a major factor in the program's effectiveness. Youngsters who have experienced numerous failures are reinforced and motivated by data indicating that they are improving their behavior. Conversely, when these data are lacking, these students frequently become unmotivated and depressed, even though their efforts are producing meaningful results.

Case Study: Elementary

This study was conducted by a first-grade teacher who was confronted with a particularly difficult class in an inner-city school. Most of her students had been late registrants for kindergarten and, because of overcrowding, had spent their kindergarten experience in an isolated room in the district's administrative office building. Consequently, the children arrived in first grade having had few interactions with older schoolchildren. In addition, their kindergarten class had started nearly a month late and they had had several teachers during the year. They were also generally a particularly immature, unskilled group, more than half living in single-parent homes. The following material is taken directly from the teacher's report of her study.

Many distractions within my classroom were caused by students who were not attending to my instructions. My students needed to learn to sit and work without talking, opening and closing their desks, walking to someone else's desk to talk, and so on. I decided to attempt a self-management technique, or a countoon, with my class. This group wanted to please me and be viewed positively by me, but they lacked the inner skills to control their behavior on their own. This technique would let them demonstrate their competence at monitoring and controlling their own behavior. I do not think they were aware of the extent of their off-task behavior. Some children have difficulty controlling their behavior without assistance from an external cue. When children are involved in collecting data on their own behavior, sometimes this act can provide enough external structure to produce dramatic results.

I started my study by collecting baseline data on five children in my group, to determine their off-task frequency. I chose five students who varied greatly in ability, behavior, background, and so forth. I recorded their behavior during seatwork three times at ten-minute intervals, and the results (Figure 11.3) showed that during a ten-minute interval, the frequency of off-task behavior averaged eight per student. I then individually informed the students that I had collected data on them and then I informed the entire group of my results without mentioning the names of the students I had observed. I tried to emphasize to them that I did not think they realized the extent of their off-task behavior. I told them I was going to set up a program whereby they would keep track of their own off-task behavior, with the hope that it would help them to increase their time on task. We then discussed, modeled, and role-played those behaviors which would be considered off-task behaviors. This behavior included talking out loud either to oneself or to a peer; doing any other activity than what I had instructed them to do; getting up from one's desk to wander around the room; or making distracting noises, either by mouth or by opening desks, rolling pencils; and so on. They realized that if they needed assistance from me, they should raise their hand, and because I have a free bathroom-break policy, they could use the bathroom if it was necessary. Students need to be taught how to record their own behavior, and so I spent considerable time in this phase of the project. Also, with students involved in collecting their behavioral data, the time I had to spend on behavior monitoring was lessened. Self-monitoring ideally helps create an internalized source of control, and changes in behavior associated with this approach are expected to be more likely to generalize both to other situations and to other behaviors.

After we had sufficiently practiced and discussed behaviors, I gave each student a countoon. My countoon had a picture of desirable behavior on it, showing an animal deeply involved in doing a worksheet. Originally I had decided to involve only five students in the study, but after a discussion with the class, I decided to give every student a countoon. My results in this study will include only the five students described in the baseline data, but I really felt that it could not hurt to have all the students involved, making them all aware of their talking and behaviors, and keeping track of their off-task times. I then instructed the students when to keep track of their

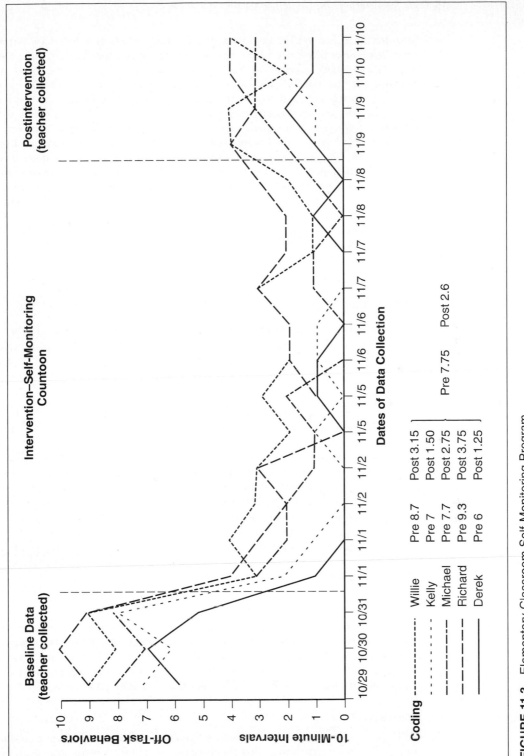

FIGURE 11.3 Elementary Classroom Self-Monitoring Program

351

behavior. Each box on the countoon was for tallying off-task behavior. After each ten-minute interval, we circled the box with a crayon so that the children could keep track of how many intervals we had done. In that way, if a student had no off-task behavior, the box was still circled to show that we had kept track of that interval. I ran the program for six days, monitoring behavior twice each day for ten minutes each. Generally this monitoring was done during math or science, in which we were working on booklets about baby animals. Several of the children almost completely quit off-task behaviors. They were excited about the program and requested that we keep track of behaviors more often. I think they really did feel they had some control over their situation. Because the results were favorable, they also received praise and points for a class party, and the atmosphere in the room improved significantly during use of the countoons. The five students for whom I had collected baseline data went from an average of eight off-task behaviors to less than three per ten-minute interval during data collection. When I did the followup data collection, without their knowledge, they did regress a little, and were a little more talkative, but overall their off-task behavior was cut in half.

Case Study: Junior High

The following study was implemented by a teacher concerned about the behavior of a student in her last-period study hall. She implemented the study with no assistance and as a project for a course in classroom management.

Background

Samuel (not the student's real name) is a retained seventh grader who has been identified as seriously emotionally disturbed. He has been receiving special education services since the first grade and has attended the same school district since kindergarten. He is functioning in the average range on both the verbal and performance scales of the WISC. His academic achievement does not match his potential. The Woodcock-Johnson Psycho-Educational Battery shows an average knowledge score, low average reading, a mild deficiency in math, and a severe deficiency in written language.

Further testing shows that he has a weakness in visual motor tasks and in visual memory. He gains most of his knowledge auditorily as he has good hearing comprehension. Language is adequate for his age. He expresses his thoughts and ideas appropriately and has good conversational skills. He placed below the fifth percentile on the Piers Harris Children Self-Concept Scale.

Classroom Problem

Samuel is in my ninth-period study hall. He has an extremely high percentage of off-task behavior, which includes talking out, drawing pictures on his assignments, distracting other students, and just generally wasting time. I have tried a variety of interventions through the quarter, including changing his seat, having him stay after school, and glaring at him. The problem continued despite these efforts.

Intervention Plan

For three days I collected baseline data on Samuel and three other students in the same study hall. The results showed that the three control students were off task an average of 6.7 percent during the 40-minute period, whereas Samuel was off task 50 percent during the same period.

I showed the graph to Samuel and told him of my concerns with his off-task behavior. We had a good informative talk, part of which was a pep talk to let him know of his cognitive and academic strengths. I told him about the class I was taking and the project I wanted to involve him in. I showed Samuel the countoon (similar to Figure 11.2) I wanted him to use for the next five days. He was to watch the clock (without having it interfere with his work) and put a plus at the end of each five-minute period that he was on task or a zero if he was off task. I would be doing the same thing, and at the end of the period we would discreetly compare our results. No one in the class would know about our project. This was extremely important to Samuel. The self-monitoring recording sheet was to be kept in his folder each day, and he would stay after school to discuss it.

Results

The first day of self-monitoring Samuel was extremely aware of the clock; it really did distract him. We discussed this after class. The next day was better, and he continued to improve the third day. During the fourth and fifth days, he had only one incident each of off-task behavior. Our comparison data were very similar. A lot of verbal feedback went along with the plan, and Samuel responded well to the praise and individual attention.

The next week Samuel knew I was taking data on him but he was no longer self-monitoring. We discussed his behavior every day and looked at the data. The results (Figure 11.4) were very gratifying to us both. Samuel actually maintained an average of 5 percent of off-task behavior the third week. He was getting an incredible amount of homework done and was receiving positive feedback from his other classroom teachers as well.

Afterthoughts

I am really excited about the results of this project. With it I was able to do in three weeks what I thought was impossible. I thought Samuel was my most difficult student and really did not think I would get dramatic results using this approach.

Self-Instruction

Although self-monitoring can provide excellent results by itself, it is often combined with strategies such as self-instruction, self-evaluation, and self-reinforcement (Mace, Brown, & West, 1987; DiGangi & Maag, 1992). Students who consistently act out in a school setting are often characterized by their inability to express or control their emotions productively. Partially because these students have had numerous failure experiences and lack confidence, they frequently respond with intense emotions when confronted by situations their peers handle quite comfortably.

One approach to helping students respond more effectively to frustration and stress is to teach them to give themselves verbal instructions that cue them to behave more appropriately. This approach is based on the concept that students who have attention-deficit hyperactivity disorder (ADHD) or who are labeled *impulsive* are less skilled than normal youngsters in using silent speech to monitor their behavior (Epstein, Hallahan, & Kauffman 1975; Meichenbaum & Cameron, 1974). When faced with a difficult problem, a normal student might say to herself or himself, "Okay, I'll try it once more and if I can't do it I'll ask the teacher for help." Students

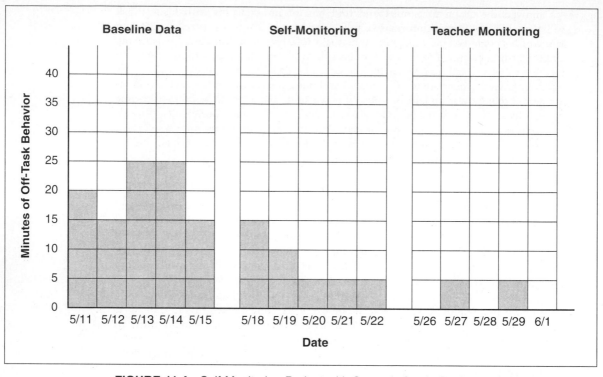

FIGURE 11.4   Self-Monitoring Project with Seventh-Grade Student with Disabilities

with behavior problems may lack the ability to monitor their behavior in this manner and therefore respond actively and unproductively when faced with a frustrating task. These students may also use negative silent speech. A student might say to herself or himself, "I'm stupid and I can't do this." This internalized statement compounds the student's problem and intensifies negative emotions.

According to the principles of rational-emotive therapy, students' behaviors can be changed by helping them make positive, thoughtful internalized statements in place of the negative, unproductive statements they often make. Research indicates that this approach can be successful in reducing students' anxiety (Warren, Deffenbacher, & Brading, 1976), improving academic performance of behavior-problem students (Lovitt & Curtiss, 1968), reducing rule-breaking behavior (Monohan & O'Leary, 1971), and responding less aggressively to oral taunts from peers (Goodwin & Mahoney, 1975).

The basic procedure involves teaching students to use silent statements to control their behavior more effectively. We can do so by providing students with specific statements that they can make when confronted with specific, frustrating situations. Students who become frustrated when attempting to solve math problems can be taught to say, "I can do this if I slow down and relax. What I have to do is first add the two numbers on the right . . . ." Similarly, a student who becomes aggressive when losing a game can be taught to say, "Okay, I didn't win this time, but that's all right. The other students will like me better if I give the ball back and go to the end of the line." We can help students develop these skills by providing them with opportunities to practice self-instruction under our supervision and on tasks they can already perform. While working on fairly simple tasks, students may initially be encouraged to make statements we provide. The students can then be asked to repeat these statements on their own. Next, they can be asked to whisper the words as they complete the task. Finally, they can be encouraged to say the words to themselves.

If you are interested in examining these procedures in more detail, you can find additional practical suggestions in Kranzler's (1974) *You Can Change the Way You Feel: A Rational-Emotive Approach,* and Workman's (1982) *Teaching Behavioral Self-Control to Students.*

A similar approach focuses both on self-talk and developing alternative methods for dealing with problem situations. Students can be asked to role-play situations in which they consistently respond in an inappropriate manner. As the role-playing unfolds, students are encouraged to replace unproductive self-talk with statements that help them control their behavior. Likewise, the teacher and/or other students provide alternative methods of responding. For example, a boy who consistently responds angrily to not being chosen immediately at recess may be asked to replace self-talk such as "Nobody likes me" or "I'm no good" with the statement, "I'll be chosen soon. I guess some students are a little better at this game than I am." The student may also be taught how to send an I-message in a class meeting to express his hurt over not being chosen or given help in learning positive social skills that make it more likely that peers will choose him to be on their team.

A final approach to self-instruction involves teaching students skills in self-relaxation. This can be accomplished by the teacher or counselor initially providing direct instruction in how to relax. Students can learn to relax using the Jacobson (1938) method of relaxing and tensing different muscle groups. More simple and less obvious methods involve teaching youngsters yogalike breathing skills or asking them to let their bodies go limp and imagine a warm, relaxing substance flowing through their body. After students have learned relaxation methods, they can be encouraged to use these methods when they experience feelings of tension or anxiety. We can assist acting-out students by providing them with cues when it is necessary for them to use relaxation procedures. We can reinforce use of these skills by using them with the entire class before or following tension-producing or exciting activities, such as tests, recesses, or assemblies.

Relaxation can also be used in association with cognitive rehearsal (a strategy similar to self-talk). Before an activity that might evoke anxiety or inappropriate student behavior, we can have students close their eyes and go into a relaxed state. We then describe the upcoming situation and the desired student behavior. Before an assembly, we might have the students envision themselves walking quietly to the gymnasium, sitting quietly during the performance, and applauding at appropriate times. When students visually practice behavior in a relaxed state before performing the activity, their behavior can be significantly improved.

SOCIAL SKILLS TRAINING

Any student who has persistent and/or serious behavior problems (including such nonaggressive behaviors such as infrequent contact with peers and infrequent participation in class discussions) is demonstrating a lack of certain social skills. Therefore, a responsible response to serious and persistent unproductive student behavior will almost always include efforts to assist the student in developing behaviors to replace those that have been the cause of concern. In their landmark book on programs serving students with serious behavior disorders, Knitzer, Steinberg, and Fleisch (1990) noted that too many programs focused on behavior control rather than on helping students add new behaviors to their repertoire. These authors argued for a greater emphasis on social skills training and other interventions to provide students with the skills to work effectively in regular classrooms.

Implementing a Social Skills Lesson

The first step is to determine what skills the student(s) need to develop. This is best determined by completing what is often called a functional analysis. Similar to Figure 9.6, a functional analysis examines the actual situation in which the behavior problems are occurring and attempts to determine the specific skills the student(s) failed to demonstrate that led to the problem. For example, a student who becomes angry and hits others when rejected at joining a game may be lacking skill in how to ask to be involved in the game or how to play the game in a way that does not alienate his peers. Similarly, a student who fails to obey reasonable adult requests may lack skills in accepting corrections or directions. As discussed earlier in this chapter, it is imperative to select specific behaviors that can be observed. It is not possible to use social skills training to change a student's "bad attitude." The student may, however, be taught more positive and productive methods for responding to corrections from adults.

The references at the end of the chapter provide numerous excellent sources for further study of social skills training. The remainder of this section provides and discusses a generic lesson outline (Figure 11.5) that can be used with either an individual student or group of students at any age level. As seen in Figure 11.5, the first step, identifying the ineffective behavior, is similar to the second step in problem solving (Figure 10.2). The second step, identifying the reason for changing the behavior, is similar to the third step in problem solving, where the student evaluates the behavior. This step is critical because if the student cannot present and accept a reason for changing the behavior, there is almost no possibility that the behavior change will have any long-lasting effect.

The third step is similar to the problem-solving step of making a plan. The difference is that in social skills training, an effort is made to specify in detail the components of the new behavior. For example, if the student is going to use positive self-talk or relaxation when confronted by a negative peer comment, the specific steps of these behaviors will need to be described.

After the positive alternative behavior has been identified and broken into its component parts, the next step is for the adult to demonstrate or model the behavior. This can often involve the student playing the role of the other person

Describe the inappropriate behavior _____

_____

_____

Rationale for a new behavior _____

_____

Describe the appropriate behavior _____

_____

_____

Skill Components

1. _____
2. _____
3. _____
4. _____
5. _____
6. _____

Model demonstration example _____

_____

_____

_____

Student practice example _____

_____

_____

_____

Natural setting practice (if different than initial practice) _____

_____

_____

_____

Homework assignment _____

_____

_____

Individual or group reinforcement strategy _____

_____

_____

FIGURE 11.5
Social Skills
Lesson Design

involved (a teacher, peer, etc.) while the person assisting the student in developing the new skill will role play the student using the new skill.

The obvious next step is to have the student practice the behavior. This will initially be done in the classroom, office, or wherever the training is taking place. The following step is crucial and is often left out. It is absolutely essential to ensure that the student has an opportunity to practice the new behavior in a setting similar to that in which he or she will have to use it. For example, if the problem occurs on the playground with peers, the new behavior would need to be practiced on the playground with peers.

The next step is to assign the student the task of attempting the new skill and reporting back to the group or individual adult regarding what happened when he or she used the new skills. Often, this will involve the student determining a specific situation in which he or she will attempt to use the new skill. Figure 11.6 provides an example of a homework form that might be given to a student.

The final step involves determining whether the student will earn a reward for using the new skills. The authors once worked with a teacher who taught a developmentally delayed first-grader a series of new behaviors and had the class

FIGURE 11.6
Social Skills
Homework Sheet

Student: __Todd_____   Date: __October 20__

Skill: __Asking for help_____

Steps: 1. Ask myself "Can I do this alone?"

2. Raise my hand.

3. Wait, I know I can wait without talking.

4. Ask in a friendly way.

_____

How did I do?

Why did I circle this? __I did all the steps.__

_____

Source: From *Skillstreaming the Elementary School Child: A Guide for Teaching Prosocial Skills* by E. McGinnis and A. P. Goldstein, 1984, Champaign, IL: Research Press. Copyright 1984 by the authors. Reprinted by permission.

mark on the board each time they saw the student using his "skill of the week." Initially, when 5 incidents of use were reported, the entire class was provided with a brief activity reinforcement. Later, this was changed to require 10 reports of his using the skill before the class earned its reward.

The authors have used the method outlined in Figure 11.5 to work with students ranging from attention-deficit disorder (ADD) first-graders to high school seniors having difficulty with anger management in dealing with teachers. Literally hundreds of teachers have completed action plans in which they used social skills training to change a student's behavior. Findings support extensive research indicating that social skills training is a powerful behavior change strategy that meets the criteria of an effective, ethical response to altering student behavior.

DEVELOPING CONTRACTS

A behavior contract is an agreement between two or more parties that indicates the manner in which one or more of the parties will behave in a given situation. Behavior contracts provide a specific, often written, agreement designating the exact behavior(s) each individual will emit. Furthermore, behavior contracts frequently indicate the specific reinforcement or punishment associated with performing or failing to perform the behaviors listed in the contract. Therefore, behavior contracting is a more structured intervention than either problem solving or self-management. Behavior contracting provides students with a structure that encourages them to perform behaviors they have been unable to display consistently without some form of external, concrete payoff or negative consequences.

> Because the behavior contract . . . is definitive, interaction among the parties is highly predictable, and each person is therefore encouraged to assume his responsibilities. The specificity of the terms makes people face up to "the games they play" and prevents the conscious use of defensive posturing, such as readily invoked excuses. Since the interaction among parties is clearly structured, a sense of security and safety appears to be an important by-product of the stratagem. (Blackham & Silberman, 1975, p. 127)

Negotiating a Contract

Unless a contract is sensitively and concisely negotiated, you may find that it fails regardless of the type of consequence involved. Contracts should ideally result from a teacher-student discussion in which you help the student describe his or her behavior, decide that it needs to be changed, and suggest a plan for making the change. When students are unable to devise a plan or when previous plans have failed to bring about the desired change, you can help them develop a more structured behavior contract.

An effective behavior contract includes a statement about each of these variables:

1. What is the contract's goal? Why has the contract been developed?
2. What specific behaviors must the student perform in order to receive the rewards or incur the punishment?

3. What reinforcers or punishers will be employed?
4. What are the time dimensions?
5. Who will monitor the behavior and how will it be monitored?
6. How often and with whom will the contract be evaluated? (Jones, 1980, p. 230)

Behavior contracts can be presented to students in many forms. Short-term contracts with elementary school children need not include each of these six components. The important factor is that the child clearly understand the contract. Figure 11.7 is an example of a form you can use to present a contract to a primary-grade child, and Figure 11.8 is a form for intermediate-grade or secondary students. Though it is not necessary to develop a written contract, putting an agreement in writing tends to clarify each party's responsibilities. Whenever possible, students should be involved in determining the terms of a contract. Teachers should also help students express their feelings about a contract. Finally, once the contract has been negotiated, the student should be able to paraphrase clearly the conditions outlined in the contract.

Selecting Reinforcement Procedures and Consequences

Once you know when a contract should be used and how to negotiate a contract with a student, the next step involves understanding the various types of consequences (reinforcers and punishers) that can be incorporated into a behavior contract.

Just as the preventive measures discussed in Parts II and III of this book should precede the corrective measures outlined in Part IV, and problem-solving approaches should be implemented before using behavioristic methods, you should begin your contractual interventions with the least restrictive and most natural types of consequences. Figure 11.9 presents a hierarchic approach to consequences used in behavior contracts. You should start by trying to use contractual agreements based on the types of reinforcers and controls at the bottom of the hierarchy. Only if these fail should you develop a contract based on higher-level reinforcers.

Examining Figure 11.9, notice that teachers should initially use reinforcers that are a normal part of the school day and are available to all students. Although token reinforcers may appear to be less natural than curtailment of activity, we constantly provide token reinforcers in the form of grades, points earned on tests, or promises to provide a reward if students behave appropriately for a designated period. Furthermore, we should, whenever possible, focus on positive behavior. Punishment in the form of curtailments of activity should be used only after natural reinforcers have proven ineffective in helping a student change a behavior. Curtailment of activity is listed as more desirable than implementing a response cost (the procedure of taking away points or other rewards when a student misbehaves) primarily because response cost is a complex intervention and should not be used unless simpler interventions fail. Curtailment of activity is placed lower on the hierarchy than are tangible reinforcers because restricting a student's behavior by requiring that he or she stay in from recess in order to complete required work is a more logical intervention than is providing the student with candy for completing a task. Furthermore, the use of tangible reinforcements suggests that the desired

I'm Leaping in to Say

If:

I can play four square

without getting in a

fight at recess

Then:

I can play with

the gerbil for

10 minutes

_____   _____   _____

Date   My Name   Teacher's Name

_____

My Friend's Name Who Will Help Me

FIGURE 11.7   Primary-Grade Contract

I've got the POWER!

Matt
_____
IS GREAT!
NOT LATE!

I WILL be on time to P.E. class, 11:00 a.m. sharp FOR 5 consecutive days . Allan
HAS OFFERED TO HELP BY walking to class with Matt . MY TEACHER WILL HELP
BY telling me how well I did each day I am on time .
TO CELEBRATE I WILL BE ABLE TO be a student helper in P.E. and referee/umpire
activities for 2 days .

_____   _____
DATE   GREAT PERSON

                               _____
                               HELPER

                               _____
                               TEACHER

FIGURE 11.8
Upper
Elementary or
Middle School
Contract

behavior is not valuable enough to warrant being displayed without a tangible payoff. This statement has subtle but potentially powerful negative consequences for long-term improvement in the student's behavior.

In the remainder of this chapter, procedures for implementing the first four types of consequences listed in Figure 11.9 are presented. Because few teachers use response-cost or tangible reinforcers, these consequences are not discussed. If you are interested in these, refer to Hill Walker's (1979) book, *The Acting-Out Child.*

Social Reinforcement

Social reinforcement refers to behaviors of other people that tend to increase the frequency with which a student emits a behavior. If a smile from you is followed by a student's continuing to work on an assignment, the smile has served as a social reinforcer. Similarly, if a child consistently returns to a group after having been chased away, the attention inherent in being chased may be viewed as a social reinforcer. Social reinforcement can be used either as a spontaneous teaching strategy for influencing students' behavior or as a consequence in a contract.

FIGURE 11.9
Behavior-
Contract
Hierarchy

Tangible reinforcement
Social, token, and activity reinforcement and response cost
Curtailment of activity
Social, token, and activity reinforcement
Activity reinforcement
Social reinforcement

When systematically using social reinforcement as a method for improving students' behavior, you should develop skill in employing a wide range of reinforcers, learn how to give reinforcement, and learn when to use it. Among the many types of social reinforcement, the most obvious involves saying positive things to students. When giving social reinforcement, be careful not to use the same word or phrase constantly. Students appreciate different, creative expressions of encouragement and appreciation. Figure 11.10 lists social reinforcers that can be used at a variety of grade levels.

Words are not the only type of social reinforcement. Many types of nonverbal social reinforcers may be used. You can share your positive feelings about students'

FIGURE 11.10
Social
Reinforcers

Praising Words and Phrases

Good	That's interesting
That's right	That's really nice
Excellent	Wow
That's clever	Keep up the good work
Good job	Terrific
Good thinking	Beautiful
That shows a great deal of work	I appreciate your help
You really pay attention	Now you've got the hang of it
You should show this to your father	Now you've figured it out
Show Grandma your picture	Very interesting
That was very kind of you	That's an interesting point
Thank you; I'm pleased with that	Nice going
Great	You make it look easy
I like that	What neat work
Exactly	I like the way you got started on your homework

Expressions	*Nearness*	*Physical Contact*
Smiling	Walking together	Touching
Winking	Sitting together	Hugging
Nodding up and down	Eating lunch together	Sitting in lap
Looking interested	Playing games with student	Shaking hand
Laughing	Working after school together	Holding hand

behavior by smiling, laughing, winking, or looking interested in what a youngster is doing. You can also reinforce students by spending time with them. Many students who have behavior problems receive little attention and affection from adults and are starved for positive attention. You can reinforce these children by walking with them, eating lunch together, joining them in playground games, or asking them to stay after school and help you with a classroom task. Physical touch is another important and effective nonverbal social reinforcer. Research (Kazdin & Klock, 1973) has demonstrated that nonverbal reinforcement in the form of smiles and touch can positively influence students' on-task behavior.

When using social reinforcement, be especially careful to reinforce specific behaviors. Teachers often use words such as *great, good, nice,* and *super* when referring to students' work or behavior. Unfortunately, this form of reinforcement does not provide the student with specific information on which aspect of behavior is being reinforced. Therefore, it is important to describe the behavior being praised. Rather than saying, "That's nice, Bill," when Bill listens attentively, you might say, "Bill, I appreciate the way you are listening to the discussion. It should help you do well on the assignment."

Although teachers must develop an extensive repertoire of social reinforcers and learn to praise specific behavior, it is perhaps even more important to learn when to reinforce students. The reason social reinforcement is frequently ineffective in changing students' behavior is that it is so often ineffectively used by teachers. Several studies have demonstrated that teachers often dispense social reinforcement at the wrong time. Walker and colleagues (1976) observed the interactions between five acting-out children and their teachers. The results showed that though the five teachers praised the acting-out child's appropriate behavior about once every hour, they attended to inappropriate behavior nine times each hour. Similarly, Walker and Buckley (1973) observed an elementary classroom teacher and found that although 82 percent of the teacher's interactions with normal children followed appropriate behavior, 89 percent of the responses to acting-out children followed inappropriate behavior. Taken together, these and other studies suggest that we should attempt to increase our use of positive social reinforcement and make this reinforcement contingent on acceptable student behavior. When an acting-out child demonstrates a positive behavior, we should try to reinforce this behavior immediately.

Social reinforcement is usually viewed as a spontaneous approach to changing students' behavior, but it can also be incorporated into behavior contracts. Because social reinforcement is inexpensive, readily available, and easy to give, we should attempt to incorporate this type of reinforcement into our initial contracts with a student. There are several approaches to take when using social reinforcement in this manner. A contract can be developed in which a student receives social reinforcement from peers or us as a consequence for making a desirable behavior change. We can also involve parents in providing social reinforcement when their child behaves appropriately at school. A contract might indicate that if a student reaches a specified behavioral or academic goal, we will send a note home to the parent and the parents will respond by providing the student with a designated number of specific positive statements.

Activity Reinforcement

Because social reinforcement is not a powerful enough reinforcer to bring about prompt or significant change for all students, we need to use other forms of reinforcers. Involvement in various preferred activities is another natural and easily dispensable reward for desirable behavior.

PROCEDURES. The first step is to list activities that students find reinforcing. Students enjoy being involved in this process and often offer creative and surprising ideas. Figure 11.11 lists classroom-activity reinforcers. The second step is to de-

FIGURE 11.11
Activity Reinforcers

Being group leader
Going first
Running errands
Collecting materials
Helping clean up
Getting to sit where he or she wants to
Taking care of class pets
Leading the flag salute
Telling a joke to the class
Being in a skit
Having a party
Making puppets and a puppet show
Doing artwork related to studies
Spending special time with the teacher
Choosing the game for recess
Getting to make puzzles
Earning an extra or longer recess
Choosing songs to sing
Working puzzle
Drawing, painting, coloring, working with clay, and so on
Choosing group activity
Taking a "good" note home to parent (arrange a reward with the parent)
Extending class recess by specified number of minutes
Visiting another class
Helping teacher
Taking 10-minute break to choose game and play with a friend, QUIETLY
Building with construction materials
Getting time to read aloud
Playing short game: tic-tac-toe, easypuzzles, connect the dots

Performing for parents
Taking a class pet home for the weekend
Leading the songs
Being team captain
Reading to the principal
Seeing a filmstrip
Getting to read a new book
Seeing a movie
Listening to music
Playing games in class
Writing on chalkboard: white or colored chalk
Playing with magnet or other science equipment
Solving codes and other puzzles
Listening to a song
Performing before a group: sing a song; tell a poem or riddle; do a dance, stunt, or trick
Being hugged, tickled, kissed, patted
Choosing a book to review for class
Selecting topic for group to discuss
Reading to a friend
Reading with a friend
Receiving the right to tutor a slower classmate
Getting free time in the library
Being asked what he or she would like to do
Listening to record or radio with earphones
Planing a class trip or project
Working in school office
Working in school library

velop a contract stipulating what the child must do to obtain the activity reinforcer. Figure 11.7 is an example of a simple contract. Whenever activity reinforcers are used, they should be paired with social reinforcement so that the social reinforcement may gradually acquire some of the reinforcing properties associated with the activity reinforcer.

The problem of delayed gratification (the student becomes frustrated because he or she must wait for the reinforcement) that is frequently associated with activity reinforcers can be dealt with by gradually extending the time a student must wait in order to receive the award. When first implementing a contract, the student can be informed that he or she can be involved in the activity immediately after performing the desired behavior. As the student's behavior improves, he or she can be informed that he or she will have to demonstrate increasingly appropriate behavior as well as wait longer before the reinforcement is provided.

An interesting approach to using activity reinforcers involves allowing students to take home school equipment they find particularly interesting. A student's contract might indicate that he or she can take a tape recorder home for two days if he or she meets the conditions of the contract. Although this type of reinforcement may at first glance appear to be a tangible reinforcer, the student uses the borrowed item but neither consumes nor acquires permanent possession of the reinforcer. The reinforcer provides the student with an opportunity to reinforce himself or herself by participation in an activity involving school property. In essence the student is involved in the reinforcing event at home rather than at school.

Social, Token, and Activity Reinforcement
Token reinforcement refers to a system in which students receive immediate reinforcement in the form of a check, chip, or other tangible item that can be traded in for reinforcement at a future time.

PROCEDURES. There are seven basic steps to implementing a token reinforcement system in the classroom. Before introducing a token system, you should determine specifically how each step will be accomplished.

   1. Determine when and with whom the program should be implemented. You might choose to employ a token system with two acting-out children whose behavior during seatwork continues to be extremely disruptive despite your attempts at instigating other types of interventions.

   2. Select the specific behaviors to be reinforced. When working with an individual student, you might state that the student will receive a token for every two minutes he or she is in his or her seat, not talking to peers, and working on the assignment. When working with several students or the entire class, it is desirable to generate a list of behaviors (the classroom rules may be suitable) that will be reinforced. It is desirable to involve students in determining the behaviors and to post the behaviors in a prominent place.

   3. Decide when tokens will be dispensed. When working with a seriously acting-out student, you will usually have to dispense the tokens whenever the desired behavior occurs. As the student begins to gain control of his or her behavior, you and the student can tally the occurrence of the desired behaviors (the tallies serve as tokens), and this total can be recorded or actual tokens can be given to the student at the end of a designated time. When employing a token system with an entire class, it is best to distribute tokens randomly. Thus, as you move around the room or work with a group, you present tokens to students who are behaving appropriately. Though you must be careful not to overlook students or unfairly focus on some students, a random reinforcement schedule is easy to administer and maintains acceptable behavior at a high rate.

4. Determine how to dispense tokens. There are numerous methods for dispensing tokens. Each student involved in the program can have a card taped on the corner of his or her desk and you can make a mark on the card each time the student displays the desired behavior. When working with small children, teachers occasionally choose to place a jar or box on each participant's desk so that tokens can be dropped into the container when the student behaves appropriately. When working with students who change classes or teachers during the day, a travel card (Figure 11.12) can be used. The desired behaviors are written on the card, and at the end of each period the student receives a check for each desired behavior displayed throughout the period.

FIGURE 11.12
Travel Card

| Student _____ Grade _____ Date _____ |

Desired Behaviors

Period	On Time to Class	Brought Necessary Materials	Handed in Assignment	Obeyed Class Rules	Participated in Class	Teacher's Signature
1						
2						
3						
4						
5						
6						
7						

5. Select a procedure for recording tokens earned. Because most token systems involve earning tokens over a specified period, it is necessary to devise a system for recording the number of tokens each child has accumulated. Likewise, because children can trade tokens in for preferred activities, a record of tokens spent and remaining must be kept.

Curtailment of Activity

Activity curtailment refers to any situation in which inappropriate student behavior is followed by removal of a desired activity. This method of altering students' behavior has been used since time began, but it has received considerable attention with formal time-out procedures.

PROCEDURES

1. Students should understand the behaviors that will lead to curtailment of activity, what activities will be curtailed, and how long the restriction will be in effect. Punishment should never be presented arbitrarily.

2. Rules on curtailment of activity should be used consistently and fairly. If fighting on the playground is followed by sitting out the next recess, this restriction should be applied to all students in every instance. You should also consider, however, whether playground facilities and activities support positive play, whether rules are clearly understood, and whether students have been taught methods for resolving inevitable playground conflicts.

3. Be aware of cases in which curtailment of activity provides a more desirable alternative than the activity itself. Students may behave inappropriately in order to receive what appears to you to be a punishment but the student views as a relatively positive consequence. A student may dawdle at work in order to stay in from recess, either because recess is perceived as undesirable or the time in the room is viewed as pleasant. Continuing to use a curtailment of activity in this situation might prevent the child from dealing with important social skill deficits that are causing problems on the playground. Therefore, the punishment would be detrimental rather than helpful.

4. Present the negative consequences in a nonpunitive, interested manner. Communicate sincere regret that a punishment is necessary. This attitude helps students accept responsibility for their behavior rather than project the blame onto you. Punishment should never be presented in anger, which only encourages the student to feel persecuted and to transfer the blame to you.

5. When presenting a curtailment of activity to a student, always inform the student which specific behavior(s) were responsible for bringing about the undesirable consequence. The student should also be reminded of the desirable behaviors that could prevent the consequences.

6. When presenting a punishment, inform the student what must be done to terminate the punishment. You might inform a student that he or she can return to the class activity after quietly completing a problem-solving form.

7. Whenever possible, a curtailment of activity should logically relate to the behavior that necessitated the punishment. If a child could not play on the play-

ground without fighting, it is logical that he or she should miss recess until he or she can develop a plan for interacting more appropriately with peers. It is not logical, though, to have children stay after school and write sentences because they fought on the playground.

8. Activity curtailment should, whenever possible, be consolidated with activities aimed at helping the student develop new skills that will prevent repeated performance of the undesirable behavior. Therefore, when being excluded from a desired activity, the student should be involved in examining the problem and developing a plan for solving it.

9. Collect data to help determine whether the curtailment of activity is effective in reducing the undesirable behavior or increasing the desired behavior. Because punishment in any form may have numerous negative side effects, it should be discontinued if data indicate that it is ineffective.

10. Punishment methods of changing students' behavior should be phased out as soon as possible and replaced by more positive approaches, such as problem solving, self-management, or social or activity reinforcement.

Group Contracts

A group contract involves a situation in which the entire group earns a reward or loses previously awarded points or privileges contingent on the entire group's behaving in a desired manner. Some writers define group contracts as including programs in which an individual student's behavior is reinforced by a desired activity for the entire group, but this technique is more accurately labeled an activity reinforcer.

PROCEDURES. In an attempt to reduce talking-out and out-of-seat behavior in a fourth-grade class, Barrish, Saunders, and Wolf (1969) developed a group contract called the Good Behavior Game. The class was divided into two teams, and students were informed that it was possible for either or both teams to win or lose. The winning team(s) received a 30-minute free period at the end of the schoolday as well as an opportunity to wear victory tags and be first in line for lunch. The game was played by having the teacher make a mark on the board each time a team member talked out or was out of seat without permission. The team with the fewest points was designated the winner. Both teams could win, however, if neither team had more than five marks. Results of this activity showed marked decreases in the undesirable behavior.

Schmidt and Ulrich (1969) reported successful implementation of a similar program in which a class was reinforced with free time when they maintained an acceptable noise level and remained in their seats. In their program, though, the class could also lose free time for violating these rules.

A more formal procedure for reinforcing on-task behavior involves providing a group reinforcement contingent on the entire group's being on task for a designated percentage of the class period. A method for implementing such a procedure has been developed and extensively researched by Greenwood, Hops, Delquadri, and Walker (1974). This systematic program, entitled PASS (Program for Academic Survival Skills), is aimed at helping students learn and demonstrate specific skills that are necessary for academic success.

In its simplest form, PASS involves these components: (1) a list of class rules (survival skills); (2) daily charting of the percentage of time these rules are followed by all class members; (3) a group reward for improvement; and (4) gradual removal of the major program components, such as the visible timing device, rules, and data display.

PASS was initially designed for use with elementary-school children, but it has also been successfully employed with young adolescents (Jones, 1980). The program involves the class in developing class rules stated in terms of specific, observable behaviors. The class is then informed that they will receive a group-activity reinforcement if they can improve the percentage of time during which all members of the class are obeying all the rules. The students receive feedback about their on-task behavior by means of a clock operated by the teacher. The clock shows a green light whenever the entire class is on task and the clock is recording, and a red light indicates that the clock has stopped because at least one student is violating one of the rules. As the class begins to follow the rules consistently more than 80 percent of the time, the frequency of reinforcement is systematically reduced and the clock light is replaced by a stopwatch. Eventually, the reinforcement becomes entirely verbal except for periodic maintenance checks and occasional activity reinforcers associated with a particularly positive check.

Group competition and group rewards have also proved effective in reducing disruptive behavior in a school cafeteria (Sherman, 1973). In this program, rules were established, and each day the class that was judged as following the rules most effectively received praise and had a star placed on a chart posted in the cafeteria. Further reinforcement was provided in the form of a special prize offered each month for the class with the most stars. Teachers on lunchroom duty were asked to ignore inappropriate behavior and praise students who followed the rules. Implementation of this program was followed by immediate reduction in disruptive behavior.

One problem that occasionally arises when implementing a group contract is that one or several students subvert the group's chance for success. When they do so, the teacher might initially implement a Glasser problem-solving discussion in order to help the student acknowledge the situation, decide whether to make a change, and develop a plan. If the student either indicates unwillingness to change or is simply unable to control his or her behavior adequately in response to a group contract, the student can be placed on an individual contract and the class can be informed that his or her behavior will not influence the class's chances of earning a reward. Although this intervention may be necessary, it tends to isolate the student. Therefore, the teacher should periodically discuss the situation with the student with the goal of including the student in the group contract.

A final approach to devising a group contract is to develop the contract during a class meeting. An excellent example of this method occurred when a graduate student of one of the author's expressed concern because students in her eighth-grade math class were averaging nearly 10 minutes before they were all seated and ready to begin the day's lesson. The teacher's initial idea was to present the students with an offer to take the entire class out for an ice cream cone on Friday if they could be ready to start class within 2 minutes after the bell rang for five consecutive days. The authors suggested, however, that students would be more likely to accomplish the goal and might need less reinforcement if they solved the problem themselves. The teacher accepted this logic and decided to present the problem to the class along with a large chart indicating the number of minutes it had taken them to settle down during the past ten days.

Because the teacher was well liked by her students and had demonstrated her competence by coming prepared with a data display, the students acknowledged that a problem existed and decided to solve it. The initial solution offered by a student and enthusiastically supported by the class was simply for everyone to be prepared every day when the bell rang. Fortunately, the teacher realized that this was an overly ambitious goal and informed the class that she would be delighted if the class could be prepared to start 2 minutes after the bell rang. The class then decided to clearly define the term *ready to start* and determined that it meant the entire class (1) being in their seats, (2) having a paper and pencil on their desk, (3) being quiet, and (4) looking at the front of the room. Finally, the class decided to borrow a stopwatch from the physical education department and to allow each member of the class to time the class for one day and mark the results on the large chart the teacher had prepared.

Not surprisingly, the student involvement served as its own reinforcement, and no one suggested any form of extrinsic reward. Results indicated that during the 5 weeks the class marked the chart, they never required more than 1 minute 45 seconds to become prepared for class. Furthermore, follow-up data collected 2 weeks after students had ceased to mark the chart indicated that this behavior had been maintained.

The effectiveness of this group contract was based on the fact that the solution responded sensitively to students' needs for competence and power while using a problem-solving approach that incorporated the basic components of a sound behavioristic intervention. When teachers are able to integrate these approaches, they will consistently find themselves able to work with their students to develop productive solutions to classroom problems.

CASE STUDY: A CONTRACT WITH A HIGH SCHOOL BAND CLASS. An excellent example of a group contract was recently presented by a high school band teacher who used a contract to reduce talking during class. In this incident, the students decided that a consequence and reward would help them change their behavior. They agreed to give up 1 minute of the break following band class for every minute they were off task. They also decided that if they could meet the goal of 30 minutes off task in 8 days they would have a buffet luncheon as a reward. Figure 11.13 presents the data associated with this intervention. The data indicate that off-task behavior reduced from 17.2 minutes per class period to 2.88 minutes per period. This teacher also found that when students are presented with the data and asked to be involved in determining the solution, dramatic results can often be obtained.

A Contract for Teaching Student Responsibility

One problem with contracts is that they too often focus on controlling student behavior rather than on helping students develop responsibility. As mentioned earlier, this problem can be minimized by using contracts as step 5 (developing a

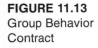

FIGURE 11.13
Group Behavior
Contract

plan) in Glasser's reality therapy approach. In addition, as presented in the section on group contracts, involving students in developing the contract and monitoring the results can also increase the likelihood that students will develop a sense of responsibility while being involved in a contract. Another method for using a contract to control student behavior while simultaneously focusing on student responsibility and an internal locus of control is to develop a contract that uses language related to responsibility.

The appendix at the end of this chapter provides a shortened example (the actual contract involved three behaviors) of a curriculum of responsibility contract. It is so named because it provides an extremely clear and specific statement regarding everyone's responsibility in assisting a student in improving several critical aspects of his school behavior. This contract is almost always used in the event that the personalized education plan (described in the next section) is ineffective.

Although excellent success has been achieved with curriculum of responsibility contracts, the authors have also found that, especially for high school students, a less time-consuming and highly effective approach for a student failing a class is to develop success or failure contracts. Figure 11.14 presents a success contract that has been used to help students determine what they will need in order to succeed in a particular class. Figure 11.15 describes a failure contract that the authors have occasionally used after all other methods have failed and the student refuses either to sign a success contract or to respond in a responsible manner to the contract. These contracts help students, parents, and teachers clarify the expectations and responsibilities of the teacher and student, as well as the support that will be provided to the student. Experience shows that this has the dual effect of encour-

FIGURE 11.14
Success Contract

I _____ have decided that I want to pass
_____ . My current grade in the class is _____ .

I understand that in order to pass this class, I need to:

1. Complete every homework assignment on time for April, May, and June.
2. Achieve a score of 80% or better on each chapter test.
3. Be a respectful contributing member of my group.
4. _____
5. _____

To help me achieve these standards to pass the class, Mr. T has agreed to provide opportunities for:

1. Retaking the chapter tests until I achieve a score of at least 80%.
2. Extra tutoring outside of regular class time.
3. Extra credit projects if all homework is completed on time.
4. _____
5. _____
6. _____

What I will need to do in addition to take advantage of these opportunities:

1. Complete my homework assignments on time.
2. Attend the Monday night Math Lab for extra assistance.
3. Ask my classmates for assistance if there is a concept I am having difficulty with and Mr. T is not available.
4. Let Mr. T know if I am having difficulties meeting the terms of this contract.
5. _____
6. _____

I will know I have succeeded when _____
_____
_____
_____

Mr. T and I will examine my progress and share it with my parents and
_____ on _____ .
       Support Person   Date

Signed

_____ _____ _____
Student   Parent   Counselor

_____ _____
Teacher   Date

I _____ am choosing to fail _____ , despite the fact that Mr. T is willing to:

1. Allow me to retake each chapter test until I achieve a score of 80% or better.
2. Provide extra tutoring outside of regular class time.
3. Allow for extra credit projects to raise by grade if all of my homework is completed on time.
4. _____ .

I am not going to complete my work, study for tests, participate in group work, or take advantage or the opportunities Mr. T and the school staff provide for me to catch up on my work and be successful on future work.

I understand that the consequences of my choosing to fail this class are:

_____
_____
_____
_____ .

Signed

_____   _____   _____
Student   Parent   Counselor

_____   _____   _____
Teacher   Principal   Date

FIGURE 11.15
Failure Contract

aging teachers to make specific changes to support the student's unique learning needs and helping the student take responsibility for his or her behavior. This has proved to be a powerful combination.

Although some teachers use a curriculum of responsibility contract, it is most often used in conjunction with a counselor or special education teacher or consultant. The next section presents a model for helping a group of educators develop a specific plan to assist a student who has failed to respond to a teacher's best efforts to implement a variety of proactive and corrective behavior change interventions.

DEVELOPING A PERSONALIZED EDUCATION PLAN

Even though current technology provides teachers with a variety of proactive and corrective methods they can implement to help students develop productive behaviors, there are obviously times when teachers need assistance. Chapter 12 provides a sequential systems approach for determining when to involve various individuals in working with students who have behavior problems. This section presents a model to develop a specific behavior change plan for students who continue to act irresponsibly despite teachers' efforts to implement many of the methods described in this book.

Like most experienced teachers, the authors have attended hundreds of staffings. The problem with many of these is that they sound more like soap operas than well-organized attempts to develop specific plans to assist a student. Not only do family factors influence student behavior but school factors also have a significant impact, and educators need to place a primary emphasis on school factors. If home factors appear to be a major issue in a particular case, this should be noted and a person can be assigned to contact the school or community agent responsible for coordinating services for families. The staffing can then return to a focus on school variables that can be altered to help the student.

To emphasize the focus on developing a specific plan for the student, the authors prefer to call staffings Personalized Education Plan (PEP) meetings. The development of such plans can be expedited by using a structured approach to staffings. An effective process includes these five steps:

1. Focus on specific student behaviors that need to be changed.
2. Determine specific interventions to bring about these changes.
3. Assign responsibility to staff for implementing each intervention.
4. Determine the data to be collected for the purpose of assessing the effectiveness of interventions.
5. Set a date to review the program.

It is suggested that you focus on no more than two behaviors and develop no more than three interventions for each behavior.

Figure 11.16 presents the form the authors used to develop a PEP. The numbers in brackets near the top of the form indicate the numbers of minutes allocated to that task. The bottom of the sheet lists those individuals who have agreed to be involved in implementing one or more of the interventions, and the mentor is the person who agrees to monitor both the implementation of and the progress achieved in using the plan. Figure 11.17 presents a PEP one of the authors helped a staff develop for a fourth-grade boy.

The authors are often asked to discuss the relationship between a Teacher Assistance Team and personalized education plans. Figure 11.18 shows the sequential relationship of various groups that work to assist students with serious behavior problems. As the figure indicates, once teachers have implemented effective classroom management methods and considered environmental factors that may be influencing a student's behavior, they are advised to seek assistance. Teacher Assistance Teams (Chalfant, Van Dusgen, Pysh, & Moultree, 1979; Gilmer, 1985, Hayek, 1987) are comprised of several teachers who meet to provide suggestions for their peers on working with students who are failing to follow school rules or making satisfactory academic progress. A form used at a TAT team meeting is found in Figure 11.19.

Although strong supporters of the idea of TATs, the authors have also found that most staff attend numerous meetings and also become frustrated when a

(3) Is Community Interaction Needed?	(7) Behavior to Change	(12) Intervention Plan	(5) Person Responsible	(3) Evaluation Data
	1.	1a. 1b.		
	2.	2a. 2b.		
Roles: Presenter Recorder Facilitator Timer				

Signed

_____	_____	_____
Teacher	Teacher	Teacher (Monitor)
_____	_____	_____
Teacher	Counselor	Principal

_____
Dated

PEP Monitor agrees to check within seven days to determine how the program is working

FIGURE 11.16
Developing a
Personalized
Education Plan
(PEP)

student is not referred for outside assistance or evaluation after they have met with a team to develop strategies to assist the student. Since the Teacher Assistance Team is usually designed to provide teachers with ideas but is not designed to develop a comprehensive plan involving other school personnel, these meetings, although valuable, often fail to provide interventions that alter a student's behavior. Ideally, this would lead to the student being referred to a Personalized Education Plan team. Realistically, school staff do not have time or energy for yet another staffing. Therefore, if only one meeting or series of meetings will be held, it is recommended that it be a PEP team that includes a building administrator, three or more teachers, and a specialist. As just mentioned, this team is responsible for coordinating the staff resources to develop a plan to involve several adults in assisting the student in improving his or her learning and/or behavior. Experience indicates that teachers find this type of planning meeting supportive and instructive and that a Personalized Education Plan team can in many ways eliminate the need for a Teacher Assistance Team.

FIGURE 11.17   PEP for Jason

Behavior to Change	Intervention	Person Responsible	Data
Failure to follow reasonable adult requests	1. Role-playing methods for following requests. Do this both with the teacher and with the class. This would include teaching Jason how to remove himself to his seat for quiet work when he cannot handle the large group work. 2. Provide Jason with frequent prompts and reinforcements for using his new skills.	CDS or Principal	Tallies of this behavior
	3. Teach students to ignore him when he is inappropriate.	Classroom teacher	
	4. Countoon with Jason showing improvement to the principal or other valued adult.	CDS or teacher	
	5. Consistent time-outs when Jason reaches the maximum allowable number of times he fails to follow a request.	Teacher	
Improved peer relationships	1. Class meeting to help students learn how to ignore and reinforce Jason.	Teacher	
	2. Have a peer be his assistant who helps him when he has not heard directions and so on.	Teacher	
	3. Perhaps Jason could tutor in a kindergarten or first-grade classroom so he could be a model rather than needing to obtain attention being inappropriate.	K or first-grade teacher and classroom teacher	
	4. Work with Jason and several students from the class on specific activities for recess.	CDS	

CASE STUDY: A FOURTH-GRADE STUDENT EXPERIENCING SERIOUS EMOTIONAL TURMOIL

This case (Jones, in press) presents a way to use the Personalized Education Plan model as a means of developing an IEP for a student experiencing more serious social-emotional issues, or responding in a more traumatized manner than students

IEP (Individualized Education Plan) MDT (Multidisciplinary Team)	Special Education
PEP (Personalized Education Plan) TAT (Teacher Assistance Team) EA (Environmental Analysis)	Regular Education

FIGURE 11.18
Alphabet Soup

for whom a PEP might be developed. This case study also shows how each of the main concepts presented in this book—changing the environment, helping the student gain control over his or her behavior, and developing positive social skills—can be incorporated into a plan to assist a girl experiencing serious social-emotional problems. This case incorporates the additional behavior change intervention of helping the student understand the social-emotional factors influencing her behav-

FIGURE 11.19
Teacher
Assistance Team
Worksheet

Name of student _____

Grade _____ Date _____

Referred by _____ Classroom teacher _____

Present _____

Perceived Problem:

Expectations for Change:

Student Strengths: Student Weaknesses:

Prior Strategies:

Brainstorming:

Follow-Up: TAT Coordinator:

ior. This is in many ways similar to helping students develop a metacognitive structure for their learning through the process of demystifying learning. This case study represents a common set of family issues, behavior problems, and skill deficits experienced by students receiving services for emotional and behavioral problems.

Cary was a 10-year-old child whose father was physically abusive to her and her mother. The father left home when Cary was age 5. Her mother was involved in several relationships, but when Cary was 8, her mother began living with one man. When Cary was 10, the man left, saying Cary and her brother were too difficult to manage. Cary's mother frequently blamed Cary for the man leaving and suggested that she would be better off leaving the children. At this point, Cary—whose referring problems included violent outbursts and highly anxious, dependent behavior, including frequent crying, physically clinging to adults, and making strange sounds—began to act like various animals and to suck her thumb and curl up in the fetal position under her desk. She also became noncompliant and responded violently to threats of time-out or suspension. Cary scored 120 on the WISC-R with almost no discrepancy between her performance and verbal scores. Her schoolwork was characterized by incompleteness, frequent careless errors, and sloppiness.

Cary's IEP included four items related to improved academic performance and two related to behavior—calmly following adult requests and a reduction in the use of animal sounds. The IEP listed placement in the behavioral disorder (BD) classroom as the intervention for changing the behaviors, and an 85 percent compliance rate and elimination of all animal sounds as the goals. There were no specific intervention plans listed for implementing the IEP behavioral goals. The major interventions being implemented with Cary were a classroom point-and-levels system and a time-out procedure. The following section describes the changes recommended during a meeting with the BD teacher, BD supervisor, social worker, parent, and building administrator. The changes were incorporated in order to develop a comprehensive treatment plan that acknowledged and responded to the behavioral and psychological aspects of Cary's condition. The recommendations (based on functional assessments conducted by the senior author) were presented to the team for discussion and the development of specific interventions. The concept and strategies of conducting a functional analysis have been presented elsewhere (Foster-Johnson & Dunlap, 1993, Lennox & Miltenberger, 1989, O'Neill, Horner, Albin, Storey, & Sprague, 1990).

Environmental Change

The staff was encouraged to work with Cary to determine the antecedent events that led to her experiencing anxiety and responding with defensive, inappropriate behaviors. The staff also examined her environment to determine antecedent events associated with her withdrawal behavior. The functional analysis indicated that Cary became agitated in response to: (1) tasks she did not believe she could complete, (2) receiving feedback through the point system, (3) harsh adult requests, and (4) the desire to express her feelings. These findings led to the following interventions.

Because Cary frequently verbalized about her failure to meet academic expectations, she was assisted in setting goals and recording her progress in three academic subjects. Cary had difficulty understanding assignments and starting her work. Therefore, she was allowed to select a "jump starter"—a student who would help her understand tasks and get started. Because the functional analysis indicated that Cary most frequently became agitated when confronted with very firm or hostile adult requests, the adults whose behaviors most frequently elicited the inappropriate behaviors were coached in providing Cary with requests in a clear but less harsh manner. Since Cary's outbursts were frequently associated with her frustration over not being allowed or able to express her feelings, the social worker assisted the adults with whom Cary interacted most frequently in accepting Cary's need to express her feelings. Since Cary also made frequent self-deprecating statements, she was encouraged to become involved in assisting younger students with artwork—an area in which Cary excelled. Finally, Cary often stroked herself or wrapped her arms around herself when anxious. She also spoke of wanting to have her "Teddy" at school. It was hypothesized that holding the animal might have a calming effect on her and she was allowed to bring the animal to school.

Contingency Management

The only contingency management methods used with Cary were the behavior point and time-out systems utilized with all students in the program. Because of the frequency with which Cary became embroiled in arguments over the assignment of points, this was modified slightly to involve Cary and her teacher in a collaborative evaluation process. Cary and the teacher both evaluated Cary's hourly academic work and behavior. They met each noon and at the end of the schoolday to discuss the assignments and to determine points received. The points needed to earn the privileges associated with each state in the levels system remained constant.

Social Skills Training

The interventions in this section included both cognitive-behavioral and social-cognitive interventions. At the same time adults were being trained to provide clear, nonaggressive requests to Cary, she practiced receiving and responding appropriately to these requests. This work initially occurred in individual skill-training sessions but was later generalized to practice in the setting in which she had previously responded inappropriately. As mentioned previously, Cary was provided assistance in evaluating her own behavior and accurately estimating her points earned. The social worker provided Cary with practice in expressing her feelings in a more acceptable, adultlike manner. This included training in anger management. Cary learned to identify the precursors to her angry outbursts and, depending on the setting, to send an I-message, utilize relaxation techniques, request a backrub, ask for quiet time, or request time for conflict negotiation.

Insight-Oriented Work

Cary frequently accused adults of not liking her, wanting her out of the room, not helping her, and so on. As part of the treatment plan, the staff was provided with skills in interpreting her statements. For example, when she accused adults of not liking her when they refocused her behavior, the adults reflected that sometimes it must feel scary to have adults appear to not like you but that they liked her and were simply asking her to use her new skills. When she began to withdraw, the staff responded by noting that they too sometimes became nervous or upset and wanted to withdraw, and they found it helpful to relax, tell someone how they were feeling, or ask to solve the problem. During her sessions with the social worker, Cary focused on her fear that her mother would abandon her, and her anger at her mother for not being nice to her. She also worked on understanding her mother's stress and needs. This was associated with attempts to involve Cary and her mother in counseling. Figure 11.20 presents a portion of the IEP and associated treatment plan developed for Cary.

FIGURE 11.20
Sample Partial
IEP and
Associated
Treatment Plan

Name: Cary

Present Level of Educational Performance

Cary completes approximately 15% of the appropriate academic work assigned to her. She is on task an average of 20% of the time. Cary makes an average of 35 animal sounds per day. She follows reasonable adult requests 55% of the time. Cary expresses anxiety by hiding under her desk and becoming highly agitated when asked to join in classroom activities. She has difficulty identifying or expressing her feelings and frequently blames others for her problems. Cary's strengths include her above average ability, her ability to test near grade level in general knowledge, reading and math, her art skills and her sensitivity to younger children.

Annual Goal

Cary will increase her rate of following adult requests and completing her assigned academic tasks. Cary will reduce her use of animal sounds and withdrawal and will increase her ability to accurately describe he feelings and her relationships with significant others.

Short-Term Objectives	Criteria	Evaluation Process	Schedule for Review
Follow reasonable adult requests	95%	Teacher counts	Monthly
Reduce animal sounds	None	Teacher counts	Monthly
Increase accurate descriptions of her own feelings	10 weekly	teacher counts, audiotapes	Quarterly
Increase positive self-statement	3 per day	Teacher observation	Quarterly
Decrease time required to begin assigned academic tasks	Within 1 minute with no negative statements	Teacher observation	Quarterly
Increase accurate statements about relationship with mother	In 8 of 10 references to the relationship	Social worker observation	Quarterly
Increase Cary's understanding of her fears and anxieities related to relationships	80% reduction in fearful statements about relationships	Teacher and social worker evaluations	Quarterly

(continued)

FIGURE 11.20
Continued

Implementation Plan

Short-Term Objectives	Intervention	Person Responsible
1. Follow reasonable adult requests	1a. Work with adults involved to provide clear positive requests (E)	EBD teacher
	1b. Social skill training for Cary on accepting adult requests (SS)	Social worker
	1c. Point system with twice daily self- and teacher evaluation (BC)	EBD teacher
2. Reduce animal sounds	2a. Allow Cary to bring a stuffed animal from home (E)	EBD teacher
	2b. Reduce anxiety through the interventions listed in objective 5 (E)	EBD teacher and staff
3. Increase accurate description of her own feelings	3a. Teach Cary to send accurate I-messages (SS)	Social worker
	3b. Training in feeling identification and verbalization (SS)	Social worker
	3c. Staff will model describing their own feelings (E)	EBD staff and social worker
4. Increase positive self-statement	4a. Teach Cary to make specific positive self-statements (SS)	Social worker
	4b. Social reinforcement for positive self-statements (BC/SS)	EBD staff
	4c. Cary will tutor during art lessons in a second-grade classroom (E)	Classroom teacher
5. Decrease time required to begin assigned academic tasks	5a. Teach Cary to set goals for each academic work session (SS/E)	EBD teacher
	5b. Select and train a peer to assist Cary when she has difficulty beginning a task (E)	EBD teacher
	5c. Teach Cary to request the assistance of her peer tutor (SS)	
	5d. Twice daily self- and teacher evaluation of academic work and its relationship to points earned (BC/SS)	EBD teacher

Short-Term Objectives	Intervention	Person Responsible
6. Increase accurate statements about relationship with mother	6a. Individual therapy sessions (I)	Social worker
	6b. Family therapy sessions with the mother (I)	Mental health center staff
7. Increase Cary's understanding of her fears and anxieties related to relationships	7a. Individual therapy sessions (I)	Social worker

Key
(E)—Environmental change   (SS)—Social skill training
(BC)—Behavior control   (I)—Insight-oriented work

CASE STUDY: A MIDDLE SCHOOL STUDENT

The following case study was presented as an action research project by a middle school teacher who was a student in one of the authors' courses. It presents an excellent example of combining self-monitoring with problem solving.

After collecting some data, I found that Manuel was off task 45 percent of the class time and talked out without raising his hand on average of 4.25 times per class period. I used time-outs following by a conference with me for over a month and Manuel had to take a time-out on 6 of 22 school days. I found that this was not working with this specific student. He was promising not to repeat the behavior and developed simple plans but the same behaviors were occurring again and again. I realized that this method was not working at all after one of the last time-outs when Manuel wrote profanity all over the plan sheet and proceeded to walk out of our conference without permission, leaving the classroom and calling me a whole string of verbally abusive names and profane words. I realized that this problem with behavior was really not directed at me, but that this student had some real anger inside him and that I was merely a convenient foil.

I telephoned Manuel's mother who was herself extremely frustrated with Manuel's attitude and behavior. She was not pleased with his disrespect, especially since I was obviously taking a lot of care and time to help her son. I explained that the phone call was not to recommend punishment at home, but, quite to the contrary, that perhaps additional attention could be paid to him. I told his mother about my plan to have a problem-solving conference with Manuel, myself, and the vice-principal. I chose the vice principal because he was trained in Glasser's problem-solving methods and seemed to have a good relationship with Manuel.

The conference between Manuel, the vice-principal, and me was held soon thereafter. We used the entire Glasser problem-solving model and made much progress. We had a lengthy discussion about Manuel's strengths and weaknesses in the classroom. We talked about what Manuel perceived was the problem and what he considered possible solutions to the problem. We also role-played a few situations that might come up and some methods to solve those problems. The vice-principal helped to make a verbal plan and Manuel paraphrased and agreed to the plan. The plan was for Manuel to spend some after-school time with me to get some missed work completed. Also, if a classroom problem arose, Manuel was to place himself in time-out at the vice-principal's office with a conference and follow-up plan made with Manuel, myself, and the vice-principal. If our original plan did not prove to be successful, we would conference again and compose a written plan or behavior contract.

It was also at this time that I mentioned that I was collecting baseline data about Manuel's behaviors and was going to do an action research project based on these bindings. I showed Manuel the graph I had made concerning one of his off-task behaviors: talking out without raising his hand. He was amazed he was disrupting the class so much. Then I showed him the other two control group individual students' data and bar graphs (without names of course). Manuel could not believe it at first, but then after some further discussion, admitted he did distract the music class and other classes more than the other students. We ended the conference with a plan to not let the rest of the classmates know about our arrangements to monitor and chart his behavior. At last I realized that some trust was being established between me and Manuel. Manuel decided that he would monitor himself for the next five days, keeping his monitoring sheet in his folder and coming in to talk with me during his study hall. We developed a self-monitoring sheet involving three behaviors: talking out without raising his hand, swearing, and not completing work. Manuel chose his three favorite colors: green, blue, and red, and we assigned each of these colors to one of the behaviors. Manuel agreed to tally a red circle each time he talked out, a blue square each time he swore, and a green triangle each time he realized he was not completing his work. We further agreed that I would keep a tally sheet to compare my observations with Manuel's.

The first day of self-monitoring, Manuel was self-conscious and did well to record his behaviors. We talked during his free period and he really enjoyed using the tally sheet and the colored pens. The second day, his behaviors were not as good as the first day and we discussed this. The third and fourth days, Manuel had less incidents of swearing and talking out. I took this opportunity to commend him on his hard work and self-control. I showed him the pre-data and how his behaviors were getting much better. On the fifth and sixth days, there were drastic changes in Manuel's behavior. By the sixth day, Manuel had also come in for help after school twice and had completed 12 of his 14 missing assignments. During the sixth-day conference, Manuel also mentioned that he had not gotten angry in class or had an urge to go to the vice-principal's office for time-out. He mentioned that he also felt he was doing much better in his other classes. Finally, we were both pleased at how similar our data were—an indication that Manuel was being responsible in this process.

As the data in Figure 11.21 indicate, this program assisted Manuel in making some significant changes in this behavior. Manuel decided that the plan had helped so much that he set it up in several other classes. The data I collected near the end of the school year indicated that Manuel was on-task 92 percent of the time during the four classes I sampled.

I received many positive comments from Manuel's other teachers about our work with self-monitoring. Also, the entire Teacher Assistance Team met and commended me on my successful work. When we telephoned his mother following his first successful week, she was extremely pleased and encouraged him to bring the tally sheets home to put on the refrigerator. She thanked me for the efforts in helping her son.

In the beginning of the trimester, I thought there was no hope for this specific student. I have now learned that I can make a positive difference and can help the

FIGURE 11.21
Data for Manuel

extremely at-risk student become successful in the school setting. In addition to the assistance I offered Manuel, I benefited from this project in many ways. I realized that I cannot possibly do it all by myself. Sometimes it takes the help of other professionals, and asking for help does not mean I am a poor teacher. I found another level of capability in my teaching that I had not utilized before.

CASE STUDY: A DISRUPTIVE HIGH SCHOOL STUDENT

The following example occurred when one of the authors was asked to assist a high school staff develop a program for a disruptive student. The student had received dozens of office referrals for relatively minor but persistent classroom disruptions and had finally been pulled out of two of his classes. The student was identified under Public Law (PL) 94-142 and had serious social cognition deficiencies. He demonstrated limited ability to understand others' perspectives and limited sense of his own efficacy and responsibility, and attributed his successes and failures to external factors. He also had few skills in developing specific plans to alter his behavior. Based on observations and interviews with parents, teachers, administrators, counselors, and the student, the following recommendations were made to the school staff to help them respond to this young man more productively. These recommendations highlight the importance of following the 10 procedures for effective curtailment of activity. They also reinforce the value of collecting data, examining the learning environment, helping students become responsible for their own behavior, and systematically assessing the effectiveness of a program developed to change a student's behavior.

RECOMMENDATIONS

1. The current and past IEPs available to me did not include any specific educational program that would assist Randy in remediating or circumventing his behavior problems. The IEP merely listed several obvious goals and an evaluation component to several but not all of the goals. Randy's school history, psychological assessment, and comments from school staff all support my belief that Randy has deficiencies in impulse control, social cognition, judgment, and problem solving. It seems necessary and appropriate that an ongoing program be developed for remediating these deficiencies. A peer counseling group, focusing on social skills and conflict resolution, or at minimum, ongoing counseling, focusing on responsibility and enhancing social cognition, would seem desirable. Additionally, the school's response to Randy's behavior problems should be adjusted so that it consistently serves a behavior change function in light of Randy's social/emotional problems. (See items 3 and 5.)

2. The school staff should keep more accurate records of Randy's behavior problems. Available records are possibly acceptable for nonidentified students but are not adequate for making IEP decisions. For example, the vice-principal indicated that during the past semester, Randy had been referred to his office "every other day." His records, however, were kept on a five-by-seven card with no trend analysis made on an ongoing or summative basis. Additionally, I was informed that Randy had been suspended once, yet Randy stated unequivocally that he had not been suspended during the previous term. I believe it is important to have a good record concerning the behavior, the class in which it occurred (and thus time of day), the time during the class (early, middle, or late), the activity in which the class was involved, preceding

events, and responses by the teacher. These data can help those involved in writing the IEP determine the environmental factors influencing Randy's behavior.

3. The school should develop a clear, concise policy regarding consequences for office referrals. It appears that most of the behaviors for which Randy is referred fall into the category of minor discipline problems. The student handbook is vague concerning the consequences for these behaviors. There is no indication as to how many referrals result in a Saturday school, suspension, or expulsion. While this policy has the advantage of providing administrative flexibility, it creates a response that can be confusing and countertherapeutic for some students. Last semester Randy spent numerous hours sitting in the office. It is very likely that besides being moderately reinforcing, the lack of clear, precise, predictable consequences was confusing for Randy and was a factor affecting his continued disruptive behavior. Indeed, the vice-principal mentioned that at one point Randy's mother was informed that "Randy would be expelled if he continued to be referred." Randy continued, however, and these consequences did not follow. An expulsion certainly would not have been the correct response given the lack of a systematic program prior to this serious consequence. The point is, however, that no predetermined guidelines were established and followed.

I recommend that a program be developed that provides Randy with a clear statement that X number of referrals will result in a Saturday school, Y number of Saturday schools will result in the next referral's being a suspension, and Z number of suspensions will mean that the next referral will result in a change of placement. This consistent policy will provide clarity, limits, and structure for Randy—important components in a responsible educational plan for him.

4. Similar to the schoolwide program, teachers should provide Randy with a clear statement about how they will respond to his violations of classroom rules. It is important that this discussion not take place unless Randy begins to develop a pattern of disruptive behavior. At this point, Randy appears to be behaving well in all of his classes. It would be undesirable and unfair to treat him in a manner suggesting that problems are expected. However, if problems arise, Randy should have a clear understanding about how they will be handled. Generally, this should involve making a polite request to stop the behavior. If Randy continues to be disruptive, he should again politely and calmly be informed that further disruptions will mean *he is choosing* to receive an office referral. If he persists, he should be informed that he has chosen a referral.

5. If Randy receives an office referral, he should not be allowed to chat with the vice-principal or sit in the office. Instead, he should be required to complete a worksheet in which he responds to a series of questions such as (a) What did you do? Be specific. Describe *your* behavior, not the behavior of others. (b) Did your behavior violate a classroom rule or disrupt the class? Describe the possible negative effect your behavior might have had on the teacher and other students. (c) Do you believe this behavior needs to be changed? (d) What can you do to help prevent this from happening again? (e) Is there any way the teacher can help you prevent this behavior and have a better class? (f) Will you attempt to follow the suggestions you have made?

Completing such a form will help Randy consider his actions in a concrete way and thus respond to the goals that should be written into his IEP. Randy needs assistance in understanding others' perspectives, taking responsibility for his own behavior, and developing plans to improve his behavior. Consequences for misbehavior should be aimed at teaching these needed skills, not merely making him sit or complete custodial work.

6. Randy needs to receive attention and praise for his positive efforts and performance. At the time of my visit, he had gone 12 days without a referral and had received only one "up slip" (note indicating improved behavior or achievement). Staff—including the vice-principal, who could serve as a good model for Randy—should be encouraged to provide Randy and his mother with specific statements about Randy's improvement.

7. The change to a 2–1–2–1–2 schedule was a wise decision. Randy begins his day with two academic courses, followed by a study hall, two more courses, lunch, and completes the day with two courses. The only possible problem I envision would be the last period.

8. Randy appears to be influenced by his peers. He admits that much of his acting out involves peers who encourage and reinforce these behaviors. When planning Randy's schedule, an attempt should be made to place him in classes with students who value appropriate behavior. It may be better to err slightly in terms of placing Randy in more challenging courses than to place him in lower courses with more disruptive peers. At this point, however, I would continue on his current schedule. He seems particularly pleased with the quality and sensitivity of his current teachers.

9. Randy should be involved in a weekly monitoring of his academic and behavioral progress in each class. His assessment should be shared and discussed with a counselor with the goal of reinforcing progress and accomplishment and developing plans for dealing with any problems.

ACTIVITIES FOR DEVELOPING SKILL IN DATA COLLECTION AND USING BEHAVIORAL INTERVENTIONS

The following activities can help you improve your skills in data collection and the use of behavioral interventions.

ACTIVITY 11.1
Clearly Defining Students' Behavior

For each of the five adjectives listed in the left-hand column, write three specific observable student behaviors that might be displayed by a student described by the adjective.

General Descriptor	Specific Behavioral Descriptor
Angry	1.
	2.
	3.
Unmotivated	1.
	2.
	3.
Hyperactive	1.
	2.
	3.

General Descriptor	Specific Behavioral Descriptor
Uncooperative	1.
	2.
	3.
Lacks social skills	1.
	2.
	3.

ACTIVITY 11.2
Discriminating between Discrete and Continuous Behavior

Determine whether each of the 10 behaviors listed is a discrete or continuous behavior. Indicate your choice by placing an *X* under the appropriate word in the right-hand column.

Behavior	Discrete	Continuous
Example: On-task		X
Sharpens pencil		
Requests to go to the bathroom		
Talks out without raising hand		
Sits with chair tilted backward		
Out-of-seat		
Refuses to obey teacher's request		
Spends time alone on playground		
Scratches arm while sitting at desk		
Hits other children		
Talks to other students during seatwork		

ACTIVITY 11.3
Implementing and Assessing a Behavioristic Intervention

Select an individual student's behavior that is detrimental to the student as well as the class. Describe the behavior in behavioral terms, collect baseline data for at least two 30-minute periods, and graph the results.

Next, select one of the procedures for developing a contract described in this chapter and develop a written contract with the student.

Implement the contract for five days. Collect and record data during all times when the contract is in effect.

At the end of five days, discuss the results with the student and determine whether to (1) continue the contract, (2) alter the contract by requiring improved behavior while reducing the reinforcement or employing a reinforcer lower on the hierarchy, or (3) discontinue the contract.

Finally, complete these statements:

The student's behavior . . . .
At the end of the five days the student said that he or she . . . .
I was surprised that . . . .
I was pleased that . . . .

SUMMARY

Even though teachers are not responsible for developing a series of sophisticated behavior change interventions, there are a variety of effective, efficient methods teachers can implement that can dramatically influence student behavior. As teachers work with an increasing number of at-risk students, they will benefit from being able to implement a variety of these methods.

Teachers will increasingly be asked to document both student behavior problems and their interventions aimed at altering student behavior. This chapter provides methods for accomplishing this important task. The chapter describes methods for helping students become involved in data collection and become more aware of and responsible for their own behavior through self-monitoring. Methods for involving students in setting goals and becoming more aware of the consequences associated with their behavior through the use of contracts have also been explored.

Experience and research with teachers (Jones, 1991) who have implemented these methods show that nearly 80 percent find they can use them in their classrooms and that the methods are effective approximately 80 percent of the time. While these teachers realize that the quality of their proactive classroom management and instruction are their major responsibility, they find that using the methods discussed in Chapters 10 and 11 can have a major positive impact on individual problem students; this is professionally rewarding and also has a positive impact on the behavior and learning of other students.

APPENDIX: Curriculum of Responsibility Contract

Name of Student: Tyler _____   Grade: 8   Date: _____

School: _____

PEP Facilitator: _____

PEP Team: _____   _____   _____

_____   _____   _____

_____   _____   _____

Goal of the Curriculum of Responsibility Contract: To encourage Tyler to follow school rules and take responsibility for his behavior in school.

Expectations for Responsible Student Behavior

In addition to following all classroom and school rules, the specific expectations that may require additional instruction, clarification, and assistance are:

1. Follow teacher directions in class without making off-task comments.
2. Use polite, appropriate language when talking to teachers and other students.

Expectation 1:

Follow teacher directions in class without making off-task comments.

Responsible Choices
Try to do my work and ask politely
  and quietly for help if I need it.
Listen quietly to my teachers and
  follow their directions.

Positive Consequences
Get my work done.
Stay out of trouble.
Learn more.
Learn better work habits.
Get high scores on my card and earn
  my reward.

Help the Teachers Will Give
Teacher will respond when I raise my hand.
If I become too upset, I can ask to return to my special education class.
Daily communication with parents via the "travel card."
Help in preparing for class sessions.

Irresponsible Choices
Talk while teacher is talking.
Make rude or attention-getting
  comments during class.
Follow teacher requests.

Negative Consequences
Return to resource room.
Receive low scores on my travel card.
Complete problem-solving form in the
  resource room.
Have my parents get a call.

Help the Teachers Will Give to Prevent Negative Consequences
Politely remind me when I am making off-task comments.
Remind me that I need to make a choice.
Help me with my problem-solving sheet.

Expectation 2:

Use polite, appropriate language when talking to teachers and other students.

Responsible Choices
Speak politely to students.

Speak politely to teachers.

When frustrated, use new skills to tell
  someone how you feel.
Ask to return to the resource room.

Positive Consequences
Be seen by other students as a
  more normal, positive student.
Help teachers teach so I can learn
  more.
Practice new skills I can use the rest
  of my life.
Learn to walk away from trouble and
  seek assistance.
Receive high scores on my card.

Help the Teachers Will Give
Complete the travel card each day.
Tell Tyler how well is he doing when he succeeds.

Provide Tyler with appropriate instructional activities.
Politely remind Tyler when he needs to speak more politely.
Politely inform Tyler that he is making a choice to return to the resource center if
   he continues any inappropriate talk.

Irresponsible Choices	*Negative Consequences*
Make rude comments to other students (particularly girls).	Receive a low score on my travel card.
Make mean or aggressive comments to other students.	Be informed that I have chosen to leave the regular class and return to my special education class.
Threaten other students.	
Hurt other students.	

Help the Teacher Will Give to Prevent Negative Consequences
Fill out their part of the travel card.
Teach new communication skills.
Allow me to leave class if I need to return to my special education class.
Tell me how well I am doing.
Tell my parents how well I am doing.

Curriculum of Responsibility Process

PEP Facilitator Agrees to:
1. Collect and share information with the student, parent, and PEP team.
2. Convene the individuals who will sign the Curriculum of Responsibility contract.
3. Review the contract with Tyler weekly.
4. Coordinate the reinforcements and communicate with Tyler's parents.

PEP Team Agrees to:
1. Consistently apply the stated teacher help, consequences, and reinforcers.
2. Provide information to the PEP facilitator regarding the efforts of the student and
   the effectiveness of the plan.
3. Complete the daily travel card.
4. Encourage Tyler as much as possible.

Parent Agrees to:
1. Keep in regular contact with the school.
2. Talk with Tyler about his school behavior and encourage him to follow the expectations written in the contract.
3. Contact the school staff if they have any concerns.
4. Encourage Tyler.

Student Agrees to:
1. Work with the PEP team to complete the Curriculum of Responsibility Contract.
2. Try to follow the contract.
3. Take the daily travel card home and show his parents.

PEP Facilitator's Signature: _____ Date: _____
Parent's Signature: _____ Date: _____
Student's Signature: _____ Date: _____
Principal's Signature: _____ Date: _____

RECOMMENDED READING

Alberto, P., & Troutman, A. (1986). *Applied behavior analysis for teachers* (2nd ed.). Columbus, OH: Charles E. Merrill.

Algozzine, B. (1987). *Problem behavior management: Educator's resource service.* Rockville, MD: Aspen.

Axelrod, S. (1983). *Behavior modification for the classroom teacher* (2nd ed.). New York: McGraw-Hill.

Camp, B., & Bash, A. (1985). *The think aloud series: Increasing social skills—A problem-solving program for children.* Champaign, IL: Research Press.

Carpenter, R., & Apter, S. (1988). Research integration of cognitive-emotional interventions for behaviorally disordered children and youth. In M. Wang, M. Reynolds, & H. Walbert (Eds.), *Handbook of special education: Research and practice: Volume 2.* New York: Pergamon.

Gloeckler, T., & Simpson, C. (1988). *Exceptional students in regular classrooms.* Mountain View, CA: Mayfield.

Goldstein, A. (1988). *The prepare curriculum: Teaching prosocial competencies.* Champaign, IL: Research Press.

Goldstein, A., & McGinnis, E. (1988). *The skillstreaming video: How to teach students prosocial skills.* Champaign, IL: Research Press.

Hazel, J., & Pederson, C. *Social skills for daily living.* Circle Pines, MN: American Guidance Service.

Jackson, N., Jackson, D., & Monroe, C. (1983). *Getting along with others: Teaching social effectiveness to children.* Champaign, IL: Research Press.

Jones, V. (1980). *Adolescents with behavior problems: Strategies for teaching, counseling, and parent involvement.* Boston: Allyn and Bacon.

Kaplan, J., & Brainville, B. (1991). *Beyond behavior modification: A cognitive-behavioral approach to behavior management in the school.* Austin, TX: Pro-Ed.

Knitzer, J., Steinberg, Z., & Fleisch, B. (1990). *At the schoolhouse door: An examination of programs and policies for children with behavioral and emotional problems.* New York: Bank Street College of Education.

McCarney, S., & Cummins, K. (1993). *The pre-referral intervention manual: The most common learning and behavior problems encountered in the educational environment.* Columbia, MO: Hawthorne Educational Service.

McGinnis, E., & Goldstein, A. (1984). *Skillstreaming the elementary school child: A guide for teaching prosocial skills.* Champaign, IL: Research Press.

McGinnis, E., & Goldstein, A. (1990). *Skillstreaming in early childhood: Teaching prosocial skills to the preschool and kindergarten child.* Champaign, IL: Research Press.

Nelson, C., & Rutherford, R. (1988). Behavioral interventions with behaviorally disordered students. In M. Wang, M. Reynolds, & H. Walbert (Eds.), *Handbook of special education: Research and practice: Volume 2.* New York: Pergamon.

Strain, P., Guralnick, M., & Walker, H. (Eds.). (1986). *Children's social behavior.* Orlando, FL: Academic Press.

Walker, H. (1979). *The acting-out child: Coping with classroom disruption.* Boston: Allyn and Bacon.

Walker, H., McConnell, S., Holmes, D., Todis, B., Walker, J., & Golden, N. (1987). *The ACCEPTS program: A curriculum for children's effective peer and teacher skills.* Austin, TX: Pro-Ed.

Walker, H., Todis, B., Holmes, D., & Horton, G. (1988). *The ACCESS program: Adolescent curriculum for communication and effective social skills.* Austin, TX: Pro-Ed.

Walker, H., & Walker, J. (1991). *Coping with noncompliance in the classroom: A positive approach for teachers.* Austin, TX: Pro-Ed.

Wolery, M., Bailey, D., & Sugai, G. (1988). *Effective teaching principles and procedures of applied behavior analysis with exceptional students.* Boston: Allyn and Bacon.

Workman, E. (1982). *Teaching behavioral self-control to students.* Austin, TX: Pro-Ed.

CHAPTER 12

Schoolwide Student Management Programs

The problem lies in one of our educational systems more glaring contradictions—the autocratic schools we use for teaching students to be responsible citizens in a democratic society. Students experiencing problems are already feeling insecure, and they do not need educators compounding their problems by making them feel even more insecure. . . . Therefore, it does not make sense for educators to use the criminal/justice model first, before employing what they were professionally prepared to use—educational and mentoring approaches.

—Forrest Gathercoal (1993)
Judicious Discipline

It is the teachers' responsibility to prevent and effectively deal with minor student misbehavior in the classroom. It is the students' responsibility to know that even though they have a right to express concern if they feel their personal or learning needs are not being met, they will not be allowed to disrupt the learning process. In order to meet these responsibilities, both teachers and students need the support provided by a clear, fair, consistent, schoolwide student management policy. School policies for handling discipline must be based on the creation of positive, productive learning environments, and a commitment to helping students develop skills they need to become responsible self-managers.

A SYSTEMS APPROACH TO MANAGING STUDENT BEHAVIOR

Disruptive students evoke responses in adults that tend to limit their patience and creativity in managing these students. Unlike students with visual impairments or learning disabilities who may evoke empathy, concern, and other sensitive responses, a student who consistently or aggressively acts out often evokes feelings of fear, anger, frustration, and confusion. These feelings are understandably associated with the desire to have the student removed from the setting for which the adult is responsible and to have someone else assume responsibility for the student. However, when this response is used too early, too frequently, or as the major means for responding, it runs counter to the needs of students and it may

violate students basic constitutional rights (Gathercoal, 1993). Students who behave in ways that disrupt the learning environment need to know there are consequences for this behavior. However, they also need assistance in developing skills
for managing their emotions in situations that are often causing them emotional
stress and pain.

To serve students who experience behavior and learning difficulties and also
to provide assistance for teachers who work with these students, it is important to
clarify the various roles and responsibilities all educators have in managing student
behavior. Likewise, it is imperative that rules and consequences for rule violation
be clear and educationally sound. In their study of 50 elementary schools in
London, Mortimore and Sammons (1987) found that "much of the variation
among schools in their effects on students' progress and development is accounted for by differences in school policies and practices" (p. 6). In their reanalysis
of the High School and Beyond Study, Wehlage and Rutter (1986) found that
so-called marginal students viewed school discipline policies as ineffective and
unfair. A report published by the Northwest Regional Educational Laboratory
entitled *Effective Schooling and At-Risk Youth: What the Research Shows* (Druian
& Butler, 1987) stated a similar finding: "Finally, it should be noted that one of
the strongest criticisms of schools made by dropouts is that the *discipline* is unfair
and arbitrary. Successful programs that serve drop-outs are characterized as having fair—though sometimes tough—programs of discipline. The programs clarify
what offenses are and what the punishment is" (p. 6). Finally, a report prepared by
the Office of Educational Research and Improvement on establishing safe, disciplined, and drug-free schools (Aleem & Moles 1993) emphasized the importance
of having "clear discipline standards that are firmly, fairly and consistently enforced" (p. 12).

The authors' experience in working with school districts to establish a clear,
fair system that creates shared responsibility for helping students with behavior
problems suggests that this can best be accomplished by creating a systems approach to managing student behavior. Nine major concepts serve as the foundation
for effectively implementing a systems approach.

MAJOR CONCEPTS IN DEVELOPING A SYSTEMS APPROACH

*Concept 1: School policies for responding to irresponsible student behavior will be
most effective when they are supported by clear school-board policies and administrative regulations.*

Because a systems approach requires that a variety of individuals be actively
involved in assisting students with behavior problems, it is likely to meet with some
resistance. Experience indicates that this model will be dramatically more effective
if it receives support and legitimacy from the highest administrative level. For
example, a school board or local educational service district can draft policy that
supports a systems approach. This central administrative support places principals
and other support staff in a more solid and positive position. Instead of being the
instigator or supporter of a policy that asks all staff to be responsible for working

effectively with students who have behavior problems, everyone involved is in the position of implementing school-board policy. This will enhance relationships between staff members and between staff and administration—factors shown to be associated with more effective responses to these students (Anderson, 1985; Gottfredson & Gottfredson, 1985). Appendix B provides an example of well-designed school-board policies and administrative regulations.

Concept 2: The teacher must initially assess his or her classroom management and instructional methods to determine whether they are consistent with best accepted practice.

As mentioned earlier, Figure 9.5 presents a form for helping teachers assess their use of effective classroom management methods. Teachers also need to determine whether the use of the instructional and motivational methods described in Chapter 6 and particularly the implementation of academic goal setting can have a significant positive impact on student learning and behavior.

Concept 3: The teacher has a responsibility to use behavior change methods aimed at altering students' behavior.

The material in Chapters 10 and 11 highlights what the authors believe are the most effective and practical methods teachers can use to fulfill this obligation. It is important that teachers keep a record of their efforts in this area. Teachers must be careful not to refer a student prior to making reasonable attempts to work with that student. Teachers who make few attempts give up their natural authority by sending two very negative messages to students: (1) they do not value the student and (2) they do not have skill in dealing with student's behavior. When a significant amount of students believe this about a teacher, the teacher is likely to have ongoing and serious classroom management problems.

Concept 4: Teachers need to receive assistance from peers in examining their efforts to help youngsters who persist in their learning and behavioral difficulties.

Because continued student failure, acting out, or withdrawn behavior evoke in teachers feelings of frustration and inadequacy, resources need to be available to assist teachers with these problems. These resources can include (1) in-service opportunities to improve their management or instructional skills; (2) observation by building, district, or contracted professionals to observe the teacher and student and to provide suggestions on how to work more effectively with the student; or (3) the creation of teacher assistance teams that offer a forum for colleagues to provide teachers with ideas for working with students who are experiencing behavior or academic difficulties (Chalfant, 1983; Chalfant, VanDusgen Pysh, & Moultrie, 1979).

Concept 5: Teachers will be more effective in helping students develop responsible behavior when the school has a clearly written and effectively communicated schoolwide student management system.

The remaining sections of this chapter focus on this component. Research on school organization that influences student behavior has consistently pointed to the importance of clearly stated school rules and consequences for irresponsible behavior. The most effective programs, however, go beyond a focus on controlling students; they attempt to examine the quality of relationships and instruction in the building and the options provided to students experiencing difficulties.

Concept 6: An effective response to students who experience ongoing problems includes a procedure for holding staffings aimed at developing specific plans to assist the student.

Whenever behavior problems persist to the point at which the student has received several office referrals or is uninvolved in the classroom despite all efforts associated with concepts 1 through 5, it is desirable to have a staffing at which teachers meet to develop a specific plan for assisting the youngster in having a more successful school experience. Even though most schools use staffings, they are seldom built into the schoolwide student management plan as a systematic method for intervening to help the student. One way to ensure that staffings occur is to indicate within the schoolwide student management plan the specific stage at which a staffing will be held. Ideally, each staffing will lead to a specific intervention plan involving several school staff. As presented in Chapter 11, these plans are called Personalized Education Plans (PEPs). Unlike an individual education plan (IEP), required for students identified as eligible for special education services, a PEP is not a legal document nor does it involve special education services. However, like IEPs, PEPs are specific plans developed to respond to the unique educational needs of a student.

Concept 7: Outside consultation should be provided when a student continues to have behavioral difficulties despite concepts 1 through 6 being employed.

School staff are often stretched to their limits and may not always be able objectively to assess attempts to help students whose behavior has consistently caused the staff frustration and anger. In addition, even though their concern and efforts may be commendable, school staff may lack skill in developing alternative interventions with students whose behavior is difficult to manage or extremely withdrawn. Because these factors may cause school staff to refer to special education or to exclude students who could function in a regular school environment, assistance should be provided to staff once it has been documented that the staff has followed district guidelines for assisting these students.

Assistance can be provided by a variety of sources. District or regional service district school psychologists or behavioral specialists can be asked to review the situation and make recommendations. It is usually desirable to have the consultant spend a sizable portion of a schoolday observing the student in classroom settings. The consultant will also need to examine the student's school file and review PEP plans and the associated data. Finally, it is often useful for the consultant to interview the student. Following this evaluation, the consultant can meet with the teachers involved and make recommendations concerning any additional interventions that appear likely to assist the student in improving behavior. The consultant might make suggestions concerning classroom management and instruction, modifications in the schoolwide student management plan, an individualized contract for the student, or additional school counseling services. The consultant may also indicate that the existing program appears to be a well-designed and reasonable response to the student's behavior and may suggest that the staff instigate a referral for special education services.

Concept 8: School personnel will better serve students with behavior problems when procedures are in place for coordinating with community resources.

A significant number of children experience emotional problems and difficulties outside of school that warrant interventions from community agencies. It is important for educators to realize that these at-risk children are viewed differently by schools and community agencies. In general, the term *at-risk* implies the threat of impending negative consequences for a child. Educational definitions of at-risk suggest a student may potentially drop out of a school program entirely. Within community agencies using clinical definitions, the term *at-risk* suggests the potential injury to a child of an emotional or mental nature that would require clinical intervention to remediate. Although many students may meet criteria in both groups, there are important distinctions between them that have significant implications. One important difference is that the educational definitions imply educational interventions, whereas clinical definitions imply clinical interventions. It is, therefore, important for educators and social service agency staff to be aware of the variation in definitions and the implications for services.

For example, if educators assume a clinical definition of the term, they may decide that there is little they can do in the way of interventions with the student. In reality, as presented throughout this book, a wide range of preventive and corrective approaches for at-risk students are available to educators that are unavailable if clinical definitions are employed. On the other hand, due to the educational nature of their primary responsibility and the training of their staff, educational institutions have a limited ability to respond to the clinical needs that some students present in the school setting. It is therefore important for school systems to understand and be able to access the community resources that exist for the at-risk student.

A concept designed to respond to the needs of these students and the institutions that serve them is interagency cooperation and collaboration. More specifically, the Youth Service Team (YST) provides a format for promoting more productive services to at-risk students. These teams provide for networking and liaison among schools, social service agencies, law enforcement, the juvenile department, and other community resources. School personnel are often in a prime position to become aware of a variety of student needs that increasingly seem to be beyond the scope of appropriate intervention in the educational system. By staffing students among a variety of agency representatives, information is shared and alternatives can be developed. This process is effective in preventing a duplication of services as well as in identifying children who might otherwise never receive services.

Interagency collaboration and cooperation provide for a more comprehensive view and coordinated planning for at-risk children and their families. They also provide for the appropriate delivery of services and promote a much more responsible model for children who have the greatest need for being held accountable for their actions.

Concept 9: Referral for special education services should be considered when other interventions have failed.

One important benefit of using a systematic continuum of services approach to responding to unproductive student behavior is that if it becomes necessary to refer the student for special education identification, much of the most important groundwork will already have been completed. Research (Smith, Frank, & Snider, 1984) indicates that when making eligibility decisions regarding students who are seriously emotionally disturbed or behavior disordered, the most frequently missing data involve information on students' actual behavior and interventions that have been implemented to alter the inappropriate behavior. At least seven states currently require that such information be available prior to a student being identified as behavior disordered or emotionally disturbed. Several other states recommend that this process be followed (Jones & Waksman, 1985). A continuum of services approach ensures that appropriate prior interventions will already have been made. Because this dramatically expedites referrals to special education, it helps alleviate a common teacher concern about the delays in processing such referrals.

Figure 12.1 provides an instrument that staff can use to examine whether their current schoolwide student management plan incorporates the key concepts described in this section. The following section presents the major components of an effective plan and this is followed by a section that examines the process for building or making a major modification in a schoolwide student management plan.

SCHOOLWIDE STUDENT MANAGEMENT PLANS

What Are They?

The most widespread response to student behavior problems in this country has been the development of schoolwide plans for managing student behavior (Duke, 1986; Duke & Jones, 1984). In the early 1980s, the State Board of Education in New York City required every city school to have a comprehensive disciplinary code listing unacceptable behaviors and the punishments teachers and administrators would administer when these occurred. A 1987 survey conducted for the Center for Educational Statistics showed that 93 percent of teachers in all grade levels stated that their school had a written discipline policy. It is interesting to note, however, that 34 percent of teachers in 1986 to 1987 still regarded their schools' discipline

FIGURE 12.1 Evaluating Your Schoolwide Student Management Plan

Component	Rating		
	Clearly Evident and Functional	Somewhat Evident or Functional	Not Evident or Functional
1. A philosophy statement.			
2. School rules and procedures are effectively taught and retaught when problems occur.			
3. A statement concerning student behaviors that can lead to a direct office referral.			

(continued)

FIGURE 12.1
Continued

Component	Rating		
	Clearly Evident and Functional	*Somewhat Evident or Functional*	*Not Evident or Functional*
4. A focus on specific teacher interventions that will be employed prior to an office referral.			
5. A requirement that all teachers teach students and provide the administration with their classroom management procedures.			
6. Classroom consequences are educational and treat students with dignity.			
7. Clear, sequential responses to office referrals.			
8. Consequences for office referrals are educational and treat students with dignity.			
9. A clear procedure for teachers to seek assistance when they have continued problems.			
10. Forms exist for communicating effectively about student behavior between staff, administration, and students.			
11. A process for developing a personalized plan for all students receiving a specified number of office referrals in a designated time frame.			
12. Data collection to determine where referrals occur and to assess the results of interventions.			

policy as not strict enough; 25 percent regarded the policy as not comprehensive enough; and 50 percent indicated it was not consistently applied (Ashwick, 1987, p. 7).

Schoolwide student management plans are essential ingredients in effective classroom management. These plans provide students with important clarity and safeguards concerning behavioral expectations and consequences. As mentioned earlier, many students who are doing poorly in school view school discipline policies as ineffective and unfair (Wehlage & Rutter, 1986). Students' attitudes toward school and their behavior can be improved by providing clarity and fairness in schoolwide student management policies (Stedman, 1985). Likewise, teachers must have the support of consequences that occur when students fail to respond to teachers' professionally responsible efforts to ensure acceptable student behavior.

Major Components of an Effective Schoolwide Student Management Program

The senior author has worked with dozens of school districts and schools to develop systematic schoolwide student management plans. His findings indicate that there are nine key components to an effective schoolwide student management plan. These components have recently been supported by Sprick's (1992) work on schoolwide student management. The components are discussed in the order in which school staff will most effectively draft a schoolwide student management plan.

Component 1: A philosophy statement.

It is often asked why the authors suggest that school staff begin by drafting a philosophy statement. There are two key reasons for this suggestion. First, the authors have never worked with a group of teachers who were not concerned about their students' learning and personal development. Therefore, they are willing and able to develop a philosophy statement that emphasizes a positive learning environment and providing students with new skills. This helps create a positive start to the process of building a schoolwide plan. Second, if a philosophy statement emphasizes issues of the personal relationships, instruction, and problem solving, this will result in a solid basis for comparing all other components of the plan. Teachers often view discipline as an issue of control, and the creation of a philosophy statement with a different focus helps provide a benchmark against which all other aspects of the discipline plan can be checked. Figure 12.2 provides an example of a philosophy statement that introduces a schoolwide student management plan.

Component 2: School rules or expectations.

All social settings need to have clear behavioral expectations in order to enhance safety and security, and developing schoolwide behavioral expectations is a central feature of developing a schoolwide plan. Like classroom rules, these will be most effective when they are initially developed by students, school staff, and parents. After their initial development, they can be discussed, accepted, and celebrated at the beginning of every year. The authors work with a number of schools whose staff begin the school year with an assembly in which key school rules and procedures are role-played. This is followed by classroom discussions in which

FIGURE 12.2
Philosophy
Statement

> The major role of the student management plan is to promote positive behavioral growth and self-management that enables students to be successful in their current and future social and educational environments. The staff at Jefferson Middle School believes that responses to student behavior problems will be most effective when they provide an opportunity for students to see adults model effective communication skills, problem solving and conflict negotiation, and when students are assisted in developing these skills. The staff also acknowledges that inappropriate student behavior is often a response to factors within the learning environment and that responses to student behavior problems include examining and modifying some aspect of the school environment. The staff at Jefferson Middle School will encourage students' success in the learning community by aiding students in developing a sense of responsibility by defining roles of students, staff, and parents and by following a clear, consistent and skill-based student management process.

students personalize the importance of these behavioral expectations. The authors work with several elementary schools who simply use the words *Be FAIR, SAFE, and KIND* as their schoolwide expectations. In his book *Judicious Discipline,* Forrest Gathercoal (1993) suggested that school rules be matched to students' constitutional rights and he suggested helping students create rules such as:

1. Act in a safe and healthy way.
2. Treat all property with respect.
3. Respect the rights and needs of others.
4. Take responsibility for learning. (pp. 80–81)

The key is that students understand and accept the standards to which they will be held accountable.

Component 3: Schoolwide procedures.

As discussed in Chapter 8, procedures differ from rules in that rather than describing general parameters for behavior, they describe specific behaviors in specific settings. Elementary school discipline plans are more likely to include rather extensive lists of schoolwide procedures. Appendix C presents an example of procedures that might be taught to elementary school students. As with rules, it is important to teach schoolwide procedures! This might be done at an assembly and through role-playing sessions conducted in hallways, the cafeteria, and the playground. The authors work with a number of schools who use a rodeo approach to teaching playground procedures. Early in the year, each class rotates through a series of events during which they learn key procedures for using that area of the playground. Procedures are also important in secondary schools. These are likely to include issues such as uses of a pass in the hallway, using school phones, tardy policies, and so on.

Component 4: The roles/responsibilities of all parties involved in managing student behavior.

How students behave is a joint responsibility of students, parents, teachers, administrators, and counselors. Therefore, an effective schoolwide student management plan clarifies the roles all parties will play in facilitating positive student behavior. In the authors' experience, this is the most important component of an effective plan and is by far the most demanding to draft and on which to reach consensus. Appendix D provides an example of the responsibilities developed by one staff with whom the senior author consulted.

One key aspect of this component that is occasionally missing is to determine which behaviors will be responded to by teachers and which involve a direct referral to an administrator. This also includes providing a clear statement regarding any behaviors that will be responded to with an immediate contact with a parent or guardian and/or a suspension. The author recently worked with a combined middle and high school whose staff was willing to move from an assertive discipline model to a problem-solving model of student management. However, during the transition, the teachers became very concerned about the lack of clear consequences for extremely disruptive behavior. It was necessary to back up and consider "bottom-line" issues about student behavior before the staff could move on to enthusiastically work on improving their skills in preventing and responding to behavior problems. To this staff, the "bottom line" involved several decisions. First, students who had verbally threatened teachers would be suspended pending a conference with the administration, student, parent, and teacher, and a conflict resolution session between the teacher and the student. Second, students who received more than five referrals in a quarter would have a PEP or curriculum of responsibility contract developed to assist them in developing improved behavior. Third, all referrals would be returned to the person who initiated the referral and would indicate the action taken by the administrator.

Component 5. Methods for creative a positive school climate and reinforcing students for desirable behavior.

Several major studies, including Rutter, Maughan, Mortimore, Ouston, and Smith's (1979) *Fifteen Thousand Hours* and Mortimore and Sammon's (1987) study on effective elementary schools, suggest that school staff are more effective in obtaining high student achievement and desirable behavior when they find ways to reinforce positive student behavior. Although teachers must be careful not to overemphasize reinforcers and thus imply that learning and positive behavior should be demonstrated in order to earn extrinsic rewards, we can find opportunities to engage students in setting goals and celebrating successes related to positive learning and behavior. The authors have seen numerous examples of such programs. The senior author worked with a middle school where each August, 50 students go on a camping retreat with several administrators, teachers, and counselors in order to set goals for the upcoming school year. Students select a theme for the year (such as "Make all the right moves") and this theme is used to decorate the building and design the school T-shirt, and is incorporated into numerous assemblies and instructional units. The year the theme was "Make all the right moves," the school was decorated with chessboards and playing pieces and students focused on goal setting and making moves that would open possibilities for their future.

Although the authors certainly prefer the type of goal setting and student involvement being used at the middle school described in the previous paragraph, several high schools with whom the senior author works have found student pride

"Mr. Johnson certainly makes no attempt to make this any easier."

and motivation increased by providing students who reach a specified grade-point average, number of days absent, and number of tardies (or who make a designated improvement in one or more of these areas) with a card good for discounts at local stores, restaurants, and recreational facilities. The percentage of discount is determined by the quality of performance or improvement in each of these areas.

Component 6: A problem-solving model that will be taught to staff and students.

It is inevitable that problems will arise whenever large groups of students are involved in exciting and at times demanding and stressful activities. Therefore, a key to an effective schoolwide student management plan is to determine how problems will be resolved. The most effective approach involves two key factors: (1) develop and teach a general model for how individuals in the building will relate to each other and (2) teach specific skills for solving problems or resolving conflicts.

First, the Ladder of Success (Figure 9.4) provides an outstanding general model for how individuals will interact with each other. School rules can be used to support the more specific concepts presented in the Ladder of Success. Second, as discussed in Chapter 10, teaching students either Glasser's problem-solving approach or a conflict management model provides the most effective means to define and implement an approach for solving problems. Again, in elementary schools, this can be facilitated by developing simple cues such as "TALK, WALK, and SQUAWK" to assist students in developing nonaggressive means for solving problems. It is important to keep in mind that, like rules and procedures, these methods will be most effective when they are taught and celebrated in some form of large group assembly and retaught and practiced in the classroom.

Component 7: A format for developing special plans (PEPs) for students who experience ongoing and/or serious behavior problems.

Teachers frequently state that their most serious concern is the few students who display serious and persistent behavior problems. Data from hundreds of schools with whom the senior author has worked indicate that a relatively small percentage of students account for a large percentage of discipline referrals. Therefore, it is imperative that a schoolwide student management plan include a statement about how the school staff will work collaboratively to develop plans to assist these few, but increasing number, of students to develop more acceptable behavior.

As indicated in Chapter 11, the development of personalized education plans is the most effective method for resolving this issue. The creation of such plans is dramatically facilitated by including in the schoolwide student management plan a statement about when such plans will be developed. For example, the plan might state that when a student receives his or her fourth referral within a nine-week period, a team will be convened to develop a PEP. Similarly, a staff might choose to write into their plan that a teacher, counselor, or administrator can instigate the process for convening a PEP meeting for any student for whom they believe a detailed plan is needed.

Component 8: Forms for communicating between teachers, administrators, and parents.

For several reasons, effective communication between all parties involved in working with student behavior problems is an essential ingredient in developing effective plans. First, as discussed in Chapter 2, most students who have persistent or serious behavior problems have become experts at "playing the system." They are adept at finding ways to have others take responsibility for their behavior and at ensuring that all parties involved in dealing with their behavior do not have the same story. Second, since student misbehavior evokes strong emotions in both parents and educators, finger pointing and blaming is more likely to occur in association with discipline issues than with almost any other issue in the school setting.

In order to minimize miscommunication, ineffective and inconsistent responses, and anger over staff responsibilities, it is important that staff develop an instrument for communicating in writing about student behavior and staff's responses to these behaviors. Figures 12.3 and 12.4 provide examples of forms for communicating among staff regarding issues of student behavior.

Component 9: Determining the role of the schoolwide student management committee.

Along with a school improvement team, the most important committee in the school may well be the schoolwide student management committee. The role of this committee is to (1) manage the development and ongoing implementation of the schoolwide student management plan, (2) coordinate dissemination of information about the plan to parents, students, and staff, (3) review data concerning discipline referrals and make a monthly presentation to the staff—including recommendations either for modification of the plan or additional activities to assist students and/or staff in developing skills needed to improve student behavior, and (4) conduct a formal review of the policy at the end of each year and work with the staff to make any necessary modifications for the following year. In discussing the type of data a committee might examine, Duke (1980) suggested the following:

1. Average daily attendance;
2. Average daily illegal absenteeism;
3. Average daily referrals to office;
4. Annual number of suspensions and breakdown according to reason;
5. Breakdown of number and type of student behavior problems;
6. Along with above breakdowns, data on race/ethnicity of students (to determine if a disproportionate number of certain groups of students are being suspended or reported for rule-breaking);

```
                                          Yellow Copy:   Gr. Level Counselor
                                          Pink Copy:     Teacher
                                          Gold Copy:     Main Office

   Student _____  Grade ___  Period ___  Teacher _____

   Step 1
   Describe the specific problem: _____
   _____
   _____


   Step 2
   Summary of step two conference with student __ /__ /__ (Date)
   _____
   _____

   Parent contacted __ /__ /__ (Date)    at _____ AM or PM
   Response _____
   _____


   Step 3
   Referred to administrator on __ /__ /__ (Date)
   Administrative action: __ Conference __ Detention __ Paper __ Suspension
   __ Parent notified __ Parent conference __ /__ /__ (Date)
   _____
   _____

   Counselor contacts were made on __ /__ /__    __ /__ /__ (Dates)
   Summary of counselor contact _____
   _____
   (Office and staff use only—not a part of student's behavioral or cumulative files)
```

FIGURE 12.3
Student Referral
Form

7. Breakdown of punishments applied to students and rate of repeated offenses;
8. Estimates by administrators, counselors, and teachers of time per day spent on discipline-related matters;
9. Breakdown of student behavior problems in special programs (i.e., alternative schools, continuation schools, etc.);
10. Sources of referrals to the office;
11. Comparative data on school discipline from (a) previous years and (b) nearby schools;
12. Number of student behavior problems occurring "in class" and "out of class" (before school, between classes, cafeteria, after school);
13. Number of students in disciplinary difficulty who transferred into the school after regular fall registration. (pp. 68–69)

THE PROCESS FOR DEVELOPING A SCHOOLWIDE STUDENT MANAGEMENT PLAN

The authors' extensive experience and discussions with several consultants who also work with schools to develop effective schoolwide student management plans

Student Name: _____   Teacher: _____
Subject: _____   Period: _____

The student's behavior has become a concern; specifically, the problem(s) is:
_____
_____

Intervention History

Intervention #1   Date: _____
Description of Intervention Attempted: _____
_____
                    Student Signature: _____

Intervention #2   Date: _____
Description of Intervention Attempted: _____
_____
                    Student Signature: _____

*Send back copy to parent after Intervention #2

Intervention #3   Date: _____
Description of Intervention Attempted: _____
_____
                    Student Signature: _____

Evaluation of Intervention Attempts: _____
_____

Office Referral   Date: _____

FIGURE 12.4
Classroom
Intervention
Form (Stanwood
Middle School)

Source: Stanwood Middle School, Stanwood, WA. Reprinted by permission.

suggest that there are five steps in developing or modifying a schoolwide student management plan.

Step 1: Select a committee.

It is most effective to develop a committee whose members represent natural constituent groups in the school. For example, in an elementary school, a committee might consist of one teacher from each grade level, along with the administrator and a counselor or other specialist. In a secondary school, a committee might be comprised of representatives from five or six curriculum areas. It is best for the committee to be comprised of four to eight members, with an administrator always being a member. It is important that the committee include both men and women and be balanced in terms of ethnic makeup. For example, especially when the student population is ethnically diverse, it is important to have a staff member of the same ethnic background as each major group of students. Finally, it is important to include veteran and newer teachers and teachers who represent varied views on student management. The authors have been asked if it is not better to keep people off the committee whose views differ dramatically from the direction the administration and staff appear to be headed. Experience clearly shows that these people have important ideas that need to be shared and that they can be more effectively integrated into a changing model of student management if they are represented in all phases of the discussions. If at least one key leader of those who oppose a change is not part of the drafting group, those who oppose change will most likely feel isolated and will consistently undermine any change. Additionally, the authors have been impressed with the frequency with which such individuals become productive members of the committee and in the end are effective advocates for important change.

The issue is often raised as to whether it is desirable to have parents and students on the drafting committee. Experience suggests that, at least during the early stages, the committee needs to be able to discuss issues that are more personal in nature than is appropriate for students and community members to hear. Staff often need to discuss feelings about lack of support by the administration, problems with the existing document, how colleagues might feel about change, and so on. Although some schools do include parents and students on the drafting group, generally the process will work more smoothly if they form a separate editing group or are assigned to some existing group. If parents and students are to be members of the drafting group, they should be added following several initial meetings of the group.

Step 2: Draft a document.

The next step is for the committee to begin drafting a document. This task is made easier if committee members have access to a variety of examples from schools similar to their own. It makes little sense to reinvent the wheel, and many functional schoolwide student management plans are available as models.

As the committee drafts, it does so using the outline presented in the previous section. Therefore, members would first draft a philosophy statement, next draft a list of rules, followed by key schoolwide behavioral procedures, and so on. It is helpful to have the word *DRAFT* printed on all draft material so colleagues do not misinterpret the draft as a final document.

Step 3: Edit the draft.

The next step is for each committee member to discuss the draft with the staff whom they represent and to work with this group to edit the draft. It is at this point that all staff have an opportunity to give input into the plan and to begin to develop a sense of ownership for it. Experience indicates that by completing the drafting process in small groups of colleagues who are more likely to work together on a regular basis, the discussions are more open and congenial and individuals have a sense of having their ideas heard.

When a section of the document has been edited by each small group, the drafting committee considers all suggestions and develops a revised draft. This draft is then returned to the small groups for approval or additional editing.

Step 4: Approve and celebrate the work.

Once all components of the document have been accepted by the small groups, it is important to present the final draft to the faculty, parents, and students for formal approval and to celebrate the communities' efforts.

Step 5: Communicate the plan.

The final step involves communicating the plan to students and parents. This may occur through an assembly, in advisory groups, in social studies classes, or in some other setting where all students will be reached. In addition, some schools hold special PTA or local school advisory sessions to provide a forum for discussing the new or revised plan. Finally, the plan is usually presented in some fashion at a back-to-school night or other standard function in which a number of parents are likely to be involved.

Staff interested in examining this process in more detail can refer to an excellent set of videotapes developed by Sprick and associates (1992). The tapes and associated manuals help a staff move through a process very similar to that just described. The chapter bibliography includes a reference for this material.

DEVELOPING A SCHOOL PLAN FOR STUDENTS AT RISK FOR SCHOOL FAILURE

A book on working with students at risk for school failure would not be complete without discussing the importance of developing a plan for assisting all students in the school to have a successful school experience. Whether they are called *school improvement plans, school excellence plans, plans for the twenty-first century,* or whatever, the key is to examine changes being considered to increase the percentage of students who make satisfactory progress toward meeting the goals established for high school graduation. The importance of developing such comprehensive plans was highlighted in *Review of Research on Ways to Attain Goal Six: Creating Safe, Disciplined, and Drug-Free Schools.* The writers noted that "it is likely that a disciplined environment will not result from a limited change in a single dimension of a school but rather will result from a multi-year, multi-model approach to change that involves simultaneous attention to curriculum and instruction, school organization, school governance, and social relations in the school" (Aleem & Moles, 1993, p. 19).

One model that is particularly helpful was developed by Segor (1990). Segor suggested that rather than start with questions such as, What are the needs of teenagers who are at risk for school failure? we should ask, What do we believe are the causes of being at risk for school failure? This helps to focus our efforts on matters directly related to school failure rather than areas that are important but tangential to or even the result of school failure. As indicated in Figure 12.5, Segor also suggested that once the key causes have been determined, the next step is to develop specific interventions that address these causes. Finally, he argued that it is essential that school staff develop indicators to determine whether the interventions in fact make a meaningful difference to students' involvement in and success at school.

Another model was created by Jim Slemp, principal at Theodore Roosevelt Middle School in Eugene, Oregon. He and his staff built their program of success for all students by categorizing their efforts as follows: (1) group activities for all students, (2) group activities for selected students, (3) individual activities for stu-

Cause	Interventions	Indicators
Competence	Mastery learning	Direction of grades
	Elimination of C, D, and F	Direction of Achievement
	Dropping pull-outs	Student self-reports
	In-class support	Teacher perceptions
Belonging	Open enrollment activities	Activity census
	Recruitment	Student self-reports
	Family SOPs	Teacher perceptions
	Homebase advisement	
Usefulness	Cooperative learning	Student self-reports
	Service requirement	Teacher perceptions
	Time spent on service	
Potency	Reality therapy	Student self-reports
	Cause and effect emphasis	Teacher perceptions
	Curriculum revisions	Parent perceptions
	Goal setting	

FIGURE 12.5
Cougar Middle School Comprehensive At-Risk Prevention Plan

Source: Reprinted from *The High School Journal,* Vol. 74, No. 1 (October/November 1990). Copyright © The University of North Carolina Press. Reprinted by permission.

dents identified as at risk for school failure, (4) activities for parents of students at risk, (5) orientation and transition programs for students moving into and out of the school, and (6) staff development. Appendix E presents the document developed by this staff and Appendix F presents an outline of the model developed at Monroe Middle School where Jim Slemp had been principal prior to moving to Roosevelt.

SUMMARY

Schoolwide student management is an important issue in many if not most schools. Students make better choices and take greater responsibility for their own behavior in schools that possess a systematic, clear, effectively communicated system for responding to inappropriate student behavior. Likewise, because a teacher's primary role is to provide excellent instruction, teachers need the support of a schoolwide student management system that removes and provides educational interventions for students who continue to disrupt classes when teachers have responsibly instructed and managed the class.

Unfortunately, schools have too often looked for and accepted simplistic, often unproven solutions for responding to unproductive student behavior. This chapter outlines the major components to a systems approach for involving a variety of school staff in accepting their responsibility for responding to disruptive student behavior. In addition, the chapter outlines and presents examples of the major components in an effective schoolwide student management (discipline) plan.

RECOMMENDED READING

Duke, D. (1980). *Managing student behavior problems.* Alexandria, VA: Association for Supervision and Curriculum Development.

Duke, D. (1986). School discipline plans and the quest for order in American schools. In D. Tattum (Ed.), *Management of disruptive pupil behaviour in schools.* New York: John Wiley & Sons.

Emmer, E., & Aussiker, A. (1987, April). *School and classroom discipline programs: How well do they work?* Paper presented at the annual meeting of the American Educational Research Association, Washington, DC.

Garden, J., Zins, J., & Curtis, M. (Eds). (1988). *Alternative educational delivery systems.* Washington, DC: National Association of School Psychologists.

Jones, V. (1984). An administrator's guide to developing and evaluating a building-wide discipline program. *National Association of Secondary School Principals Bulletin, 68,* 60–73.

Segor, R. (1990, October/November). Theory driven assessment for at-risk prevention programs. *High School Journal, 74*(1), 64–72.

Sleeter, C. (Ed.). (1991). *Empowerment through multicultural education.* New York: State University of New York Press.

Sprick, R. (1990). *Playground discipline: Positive approaches for recess supervision. A video inservice program for principals, teachers, and playground supervisors.* Eugene, OR: Teaching Strategies, Inc.

Sprick, R., & Colvin, G. (1992). *Bus discipline: A positive approach.* Eugene, OR: Teaching Strategies, Inc.

Sprick, R., Sprick, M., & Garrison, M. (1992). *Foundations: Establishing positive discipline policies.* Longmont, CO: Sopris West.

An Activity for Teaching the Concept of Learning Differences

The goal of this activity is to have students learn that individuals vary in their ability to complete tasks and that this is indicative of one type of special ability. Students are given the star (shown on the next page) and a small mirror (5" × 7" mirrors work well). The activity is completed in dyads, with one partner being the drawer while the other holds the mirror and holds a piece of paper over the star so the person drawing can see the star only by looking in the mirror. The partners who will be drawing are asked to place their pencil on the character's face at the top of the star and, without lifting their pencil, and staying within the lines, to draw as straight a line as possible around the inside of the star. The partner who is assisting is asked to help his or her partner by moving the mirror as needed to provide a clear view of the star and to listen and watch their partner as he or she completes the task. After most individuals have completed the task, the partners are asked to exchange roles and the other person completes the drawing task.

When both members have completed the task, the teacher can ask students to describe some of what they heard and saw as they observed their partner. The teacher may also want to show examples of drawings that demonstrate that some students found the work easy while others found it very difficult. This can lead into a discussion about how different people find different tasks easier or more difficult. This can be followed by a discussion concerning how people respond to frustration, and that it is the teacher and peers' role to assist anyone who is having difficulty with a task.

Mukilteo School District: Student Rights and Responsibilities

Mukilteo School District Board of Directors views the school as a place to experience academic and social success. Success contributes to positive student self-esteem which in turn translates into positive student behavior. By providing opportunities for students to learn concepts, practice skills and experience academic success, we create an environment which promotes academic and social success.

Our program focuses on developing each student as a competent self-disciplined learner. This requires learning decision-making skills; thus our emphasis is on identifying and defining problem behaviors, problem-solving skills, and prevention measures. These are built within an atmosphere of self-respect, respect for one another, and respect for the learning environment. School District policies, including rights and responsibilities, and student conduct procedures are designed to provide boundaries within which individuals find security, yet freedom to develop self-discipline. Emphasis is placed on positive behaviors, growth and behavior-related consequences. The Board strongly supports the application of the positive approach to discipline. The

Board does not believe in the application of corporal punishment as a disciplinary action. It is important for all persons (i.e., students, teachers, administrators, and parents) to be responsible for their actions.

Students, parents, and all staff must simultaneously work to support the rights of students while helping students accept responsibility for their academic and social growth.

To implement this positive approach to discipline, the Mukilteo school District Board of Directors approves this Student Rights and Responsibilities Handbook as policy of the District.

STUDENT RIGHTS AND RESPONSIBILITIES

The philosophy and policies of Mukilteo School District respect and protect the general rights of all students and parents provided by the Constitution of the United States. In addition, these policies establish certain student rights and corresponding responsibilities within our educational framework.

Students have a right to:
a. A school climate which continually affirms the worth and diversity of all students.
b. Know specific learning expectations in both academic areas and behavior.
c. An environment which expects appropriate high levels of student achievement and high standards for self-management.
d. Opportunities for personal success in academic and social areas.
e. An instructional approach in each class, subject or assignment which varies the time for learning according to the needs of each student and the complexity of the task.

Students have a responsibility to:
a. Behave in such a manner as to reinforce a positive school climate.
b. Strive to meet these specific expectations.
c. Strive for academic achievement and self-management at the highest appropriate level for themselves.
d. Participate fully in opportunities as they arise.
e. Respond in a timely fashion with their highest quality performance on every occasion.

Source: Mukilteo School District, Mukilteo, WA. Reprinted by permission.

Students have a right to:

f. Share with District staff the responsibility for their education.

g. Expect that instructional assignment will be determined directly through assessment of then knowledge and skills.

h. Expect that educational progress will be certified when mastery has been demonstrated.

i. A systematic process for planning and providing instruction appropriate to each student.

j. A system for assessing current student skills/learning prior to instructional assignment.

k. An instructional system where the objectives, instructional materials, and skills tested are aligned.

l. Be provided with correctives, when mastery is not attained, until mastery is attained.

m. A school environment which considers individual differences when providing educational opportunities and when dealing with student behavior, and which does not prescribe automatic consequences for particular forms of misconduct.

n. Students have the right to equal educational opportunity.

o. Students have the right to an environment which is free of any form of harassment.

Students have a responsibility to:

f. Demonstrate the acceptance of this responsibility by active participation in each class, course, and assignment.

g. Perform at the highest possible level within the assessment system.

h. Strive for mastery in all assignments, classes, and courses.

i. Take advantage of all instructional opportunities as they are presented.

j. Perform at the highest possible level.

k. Perform at the highest possible level.

l. Maintain an achievement oriented attitude while in attendance at school.

m. Know school and District rules and adhere to those rules.

n. Students have the responsibility to demonstrate respect for others.

o. Students have the responsibility of not harassing others.

DISTRICT RESPONSIBILITIES

To implement our commitment to the development of student academic and social growth through the process of providing opportunities and developing self-discipline and individual responsibility in a positive way, school district personnel will:

a. Demonstrate respectful and positive attitudes as models for our students to follow;

b. Define and consistently hold high expectations of students, academically and behaviorally;

c. Be consistent and appropriate with students, individually and collectively;

d. Maintain the dignity and self-esteem of students;

e. Promote healthy, helping relationships between students and staff;

f. Use problem-solving skills to resolve conflicts and problems;

g. Deal with issues and observable behaviors only;

h. Create an atmosphere of respect for all;

i. Give students alternatives to develop decision-making skills;

j. Communicate with parents when concerns arise regarding their students;

k. Provide students opportunities for success in academic and social growth;

l. Vary the time for learning for students according to the needs of each student and the complexity of the task;

m. Assess current student skills prior to instructional assignment;

n. Provide correctives when students do not attain mastery;

o. Use the positive approach to discipline to change behavior rather than punishment; and

p. Demonstrate in daily activities a consistent adherence to the District's Equal Educational Opportunity policy.

SCHOOL DISTRICT RULES

The Mukilteo School District believes that students can learn and can be taught to manage their own behavior. With that belief, the District has established three general rules of conduct that guide behavior of students:

Students will respect the rights and property of themselves and others;

Students will behave in such a manner as to create a positive learning environment; and

Students will respect the health and safety of others.

Individual schools and classrooms may develop more specific rules for students. These rules will also be consistent with Board policy and philosophy.

When students do not adhere to these three basic District rules and the rules of their specific building, the District will utilize the positive approach to discipline described herein.

These rules are in effect at all events sponsored by the Mukilteo School District including after school and off campus events.

THE POSITIVE APPROACH

In our endeavor to focus on academic and social growth, staff will follow a process for positively directing students in behavior change. Our goal is to help students to be responsible, self-disciplined individuals.

Involvement Phase

The purpose of the Involvement Phase is to encourage each staff member to analyze his/her behavior as a positive model for students. The development of genuine interest in students and the building of student/teacher rapport is the most critical component of the program.

Students have the right to expect praise, recognition, and open, honest communication at all times. Administrators, teachers, and other district personnel should reflect on how they are perceived by students; whether the relationships they have developed can lead to mutual respect, and ultimately to self-discipline. Staff members should ask the questions: "Am I modeling constructive behavior? Is my behavior effective with individual students? Am I giving individual students proper recognition and praise? Am I being open and honest in my communication with individual students?"

The Redirection Phase

In this Redirection Phase, the student is guided toward:

- Understanding his/her own misconduct or inappropriate behavior;
- Judging why the action was not a good decision, and
- Devising a plan and commitment to behavior change.

Steps in the process might include:

a. Asking the student to acknowledge the *behavior* or misconduct. This checks to see if his/her description matches the staff member's perception.

b. Asking the student if the behavior is against the rules. It is important that the *student* makes the *value* judgment about his/her behavior.

c. Helping the student understand why the behavior is inappropriate and/or unacceptable as well as determine the effect and consequences of his/her behavior.

d. Helping the student *make a plan* and commitment to change that behavior by exploring alternatives to the behavior observed.

The Time-Out Phase

The purpose of the Time-Out Phase is to remove the student from the area or situation where the difficulty is occurring, to direct the student in understanding his/her behavior, and to consider what steps can be followed if the student continues with unacceptable, irresponsible behavior.

If inappropriate behavior continues, the student is separated from the class or school activities until the student offers an acceptable plan to act more responsibly. The intent of this step is not to be punitive but to help the student evaluate his/her own behavior and plan better ways to act in the classroom and/or on campus.

It the student is disruptive when in time-out and/or refuses to plan a better way to behave, he/she will receive assistance in developing an acceptable plan for improvement of behavior in order to return to class/school activities.

Parents are notified of the student's behavior in accordance with building procedures when their student's behavior warrants a time-out.

The sending staff member will have an exit conference with the student to ensure an understanding of the plan for change in behavior. This conference takes place after the student has made some commitment to change behavior in a positive direction. It is also designed to assist the student in focusing upon more appropriate decisions regarding his/her behavior.

If the student cannot control his/her behavior and disrupts the Time-Out, parent(s) will be called to take the student home.

The student may return to school after a parent conference (by telephone or in person, whichever is appropriate for the incident) and the student has made a commitment to follow the District, school, and classroom rules. Upon his/her return, the student remains obligated to complete an acceptable plan and exit conference from Time-Out.

If the student cannot maintain or control his/her behavior at an acceptable level the student stays home until he/she can make a commitment to return and follow rules. Every attempt will be made to enlist the cooperation of the parents again at this point.

The District may pursue more formal discipline procedure if:

a. The student does not make an appropriate commitment to improve his/her behavior;

b. The student behaves in a manner which disrupts the educational process or poses a threat to safety; or

c. The parent's cooperation is lacking.

APPENDIX **C**

Possible Procedures for Common Areas in an Elementary School

PLAYGROUND

GOAL: Students will play safely in all games and on all equipment.

Responsible Playground Behavior:

**1. Rough play is not allowed on the playground.

**2. When the bell rings, students are to stop what they are doing and should line up quickly.

**3. Students will settle differences peacefully using "Stop/Think/Plan" (STP).

4. Students will show respect for others and follow instructions given by staff.

5. Students will stay outside in the morning before school, and during all recesses, unless they have a "pass."

6. Students will stay out of ditches, off hills, and away from puddles and mud.

7. Students will leave rocks, bark, sticks, and other dangerous objects alone.

8. Students will play only on playground areas, not in courtyard, grassy areas, or bushes.

9. Students will show pride in their school by keeping the building and grounds free of litter.

10. Students will take turns on equipment (e.g., 25 swings on swings).

Note: Items marked with ** indicate expectations that students must understand fully and immediately.

Source: Sprick, R. *Responsibility and Discipline Manual: Elementary Sample.* Eugene, OR: Teaching Strategies, Inc. Reprinted by permission.

11. Students will not chew gum and candy on playground.
12. Students will leave knives and other unsafe objects at home along with radios, tape players, hard balls, and toys.
13. Students in grades K–3 will stay off monkey bars until the first bell during the lunch hour.
14. Students will leave the playground immediately after school and not return until after 3:00 P.M.
15. During school, students will not leave the playground for any reason without a note signed by their parent and/or their teacher and the principal. The note must be shown to the person on duty.

RESTROOMS

GOAL: The restrooms at Lincoln Elementary will be clean and safe.

Responsible Hallway Behavior:
**1. Use restrooms during recess, before the last bell rings.
**2. If restrooms must be used during class, students must have a restroom pass.
**3. Use restrooms appropriately and leave them clean.
  4. Put toilet paper in the toilet. Put all other paper in the garbage can.
  5. Flush the toilet.
  6. Leave stalls unlocked after use.
  7. Wash your hands.

HALLS

GOAL: The halls and breezeways will be a safe and quiet environment where people interact with courtesy and respect.

Responsible Hallway Behavior:
**1. Students will move safely through the hallways.
**2. Normal speaking voices will be used in the hallway. (If someone is too far away to hear, move close enough to speak in a normal voice.)
  3. During class time, students must have a signed pass to be in the halls.
  4. Everyone will be treated with respect.
  5. If an adult asks to speak with you, stop and talk with that person.

6. If an adult requests that you correct a behavior, do what the adult asks you to do.
7. No student should be in the halls prior to 8:15 A.M. unless escorted by an adult.
8. Students should go directly home after dismissal from class.

LUNCHROOM

GOAL: The lunch line and lunch area will be a safe and clean environment where people interact with courtesy and respect.

Responsible Cafeteria Behavior:

Coming to Lunch and Lunch Line:
**1. While in line, students will keep hands, feet, and objects to themselves.
**2. Students will use quiet voices in the lunch line.
  3. Students are to be escorted to the lunch area in two lines; "buyers and bringers." Buyers' line is closest to the learning center. Bringers' line is closest to the lunch tables.
  4. Monitors will walk quietly and stand in the lunch monitor line.
  5. Students will buy lunch, milk, or snacks before they sit down.

Lunch Area Procedures:
**1. Students will use quiet voices when talking.
**2. Students will keep hands, feet and objects to themselves.
  3. Students will stay in their seats and raise their hands to get help.
  4. Students will eat quietly and use good manners.
  5. Students will walk in the lunch area.
  6. Everyone will treat others with respect.

Dismissal:
**1. Students will clean up their own area.
**2. When the bell rings, the supervisor will check each table and dismiss students if the table and floor are reasonably clean.
  3. Slow eaters will be reassigned to overflow tables.
  4. When dismissed, students will walk quietly to the north door of the cafeteria.
  5. Lunch boxes will be left in the playground area where classes line up.
  6. Students are to remain on the playground unless they are given a pass to enter the building.

ASSEMBLIES

GOAL: Lincoln students will demonstrate respectful behavior during assemblies by listening, participating and following directions.

Responsible Assembly Behavior:

**1. When the leader goes to the microphone and says, "May I have your attention please," stop talking and look at the person at the microphone.

**2. Listen carefully.

3. Students will follow their teacher's directions regarding where to sit.

4. Everyone will wait quietly for the program to begin. Quiet talking will be allowed until the program is ready to begin.
5. Communicate with the performers with your eyes and ears.
6. Never boo, whistle, yell, or put someone down.
7. At the end of the program, the leader will conclude the assembly by thanking the performers.
8. Students will remain seated until the teacher gives them the signal to stand and follow the teacher from the assembly area.

APPENDIX D

Responsibilities for Student Behavior

The Student Has the Responsibility to:

1. Participate in learning and complete classroom assignments on time.
2. Respect the rights, feelings, and property of everyone.
3. Follow classroom and school expectations.
4. Follow the directions of all staff members, guests, and substitutes.
5. Come to class on time and prepared.
6. Settle conflicts in a nonviolent way.
7. Keep our school clean.
8. Be courteous, responsible, and act in a safe manner.
9. Read and understand the *Student's Rights and Responsibility Handbook*.

Students have the right to express their concerns through their parents or by getting an appointment with the school counselor or an administrator.

Parents and/or guardians are encouraged to participate with the George Middle School staff in the education of our students. With the cooperation and support of the home, the school can effectively help a student reach his or her fullest potential.

The Home Can Support Their Child's Success in School by Taking the Responsibility to:

1. Understand and support GMS student behavior expectations and consequences.
2. Encourage a positive attitude toward learning.
3. Encourage school success by ensuring attendance and conformance with the rules and regulations of the school and school district as required by law.
4. Communicate with the school when they anticipate or see a student learning problem and/or behavior problem developing.

Source: George Middle School, Portland, Oregon. Reprinted by permission.

5. Respond in a cooperative and timely manner with the school and staff members in working to solve and/or modify student behavior.

6. Read and discuss the GMS discipline plan and the *Student's Rights and Responsibilities Handbook* with your student.

The Teacher Has the Responsibility to:

1. Teach, model, review, post, and enforce the expectations of the school and individual classroom.
2. Maintain a positive learning environment.
3. Implement and document a minimum of three intervention actions such as having a problem-solving conference with students, writing behavior plans, notifying parents, classroom consequences, referral to conflict managers, and/or curriculum modification prior to writing a referral (except in extreme cases).
4. Seek assistance from available building resources whenever established classroom procedures are not effective with individual students and/or within certain classroom situations.
5. Maintain a place in his or her classroom where students can be timed-out in an alternative place in another classroom. A time-out will include a problem-solving component.
6. Develop a problem-solving form for use by student in time-out. This form will also serve as documentation.
7. Request a staffing when the above interventions have not been successful.

Referrals Administrative Staff Will Respond to:

1. Staff referrals, following required teacher interventions for continual classroom problems (i.e., defiance of authority and chronic rule violation poor behavior choices in common areas).
2. Fighting, and/or assault.*
3. Weapons, explosives, dangerous objects.**
4. Serious or chronic threats or harassment of peers.*
5. Skipping class or school.
6. Leaving school without permission.
7. Vandalism.
8. Smoking or chewing tobacco.

9. Under the influence use, transfer, sale or possession of alcohol, drugs, or drug paraphernalia.**
10. Battery committed toward a staff member. If investigation shows a student committed battery on a teacher and the teacher so recommends, the student will not be returned to said teacher's classroom.**
11. Using abusive language directed toward a staff member.*

The Student Management Specialist Has the Responsibility to:

1. Provide appropriate, consistent intervention consequences as identified in the level of consequences.
2. Communicate staff/student/parent responsibilities effectively and consistently.
3. Help monitor at-risk students and/or students who chronically misbehave.
4. Demonstrate a leadership role in establishing staffings and initiating personalized education plans.
5. Provide clear feedback to staff and parents.
6. Follow district policy, as well as state and federal laws.
7. Be a member of the school disciplinary committee and participate in the planning and implementation of student, staff, and parent discipline instructional activities.
8. Mediate conflicts between students or between student and teachers.
9. Assist teachers by visiting classrooms to provide consultation regarding problems with individual students or groups of students.

Administrative responses will be consistent with district policy as stated in the *Students Rights and Responsibility Handbook* and will emphasize teaching students new skills for resolving the problems that led to a student management referral.

Administrative Responses to Discipline Referrals:

1. Counsel with student.
2. Notify parent or guardian.
3. Assign one or more days of noon detention.
4. Assign one or more days of after-school detention.

---

*The teacher has the option of removing the student from class immediately.

**The student should be immediately removed from the classroom and/or school until an investigation is conducted.

5. Arrange for student to see the counselor, the student services specialist, or the drug and alcohol counselor.
6. Refer to conflict manager program.
7. Assign one or more days of in-school suspension.
8. Implement and monitor a trip card.
9. Develop and implement a student contract.
10. Develop and implement a personalized education program.
11. Arrange for a staffing.*
12. Arrange a conference with parent, student, and teacher.*
13. Change student's schedule.
14. Deny student involvement in school activities.
15. Invoke minor suspension.
16. Invoke major suspension.
17. Refer student for alternative placement.

The Principal Has the Responsibility to:

1. Facilitate and lead in the establishment of a consistent school student management plan.
2. Provide for yearly staff review of the school discipline plan prior to June 1 and make necessary revisions.
3. Distribute copies of school discipline plan to staff, parents, and students by the second week of school.
4. Provide funding for discipline program activities in the school budget.
5. Facilitate the planning and implementation of student, staff, and parent discipline instructional activities.
6. Approve individual teacher's classroom expectations.
7. Be a member of the school discipline committee.
8. Select appropriate consequences, which may include administrative staffings, for students who have committed major violations.
9. Protect the due process rights of those involved in disciplinary matters.
10. Communicate effectively with students, staff members, and parents.
11. Represent the school's position regarding all disciplinary matters.

12. Follow district policy and guidelines, state and federal laws, and keep staff advised of changes.
13. Provide an opportunity for review of discipline decisions.

The Counselor, Student Services Specialist and Drug and Alcohol Counselor will respond to:

Behaviors
1. Attendance problems
2. Academic performance
3. Lack of materials
4. Family concerns
5. Peer problems
6. Conflicts (student/student or student/teacher)
7. Suspected physical/sexual/emotional abuse
8. Suspected chemical use or abuse
9. Needs of students dealing with personal issues

Actions
1. Conduct individual student conferences.
2. Assist in or initiate parent contacts or conferences.
3. Consult with teachers.
4. Assist in or initiate meetings for at-risk students (may include teachers, support staff, administrators, parents, agency representatives).
5. Referral for special education.
6. Referral for alternative education.
7. Referral to outside agency or services.
8. Referral to support groups.
9. Referral to conflict managers.
10. Assist in student/student or student/teacher mediation.
11. Implement and/or monitor student contracts and trip cards.
12. Assist in administering District Drug and Alcohol Discipline Policy.
13. Prepare, consult on, or teach lessons to target specific areas of behavioral expectations (attendance, school rules, etc.).
14. Provide clear feedback to staff and parents.

---

*Should a parent meeting be necessary, teachers will be given one workday notice by the administrative staff. Teachers may request representation at the meeting if it appears a complaint is being made that could result in disciplinary action toward the teacher. A teacher may request that a conference be held between the teacher, the student and/or the parent, and the administrative staff representative prior to the student returning to class or within a reasonable time thereafter when all needed parties are available. This conference will be done without disrupting the teacher's class instruction time.

Roosevelt Middle School Plan for Students At Risk

GROUP ACTIVITIES FOR ALL STUDENTS

Group activities for all students should be designed to create a positive school atmosphere which is necessary for all students to have success. These types of activities should reflect a commitment by school staff to provide a more personalized environment for all students. The activities should also provide an opportunity for the staff to determine the needs of identified at risk students and to become aware of additional students who were not identified.

The following are examples of activities that could form the foundation for the development of an at risk program but should not be considered as the complete program.

Who:
- Trained school personnel such as regular classroom teachers, counselors, administrators, or outside consultants.
- All students in the school.

What:

Sample Activities:
- Teachers use a variety of teaching strategies in all classes
- Youth Service Program
- Staff Agreement regarding IEP students in regular classes
- TAG Program
- Mini-classes
- Conferences
- Refusal Skills Training
- Positive Recognition Program
- Curriculum structure appropriate for age level
- Summer Visitation Program
- Notes and calls home
- Mentorship Program

- Displays of students' work
- Student Leadership Plan
- Variety of special events and Guide activities
- Student responsibilities within school setting

Activities like these could take place in the following types of groups:

- Regular classes
- Advisor/advisee groups
- Counseling groups
- Interest groups (before, during, and after school)
- Informal groups at break, lunch, etc.
- Choice of classes
- Increased amount of heterogeneous classes
- School racial harassment policy

GROUP ACTIVITIES FOR SELECTED STUDENTS

Group activities for selected students should be designed to provide opportunities for class involvement with at-risk students in a caring environment.

Who:
- Selected teachers, administrators, teacher aides, parents, classified, senior citizens, volunteers, and peer tutors.
- Those involved should be both responsive to the needs of at risk students and trained in working with them.
- Identified at risk students based on building screening process.

What:

Sample Activities or Approaches:
- Informal lunches by invitation
- Special-interest groups based on student interest (before school, after school, lunch or break)

Source: Jim Slemp, Principal, Roosevelt Middle School, Eugene, OR. Reprinted by permission.

- Counselor-led groups (both on staff and community)
- Academic skills classes
  a. Writing/Science lab
  b. Continuous Progress Program in Reading and Math
  c. Study Skills class
  d. Skills Center
- Bridge the Gap class
- Homework Club
- Transportation support

INDIVIDUAL ACTIVITIES FOR IDENTIFIED AT-RISK STUDENTS

Individual activities for identified at-risk students should be designed to facilitate a sense of belonging (someone cares) and to strengthen belief in oneself.

Who:

- Selected teachers, administrators, teacher aides, parents, classified, senior citizens, volunteer, and peer tutors.
- Those involved should be both responsive to the needs of at-risk students and trained in working with them.
- Identified at-risk students based on building screening process.

What:

Sample Activities or Approaches:
- Mentor Program
- Spotlight-a-Student (biographical information posted in staff room, encourage extra support, hugs, etc.)
- Encourage informal out of class involvement with at risk students (legitimize staff member leaving school with students)
- Take students on special trips
- Provide connections with minority organizations within the community
- Encourage after school activities
- Student mentors (peer counseling and peer tutoring programs)

- Tutoring—cross-grade level
- Monitor and update at-risk profile sheets
- Disseminate useful information to staff when child is at risk (color code to heighten sensitivity to confidential information or use sealed envelopes)
- Have staffings on every at-risk student
- Positions or responsibility within the school
- Counselor one-to-one contacts
- Information library for substance abuse issues
- Have money available for basic needs
- Impact Program
- D.A.R.T training

ACTIVITIES FOR PARENTS OF AT-RISK STUDENTS

Activities for parents of at-risk students should be designed to provide a connection between the home and the school which will encourage parents to support their children.

Who:

- School staff (administrators, counselors, teachers, classified, mentors), at-risk coordinator, community school coordinator, home/school worker, consultants.
- Parents of identified students

What:

Sample Activities:
- Parenting skills classes—during the day and in the evening
- Home/school visits
- Social worker services
- Communication from mentors
- Conference times available in the evening
- Parent workshops on age appropriate issues
- Newsletter articles
- Parent breakfast and visitations (special invitations)
- 8–5 school day

Components of the Monroe Middle School Plan for Students At Risk for School Failure

PHILOSOPHY AND GOALS

At Monroe Middle School we are committed to provide for the success of all students. Failing to meet the needs of any student, by default, is a failure for all. For an increasing number of students, schools and teachers make the difference between their success and failure. These students we define as being *at-risk*.

Providing for the opportunity for all students to succeed is the only way for a school to achieve excellence. To achieve this kind of excellence requires special understanding and extra time and effort with the at-risk student.

To meet our commitment to provide success for our students, we intend to focus on the following goals. These goals are the basis of the programs and activities described in the rest of this plan. Our entire program focuses on meeting the needs of our students, but the specific programs described in this document will be coordinated by our administrators and counselor in such a way as to particularly focus on at-risk students.

1. To improve the self-esteem of all students.
2. To provide a program where students feel a sense of belonging and success.
3. To provide for students' academic success realizing that to do this we must concern ourselves with those social and psychological factors that largely control the ability or readiness to achieve academically.
4. To work with parents in an effort to increase students' success in school.
5. To seek additional time and resources for staff allocation and budgeting.
6. To increase the quality of at-risk students' lives and potential for their futures.

7. To join with the community at large to work for the success of at-risk students.
8. To develop a closely monitored system for coordination of programs within our school community and the community at large for at-risk students.

Selected Program Components

1. Guide groups that include a study skills curriculum, notebook monitoring, community projects, etc.
2. A mentor program that encourages staff to serve as a mentor for a student experiencing ongoing school difficulties.
3. Homework assignments given only on Friday, Tuesday, and Thursday, with teachers being available before school on Monday, Wednesday, and Friday to provide students with assistance on homework.
4. Continuous progress monitoring in math and reading for all students.
5. A peer tutoring program.
6. Mini-classes to provide short-term high-interest learning experiences.
7. The use of a "K" grade—"a grade that can be awarded to those students who, in the judgment of the teacher, are working to the best of their abilities, but have fallen below a grade average of 'C' In a noncontinuous progress class. By awarding a passing grade rather than a 'D' or 'F,' we hope to communicate to the student and parent(s) that we appreciate and applaud the student's sustained efforts to do his/her best work commensurate with his/her ability."
8. Weekly attendance staffings for students absent 5 out of any 20 school days.

Source: James Monroe Middle School, Eugene, OR. Reprinted by permission.

9. A variety of incentive and reward programs.
10. An extensive drug and alcohol program.
11. Teachers "shadow" students for a day and report on their perception of how it felt to be a student.
12. Home visits for all incoming sixth graders and all new students.
13. A student "buddy"/guide program for all new students.
14. Followup interviews with new students at the end of the first, second, and sixth weeks and with their parents after the first two weeks.
15. A focus on heterogeneous grouping in all block classes with an emphasis on adjusting assignments to students' ability levels.
16. A 5-day summer day camp for 20 at-risk entering sixth graders to give them a head start on school.
17. Weekly and daily academic and behavior monitoring for students who benefit from this added structure.
18. Team meetings include an agenda item focusing on individual students needing special assistance.
19. An "Attendance Club"—a weekly support group for students experiencing attendance problems.
20. In-school suspension utilized whenever possible in lieu of out-of-building suspension.
21. Extensive home contacts concerning students' positive progress.
22. A parenting class to teach parents basic parenting skills.
23. A home-school liaison staff member.
24. Twice yearly parent-student-staff breakfast.
25. Extensive programs for transitioning students from elementary to middle school and from middle school to high school.

Adams, R., & Biddle, B. (1970). *Realities of teaching: Explorations with videotape.* New York: Holt, Rinehart and Winston.

Aiello, J., & Jones, S. (1971). Field study of the proxemic behavior of young school children in three subcultural groups. *Journal of Personality and Social Psychology, 19,* 351–356.

Aikin, M. (1942). *The story of the eight-year study, Vol. 1.* New York: Harper and Row.

Akita, J., & Mooney, C. (1982). *Natural helpers: A peer support program.* Seattle, WA: Roberts and Associates.

Alberto, P., & Troutman, A. (1986). *Applied behavior analysis for teachers: Influencing student performance* (2nd ed.). Columbus, OH: Charles E. Merrill.

Aleem, D., & Moles, O. (1993). *Review of research on ways to attain goal six: Creating safe, disciplined, and drug-free schools.* Washington, DC: OERI.

American Association of University Women Educational Foundation. (1992). *The AAUW report: How schools shortchange girls.* Washington, DC: National Education Association.

American Council on Education and Education Commission of the States. (1988). *One-third of a nation.* Washington, DC: Author.

Anderson, C. (1982). The search for school climate: A review of the research. *Review of Educational Research, 52,* 368–420.

Anderson, C. (1985). The investigation of school climate. In G. Austin & H. Garber (Eds.), *Research on exemplary schools.* New York: Academic Press.

Anderson, L., Brubaker, N., Alleman-Brooks, J., & Duffy, G. (1984). *Making seatwork work* (Research Series No. 142). East Lansing: Michigan State University, Institute for Research on Training.

Anderson, L., Evertson, C., & Brophy, J. (1979). An experimental study of effective teaching in first grade reading groups. *Elementary School Journal, 79,* 193–223.

Anderson, L., & Prawat, R. (1983). Responsibility in the classroom: A synthesis of research on teaching self-control. *Educational Leadership, 12,* 62–66.

Angus, M. J., Evans, K. W., & Parkin, B. (1975). *An observational study of selected pupil and teacher behavior in open plan and conventional design classrooms.* Australian Open Area Project (Tech. Rep. No. 4). Perth: Educational Department of Western Australia.

Ashcroft, L. (1987). Defusing "empowerment": The what and the why. *Language Arts, 64,* 142–156.

Asher, S., & Markell, R. (1974). Sex differences in comprehension of high- and low-interest reading material. *Journal of Educational Psychology, 66,* 680–687.

Ashwick. H. (1987, April). Public school teacher perspectives on school discipline. *OERI Bulletin.* Washington, DC: U.S. Department of Education, Office of Educational Research and Improvement.

Aspy, D., & Roebuck, R. (1977). *Kids don't learn from people they don't like.* Amherst, MA: Human Resource Development Press.

Axline, V. (1947). *Play therapy.* Boston, Houghton Mifflin.

Bandura, A. (1969). *Principles of behavior modification.* New York: Holt, Rinehart and Winston.

Bandura, A. (1977). *Soocial learning theory.* Englewood Cliffs, NJ: Prentice Hall.

Banks, J. (1988). *Multiethnic education: Theory and practice.* Boston: Allyn and Bacon.

Banks, J., & McGee Banks, C. (1993). *Multicultural education: Issues and perspectives* (2nd ed.). Boston: Allyn and Bacon.

Barrish, H., Saunders, M., & Wolf, M. (1969). Good behavior game: Effects of individual contingencies for group consequences on disruptive behavior in a classroom. *Journal of Applied Behavior Analysis, 2,* 119–124.

Bastian, L., & Taylor, B. (1991). *School crime: A national crime victimization survey report.* Washington, DC: U.S. Department of Justice, Bureau of Justice Statistics.

Bauer, E. (1973). Personal space: A study of blacks and whites. *Sociometry, 36,* 402–408.

Becker, W., Engelmann, S., & Thomas, D. (1975). *Teaching 1: Classroom management.* Champaign, IL: Research Press.

Belenky, M., Clinchy, B., Goldberger, N., & Tarule, J. (1986). *Women's ways of knowing: Development of self, body and mind.* New York: Basic Books.

Bell, C. (1985). *Explaining the progressively decreasing scores on Comprehensive Tests of Basic Skills (CTBS) of the school children of the District of Columbia Public Schools as they progress from elementary school into high school.* Alexandria, VA: ERIC Document Reproduction Service, ED 226 234.

Bennett, C. (1986). *Comprehensive multicultural education* Boston: Allyn and Bacon.

Berliner, D. (1979). Tempus educare. In P. Peterson and H. Walberg (Eds.), *Research on teaching: Concepts, findings and implications.* Berkeley, CA: McCutchan.

Berliner, D. (1984). The half-full glass: A review of research on teaching. In P. Hosford (Ed.), *Using what we know about teaching.* Alexandria, VA: Association for Supervision and Curriculum Development.

Bernard, H. (1973). *Child development and learning.* Boston: Allyn and Bacon.

Blackham, G., & Silberman, A. (1975). *Modification of child and adolescent behavior.* Belmont, CA: Wadsworth.

Blase, J. (1986). A qualitative analysis of sources of teacher stress. *American Educational Research, 23,* 13–40.

Bloom, B. (Ed.). (1956). *Taxonomy of educational objectives, handbook I: Cognitive domain.* New York: David McKay.

Bolstad, O., & Johnson, S. (1972). Self-regulation in the modification of disruptive classroom behavior. *Journal of Applied Behavior Analysis, 5,* 433–454.

Borg, W. (1980). Time and school learning. In C. Denham & A. Lieberman (Eds.), *Time to learn.* Washington, DC: National Institute of Education.

Boyer, E. (1983). *High school: A report on secondary education in America.* New York: Harper and Row.

Broden, M., Hall, R., & Mitts, B. (1971). The effect of self-recording on the classroom behavior of two eighth-grade students. *Journal of Applied Behavior Analysis, 4,* 191–199.

Bronfenbrenner, U. (1970). *Two worlds of childhood: U.S. and U.S.S.R.* New York: Russell Sage.

Brophy, J. (1981). Teacher praise: A functional analysis. *Review of Educational Research, 51,* 5–32.

Brophy, J. (1982). Classroom management and learning. *American Education, 18,* 20–23.

Brophy, J. (1983). Research on the self-fulfilling prophecy and teacher expectations. *Journal of Educational Psychology, 75,* 631–661.

Brophy, J. (1986a, April). *Teacher effects research and teacher quality.* Paper presented at the annual meeting of the American Educational Research Association, San Francisco.

Brophy, J. (1986b, April). *Socializing students' motivation to learn.* Paper presented at the annual meeting of the American Educational Research Association, San Francisco.

Brophy, J. (1987). Synthesis of research on strategies for motivating students to learn. *Educational Leadership, 45,* 40–48.

Brophy, J., & Evertson, C. (1976). *Learning from teaching: A developmental perspective.* Boston: Allyn and Bacon.

Brophy, J., & Good, T. (1971). Teacher's communication of differential expectations for children's classroom performance: Some behavior data. *Journal of Educational Psychology, 61,* 365–374.

Brophy, J., & Good, T. (1974). *Teacher-student relationships: Causes and consequences.* New York: Holt, Rinehart and Winston.

Brophy, J., Rohrkemper, M., Rashid, H., & Goldberger, M. (1983). Relationships between teacher's presentations of classroom tasks and students' engagement in those tasks. *Journal of Educational Psychology, 75,* 544–552.

Bryan, J., & Locke, E. (1967). Goal setting as a means to increase motivation. *Journal of Applied Psychology, 51,* 274–277.

Burger, H. (1972). Ethno-lematics: Evoking "shy" Spanish-American pupils by cross-cultural mediation. *Adolescence, 6,* 61–76.

Burrows, C. (1973). *The effects of a mastery learning strategy on the geometry achievement of fourth and fifth grade children.* Unpublished doctoral dissertation, Indiana University.

Bush, R. (1954). *The teacher-pupil relationship.* Englewood Cliffs, NJ: Prentice Hall.

Butler, J. (1993). *Transforming the curriculum: Teaching about women of color.* In J. Banks & C. McGee Banks (Eds.), *Multicultural education.* Boston: Allyn and Bacon.

Butler, K. (1984). Working your curriculum with style. *Challenge, 2,* 38–42.

Butler, R., & Nisan, M. (1986). Effects of no feedback, task-related comments, and grades on intrinsic motivation and performance. *Journal of Educational Psychology, 78,* 210–216.

Cahoon, P. (1988). Mediator magic. *Educational Leadership, 45,* 93–94.

Canter, L. (1976). *Assertive discipline.* Los Angeles: Lee Canter Associates.

Carnegie Council on Adolescent Development. (1989). *Turning points: Preparing American youth for the 21st century.* Washington, DC: Author.

Carpenter, R., & Apter, S. (1988). Research integration of cognitive-emotional interventions for behaviorally disordered children and youth. In M. Wang, M. Reynolds, & H. Walberg (Eds.), *Handbook of special education: Research and practice* (pp. 155–169). New York: Pergamon.

Chalfant, J. (1983). *Identifying LD students: Guidelines for decision making.* (ERIC Document Reproduction Service No. ED 258390).

Chalfant, J., VanDusgen Pysh, M., & Moultrie, R. (1979). Teacher assistance teams: A model for within-building problem solving. *Learning Disability Quarterly, 2,* 85–96.

Chamberlain, D. (1942). *Did they succeed in college?* (Vol. 4). New York: Harper & Row.

Coats, W., & Smidchens, U. (1966). Audience recall as a function of speaker dynamism. *Journal of Educational Psychology, 57,* 189–191.

Coleman, J. (1966). *Equality of educational opportunity.* Washington, DC: U.S. Department of Health, Education and Welfare, Office of Education.

Collins, K. (1971). A strategy for mastery learning in modern mathematics. In J. Block (Ed.), *Mastery learning: Theory and practice.* New York: Holt, Rinehart and Winston.

Combs, A., & Taylor, C. (1952). The effect of the perception of mild degrees of threat on performance. *Journal of Abnormal and Social Psychology, 47,* 420–424.

Cooper, H., & Good, T. (1983). *Pygmalion grows up.* New York: Longman.

Cooperman, M. (1975). Field-dependence and children's problem-solving under varying contingencies of predetermined feedback. *Dissertation Abstracts International, 35,* 2040–2041.

Coopersmith, S. (1967). *The antecedents of self-esteem.* San Francisco: W. H. Freeman.

Cormany, R. (1975). *Guidance and counseling in Pennsylvania: Status and needs.* Lemoyne, PA: ESEA Title II Project, West Shore School District.

Corno, L. (1979). A hierarchical analysis of selected naturally occurring aptitude-treatment interactions in the third grade. *American Educational Research Journal, 16,* 391–409.

Costello, C. (1964). Ego-involvement, success and failure: A review of the literature. In H. J. Eysenck (Ed.), *Experiment in motivation.* New York: Macmillan.

Covington, M., & Beery, R. (1976). *Self-worth and school learning.* New York: Holt, Rinehart and Winston.

Covington, M., Spratt, M., & Omelich, C. (1980). Is effort enough, or does diligence count too? Student and teacher reactions to effort stability in failure. *Journal of Educational Psychology, 72,* 717–729.

Currence, C. (1984, February 29). School performance tops list of adolescent worries. *Education Week, 3,* 8.

Curwin, R., & Fuhrmann, B. (1975). *Discovering your teaching self: Humanistic approaches to effective teaching.* Englewood Cliffs, NJ: Prentice Hall.

Curwin, R., & Mendler, A. (1988). *Discipline with dignity.* Reston, VA: Association for Supervision and Curriculum Development.

Daum, J. (1972). *Proxemics in the classroom: Speaker-subject distance and educational performance.* Paper presented at the annual meeting of the Southeastern Psychological Association.

Davidson, H., & Lang, G. (1960). Children's perceptions of their teachers' feelings toward them. *Journal of Experimental Education, 29,* 109–118.

DeCharms, R. (1976). *Enhancing motivation.* New York: Irvington.

DeCharms, R. (1984). Motivation in educational settings. In R. Amos & C. Ames (Eds.), *Research on motivation in education, Vol. I: Student motivation.* New York: Academic Press.

Deci, E. (1971). Effects of externally mediated rewards on intrinsic motivation. *Journal of Personality and Social Psychology, 18,* 105–115.

Deci, E. (1972). The effects of contingent and noncontingent rewards and controls on intrinsic motivation, *Organizational Behavior and Human Performance, 8,* 217–229.

Deal, E., Nezlek, J., & Sheinman, L. (1981). Characteristics of the rewarder and intrinsic motivation of the rewardee. *Journal of Personality and Social Psychology, 40,* 1–10.

Delefes, P., & Jackson, B. (1972). Teacher-pupil interaction as a function of location in the classroom. *Psychology in the Schools, 9,* 119–123.

Denham, C., & Lieberman, A. (Eds.). (1980). *Time to learn.* Washington, DC: National Institute of Education.

Diaz-Rico, L. (1993). From monocultural to multicultural teaching in an inner-city middle school. In A. Woolfolk (Ed.), *Readings and cases in educational psychology.* Boston: Allyn and Bacon.

DiGangi, S., & Maag, J. (1992). A component analysis of self-management training with behaviorally disordered youth. *Behavioral Disorders, 17,* 281–290.

Dorman, G. (1981). *Middle grades assessment program.* Chapel Hill, NC: Center for Early Adolescence.

Doyle, W. (1983). Academic work, *Review of Educational Research, 53,* 159–199.

Doyle, W. (1984). How order is achieved in classrooms. *Journal of Curriculum Studies, 16,* 259–277.

Doyle, W. (1986). Classroom organization and management. In M. C. Wittrock (Ed.), *Handbook of research on teaching* (3rd ed.). New York: Macmillan.

Drabman, R., & Lahey, B. (1974). Feedback in classroom behavior modification: Effects on the target child and her classmates. *Journal of Applied Behavior Analysis, 7,* 591–598.

Drabman, R., Spitalnik, R., & O'Leary, K. (1973). Teaching self-control to disruptive children. *Journal of Abnormal Psychology, 82,* 10–16.

Dreikurs, R., & Cassel, P. (1972). *Discipline without tears: What to do with children who misbehave.* New York: Hawthorn.

Dreikurs, R., Grunwald, B., & Pepper, F. (1971). *Maintaining sanity in the classroom: Illustrated teaching techniques.* New York: Harper and Row.

Dreikurs, R., Grunwald, B., & Pepper, F. (1982). *Maintaining sanity in the classroom: Classroom management techniques* (2nd ed.). New York: Harper and Row.

Druian, G., & Butler, J. (1987). *Effective schooling and at-risk youth: What the research shows.* Portland, OR: Northwest Regional Educational Laboratory.

Dryfoos, J. (1990). *Adolescents at risk: Prevalence and prevention.* New York: Oxford University Press.

Duckworth, E. (1964). Piaget rediscovered. In R. E. Ripple & V. N. Rockcastle (Eds.), *Piaget rediscovered: A report of the conference on cognitive skills and curriculum development.* Ithaca, NY: Cornell University, School of Education.

Duke, D. (1980). *Managing behavior problems.* New York: Columbia University Teachers College Press.

Duke, D. (1986). School discipline plans and the quest for order in American schools. In D. Tattum (Ed.), *Management of disruptive pupil behaviour in schools.* New York: John Wiley & Sons.

Duke, D., & Jones, V. (1984). Two decades of discipline—Assessing the development of an educational specialization. *Journal of Research and Development in Education, 17,* 25–35.

Dunn, K., & Dunn, R. (1987). Dispelling outmoded beliefs about student learning. *Educational Leadership, 44,* 55–62.

Dunn, R. (1983). Learning style and its relation to exceptionality at both ends of the spectrum. *Exceptional Children, 49,* 496–506.

Dunn, R., Beaudry, J., & Klavas, A. (1989). Survey of research on learning styles. *Educational Leadership, 46,* 50–58.

Dunn, R., Cavanaugh, D., Eberle, B., & Lenhausem, R. (1982). Hemispheric preference: The newest element of learning style. *American Biology Teacher, 44,* 291–294.

Durkin, D. (1981). Reading comprehension instruction in five basal reader series. *Reading Research Quarterly, 16,* 515–544.

Dweck, C. (1975). The role of expectations and attributions in the alleviation of learned helplessness. *Journal of Personality and Social Psychology, 31,* 674–685.

Ebbeck, M. (1984). Equality for boys and girls: Some important issues. *Early Childhood Development and Care, 18,* 119–131.

Eccles, J., & Wigfield, A. (1985). Teacher expectations and student motivation. In J. Dusek, V. Hall, & W. Meyer (Eds.), *Teacher expectancies.* Hillsdale, NJ: Erlbaum.

Edmonds, P. (April 4, 1994). 1 million victims and counting. *USA Today.*

Eisner, E. (1984). Can educational research inform educational practice? *Phi Delta Kappan, 65,* 447–452.

Elem, S., Rose, L., & Gallup, A. (1992). The 24th Annual Gallup/Phi Delta Kappa Poll of the public's attitudes toward the public schools. *Phi Delta Kappan, 74,* 41–53.

Elkind, D. (1967). Egocentrism in adolescence. *Child Development, 38,* 1025–1034.

Elkind, D. (1981). *The hurried child: Growing up too fast too soon.* Reading, MA: Addison-Wesley.

Emmer, E. (1994, April). *Teacher emotions and classroom management.* Paper presented at the annual meeting of the American Educational Research Association, New Orleans, LA.

Emmer, E., & Aussiker, A. (1987, April). *School and classroom discipline programs: How well do they work?* Paper presented at the annual meeting of the American Educational Research Association, Washington, DC.

Emmer, E., Evertson, C., & Anderson, L. (1980). Effective management at the beginning of the school year. *Elementary School Journal, 80,* 219–231.

Emmer, E., Evertson, C., Sanford, J., Clements, B., & Worsham, M. (1981). *Organizing and managing the junior high school classroom.* Austin, TX: Research and Development Center for Teacher Education.

Englander, M. (1982). Teacher management of classroom misbehavior. In J. Harris & C. Bennett (Eds.), *Student discipline.* Bloomington: University of Indiana.

Englander, M. (1986). *Strategies for classroom discipline.* New York: Praeger.

Epanchin, B. C., & Paul, J. (1982). *Casebook for educating the emotionally disturbed.* Columbus, OH: Charles E. Merrill.

Epstein, M., Hallahan, D., & Kauffman, J. (1975). Implications of the reflectivity-impulsivity dimension for special education. *Journal of Special Education, 9,* 11–25.

Erikson, E. (1963). *Childhood and society* (2nd ed.). New York: Norton.

Erikson, E. (1968). *Identity, youth, and crisis.* New York: Norton.

Evertson, C. (1985). Training teachers in classroom management: An experimental study in secondary school classrooms. *Journal of Educational Research, 79,* 51–58.

Evertson, C. (1989). Improving elementary classroom management: A school-based training program for beginning the year. *Journal of Educational Research, 83,* 82–90.

Evertson, C., & Emmer, E. (1982a). Effective management at the beginning of the school year in junior high school classes. *Journal of Educational Psychology, 74,* 485–498.

Evertson, C., & Emmer, E. (1982b). Preventive classroom management. In D. Duke (Ed.), *Helping teachers manage classrooms.* Alexandria, VA: Association for Supervision and Curriculum Development.

Evertson, C., Emmer, E., Sanford, J., & Clements, B. (1983). Improving classroom management: An experiment in elementary school classrooms. *Elementary School Journal, 84,* 173–188.

Feather, N. (Ed.). (1982). *Expectations and actions.* Hillsdale, NJ: Erlbaum.

Feitler, F., & Tokar, E. (1992). Getting a handle on teacher stress: How bad is the problem? *Educational Leadership, 49,* 456–458.

Ferrell, J. (1971). The differential performance of lower class, preschool, Negro children as a function of sex of E, sex of S, reinforcement condition, and level of field dependency. *Dissertation Abstracts International, 32,* 3028B–3029B.

Fewer than 5 percent??? *The New York Times,* August 27, 1990.

Finn, J. (1989). Withdrawing from school. *Review of educational Research, 59,* 117–142.

Fisher, C., Berliner, D., Filby, N., Marliave, R., Cahen, L., & Dishaw, M. (1980). Teaching behaviors, academic learning time, and student achievement: An overview. In C. Denham & A. Lieberman (Eds.), *Time to learn.* Washington, DC: National Institute of Education.

Fisher, C., Filby, N., Marliave, R., Cahen, L., Dishaw, M., Moore, J., & Berliner, D. (1978). *Teaching behaviors, academic learning time and student achievement* (Report of Phase III–B, Beginning Teacher Evaluation Study. Tech. Rep. V–1). San Francisco: Far West Laboratory for Educational Research and Development.

Flanders, N., & Amidon, E. (1967). *The role of the teacher in the classroom,* Minneapolis: Minneapolis Association for Productive Teaching.

Flanders, N., Morrison, B., & Brode, E. (1968). Changes in pupil attitudes during the school year. *Journal of Educational Psychology, 59,* 334–338.

Foster-Johnson, L., & Dunlap, G. (1993). Using functional assessment to develop effective, individualized interventions for changing behaviors. *Teaching Exceptional Children, 25.*

Freiberg, H. (1993). A school that fosters resilience in inner-city youth. *Journal of Negro Education, 62,* 364–376.

Freiberg, H., Huang, S., Stein, T., & Waxman, H. (1994, April). *The effects of classroom management on student learning in inner city elementary schools.* Paper presented at the annual meeting of the American Educational Research Association, New Orleans, LA.

Freiberg, H., Prokosch, N., Treister, E., & Stein, T. (1990). Turning around five at-risk elementary schools. *School Effectiveness and School Improvement, 1,* 5–25.

Frericks, A. (1974, March). *Labeling of students by prospective teachers.* Paper presented at the American Educational Research Association Convention, Chicago.

Galloway, D., & Goodwin, C. (1987). *The education of disturbing children.* London: Longmans.

Gallup, A. (1984). The Gallup poll of teachers' attitudes toward the public schools. *Phi Delta Kappan, 66,* 97–101.

Gallup, A., & Clark, D. (1987). The 19th annual Gallup Poll on the public's attitudes toward the public schools. *Phi Delta Kappan, 69,* 17–30.

Gallup, A., & Elam, S. (1988). The 20th annual Gallup Poll of the public's attitudes toward the public schools. *Phi Delta Kappan, 70,* 33–46.

Gallup, G. (1984). The 16th annual Gallup Poll of the public's attitudes toward the public schools. *Phi Delta Kappan, 66,* 23–38.

Gardner, H. (1983). *Frames of mind: The theory of multiple intelligence.* New York: Basic Books.

Gardner, H. (1993). *Multiple intelligence: The theory into practice.* New York: Basic Books.

Gathercoal, F. (1993). *Judicious discipline* (3rd ed.). San Francisco: Caddo Gap Press.

Gay, G. (1993). Ethnic minorities and educational equality. In J. Banks & C. Banks (Eds.), *Multicultural education.* Boston: Allyn and Bacon.

Gay, G., & Abrahams, R. (1973). Does the pot melt, boil, or brew? Black children and white assessment procedures. *Journal of School Psychology, 11,* 330–340.

Gibb, J. (1964). Climate for trust formation. In L. Bradford, J. Gibb, & K. Beene (Eds.), *T-group theory and laboratory method.* New York: Wiley.

Gilliam, H., & Van Den Berg, S. (1980). Different levels of eye contact: Effects on black and white college students. *Urban Education, 15,* 83–92.

Gilmer, J. (1985). *Factors related to the success and failure of teacher assistance teams in elementary schools.* Unpublished doctoral dissertation, University of Arizona, Tucson.

Ginott, H. (1972). *Teacher and child.* New York: Macmillan.

Glasser, W. (1965). *Reality therapy.* New York: Harper and Row.

Glasser, W. (1969). *Schools without failure.* New York: Harper and Row.

Glasser, W. (1985). *Control theory in the classroom.* New York: Harper and Row.

Glasser, W. (1988). On students' needs and team learning: A conversation with William Glasser. R. Brandt (Ed.), *Educational Leadership, 45,* 38–45.

Glasser, W. (1990). *The quality school: Managing students without coercion.* New York: Harper and Row.

Good, T. (1979). Teacher effectiveness in the elementary school. *Journal of Teacher Education, 30,* 52–64.

Good, T. (1983). Classroom research: A decade of progress. *Educational Psychologist, 18,* 127–144.

Good, T. (1986). Recent classroom research: Implications for teacher education. In D. Smith (Ed.), *Essential knowledge for beginning educators.* Washington, DC: American Association of Colleges for Teacher Education.

Good, T., & Beckerman, T. (1978). Time on task: A naturalistic study in sixth grade classrooms. *Elementary School Journal, 78,* 193–201.

Good, T., & Brophy, J. (1973). *Looking in classrooms.* New York: Harper and Row.

Good, T., & Brophy, J. (1974). Changing teacher and student behavior: An empirical investigation. *Journal of Educational Psychology, 66,* 390–405.

Good, T., & Brophy, J. (1984). *Looking in classrooms* (3rd ed.). New York: Harper and Row.

Good, T., & Brophy, J. (1987). *Looking in classrooms* (4th ed.). New York: Harper and Row.

Good, T., & Brophy, J. (1994). *Looking in classrooms* (6th ed.). New York: Harper and Row.

Good, T., Ebmeier, H., & Beckerman, T. (1978). Teaching mathematics in high and low SES classrooms: An empirical comparison. *Journal of Teacher Education, 29,* 85–90.

Good, T., & Grouws, D. (1979). The Missouri mathematics effectiveness project. *Journal of Educational Psychology, 71,* 355–362.

Good, T., & Power, C. (1976). Designing successful classroom environments for different types of students. *Journal of Curriculum Studies, 8,* 47–52.

Goodlad, J. (1983a). A study of schooling: Some findings and hypotheses. *Phi Delta Kappan, 64,* 465–470.

Goodlad, J. (1983b). A study of schooling: Some implications for school improvement. *Phi Delta Kappan, 64,* 552–558.

Goodlad, J. (1984). *A place called school: Prospects for the future.* New York: McGraw-Hill.

Goodwin, S., & Mahoney, M. (1975). Modification of aggression through modeling: An experimental probe. *Journal of Behavior Therapy and Experimental Psychiatry, 6,* 200–202.

Gordon, T. (1970). *Parent effectiveness training: The tested new way to raise responsible children.* New York: Wyden.

Gordon, T. (1974). *Teacher effectiveness training.* New York: Wyden.

Gottfredson, G., & Gottfredson, D. (1985). *Victimization in schools.* New York: Plenum Press.

Gray, R., Graubard, P., & Rosenberg, H. (1974, November). Little brother is changing you. *Psychology Today, 7,* 42–46.

Greenwood, C., & Hops, H. (1976). *Generalization of teacher praising skills over time and setting: What you teach is what you get.* Paper presented at the 54th Annual Convention of the Council for Exceptional Children, Chicago.

Greenwood, C., Hops, H., Delquadri, J., & Walker, H. (1974). *PASS: Program for academic survival skills.* Eugene: Center at Oregon for Research in the Behavioral Education of the Handicapped.

Gregorc, A. (1982). *An adult's guide to styles.* Maynard, MA: Gabriel Systems.

Grossman, H. (1984). *Educating Hispanic students: Cultural implications for instruction, classroom management, counseling, and assessment.* Springfield, IL: Thomas.

Gump, P. (1967). *The classroom behavior setting: Its nature and relation to student behavior* (Report No. BR–

5–0334). Washington, DC: Office of Education, Bureau of Research. (ERIC Document Reproduction Service No. EDO15515)

Hale, J. (1981). Black children: Their roots, culture, and learning styles. *Young Children, 36,* 37–50.

Hale-Benson, J. (1986). *Black children: Their roots, culture and learning styles* (rev. ed.). Baltimore, MD: Johns Hopkins University Press.

Haley, P., & Berry, K. (1988). *Home and school as partners: Helping parents help their children.* Andover, MA: Regional Laboratory for Educational Improvement of the Northeast and Islands.

Hall, R., Lund, D., & Jackson, D. (1968). Effects of teacher attention on study behavior. *Journal of Applied Behavior Analysis, 1,* 1–12.

Hargreaves, D. (1982). *The challenge for the comprehensive school.* London: Routledge and Kegan Paul.

Harmin, M., Kirschenbaum, H., & Simon, S. (1973). *Clarifying values through subject matter.* Minneapolis: Winston Press.

Hawkins, D., Doueck, H., & Lishner, D. (1988). Changing teaching practices in mainstream classrooms to improve bonding and behavior of low achievers. *American Educational Research Journal, 25,* 31–50.

Haycock, K. (June, 1990). *Closing remarks.* Presentation at the AAHE/College Board Conference on Mainstreaming University/School Partnerships, Chicago.

Hayek, R. (1987). The teacher assistance team: A pre-referral support team. *Focus on Exceptional Children, 20,* 1–7.

Henry, J. (1963). *Culture against man.* New York: Random House.

Heward, W., & Orlansky, M. (1980). *Exceptional children.* Columbus, OH: Charles E. Merrill.

High-school drop-out rates??? *The New York Times,* May 1, 1990.

Hill, K., & Wigfield, A. (1984). Test anxiety: A major educational problem and what can be done about it. *Elementary School Journal, 85,* 105–126.

Hodgkinson, H. (1985). *All one system: Demographics of education, kindergarten through graduate school.* Washington, DC: Institute for Educational Leadership.

Hosford, P. (1984). *Using what we know about teaching.* Alexandria,

VA: Association for Supervision and Curriculum Development.

Howard, E. (1981). School climate improvement—Rationale and process. *Illinois School Research and Development, 18*, 8–12.

Huggins, P. (1993). *The assist program: Multiple intelligence lessons.* Longmont, CO: Sopris West.

Hunter, M. (1981). *Increasing your teaching effectiveness.* Palo Alto, CA: Learning Institute.

Hutzell, R., Platzek, D., & Logue, P. (1974). Control of symptoms of Gilles de la Tourette's Syndrome by self-monitoring. *Journal of Behavior Therapy and Experimental Psychiatry, 5*, 71–76.

Hyman, I., & D'Alessandro, J. (1984). Good old-fashioned discipline: The politics of punitiveness. *Phi Delta Kappan, 66*, 39–45.

Jackson, P. (1968). *Life in classrooms.* New York: Holt, Rinehart and Winston.

Jacobson, E. (1938). *Progressive relaxation.* Chicago: University of Chicago Press.

Jencke, S., & Peck, D. (1976). Is immediate reinforcement appropriate? *Arithmetic Teacher, 23*, 32–33.

Johnson, D. (1979). *Educational psychology.* Englewood Cliffs, NJ: Prentice Hall.

Johnson, D., & Johnson, R. (1987). *Learning together and alone: Cooperative, competitive, and individualistic learning* (2nd ed.). Englewood Cliffs, NJ: Prentice Hall.

Johnson, D., Johnson, R., & Johnson-Holubec, E. (1986). *Circles of learning: Cooperation in the classroom.* Edina, MN: Interaction Book Co.

Johnson, D., Johnson, R., & Johnson-Holubec, E. (1988). *Cooperation in the classroom.* Edina, MN: Interaction Book Co.

Johnson, D., Marayama, S., Johnson, R., Nelson, D., & Skon, L. (1981). Effects of cooperative, competitive, and individualistic goal structures on achievement: A meta-analysis. *Psychological Bulletin, 89*, 47–62.

Johnson, R. & Johnson, D. (1985). *Cooperative learning: Warm-ups, grouping strategies and group activities.* Edina, MN: Interaction Book Co.

Johnson, S. (1970). Self-reinforcement versus external reinforcement in behavior modification with children. *Developmental Psychology, 3*, 147–148.

Johnson, S., & Martin, S. (1973). Developing self-evaluation as a conditioned reinforcer. In B. Ashem & E. Poser (Eds.), *Behavior modification with children.* New York: Pergamon.

Johnston, L. (1994). *Monitoring the future study: 1993 data.* Ann Arbor, MI: Institute for Social Research, University of Michigan.

Jones, F. (1987). *Positive classroom discipline.* New York: McGraw-Hill.

Jones, V. (1973). A junior high school program for emotionally disturbed children. In J. McDonnel, H. Fredericks, V. Baldwin, W. Moore, R. Crowley, R. Anderson, & K. Moore (Eds.), *Impact 7 of the Title VI programs in the state of Oregon, September 1972–August 1973.* Monmouth: Teaching Research.

Jones, V. (1980). *Adolescents with behavior problems: Strategies for teaching, counseling, and parent involvement.* Boston: Allyn and Bacon.

Jones, V. (1983). Current trends in classroom management: Implications for gifted students. *Roeper Review, 6*, 26–30.

Jones, V. (1984). An administrator's guide to developing and evaluating a building-wide discipline program. *National Association of Secondary School Principals Bulletin, 68*, 60–73.

Jones, V. (1991). Experienced teachers' assessment of classroom management skills presented in a summer course. *Journal of Instructional Psychology, 18*, 103–109.

Jones, V. (in press). Developing a comprehensive treatment plan for students with emotional and/behavioral disorders. *Teaching Exceptional Children.*

Jones, V., & Waksman, S. (1985). *A suggested procedure for the identification of and provision of services to seriously emotionally disturbed students: Technical assistance paper 5.* Salem: Oregon State Department of Education.

Joyce, B., & Weil, M. (1986). *Models of teaching* (3rd ed.). Englewood Cliffs, NJ: Prentice Hall.

Kagan, S. (1988). *Cooperative learning: Resources for teachers.* Laguna Niguel, CA: Resources for Teachers.

Kahle, J. (1990). Why girls don't know. In M. Rowe (Ed.), *What research says to the science teacher: The process of knowing.* Washington, DC: National Science Testing Association.

Kaufman, P., Bradby, D., & Owings, J. (1992). *National longitudinal study of 1988: Characteristics of at-risk students in NELS: 88.* Washington, DC: U.S. Office of Education, Office of Educational Research and Improvement.

Kaufman, P., McMillen, M., & Bradby, D. (1992). *Dropout rates in the United States: 1991.* Washington, DC: U.S. Printing Office.

Kazdin, A. (1973). The effect of vicarious reinforcement on attentive behavior in the classroom. *Journal of Applied Behavior Analysis, 6*, 71–78.

Kazdin, A., & Klock, J. (1973). The effect of nonverbal teacher approval on student attentive behavior. *Journal of Applied Behavior Analysis, 6*, 643–654.

Kelley, E. (1980). *Improving school climate: Leadership techniques for principals.* Reston, VA: National Association of Secondary School Principals.

Kelley, E. (1981). Auditing school climate. *Educational Leadership, 39*, 180–183.

Kennedy, B. (1968). *Motivational effect of individual conferences and goal setting on performance and attitudes in arithmetic.* (Report No. UW-WRDCCL-TR-61). Washington, DC: Office of Education, Bureau of Research. (ERIC Document Reproduction Service No. ED 032113).

Kerman, S., & Martin, M. (1980). *Teacher expectations and student achievement.* Bloomington, IN: Phi Delta Kappa.

Klein, R., & Schuler, C. (1974, April). *Increasing academic performance through the contingent use of self-evaluation.* Paper presented at the annual meeting of the American Educational Research Association, Chicago.

Kleinfeld, J. (1972). *Instructional style and the intellectual performance of Indian and Eskimo students.* Project No. I-J-027 (Final Report). Washington, DC: Office of Education, U.S. Department of Health, Education, and Welfare.

Kleinfeld, J. (1975). Effective teachers of Indian and Eskimo students. *School Review, 83*, 301–344.

Knitzer, J., Steinberg, Z., & Fleisch, B. (1990). *At the schoolhouse door: An* examination of programs and policies for children with behavioral and emotional problems. New York: Bank Street College of Education.

Kohl, H. (1967). 36 children. New York: New American Library.

Kolb, D. (1978). Learning style inventory technical manual. Boston: McBer.

Kounin, J. (1970). Discipline and group management in classrooms. New York: Holt, Rinehart and Winston.

Kounin, J., & Gump, P. (1961). The comparative influence of punitive and non-punitive teachers upon children's concept of school misconduct. Journal of Educational Psychology, 52, 44–49.

Kranzler, G. (1974). You can change the way you feel: A rational-emotive approach. Eugene: Published by author, Counseling Department, University of Oregon.

Krathwohl, D., Bloom, B., & Masia, B. (1964). Taxonomy of educational objectives, handbook II: Affective domain. New York: David McKay.

Kuykendall, C. (1992). From rage to hope: Strategies for reclaiming Black and Hispanic students. Bloomington, IN: National Education Service.

LaBenne, W., & Green, B. (1969). Educational implications of self-concept theory. Pacific Palisades, CA: Goodyear.

Lee, V. (1991, August). Sexism in single-sex and co-educational secondary school classrooms. Paper presented at the annual meeting of the American Sociological Association, Cincinnati, OH.

Lennox, D., & Miltenberger, R. (1989). Conducting a functional assessment of problem behavior in applied settings. Journal of the Association of Persons with Severe Handicaps, 14, 304–311.

Lepper, M. (1981). Intrinsic and extrinsic motivation in children: Detrimental effects of superfluous social controls. In A. Collins (Ed.), Aspects of the development of competence: The Minnesota symposia on child psychology (Vol. 14). Hillsdale, NJ: Erlbaum.

Lepper, M., & Greene, D. (1975). Turning play into work: Effects of adult surveillance and extrinsic rewards on children's intrinsic motivation. Journal of Personality and Social Psychology, 31, 479–486.

Lewis, A. (1990). Making it in the middle: The why and how of excellent schools for young urban adolescents. New York: The Edna McConnell Clark Foundation.

Lewis, R., & St. John, N. (1974). Contribution of cross-racial friendship to minority group achievement in desegregated classrooms. Sociometry, 37, 79–91.

Lightfoot, S. L. (1983). The good high school. New York: Basic Books.

Lindelow, J., & Mazzarella, J. (1981). School climate. (Contract No. 400–78–0007). Washington, DC: National Institute of Education. (ERIC Document Reproduction Service No. EA 014 193).

Lipsitz, J. (1984). Successful schools for young adolescents. New Brunswick, NJ: Transaction Books.

Long, N., Morse, W., & Newman, R. (Eds.). (1971). Conflict in the classroom (2nd ed.). Belmont, CA: Wadsworth.

Lovitt, T., & Curtiss, K. (1968). Effects of manipulating an antecedent event on mathematics response rate. Journal of Applied Behavior Analysis, 1, 329–333.

Luce, S., & Hoge, R. (1978). Relations among teacher rankings, pupil-teacher interactions, and academic achievement: A test of the expectancy hypothesis. American Educational Research Journal, 15, 489–500.

McCarthy, B. (1987). The 4-MAT system: Teaching to learning styles with right/left mode techniques. Barrington, IL: Excel.

McCarthy, B., Leflar, S., & McNamara, M. (1987). The 4-MAT workbook: Guided practice in 4-MAT lesson and unit planning. Barrington, IL: Excel.

McCaslin, M., & Good, T. (1992, April). Compliant cognition: The misalliance of management and instruction goals in current school reform. Educational Researcher, 4–17.

McDonald, F. (1976). Research on teaching and its implications for policy making: Report on phase II of the beginning teacher evaluation study. Princeton, NJ: Educational Testing Service.

McEwan, B. (Ed.). (1991). Practicing judicious discipline: An educator's guide to a democratic classroom. Davis, CA: Caddo Gap Press.

McGinley, P., & McGinley. (1970). Reading groups as psychological groups. Journal of Experimental Education, 39, 35–42.

McKenzie, T., & Rushall, B. (1974). Effects of self-recording on attendance and performance in a competitive swimming training program. Journal of Applied Behavior Analysis, 7, 199–206.

McLaughlin, T., & Gnagey, W. (1981, April). Self-management and pupil self-control. Paper presented at the annual meeting of the American Educational Research Association, Los Angeles.

Mace, F., Brown, D., & West, B. (1987). Behavioral self-management in education. In C. Maher, & J. Zins (Eds.), Psychoeducational interventions in the schools. New York: Pergamon.

Madsen, C., Becker, W., & Thomas, D. (1968). Rules, praise, and ignoring: Elements of elementary classroom control. Journal of Applied Behavior Analysis, 1, 139–150.

Maehr, M., & Sjogren, D. (1971). Atkinson's theory of achievement motivation: First step toward a theory of academic motivation. Review of Educational Research, 41, 143–161.

Maher, C. (1987). Involving behaviorally disordered adolescents in instructional planning: Effectiveness of the GOAL procedures. Journal of Child and Adolescent Psychotherapy, 4, 204–210.

Mahoney, M. (1974). Cognition and behavior modification. Cambridge, MA: Ballinger.

Mansfield, W., Alexander, D., & Farris, E. (1991). Teacher survey on safe, disciplined, and drug-free schools. Washington, DC: U.S. Department of Education, National Center for Educational Statistics.

Maple, F. (1977). Shared decision making. Beverly Hills, CA: Sage.

Maslow, A, (1968). Toward a psychology of being. New York: D. Van Nostrand.

Mastin, V. (1963). Teacher enthusiasm. Journal of Educational Research, 56, 385–386.

Matheny, K., & Edwards, C. (1974). Academic improvement through an experimental classroom management system. Journal of School Psychology, 12, 222-232.

Mendler, A. (1992). What do I do when . . . ? How to achieve discipline with *dignity in the classroom*. Bloomington, IN: National Educational Services.

Meichenbaum, D., & Cameron, R. (1974). The clinical potential of modifying what clients say to themselves. In C. Mahoney & C. Thorenson (Eds.), *Self-control: Power to the person*. Monterey, CA: Brooks/Cole.

Meyen, E. (Ed.). (1982). *Exceptional children in today's schools: An alternative resource book*. Denver: Love.

Monohan, J., & O'Leary, K. (1971). Effects of self-instruction on rule-breaking behavior. *Psychological Reports, 29*, 1059–1066.

Morgan, M. (1984). Reward-induced decrements and increments in intrinsic motivation. *Review of Educational Research, 54*, 5–30.

Morris, J. (1978). *Psychology and teaching: A humanistic view*. New York: Random House.

Morrison, A., & McIntrye, D. (1969). *Teachers and teaching*. Baltimore: Penguin.

Morse, W. (1964). Self-concept in the school setting. *Childhood Education, 41*, 195–198.

Morse, W. (1985). *The education and treatment of socioemotionally disturbed children and youth*. Syracuse, NY: Syracuse University Press.

Mortimore, P., & Sammons, P. (1987). New evidence on effective elementary schools. *Educational Leadership, 45*, 4–8.

Moskowitz, G., & Hayman, J. (1976). Success strategies of inner-city teachers: A year-long study. *Journal of Educational Research, 69*, 283–289.

Mosley, A., & Smith, P. (1982). What works in learning? Students provide the answers. *Phi Delta Kappan, 60*, 273.

Muldoon, J. (1955). The concentration of liked and disliked members in groups and the relationship of the concentration to group comprehensiveness. *Sociometry, 18*, 73–81.

Nash, R. (1963). Corporal punishment in an age of violence. *Educational Theory, 13*, 295–308.

National Center for Educational Statistics. (1988). *National Education Longitudinal Study of 1988*. Washington, DC: U.S. Department of Education.

National Council of LaRaza. (1991). *State of Hispanic America*. Washington, DC: Author.

National Education Association. (1988). *Conditions and resources of teaching: A special report by NEA*. Washington, DC: National Education Association. (ERIC Document Reproduction Service No. ED 316524).

Nelson, C., & Rutherford, R. (1988). Behavioral interventions with behaviorally disordered students. In M. Wang, M. Reynolds, & H. Walberg (Eds.), *Handbook of special education: Research and practice* (pp. 155–169). New York: Pergamon.

Nguyen, T. (1987). Positive self-concept in the Vietnamese bilingual child. In M. Dao (Ed.), *From Vietnamese to Vietnamese American: Selected articles*. San Jose, CA: Division of Special Education and Rehabilitative Services, San Jose State University.

Nichols, P. (1984). Down the up staircase: The teacher as therapist. In J. Grosenick (Ed.), *Interventions in behavioral disorders*. Des Moines: Special Educational Division, State Department of Education.

Norman, J., & Harris, M. (1981). *The private life of the American teenager*. New York: Rawson, Wade.

O'Leary, D., Becker, W., Evans, M., & Saudargas, R. (1969). A token reinforcement program in public school: A replication and systematic analysis. *Journal of Applied Behavior Analysis, 2*, 3–13.

O'Leary, D., & O'Leary, S. (Eds.). (1977). *Classroom management: The successful use of behavior modification* (2nd ed.). New York: Pergamon Press.

O'Neill, R., Horner, R., Albin, R., Storey, J., & Sprague, J. (1990). *Functional analysis: A practical guide*. Baltimore: Paul H. Brookes.

Page, E. (1958). Teacher comments and student performance. *Journal of Educational Psychology, 49*, 172–181.

Pascarella, E., Walberg, H., Junker, L., & Haertel, G. (1981). Continuing motivation in science for early and late adolescents. *American Educational Research Journal, 18*, 439–452.

Patterson, G. (1971). Behavioral intervention procedures in the classroom and in the home. In A. E. Berzin & S. L. Garfield (Eds.), *Handbook of psychotherapy and behavior change: An empirical analysis*. New York: Wiley.

Peterson, P., & Swing, S. (1982). Beyond time on task: Students' reports of their thought processes during classroom instruction. *Elementary School Journal, 82*, 481–491.

Phelan, P., Davidson, A., & Cao, H. (1992). Speaking up: Students' perspectives on school. *Phi Delta Kappan, 73*, 695–704.

Piaget, J. (1977). The role of action in the development of thinking. In W. F. Overton & J. M. Gallagher (Eds.), *Knowledge and development* (Vol. 1). New York: Plenum Press.

Porter, A., & Brophy, J. (1988). Synthesis of research on good teaching. *Educational Leadership, 45*, 74–85.

Postman, M., & Weingartner, D. (1969). *Teaching as a subversive activity*. New York: Delacorte.

Presseisen, B. (Ed.), (1988). *At-risk students and thinking: Perspectives from research*. Washington, DC: National Education Association.

Price, G. (1980). Which learning style elements are stable and which tend to change? *Learning Styles Network Newsletter, 1*, 1.

Purkey, W. (1970). *Self-concept and school achievement*. Englewood Cliffs, NJ: Prentice Hall.

Purkey, W., & Novak, J. (1984). *Inviting school success: A self-concept approach to teaching and learning* (2nd ed.). Belmont, CA: Wadsworth.

Quigley, B. (1987). *The registers: An analysis of non-participation in adult basic education*. Unpublished doctoral dissertation, Northern Illinois University.

Ramirez, M., & Castaneda, A. (1974). *Cultural democracy, bicognitive development, and education*. New York: Academic Press.

Reardon, F., & Reynolds, R. (1979). A survey of attitudes toward corporal punishment in Pennsylvania schools. In I. Hyman & J. Wise (Eds.), *Corporal punishment in American education*. Philadelphia: Temple University.

Regan, W. (1966). *Modern elementary curriculum*. New York: Holt, Rinehart and Winston.

Reisman, F. (1964). The strategy of style. *Teachers College Record, 64*, 484–495.

Renzulli, J. (1983, April). *The assessment and applications of learning style preferences: A practical approach for classroom teachers*. Paper presented at the annual meeting of the American Education Research Association, Montreal.

Rist, R. (1970). Student social class and teacher expectations: The self-fulfilling prophecy in ghetto education. *Harvard Educational Review, 40,* 411–451.

Roberts, D. (1986). *Recognizing and reporting child abuse and neglect.* Salem, OR: Department of Human Resources.

Roderick, T. (1988). Johnny can learn to negotiate. *Educational Leadership, 45,* 86–90.

Roehler, L., Duffy, G., & Meloth, M. (1987). The effects and some distinguishing characteristics of explicit teacher explanation during reading instruction. In J. Niles (Ed.), *Changing perspectives on research in reading/language processing and instruction.* Rochester, NY: National Reading Conference.

Rohrkemper, M., & Bershon, B. (1984). Elementary school students' reports on the causes and effects of problem difficulty in mathematics. *Elementary School Journal, 85,* 127–147.

Rose, S. (1983). Promoting social competence in children: A classroom approach to social and cognitive skill training. In C. W. LeCroy (Ed.), *Social skills training for children and youth.* New York: Haworth Press.

Rose, T. (1984). Current uses of corporal punishment in American public schools. *Journal of Educational Psychology, 76,* 427–441.

Rosenholtz, S., & Simpson, C. (1984). Classroom organization and student stratification. *Elementary School Journal, 85,* 21–37.

Rosenshine, B. (1976). Classroom instruction. In N. Gage (Ed.), *The psychology of teaching methods.* National Society for the Study of Education. Chicago: University of Chicago Press.

Rosenshine, B. (1980). How time is spent in elementary classrooms. In C. Denham & A. Lieberman (Eds.), *Time to learn.* Washington, DC: National Institute of Education.

Rosenshine, B. (1983). Teaching functions in instructional programs. *Elementary School Journal, 83,* 335–351.

Rosenshine, B., & Furst, N. (1973). The use of direct observation to study teaching. In R. Travers (Ed.), *Second handbook of research on teaching.* Chicago: Rand McNally.

Rosenthal, R. (1973). The Pygmalion effect lives. *Psychology Today, 7,* 56–63.

Rosenthal, R., & Jacobson, L. (1968). *Pygmalion in the classroom: Teacher expectation and pupils' intellectual development.* New York: Holt, Rinehart and Winston.

Rotter, J. (1966). Generalized expectancies for internal versus external control of reinforcement. *Psychological Monographs, 80,* 1–28.

Rowe, M. (1974). Wait-time and rewards as instructional variables, their influence on language, logic, and fate control: Part one, Wait-time. *Journal of Research in Science Teaching, 11,* 81–94.

Rowe, M. (1978). Wait, wait, wait. *School Science and Math, 78,* 207–216.

Runkel, P., Lawrence, M., Oldfield, S., Rider, M., & Clark, C. (1971). Stages of group development: An empirical test of Tuckman's hypothesis. *Journal of Applied Behavioral Science, 7,* 180–193.

Rutter, M., Maughan, B., Mortimore, P., Ouston, J., & Smith, A. (1979). *Fifteen thousand hours.* Cambridge, MA: Harvard University Press.

Sadker, D., & Sadker, M. (1985). Is the o.k. classroom o.k.? *Phi Delta Kappan, 66,* 358–361.

Sadker, D., Sadker, M., & Thomas, D. (1981). Sex equity and special education. *Pointer, 26,* 33–38.

Sanford, J., Emmer, E., & Clements, B. (1983). Improving classroom management. *Educational Leadership, 41,* 56–60.

Schmidt, G., & Ulrich, R. (1969). Effects of group contingent events upon classroom noise. *Journal of Applied Behavior Analysis, 2,* 171–179.

Schmuck, R. (1963). Some relationships of peer liking patterns in the classroom to pupil attitudes and achievement. *School Review, 71,* 337–359.

Schmuck, R. (1966). Some aspects of classroom social climate. *Psychology in the Schools, 3,* 59–65.

Schmuck, R., & Schmuck, P. (1974). *A humanistic psychology of education: Making the school everybody's house.* Palo Alto, CA: National Press Books.

Schmuck, R., & Schmuck, P. (1975). *Group processes in the classroom.* Dubuque, IA: Wm. C. Brown.

Schmuck, R., & Schmuck, P. (1992). *Group processes in the classroom*

(6th ed.). Dubuque, IA: Wm. C. Brown.

Schunk, D. (1983). Reward contingencies and the development of children's skills and self-efficacy. *Journal of Educational Psychology, 75,* 511–518.

Schutz, W. (1966). *The interpersonal underworld.* Palo Alto, CA: Science and Behavior.

Schwebel, A., & Cherlin, D. (1972). Physical and social distancing in teacher-pupil relationships. *Journal of Educational Psychology, 63,* 543–550.

Segor, R. (1990). Theory driven assessment for at-risk prevention programs. *High School Journal, 74,* 64–72.

Selman, R. (1980). *The growth of interpersonal understanding: Developmental and clinical analyses.* New York: Academic Press.

Serbin, L. (1973). A comparison of teacher responses to the pre-academic and problem behavior of boys and girls. *Child Development, 44,* 796–804.

Sgan, M. (1967). Social reinforcement, socioeconomic status, and susceptibility to experimenter influence. *Journal of Personality and Social Psychology, 5,* 202–210.

Shade, B. (1989). Afro-American cognitive patterns: A review of the research. In B. Shade (Ed.), *Cultural, style and the educative process.* Springfield, IL: Charles C. Thomas.

Sharan, S., & Sharan, Y. (1976). *Small group teaching.* Englewood Cliffs, NJ: Educational Technology.

Sherman, A. (1973). *Behavior modification: Theory and practice.* Belmont, CA: Wadsworth.

Silberman, C. (1970). *Crisis in the classroom: The remaking of American education.* New York: Random House.

Simpson, R. (1962). Parental influence, anticipatory socialization, and social mobility. *American Sociological Review, 27,* 517–522.

Sirotnik, K. (1982). The contextual correlates of the relative expenditures of classroom time on instruction and behavior: An explanatory study of secondary schools and classes. *American Educational Research Journal, 19,* 275–292.

Sizer, T. (1984). *Horace's compromise: The dilemma of the American high school.* Boston: Houghton Mifflin.

Slavin, R. (1983). *Cooperative learning.* New York: Longman.

Slavin, R. (1987). Cooperative learning and the cooperative school. *Educational Leadership, 45,* 7–13.

Slavin, R. (1988). Cooperative learning: A best-evidence synthesis. In R. E. Slavin (Ed.), *School and classroom organization.* Hillsdale, NJ: Erlbaum.

Slavin, R., Karweit, N., & Madden, N. (1989). *Effective programs for students at risk.* Boston: Allyn and Bacon.

Slavin, R., Maddin, N., & Leavey, M. (1984). Effects on team-assisted individualization on the mathematics achievement of academically handicapped and non-handicapped students. *Journal of Education Psychology, 76,* 813–819.

Sleeter, C. (Ed.). (1991). *Empowerment through multicultural education.* New York: Albany State University Press.

Smith, C., Frank, A., & Snider, B. (1984). School psychologists' and teachers' perceptions of data used in the identification of behaviorally disordered students. *Behavioral Disorders, 10,* 27–32.

Soar, R., & Soar, R. (1979). Emotional climate and management. In P. L. Peterson & H. J. Walberg (Eds.), *Research on teaching.* Berkeley, CA: McCutchan.

Soar, R., & Soar, R. (1980). Setting variables, classroom interaction and multiple pupil outcomes. *JSAS Catalog of Selected Documents in Psychology, 10,* 2110.

Spencer-Hall, D. (1981). Looking behind the teacher's back. *Elementary School Journal, 81,* 281–289.

Sprick, R. (1990). *Playground discipline: Positive techniques for recess supervision.* Eugene, OR: Teaching Strategies.

Sprick, R., Sprick, M., & Garrison, M. (1992). *Establishing positive discipline policies.* Longmont, CO: Sopris West.

Squires, D., Huitt, & Segars. (1983). *Effective schools and classrooms: A research-based perspective.* Alexandria, VA: Association for Supervision and Curriculum Development.

Stallings, J. (1975). Implementation and child effects of teaching in follow-through classrooms. *Monographs of the Society for Research in Child Development, 40,* 7–8.

Stallings, J. (1976). How instructional processes relate to child outcomes in a national study of the follow-through. *Journal of Teacher Education, 37,* 43–47.

Stallings, J. (1984). *An accountability model for teacher education.* Nashville, TN: George Peabody College for Teachers, Vanderbilt University, Stallings Teaching and Learning Institute.

Stallings, J., & Mohlman, G. (1981). *Principal leadership style, school policy, teacher change and student behavior in eight secondary schools* (Final Report). Washington, DC: National Institute of Education.

Stedman, L. (1985). A new look at the effective schools literature. *Urban Education, 20,* 295–326.

Steiner, C. (1977). *The original warm fuzzy tale.* Sacramento, CA: Jalmar Press.

Stevens, D. (1971). Reading difficulty and classroom acceptance. *Reading Teacher, 25,* 52–55.

Stinchcombe. A. (1964). *Rebellion in high school.* Chicago: Quadrangle.

Stipek, D. (1988). *Motivation to learn: From theory to practice.* Englewood Cliffs, NJ: Prentice Hall.

Sullivan, (1988). Special study groups: Motivating underachievers. *Middle School Journal, 19,* 20–21.

Suzuki, B. (1980). *An Asian-American perspective on multicultural education: Implications for practice and policy.* Paper presented at the Second Annual Conference of the National Association for Asian and Pacific American Education, Washington, DC.

Swift, M., & Spivack, G. (1975). *Alternative teaching strategies: Helping behaviorally troubled children achieve.* Champaign, IL: Research Press.

Tetreault, M. (1993). Classrooms for diversity: Rethinking curriculum and pedagogy. In J. Banks & C. McGee Banks (Eds,), *Multicultural education.* Boston: Allyn and Bacon.

Thomas, D., Becker, W., & Armstrong, M. (1968). Production and elimination of disruptive classroom behavior by systematically varying teacher's behavior. *Journal of Applied Behavior Analysis, 1,* 35–45.

Thomas, J., Presland, I., Grant, M., & Glynn, T. (1978). Natural rates of teacher approval and disapproval in grade 7 classrooms. *Journal of Applied Behavior Analysis, 11,* 91–94.

Thompson, R., White, K., & Morgan, D. (1982). Teacher-student interaction patterns in classrooms with mainstreamed mildly handicapped students. *American Educational Research Journal, 19,* 220–236.

Tobias, S. (1979). Anxiety research in educational psychology. *Journal of Educational Psychology, 71,* 573–582.

Tobin, K. (1987). The role of wait time in higher cognitive level learning. *Review of Educational Research, 57,* 69–95.

Travers, R. (1967). *Essentials of learning* (2nd ed.). New York: Macmillan.

Truax, C. & Tatum, C. (1966). An extension from the effective psychotherapeutic model to constructive personality change in pre-school children. *Childhood Education, 42,* 456–462.

Trupin, E., Low, B., Forsyth-Stephens, A., Tarico, V., & Cox, G. (1988). *Forgotten children—A systems analysis.* Seattle, WA: Division of Community Psychiatry, Department of Psychiatry and Behavioral Sciences, University of Washington.

Tuckman, B. (1965). Developmental sequence in small groups. *Psychological Bulletin, 63,* 384–489.

Turnbaugh, A. (1986). A view from the center. *National Center on Effective Secondary Schools Newsletter, 1,* 8–10.

United States Department of Education. (1993, February). *Fall 1990 elementary and secondary school civil rights survey: Revised national statistical estimates.* Washington, DC: Office of Civil Rights.

United States Department of Education. (1993). *Reaching the goals. Goal 6: Safe, disciplined, and drug-free schools.* Washington, DC: Office of Educational Research and Improvement.

Veenman, S. (1984). Perceived problems of beginning teachers. *Review of Educational Research, 54,* 143–178.

Walberg, H. (1988). Synthesis of research on time and learning. *Educational Leadership, 45,* 76–85.

Walberg, H., & Anderson, G. (1968). The achievement-creativity dimension and classroom climate. *Journal of Creative Behavior, 2,* 281–292.

Walker, H. (1979). *The acting-out child: Coping with classroom disruption.* Boston: Allyn and Bacon.

Walker, H., & Buckley, N. (1973). Teacher attention to appropriate and inappropriate classroom behavior: An individual case study. *Focus on Exceptional Children,.5,* 5–11.

Walker, H., Hops, H., & Fiegenbaum, E. (1976). Deviant classroom behavior as a function of combinations of social and token reinforcement and cost contingency. *Behavior Therapy, 7,* 76–88.

Walker, H., Hops, H., Greenwood, C., Todd, N., & Garrett, B. (1977). *The comparative effects of teacher praise, token reinforcement, and response cost in reducing negative peer interactions* (CORBEH Report #25). Eugene: Center at Oregon for Research in the Behavioral Education of the Handicapped, University of Oregon.

Wang, M., Haertel, G., & Walberg, H. (1993). Toward a knowledge base for school learning. *Review of Educational Research, 63,* 249–294.

Ward, B., & Tikunoff, W. (1976). The effective teacher education program: Application of selected research results and methodology to teaching. *Journal of Teacher Education, 27,* 58–63.

Ware, B. (1978). What rewards do students want? *Phi Delta Kappan, 59,* 355–356.

Warren, R., Deffenbacher, J., & Brading, P. (1976). Rational-emotive therapy and the reduction of test anxiety in elementary school students. *Rational Living, 11,* 26–29.

Wayson, W., & Pinnell, G. (1982). Creating a living curriculum for teaching self-discipline. In D. Duke (Ed.), *Helping teachers manage classrooms.* Alexandria, VA: Association for Supervision and Curriculum Development.

Weber, K. (1982). *The teacher is the key: A practical guide for teaching the adolescent with learning difficulties.* Denver: Love.

Wehlage, G. (1983). *Effective programs for the marginal high school students: PDK fastback 197.* Bloomington, IN: Phi Delta Kappa Educational Foundation.

Wehlage, G., & Rutter, R. (1986). Dropping out: How much do schools contribute to the problem? *Teachers College Record, 87,* 374–392.

Wehlage, G., Rutter, R., Smith, G., Lesko, N., & Fernandez, R. (1989). *Reducing the risk: Schools as communities of support.* Philadelphia: Falmer Press.

Wei, T. (1980). *Vietnamese refugee students: A handbook for school personnel* (2nd ed.). ERIC ED 208 109.

Weiner, B. (1979). A theory of motivation for some classroom experiences. *Journal of Educational Psychology, 71,* 3–25.

White, M. (1975). Natural rates of teacher approval and disapproval in the classroom. *Journal of Applied Behavior Analysis, 8,* 367–372.

White, R. (1959). Motivation reconsidered: The concept of competence. *Psychological Review, 66,* 478–481.

Whitehead, B. (1993, April). Dan Quayle was right. *The Atlantic Monthly,* 47–84.

Wineburg, S. (1987). The sulf-fulfilling prophecy. *Educational Researcher, 16,* 28–37.

Wittcock, M. (Ed.). (1986). *Handbook of research on teaching* (3rd ed.). New York: Macmillan.

Wlodkowski, R. (1978). *Motivation and teaching: A practical guide.* Washington, DC: National Education Association.

Wood, F., & Johnson, G. (1982). *Staff development and the /I/D/E/A/ school improvement project.* Dayton, OH: Institute for Development of Educational Activities.

Wood, M. (1975). *Developmental therapy.* Baltimore: University Park Press.

Wood, M., & Long, N. (1991). *Life space intervention: Talking with children and youth in crisis.* Austin, TX: Pro-Ed.

Workman, E. (1982). *Teaching behavioral self-control to students.* Austin, TX: Pro-Ed.

Wragg, E. (Ed.). (1984). *Classroom teaching skills.* New York: Nichols.

Yando, R., & Kagan, J. (1968). The effect of teacher tempo on the child. *Child Development, 39,* 27–34.

NAME INDEX